THE
BIG
BOOK
OF
MATH &
PHYSICS

THE BIG BOOK OF MATH & PHYSICS

Patricia Barnes-Svarney | Thomas E. Svarney | P. Erik Gundersen

FALL RIVER PRESS

New York

FALL RIVER PRESS

New York

An Imprint of Sterling Publishing
387 Park Avenue South
New York, NY 10016

This 2012 edition published by Fall River Press
by arrangement with Visible Ink Press LLC.

ISBN 978-1-4351-3321-1

For information about custom editions, special sales,
and premium and corporate purchases,
please contact Sterling Special Sales at 800-805-5489
or specialsales@sterlingpublishing.com.

Manufactured in the United States of America

2 4 6 8 10 9 7 5 3 1

www.sterlingpublishing.com

Contents

MATH BASICS

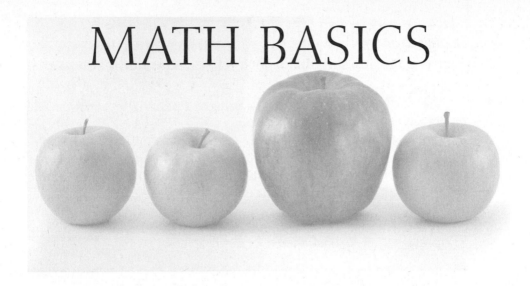

BASIC ARITHMETIC

What is **arithmetic**?

Arithmetic is a branch of mathematics that deals with numerical computation—specifically computation using integers, rational numbers, real numbers, or complex numbers—with the computations simple to complex. The word arithmetic has its roots in the Greek word for "to count" (*arithmeein*; also *arithmos*, or "number").

Arithmetic contains all the rules for combining two or more numbers. In most cases, when mathematicians talk about elementary arithmetic, they are speaking of those subjects most of us learned in grade school: addition, subtraction, multiplication, and division being the most common; and fractions, geometry and measurements, ratios and proportion, simple probabilities, and algebra examined in more advanced levels. For even more advanced students, such arithmetic lessons as congruence calculation, root extraction, power computations, and advanced factorizations are often presented.

Are there **more advanced concepts** in arithmetic?

Yes, arithmetic can even be more advanced than the ideas mentioned above. For example, higher arithmetic is the archaic term for *number theory*, which is the study of the properties of integers, or whole numbers ($0, \pm 1, \pm 2...$). It can include simpler arithmetic concepts to more complex, such as diophantine equations (for more information about these equations, see "Algebra"), prime numbers (see below), and functions such as the Riemann hypothesis (for more about Friedrich Bernhard Riemann, see "Geometry and Trigonometry").

There are other more advanced ideas in arithmetic, too. For example, *modular arithmetic* is known as the arithmetic of congruences (see below). The *model theory*

discusses the existence of "non-standard" models of arithmetic. And *floating-point arithmetic* is performed on real numbers by computers or other automated devices.

What is **arithmetic progression**?

Arithmetic progression is one of the simpler types of series in mathematics. It is usually in the form of $a, a + d, a + 2d, a + 3d$, and so on, in which a is the first term and d is the constant difference between the two successive terms. A progression is also seen as these numbers are added, as in $a + (a + d) + (a + 2d) + (a + 3d) +,..., (a + [n + 1]d)$. An example of an arithmetic progression would be $2 + 6 + 10 + 14 +...$, in which d is equal to 4.

What do **computers and arithmetic** have in **common**?

Computers and arithmetic have a great deal in common. *Arithmetical operations* are actually digital computer operations in which the numerical quantities are computed, either through adding, subtracting, multiplying, dividing, or otherwise comparing. *Arithmetical instructions* give a computer program direction to perform an arithmetic operation on specific types of data, such as addition, subtraction, multiplication,

and division. The sections of the computer that carry out these computations and other logic operations are called *arithmetical units* (or arithmetic sections). (For more information about computers and math, see "Math in Computing.")

Computers have become such an everyday part of our lives that we hardly think about them. Yet the mathematical concepts that lie behind their operations are staggering.

ALL ABOUT NUMBERS

What is a **number**?

The term number can be defined in many ways, including a sizable collection of people or things, and even an indefinite quantity or collection. In mathematics, a number, or numeral, is usually defined as a symbolic representation of a specific quantity or place in a sequence; to most people, the most familiar numbers are 1, 2, 3, 4, 5, and so on.

What is a **decimal system**?

The *decimal system* uses the base 10 notation system to represent real numbers. A *decimal expansion* is the expression of a number within the decimal system, such as 1, 15, 359, 18.7, and 3.14159. Each number within the system is called a *decimal digit*. (Such decimal notation—or a numbering notation based on decimals—was first used in India around 594.) The *decimal point* is represented by a period placed to the right of a unit's place in a decimal number. It is interesting to note that a comma is used in continental Europe to denote a decimal point, such as 3,25 (translated as 3.25 as a decimal point), which in this case would logically be called the *decimal comma*.

What is currently the most **common numeration system**?

The most common numeration system in use today is the Hindu-Arabic. This set of numerals has ten digits in a place value decimal system, which is a fancy way of saying that a decimal system—one based on tens—is an integral part of the system and that each number has a certain value depending on its place in the list of numbers.

How did the **Hindu-Arabic numerals** spread to **Europe**?

Hindu-Arabic numerals (often less accurately called Arabic numerals or numbers) had their roots in India before 300 B.C.E. From there, the use of Indian numerals followed

3

One of the earliest and most common devices developed for making everyday calculations was the abacus, which was still being used in Europe as late as the 15th century.

the more western trade routes to Spain and Northern Africa that were taken by the Arabic/Islamic peoples; this consequently resulted in the expanded use of these symbols.

It took several more centuries for the idea to spread to Europe. Although the Spanish used some Hindu-Arabic symbols as early as the late 900s, records of a more extensive use of these symbols occurred around 1202. Italian mathematician Leonardo of Pisa (also known as Fibonacci, c. 1170–c. 1250) introduced the Hindu-Arabic numbers in his book *Liber Abaci* (*The Book of the Abacus*). The acceptance of such a numbering system was difficult. For example, in some places in Italy, it was forbidden to use anything but Roman numerals. By the late 15th century, most people in Europe were still using an abacus and Roman numerals.

The 16th century was the turning point, with European traders, surveyors, bookkeepers, and merchants spreading the use of the Hindu-Arabic numerals. After all, it took longer to record data using Roman numerals than with Hindu-Arabic numbers. The advent of the printing press also helped by standardizing the way the Hindu-Arabic numbers looked. By the 18th century, the "new" numeration system was entrenched, establishing a system that dominates the way we work with and perceive numbers in the 21st century.

How did the **Hindu-Arabic numbers evolve**?

The evolution of the Hindu-Arabic numbers was not a straight line from India to Arabia and on to Europe. In between, the Arab cultures had more than one number system to contend with, including at least three different types of arithmetic: finger-reckoning arithmetic (counting on fingers), a sexagesimal system with numbers written in letters of the Arabic alphabet, and Indian numeral arithmetic.

The evolution of the Hindu-Arabic numbers continued throughout time and includes some good reasons for why our numbers look as they do today. For example, historians believe that between 970 and 1082, the numbers 2 and 3 changed signifi-

	1	2	3	4	5	6	7	8	9	10	0
Babylonian	˥	˥˥	˥˥˥	˥˥˥˥	˥˥˥˥˥	˥˥˥˥˥˥	˥˥˥˥˥˥˥	˥˥˥˥˥˥˥˥	˥˥˥˥˥˥˥˥˥	◄	
Egyptian	ı	ıı	ııı	ıııı	ııııı	ıııııı	ııııııı	ıııııııı	ııııııııı	∩	
Greek	A	B	Γ	Δ	E	F	Z	H	Θ	I	
Ancient Chinese	一	二	三	四	五	六	七	八	九	十	
Maya	•	••	•••	••••	▬	⎯̇	⎯̈	⎯⃛	⎯⃜	═	⬭
Hindu	?	?	?	?	?	?	?	?	?	?	○
Hindu-Arabic 15th century	/	2	3	ℓ	4	6	⌐	8	9	/0	○
Modern Hindu-Arabic	1	2	3	4	5	6	7	8	9	10	0

Different cultures generally employed one of two strategies when creating symbols for numbers: multiple marks that indicated single numbers or multiples of fives or tens (e.g., Babylonian, Egyptian, Mayan), or a more abstract system using a single symbol for the numbers one through nine, with numbers then being shifted over one or more places to indicate multiples of ten, hundreds, etc. (e.g., Hindu, Hindu-Arabic).

cantly, rotating 90 degrees from their original written position. This is thought to be due to how scribes worked: Sitting cross-legged, they wrote on a scroll they wound from right to left across their body. This caused them to write from top to bottom, not our usual right to left; the script was then rotated when the scroll was read.

What do **integers include**?

Integers include the whole numbers (also called positive integers or natural numbers), negative whole numbers (also called negative integers or the negatives of the naturals), and zero. Numbers such as 3/4, 5.993, 6.2, −3.2, and pi (π; or 3.14 …) are *not* considered integers. Only integers are used when speaking of odd and even numbers (zero is considered to be an even number; for more about zero, see below).

How are **numbers classified**?

The set of natural numbers are also called integers—or counting or whole numbers—which are usually defined as the positive and negative whole numbers, along with zero (0). But many times, mathematicians do not use the term "natural numbers," and instead define numbers based on the following terminology and/or symbols:

Group	Name	Symbol
...,−3,−2,−1, 0, 1, 2, 3...	integers	Z (after the German word *Zahl*, for "number")
1, 2, 3...	positive integers (or often referred to as natural numbers)	Z+ or N
−1, −2, −3...	negative integers	Z−
0, 1, 2, 3 ...	nonnegative integers (or often referred to as whole numbers)	Z* (Z-star)
0, −1, −2, −3 ...	nonpositive integers	(no symbol)

What is a **place value**?

The *place value*, or "rule of position," are numbers whose value depends on the place or position they occupy in a written numerical expression. In the Hindu-Arabic counting system, the numerals 1, 2, 3, 4, 5, 6, 7, 8, 9, and 0 have certain specific place values. For example, the number 7 represents 7 (7 units), 70 (as 7 tens), 700 (as 7 hundreds), and so on—the 7's values based on their position in the numerical expression.

What are some of the **highest numbers** we know?

Numbers can go on forever—in other words, there are an infinite number of numbers—so no one will ever reach the "highest number." The highest numbers with which we are most familiar (and can comprehend) include million, billion, and trillion, often referring to such quantities as the number of miles to the outer planets or the federal budget deficit. These larger numbers are usually separated by comma at the thousands, millions, trillions, etc. place values. For example, for 3,490, the comma is after the thousand place value; for 1,384,993, after the million and thousand place value. Larger numbers written for technical papers are sometimes expressed with spaces; for example, 11 384 443 is equivalent to 11,384,443.

What are the various **scales** used by countries to **label big numbers**?

Not every country labels the highest numbers in the same way. Depending on the country, they use either the *short scale* or the *long scale*. The short scale is taught in American school systems, thus it is thought to be used exclusively in the United States. Other countries, including most of continental Europe, use the long scale. And several countries, including China, have large number naming systems that are even different than the long and short scales.

For example, in the American system, denominations above 1,000 million (or the American billion) are 1,000 times the preceding one (for example, one trillion is 1,000 billion; one quadrillion is 1,000 trillion). In the British system, the first denomination above 1,000 milliards (the British billion) is 1,000,000 times the preceding one (for example, one trillion is 1,000,000 billion; one quadrillion is 1,000,000 trillion). The American system is based on the French system, which the French ironically no longer follow. Their larger number names now correspond to the British system, as do those of many other countries in Europe.

American and British Naming Systems for Large Numbers

American Name	British Name	Number (in powers of ten)
billion	milliard	10^9
trillion	billion	10^{12}
quadrillion	—	10^{15}
quintillion	trillion	10^{18}
sextillion	—	10^{21}
septillion	quadrillion	10^{24}
octillion	—	10^{27}
nonillion	quintillion	10^{30}
decillion	—	10^{33}
undecillion	sextillion	10^{36}
duodecillion	—	10^{39}
tredecillion	septillion	10^{42}
quattuordecillion	—	10^{45}
quindecillion	octillion	10^{48}
sexdecillion	—	10^{51}
septdecillion	nonillion	10^{54}
octodecillion	—	10^{57}
novemdecillion	decillion	10^{60}
vigintillion	—	10^{63}
—	undecillion	10^{66}
—	duodecillion	10^{72}
—	tredecillion	10^{78}
—	quattuordecillion	10^{84}
—	quindecillion	10^{90}
—	sexdecillion	10^{96}
—	septendecillion	10^{102}
—	octodecillion	10^{108}
—	novemdecillion	10^{114}
—	vigintillion	10^{120}
centillion	—	10^{303}
—	centillion	10^{600}

What are a googol and a googolplex?

The "googol" is the invention of Milton Sirotta, the eight-year-old nephew of mathematician Edward Kasner (1878–1955), who once asked the young boy to name the number 1 followed by 100 zeros (10 to the 100th power or 10^{100}). It is also seen as "10 duotrigintillion" on the short scale, and ten thousand sexdecillion on the long scale (for more about scales, see elsewhere in this chapter). Since a googol is an incredibly large number, there is little it can represent. Although one might think it would represent some collection of astronomical entities, such as the number of elementary particles in the universe, it does not. Scientists estimate only about 10 to the 80th power (10^{80}) such particles exist. Googol was soon followed by *googolplex*, a name thought to be invented by Kasner, and said to equal 10 to the power of googol (or 1 followed by 10 to the power of 100 zeros or one followed by a googol of zeros).

No one has ever seen such large numbers printed out. And although it is true that computer processing power doubles about every one to two years—and the use of computer networks across the Internet even faster—it is still too early to print the number represented by a googol or a googolplex. Thus, many ask why begin at all, since attempts to do so will soon be overtaken by faster processors? In fact, it is estimated that it will take another 500 years before such an endeavor is achieved—but with the advancement of computer processing, in ten years, the number of years will no doubt be even less.

What are **non-vanishing** and **vanishing numbers**?

A non-vanishing number is just as the term implies: A quantity that is non-zero everywhere. For example, in the expression $x^4 + 1$, the answer will never be zero (even when x is zero or a negative number). The answer for the expression x^2 is called "vanishing" because if $x = 0$, the expression's answer "vanishes" to zero.

What are **rational, irrational**, and **real numbers**?

Rational, or fractional, numbers are most often regarded as divisions (or ratios) of integers. By creating a fraction (dividing one integer by another), a rational number produces either a number that "ends" or repeats decimals. For example, 1/4 equals the decimal equivalent of 0.25; 1/3 is equivalent to 0.33333 ... Both of these are rational numbers. (For more information about fractions, see below.)

On the other hand, *irrational numbers* are all the numbers that can be written as non-repeating, non-finite (or non-terminating) decimals. Also called non-rational numbers, they include the decimal equivalent of pi (or 3.141592 ...). Finally, if you

put the rational and irrational numbers together, they form the *real numbers*. Most numbers we use in our everyday lives are real numbers.

What are **imaginary numbers**?

The "opposite" of real numbers are (logically enough) called *imaginary numbers*. In particular, they are all non-zero multiples (real numbers) of the square root of –1, also called *i*, with the formula defined as follows:

$$i = \sqrt{-1}$$

$$\text{then } i^2 = (\sqrt{-1})^2 = -1$$

The $\sqrt{-1}$ does not have a position on a number line; and no number can be squared to get –1. (If you square a positive number, the result is positive; if you square a negative number, the result is also a positive number.) Thus, in order to square a number to get a negative one, mathematicians invented the imaginary number *i*.

Can there be **more than one type of number**?

Yes, numbers can be classified as more than one type, and it's not always easy to keep them straight. The following lists some ways to better understand the plethora of number types:

- A rational number is not always an integer: 4/1 is an integer, but 2/3 is not; but an integer is always a rational number—because it can be represented by a fraction by putting the integer over 1, or /1, such as 2/1 or 234/1.

- A number can either be rational or irrational but not both.

- The number for pi (3.141592…) is irrational (the decimal does not repeat) and real.

- 0.25 is considered rational (the numbers terminate) and real.

- The fraction 5/3 is rational (it's a fraction) and real.

- The number 10 can be explained using many terms, including a counting number, whole number, integer, rational, and real.

How do **regular** and **non-regular numbers** differ?

Regular and non-regular numbers are actually other terms for rational numbers. Regular numbers are positive integers that have a finite decimal expansion. In other words, a number that seems to "end." For example, one quarter (1/4) is equal to the decimal equivalent of 0.25, in which the numbers end with the "5." A non-regular

9

number is one that includes repeating decimals—numbers that seem to go on forever. For example, one third (1/3) is equal to the decimal equivalent of 0.3333..., in which the number 3s go on indefinitely.

How do you perform **imaginary numbers computations**?

Imaginary numbers come in handy to do many computations, especially something called *simplification*. Here are some "simple" examples of how to use imaginary numbers:

To simplify the square root (or *sqrt*) of -25:
$$\sqrt{-25} = \sqrt{-25} \times -1 = \sqrt{-25} \times \sqrt{-1} = 5i$$

To simplify $2i + 4i$:
$$2i + 4i = (2 + 4)i = 6i$$

To simplify $21i - 5i$:
$$21i - 5i = (21i - 5i) = 16i$$

To multiply and simplify $(2i)(4i)$:
$$(2i)(4i) = (2 \times 4)(ii) = (8)(i^2) = (8)(-1) = -8$$

Who first came up with the idea of imaginary numbers?

The origin of *i* is difficult to trace. Some historians give credit to Italian physician and mathematician Girolamo Cardano (1501–1576; in English, known as Jerome Cardan). In 1545, he is said to have started modern mathematics, first mentioning not only negative numbers but imaginary numbers in his Latin treatise, *Ars Magna* (*The Great Art*). But Cardano did not consider the imaginary numbers as the real mathematical objects we do today. To him, they were merely convenient "fiction" to classify certain polynomial properties, describing how their roots would behave when he pretended they even *had* roots.

Eighteenth-century Swiss mathematician Leonhard Euler, who published over 70 volumes on mathematics in his lifetime, was one of the greatest contributors to the discipline that ever lived. Euler developed important concepts in such areas as geometry, calculus, trigonometry, algebra, hydrodynamics, and much more. He also created the concept of the imaginary number that is the square root of –1.

Most agree that around 1777, Swiss mathematician Leonhard Euler (1707–1783) used "i" and "–i" (negative i) for the two different square roots of –1, thus eliminating some of the problems associated with notation when putting polynomials into categories. (He is also credited with originating the notation $a + bi$ for complex numbers.) Much to the consternation of many past and present mathematicians, *i* and *–i* were called "imaginary," mainly because the number's function at the time of Euler was not clearly understood. When German mathematician, physicist, and astronomer Johann Friedrich Carl Gauss (1777–1855) used them for the geometric interpretation of complex numbers as points in a plane, the usefulness of imaginary numbers became apparent.

What are complex numbers?

Complex numbers have two parts: the "real" part (any real number) and an "imaginary" part (any number with an *i* in it). The standard complex number format is "*a + bi*," or a real number plus an imaginary number. It is also often seen as $x + iy$, because while real numbers are viewed on a line, complex numbers are viewed graphically on an Argand (or polar) coordinate system: The imaginary numbers make up the vertical (or *y*) axis as *iy*, while the horizontal (or *x*) axis is occupied by

real numbers. (For more information about coordinate systems, see "Geometry and Trigonometry.")

What is the **polar form** of a **complex number**?

The polar form of a complex number is equal to a real number expressed as a angle's cosine, and the imaginary number (i) times the same angle's sine, with the angle expressed in radians (for more about angles, sines, cosines, and polar forms, see "Geometry and Trigonometry"). This is seen in equation form as: $r(\cos \theta + i \sin \theta)$, in which r is the radius vector, θ is the angle, and i is the imaginary number.

Is there such a thing as a **perfect number**?

Yes, there is such a thing as a perfect number, but it is not what we think of as true perfection. To mathematicians, perfect numbers are somewhat rare because they are few and far between. They are defined as a natural number (or positive integer) in which the sum of its positive divisors (or the bottom number in a fraction that divides the number to equal another whole number, and includes 1 but not the number itself) is the number itself. For example, 6 is considered a perfect number because its divisors are 1, 2, and 3—or $1 + 2 + 3 = 6$. The next perfect numbers are 28 ($1 + 2 + 4 + 7 + 14$), 496, 8128, 33550336, 8589869056, 137438691328, 2305843008139952128, and so on—with larger and larger perfect numbers being discovered, especially with the help of faster and more memory-packed computers. (For more about perfect numbers, see Mersenne primes, elsewhere in this chapter.)

What is meant by **one-to-one correspondence**?

A one-to-one correspondence means as the words imply: that the number of objects, numbers, or whatever is the same as the set of other objects, numbers, or whatever. (In set theory, the one-to-one correspondence means something different; for more about set theory, see "Foundations of Mathematics.")

Everyone has no doubt had contact with one-to-one correspondence without even thinking about it. For example, there is a one-to-one correspondence of the number 10 to the number of fingers on both hands (ten). Counting a deck of cards is a one-to-one correspondence—each number, from 1 to 52, representing a card in the deck. When you compare two decks of cards, putting the cards side-by-side to equal 52 in each deck, this could also be considered a one-to-one correspondence.

Not everything is counted in such a way. For example, when mathematicians want to know the size of an unknown quantity, they put the unknown quantity in a one-to-one correspondence with a known quantity.

Do numbers continue to infinity?

When most of us think of infinity, we envision the universe continuing on forever; and in mathematics, we often think of numbers that are never-ending. Sometimes it is difficult to understand infinity since our own lives—and most of our experiences—are finite (eventually end). Infinity is a mind-boggling concept.

There are several rules to mathematical infinity—the three most important are: no matter how high you count numbers, you can always count higher; no matter what length you draw parallel lines, they will never meet; and when starting with a line, dividing it in half, then dividing that in half, and so on, you will never stop dividing the resulting line segment.

Even though scientists and mathematicians agree that infinity exists theoretically, it is often a difficult concept to understand and accept. Is it true that the number of particles in the universe are infinite? Does the universe continue on forever? Do parallel lines eventually meet at a place we have yet to discover? If a particle is infinitely divided, just how small can an atomic particle become? And to add to the unimaginable explanations, German mathematician George (Georg) Ferdinand Ludwig Philipp Cantor (1845–1918) mathematically reasoned out that not only do infinities come in different sizes, but there are an infinite number of infinities.

What are **ordinal** and **cardinal numbers**?

In common arithmetic terms, *cardinal numbers* are those that express amounts; they are also used in simple counting or to answer the question of quantity (how many). They can be nouns (try counting to *ten*); as pronouns (*ten* were discovered); or adjectives (*ten* cats). Specifically, the term is from the Latin *cardin*, meaning "stem" or "hinge," thus meaning the most important or principal numbers with others depending (hinging) on those numbers. We are most familiar with the cardinal numbers as our counting numbers or the Hindu-Arabic numeration system—1, 2, 3, and so on.

Ordinal numbers are much different. In common, arithmetic terms, ordinal numbers are adjectives that describe the numerical position of an object, such as first, second, third, and so on. They are used to show the order of succession for objects (*second* chair), names (*second* month), or periods of time (*2nd* century).

Note that cardinal and ordinal numbers are easily divided. For example, in the Hindu-Arabic numeration system, the cardinal numbers may be read as ordinals, such as May 10 being read as "May tenth." Such differences are even harder to distinguish when it comes to Roman numerals. Most of the time, these numerals are considered cardinal numbers (I, II, III, etc.), but they can also be ordinal numbers in certain con-

13

tents, such as Henry the VIII (Henry the Eighth). Roman numerals can even contain ordinal suffixes, such as the IXth Dynasty.

Ordinal and Cardinal Numbers and Symbols

Hindu-Arabic Symbol	Roman Symbol	Cardinal Number Name	Ordinal Number Name	Ordinal Symbol
0	n/a	zero/naught/cipher		
1	I	one	first	1st
2	II	two	second	2d/2nd
3	III	three	third	3d/3rd
4	IV	four	fourth	4th
5	V	five	fifth	5th
6	VI	six	sixth	6th
7	VII	seven	seventh	7th
8	VIII	eight	eighth	8th
9	IX	nine	ninth	9th
10	X	ten	tenth	10th
11	XI	eleven	eleventh	11th
12	XII	twelve	twelfth	12th
13	XIII	thirteen	thirteenth	13th
14	XIV	fourteen	fourteenth	14th
15	XV	fifteen	fifteenth	15th
16	XVI	sixteen	sixteenth	16th
17	XVII	seventeen	seventeenth	17th
18	XVIII	eighteen	eighteenth	18th
19	XIX	nineteen	nineteenth	19th
20	XX	twenty	twentieth	20th
30	XXX	thirty	thirtieth	30th
40	XL	forty	fortieth	40th
50	L	fifty	fiftieth	50th
60	LX	sixty	sixtieth	60th
70	LXX	seventy	seventieth	70th
80	LXXX	eighty	eightieth	80th
90	XC	ninety	ninetieth	90th
100	C	one hundred	one hundredth	100th
400	CD	four hundred	four hundredth	400th
500	D	five hundred	five hundredth	500th
900	CM	nine hundred	nine hundredth	900th
1,000	M	one thousand	one thousandth	1,000th

Why are the **terms cardinal** and **ordinal** sometimes **confused** in mathematics?

Cardinal and ordinal numbers are sometimes confused because they have two distinct mathematical definitions. The cardinal numbers in the numbering system should not be confused with cardinal numbers in set theory, in which any method of counting sets using a cardinal number gives the same result. Likewise, the ordinal numbers in arithmetic should also not be confused with ordinal numbers in set theory: Such numbers, often called ordinals for short, are the order type of a well ordered set. They are divided into two types: finite and transfinite ordinals. (For more about sets, ordinals, and cardinal numbers, see "Foundations of Mathematics.")

MORE ABOUT NUMBERS

What is **congruence**?

In reference to numbers, congruence is the property of two integers having the same remainder upon division by another integer. The term also is often used in geometry to describe a property of geometric formations (for more information about congruence in geometry, see "Geometry and Trigonometry"). Still another way of using congruence is in number theory, in which modular arithmetic is the arithmetic of congruences, which is sometimes informally called "clock arithmetic."

How does **modular arithmetic** work?

In modular arithmetic, numbers "wrap around" when they reach a fixed quantity. This is also called the *modulus*—thus the name modular arithmetic—with the standard way of writing the form as "mod 12" or "mod 2."

In this case, if the two numbers b (also called the base) and c (also called the remainder) are subtracted ($b - c$), and their difference is a number integrally divisible by m, or ($b - c$)/m, then b and c are said to be congruent modulo m. Mathematically, "b is congruent to c (modulo m)" is written as follows, with the symbol for congruence (\equiv):

$b \equiv c \pmod{m}$

But if $b - c$ is not integrally divisible by m, then it is said, "b is not congruent to c (modulo m)," or

$b \not\equiv c \pmod{m}$

More formally, modular arithmetic includes any "non-trivial homomorphic image of the ring of integers." We can interpret this interesting definition using a clock. The modulus would be the number 12 on the clock (arithmetic modulo 12), with an asso-

We can look to the familiar face of a clock to illustrate the concept of "clock arithmetic" or modulo 12. With clocks, we can count through 11 before getting to 12, where we start over again at zero. Thus, if it is 7 o'clock and we add 6 hours, we get 1 o'clock, not 13 o'clock.

ciated ring labeled C_{12} and the allowable numbers being 0, 1, 2, 3, 4, 5, 6, 7, 8, 9, 10, and 11. Another example is arithmetic modulo 2, with an associated ring of C_2, or allowable numbers of 1 and 2.

What is the **Fibonacci sequence**?

Italian mathematician Leonardo of Pisa (c. 1170–c. 1250; also known as Fibonacci, or "son of Bonacci," although some historians say there is no evidence that he or his contemporaries ever used the name) may be known for helping to introduce Hindu-Arabic numerals to Europe (for more information about Fibonacci and numerals, see elsewhere in this chapter), but he also is famous for the sequence of numbers he discovered. This sequence—initially pursued as an exercise to determine how fast a pair of rabbits can reproduce per year—is formed by adding the two preceding numbers to find the next number, starting with a pair of ones. Thus, the Fibonacci numbers in this sequence are 1, 1, 2, 3, 5, 8, 13, 21, 34, 55, 89, 144, 233, 377, and so on; or

$$1 + 1 = 2$$
$$2 + 1 = 3$$
$$3 + 2 = 5$$
$$5 + 3 = 8$$
$$8 + 5 = 13$$
$$13 + 8 = 21$$
$$21 + 13 = 34$$
$$34 + 21 = 55$$
$$55 + 34 = 89$$
$$89 + 55 = 144$$
$$144 + 89 = 233$$
$$233 + 144 = 377, \text{ and so on.}$$

What are **prime** and **composite numbers**?

There are many definitions of *prime numbers*—and they all mean the same thing in translation. For example, prime numbers are defined as positive integers (natural numbers) that are greater than 1 and have only 1 and the prime number as divisors

What are some examples of "clock arithmetic"?

As stated above, the clock would be considered arithmetic modulo, with calculations including such statements shown below (Note: In all of the first calculations, the equal sign can be replaced with the congruence sign ≡, or three lines instead of the two for an equal sign.):

$$11 + 1 = 0, \text{ also written as } 11 + 1 \equiv 0 \ (\text{mod } 12)$$

$$7 + 8 = 3, \text{ also written as } 7 + 8 \equiv 3 \ (\text{mod } 12)$$

$$5 \times 7 = 11, \text{ also written as } 5 \times 7 \equiv 11 \ (\text{mod } 12)$$

(factors). Another definition is an integer greater than 1, in which its only positive divisors are 1 and itself. Still yet another definition is that a prime is a natural number that has exactly two distinct natural number divisors, 1 and itself. For instance, the prime numbers less than 20 are 2, 3, 5, 7, 11, 13, 17, and 19. All other integers greater than 1 that are not prime numbers are called *composite numbers*.

There are other rules concerning prime and composite numbers. The number 1 is unique, and is not considered a prime or composite number. And one of the basic theorems of arithmetic is that any positive integer is either a prime or the product of a unique set of prime numbers. For example, the number 12 is not a prime, but it has a unique "prime calculation" written as: $2 \times 2 \times 3$.

What is the **Sieve of Eratosthenes**?

The smallest prime numbers—those less than 1 million—can be determined using something invented circa 240 B.C.E.: the Sieve of Eratosthenes (note: the largest primes are found using *Lagrange's Theorem* from group theory studies). This method was named after astronomer and mathematician Eratosthenes of Cyrene (276–196 B.C.E.), who was actually more famous for calculating the circumference of the Earth than for his work with prime numbers.

To determine primes using this method, make a list of all the integers less than or equal to n (numbers greater than 1) and get rid of all the multiples of all primes less than or equal to the square root of n. The numbers that are left are all primes. For example, to determine primes less than 100, start with 2 as the first prime; then write all odd numbers from 3 to 100 (there is no need to write the even numbers). Take 3 as the first prime and cross out all its multiples in the numbers you listed. Take the next number, 5, and then 7, and cross out all their multiples. By the time you reach 11, many numbers will be eliminated and you will have reached a number greater than the square root of 100 (11 is greater than 10, the square root of 100). Thus, all the numbers you have left will be primes.

What are the **first 100 prime numbers**?

The first 100 prime numbers are as follows:

2	3	5	7	11	13	17	19	23	29
31	37	41	43	47	53	59	61	67	71
73	79	83	89	97	101	103	107	109	113
127	131	137	139	149	151	157	163	167	173
179	181	191	193	197	199	211	223	227	229
233	239	241	251	257	263	269	271	277	281
283	293	307	311	313	317	331	337	347	349
353	359	367	373	379	383	389	397	401	409
419	421	431	433	439	443	449	457	461	463
467	479	487	491	499	503	509	521	523	541

What is the **Reimann zeta-function**?

German mathematician Georg Friedrich Bernhard Riemann (1826–1866) was responsible for the Riemann zeta-function—the master of all the L-functions that would reveal how the prime numbers are distributed. (There are two types of L-functions—algebraic and transcendental—classified according to their degree, including the zeta-function.) Involved in all of this is the Riemann Hypothesis, an important unsolved mathematical problem. The Riemann Hypothesis is an example of something that should be true for every L-function. In 2008, researchers exhibited the first example of a third degree transcendental L-function—with the researchers' studies showing that some conditions could be confirmed in the Riemann Hypothesis. Now scientists hope these L-functions will help interpret many connections between different areas of mathematics.

Are there **different** types of **prime numbers**?

Yes, there are different types of prime numbers, including the following:

- *Mersenne primes*—See below for an explanation.

- *Twin primes*—Primes of the form p and $p + 2$ (in other words, they differ by two); discovering such a prime involves finding two primes.

- *Factorial/primorial primes*—Primorial primes are of the form $n\# \pm 1$; factorial primes are of the form $n! \pm 1$.

- *Sophie Germain primes*—This is an odd prime p for which $2p + 1$ is also a prime. It was named after Sophie Germain (1776–1831), who proved that the first case of Fermat's last theorem for exponents was divisible by such primes.

Other names for prime numbers are mainly for descriptive purposes. For example, in 1984, mathematician Samuel Yates defined a *titanic prime* to be any prime with at least one thousand digits. In the past few decades since his definition, there have been over a thousand times more such primes discovered. Yates also coined the term *gigantic prime* to indicate a prime with at least 10,000 digits. Thanks to advances in computer technology, a great deal of prime number generation has happened in the past decade, including surpassing 10,000 digits into the millions. To date, the largest prime number known was uncovered in 2009—a (Mersenne) prime number with 12,978,189 digits, written shorthand as 2 to the power of 43,112,609, minus 1. As to whether mathematicians will eventually find a one billion digit prime number, often referred to as a bevaprime, is no doubt only a matter of time.

What **special number** was recently **factored**?

In 2007, mathematicians from three institutions worked for eleven months to churn out the prime factors of a well-known, hard-to-factor number—which turned out to be 307 digits long. It was also called a "special number," because it has a special mathematical form: close to a power of two. Mathematicians know it's relatively easy to identify large prime numbers, but factoring (breaking down) a number into its prime components is very difficult. But the applications may be worth the time spent, especially for those people who work to safeguard our computer information with special encryption techniques. As for the next iteration to factor, scientists hope it won't be long before this record is broken.

What is the **story** behind the **Mersenne primes**?

Mersenne primes (or Mersenne numbers) are connected to prime numbers. They are from the form $2^p - 1$, in which p is a prime; or said another way, when $2^p - 1$ is prime, it is said to be a Mersenne prime.

Centuries ago, many mathematicians believed that numbers from the form $2^p - 1$ (they actually used the form $2^n - 1$, which is the same as the $2^p - 1$ used today) were prime for all primes p. By the 16th century, it was proven that $2^{11} - 1 = 2,047$ was not prime. By 1603, Pietro Cataldi (1548–1626) correctly discovered that $p = 17$ and $p = 19$ were both prime, but he was wrong to add 23, 29, and 37 to his prime numbers list. Soon others discovered his errors, including French mathematician Pierre de Fermat (1601–1665) in 1640, and Swiss mathematician Leonhard Euler (1707–1783) in 1738.

The hunt for primes continued. The name "Mersenne" actually came from French priest, Father Marin Mersenne (1588–1648) who in 1644 referred to such numbers in the preface to his book *Cogitata Physica-Mathematica*. He believed that these special primes were: $p = 2, 3, 5, 7, 13, 17, 19, 31, 67, 127$, and 257. But like earlier attempts at determining prime numbers, many of Mersenne's numbers were in error. It took three centuries more to check Mersenne's range of numbers, and by 1947, the correct list of

Mersenne primes were: p = 2, 3, 5, 7, 13, 17, 19, 31, 61, 89, 107 and 127. Interestingly enough, even though Mersenne incorrectly stated certain numbers belonged to this group—he probably didn't verify all the numbers on his list—his name is still attached to the numbers.

#	Prime	Mersenne Prime	# of digits	Year Discovered
1	2	3	1	c. 500 B.C.E.
2	3	7	1	c. 500 B.C.E.
3	5	31	2	c. 275 B.C.E.
4	7	127	3	c. 275 B.C.E.
5	13	8,191	4	1456
6	17	131,071	6	1588
7	19	524,287	6	1588
8	31	2,147,483,647	10	1772
9	61	2,305,843,009,213,693,951	19	1883
10	89	618970019...449562111	27	1911
11	107	162259276...010288127	33	1914
12	127	170141183...884105727	39	1876
13	521	686479766...115057151	157	1952
14	607	531137992...031728127	183	1952
15	1,279	104079321...168729087	386	1952
16	2,203	147597991...697771007	664	1952
17	2,281	446087557...132836351	687	1952
18	3,217	259117086...909315071	969	1957
19	4,253	190797007...350484991	1,281	1961
20	4,423	285542542...6085880607	1,332	1961
21	9,689	478220278...225754111	2,917	1963
22	9,941	346088282...789463551	2,993	1963
23	11,213	281411201...696392191	3,376	1963
24	19,937	431542479...968041471	6,002	1971
25	21,701	448679166...511882751	6,533	1978
26	23,209	402874115...779264511	6,987	1979
27	44,497	854509824...011228671	13,395	1979
28	86,243	536927995...433438207	25,962	1982
29	110,503	521928313...465515007	33,265	1988
30	132,049	512740276...730061311	39,751	1983
31	216,091	746093103...815528447	65,050	1985
32	756,839	174135906...544677887	227,832	1992
33	859,433	129498125...500142591	258,716	1994

#	Prime	Mersenne Prime	# of digits	Year Discovered
34	1,257,787	412245773...089366527	378,632	1996
35	1,398,269	814717564...451315711	420,921	1996
36	2,976,221	623340076...729201151	895,932	1997
37	3,021,377	127411683...024694271	909,526	1998
38	6,972,593	437075744...924193791	2,098,960	1999
39	13,466,917	924947738...256259071	4,053,946	2001
40	20,996,011	125976895...855682047	6,320,430	2003
41*	24,036,583	299410429...733969407	7,235,733	2004
42*	25,964,951	122164630...577077247	7,816,230	2005
43*	30,402,457	315416475...652943871	9,152,052	2005
44*	32,582,657	124575026...053967871	9,808,358	2006
45*	37,156,667	202254406...308220927	11,185,272	2008
46*	42,643,801	169873516...562314751	12,837,064	2009
47*	43,112,609	316470269...697152511	12,978,189	2008

*Mersenne primes are not always discovered in order, as is the case here. There may be undiscovered Mersenne primes between the 40th and 47th, so the numbers here after 40 are provisional only.

What is **GIMPS**?

GIMPS stands for the Great Internet Mersenne Prime Search, a program started in January 1996 to discover new world-record-sized Mersenne prime numbers. It harnesses the power of the Internet—and thousands of small computers belonging to public and private concerns.

This worldwide volunteer computing project made history in 2009, when the Electronic Frontier Foundation awarded GIMPS a $100,000 Cooperative Computing Award. The award was for the August 23, 2008 discovery of the 47th known Mersenne prime (M47). This huge 12,978,189 digit number was found on a University of California (Los Angeles) computer in the GIMPS PrimeNet network. So far, the GIMPS project has discovered thirteen Mersenne primes, with the latest—the 47th found by Odd Magnar Strindmo from Melhus, Norway—on April 12, 2009.

Not only do the volunteers with GIMPS search for the elusive record Mersenne primes, but it also is used to verify others found. For example, by July 2010, seven years after the 40th known Mersenne prime was discovered, GIMPS members double-checked all the smaller Mersenne primes, and found no other primes. Thus, the "40th known Mersenne prime" became the "40th Mersenne prime."

The collaboration is still going on and, in fact, there are other awards for finding the various prime numbers. There are still two Cooperative Computing Awards up for grabs: the EFF award of $150,000 to the first person or group who discovered a prime

with at least 100 million digits. Another is the CCA for discovering a prime with at least a billion digits, a prize worth $250,000.

GIMPS uses around 8 MB of memory and 10 MB of disk space per personal computer, and the computer should be on most of the time. If you decide to join the GIMPS group, be patient—a test can take a while to complete. To find out how you can get involved with GIMPS, get on your computer, log on to the Internet, and type http://www.mersenne.org/prime.htm into your browser. You'll find directions for downloading the correct software right on the GIMPS site.

What **hypothesis** concerning **prime numbers** has finally been **proven**?

There are numerous hypotheses about prime numbers that have yet to be resolved. For example, since Euclid's time, it's been known that the sequence of prime numbers is infinite, but it is still unknown if an infinity of prime numbers p exists, such that $p + 2$ is also a prime number. And another one is that, on average, there are as many prime numbers for which the sum of decimal digits is even as prime numbers for which it is odd—or, more simply put, that the sum of digits of prime numbers is evenly distributed. This hypothesis was proposed by Russian mathematician Alexandre Gelfond in 1968, and now, it has been proven to be true. Why study such complex theories about prime numbers? Like many things in mathematics, such studies—besides being exciting to theoretical mathematicians—have important implications and applications in digital simulations and cryptography.

What are **exponents**?

Exponents are actually shorthand for multiplications, and represent the number of times a number is being multiplied—called the *base*. For example, $(9) \times (9) = 9^2$, or $9 \times 9 \times 9 = 9^3$.

Another way to describe this process is called "raising to a power," in which the exponent (a number as a superscript) is the "power." For example, 9^3 is "nine raised to the third power." It is also easier to write larger numbers with exponents. For instance, instead of writing $xxxx$, we can write x^4. (For more information about exponents, see "Algebra.")

How can we **simplify** various **expressions** using **exponents**?

The following are ways to solve simple mathematical expressions with the same base:

To multiply two numbers with different exponents, add the exponents:
$(x^2)(x^4) = (xx)(xxxx) = xxxxxx = x^{2+4} = x^6$

To raise a number with a power, multiply the exponents:
$(x^3)^3 = (x^3)(x^3)(x^3) = (xxx)(xxx)(xxx) = xxxxxxxxx = x^{(3 \times 3)} = x^9$

What **common mistake** is often made in **exponential equations**?

Unlike multiplication, exponents do not "distribute" over addition. For example, $(2 + 5)^2$ *does not* mean $2^2 + 5^2 = 4 + 25 = 29$. In this case, you add the numbers in the parentheses first, then square that number. The true answer to this equation is $(2 + 5)^2 = 7^2 = 49$.

What is a **base** in mathematics?

The term "base" has many meanings in the English language, including several that apply to the field of mathematics. When talking about sets, bases are the open sets whose union forms an abstract entity called a topological space. In geometry, the base represents the side of a polygon or polyhedron that is perceived as its bottom; when referring to an isosceles triangle, the base is the side that differs in length from the other two (thus, the base angles include the side that is thought of as the base). Algebraists also use the term base to describe either the number used with an exponent to create a power, such as $3^4 = 81$; or to write the same number as a subscript to a logarithm, such as $\log_3 81 = 4$. (For more information about logarithms, see "Algebra.")

One of the more familiar uses of the term base in mathematics deals with our numbering system, in which a base is a natural number whose powers are added to produce a specific number. For example, using 10 as a base, the number 2583.789 is actually $(2 \times 10^3) + (5 \times 10^2) + (8 \times 10^1) + (3 \times 10^0) + (7 \times 10^{-1}) + (8 \times 10^{-2}) + (9 \times 10^{-3})$.

How do you **convert** from the **binary to decimal system**—and vice versa?

Besides the decimal system, one of the most familiar number systems is the binary numeration system; this is mainly because of its use in computers (for more about computers, see "Math in Computing"). In a binary numeration system, only 1 and 0 are used, or a base 2 system. Converting between binary and decimal systems is fairly simple; just remember that each digit in the binary number represents a power of two.

The first column in the base two math is the *units column*, then the twos, fours, eights, etc. columns, all of which can only be filled with 0s or 1s. Since there is no single digit that stands for "2" in base 2, when you get to what stands for 2, you put a 1 in the 2's column and a 0 in the units column, creating one 2 and no 1s. Thus, the base ten "two" (2_{10} or just 2 in decimal form) is written in the binary as 10_2; a 3 (3_{10}, or just 3 in decimal form) in base 2 is actually "one 2 and one 1," or 11_2. The number 4 is actually 2×2, so you eliminate the 2's and unit columns and put a 1 in the 4s column. Thus, 4_{10} (or just 4 in decimal form) is written in binary form as 100_2. To see how computers "translate" decimal to binary numbers, here are the first ten conversions:

Decimal	Binary	Explanation
0	0	no 1s
1	1	one 1
2	10	one 2 and no 1s
3	11	one 2 and one 1
4	100	one 4, no 2s, and no 1s
5	101	one 4, no 2s, and one 1
6	110	one 4, one 2, and no 1s
7	111	one 4, one 2, and one 1
8	1000	one 8, no 4s, no 2s, and no 1s
9	1001	one 8, no 4s, no 2s, and one 1
10	1010	one 8, no 4s, one 2, and no 1s

How do you **express** certain numbers in **powers of ten** notation?

A number in power of ten notation is represented as a base number (or *mantissa*) times ten raised to some power (or *exponent*). This means the mantissa is multiplied by ten times the number of times the power indicates. For example, in the equation 32×10^4, the 32 is the mantissa multiplied by $10 \times 10 \times 10 \times 10$. This would equal 320,000.

Power of ten notation can also be used to express the same number in various ways. For example, the distance from the Earth to the Sun averages 93,000,000 miles. This can be represented by the following:

93,000,000

93×10^6

9.3×10^7

or 0.93×10^8, and so on.

Why do mathematicians and scientists often use **scientific notation**?

Scientific notation is a way of making larger and smaller numbers used in the scientific field easier to write, read, and take up less space in calculations. Scientists generally pick the power of ten that is multiplied by a number between 1 and 10 to express these numbers. For example, it is easier to write 0.00023334522 as 2.3334522×10^{-4}. To apply this to a scientific example, take the case of the average distance between the Earth and Sun, written in scientific notation as 9.3×10^7 miles—mathematically much easier to work with than the larger number it represents.

The following are several examples of large and small numbers in powers of ten notation similar to numbers used in scientific notation (note: numbers that are extremely small in scientific notation will have negative exponents):

748,000 can be represented by 7.48×10^5

245 can be represented by 2.45×10^2

The average distance between the Earth and the Sun is most easily expressed using powers of ten as 9.3×10^7.

−45,000 can be represented by $−4.5 \times 10^4$
0.025 can be represented by 2.5×10^{-2}
−0.0036 can be represented by $−3.6 \times 10^{-3}$
0.0000409 can be represented by 4.09×10^{-5}
0.0000000014 can be represented by 1.4×10^{-9}

What **prefixes** define the **powers of ten**?

Many standard prefixes are used to represent powers of ten, most of which are employed quite frequently to express various units. We are all familiar with some of them, including kilo- (from the Greek *chilioi*, or "a thousand"), milli- (from the Latin *mille*, or "thousand"), and micro- (from the Greek *mikros*, or "small"). The following chart defines some prefixes representing the powers of ten:

Multiple	Name
10^{18}	exa
10^{15}	peta
10^{12}	tera
10^9	giga
10^6	mega
10^3	kilo
10	deka
10^2	hecto

25

Multiple	Name
10^{-1}	deci
10^{-2}	centi
10^{-3}	milli
10^{-6}	micro
10^{-9}	nano
10^{-12}	pico
10^{-15}	femto
10^{-18}	atto

THE CONCEPT OF ZERO

What is a **placeholder**?

A *placeholder* is a number that, as the name implies, holds a place. Initially, various cultures used a placeholder—often a dot or a space—to show an empty spot or place not used in a numeral (or other way of counting). This was in place of what we now call a zero (0), a symbol that is not only a placeholder, but an essential number in our numeration system.

What are the **definitions** of **zero** and **non-zero**?

Those who use the Hindu-Arabic numeration system are all familiar with the concept of "zero" (0) and its importance. The symbol "zero" represents a valuable placeholder; it is also the additive identity element of an algebraic system (when a number and its additive inverse add up to 0); and finally, it is the starting point in measurements. The zero symbol is also called a cipher (no relation to sending secret messages) or the symbol for the absence of quantity, although be aware that cipher can also mean any Hindu-Arabic numeral. (Interestingly enough, the name "zero" is derived from the Arabic *sifr*, which means "cipher.") In other words, zero is naught (nothing, or from the Old English, nāwiht, meaning "not" [na] and "thing" [wiht]).

Mathematicians also use the word *non-zero* to represent a quantity that does not equal zero. A real non-zero number must either be positive or negative; a complex non-zero number can be the real or imaginary part of the equation. (For more information about complex numbers, see above.)

What is an **indeterminate number**?

Like many other fields, mathematics has terms that sometimes confuse or overlap. For example, it is interesting to note that there *is* such a number as 0/0, which is

called an *indeterminate* number. But be careful: This is not the same as an undefined number. If an indeterminate number comes up somewhere, you never know the value for your specific case—and you can conceivably give it any number of values. Confusing? Don't worry, you're not alone. It is one of those quandaries that often baffles the best mathematicians.

BASIC MATHEMATICAL OPERATIONS

What does an **equal sign represent**?

In standard arithmetic terms, the equal sign (=) is a symbol that represents two amounts with the same value. For example $7 = 7$; or $3 + 4 = 7$. When something is not equal, the sign is \neq, as in $2 \neq 3$ or $3 + 7 \neq 12$.

In a line of computer code, the equal sign can mean something much different. For example, for codes used under certain conditions, such as a JavaScript-reading computer, a single equal sign in a line of script means "is." There is even a double equal sign (= =) that means "is equal to," an important difference when writing code for the computer. In addition—and confusing as it may seem—the computer codes for "not equal" are different, and include ! = and / =.

What is **addition**?

Addition is an operation in which two numbers, called the *addends*, produce a third number called the *sum*. Natural numbers are added by starting with the first addend and counting as many more numbers as the second addend. For example, for $2 + 4$, you would think 2, 3 (as the first number after 2), 4 (as the second number), 5 (as the third number), and 6 (as the fourth number), thus the numbers add up to 6. Not all numbers are added in the same way as natural numbers.

What does **carry mean in addition**?

In addition, *carry* defines a way in which larger numbers are added. In this arithmetic operation, there is a shifting of leading digits into the next column to the left when the sum of that column exceeds a single digit. For example, carrying is evident in the following operation in the base 10 numbering system (adding addends 234 and 168 giving the sum 402):

$$\begin{array}{r} {\scriptstyle 1\ 1} \\ 234 \\ +\ 168 \\ \hline 402 \end{array}$$

27

When was the equal sign introduced into mathematics?

The equal sign (=) is a relatively "new" invention in mathematics. It was first used by British mathematician Robert Recorde (1510–1558; also seen erroneously as Record), in his book *The Whetstone of Witte* (1557), the first algebra book introduced in England. In it, he justifies using two parallel line segments "…bicause noe 2 thynges can be moare equalle (sic)…" ("because no two things can be more equal than parallel lines"). It was not an immediately popular symbol, though, with mathematicians continuing to use a range of symbols for equal, including two vertical parallel lines (‖) used by Wilhelm Xylander in 1575, and *ae* or *oe* (both from the word *aequalis*, the Latin for "equal"). But for the most part, the word "equal" was written in an equation until around 1600, when Recorde's symbol became more readily accepted, and it continues to be so today.

By adding the same columns, starting in the right hand column, 8 + 4 is 12, a number larger than 9, the highest number than can exist in that spot; carry the amount of ten to the next column, leaving 2; add 3 + 6 + 1 (which carried, represents 10 for this column), which equals 10, again a number larger than 9. Again, carry the one to the next column leaving 0; add the 2 + 1 + 1 (carried) equals 4. All total, the sum is 402.

How do you **subtract numbers**?

Subtraction is the "opposite" (or in set theory, the inverse) of addition: In its simplest form, one whole number is essentially taken away from another whole number. When you subtract numbers, you are answering the question of how many are left. For example, if 23 people leave a building that has 123 people (123 – 23), there would be 100 people left in the building.

What does **borrow mean** in **subtraction**?

Like "carry" in addition, to "borrow" in subtraction means to take amounts from one number and assign them to the next. In this procedure, the 10 is borrowed from the next higher digit column in order to obtain a positive difference in the nearby column. For example, borrowing is evident in the following operation in the base 10 numbering system (1,234 minus 567, giving the result of 667):

$$\begin{array}{r} 1\overset{1}{2}\overset{12}{\cancel{3}}\overset{1}{4} \\ -\ 567 \\ \hline 667 \end{array}$$

When you subtract the same columns, starting in the right hand column, the 4 is too small to subtract from 7; therefore, you need to borrow 10 from the column to the left, boosting the number 4 to 14. The column to the left then loses ten, and 2 is left. Again, the 2 is too small to subtract from 6, so 10 is borrowed from the next column to the left, boosting the number 2 to 12. The last number to the left is dropped down by 10, giving 11; the 5 is subtracted from the 11, resulting in 6 in that column.

Where did the **symbols plus** (+) and **minus** (−) **originate**?

One of the first books to use the plus and minus signs was written in 1489, Johann Widmann's (c. 1460–?) *Mercantile Arithmetic*. Originally, he used the signs + and – to indicate excesses and deficits (what we would call credit and debit) in business dealings. But some historians believe the + sign initially evolved from the French *et*, or "and," because the "e" and "t" resemble the + sign.

Although they were probably used before in general mathematics, the first person known to have used the + and − symbols in writing algebraic expressions lived in the early 1500s: the Dutch mathematician Vander Hoecke. The symbols finally went into general use in England when Robert Recorde's (1510–1558; also seen erroneously as Record) book *The Whetstone of Witte* was published; this is the same book responsible for bringing the equal (=) sign to the forefront of mathematics (see above).

What is **multiplication**?

Multiply comes from the Latin roots *multi* ("many") and *pli* ("folds"). English poet Geoffrey Chaucer (c. 1340–1400) may have used the word first as a verb in his *A Treatise on the Astrolab* (1391). In multiplication, two natural numbers are multiplied together (the numbers are called *factors*; the less used terms for two such numbers are multiplicand and multiplier) producing what is called a *product*. Multiplication is actually a form of repeated addition. For example, 2×3 means $2 + 2 + 2$ (or 6).

What are **multiplication tables**?

Multiplication tables are just as the name implies: a table of multiplication. Most of these tables have a specific purpose: mainly to multiply numbers in the rows and columns by each other to find a product.

English poet Geoffrey Chaucer may have used the word "multiplication" first as a verb in his *A Treatise on the Astrolab* (1391).

One of the simplest multiplication tables deal with the whole numbers. Here is one example:

0	1	2	3	4	5
1	1	2	3	4	5
2	2	4	6	8	10
3	3	6	9	12	15
4	4	8	12	16	20

Where did the **symbols** for **multiplication originate**?

The 17th century seems to have been the century when the basic mathematical symbols were developed. The best reasons for the development of such symbols make sense: they were faster and easier to write, took up less written space, and helped the printing process. Although the use of these symbols would eventually be standard—so everyone would understand the meaning of certain mathematical operations—it took a while for this to happen.

For example, in 1686, German mathematician Gottfried Wilhelm Leibniz (1646–1716) was using the symbol ∩ for multiplication and ∪ for division. Eventually, English mathematician and scientist Thomas Harriot (also seen as Hariot; 1560–1621) used the dot to indicate multiplication in his treatise *Artis anayticae praxis*, published posthumously in 1631. (He also developed the greater than [>] and less than [<] symbols). That same year, English mathematician William Oughtred (1575–1660) used the symbol "x" for multiplication in his book, *Clavis mathematicae*, in which he was also the first to mention the plus-minus symbol (\pm).

Today, we use a number of symbols for multiplication operations. The most common symbols are \times, *, ·, and (), as in 2×3, 2*3, 2 · 3, and (2)(3).

How is the term **inverse** used in **arithmetic operations**?

Inverse operations are those that "undo" another operation. In particular, subtraction is the inverse of addition because $a + b - b = a$; division is also the inverse operation to multiplication.

The *inverse of a number* can be expressed as follows: The additive inverse of a real or complex number a is the number that, when added to a, equals 0. In multiplication, the multiplicative inverse of a is the number that, when multiplied by a, equals 1.

What is **division**?

The word divide comes from the Latin root *vidua* (referring to a separation; the word "divide" shares its major root with the word "widow") and *di*, a prefix that is a contrac-

Why can't you divide by zero?

Dividing by zero is like the old saying, "You can't get something from nothing." Mathematically speaking, it's the same way: You can't "divide by nothing." In fact, when something is divided by zero, the answer is always undefined.

Here are a few ways of looking at this: There is a rule in arithmetic that a(b/a) = b. So if we say that 1/0 = 5, then 0(1/0) = 0 × 5 = 0. In other words, if you could divide by 0, this rule would not work. Another way to look at the "no to 0 as a divisor" problem is through multiplication: if 10/2 = 5, we know that 5 × 2 = 10; the same for 5/1 = 5, thus we know that 5 × 1 = 5. But if you take 5/0, that would mean that the answer times 0 would equal 5, but anything times 0 is equal to zero. Because there is no answer to this dilemma, mathematicians say you can't divide by zero.

tion of *dis*, meaning "apart" or "away." In division, the number being divided is called the *dividend*, while the number dividing is called the *divisor*. The end result is called the *quotient*. For example, in 20/5 = 4, 20 is the dividend, 5 the divisor, and 4 the quotient.

Division in mathematics is a relatively new concept for the masses; it was only taught at university levels after the 16th century. The first to offer division to the public was German mathematician Adam Ries (1492–1559; also seen as Risz, Riesz, Riese, or Ris) in his work *Rechenung nach der lenge, auff den Linihen vnd (sic) Feder*, often shortened to *Practica*. His work reached more people for an important reason: Instead of the usual practice of writing a mathematical book in Latin, he wrote his book in German, thus reaching a wider audience.

Where did the **symbols for division originate**?

The history behind the division symbols is long and complicated. The following lists how the major ones developed:

Closed parentheses—The arrangement "8)24" was used by Michael Stifel (1486 or 1487–1567) in *Arithmetica integra*, published in 1544. It eventually evolved into the closed parentheses, such as (8)(4).

The obelus—By 1659, Swiss mathematician Johann Heinrich Rahn (1622–1676) introduced the division symbol (÷, called an *obelus*) in his book *Teutsche Algebra*, a combination of ":" and "–". (This division symbol was used by many writers before Rahn as a minus sign.) In 1668, when Rahn's book was translated into English, with additions by English mathematician John Pell (1610–1685), the division symbol was retained. Some say Pell great-

ly influenced Rahn to develop the symbol, but most historians agree that there is little evidence of such a connection.

Slash—Another sign for division (/), the slash is actually first used for fractions, such as 2/3 or 1/2. It can be extended into other, larger or smaller numbers, such as 123/112 and 0.112/0.334. Little is known about its origins, but it is known that this symbol was sometimes used for subtraction, until it became standard practice for representing division.

How did the **symbols** for **long division** develop?

In the 19th century, U.S. textbooks typically showed long division with the divisor, dividend, and quotient on the same line, separated by parentheses, as 36)108(3. In the same century, in examples of short division, a vinculum (line) was placed under the dividend, with the vinculum almost attached to the bottom of the parenthesis. The quotient was written under the vinculum, as per the following:

$$5\overline{)455}$$
$$91$$

By late in the 19th century, the vinculum is almost attached to the top of the parenthesis and the quotient is written above the vinculum, as per the following:

$$91$$
$$5\overline{)455}$$

These symbols are similar to what we see in our elementary dealings with long division, but our vinculum is attached to the parenthesis. Interestingly enough, there is no name for the symbol used for long division ($\overline{)}$).

What is the **least common multiple** and **denominator**?

The smallest common multiple (whole number) of two or more whole numbers is called the *lowest (or least) common multiple (LCM)*. For example, for the numbers 3 and 8, the multiples of 8 are 8, 16, 24, 32, and so on; the multiples of 3 are 3, 6, 9, 12, 15, 18, 21, 24, 27, and so on. Therefore, the LCM of 3 and 8 is 24.

The least common denominator (or LCD) is mainly used to carry out the addition or subtraction of fractions. In order to do these operations, the fractions need to have the same denominator. (For more information about fractions, see below.) The easiest way to work on such calculations is to determine the lowest number possible for the denominator—a number called the least common denominator (LCD)—which is actually the common factor by which two numbers are divisible. For example, to add 1/6 and 1/8, we have to find the least common multiple of the denominators. In this case, the number is 24: Multiply 1/6 × 4/4 and 1/8 × 3/3, to change each addend to

some number of "24ths"; or $1/6 \times 4/4 = 4/24$; and $1/8 \times 3/3 = 3/24$. Thus, $1/6 + 1/8 = 4/24 + 3/24 = (4+3)/24 = 7/24$.

What is the **root** of a number?

The root of a real or complex number is a number that, when raised to some exponent (or multiplied by itself the number of times indicated by the exponent), equals the original number. Most people are familiar with square and cube roots. There are actually many other such roots, including the real fourth roots, real fifth roots, and so on, and roots associated with complex numbers. For example, the real fourth roots of 16 are 2 and –2; the real fifth root of –32 is –2.

What are **square** and **square roots**?

When you multiply a real or complex number by itself, you are actually squaring that number. Mathematicians express the square of a number using the superscript 2, or, for example, 2^2. The square of a real number is always positive, whether the number is 2^2 (= 4) or -2^2 (= 4; a negative times a negative equals a positive real number).

A square root is a number that when multiplied by itself equals a specific product. For example, if $t^2 = s$, then $t = \pm \sqrt{s}$, in which t is the square root and s is a positive number. For example, the two square roots of 16 ($\sqrt{16}$) are 4 and -4, as $4^2 = 16$ and $-4^2 = 16$.

What are a **cube** and **cube root**?

Much like a square, a cube is when you multiply a real or complex number by twice itself (making a total of three numbers). Mathematicians express the cube of a number using the superscript 3; or, for example, 2^3, or $2 \times 2 \times 2$. Unlike a square of a number, the cube of a number will not always be positive, such as $-3 \times -3 \times -3$, which equals -9.

A cube root is a number that when multiplied by itself two more times has the product of s, in which $t^3 = s$. For example, the cube root of 125 (s) is 5 (t), or written as $\sqrt[3]{125} = 5$; the cube root of -125 is -5.

What does a **factor** and **factorization** mean?

A *factor* is a portion of a quantity that when multiplied by other factors gives the entire quantity (or product). In order to determine such factors (or divisors), you have to use *factorization* (also called *factoring* or *to factor*). When factoring an integer, it is referred to as prime factorization; when factoring a polynomial, it is called polynomial factorization.

What is **prime factorization**?

Many of us are most familiar with prime factorization, which is a way of taking a number and breaking it down into its constituent primes. An example of prime factorization is as follows: One finds the "simplest" representation of the given quantity in terms of smaller parts—in the case of 15, the factors would be 1, 3, 5, and 15 (essentially, all the numbers that will divide integrally into 15). Not that prime factorization is always that easy. Larger numbers make it more difficult to factor, and many sophisticated prime algorithms have been devised for larger—and different types—of numbers.

What does the **greatest common factor** mean?

The *greatest common factor* (or GCF; sometimes called highest common factor) of two whole numbers is the largest whole number that is a factor of both. Take, for example, the numbers 12 and 15: The factors of 12 are 1, 2, 3, 4, 6, and 12; the factors of 15 are 1, 3, 5, and 15. Therefore, the common factors—or numbers in both lists of factors—are 1 and 3; therefore, the greatest (highest) common factor is 3.

There is another method used to discover the GCF: listing the numbers' prime factors, then multiplying those numbers. For example, the prime factorization of 12 and 15 are: $2 \times 2 \times 3 = 12$ and $3 \times 5 = 15$. Notice that the prime numbers have 3 in common; thus, the GCF is 3.

An example with larger numbers is to find the GCF of 36 and 54. Working it out by the first method, the factors of 36 are 1, 2, 3, 4, 6, 9, 12, 18, and 36; the factors of 54 are 1, 2, 3, 6, 9, 18, 27, and 54. The greatest (or highest) common factor of both numbers is 18. To work it out using prime factorization, the prime factorization of 36 is $2 \times 2 \times 3 \times 3$; the prime factorization of 54 is $2 \times 3 \times 3 \times 3$. Both these factorizations have one 2 and two 3s in common; thus, we multiply those common numbers, or $2 \times 3 \times 3 = 18$.

FRACTIONS

What are **proper** and **improper fractions**?

The word "fraction" to most of us means a part of something; in mathematics, it represents a type of numeral, in most cases the quotient of two integers, with the top number called the *numerator* (the number of parts) and the bottom number the *denominator* (how many parts the whole is divided into). Written, the numerator and denominator are separated by a "/" or "—". A fraction is usually denoted by a/b, in which "a" and "b" are whole numbers and "b" is not equal to zero (for the explanation of why you cannot divide by zero, see above).

A rational number between 0 and 1 can be represented by fractions (by the division of two numbers). If the quotient is less than one, such as 1/2 or 2/5, then it is

Proper fractions are used to express parts of a whole. For example, in this photo there are four apples but only one red apple. One in four, or 1/4, of the apples is a red apple. In an improper fraction, the numerator is larger than the denominator, such as 4/3 or 3/2.

called a *proper fraction*; if the quotient is greater than one—or in other words, if the numerator of a fraction is larger than the denominator, such as 23/7—it is called an *improper fraction*.

How are **fractions converted to decimals** and vice-versa?

In the most commonly used place value, the decimal system, numbers smaller than 1 can be expressed as fractions, called *decimal fractions*. In this system, the decimal fractions are expressed in terms of tenths, hundredths, thousandths, and so on. For example, for the fraction 1/2, or 1 divided by 2, the decimal fraction is 0.5; and vice versa, the decimal fraction 0.5, or 5/10ths, is equal to 1/2.

Not all fractions are so easily converted to decimals. It depends on the type of number, especially if it is an irrational or rational number. Some decimal fractions include an infinite number of decimal places to be expressed exactly; something that is not possible as far as we know (who can write an infinite number of numbers?). And some decimal fractions repeat forever, such as 1/3 = 0.3333....

What are the **rules** for **adding and subtracting fractions**?

When adding fractions, the denominators need to be the same, but you can't add the denominators to get the answer. Simply put, if the denominators are already the same, the fractions are simple to add, such as 1/3 + 1/3 = (1 + 1)/3 = 2/3. If the denominators are not the same, find the common denominator by multiplication. For example, 1/2 + 1/3 = 3/6 + 2/6 = (3 + 2)/6 = 5/6.

When subtracting fractions, the denominators again need to be the same; and you can't add (or subtract) the denominators to get the answer. If the denominators are the same, subtract the fractions, such as $2/3 - 1/3 = (2 - 1)/3 = 1/3$. If the denominators are not the same, find the common denominator by multiplication, such as $1/2 - 1/3 = 3/6 - 2/6 = (3 - 2)/6 = 1/6$.

What are the **rules** for **multiplying and dividing fractions**?

As to be expected, there are rules for multiplying and dividing fractions. Multiplication of factions is very straight forward—just multiply the numerators and denominators, then simplify the resulting fraction, if needed (or if you can). For example, $2/5 \times 4/7 = (2 \times 4) / (5 \times 7) = 8/35$ (this number cannot be simplified).

Division of fractions entails one main rule: You need to flip over, or invert, the "divisor" fraction (the fraction on the bottom) to get the result (this is also called the reciprocal of the fraction; see below). Here are the steps: First change the division sign to a multiplication sign after inverting the fraction to the right of the sign. Multiply the numerators and denominators and write the result. You can then simplify or reduce the fraction if needed. For example, $1/2 \div 1/4 = 1/2 \times 4/1 = 4/2$. This number can be simplified to 2.

How are **decimal fractions added, subtracted, multiplied, and divided**?

Decimal fractions are added, subtracted, multiplied and divided much like whole numbers—but with decimal differences. The following gives some examples: Adding such numbers as $0.3 + 0.2$ is simple: $0.3 + 0.2 = 0.5$. Adding whole and decimal fractions is also easy: $2.4 + 5 = 7.4$. These numbers are also easy to subtract, such as $0.3 - 0.2 = 0.1$. Multiplication and division are also similar to regular numbers, although the placement of the decimal point is ever-important. For example, multiplying $24.45 \times 0.002 = 0.0489$; dividing the same numbers $24.45/.002 = 12,225$. (It's interesting to note here a "mathematical surprise": In the last example, dividing the small numbers equaled a much larger number—the opposite of what most of us would expect.)

What are unit fractions and how are they tied to ancient Egypt?

A *unit fraction* is one that has a numerator of 1, such as 1/2, 1/4, and 1/43545. One of the earliest discussions of unit fractions—a table of representations of 1/n—was found on the famous Rhind papyrus (also called the Rhind Mathematical Papyrus), dated to around 1650 B.C.E. This record—a table copied by the Egyptians from another papyrus dated 200 years earlier—represented a sum of distinct unit fractions for odd "n" numbers between 5 and 101. To write a certain fraction, they would add combinations of 1/n. For example, instead of writing 2/5, they wrote 1/3 + 1/15; for 2/29, they wrote 1/24 + 1/58 + 1/174 + 1/232.

Because of the Rhind papyrus discovery, the sums of unit fractions are now called *Egyptian fractions*. No one truly knows why the Egyptians chose this method for representing fractions, but some historians believe it was a "wrong turn" in Egyptian mathematical history. Whatever the reason, the Egyptians (apparently successfully) used this system for 2,000 years.

How do you **reduce a fraction**?

To reduce a fraction, there are three general steps: factor the numerator, factor the denominator, and cancel out the *fractional mixes* that have the value of one. The leftover number is the reduced fraction. For example, to reduce 16/56, factor the numerator ($16 = 2 \times 2 \times 2 \times 2$) and factor the denominator ($56 = 2 \times 2 \times 2 \times 7$); eliminate the 2s (2/2 equals 1):

$$\frac{16}{56} = \frac{2 \times 2 \times 2 \times 2}{2 \times 2 \times 2 \times 7} = \frac{2}{7}$$

How do you find an **equivalent fraction**?

An equivalent fraction—also called a "building fraction"—is the reverse of reducing the fraction: Instead of searching for the 1 in the fractional mix that you can reduce, you insert a 1 and build the fractions. For example, find the equivalent fraction for 1/4, using the number 3, multiply the numerator and denominator by 3 (3/3 = 1); 1/4 × 3/3 = 1 × 3/ 4 × 3 = 3/12; therefore the equivalent fraction in this case is 1/4 = 3/12 (the equal sign is used to represent equivalent fractions).

What is the **reciprocal** of a number?

The reciprocal of a number is obtained when a given number is divided into 1: the results are called the reciprocal of that number. For example, the reciprocal of 6 is 1

divided by 6, or 1/6. Reciprocals come in most handy when dividing fractions (see above to learn more about dividing fractions).

FOUNDATIONS OF MATHEMATICS

FOUNDATIONS AND LOGIC

What are the **foundations of mathematics**?

The foundations of mathematics include how to formulate and analyze the language (you have to "speak" the right mathematical language to make meaningful mathematical statements), axioms (a statement accepted as true without proof), and developing logical methods in all mathematical studies. The most basic mathematical concepts in the foundations include numbers, shapes, sets, functions, algorithms, axioms, definitions, and proofs.

Why do so many **philosophers study** the **foundations of mathematics**?

There are three underlying reasons why philosophers often study the foundations of mathematics. First, these foundations have always been a part of scientific thought, with the abstract nature of mathematical objects offering unusual and often unique philosophical quandaries. Second, the subject offers a high level of technical sophistication, allowing philosophers to develop connections between models and patterns, laying the groundwork for many other sciences. And finally, the foundations of mathematics provides ways for philosophers (and mathematicians) to try out general philosophical doctrines in a specific scientific context.

What is **logic**?

Although it closely resembles mathematics (and is sometimes used as a basis for it), logic is a branch of knowledge or inquiry that is separate from mathematics and the sciences, but is still used by both fields in various ways. Simply put, logic is described

A bust of the Greek philosopher Aristotle, whose work *Organon* is the earliest known to introduce systematic logic, the foundation of mathematical logic.

as the systematic study of well-founded inference, in which there is a definite distinction between logical validity (also known as the formal properties of the inference process) and truth. This also means that a true result may come from an invalid argument (see below for definition of an argument). For example, "all cats are cute; Fluffer is a cat; therefore, Fluffer is cute," is a valid inference; whereas, "all cats are cute; Fluffer is cute; therefore, Fluffer is a cat," is an invalid inference, even if Fluffer really is a cat.

What is the **historical basis** for **mathematical logic**?

Most mathematicians believe that systematic logic began with Aristotle's collection of works titled *Organon* (*Tool*), in which he introduced his ideas on logic. In particular, Aristotle used general forms to describe logic, such as if all x are y; and all y are z; then all x are z. He presented three laws basic to all valid thought: the law of identity, or A is A (for example, an acorn will always yield a oak tree and nothing else); the law of contradiction, or A cannot be both A and not A (for example, an honest woman cannot be a thief); and the law of the excluded middle, or either or, in which A must either be A or not A (for example, a dog can be brown or not brown). In fact, author Ayn Rand divided her novel *Atlas Shrugged* into three parts after these three principles, as a tribute to Aristotle.

Was **mathematics** always based on a **logical foundation**?

No, not all of mathematics was always based on a logical foundation, but some ancient cultures did develop certain aspects of logic in their thought. The Greeks were probably one of the first cultures to understand logic's role in mathematics and philosophy, and studied the subject extensively. For example, geometry, as presented by Greek mathematician Euclid (c. 325–c. 270 B.C.E.), had some foundations in logic. Greek scientist and philosopher Aristotle's (384–322 B.C.E.) rules for syllogisms were also based on logic, and he wrote the first systematic treatise on logic. But his logic works were based on ordinary language—making them a matter of interpretation and subject to ambiguities.

It was not until the development of calculus that most of mathematics was put on a logical foundation. By the 17th century, people like German mathematician Gottfried Wilhelm Leibniz (1646–1716) began to demand a more regular and symbolic

What is an argument?

In logic, an argument is not a "heated discussion," although some mathematicians may argue over the validity of certain mathematical arguments. In this sense, an argument is a list of statements called *premises*, followed by a statement called the *conclusion*. Generally, an argument is valid if the conjunction of its premises implies its conclusion; stated differently, validity means that if all the premises are true, then so is the conclusion. But remember: The validity of an argument does not guarantee the truth of its premises, and thus it does not guarantee the truth of its conclusion. It only guarantees that if the premises are true, the conclusion will be true.

way to express logic. Logic truly became a part of mathematics around the mid–19th century, especially with the 1847 publication of English mathematician George Boole's (1815–1864) *The Mathematical Analysis of Logic* and English mathematician Augustus De Morgan's (1806–1871) *Formal Logic*. Thus, mathematics began to encompass symbolic logic, with precise rules to manipulate those symbols (see below for more about symbolic logic).

Of course, nothing is perfect, although mathematicians in the late 19th and early 20th centuries hoped it would be. They believed that all of mathematics could be described using symbolic logic and made purely formal. But in the 1930s, Austrian-American mathematician and logician Kurt Gödel (1906–1978) put a damper on such an idea by showing that not all truths could be derived by a formal logic system.

What were **Aristotle's contributions** to logic?

Aristotle contributed syllogisms and propositions to the world of logic—in other words, the verbal versions of the formal deductive rules for logic. Aristotle believed that any logical argument could be explained in these standard forms. Today, we call these ideas Aristotelian logic, whereas Aristotle would have called it "analytics;" he would have referred to the term "logic" as "dialectics." Although syllogisms are attributed to Aristotle, no doubt others came up with the same ideas with different ways of expressing them. But his teachings were well-known, even in his time. Thus, syllogistic logic would dominate Western cultural thought for more than 2,000 years.

Aristotle's six books—*Categories*, *On Interpretation*, *Prior Analytics*, *Posterior Analytics*, *Topics*, and *On Sophistical Refutations*—were compiled around 1 B.C.E. Some historians don't believe all the writings should be totally attributed to Aristotle, but were changed over time by teachers, lecturers, and students who studied his works. It is also thought that the books were used extensively in the school founded by Aristotle at the Lyceum (a form of educational school). The collection of books is often

An example of a syllogism.

called the *Organon*, the name given by the followers of Aristotle (often referred to as the Peripatetics).

What are **subjects and predicates** found in Aristotelian logic?

Aristotelian logic is more like an English lesson: one subject and one predicate are used in a sentence (called a proposition). The *subject* is usually an individual entity (an object, house, city, man, animal); or it may be a class of entities (objects, houses, cities, men, animals). The *predicate* is the property or mode of existence that does or does not exist with a given subject. For example, a singular plant (subject) may or may not be blooming (predicate); all houses (subject) may or may not have two stories (predicate).

What do the terms **propositions and syllogisms** mean in Aristotelian logic?

There is a great deal to Aristotelian logic—too much to mention in this text. But overall, there are some general terms and properties. For example, propositions are sentences with two terms—a grammatical subject and predicate. A proposition has the properties of quality and quantity only. They can either be a negative or positive proposition in terms of quality; in terms of quantity, they are either universal or particular propositions. That means the four types of propositions are: universal affirmative (for example, "all men are mortal"); universal negative (for example, "no men are mortal"); particular affirmative (for example, "some men are strong"); and particular

What erroneous logic statement is often attributed to Aristotle?

It's interesting to note that the classical syllogism is, "All men are mortal. Socrates is a man. Therefore Socrates is mortal." But in reality, this is wrong, and is actually called a *Peripatetic syllogism*, a form not used by Aristotle. In fact, in Aristotelian logic, there are no singular terms. A more apt statement of Aristotelian logic would be "If all men are mortal, and all Greeks are men, then all Greeks are mortal." To break part of this sentence down, in "All Greeks are men," the "Greeks" is the subject, and the "men" is the predicate.

negative (for example, "some men are not mortal"). In most texts, these four proposition types are denoted by the letters *A*, *E*, *I*, and *O*, respectively.

Syllogisms are composed of two premises and a conclusion; the conclusion comes from the two premises in a certain way. Apparently, Aristotle liked to name his logical offerings, so each word in the syllogism has a label. He said that each premise must have a term in common, which he called the *middle term*. The other terms he called *extreme terms*, divided into the *major term*, or the predicate of the conclusion and *minor term*, or subject of the conclusion. And logically, of course, the premise with the minor term is called the *minor premise*, and the one with the major term is called the *major premise*. Aristotle further divided the syllogisms into *perfect syllogisms* ("…which needs nothing other than what has been stated to make plain what necessarily follows…") and *imperfect syllogisms* ("…needs either one or more propositions, which are indeed the necessary consequence of the terms set down, but have not been expressly stated as premises…").

Who invented a way of analyzing syllogisms?

In 1880, English logician John Venn (1834–1923) presented a method to analyze syllogisms, now known as Venn diagrams. Venn initially criticized such diagrams in works by his contemporaries, especially those of English mathematicians George Boole (1815–1864) and Augustus De Morgan (1806–1871). But in 1880, Venn introduced his own, now famous, version of the diagrams in his paper *On the Diagrammatic and Mechanical Representation of Prepositions and Reasonings*. By 1881, along with correcting Boole's work, Venn further elaborated on the diagrams in his book, *Symbolic Logic*. Today we are most familiar with Venn diagrams in connection with understanding sets.

Although Venn is credited with the diagrams, he was not the first person to use such geometric methods to represent syllogistic logic. German mathematician Gottfried Wilhelm Leibniz (1646–1716) used such graphic representations in his work. And even Swiss mathematician Leonhard Euler (1707–1783) is known to have presented diagrams that had a definite "Venn-ish" look a century before John Venn.

43

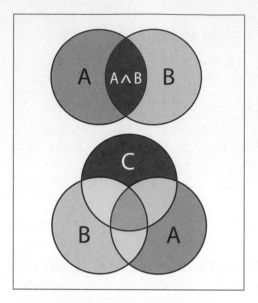

In these examples of Venn diagrams, the top illustration represents an order-two diagram, and the bottom is an order-three diagram.

What are some **examples** of **Venn diagrams**?

Venn diagrams are schematic illustrations used in logic theory to show collections of sets and the relationship between them. Overlapping circles represent the sets (or the subjects and predicates in syllogistic logic); the standard way of presenting such diagrams include the intersection of two (order-two diagram) to three (order-three diagram) circles. Based on what circles intersect and the areas shaded, a conclusion about the sets may then be read directly from the diagram. Such illustrations can include the union of two sets, the intersection of two sets, the complement of a set, and the complement of the union of two sets. (For more information about sets, see "Set Theory," below.)

MATHEMATICAL AND FORMAL LOGIC

What is **mathematical logic**?

Mathematical logic is not the logic of mathematics, but is really the mathematics of logic composed of those parts of logic that can be modeled mathematically. Overall, it was invented to understand and present the work of Austrian-American mathematician and logician Kurt Gödel (1906–1978) and his interpretation of the foundations of mathematics in the early 20th century. Although mathematicians use mathematical logic to have rational and reasonable discussions of the many issues in the foundations of mathematics, not everything is agreed upon.

What is **intuitionism**?

There are some people within philosophy and mathematics who reject the formalism of mathematics and believe in *intuitionism*, which says that words and formulas have significance only as a reflection of the mind's activity. Intuitionists believe that a theorem is meaningful only if it represents a mental construction of a mathematical or logical entity. This is different from the classical approach that states that the exis-

What contributions did David Hilbert make to mathematics?

German mathematician David Hilbert (1862–1943) contributed a great deal to mathematical logic, as well as mathematics in general. In 1890 his proof of the theorem of invariants replaced earlier work on the subject and paved the way for modern algebraic geometry; by 1897, his algebraic number theory lead to many developments in that field. His contributions also included discoveries in number theory, mathematical logic, differential equations, multivariable calculus, Euclidean geometry, and even mathematical (theoretical) physics.

Hilbert is most well-known for presenting "Hilbert's problems," which originally were a set of 23 unsolved mathematical problems that he hoped would eventually lead to many more disciplines within the field of mathematics. His idea worked: As mathematicians attempted to solve the problems, their efforts led to mathematical discoveries in the 20th century, although a number of the problems have yet to be solved.

tence of an entity can be proven by refuting its non-existence. For example, if you said "A or B" to an intuitionist, he or she believes that either A or B can be proved; but if you said, "A or not A," this is not allowed, since you cannot assume that it is always possible to either prove or disprove statement A.

What is a **proposition** in **mathematical logic**?

A *proposition* in mathematical logic is a statement that can be proven to be either true or false. For example, if you say, "the bear is black," that is a proposition; but the statement "the bear is x," cannot be true or false until a particular value for x is chosen; therefore, it is not a proposition.

What is **symbolic logic**?

Symbolic logic (also called formal logic) is mainly concerned with the structure of reasoning. It determines the meaning and relationship of statements used to represent specific mathematical concepts and provides a means to compose proofs of statements. Symbolic logic draws most notably on set theory. It uses variables combined by operations such as *not* or *and*, and assigns symbols to such ("~" and "&", respectively).

What is **propositional calculus**?

Propositional calculus is not the calculus most of us hear about, but is considered by many to be the foundation of symbolic logic. (Actually, the term "calculus" is a generic name for any area of mathematics that deals with calculating; thus, arithmetic could

be called the "calculus of numbers.") Also known as truth-functional analysis, sentential calculus, or the calculus of propositions (or as seen above, any declarative sentence that is either true or false), propositional calculus deals with statements that can be assigned *truth values*. In general, it uses symbols to denote logical operators (such as *and* and *or*), and parentheses for grouping formulas.

What are **truth values** and **truth functions**?

As seen above, when discussing propositional calculus, a proposition is any declarative sentence that is either true (T) or false (F). Mathematicians refer to T or F as the *truth value* of the statement.

The combinations of such statements are known as *truth functions*, with their true values determined from the overall true values of their contents. Truth-functional analysis includes the following logical operators:

Negation—The negation of a statement is false if the original statement is true, and true if the original statement is false; it refers to "it is not the case that" or simply "not" in natural language.

Conjunction—The conjunction of two statements is true only if both are true and false in all other instances; it refers to "and" in natural language.

Alteration—Alteration (or disjunction) of two statements is false only if both are false and true in all other instances; it refers to "or" (and "either … or") in natural language.

Conditional—Conditional (or implication) is false only if the antecedent is true and the consequent is false, and is true in all other instances; it refers to "if … then" or "implies" in natural language.

Biconditional—Biconditional (double implication or bi-implication) is true only if the two statements have the same value, either true or false; it refers to "if and only if…" in natural language.

What is a **truth table**?

A truth table is a two-dimensional array of truth values derived by determining the validity of arguments through assigning all possible combinations of truth values to the statements. This simple form of logic depends on a combination of certain statements, using terms such as "not" or "and," along with the input values.

The first columns correspond to the possible input values and the last columns to the operations being performed; the rows list all possible combinations of true (T) or false (F) inputs, together with the corresponding outputs. The following is a truth table for the three most common binary operations of logic ("if…then," "or," "and"), using *s* and *t* as the statements:

> ## Why are truth tables important to computers?
>
> In many ways, truth tables are directly connected to digital logic circuits; in the case of computers, the terms would be AND, OR, NAND, NOR, NOT, XOR, or the "gates" that open and close in response to such terms. In such a circuit, values at each point can take on values of only true (1) or false (0); this is also known as the computer binary system. In general, there is also a *three-valued logic*, in which possible values are true, false, and "undecided." A further generalization called *fuzzy logic* examines the "truth" as a continuous quantity ranging from 0 to 1. (For more about fuzzy logic and computers, see "Math in Computing.")

s	t	if s, then t	s or t	s and t
T	T	T	T	T
T	F	F	T	F
F	T	T	T	F
F	F	T	F	F

What are **logical operators** in **truth tables**?

Logical operators in truth tables include such words as "and" or "or," which are all represented by certain symbols (for more about logical operators in predicate calculus, see below). For example, "and" (also called the conjunction operator) is also referred to as a *binary operator*. It is one of the most useful logical operators, as in "p AND q", represented by the symbols ∧ or &. The "or" (also called the disjunction operator) is also a binary operator, as in "p OR q", and represented by the symbols ∨ and |. The "not" (also called the negation or inversion) operator is known as a *unary operator*, and is represented by the symbols ~ or ¬ (in computer programming, NOT is often represented by the !). The "implies" (or implication operator) is also a binary operator; its symbols include ∴, ⊃, and Ã.

But note: Not all logical operators seem to represent words the way we are accustomed to using them, and many times they seem to contradict their proper definitions. But in a truth table, the logical operator means what it means—without the usual nuances of the English language.

What is a **formula**?

In mathematics, a formula is generally a rule, principle, or fact that is displayed in terms of mathematical symbols. (Although the Latin plural form of formula is "formulae," "formulas" is the accepted common use in mathematics.) These equations express a definite, fixed relationship between certain quantities (usually expressed by

letters), with their relationship indicated by algebraic symbols. For example, scientist Albert Einstein's famous $E = mc^2$ is a formula representing energy (E) equal to mass (m) times the speed of light (c) squared. The word "formula" is also used in logic; it is written as a propositional or sentential formula, or "a formula in propositional calculus is one that uses 'and,' 'or,' and so on."

What is **predicate calculus**?

Predicate calculus (also called first-order logic, functional calculus, or quantification theory) is a theory in symbolic logic that uses statements such as "there exists an object such that…" or "for all objects, it is the case that…". It is a much more solid theory than propositional calculus, taking the interrelationship between sentences much further, but it is weaker than certain branches of mathematics, such as arithmetic and set theory.

What is a **quantifier** in **predicate calculus**?

A sentence or many sentences containing a variable (such as x) can be made into true or false propositions simply by using a *quantifier*. The quantifier actually assigns a truth value to the sentence, depending on the set of values allowed for that variable. There are two major quantifiers: the existential and universal quantifiers, which are

represented by the logical operator symbols of ∀ and ∃, respectively, although there are more exotic types of logic that use different quantifiers.

How is **predicate calculus interpreted**?

Predicate calculus may be a general system of logic, but it accurately expresses a large variety of assertions and provides many types of reasoning. It is definitely more flexible than Aristotle's syllogisms and more useful (in many cases) than propositional calculus.

Predicate calculus makes heavy use of symbolic notation, using lower-case letters $a, b, c, ..., x, y, z, ...$ to denote the subject (in predicate calculus, often referred to as "individuals"); upper-case letters $M, N, P, Q, R, ...$ to denote predicates. The simplest of assertions are formed by moving the predicate with the subject.

For example, using the "all" quantifier means that when you have an arbitrary variable, you must prove something true about that variable, and then prove that it does not matter what variable you chose, it will always be true. Thus, from propositional calculus, the sentence, "All humans are mortal," becomes in predicate calculus, "All things x are such that, if x is a human, then x is a mortal." This sentence may also be written symbolically under predicate calculus. (To compare, the sentence "x is a human" is not a statement in propositional calculus [see above] because it involves an unknown entity x; therefore, a truth value cannot be assigned without knowing what x represents.)

What are **logical operators** in **predicate calculus**?

Predicate calculus commonly uses seven special symbols—called *logical operators*—to express a formula (in this case, a formula is a meaningful expression built up from atomic formulas by repeated application of the logical operators). The following table lists the symbols and their meanings. (Note: Many of these symbols are also used as logical operators in truth tables; see below.)

Logical Operators in Predicate Calculus

Symbol	Name	Usage	Meaning*
&	conjunction	... & ...	"both ... and ..."
∨	disjunction	... ∨ ...	"either ... or ... (or both)"
~	negation	~...	"it is not the case that ..."
⊃	implication	... ⊃ ...	"if ... then ..."
≡	bi-implication	... ≡ ...	"... if and only if ..."
∀	universal quantifier	∀x ...	"for all x, ..."
∃	existential quantifier	∃x ...	"there exists x such that ..."

*Where x is any variable

What is the **atomic formula** of **predicate calculus**?

The atomic formula of predicate calculus is when a predicate and special case of a subject (individual) are written together. For example, if M is the predicate "to be a human," and b is the subject (individual) "Socrates," then Mb means the assertion "Socrates is a human." This atomic formula is phrased "b is the argument of M." Thus, M, as the predicate, may be applied to any subject, and that subject is then an argument of M. But if c is the subject "Vermont," then Mc is a false assertion, because Vermont is not a human. Some predicates require more than one argument, thus, you can have formulas such as Mxy.

What is an **algorithm**?

The word "algorithm" is a distortion of Muhammad ibn Musa al-Khuwarizmi's name (783–c. 850; also seen as al-Khowarizmi and al-Khwarizmi), the Persian mathematician who wrote about algebraic methods. In general, an algorithm is a specific set of instructions that, if followed correctly, will lead to a recognizable end result. Simply put, a recipe is an example of an algorithm. For example, if there are two different recipes for making apple pie—one calling for cutting fresh apples for the filling, the other calling for apples from a can—the end results will be the same: an apple pie.

In mathematics, most algorithms include a finite sequence of steps that repeat, or require decisions using logic and comparisons until the final result is found (often called a computation). The best example is the long-division algorithm, in which the remainders of partial divisions are carried to the next digit or digits. For example, in the division of 1,347 by 8, a remainder of 5 in the division of 13 by 8 is placed in front of the 4, and 8 is then divided into "54," and so on. More advanced use of algorithms are found in a type of logic called metamathematics (see below).

What is **metamathematics**?

Metamathematics is the study of mathematical reasoning in a general and abstract way, usually by trying to understand how theorems are derived from axioms. Thus, it is often called proof theory (for more information about axioms, see below). It does not study the objects of a particular mathematical theory, but examines the mathematical theories themselves with respect to their logical structure. Metamathematics is also used in logic to study the combination and application of mathematical symbols; this is often referred to as metalogic.

What is **Gödel's incompleteness theorem**?

Austrian-American mathematician and logician Kurt Gödel (1906–1978) is best known for his studies in mathematical logic—in particular for his "incompleteness

theorem" presented in 1931. This theorem shows that an infinite number of propositions that cannot be derived from axioms of a system may be proved by metamathematical means external to mathematics. In other words, mathematics abounds with questions that have a "yes or no" nature; the incompleteness theory suggests that such questions will always exist.

What does the **philosophy of mathematics** mean?

The philosophy of mathematics, or mathematical philosophy, may seem like the same thing. But to mathematicians,

Austrian-American mathematician and logician Kurt Gödel is best known for his studies in mathematical logic.

mathematical philosophy means many areas of study, such as ethics, logic, or metaphysics. The philosophy of mathematics is actually a branch of philosophy that studies the philosophical assumptions, implications, and foundations of the mathematics world. This branch of philosophy gives us an idea of just how mathematics fits into our modern world.

These philosophies tell us a great deal about the state of modern mathematics and logic. Like many abstract and complex studies, philosophies come and go; some good, some seemingly on the mathematical fringe. Currently, there is no single philosophy that truly defines our mathematical and logic foundations, especially when it comes to combining both mathematical knowledge and the application of mathematics to physical reality.

What are **some philosophies** of **mathematical logic**?

Over the centuries, there have been many mathematicians who have tried to figure out the complexity of mathematics. Fast-forward to modern times, and one finds that mathematical knowledge and logic have dramatically changed. In particular, in the late 20th and early 21st centuries, the development of predicate calculus and the digital computer has had a great impact on these studies. And out of these ideas—not to mention centuries of mathematics and logic groundwork—are some of the more interesting philosophical doctrines of mathematical thought:

- *Formalism* is the idea that mathematics is truly formal; therefore, it is only concerned with the algorithmic manipulation of symbols. In formalism, predicate calculus does not denote predicates—or anything else—meaning mathematical objects do not exist at all. This definitely fits into today's

world of computers, especially in the field of artificial intelligence. But this philosophy does not take into account human mathematical understanding, not to mention mathematical applications in physics and engineering.

- *Set-theoretical Platonism* sounds as if mathematicians are regressing back to Plato's time. In reality, this philosophy is based on a variant of the Platonic doctrine of recollection, in which we are born possessing all knowledge and our realization of that knowledge is contingent on our discovery of it. In the set-theoretical Platonism, infinite sets exist in a non-material, purely mathematical realm. By extending our intuitive understanding of this realm, we can cope with the problems such as those encountered by the Gödel incompleteness theorem. But this philosophy, like the others, has a seemingly infinite number of gaps, especially the question of how can a theory of infinite sets be applied to a finite world.

- *Constructivism* was a "fringe" movement at the turn of the 21st century. Constructionists believe that mathematical knowledge is obtained by a series of purely mental constructions, with all mathematical objects existing only in the mind of the mathematician. But constructivism does not take into account the external world, and when taken to extremes, it can mean that there is no possibility of communication from one mind to another. This philosophy also runs the chance of rejecting the basic laws of logic. For example, if you have a mathematical problem with a yes or no nature, with the answer unknown, neither "yes" nor "no" is in the mind of the mathematician. This means that a disjunction is not a legitimate mathematical assumption—and thus, ideas such Aristotle's law of the excluded middle ("either or") are cast aside. And not many modern mathematicians want to throw out centuries of logic.

- *Structuralism* holds that mathematical theories describe structures—and that mathematical objects are defined by their place in such structures, but have no intrinsic properties. For example, if one knows that the number 1 is the first whole number after 0, then that is all that needs to be known. Even though it sounds simple, structuralism only relates to "… what kind of entity a mathematical object is, not to what kind of existence mathematical objects or structures have…" Thus, it has some interesting interpretations in philosophy.

- *Fictionalism* sounds like something you read that's the opposite of non-fiction, but it's actually a type of mathematical philosophy proposed around 1980. But in a way, the mathematician who brought out the proposal of fictionalism, Hartry Field, was talking about fiction after all: He believed that mathematics was dispensable, and should be considered "…as a body of falsehoods not talking about anything real." This type of logic has not been readily accepted, as there are some logic and statement problems inherent in his philosophy.

- *Social realism*, or social constructivism, proposes that mathematics is mainly a construct of culture that is subject to change or even correction. It's often said that this idea is the opposite of how mathematicians treat their field—that mathematics is more pure and objective. Social realism theorists believe this isn't true, that mathematics is grounded by much uncertainty, and grows, like things in nature, through a sort of mathematical evolution.

AXIOMATIC SYSTEM

What are **axioms** and **postulates**?

These two words are often treated as the same: in fact, some mathematicians consider the word *axiom* a slightly archaic synonym for *postulate*. Although both are considered to be a proposition (statement) that is true without proof, there are subtle differences.

An axiom in mathematics refers to a general statement that is true without proof, and is often related to equality, such as "two things equal to the same thing are equal to each other," and those related to operations. They should also be consistent—or it should not be possible to deduce any contradictory statements from the axiom.

A postulate is also a proposition (statement) that is true without proof, but it deals with specific subject matter, such as the properties of geometric figures. Thus, it is not

as general as an axiom. For example, Euclidean geometry is based on the five postulates known, of course, as Euclid's postulates. (See below; for more about Euclid, see "Geometry and Trigonometry").

What is an **axiomatic system**?

An axiomatic system is a logical system that has a definite set of axioms; from these axioms, theorems can be derived. In each system, propositions (statements) are proved on the basis of a limited number of axioms or postulates—all with a few undefined terms. The other terms are defined on the basis of the undefined terms. One of the first axiomatic systems was Euclidean geometry.

Overall, an axiomatic system has several basic components: the undefined terms of the system (primitives); well-formed formulas, or how symbols are put into the system based on certain allowed rules, sometimes called defined terms; axioms, or what is also known as "self-evident truths" of the system; theorems, or statements that are proved based on axioms or other proven theorems; and finally, the rules of inference, or those that allow moves from certain formulas to other formulas.

How are some parts of an **axiomatic system further defined**?

There are several terms that further define an axiomatic system. All of them are slightly intertwined, depending on the system.

The absence of contradiction—or the ability to prove a proposition (statement) and its negative are both true—is known as *consistency*. Independence is not necessary to an axiomatic system, but consistency is definitely necessary. The opposite of consistency in an axiomatic system is inconsistency.

An axiomatic system is called *independent* if no other axioms can be derived (or proved) from other axioms in the system; in other words, the entire axiomatic system will be termed independent if all of its underlying axioms are independent. The inde-

A page from Euclid's *Elements*, found near Oxyrhynchus, Egypt, c. 1896, is currently kept at the University of Pennsylvania.

pendence of a system is usually determined after the consistency. An axiomatic system that is *dependent* has some axioms that are redundant; this is also called redundancy.

An axiomatic system is *complete* if no additional axiom can be added to the system without making the new system dependent or inconsistent. In other words, the aim is to prove or disprove any statement about the objects in the system from the axioms alone. In complete systems, every true proposition about the defined and undefined terms can be proved from the axioms. Systems with the logic based on true or false propositions connected by "and," "or," and "not" are complete, as are those that include quantifiers. More complex systems, such as set theory, are not considered complete.

What is an **undefined term**?

In terms of axiomatic systems, undefined terms are also called *primitives*. And although it sounds like "double-speak," these primitives are object names, but the objects they name are left undefined. (The axioms are statements within the system that make assertions about the primitives.) If a meaning is attached to a primitive, it is called an *interpretation*.

Undefined terms are also found in a mix of axiomatic systems and geometry, in which definitions are formed using known words or terms to describe a new word. There are three words in geometry that are not formally defined—point, line, and plane—because they cannot be described without using words that are themselves undefined. These terms are fundamentally important in the study of geometry,

55

because they are needed to further describe even more complex objects such as circles and triangles. (For more about geometry, see "Geometry and Trigonometry.")

What are **theorems, corollaries**, and **lemmas**?

In mathematics and logic, a *theorem* is a statement demonstrated to be true by accepted mathematical operations and arguments. In general, a theorem is usually based on some general principle that makes it part of a larger theory; it differs from an axiom in that a proof is required for its acceptance. Some of the more well-known theorems are named after their discoverers, such as the Pythagorean theorem (involving right triangles) and Fermat's last theorem. It is interesting to note that American Richard Feynman (1918–1988), one of the most brilliant physicists of the 20th century, stated that any theorem, no matter how difficult to prove in the first place, is viewed as "trivial" by mathematicians once it has been proved. Thus, according to Feynman, there are only two types of mathematical objects: trivial ones and those that have not yet been proved.

A *corollary* is a theorem that has been proved in only a few steps from an established theorem, or one that follows as a direct consequence of another theorem or axiom. And finally, a *lemma* is a theorem proved as a preliminary or intermediate step in the proof of another, more basic theorem; or a brief theorem used to prove a larger theorem.

What is a **proof**?

A proof is simply the process of showing a theorem to be correct, although the process itself might not be simple. These mathematical arguments are often quite rigorous, and they are used to demonstrate the truth of a given proposition. The result of the proven statement is a theorem.

Are there **different types of proofs**?

There are several different types of proofs in mathematical logic. *Direct proofs* are based on rules that result in one true proposition from two propositions. They show that a given statement is true by simply combining existing theorems with or without some mathematical manipulations. For example, if you have two sides of a triangle with the same length, a definition and theorem show that a line bisecting their vertex produces two congruent triangles—a direct proof that the angles at the other two vertices have the same size.

In logic, *indirect proofs* are also called "proofs by contradiction," and are known in Latin as *reductio ad absurdum* ("reduced to an absurdity"). This type of proof initially assumes that the opposite of what you are trying to prove is true; from this assumption, certain conclusions can be drawn. One then searches for a conclusion

> ### What are some well-known axiomatic systems?
>
> **O**ne of the most well-known axiomatic systems was developed by the Greek mathematician Euclid (c. 325–c. 270 B.C.E.). He presented 13 books of geometry and other mathematics, titled *Elements* (or *Stoicheion* in Greek). Included in these books were theorems about geometry and numbers derived from five postulates about points, lines, circles, and angles, four axioms about equality, and one axiom stating "the whole is greater than the part." A more modern axiomatic system is the axiomatic set theory, which is based on eight axioms and three undefined terms.

that is false because it contradicts given or known information. Sometimes, a given piece of information is contradicted, which shows that, since the assumption leads to a false conclusion, the assumption must be false. If the assumption is false (the opposite of the conclusion one is trying to prove), then it is known that the goal conclusion must be true. All of this has therefore been shown "indirectly."

Finally, a *disproof* is a single instance that contradicts a proposition. For example, the disproof of "all primes are odd" is the true statement "the number 2 is a prime and not odd." If a disproof exists for a proposition, then the statement is false.

How are **computers** involved in determining **proofs**?

Numerous mathematicians and computer scientists are adapting computer systems to automate proofs, a computer process called automated theorem proving (ATP) or automated deduction, currently the most well-developed subfield of automated reasoning. In the 1970s, the first attempts were made to prove a theorem by computer. The so called four-color theorem was attempted by an ATP computer, which involved the theorem's mapping problem: Using no more than four colors, the computer had to color regions of a map so that no two adjacent regions had the same color. Its proof relied on meticulous computer testing of many separate cases, all of which cannot be verified by hand.

Yet another more recent automated theorem prover is the *Vampire*, developed in the Computer Science Department at the University of Manchester by Andrei Voronkov and Kryštof Hoder (and previously with Alexandre Riazanov). To date, this ATP computer has won the "world cup for theorem provers," also called the CADE ATP System Competition (International Conference on Automated Deduction [CADE], associated with the Association for Automated Reasoning) eleven times.

Although becoming less and less in numbers, some mathematicians (mostly purists) do not believe these computer-assisted proofs are valid. Not only could numbers be wrong, but the logic entered into the computer may not be correctly interpret-

ed by the computer. They believe that only humans can understand the nuances and have the intuition needed to develop a theorem's proof. But this is also often a proof's dilemma: Many proofs would take decades—and reams of paper—to finish and prove, if you could prove them at all.

Have any **recent proofs** been discovered?

It seems that as long as there are mathematicians, there will always be someone who tries to solve mathematical questions using proofs. For example, a researcher at the Georgia Institute of Technology recently came up with a new proof, using a game-type scenario, that real numbers are not countable. Another researcher uncovered the proof of the Poincaré conjecture, or that the three-sphere is the only type of bounded three-dimensional space possible that contains no holes, a conjecture first proposed by H. Poincaré in 1953. And what is the dream of some mathematicians? To eventually have formal proofs of all the central theorems in mathematics right at their fingertips, something some have compared to DNA sequencing—as in the "sequencing of the mathematical genome."

What is **deduction** and **induction** and how are they used in mathematics?

Deduction in logic is when conclusions are drawn from premises and syllogisms (for more information on these terms, see above). In this instance, a deduction is a form of inference or reasoning such that the conclusion is true if the premises are true; or, based on general principles, particular facts and relationships are derived. Deductive logic also means the process of proving true statements (theorems) within an axiomatic system; if the system is valid, all of the derived theorems are considered valid. For example, if it is known that all dogs have four legs and Spot is a dog, we logically deduce that Spot has four legs; other examples of deductive reasoning include Aristotle's syllogisms.

Induction is a term usually used in regards to probability, in which the conclusion can be false even when the premises are true. In contrast to deduction, the premise gives grounds for the conclusion, but does not necessitate it. Inductive logic generates "correct" conclusions based on observation or data. (But note that not all inductive logic leads to correct generalizations, making the validity of many such arguments probabilistic or "iffy" in nature.)

One can see how both these processes work in the scientific world, especially in the scientific method, in which general principles are inferred from certain facts. For example, by observation of events (induction) and from principles already developed (deduction), new hypotheses are formulated. Hypotheses are then tested by applications; and as the results satisfy the conditions of the hypotheses, laws are developed by induction. Future laws are then often developed, many of them determined by deduction.

What are some examples of paradoxes throughout history?

The oldest paradoxes may be from the Greek Epimenides the Cretan (lived sometime during the 6th century B.C.E.), who stated, "All Cretans are liars." If this statement is true—and any other culture you would care to put in the Cretans' place—then the implication is that the statement is a lie. This is also called the "Liar's paradox."

The number of paradoxes continued almost *ad infinitum* since then. Some of the more popular ones include those listed as *Zeno's paradoxes*. They were named after Greek philosopher Zeno of Elea (c. 490 B.C.E.), a disciple of the philosopher Parmenides, who believed that reality was an absolute, unchanging whole—and, thus, many things we take for granted, such as motion, were simply illusions. In order to defend his master's highly debated philosophy, Zeno developed his paradoxes. Most of Zeno's paradoxes are still highly debated by modern mathematicians and philosophers, thus proving another paradox: Nothing truly changes throughout history—or does it?

What is a **conclusion** in logic?

A conclusion is a statement (proposition) found by applying a set of logical rules (syllogisms) to a set of premises. In addition, the final statement of a proof is called the proof's conclusion. For example, in a statement that includes "if … then," the result following the "then" in the statement is called the conclusion.

What is *modus ponens*?

The Latin term *modus ponens* means "mode that affirms," or in the case of logic, stands for the rule of detachment. This rule (also known as a rule of inference) pertains to the "if…then" statement and forms the basis of most proofs: "If p then q," or if p is true, then the conclusion q is true. Or simply, it is often seen as the following:

If p, then q.

p. Therefore, q.

To see this another way:

p ⇒ q: 'If it is raining, then there are clouds in the sky."

p: "It is raining."

q: "There are clouds in the sky."

There are several ways to break down the *modus ponens*. The argument form has two premises: The "if-then" (or conditional claim), or namely that p implies q; and that p (called the antecedent of the conditional claim) is true. From these two

premises it can be logically concluded that q (called the consequent of the conditional claim) must be true as well; in other words, if the antecedent of a conditional is true, then the consequent must be true.

What is a **fallacy**?

A fallacy is an incorrect result—in this case, one arrived at through misleading reasoning when examining a logical argument. One of the more common fallacies in logic is thinking incorrectly that if "p implies q" is true, "then q implies p" is also true. The idea of such invalid arguments was well-known in the past: With Greek mathematician Aristotle's syllogisms, an argument was valid if it adhered to all the laws; to be false, it only needed to break one law. Euclid, another Greek mathematician, was known to have written an entire book on fallacies in geometry, but the book has since been lost.

English logician, philosopher, and mathematician Bertrand Russell came up with a puzzling paradox involving sets.

What is a **paradox**?

In logic, paradoxes are statements that seem to be self-contradictory or contrary to one's expectations. These arguments imply both a proposition and its opposite. One of the most famous paradoxes was stated by English logician Bertrand Russell (1872–1970) in 1901 dealing with sets: "If sets that are not members of themselves are normal, is the set of normal sets itself normal?" (For more information about Russell's paradoxes in set theory, see below.)

What are some **paradoxes** that deal with **space and time**?

There are numerous paradoxes that deal with the counterintuitive aspects of continuous space and time. One of the most well-known is the *dichotomy (or racetrack) paradox*. Before an object can travel a distance *d*, it must keep traveling "in halves." In terms of the racetrack, in order to reach the end of the course, a person would have to first reach the halfway mark, then the halfway mark of the remaining half, then the halfway mark of the final fourth, then of the final eighth, and so on *ad infinitum* (to infinity). Therefore, the distance can never truly be traveled to reach the end of the racetrack.

When is a paradox not a paradox?

There are many proposed paradoxes that are not really one—even though they sound like it. One just-for-fun, simple example of a non-paradox can be called a "friends" paradox. Brought out in a study on friendships by sociologists Scott L. Feld, it demonstrates the seeming paradox of why your friends seem to have more friends than you do. Follow us here: There are 12 people who have a friend who has 12 friends, but there is only one person who has a friend who has only one friend. There is also no one who has a friend who doesn't have any friends. There is only one friend who has 12 friends. Thus, the number 12 gets counted only once when you compute the average number of friends that people have, but it gets counted 12 times when you calculate the average number of friends that their friends have. Thus, it seems like a paradox that your friends have more friends than you do, when in reality, it's merely that you're more likely to be friends with someone who has more friends than with someone who has fewer friends. If you're totally confused, don't worry. That's the nature of logic and the paradox.

The *Achilles and the tortoise paradox* is a version of the tortoise and the hare, but with a very different resolution than the well-known fable. In this paradox, Achilles gives the slower tortoise a head start; Achilles starts when the tortoise reaches point *a*. But by the time Achilles reaches *a*, the tortoise has already moved beyond that point, to point *b*; when Achilles reaches *b*, the tortoise is at point *c*, and so on *ad infinitum*. Since this process goes on forever, Achilles can never catch up with the tortoise.

Another paradox is *the arrow paradox*. In this case, an arrow in flight has a certain position at a given instant in time, but that is indistinguishable from a motionless arrow in the same position. So how is the arrow's motion perceived?

Finally, one of the most interesting and insightful paradoxes is attributed to Socrates—thus, the *Socrates' paradox*. It is based on Socrates' statement, "One thing I know is that I know nothing."

SET THEORY

What is **set theory**?

Set theory is the mathematical theory of sets and is associated with logic; it is also considered the study of sets (collections of objects or entities that can be real or concepts) and their properties. (For more about sets, see below.) Under formal set theory, three primitives (undefined terms) are used: *S* (the set), *I* (the identity), and *E* (the

element). Thus, the formulas *Sx, Ixy, Exy* mean "x is a set," "x is identical to y," and "x is an element of y," respectively.

Overall, set theory fits in with the aims of logic research: to find a single formula theory that will unify and become the basis for all of mathematics. And as it turns out, sets lead directly to a vast amount of data encompassing all of modern mathematics. There are also a number of different set theories, each having its own rules and axioms. No matter what version, set theory is not only important to mathematics and logic, but to other fields as well, such as computer technology, and atomic and nuclear physics.

What are **naïve** and **axiomatic set theory**?

The naive set theory is not one that takes everything for granted. It is actually a branch of mathematics that attempts to formalize the nature of the set using the fewest number of independent axioms possible. But it is not the answer to formalizing sets, as it quickly leads to a number of paradoxes. Because of this, mathematicians use a more formal theory called the *axiomatic set theory*, which is a version that uses axioms taken as uninterpreted rather than as formalization of pre-existing truths.

What is **Russell's Paradox**?

Russell's Paradox is one of the most famous of the set theory paradoxes. It first appears when studying the naive set theory: In this case, *R* is the set of all sets that are not members of themselves; from there, *R* is neither a member of itself nor a member of itself. The paradox sets in when you try to reason how a set appears to be a member of itself if and only if it is not a member of itself. Symbolically, it is expressed as follows:

$$R = \{x : x \notin x\} \text{ then,}$$
$$R \in R \text{ iff } R \notin R$$

Discovered by Welsh mathematician and logician Bertrand Arthur William Russell (1872–1970) in 1901, the paradox sparked a great deal of work (and controversy) in logic, set theory, and especially in philosophy and foundations of mathematics. The reason why it became so important was its affect on mathematics: It created problems for those who based mathematics on logic, and it also indicated that something was wrong with Georg Cantor's intuitive set theory.

What is a **set**?

Simply put, a set is a collection of objects or entities; these are called the *elements* of the set. The number of elements in a set can be large, small, finite, or infinite. The informal notation used for sets is sometimes seen as $x = \{y, z, ...\}$, with brackets used

> ### Who developed set theory?
>
> **G**erman mathematician George (Georg) Ferdinand Ludwig Philipp Cantor (1845–1918) is most well-known for his development of set theory. His *Mathematische Annalen* was a basic introduction to set theory, in which he built a hierarchy of infinite sets according to their cardinal number. In particular, using one-to-one pairing, he showed that the set of real numbers has a higher cardinal number than does the set of rational fractions.
>
> Unlike most subjects in mathematics, Cantor's set theory was his creation alone. But like many brilliant, revolutionary thinkers throughout history, his ideas were highly criticized by his contemporaries. This strong opposition contributed to the multiple nervous breakdowns he suffered throughout the last 33 years of his life, which ended tragically in a mental institution.

to contain the elements within the set. It is stated as, "x is a set consisting of the elements y, z, and so on." But more commonly, sets are seen as capital letters and elements as lowercase letters, such as *a* is an element of set *A*.

How do you **interpret sets**?

There are several ways to look at sets. Two sets (or more) are considered identical if, and only if, they have the same collection of objects or entities. This is a principle known as *extensionality*. For example, the set $\{a, b, c\}$ is considered to be the same as set $\{a, b, c\}$, of course, because the elements are the same; the set $\{a, b, c\}$ and the set $\{c, b, a\}$ are also the same, even though they are written in a different order.

It becomes more complex when sets are elements of other sets, so it is important to note the position of the brackets. For example, the set $\{\{a, b\}, c\}$ is distinct from the set $\{a, b, c\}$ (note that the brackets differ); in turn, the set $\{a, b\}$ is an element of the set $\{\{a, b\}, c\}$. (It is a set included between the outside brackets.)

Another example that shows how sets are interpreted includes the following: If *B* is the set of real numbers that are solutions of the equation $x^2 = 9$, then the set can be written as $B = \{x: x^2 = 9\}$, or *B* is the set of all *x* such that $x^2 = 9$. Thus *B* is $\{3, -3\}$.

What are **open** and **closed sets**?

Formally, an *open set* is one in which every element in the set has a *neighbor* in the set or does not include its boundary. A *closed set* is one that does include a boundary of a set, or one where some elements have neighbors not in the set.

63

What is a **null** or **empty set**?

A null or empty set contains no elements; an empty set is considered to be a subset of every other set. The opposite of an empty set is, logically, a *nonempty* set, or one that is not empty. The notations for empty set are { } and ∅, but not (), as it is sometimes written in texts. Interestingly enough, an empty set is considered to be both open and closed for any set X.

What is the **set theory approach to arithmetic**?

The set theory approach to arithmetic is defined in terms of the non-negative whole numbers 0, 1, 2, 3, These numbers are identified with specific sets based on the placement and number of brackets. For example, mathematicians identify 0 with the empty set { }; 1 is identified with {{ }}; 2 is identified with {{}, {{}}}; 3 is identified with {{ }, {{ }}, {{ }, {{ }}}}, and so on (each bracket an interpretation of the empty set and 1, or {{}}).

What are the **basic symbols** used to **operate on sets**?

When set theory founder Georg Cantor developed the symbols for sets, he used a single horizontal overbar to denote a set with no structure besides order; thus, it represented the order type of the set. A double bar meant that there was no order from the set, also called the cardinal number of the set (see below).

The more common symbols accepted in today's set theory include the following:

Symbols Used to Operate Sets

Symbol	Meaning
∩	"and" or intersection (the intersection of two sets)
∪	"or" or union (the union of two sets)
∈	set membership (such as $a \in S$ in which a is an element of the set S) and subset (such as $A \in B$ or every element of A is also an element of B)
⫾	not a set membership (such as $a \, ⫾ \, S$, in which a is not an element of S; this symbol is larger and thicker than set membership
∅	empty or null set (a set with no elements)
{}	braces or brackets (to enclose the listed elements of a set; empty brackets are called an "empty set," or a set with no elements)
\|	such that, as in {x \| x is a rational number}, is a set "x, such that x is a rational number"
:	also used as "such that"
∉	is not an element of
⊆	is a subset of (as in $A \subseteq B$)
⊂	is a proper subset of
⊄	is not a proper subset of
A'	complement of A

How are some **symbols used** in **operations on sets**?

There are many ways to operate on sets. The following lists some of the more simple operations on sets, in which E, F, and G are sets:

$E \cap F = F \cap E$

$E \cup F = F \cup E$, in which both are commutative operations;

$(E \cap F) \cap G = E \cap (F \cap G)$

$(E \cup F) \cup G = E \cup (F \cup G)$, in which both are associative operations;

$(E \cap F) \cup G = (E \cup G) \cap (F \cup G)$

$(E \cup F) \cap G = (E \cap G) \cup (F \cap G)$, in which both are distributive operations.

What are the **basic set operations**?

There are several basic set operations, the most common being the intersection of sets, union of sets, and the complement of sets. The following lists these operations (note: the first two operations obey the associative and communtative laws, and together they obey the distributive law):

Intersection—The intersection of two sets is the set of elements common to the two sets. For example, the intersection of sets A and B is the set of elements common to both A and B. This is usually written as $A \cap B$. Thus, if $A = \{1, 2, 3, 4\}$ and $B = \{3, 4, 5\}$, then the intersection of A and B would be $\{3, 4\}$.

Union—The union of sets is the combining of members of the sets. For example, the union of two sets A and B is the set obtained by combining members of sets A and B. This is usually written as $A \cup B$. Thus, if $A = \{1, 2, 3, 4\}$ and $B = \{3, 4, 5\}$, then the union of A and B would be $\{1, 2, 3, 4, 5\}$.

Complement or complementation—When the set of all elements under consideration must be specified, it is called the universal set. And if the universal set is $U = \{1, 2, 3, 4, 5\}$ and $A = \{1, 2, 3\}$, then the complement of A (or A') is the set of all elements in the universal set that are not A, or $\{4, 5\}$. The intersection between a set and its complement is the empty or null set (\varnothing); the union of a set and its complement is the universal set.

What are **cardinal** and **ordinal numbers** and **finite sets** in set theory?

Cardinal and ordinal numbers are used in reference to numbers: Ordinal numbers are used to describe the position of objects or entities arranged in a certain sequence, such as first, second, third, and so on; cardinal numbers are natural numbers, or 0, 1, 2, 3, and so on. (For more information about cardinal and ordinal numbers, see "Math Basics.")

But cardinal numbers used in set theory describe the number of members in a set. Both ordinal and cardinal numbers are further used to describe infinite sets, and are

prefaced with "first ordinal" or "first cardinal" infinities. The first ordinal infinity applies to the smallest number greater than any finite ordered set of natural numbers. The first cardinal infinity applies to the number of all the natural numbers. (For more about infinite sets, see below.)

A *finite set* is one that is not infinite; it can be numbered from 1 to n, for some positive integer n. This number n is also called the set's cardinal number; thus, for a certain set A, the cardinality is denoted by *card(A)*. There are a number of rules to cardinal numbers and finite sets. For example, if two sets bisect, then they are said to have the same cardinality (or power). The empty set is considered to be a finite set, with its set's cardinal number being 0.

What is a **universal set**?

A universal set actually applies to sets that are not universal, but are chosen from a specific type of entity, such as sets of numbers or letters. Thus, the set of all the elements in a set theory problem are collectively called the universal set. In reality, the "set of all things" does not exist because there is no largest or all-inclusive set, and so the true universal set is not recognized in standard set theory.

What is a **subset** and **proper subset** in set theory?

Simply put, a *subset* is a portion of a set. If set B is a subset of set A, then all elements of set B are also elements in set A. If A and B are equal, then both sets are subsets of themselves; the empty set is also considered a subset of every other set. A *proper subset* is a subset other than the set itself.

When is a set a **superset**?

A superset is one that contains all the elements of a smaller set. For example, if B is a subset of A, then A is a superset of B; in other words, A is a superset of set B if every element in B is in A. Like a proper subset, there are also proper supersets (or a superset that is not the entire set).

What does it mean if **a set is countable**?

If a set is countable (or denumerable), it means that it is finite. This also means that the set's members can be matched in a *one-to-one correspondence*, in which each element in one set is matched exactly with one element in the second, and vice versa, with all the natural numbers, or with a subset of the natural numbers. Mathematicians often say, "A and B are in one-to-one correspondence," or "A and B are bijective." (For more about one-to-one correspondence, see "Math Basics.") In set theory, all finite sets are considered to be countable, as are all subsets of the natural numbers and integers. But sets such as real numbers, points on a line, and complex numbers are not countable.

What is Zermelo's axiom of choice?

Although it sounds like something on a Greek restaurant menu, Zermelo's axiom of choice is actually a fundamental axiom in set theory. It states that given any set of mutually exclusive nonempty sets, there is at least one set that contains exactly one element common with each of the nonempty sets.

This was one of David Hilbert's problems that needed to be solved by mathematicians of his day (for more about David Hilbert, see elsewhere in this chapter, and in "History of Mathematics"). German mathematician Ernst Friedrich Zermelo (1871–1953) took on the task, and in 1904 he developed what is called the well-ordering theorem, which says every set can be well ordered based on the axiom of choice.

This brought fame to Zermelo, but it was not accepted by all mathematicians who balked at the lack of axiomatization of set theory (for more about axiomatic set theory, see above). Although he finally did axiomatize set theory and improve on his theorem, there were still gaps in his logic, especially since he failed to prove the consistency in his axiomatic system. By 1923, German mathematician Adolf Abraham Halevi Fraenkel (1891–1965) and Norwegian mathematician Albert Thoralf Skolem (1887–1963) independently improved Zermelo's axiomatic system, resulting in the system now called *Zermelo-Fraenkel axioms* (Skolem's name was not included, although another theorem is named after him). This is now the most commonly used system for axiomatic set theory.

What is **combinatorics**?

Combinatorics is a branch of mathematics—overall called combinatorial mathematics—that studies the enumeration, combination, and permutation of sets and the mathematical relations that involve these properties, defined as:

Enumeration—Sets can be identified by the enumeration of their elements; in other words, determining (or counting) the set of all solutions to a given problem.

Combination—Combination is how to count the many different ways elements from a given set can be combined. For example, the 2-combinations of the 4-set {A,B,C,D} are {A,B}, {A,C}, {A,D}, {B,C}, {B,D}, {C,D}.

Permutation—Permutation is the rearrangement of elements of a set into a particular order, often a one-to-one correspondence. The number of permutations of a particularly sized set with n members is written as the factorial $n!$. For example, a set with 4 members would have 4 in first place to 1 in the last

place. This would equal $4 \times 3 \times 2 \times 1 = 4!$, or 24, permutations of 4 members. (For more information about factorials, see "Algebra.")

What is an **ordered pair**?

An ordered pair is two quantities—usually written as (a, b)—that have a significant order; thus, (a, b) does not equal (b, a). Ordered pairs are used in set theory to define members in a function.

Ordered pairs are also valuable in linear equations and graphing, in which the x coordinate is the first number and the y coordinate is the second number, or (x, y). They are used on a grid to locate a point. (For more information about ordered pairs and graphs, see "Geometry and Trigonometry.")

How do **functions pertain** to **sets**?

A function in sets pertains to a correspondence between two sets, called the *domain* and *range*; each member of the domain has exactly one member of the range. It is often called a many-to-one (or sometimes one-to-one) relation. For example, f = {(1,2), (3,6), (4, –2), (8,0), (9,6)} is a function, with each set of numbers being ordered pairs. This is because it assigns each member of the set {1, 3, 4, 8, 9} exactly one value in the set {2, 6, –2, 0, 6}. It never has two ordered pairs with the same x and different y values. In this case, the domain is {1, 3, 4, 8, 9} and the range is {2, 6, –2, 0, 6}.

To show an example that is *not* a function, f = {(1,8), (4,2), (3,5), (1,3), (6,11)} is *not* a function because it does not assign each member of the set exactly one value: It assigns $x = 1$ to both $y = 8$ and $y = 3$, or it has two ordered pairs that have the same x values to two different y values, (1, 8) and (1, 3). (For more information about functions, see "Algebra.")

The expanses of the universe seem infinite to us, but in mathematics the concept of infinity reaches even beyond the edges of the universe toward numbers that are inconceivably large.

How else is the **term function used**?

Unfortunately (as with many mathematical terms), there is often more than one function for the word "function." For example, contrary to the definition above, function can also mean the relationships that map single points in the domain to multiple points in the range—called *multivalued functions*—mainly used in the theory of complex functions. To further confuse matters, there are also functions called non-multivalued functions.

What are some strange characteristics of infinity?

There are some strange ideas about infinity—the most interesting one being that it's not just a bunch of numbers that go on forever. There are certain properties, too. For example, infinity doesn't always equal infinity; and infinity minus infinity does not equal zero; or even infinity over infinity (infinity/infinity) does not equal one. Why don't the "normal" rules of mathematics apply here? The biggest problem is infinity itself—or is it "themselves"? After all, one infinity in the questioned equation may be larger than the other—and you wouldn't know.

There is also the paradox of infinity. For example, take the following two sequences:

$ab = 1, 2, 3, 4, 5, 6 \ldots$
$cd = 2, 4, 6, 8, 10 \ldots$

ab contains all natural numbers, while *cd* contains all even natural numbers. Although you would think *cd* would have half the number of terms, and thus would be a "smaller" infinity, they both have an infinite number of terms—thus the paradox of infinity. That is because most of us think of infinity as a number rather than a concept.

Where did the **symbol** for **infinity originate**?

Infinity is represented by the symbol ∞, a sign introduced by John Wallis in 1655 in his treatise, "De sectionibus conicus." Historians believe that Wallis, a classical scholar, adopted the sign from the late Roman symbol for "1,000." Whether it was from there or another source, the result was (and remains) the same: "a figure-eight on its side," as many people call the infinity symbol.

Are there **different types of infinity in mathematics**?

At the end of the nineteenth century, German mathematician George (Georg) Ferdinand Ludwig Philipp Cantor (1845–1918) showed that different orders of infinity existed and that the infinity of points on a line was of a greater order than that of prime numbers. Since that time, mathematicians have managed to divide the topic of infinity into even more precise terms.

To most of us, the universe represents infinity, but in mathematics, infinity is the unbounded quantity that is greater than every real number. In fact, it is called *potential infinity* in mathematics, in which the potential for infinity exists with natural numbers because you can always mention a number greater than any given number. *Directed infinity* applies to an infinity in direction *z* and is an infinite numerical quan-

tity that is a positive real multiple of the complex number z; a directed infinity with an unknown direction is known as a *complex infinity*. Still another "type" of infinity in mathematics is *completed infinity*, which refers to the size of an infinite set (such as all the points on a line).

ALGEBRA

THE BASICS OF ALGEBRA

What is the **origin** of the word **"algebra"**?

The word "algebra" comes from the title of the book *Al jabr w'al muqābalah*, by Persian mathematician Muhammad ibn Musa al-Khuwarizmi (783–c. 850; also seen as al-Khowarizmi or al-Khwarizmi). The book is roughly translated as *Transposition and Reduction*, in which he explained the basics of algebraic methods.

What **early mathematicians** are thought to be responsible for originating the use of **algebraic methods and ideas**?

To some scholars, Greek (Hellenic) mathematician Diophantus (c. 210–c. 290) is considered the "father of algebra," as he developed his own algebraic notation. His words were noted and preserved by the Arabs; the translation of his words into Latin in the 16th century led to many algebraic advances. In more "modern" times, French mathematician François Viète (1540–1603; also known by his Latin name, Franciscus Vieta) is often credited as the "founder of modern algebra." (For more information about Diophantus and Viète, see below.)

What is **algebra**?

Depending on whether one is a student or a professional mathematician, the word can mean either of the following (both of which are further described elsewhere in this chapter). *School algebra* is what mathematicians refer to as the algebra we learn in middle and high school and call "arithmetic." But for most of people, algebra means

solving polynomial equations with one or more variables; the solutions to such equations are often obtained by the operations of addition, subtraction, multiplication, division, raising to a power, and extracting a root. (For more information about all these operations, see "Math Basics."). This also includes determining the properties of functions and graphs.

But mathematicians use the word "algebra" most often in reference to the abstract study of number systems and operations within them, such as groups, rings, and invariant theory. This is called *abstract algebra*.

How else is the **word algebra used**?

Algebra may be defined as the subjects of arithmetic and abstract algebra, but there are other meanings. These algebras involve vectors and matrices, the algebra of real numbers, complex numbers, and quaternions (an operator or factor that changes one vector into another). There are also those exotic algebras "invented" by mathematicians—usually named after the inventor—with the majority not truly understood except, perhaps, by their creators.

ALGEBRA EXPLAINED

What is an **expression** in mathematics?

An expression in mathematics is a statement that uses either numbers, variables, or both. For example, the following are all mathematical expressions:

y

4

$6 - 4$

$5 \times x - 7$

$4 + 5 \times (3 - 2)$

$x + 4 \times (7 - x)$

In order to write an expression from a written mathematical problem, one has to interpret the text. For example, one person weighs 100 pounds and another weighs y pounds; the expression for their combined weights would be $100 + y$.

What are **equations**?

In its simplest form, an equation is represented by expressions written with an equal sign in between; the two entities on either side are equal to each other. They are among the simplest mathematical problems most people deal with; in fact, most people have solved equations in their daily lives without realizing it. For example, when

students first learned addition in school, they typically work on equations such as: ___ + 5 = 7, in which the blank needs to be filled. This problem could also be expressed as $x + 5 = 7$, a simple equation. In this case, the equation is solved when x equals 2. The following are also equations:

$6 = 6$

$x = 8$

$y + 8 = 14$

$x - 4 = 15 - x$

$5xy = 8xy^2 + 4$

There are also some fundamental properties of equations that are good to know. They include symmetric properties (if $a = b$, then $b = a$); substitution (if $a = b$, then a may be replaced by b); addition (if $a = b$, and c is a number, then $a + c = b + c$); and multiplication (if $a = b$, and c is a number, then $a \times c = b \times c$).

What are **algebraic equations**?

An *algebraic equation*, as with the equations defined above, is a statement in which two numbers, letters, or expressions are equal. But algebraic equations take the idea even further: Most of the time, you are trying to simplify the numbers and one (or more) variables in the equation. They can further be defined as any combination of variables or constants linked together by any operation—addition, subtraction, multiplication, division (except division by zero). This type of algebraic equation is often referred to as a polynomial (see elsewhere in this chapter for more about polynomials).

Who was the **first** to **write and solve** general algebraic **equations**?

French mathematician François Viète (1540–1603; also known as Franciscus Vieta, his Latin name) is often referred to as the "founder of modern algebra." He was not a professional mathematician, but contributed a great deal to the understanding and spread of modern symbolic algebra. Although some of his work paid tribute to ancient mathematical traditions, Viète created a kind of "new math." It was not one based on the traditional geometric visualizations, but rather expressed as abstract formulas and general rules. But Viète still divided algebra into distinct branches partially derived from Greek mathematics: *zetetics* (translating a problem into an equation), *poristics* (proving theorems through equations), and *exegetics* (solving equations). He also was the first to combine algebra with geometry and trigonometry. (For more about Viète, see "Geometry and Trigonometry.")

What are **variables** in algebraic equations?

Variables are the symbols (usually a letter such as x or y) used in algebraic equations that represent an unknown number—and on whose value a function, polynomial, and

You can use algebra to solve word problems by converting known and unknown data into figures and variables. For instance, a word problem might involve two trains, one going 120 mph and one traveling at 112 mph. If the first train is 250 miles from a destination and the second train is 220 miles from the same destination, which train will arrive first?

so on, depends. Variables remain unknown until the equation is solved; thus, they are sometimes referred to as *unknowns* in an algebraic equation.

It is not always easy to work with variables, as there are so many letters used throughout various equations. But in many mathematical and scientific texts, there are some variables that are customary to use. They are listed as follows:

n indicates natural numbers or integers

x represents real numbers

z stands for complex numbers.

What are some **other terms** used in dealing with **algebraic equations**?

There are many terms in algebra, including those dealing with equations. The following lists some of the more common ones:

Equality and *inequality*—An equality is a mathematical statement that shows the equivalence of two quantities. For example, if a is equal to b, it is written as the equality $a = b$. An inequality is just the opposite: a does not equal b, or $a \neq b$.

Formula—A formula is a rule, fact, or principle expressed in terms of mathematical symbols, including equations, equalities, identities, or inequalities.

(Note: the plural of formula in Latin is "formulae," but it is more readily accepted today as "formulas.")

Identity—An identity is a mathematical relationship equating one quantity to another that initially may appear to differ; it also means an equation that is always true, such as the Pythagorean theorem (for more about identities, see below).

How are **word problems** expressed as **equations**?

There seem to be a gazillion word problems out there—just ask anyone taking such tests in grade or high school! The one thing most have in common is that they can be expressed as an equation—many as algebraic equations—in which there are known and unknown quantities. In almost all instances, there are key words that lead the reader to determine not only the numbers and variables, but what operations to use in the equation to determine the answer. The following lists some simple key words and the corresponding operation:

Common Key Words Used in Word Problems

Key Words	Operation	Examples
sum, total, more than	addition	The sum of my weight and 10 equals 130 ($y + 10 = 130$); the groceries at one store were \$3.00 while the total for two stores was \$4.00 ($y + 3 = 4$); seven more than the price is \$126 ($y + 7 = 126$)
difference, discrepancy	subtraction	The difference (or discrepancy) between her age and her sister's age, who is 30, is 10 ($y - 30 = 10$)
times, multiplied by	multiplication	Three times his brother's age is 6 ($3 \times y = 6$); eight multiplied by her weight is 96 ($y \times 8 = 96$); the product of his weight and 6 is 36 ($y \times 6 = 36$)

What are **independent** and **dependent variables** in algebra?

Variables can be broken down into independent and dependent variables. An independent variable is a quantity that increases or decreases (is variable), or that has an infinite number of values in the same expression. For example, in the expression $x^2 + y^2 = r^2$, x and y are variables. A dependent variable is a quantity that varies, but is produced by changes in the independent variable. In other words, the dependent variable's value is dependent on the independent variable. For example, in the expression $f(x) = y$, x is the independent variable and y is a dependent variable (because y is dependent on the value of x).

François Viète was the first to write and solve general algebraic equations by introducing the systematic use of letters as algebraic symbols.

Are there **differences** between **independent and dependent variables** in mathematics and statistics?

Yes, there are subtle differences between these two types of variables in mathematics and statistics. In mathematics, independent variables are those whose value determines the value of other variables; in statistics, they are a manipulated variable in an experiment or study whose presence or degree determines the change in the dependent variable.

Dependent variables in mathematics are those variables whose value is determined by an independent variable; in statistics, they are the observed variables in an experiment or study whose changes are determined by the presence or degree of one or more independent variables. (For more information about variables in statistics, see "Applied Mathematics.")

What is a **solution**?

When an equation has a variable, the number that replaces the unknown and makes the equation true is called a *solution*. For example, for the equation $(5 \times y) + 2 = 12$, y would be 2, or "2" is the solution that makes the equation true. Working it out would be: $(5 \times 2) + 2 = 12$; $10 + 2 = 12$; and finally, $12 = 12$. Remember, when finding a solution for an equation, one must follow any parentheses, exponents, multiplications, divisions, additions, and subtractions in the correct order of operation.

How do you **simplify** an algebraic equation?

The best way to *simplify* an equation is to combine like terms, which makes the equation simpler to solve. Numbers may be combined, as well as any terms with the same variable.

Terms can be combined either by adding or subtracting variables of the same kind. One can also use multiplication and division to simplify an equation by multiplying or dividing each side by the same number (except 0). The following are some examples:

- Add the like terms: $4x + 3x = 14$, simplifies to $7x = 14$.
- The equation $4 + 8x + 10 - 4x - 2 = 20$ can be simplified by combining the like terms, which gives the simplified result $12 + 4x = 20$.

How did symbols for unknowns and knowns in algebraic equations develop?

In 1591, François Viète was the first to write and solve general algebraic equations by introducing the systematic use of letters as algebraic symbols. He used vowels (a, e, i, o, u) for the unknowns and consonants (the rest of the alphabet) for the coefficients (or knowns).

But it was René Descartes who introduced a new way of using letters in the alphabet in his work, *La Gèometrie*. He used the letters at the end of the alphabet (x, y, ...) for unknowns and beginning of the alphabet (a, b, ...) for knowns (in many instances, these letters are italicized). This standard is still in algebraic use today.

- If necessary, do a combination of addition, subtraction, multiplication, or division. For example, the equation $2x - 2 = 4x + 3$, simplifies to $2x = 4x + 5$ (by adding 2 to both sides); then subtract $2x$ from both sides, simplifying to $0 = 2x + 5$. (Note: Since subtracting any number is the same as adding its negative, it is often more helpful to replace subtractions with additions of a negative number.) Finally, subtract 5 from both sides (or $2x = -5$) divide both sides by 2, resulting in the solution of $x = -5/2$ (or -2.5).

- To simplify expressions raised to a power, certain rules should be followed. For example, for $(x + 3)^2 - 4x$, square $x + 3$, or $(x + 3)(x + 3)$, first squaring the first term (x squared equals x^2), then the second (3 squared equals 9), then multiply and add the inner and outer terms together ($3x + 3x = 6x$). By combining like terms, the entire equation results in the simplified expression $x^2 + 6x + 9 - 4x$, which finally equals $x^2 + 2x + 9$.

What is the **order of operations** when you **simplify** an algebraic equation?

There is a certain order to working out an algebraic equation. The following lists the operations in their correct order:

- First: do what is inside the parentheses

- Second: do the exponents

- Third: do all the multiplications and divisions from left to right

- Finally: do all the additions and subtractions from left to right

There are also rules when it comes to grouping in algebraic equations—especially when working with parentheses. When an expression has parentheses within paren-

theses, work from the inside out, removing the innermost parentheses first. And remember—if there is a positive sign in front of the parentheses, it does not change any sign inside the parentheses; if there is a negative sign in front of the parentheses, it *will* change all the signs within the parentheses.

What are some **examples** of algebraic **equation solutions**?

The following lists some simple solutions to selected algebraic equations:

- Solve for the equation $4x - 4 = 12$

 add 4 to each side: $4x = 16$

 divide both sides by 4: $x = 16/4$

 solve for x: $x = 4$

- Solve for the equation $(x + 3)^2 - 4x = (x—1)^2 + 3$

 expand each side by doing the operations in the parentheses: $x^2 + 2x + 9 = x^2 - 2x + 4$

 then add $-x^2$ to each side (another way of subtracting):

 $2x + 9 = -2x + 4$

 then add $2x$ to each side: $4x + 9 = 4$

 then add -9 to each side: $4x = -5$

 then multiply each side by 1/4 (divide by 4): $x = -5/4$

What are **functions**?

Functions are mathematical expressions describing the relationship between variables and involve only algebraic operations. If there is one independent variable, the dependent variable, for example y, can be determined through the function. This is often seen written as $y = f(x)$, spoken as, "y equals f of x" (functions also use notation with x; for example, $f(x) = 2x + 1$ is a function). Functions within equations are also common; for example, in the equation $-x^2 + y = 3$, the y represents a function of x. To see this, note that this equation can also be written as $y = 3 + x^2$.

Functions do not always have to be in terms of $f(x)$. They can just as easily be termed $g(x)$, depending on the equation. But note: The equation $x^2 + y^2 = 9$ is *not* a function, as x and y are both independent variables.

Are there different **types of functions**?

Yes, there are different types of functions—so many, in fact, that the topic of "functions" is a book in itself. In particular, algebraic equations include polynomial and rational expression functions. For example, polynomial equations include linear (first

degree) functions, such as $f(x) = 2x$; a quadratic (second degree) function example is $f(x) = x^2$ (for more about polynomials and degrees, see below).

But "algebraic and polynomial functions" are not the only use of the term "function"—so don't get confused. There are also non-algebraic functions called exponential functions, and the inverses of exponential functions, called logarithmic functions. Set theory emphasizes the use of functions (for more about functions and sets, see "Foundations of Mathematics"); and there are trigonomic functions that include the relationships of sine, cosine, and tangent functions (for more information about trigonometry, see "Geometry and Trigonometry"). There also are continuous or discontinuous functions, transcendental functions, and even real and complex functions (all this may or may not be connected to algebra). The list goes on, and it is easy to see that mathematicians love the word "function."

What is a **coefficient**?

In an algebraic equation, a coefficient is simply a multiplicative factor. In the majority of cases, the coefficient is the numerical part (most often a constant) of the equation. Thus, it is called a numerical coefficient. For example, in $3x = 6$, the coefficient is 3; in $-3x = 6$, the coefficient is -3, as the coefficient takes on the sign of the operation. Terms such as xy may not appear to have a numerical coefficient, but it is 1—a number that is not written, but assumed.

Coefficients do not have to be just numbers: In the equation $5x^3y$, the coefficient of x^3y is 5. But in addition, the coefficient of x is $5x^2y$, and the coefficient of y is $5x^3$. Coefficients are also seen in functions; for example, in the function $f(x) = 2x$, the 2 is the coefficient.

What is a **diophantine equation**?

The first mention of diophantine equations was by Greek (Hellenic) mathematician Diophantus (c. 210–c. 290 c.e.). In his treatise *Arithmetica*, he solved equations with several variables for integral solutions—or what we call diophantine equations today. These are represented by one equation with at least two variables, such as x and y, and whose solutions have to be whole numbers (or integers). These equations either have no solutions, or an infinite or finite number of solutions. *Dio-*

A 1621 Latin edition of Greek mathematician Diophantus's *Arithmetica*.

79

phantine analysis is the mathematical term for how to determine integer solutions for such algebraic equations.

What is a **linear equation**?

As the term suggests, linear equations have to do with lines; and in algebra, a linear equation means certain equations (or functions) whose graph is a line (for an extensive explanation of graphs, see "Geometry and Trigonometry"). More specifically, in algebra, a linear equation is one that contains simply the variable, which makes them one of the simplest types of equations. For example, a linear equation in one variable has one unknown (the variable) represented by a letter; this letter, usually x, is always to the power of 1, meaning there is no x^2 or x^3 in the equation.

For instance, $x + 3 = 9$ is a simple linear equation. To solve such an equation, one must either add, subtract, multiply, and/or divide both sides of the equation by numbers and variables—and do this in the correct order—to end up with a solution: a single variable and single number on opposite sides of the equals sign. In this case, the solution to the linear equation is $x = 6$.

Finally, linear equations can be further broken down. For example, in the linear equation $ax + by + cz + dw = h$, in which a, b, c, and d are known numbers and x, y, z, and w are unknown numbers, if $h = 0$, the linear equation is said to be *homogeneous*.

What is the **absolute value** of a number?

The absolute value of a real number is the number stripped of any negative value. Therefore, the absolute value of a number will always be greater than or equal to zero. (Formally, the absolute value is considered the distance of a number from zero on a number line.) The symbol for "absolute value" is the number inside two parallel vertical lines (| |). For example, the absolute value of x is given by $|x|$. If the number is negative within the absolute value sign, it will automatically become positive. In numerical form, $|3|$ equals 3 and $|-3|$ equals 3.

When discussing complex numbers, the absolute value often means squaring the numbers, then taking the square root of those numbers. For example, the common way of writing complex equations is $z = a + bi$; the absolute value of z becomes $|z| = \sqrt{a^2+b^2}$. For instance, if $z = 3 - 4i$, then $|z| = \sqrt{3^2+4^2}$; $|z| = 5$.

What is a **system of equations**?

A system of equations is any set of simultaneous equations—two or more—that are intertwined and have to be determined together. They are usually a finite set of equations with the same unknowns, all of which have common solutions. A set of linear equations is said to be a *linear system*, while a set of homogeneous linear equations is called a *homogeneous linear system*. The number of equations is finite, meaning the solutions don't go

on forever like some with billions of answers. But a word of caution: Some problems use systems with hundreds of equations and just about the same number of variables.

ALGEBRAIC OPERATIONS

What are the **common** types of mathematical **operations**?

Operations are ways to obtain a single entity from one or more entities by manipulating numbers (and letters) in certain ways. They include the *elementary operations* most of us are familiar with: addition, subtraction, multiplication, division, cubing, squaring, and integer root extraction. There are numerous types of other operations, including *binary operations*, in which two quantities or expressions x and y interact in set theory (for more about set theory, see "Math Basics").

What is the algebraic concept of **inverse**?

"Inverses" in algebra are operations (or numbers) that "undo" each other. For example, if one multiplies 4 times its inverse, or 1/4, the solution is 1; thus, the rule for multiplicative inverse for x (with $x \neq 0$) is $1/x$, as in $x(1/x) = 1$. In addition, if you add -4 to 4, you get zero (0); thus, the additive inverse of x is $-x$, as in $x + (-x) = 0$.

What are **identity** and **conditional equations**?

Identity and conditional equations are ways in which numbers associate with each other. When an equation is true for every value of the variable, then the equation is called an identity equation. It is often denoted as I or E (the E is from the German *Einheit*, or "unity"). For example, $3x = 3x$ is an identity equation, because x will always be the same number. Zero is the identity element for addition, because any number added to 0 does not change the value of any of the other numbers in the operation (or $x + 0 = x$). The number 1 is the identity element of multiplication, as any number in an operation multiplied by 1 does not change the value of that number. Multiple identity is often written as $x \times 1 = x$.

When an equation is false for at least one value, it is called a conditional equation. For example, $6x = 12$ is conditional because it is false when $x = 3$ (and any number other than 2). In other words, if at least one value can be found in which the equation is false (or the right side is not equal to the left side) then the equation is called a conditional equation.

How do **numbers associate** with each other?

Generally in mathematics, there are certain properties of operations that determine how numbers associate with each other. *Closure* is a property of an operation that

reveals how numbers associate with each other; in particular, when two whole numbers are added, their sum will be a whole number. Closure as a property of multiplication occurs when two whole numbers are multiplied and their resulting product is a whole number.

An *associative* property means that for a given operation that combines three quantities (two at a time), the initial pairing of the quantities is arbitrary. For example, when doing an addition operation, the numbers can be combined in two ways: $(a + b) + c = a + (b + c)$. Thus, when adding the numbers 3, 4, and 5, this means that they may be combined as $(3 + 4) + 5 = 12$ or $3 + (4 + 5) = 12$. Following the same logic for multiplication, the associative law states that $(a \times b) \times c = a \times (b \times c)$. In fact, in an associative operation, the parentheses that indicate what quantities are to be first combined can be omitted; an example of the associative law for addition is $3 + 4 + 5 = 12$, and for multiplication, $2 \times 3 \times 4 = 24$. But not all operations are associative. One good example is division: You can't divide in the same way as you added or multiplied above. For example, the result of dividing three numbers differs. The operation $(96 \div 12) \div 4 = 2$ is not the same as $96 \div (12 \div 4) = 32$.

Like the associative property, the *commutative property* is another way of looking at how numbers associate with each other in operations. In particular, this law holds that for a given operation that combines two quantities, the order of the quantities is arbitrary. For example, in addition, adding $4 + 5$ can be written either as $4 + 5 = 9$ or $5 + 4 = 9$, or expressed as $a + b = b + a$. When working on a multiplication operation, the same rule applies, as in $a \times b = b \times a$. Again, not all operations are commu-

tative. For example, subtraction is not, as $6 - 3 = 3$ is not the same as $3 - 6 = -3$. Division also is not commutative, as $6 \div 3 = 2$ is not the same as $3 \div 6 = 1/2$.

The final property of an operation is the *distributive property*. In this rule, for any two operations, the first is distributive over the second. For example, multiplication is distributive over addition; for any numbers a, b, and c, $a \times (b + c) = (a \times b) + (a \times c)$. For the numbers 2, 3, and 4, you would have $2 \times (3 + 4) = 14$ or $(2 \times 3) + (2 \times 4) = 14$. Formally, there is a right and left distribution—left is listed above; right is $(a + b) \times c = (a \times c) + (b \times c)$. In most cases, both are commonly referred to as distributivity. Again, not all operations are distributive. For example, addition is not distributive over multiplication, as in $a + (b \times c) \neq (a + b) \times (a + c)$.

What is the **factorial of a number**?

A factorial is the product of consecutive natural numbers for all integers greater than or equal to 0. Factorials usually start with 1; the symbol for factorial is an exclamation point (!). For example, 4 factorial (4!) is $1 \times 2 \times 3 \times 4$, or 24. In the numerical system, consecutive factorials are 1 (1! = 1), 2 (2! = 1×2), 6 (3! = $1 \times 2 \times 3$), 24 (4! = $1 \times 2 \times 3 \times 4$), 120 (5! = $1 \times 2 \times 3 \times 4 \times 5$), 720 (6! = $1 \times 2 \times 3 \times 4 \times 5 \times 6$), 5040 (7! = $1 \times 2 \times 3 \times 4 \times 5 \times 6 \times 7$), 40,320 (8! = $1 \times 2 \times 3 \times 4 \times 5 \times 6 \times 7 \times 8$), 362,880 (9! = $1 \times 2 \times 3 \times 4 \times 5 \times 6 \times 7 \times 8 \times 9$), and so on.

There are two additional rules: The number 0 factorial (0!) = 1; and the factorial values for negative integers are not defined. Factorials are most often used in reference to counting numbers, statistics (especially in probability calculations), calculus, and physics.

EXPONENTS AND LOGARITHMS

What is an **exponent** in terms of algebra?

An exponent is actually raising a number to a certain power; this is written as a superscript to the right of a real number, such as 3^4, expressed as "three raised to the fourth power," or "three with an exponent of four." (For more information on exponents, see "Math Basics.") The exponent represents the number of times a number is being multiplied. The above example actually means "$3 \times 3 \times 3 \times 3$," which is equal to 81. The powers can be an integer (negative or positive numbers), real number, or even a complex number. This can also be thought of as taking the quantity b, the base number, to the power of another quantity often called e, the exponent. (In many computer-oriented texts, this is written as $b \wedge e$.)

Exponents are important to algebra as they are often included in most algebraic equations. The process of performing the operation of raising to a power is known as

exponentiation. Exponents are also often associated with functions. For example, in the function $f(x) = x^2$, the 2 is the exponent.

What is a **base** in algebra?

The base is used in algebra in connection with powers. In fact, it is called the base of a power—or the number that is used as a factor a given number of times. In the example above, 3^4, 3 is the base. The base can either be the number used with an exponent to create a power, such as the 3 in 3^4; or a number written as a subscript, such as with a logarithm, for example, $\log_a x$, in which a is the base number. (See below for more information about logarithms; for more information about bases, see "Math Basics").

What are some **simple rules** of **exponents**?

There are several simple rules when it comes to exponents. These include the following:

- The equation $x^1 = x$ (or a number raised to the 1 power is the number itself; this is also called the "rules of 1").

- The equation $x^0 = 1$ (unless $x = 0$, then this is referred to as undefined; this is also called the "zero rule").

- A number without an exponent has an exponent of 1, as in $20 = 20^1$.

- A negative exponent means to divide by that number of factors instead of multiplying. For example, 3^{-3} is equal to $1/(3^3)$. But there is a restriction to this rule: $x^{-n} = 1/x^n$ only when x is not zero; if x is 0, then x^{-n} is undefined.

What are some **rules** for **combining exponents**?

There are also rules for combining exponents (also called the *laws of indices*):

- To multiply exponents with identical bases, add the exponents, such as $3^2 \times 3^3 = 3^5$ (3 is the base).

- To multiply like exponents, combine terms, such as $10^2 \times 2^2 = (10 \times 2)^2 = 400$.

- To divide identical bases, subtract the exponents, such as $10^3/10 = 10^{3-1} = 10^2 = 100$ (the denominator 10 has an assumed exponent of 1).

What are the **connections between logarithms and algebra**?

Logarithms are the numbers of the power to which a base must be raised in order to get a given positive number. For example, the logarithm of 100 to the base 10 is 2, or $\log_{10} 100 = 2$; this is because $10^2 = 100$. *Common logarithms* are positive numbers that use the number 10 as the base; they are written as $\log x$. Those using the number

symbolized by *e* as the base are called *natural logarithms* (also phrased as logarithms with a base *e*); the natural logarithm of a number *x* is written as ln *x*.

What's the connection? Because logarithms are really exponents, they satisfy all the usual rules of exponents. Consequently, tedious and long algebraic calculations such as those involving multiplication and division can be replaced by the simpler processes of adding or subtracting the corresponding logarithms. In general, logarithmic tables are usually used for this purpose—although calculators, computers, and Internet mathematics and computational sites usually replace the need for such tables.

Even the simple act of cranking up your sound system involves math. The decibel scale used by your loudspeakers and amplifiers employs the concept of logarithms.

What was the **progression** of **logarithm development**?

The invention of logarithms was a long process, starting with Scottish mathematician John Napier (1550–1617; also known as Laird of Merchiston), who first came up with the idea of logarithms in 1594. But the actual invention and announcement of logarithms would take another 20 years: In 1614, Napier would publish *Mirifici logarithmorum canonis descripto* (*Description of the Wonderful Canon of Logarithms*), offering tables and rules for their use.

Not long afterward, in 1617, English mathematician Henry Briggs (1561–1630) published *Logarithmorum chilias prima* (*Logarithms of Numbers from 1 to 1,000*), introducing the concept of common logarithms—or logarithms based on the powers of ten. And finally, independently from Briggs and Napier came Swiss mathematician Joost Bürgi (1552–1632), who in 1620, presented *Arithmetische und geometrische progress-tabulen*, a German work presenting the discovery of logarithms.

The discoveries differed in several ways: Napier's approach was algebraic; Bürgi's was geometric. There were differences from the common and natural logarithms used today. And neither Napier nor Bürgi mentioned the concept of a logarithmic base—something that Briggs presented.

By 1624, Briggs would write *Arithmetica logarithmica* (*The Arithmetic of Logarithms*), extending his common log tables from 1 to 20,000 and from 90,000 to 100,000. But the work on logarithms did not end with Napier, Briggs, or Bürgi. Natural logarithms eventually evolved out of Napier's original work. And defining loga-

rithms as exponents was finally recognized by English mathematician John Wallis (1616–1703), who presented them in his 1685 publication *De algebra tractatus* (*Treatise of Algebra*).

For what **other invention** was **John Napier** known?

Scottish mathematician John Napier may have been known for his contributions toward logarithms, but was also the inventor of a tool called Napier's Bones (also called Napier's Rods). These were multiplication tables inscribed on strips of animal bone or wood. Wilhelm Schickardt would eventually build the first calculating machine based on Napier's Bones, a device that could add, subtract, and—with help—multiply or divide.

Napier was also the "instigator" in another discovery: In 1621, English mathematician and clergyman William Oughtred (1575–1660) used Napier's logarithms as the basis for the slide rule (a ruler-like instrument used long before hand-held calculators came in vogue). Oughtred not only invented the standard rectilinear slide rule, but also the circular slide rule, which was an extremely useful tool that remained in common usage for more than three hundred years. (For more about Oughtred, see "Math Basics.")

What are the **properties of logarithms**?

Logarithms have certain properties depending on interpretations of an equation. The following lists some of the most common properties (these rules are the same for all positive bases):

- $\log_a 1 = 0$, because $a^0 = 1$. For example, in the equation $14^0 = 1$, the base is 14 and the exponent is 0. Because a logarithm is an exponent, this would mean the equation can be written as a logarithmic equation, or $\log_{14} 1 = 0$ (zero is the exponent).

- $\log_a a = 1$, because $a^1 = a$. For example, in the equation $3^1 = 3$, the base is 3 and the exponent is 1; the result is 3, with the corresponding logarithmic equation being $\log_3 3 = 1$.

- $\log_a a^x = x$, because $a^x = a^x$. For example, $3^4 = 3^4$, with the base as 3. The logarithmic equation becomes $\log_3 3^4 = 4$.

What are some **examples** of **logarithm use**?

Logarithms are used in many areas of science and engineering, especially in those areas in which quantities vary over a large range. For example, the decibel scale for the loudness of sound and the astronomical scale of stellar brightness are both logarithmic scales.

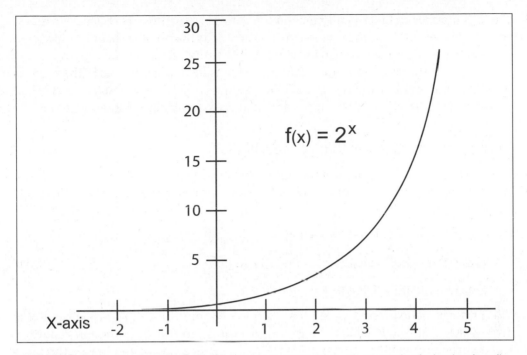

$$f(x) = 2^x$$

In this example of an exponential function, when 2 is raised to the power of x, the line representing the function always lies above the x axis.

What is an **exponential function**?

Along with exponents come exponential functions, or the relationship between values of a variable and the numbers formed by raising some positive number to the power of those values. In functional notation, an exponential function is written $f(x) = a^x$, in which a is a positive number; for example, the function $f(x) = 2^x$ is an exponential function.

In logarithmic terms, an exponential function is most commonly written as exp (x) or e^x, in which e is called the base of the natural logarithm. These types of functions are usually shown on a graph. (For more information about graphs, see "Geometry and Trigonometry.") As a function of the real variable x, the resulting graph of e^x is always positive, or above the x axis and increasing from left to right. Although the line of such a function never touches the x axis, it gets very close to it.

What is *e* in terms of **logarithms**?

No, e is not the code name in a James Bond movie. When talking about logarithms (or logs), in the majority of mathematical circles, it means the base of the natural logarithm. It is yet another irrational, transcendental number (such as pi, or π) that has a plethora of names: It has been called everything from the logarithmic constant and

Napier's number to Euler's constant and the natural logarithmic base. One of the best ways to define e is to use the expression $(1 + x)^{(1/x)}$; e is the number that this expression approaches as x gets smaller and smaller. Substituting in values for x gives you the idea: if $x = 1$, the result is 2; if $x = 0.5$, the result is 2.25; when $x = 0.25$, the result is 2.4414...; if $x = 0.125$, the result is 2.56578 ...; if $x = 0.0625$, the result is 2.63792...; and so on. This is why approximations are often used in solving equations using e.

What are the **rules** for **combining logarithms**?

There are certain rules for combining logarithms. In the following cases, let a be a positive number that does not equal 0; n be a real number; and u and v be positive real numbers:

Logarithmic Rule 1: $\log_a(uv) = \log_a(u) + \log_a(v)$

Logarithmic Rule 2: $\log_a(u/v) = \log_a(u) - \log_a(v)$

Logarithmic Rule 3: $\log_a(u)^n = n\log_a(u)$

This can be expressed as follows: In rule one, multiplication inside the log is turned into addition outside the log (and vice versa); in rule two, division inside the log is turned into subtraction outside the log (and vice versa); and in rule three, an exponent on anything inside the log can be moved to the front of the log as a multiplier (and vice versa). But remember, these rules only apply if the bases are the same. For example, because the bases are not the same in $\log_a(u) + \log_b(v)$, this expression can't be simplified.

How do you **expand logarithms**?

Like an algebraic expression, it is possible to expand logarithms, which is a way of "picking apart" an expression. The following lists two examples of expanding a logarithmic expression:

- To expand $\log_2(3x) = \log_2(3) + \log_2(x)$

- To expand $\log_2(12/x) = \log_2(12) - \log_2(x)$

Is it possible to **simplify logarithms**?

Yes, as in algebraic equations, it is possible to simplify logarithms, but in different ways. The following lists some examples:

- To simplify $\log_3(x) + \log_3(y) = \log_3(xy)$

- To simplify $\log_3(6) - \log_3(4) = \log_3(6/4)$

- To simplify $2\log_3(x) = \log_3(x^2)$

How can the **base** of logarithms be **changed**?

The base of logarithms can be changed from one that is not 10 or e to an equivalent logarithm with base 10 or e. The following gives the formula for such a transition, in which a, b, and x are real positive numbers (but neither a nor b are equal to 1, and x is greater than 0):

Convert $\log_a x$ to the base b by using the formula $(\log_b x)/(\log_b a)$.

How are **equations with exponents** and **logarithms solved**?

The way to solve an exponential equation is relatively easy: Take the log of both sides of the equation, then solve for the variable. For example, to solve for x in the equation $e^x = 60$.

1. First, take the natural log (ln) of both sides:
 $\ln(e^x) = \ln(60)$

2. Simplify using the logarithmic rule #3 (see above) for the left side:
 $x \ln(e) = \ln(60)$

3. Then simplify again, since $\ln(e) = 1$ to:
 $x = \ln(60) = 4.094344562$

4. And finally, check your answer (using log tables or your calculator) in the original equation $e^x = 60$:
 $e^{4.094344562} = 60$ is definitely true.

The way to solve a logarithmic equation is equally easy: Just rewrite the equation in exponential form and solve for the variable. For example, to solve for x in the equation $\ln(x) = 11$:

1. First, change both sides so they are exponents of the base e:
 $e^{\ln(x)} = e^{11}$

2. When the bases of the exponent and logarithm are the same, the left part of the equation becomes x, thus, it can be written:
 $x = e^{11}$

3. To obtain x, determine the solution for e^{11}, or
 x is approximately 59,874.14172.

4. And finally, check your answer (using tables or your calculator) in the original equation $\ln(x) = 11$:
 $\ln(59,874.14172) = 11$ is definitely true.

POLYNOMIAL EQUATIONS

What is a **polynomial**?

In its simplest form, a polynomial is a mathematical equation that involves a sum of powers in one or more variable, all multiplied by coefficients. In such equations, variables and numbers on both sides of the equal sign are considered polynomials. For example, by expanding out the expression $(x - 2)^3$ (or multiplying out the equation) we discover that $(x - 2)^3 = x^3 - 6x^2 + 12x - 8$, which is a polynomial equation.

Are there other **ways** of **describing polynomials**?

Yes, there are other ways to describe polynomials. In particular, a polynomial with only one variable is called a *univariate polynomial*. A *multivariate polynomial* is one with more than one variable. There are other terms to further define polynomials, including the following:

Monomial—A monomial is a one-term polynomial (*mono* means "one"). For example, $3x$ is a monomial.

Binomial—A binomial is a two-term polynomial (*bi* meaning "two"). For example, $3x^2 - 10$ is a binomial.

Trinomial—A trinomial is a three-term polynomial (*tri* means "three"). For example, $4x^3 + 3x + 6$ is a trinomial.

What is the **degree** of a **polynomial equation**?

The highest order power (or exponent) used in a univariate polynomial is called its *polynomial degree* or *order*; it is also defined as the largest (or maximum) sum of exponents that appear on the variables in the equation's terms. Commonly, the word "degree" is used more frequently because "order" has another meaning when discussing polynomials.

You can also talk about degrees in reference to monomials, binomials, and trinomials. The degree of a monomial is the sum of the degrees of the variable in the equation; the degrees of the other polynomial equations are the greatest of the degrees in terms after the equation has been simplified. For example, a third degree trinomial equation is $x^3 - 3x - 2 = 0$.

What are **quartic equations**?

Quartic equations are polynomial equations whose highest power of the unknown variable is four. Or put another way, quartic equations are algebraic equations whose highest exponent (or degree or order) is four. But take note: Quartic equations are *not* the same as quadratic equations—or second degree equations in one variable—so don't mix them up.

What are the **names** of polynomial equations with **different degrees**?

The polynomial equations with different degrees (or orders)—especially the lowest degrees—are as follows:

- *first degree* (1) polynomial = linear
- *second degree* (2) polynomial = quadratic
- *third degree* (3) polynomial = cubic
- *fourth degree* (4) polynomial = quartic
- *fifth degree* (5) polynomial = quintic
- *sixth degree* (6) polynomial = sextic

How do you **multiply polynomial equations**?

To multiply two monomials, multiply the coefficients and then multiply the variables (and when multiplying the variables, keep the variables and add the exponents). The following are several examples of multiplying various polynomial equations:

Multiplying monomials:

$$(5x)(6x^2)$$
$$= (5 \times 6)(x^{2+1}) \text{ (multiply the numbers and add the exponents)}$$
$$= 30x^3$$

Multiplying a monomial and polynomial (binomial):

$$4y(2y-8)$$
$$= 4y(2y) - 4y(8) \text{ (multiply } 4y \text{ times both terms)}$$
$$= 8y^2 - 32y \text{ (depending on what is on the other side of the equation, you can further simplify by dividing by 8, or } y^2 - 4y)$$

Multiplying polynomials:

$$6y^3(8y^6 + 5y^4 - 3y^3)$$
$$= 6y^3(8y^6) + 6y^3(5y^4) - 6y^3(3y^3)$$
$$= 48y^9 + 30y^7 - 18y^6$$

How do you **divide polynomials**?

To divide a polynomial by a monomial, divide each term in the polynomial by the monomial (to divide monomials, we divide the coefficients and then subtract the exponents) or:

$$(A + B + C)/M = A/M + B/M + C/M$$

For example, to solve the equation
$$10x^5/2x^3 = (10/2) (x^{5-3}) = 5x^2$$

What does **factoring polynomials** mean?

When a polynomial is written as the product of two or more polynomial equations, the polynomial has been factored. This allows a complicated polynomial to be broken up into easier, lower degree pieces; and it makes the equation easier to solve. One way to look at it is that factoring a polynomial is the opposite process from multiplying polynomials.

One of the most basic ways to factor a polynomial is similar to factoring a number. When a number is factored, the result will be the prime factors that multiply together to give the number (for example, $6 = 2 \times 3$, or $12 = 2 \times 2 \times 3$; see "Math Basics" to learn more about prime factors). With polynomials, this is often called "taking out a common factor": If every term in a polynomial expression has several factors, and if every term has at least one factor that is the same, then that factor is called a *common factor*. If this is the case, then the common factor can be removed from every term and multiplied by the whole remaining expression.

For example, for the equation $2x^2 + 8x$, the first term has factors of 2 and x, while the second term has factors of 2, 4, and x. The common factors are 2 and x, making $2x$ the overall common factor. This makes the expression equal to $2x(x + 4)$. Thus, it is easy to see that when a polynomial is factored, it results in simpler polynomials that can be multiplied together to give the initial polynomial.

What is the **difference** and **sum of cubes**?

When factoring polynomials, there is the difference and sum of cubes. The *difference of cubes* takes the form: $a^3 - b^3$, and can be factored into $(a - b)(a^2 + ab + b^2)$. Thus, if an expression resembles $a^3 - b^3$, then $(a - b)$ is a factor; use long division to find the remaining factor(s).

The *sum of cubes* takes the form $a^3 + b^3$, and can be factored into $(a + b)(a^2 + ab + b^2)$. Thus, if an expression resembles $a^3 + b^3$, then $(a + b)$ is a factor. Again, use long division to find the remaining factor(s).

How do you find the **roots of a polynomial**?

Finding the root, also called a zero, of a polynomial is one way to solve for the equation. In other words, the root of an equation is simply a number (or numbers) that solves the equation.

For example, for second degree polynomials, we can find the roots by *completing the square*. Picking apart an equation is the best way to see this:

1. $3x^2 - 4x + 1 = 0$

2. $(1/3)(3x^2 - 4x + 1) = (1/3)0$ (making the coefficient of the x^2 term into a 1)

3. $x^2 - (4/3)x + 1/3 = 0$

What is a perfect square?

There are many equations that can be factored into a perfect square. Any expression written in the form $x^2 + 2ax + a^2$ is a perfect square—an expression written as [something]2. To determine if an expression is a perfect square, first see if the constant term is a square number—in other words, can you take the square root of it and get an integer for an answer. If so, determine if the square root of the constant, multiplied by 2 gives the coefficient of the linear term (or the x term). If it does, the original expression may be factored into a perfect square. (Note: The above procedure only works when the coefficient of x^2 is 1.)

For example, in the equation $x^2 + 8x + 16$, the constant term (16) is already a perfect square (the square root of 16 is 4). Since $2(4) = 8$, the original expression can be written as a perfect square. Because we know $x^2 + 2ax + a^2$ is a perfect square, and equals $(x + a)^2$, by substituting the common factor 4 into the equation, we find that $x^2 + 8x + 16 = (x + 4)^2$.

4. $(x^2 - (4/3)x) + 1/3 - 0$ (group the x and x^2 terms together)

5. $(x^2 - (4/3)x + (-2/3)^2) - (-2/3)^2 + 1/3 = 0$ (determine the coefficient of the x term, divide it by 2 and then square; add and subtract that term)

6. $(x - 2/3)^2 - 4/9 + 1/3 = 0$

7. $(x - 2/3)^2 - 1/9 = 0$ (add together the $4/9 + 1/3$ by converting the denominator to 9, in which 1/3 becomes 3/9)

8. $(x - 2/3)^2 = 1/9$ (move the 1/9 to the other side of the equation by subtracting it from both sides)

9. $x - 2/3 = 1/3$ or $x - 2/3 = -1/3$

That means that $x = 1$ or $x = 1/3$ are the two roots that make the equation true (just substitute either number into the initial equation to see that they are both true).

What are **examples of polynomials** with **one root** and **no roots**?

The following is an example of a polynomial with only one root:

$x^2 + 6x + 9 = 0$

$(x^2 + 6x + (6/2)^2) - (6/2)^2 + 9 = 0$

$(x + 3)^2 - 9 + 9 = 0$

$(x + 3)^2 = 0$

$x + 3 = 0$

$x = -3$, or the polynomial has only one root $x = -3$

But not all polynomials have roots. The following is an example of a polynomial with no root:

$2x^2 - 6x + 8 = 0$

$(1/2)(2x^2 - 6x + 8) = (1/2)0$

$x^2 - 3x + 4 = 0$

$(x^2 - 3x + (-3/2)^2) - (-3/2)^2 + 4 = 0$

$(x - 3/2)^2 - 9/4 + 4 = 0$

$(x - 3/2)^2 + 7/4 = 0$

$(x - 3/2)^2 = -7/4$

Because a real number squared is greater than or equal to 0, that means $(x - 3/2)^2$ will always be greater than or equal to 0. Therefore, the answer can't be $-7/4$, a negative number, and there are no real roots for this polynomial.

What is a **quadratic equation**?

A quadratic equation is a second degree (order) polynomial equation, thus it is guaranteed to have two solutions, both of which may be real or complex. This is seen in the standard form $ax^2 + bx + c = 0$.

The roots of x can be found in the equation by factoring and completing the square (a method of transforming a quadratic equation so that it is in the form of a perfect square). For example, to solve the equation $x^2 - 3x = 4$ by factoring, you would do the following:

First, write the equation in standard quadratic equation form:

$$x^2 - 3x - 4 = 0$$

Then factor the form:

$$(x - 4)(x + 1) = 0$$

In order for these numbers to equal zero, we determine that for $(x - 4)$, x would be 4; and for $(x + 1)$, x would equal –1. Thus, the solutions are 4 and –1.

Can all **quadratic equations be solved by factoring**?

Don't be fooled: Not all quadratic equations can be solved by factoring. For example, $x^2 - 3x = 3$ is not solvable with this method. One way to solve quadratic equations is by completing the square; still another method is to graph the solution (a quadratic graph forms a parabola—a U-shaped line seen on the graph). But one of the most well-known ways is by using the quadratic formula (see below).

For example, if we want to find the roots of the polynomial $x^2 + 2x - 7$, we can replace the "corresponding" numbers from the initial equation into the quadratic equation; thus, $a = 1$, $b = 2$, and $c = -7$. Substituting these numbers into the quadratic formula, we solve for:

$$\frac{-2 + \sqrt{2^2 - 4(1)(-7)}}{2(1)}$$

$$\frac{-2 - \sqrt{2^2 - 4(1)(-7)}}{2(1)}$$

That equals

$$\frac{-2 \pm \sqrt{32}}{2} = -1 \pm 2\sqrt{2}$$

What is the **discriminant** of a **quadratic equation**?

In the quadratic equation $ax^2 + bx + c = 0$, the value of $b^2 - 4ac$ is the discriminant—the same numbers and letters that are under the square root sign of the quadratic formula. This is actually the products of the squares of the polynomial root differences. In other words, this quantity characterizes certain properties of the quantity's roots. The discriminant is often used for such mathematical concepts as metrics, modules, quadratic fields, and polynomials.

MORE ALGEBRA

What is an **array**?

A mathematical array is a list of lists, or a rectangular arrangement of objects; it is a useful way of keeping a collection of things. Arrays are orderly arrangements of objects in columns and rows, with the objects most often being numbers. For example, the most common arrays are two dimensional with a certain amount of rows and columns:

$$\begin{vmatrix} 3 & 0 & 1 \\ -2 & 4 & 0 \end{vmatrix}$$

In this case, this is a 2-by-3 array (rows are always mentioned before columns). The order of numbers and/or elements in an array may sometimes, but not always, be significant (as it is in a matrix; see below).

What is a **matrix**?

A matrix is a concise way of representing and working with linear transformations; also, it is a rectangular array or grid of numbers or variables that allows the user to perform certain mathematical operations. They are usually symbolized as large parentheses or two large pair of parallel double lines surrounding the array of numbers or variables. These numbers can be manipulated to solve systems of equations or problems with many different variables or numbers, by addition, subtraction, multiplication or other methods. Each row and column of a given matrix must have the same number of elements.

Any time one has a list of numbers, or a table of numbers in a specific order, concerning anything at all (prices, grades, populations, coordinates of points, production tables ...), it can be considered to be a matrix. When the idea of the matrix was first conceived, its development dealt with transformation of geometric objects and solution of systems of linear equations. Historically, the early emphasis was on the determinant (see below), not the matrix; today, especially in linear algebra, matrices are considered first.

Who **invented matrices**?

Although a simple form of matrices may have been used by the Mayans (and maybe other cultures; see below), the true mathematical use of a matrix was first formulated around 1850, by English mathematician, poet, and musician James Sylvester (1814–1897). In his 1850 paper, Sylvester wrote, "For this purpose we must commence, not with a square, but with an oblong arrangement of terms consisting, suppose, of m lines and n columns. This will not in itself represent a determinant, but is, as it were, a Matrix out of which we may form various systems of determinants by fix-

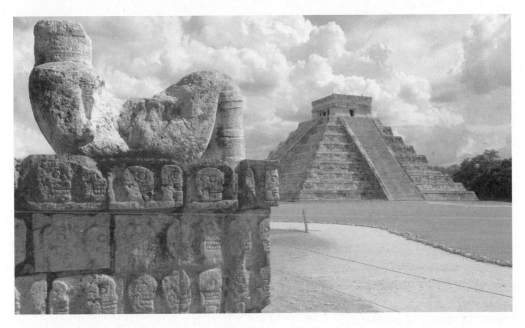

The ancient Mayans may have been among the first cultures to use a simple form of matrices.

ing upon a number p, and selecting at will *p* lines and *p* columns, the squares corresponding of *p*th order." In this case, Sylvester used the term matrix to describe its conventional use, or "the place from which something else originates."

But the matrix story was not all about Sylvester. In 1845, Sylvester's collaborator, English mathematician Arthur Cayley (1821–1895), used a form of matrices in his work, *On the Theory of Linear Transformations*; by 1855 and 1858, Cayley began to use the term "matrix" in its modern mathematical sense. Although he was an avid mountaineer and a lawyer for close to a decade and a half (which is how he met Sylvester), during his free time Cayley published more than 200 mathematical papers. He also contributed a great deal to the field of algebra, initiated analytic geometry of n-dimensional spaces, and developed the theory of invariants, among other mathematical feats.

Sylvester also remained brilliant throughout his life. He founded the *American Journal of Mathematics* in 1878; and at the ripe age of 71, he invented the theory of reciprocants (differential invariants).

What are some **examples of a matrix**?

The dimensions of a matrix are the number of rows (horizontal numbers) and columns (vertical numbers); it is written as the rows first, columns second. The following are some simple examples of matrices—all differing in dimensions:

A 3 by 2 (3 × 2) matrix:

$$\begin{bmatrix} 1 & 2 \\ 3 & 4 \\ 5 & 6 \end{bmatrix}$$

A 2 by 3 (2 × 3) matrix:

$$\begin{bmatrix} 1 & 2 & 3 \\ 4 & 5 & 6 \end{bmatrix}$$

A 4 by 4 (4 × 4) matrix (when the row and column dimensions are the same, it is called a "square matrix"):

$$\begin{bmatrix} 1 & 2 & 3 & 4 \\ 5 & 6 & 7 & 8 \\ 9 & 1 & 2 & 3 \\ 4 & 5 & 6 & 7 \end{bmatrix}$$

How do you **add matrices**?

It is pretty easy to add matrices. For example, for (1 2) + (–1 –2), you add the matrices, (or in this case, row numbers), simply by adding the corresponding terms in each matrix. Thus, the matrix of (1 2) + (–1 –2) = (1–1 2–2) = (0 0).

What is the **identity matrix**?

The identity matrix is the n-by-n matrix that has all ones down the main diagonal and zeroes everywhere else; it must also be a square. The following is the identity matrix:

$$\begin{bmatrix} 1 & 0 & 0 \\ 0 & 1 & 0 \\ 0 & 0 & 1 \end{bmatrix}$$

Or in more formal and explicit terms:

$$\begin{bmatrix} 1 & 0 & \cdots & 0 \\ 0 & 1 & \cdots & 0 \\ \vdots & \vdots & \ddots & \vdots \\ 0 & 0 & \cdots & 1 \end{bmatrix}$$

What happens when you **multiply a matrix** by the **identity matrix**?

When you multiply any n-by-n matrix by the identity matrix, you get that same matrix back again. Therefore, let the letter I represent the n-by-n identity matrix, and A rep-

> ### Did the Mayans know about matrices?
>
> Some scientists believe that the Mayan culture had a good working idea about matrices long before they became a part of mathematics. It is thought that the Mayans discovered how to place a set of "numbers" in columns and rows, then performed diverse operations on them, such as a method of adding and subtracting along diagonals to solve "equations" with unknown quantities. They may have even used the matrices for multiplication, division, and calculations of square and cubic roots on a matrix array by using a series of dots in a matrix to perform the operations. And there is evidence of these mathematical squares on their monuments, paintings, and even garments, including those of the Mayan priests and on crests of higher officials. But not everyone agrees with this notion; some scientists believe that the Mayan grids are merely mimicking objects in nature, such as the back of a turtle's shell.

resent any other n-by-n matrix; then we have $A \times I = A$ and $I \times A = A$. This is much like the situation in the real numbers: $x \times 1 = x$ and $1 \times x = x$.

How are **matrices used**?

Matrices are used in a multitude of fields, from mathematics and science to certain humanities fields. For example, they are used in physics to determine the equilibrium of rigid bodies; in graph theory, fractals, and solutions of systems of linear equations in mathematics; and in forest management, computer graphics, cryptology—even electrical networks.

ABSTRACT ALGEBRA

What is **abstract algebra**?

Abstract algebra is a collection of mathematical topics that deal with algebraic structures rather than the usual number systems. These structures include groups, rings, and fields; branches of these topics include communtative and homological algebras. In addition, linear algebra and even elementary number theory (see "Math Basics") are often included under abstract algebra.

What is an **algebraic structure**?

An algebraic structure is made up of a set (collection of objects called elements; for more information about sets, see "Foundations of Mathematics") together with one or

99

more operations on the set that satisfy certain axioms. The algebraic structures get their names depending on the operations and axioms. For example, algebraic structures include fields, groups, and rings—and many other structures with strange names such as loops, monoids, groupoids, semigroups, and quasigroups.

What is a **field**?

A field is an algebraic structure that shares the common rules for operations (addition, subtraction, multiplication, and division, except division by zero) of the rational, real, and complex numbers (but not integers, see below under "ring"). A field must have two operations, must have at least two elements, and must be commutative, distributive, and associative (see above for definitions). Formerly called "rational domain," a field in both French (*corps*) and German (*Körper*) appropriately means "body." A field with a finite number of members is called a *Galois* or *finite field*. Fields are useful to define such concepts as vectors and matrices.

What is a **group** in **abstract algebra**?

A group, usually referred to as *G*, is a finite or infinite set of elements together with a binary operation (often called the group operation) that together satisfy the four fundamental properties—closure, associativity, and the identity and inverse properties (for more information about these properties, see elsewhere in this chapter). A great many of the objects investigated in mathematics turn out to be groups, including familiar number systems—such as the integers, rational, real, and complex numbers under addition; non-zero rational, real, and complex numbers under multiplication; non-singular matrices under multiplication; and so on. The branch of mathematics that studies groups is called group theory, an important area of mathematics that has many applications to mathematical physics (such as particle theory).

What is a **ring**?

A ring is an algebraic structure (some definitions say a set) in which two binary operators (addition and multiplication) in various combinations must satisfy either the additive associative, commutative, identity, and inverse properties, the multiplicative associative property, or the left and right distributivity properties. For example, the elements of one operation, such as addition, must form a group that is commutative, also known as an abelian group. The multiplicative operation must produce unique answers that have the associative property. These two operations are further connected by requiring the multiplication to have a distributive property with respect to the addition. This can be written as follows, with *a*, *b*, and *c* elements of the ring:

$$a \times (b + c) = (a \times b) + (a \times c) \text{ and } (b + c) \times a = (b \times a) + (c \times a)$$

Rings are usually named after one or more of their investigators. But such a practice usually makes understanding the properties of the various associated rings difficult for anyone other than the mathematician working on the ring.

What is **linear algebra**?

Linear algebra is the study of linear sets of equations. It encompasses their transformation properties, and includes the analysis of rotations in space, least squares fitting, and numerous other problems in mathematics, physics, and engineering.

What is **Boolean algebra**?

Boolean algebra is an abstract mathematical system used to express the relationship between sets (groups of objects or concepts; see "Math Basics"). It is important in the study of information theory, the theory of probability, and the geometry of sets. The use of Boolean notation in electrical networks aided the development of switching theory and the eventual design of computers.

It was English mathematician George Boole (1815–1864) who first developed this type of logic by demonstrating the algebraic manipulation of logical statements, showing whether or not a statement is true, and showing how a statement can be made into a simpler, more convenient form without changing its overall meaning. Today, this way of looking at logic is called Boolean algebra.

Boolean algebra did not end there: In 1881, the English logician and mathematician John Venn (1834–1923) interpreted Boole's work and introduced a new way of diagramming Boole's notation in his treatise, *Symbolic Logic*. This was later refined by the English mathematician Charles Dodgson (1832–1898), better known as the writer of *Alice's Adventures in Wonderland* (under the pseudonym Lewis Carroll). Today when studying sets, we call this method not the Boole, Carroll, or Dodgson diagram, but the Venn diagram. Thus, Boolean notation demonstrates the relationship between groups, indicating what is in each set alone, what is jointly contained in both, and what is present in neither.

Though Charles Dodgson is more commonly known as the author of *Alice's Adventures in Wonderland* under the pen name of Lewis Carroll, he was also a brilliant mathematician. Among other accomplishments, he devised ways to refine Boolean algebra notations.

How is algebra used to solve problems in various fields— in mathematics and otherwise?

Algebra has been used extensively to solve a myriad of mathematical and scientific problems in recent years. For example, a problem that has plagued two mathematical areas—topology and algebra—was recently solved: the relationship between different mathematical structures. First formulated by German mathematician Friedrich Hirzebruch in the mid-20th century, the problem was to determine which numbers were topological invariants of complex-algebraic varieties (or the zero-sets of polynomials). The researchers found that no such numbers were topologically invariant, and thus, the numbers depend on the algebraic structure of the variety, not the topological properties. Still another study used algebra in the field of DNA hybridization—a process central to most biotechnological devices that monitor changes in cells' gene expressions. Based on their calculations and applications of algebra within their model, the researchers were able to monitor cellular changes.

Why are mathematicians so interested in **transcendental numbers**?

Transcendental numbers are those that are not the root of any integer polynomial, or that are not an algebraic number of any degree. Thus all transcendental numbers are irrational (rational numbers are algebraic numbers of degree one). The importance of such numbers translates through more than two millennia of history: For example, they provided the first proof that circle squaring was insoluble, which is one of the geometric problems that has baffled mathematicians throughout antiquity.

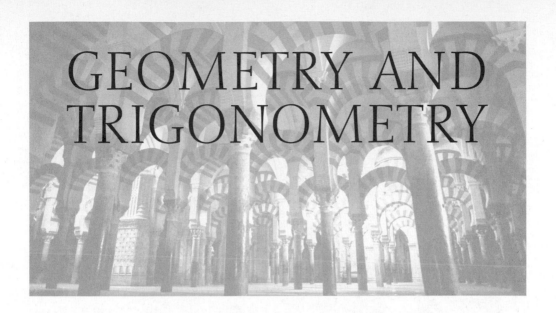

GEOMETRY AND TRIGONOMETRY

GEOMETRY BEGINNINGS

What is **geometry**?

Geometry is the study of figures or objects in space—of a certain number of dimensions and types—and focuses on the properties and measurements of points, lines, angles, surfaces, and solids of those objects (or sometimes even the space around them). The word *geometry* is from the Greek words for "earth" and "to measure" (*geometria,* broken down into *gë* and *metreein,* respectively). A person who studies geometry is called a geometer or geometrician.

What are the **divisions** found within the **field of geometry**?

The geometry field has several distinct divisions, including:

Plane geometry—This includes common features such as circles, lines, triangles, and polygons.

Solid geometry—This also includes such figures as circles and lines, as well as polyhedrons.

Spherical geometry—This includes shapes such as spherical triangles (see below) and polygons.

Analytic geometry—Also called coordinate geometry, this includes the study of figures in terms of their positions, configurations, and separations.

There are other types of geometry, too, including projective geometry and non-Euclidean geometry. Most of these are more complex forms of geometry that each have their own special reasons for use.

When did **geometry originate**?

The field of geometry was probably developed by several cultures over millennia, but only in crude, elementary forms. Some of the first to actually work with geometry were the cultures of the Mesopotamian region around 3500 B.C.E. (especially the Babylonians). They were the earliest peoples to know about what is now called the Pythagorean theorem (in fact, the Greek mathematician and philosopher Pythagoras of Samos [c. 582–c. 507 B.C.E.] may have actually learned about this theorem in his travels to the east), and they possessed all the theorems of plane geometry that the Greeks attributed to Thales. The Egyptians came next, using geometric methods mainly for construction of huge monuments. This included the sundry pyramids and monuments of the region, some of which still dot the landscape today—a tribute to their builders who used geometric techniques.

The Greek mathematician Pythagoras may have learned about the geometric principals that led to his famous theorem during his travels to such places as Babylon.

Were the **Greeks** involved in **geometry**?

The Greeks were known to have extensive knowledge of geometry, producing many great geometers. With this and other contributions in mathematics, the Greeks profoundly changed the approach and character of the entire mathematical field. It is thought that Thales of Miletus (c. 625–c. 550 B.C.E.; Ionian) first introduced geometry to the Greeks. As a merchant traveler, he was exposed to the Babylonian concept of measurement, from which practices sprang geometry. Thales used his geometric knowledge to solve problems such as the height of the pyramids and the distance of ships from the shoreline.

Greek geometer Hippocrates of Chios (470–410 B.C.E.) was one of the first to present an axiomatic approach to geometry, as well as the first to work on the elements almost a century before Euclid (see below). Hippocrates may have worked on geometry and such problems as squaring the circle, but he lacked common sense and was duped by many people.

Zeno of Elea (c. 490–c. 425 B.C.E.) raised questions about lines, points, and numbers—all part of geometry—with his many paradoxes (for more information about Zeno and his paradoxes, see "Foundations of Mathematics"). Another important figure

What are the five postulates of Euclid?

Euclid was also famous for his postulates, propositions (statements) that are true without proof and deal with specific subject matter, such as the properties of geometric objects (for more information about postulates, see "Foundations of Mathematics"). Along with definitions, Euclid began his text *Elements* with five postulates. These postulates are as follows (some of which may seem obvious to us now, but in Euclid's time they had yet to be formally recorded):

- It is possible to draw a straight line from any point to another point.
- It is possible to produce a finite straight line continuously in a straight line.
- It is possible to describe a circle with any center and radius.
- All right angles are equal to one another.
- Given any straight line and a point not on it, there "exists one and only one straight line which passes" through that point and never intersects the first line, no matter how far the lines are extended. Another way to say this is: One and only one line can be drawn through a point parallel to a given line. This is also called the parallel postulate.

Mathematicians first believed this last postulate could be derived from the first four, but they now consider it to be independent of the others. In fact, this postulate leads to Euclidean geometry, and eventually to many non-Euclidean geometries that are made possible by changing the assumption of this fifth postulate.

Like many early attempts at explaining mathematics, not all these postulates tell the entire geometric story. There were still a large number of gaps, many of which were gradually filled in over time.

is Eudoxus of Cnidus (408–355 B.C.E.), who worked on geometric proportions and theories for determining areas and volumes.

Others followed these geometers, including Archimedes (c. 287–212 B.C.E.; Hellenic), who worked on mechanics and took the first steps toward integral calculus. Apollonius of Perga (262–190 B.C.E.), or the "great geometer," first named and presented theories on conic sections in his book *Conics,* and he introduced the terms "parabola," "ellipse," and "hyperbola." There was also Pappus of Alexandria (290–350), who presented the basis for modern projective geometry (the geometry that deals with incidences, or whether elements such as lines, planes, and points coincide or not).

What **Greek mathematician** wrote the book *Elements*?

The Greek mathematician and geometrician Euclid (c. 325–c. 270 B.C.E.) made some of the most significant improvements to geometry in his time. (For more about

Euclid, see "Foundations of Mathematics.") One contribution was his collection of 13 books on geometry and other mathematics, titled *Elements* (or *Stoicheion* in Greek). This work has been called the world's most definitive text on geometry. The first six books offer elementary plane geometry, with sections on triangles, rectangles, circles, polygons, proportions, and similarities; the rest of the books present other mathematics of his day, including the theory of numbers (books 7 to 10), solid geometry, pyramids, and Platonic solids. These books were used for centuries in western Europe; in fact, the elementary geometry many students learn in high school today is still largely based on Euclid's ideas on the subject.

What is **Euclidean geometry**?

Euclidean geometry is named after Euclid, the famous Greek mathematician. It is geometry mostly based on Euclid's fifth postulate—the parallel postulate—and is sometimes called parabolic geometry. Plane geometry is described as two-dimensional Euclidean geometry, while three-dimensional Euclidean geometry is known as solid geometry.

What was **François Viéte's contribution** to geometry?

French mathematician François Viète (or Franciscus Vieta, in Latin; 1540–1603), although thought of as the "founder of modern algebra," also introduced a connection between algebra, geometry, and trigonometry. He also included trigonometric tables in his *Canon Mathematicus* (1571), along with the theory behind their construction. (For more about Viète, see "Algebra.")

French mathematician and physicist Gaspard Monge was the first to lay down ideas about modern descriptive geometry.

What was **Gaspard Monge**'s connection to geometry?

French mathematician, physicist, and public official Gaspard Monge (also known as Comte de Péluse; 1746–1818) was the first to lay down ideas about modern descriptive geometry, a field that is essential to mechanical and architectural drawing. He is also called the founder of differential geometry. As one of the founders of the école Polytechnique, he served as professor of descriptive geometry, and around 1800 published the first textbook on the subject based on his lectures, aptly called *Géométrie descriptive*. Today, the system

How do we interpret dimensions in everyday life?

We are all familiar with dimensions around us, although we may not be aware of them. Most people are familiar with the ideas of two- (such as a drawing on paper) and three-dimensional objects (ordinary objects, including an apple or a car, exist in three-dimensional space), but there are others as well.

Zero dimension can be thought of as a point in space. One dimension can be visualized by a line or a curve in space. Another way of understanding one dimension is with time, something we think of as consisting of only "now," "before," and "after." Because the "before" and "after"—regardless of whether they are long or short—are actually extensions, time becomes similar to a line (as in "timeline")—or a one-dimensional object.

Two dimensions are defined by two coordinates in space, such as a rectangle. One of the most obvious two-dimensional objects we see all around us are paintings and photographs—although they represent a three-dimensional object. Even this page you are reading can be considered a two-dimensional object, though strictly speaking, the thickness of the paper gives it a third dimension. Three dimensions are considered the space we occupy, as three dimensions give everything around us depth. Our binocular vision allows us to see depth (things in three dimensions), which is why everything becomes "flat" or two-dimensional when we view the world through just one eye.

One can also conceive of four or more dimensions, but there are few common examples. Most hyper-dimensional aspects are used by mathematicians, various scientists, and even economists. They need such dimensional analysis for their complex mathematics, such as for modeling weather patterns or the ups and downs of the stock market.

In Euclidean space, distance is defined by certain "rules": The distance between two points is positive, unless they are the same points; the distance from points a to b will be the same as from b to a; and the distance between the points does not change if they are totally shifted over in one direction (such a sliding over of the points is called *translation*; for more on this, see elsewhere in this chapter). In addition, the Pythagorean theorem is valid for three points that are the vertices (the intersection points of the sides of an angle) of a right triangle.

What are some of the **basic "building blocks"** of geometry?

There are several basic "building blocks" of geometry, all of which have to do with the objects we often see in geometry. A zero-dimensional object that is specifically located in n-dimensional space using n coordinates is called a *point*. The idea of a point may

once called "géométrie descriptive" is now known as orthographic projection, a graphical method used in modern mechanical drawing.

BASICS OF GEOMETRY

What is a **mathematical space**?

Outer space may be the "final frontier" to some people, but back on Earth there are also numerous types of space in mathematics. For the most part, mathematical space consists of points, sets, or vectors. Each space and the members of that space obey certain mathematical properties. Most spaces are named after their principal investigator, including Euclidean and Minkowski space. One of the most general types of mathematical spaces is called the topological space.

How is a **dimension described** in mathematics?

In mathematics, a dimension is the number of coordinates (or parameters) required to describe points of—or even points on—a mathematical object (usually geometric in nature). The dimension of an object is often referred to as its dimensionality. (For more about coordinates, see elsewhere in this chapter; for more about dimensions and science, see "Math in the Natural Sciences.")

Each dimension represents points in space—from a single to multiple points. The concept of dimension is important in mathematics, as it defines a geometric object conceptually and/or visually. In fact, the idea of dimensions can even be applied to abstract objects that can't be directly visualized. Mathematicians most often display such dimensions on graphs using a single point (for example, x) to represent one dimension; two points (usually x and y, or an ordered pair) to represent two dimensions; and three points (usually x, y, z) for three dimensions. The four- (and higher) dimensional analogs of three-dimensional objects often retain the prefix "hyper-" such as hypercube and hyperplane. The basic geometric structures of higher-dimensional geometry—the line, plane, space, and hyperspace—all consist of an infinite number of points arranged in specific ways.

What is **Euclidean space**?

Euclidean (also seen as Euclidian) space is often called Cartesian space, or more simply, *n-space*. It is made up of n dimensions and is a set of points, with each point represented by a coordinate of n components. Space with two to three dimensions—and that does not use Einstein's and others' ideas of relativistic physics—are considered Euclidean space.

How is a curve defined in geometry?

A curve is a continuous collection of points drawn from one-dimensional space to *n*-dimensional space; it is also considered an object that can be created by moving a point. But note: Our usual use of the word "curve" does not mean a straight line, but in mathematics, a line or triangle is often referred to as a curve.

Different forms of geometry define curves in various ways. Analytic geometry uses plane curves—such as circles, ellipses, hyperbolas, and parabolas—which are usually considered as the graph of an equation or function. The properties of these curves are largely dependent on the degree of the equation in the case of algebraic curves (curves with algebraic equations) or on the particular function, as in the case of transcendental curves (curves whose equations are not algebraic). Even more complex are space curves, all of which require special techniques used only in differential geometry.

be obvious to most people, but for mathematicians, describing and dealing with points is not straightforward. For example, Euclid once gave a vague definition of a point as "that which has no part."

Euclid also called the *line* a "breadthless length," and further called a straight line one that "lies evenly with the points on itself." Modern mathematicians define lines as one-dimensional objects (although they may be part of a higher-dimensional space). They are mathematically defined as a theoretical course of a moving point that is thought to have length but no other dimension. They are often called straight lines, or by the archaic term, a right line, to emphasize the fact that there are no curves anywhere along the entire length. It is interesting to note that when geometry is used in an axiomatic system, a line is usually considered an undefined term (for more about axiomatic systems, see "Foundations of Mathematics"). In analytic geometry, a line is defined by the basic equation $ax + by = c$, in which a, b, and c are any number, but a and b can't be zero at the same time.

A *line segment* is the shortest curve—which is actually straight—to connect two different points. It is a finite portion of an infinite line. Line segments are most often labeled with two letters corresponding to the endpoints of the line segment, such as a and b, and written as ab.

Distance is the length of the path between two points, or the length of a segment, for example, between points a and b. When talking about the distance between any two points associated with a and b (as real numbers) on a number line, distance becomes the absolute value of $b - a$ ($|b - a|$).

Another basic building block is the *ray*. Think of a ray as a laser beam: It originates at one point and continues in one direction toward infinity. A ray is defined as part of a

line on one side of a point, and includes that point. Two letters are needed to name a ray. For example, Ray *AB* is defined by point *A*, where it begins, and point *B*, the point the ray goes through. (But note: Ray *AB* is not the same as ray *BA*.) If the initial point is not included, the resulting figure is called a *half line*. In geometry, a ray is usually considered a half-infinite line with one of the two points *A* and *B* taken to be at infinity.

What does the word **parallel** mean in geometry?

In geometry, parallel means two lines in two-dimensional Euclidean space that do not intersect; or two lines in the same plane that never meet and that maintain the same distance from each other at every point. In three-dimensional Euclidean space, these lines also do not intersect, maintaining a constant separation between points closest to each other on the two lines. In analytic geometry, parallel means those lines with the same slope, as well as other curves with the same slope for every *x* value. The symbol for parallel lines is ||. For example, *A* || *B* means that line *A* is parallel to line *B*.

What is an **angle**?

An angle is a major concept in both geometry and trigonometry. An angle is formed by two rays that begin at the same point; a *straight angle* is one in which the two rays lie on the same line. It can also be described as two planes coming from a common line.

Angles are named in several ways: a capital letter at its vertex (the common points for both rays, see illustration, ∠B), a small letter within the angle, a number within the angle, or by three capital letters (ABC or CBA, with the middle letter representing the vertex and the other two points the rays). The two rays that form the angle are called the sides of the angle, such as side BA and side BC.

How are **angles measured**?

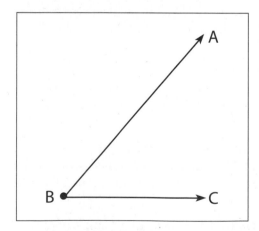

Angle ABC is formed by rays BA and BC linked at point B.

Angles are measured in two major ways: degrees and radians. Similar to degrees on a temperature scale, *degrees* in mathematics—especially when discussing angles—are usually denoted by the symbol °; they are divided into 60 arc minutes, and arc minutes are divided into 60 arc seconds. The multiples of 60 are thought to be connected to the Babylonian's sexagesimal number system (one based on the number 60), in which the year was composed of 360 days (or 12 months at 30 days each). If the vertex of an angle and one side are fixed and the

The angles of a circle are typically measured either in degrees or radians (rad). There are 360 degrees in a circle, or $2\pi \times 1$ rad.

The four basic types of angles are straight, acute, obtuse, and right.

other side is rotated about the vertex, it sweeps out a circle of 360° with each complete rotation. Said another way, a full rotation is 360 degrees.

Radians (denoted as rad) are real numbers represented as an angle; they are the central angle of a circle determined by two radii and an arc joining them. In degrees, a radian is about 57.29578 degrees or $180/\pi$ degrees, because a semicircle contains π radians. For example, $\pi/6$ is equal to a 30 degree angle; because a straight angle is π radians (or 180°), if you divide 180 by 6, (or $\pi/6$), it is equal to 30 degrees. Radians are most often used in probability and statistics, or calculus, especially to obtain the derivative of trigonometric functions.

How are the **simplest angles** classified?

Angles are usually expressed in terms of "rotation," in which a full rotation is equal—in most cases—to a 360 degree circle. Half of a full rotation is called a *straight angle;* a quarter of a full rotation is called a *right angle* (90 degrees). An angle less than a right angle is called an *acute angle;* an angle greater than a right angle is called an *obtuse angle.*

What are **other types of angles**?

There are numerous other types of angles, some of which are examined in the following list:

Adjacent angle—Adjacent angles are two angles side-by-side that have a common vertex (endpoint) and ray; angles are adjacent if a common line is between the other sides.

111

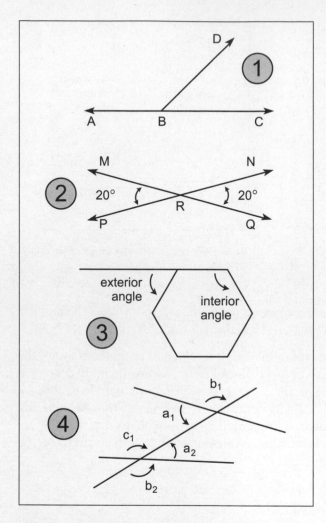

Among the types of angles are: 1. adjacent angles; 2. vertical (congruent) angles; and 3. exterior and interior angles. In illustration 4 we see alternate interior angles (a_1 and a_2), alternate exterior angles (b_1 and b_2), and corresponding angles (b_1 and c_1).

Vertical angles—Vertical angles are two angles whose sides form two pairs of opposite rays; because of this, vertical angles have no sides in common and are directly across from one another. They are also considered a pair of opposite congruent angles where two lines intersect. Vertical angles include intersecting lines that define a plane, with the vertical angles always in the same plane.

Congruent angles—Congruent angles have the same size and shape; vertical angles are considered to be congruent.

Exterior and interior angles—Interior angles are those inside a polygon, such as a triangle; exterior angles are outside the polygon formed by extending one ray (side) outside the polygon from a vertex.

Alternate and corresponding angles—A pair of angles that lie on opposite sides and opposite ends of a transversal (a line that cuts two or more lines in the same plane) are called alternate angles; both these angles are equal if the lines cut by the transversal are parallel. They are also broken into alternate interior angles (the "inside" angles) and alternate exterior angles (the "outside" angles). For two parallel lines, the alternate interior and exterior angles are equal—or congruent. Corresponding angles are pairs of angles that lie on the same sides and ends of a transversal.

Dihedral angle—A dihedral (meaning "two bases") angle is one of the four angles formed where two non-parallel planes meet.

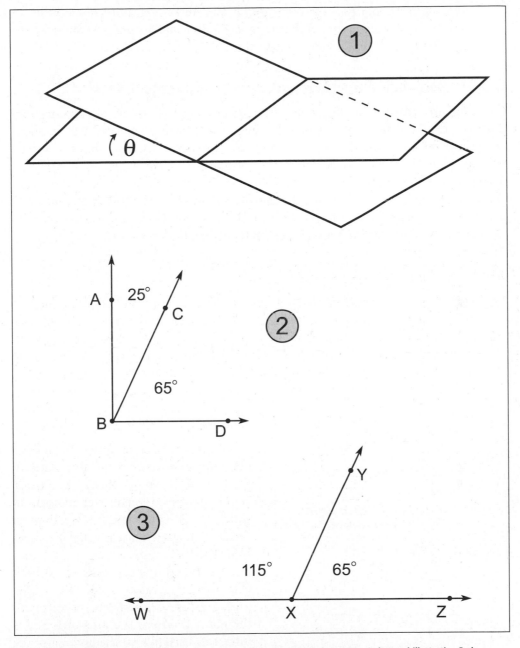

In the above, illustration 1 shows dihedral angle θ; illustration 2 shows complementary angles; and illustration 3 shows supplementary angles.

Complementary angles—Two angles that add up to a right angle are complementary. For example, the two acute angles in a right triangle are always considered complementary, as their sum adds up to 90 degrees of the right triangle.

113

Supplementary angles—Two angles that add up to a straight angle (180 degrees) are supplementary. If the angles are both supplementary to the same angle, then the two angles are congruent.

What are **perpendicular, orthogonal, normal,** and **tangent lines**?

Lines are also classified by their relationship to other angles and lines. *Perpendicular lines* are two lines, segments, or rays that intersect to form a right (90 degree) angle. *Orthogonal lines* are another way of saying lines are perpendicular—but it is mostly used in terms of functions, transformations, and vectors in other mathematical fields. *Normal lines* are perpendicular lines where each line is perpendicular to a curve (including a line) or a surface (including a plane). And finally, a line is considered to be *tangent* to a circle if it intersects the circle at exactly one point—also called the *point of tangency*. Such lines are also called tangential lines.

What does the term **bisect** mean?

The term "bisect" is important in geometry; it means to cut into two (or divide into half), mainly lines (or two-dimensional figures) and angles. To compare, a bisected line segment means finding the plane, line, or point that is the midpoint of the line segment. This is also called a segment bisector. An angle bisector is a ray in the interior of an angle that forms two equal angles. First locate the point on each ray that is equally distant from the vertex; then draw a third point equally distant from each of the first two rays. A line that extends through the third point and the vertex is the angle bisector.

To draw a bisector, follow the following sequence (as per the illustration): First, draw an angle; then draw an arc centered at the vertex (endpoint), in which B and C are the intersections of the arc and angle lines at equal distances from the vertex; next draw an arc centered at B and one centered at C—both with the same radii—inside the angle; finally, extend a line from the vertex to the point D where the arcs of B and C intersect—making AD the bisector of the angle at A.

Examples of a perpendicular line (top), normal lines (middle), and tangential lines (bottom), with point M being the point of tangency.

What are **geometric postulates**?

Similar to other parts of mathematics, there are many geometric postulates, or

statements that are assumed to be true without proof. From these postulates, theorems—another type of mathematical statement—can be proven (in addition, theorems are proven by definitions or previously proven theorems). An example of a postulate in geometry is, "Through any two points there is exactly one line." Another is, "If two points lie in a plane, then the entire line containing those two points lies in the plane."

What are **proofs** and **theorems** in geometry?

Proofs are extremely important to geometry. Similar to other divisions of mathematics, proofs are defined as sequences of justified conclusions used to prove the validity of an "if-then" statement. (For more information about postulates, theorems, and undefined terms, see "Foundations of Mathematics.")

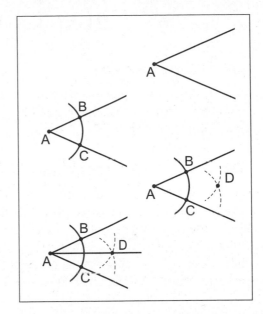

To determine a bisector, follow these steps from top to bottom: Draw an angle; draw an arc from the angle's vertex that touches the two angle lines; draw two more arcs from the points where the first arc meets the angle lines; draw a line from point A to point D.

There are essentially five steps in showing that any proof is a good proof: state the theorem to be proved; list what information is available; draw an illustration (if possible) to represent the information; state what is to be proved. Finally, develop a system of deductive reasoning, especially concentrating on statements that are accepted to be true; along with the true statements, add any necessary undefined terms.

In geometry, in order to prove a theorem, you need to use definitions, properties, rules, undefined terms, postulates, and (possibly) other theorems. And like hyperlinking to other text with Internet links, such theorems can be used throughout geometry (and other mathematics) in the proofs of other new, more difficult theorems.

What is an **indirect proof**?

Direct proofs start with a true statement and then set out to prove that a conclusion is true. But there is also a method called the indirect proof in which indirect reasoning is used. First, assume that the conclusion is false; then show that this assumption leads to a contradiction of the hypothesis or some other accepted fact, such as a postulate or theorem. Therefore, if the assumption is proved false, the conclusion has been proved—indirectly—to be true.

PLANE GEOMETRY

What is **plane geometry**?

Plane geometry is simply the study of two-dimensional figures in a plane. Most mathematicians further define the plane as Euclidean (for more information about Euclidean geometry, see above). It examines such objects as circles, lines, and polygons.

What does a **"plane"** mean in geometry?

A plane—in geometry or any other field of mathematics—means a surface such that a straight line joining any two of its points lies totally in that surface. A plane is considered to be two-dimensional; when a plane is discussed with higher dimensions, it is called a hyperplane. Thus, in the majority of mathematical discussions, a plane can be thought of as a two-dimensional group of points that reach out to infinity in all directions (for more information about dimensions, see above).

How is the term **"surface"** used in mathematics?

When most of us think of the word "surface" we often envision our own world—the thin outer crust of soil and rock we walk and live on. In engineering, the term means the outer part (or the skin with a thickness of zero) of a body. In science it can apply to a plethora of objects, from geologic structures to micrometer-sized particles.

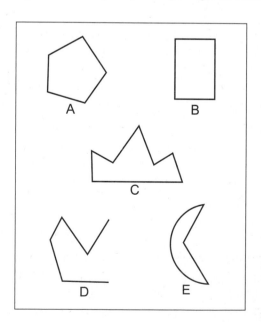

In mathematics, "surface" also has numerous meanings. The most common denotes a two-dimensional topological space or three-dimensional Euclidean space. A surface in mathematics can be complicated and complex, such as in certain fractals, or extremely simple, such as in a plane.

What is a **polygon**?

The word polygon means "many angles" (Greek *poly* for "many"; *gonis* for "angle"). It is a closed figure in a plane made up of line segments (straight with no curves) that intersect only at their vertices (endpoints). In other words, no sides (lines) can touch each other except at endpoints. A polygon has the same number of sides as it has vertices.

Examples A, B, and C above are polygons, while examples D and E are not.

What are the **names** given to **regular polygons**?

Polygons are classified according to the number of sides they have. A polygon with n sides is called an n-gon. The following lists some of the names of polygons, depending on the number of sides. It is also possible to substitute "n-gon," when the name is not known (for example 14-gon or 20-gon).

Names for Regular Polygons

Sides	Polygon Name
3	trigon or triangle
4	quadrilateral or tetragon
5	pentagon
6	hexagon
7	heptagon
8	octagon
9	nonagon or enneagon
10	decagon
11	hendecagon or undecagon (even less frequently as unidecagon)
12	dodecagon
13	tridecagon or triskaidecagon
14	tetradecagon or tetrakaidecagon
15	pentadecagon or pentakaidecagon
16	hexadecagon or hexakaidecagon
17	heptadecagon or heptakaidecagon
18	octadecagon or octakaidecagon
19	enneadecagon or enneakaidecagon
20	icosagon
30	triacontagon
40	tetracontagon
50	pentacontagon
60	hexacontagon
70	heptacontagon
80	octacontagon
90	enneacontagon
100	hectogon or hecatontagon
1,000	chiliagon
10,000	myriagon

Some texts list a two-sided polygon as a "digon," but this is only meant for theoretical mathematics. If you feel like making up your own name, try constructing some

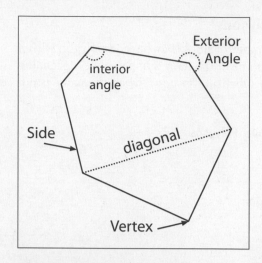

The parts of a polygon.

sided polygons. For example, a 46-sided polygon could be called a tetracontakaihexagon, or a combination of "tetracontagon" + "kai" (often used in combining names) + "hexagon." To shorten such long names, mathematicians often use "n-gon" to simplify matters; thus, 46 would be 46-gon a much easier name to remember and even say.

What are some **divisions of polygons**?

There are two major divisions of polygons: *Regular polygons* are convex polygons with equal sides and length; thus, all sides and angles are congruent (equal). For example, one of the most famous regular octagons is the stop sign used along roads in the United States: a closed polygon with eight equal sides. The naming of the various polygons can be challenging, though. For example, a polygon called a regular triangle is also called an equilateral triangle; another name for the polygon called a regular quadrilateral is a square. *Irregular polygons* are those with sides of differing lengths and variable angles. Therefore, unless all the sides of the polygon are of the same length and all the angles are of the same measure, the polygon is said to be irregular.

But don't be fooled: The names for the various polygons—such as hexagon, nonagon, and pentagon, depending on number of sides—don't just apply to the regular polygons, but rather to *any* two-dimensional closed figure with the number of sides as described by its name. For example, the two figures shown on page 185 are both polygons—A is a regular hexagon and B is an irregular hexagon.

Polygons are described in other ways, too. *Convex polygons* are those in which every line drawn between any two points inside the polygon lie entirely within the figure. Opposite from the convex polygons are the *concave polygons*—those that are essentially "caved in," with some of the sides bent inward. If a line is drawn between two points inside a concave polygon, the line often passes outside the figure. Another type of polygon is a *star polygon,* in which a star figure is drawn based on equidistant points connected on a circle.

What are **triangles** and how are they **classified**?

Triangles (or "three angles") are polygons with three sides. A triangle's three line segments (or sides) are joined together at three vertices (endpoints). For all triangles, the sum of a triangle's three interior angles is equal to a straight angle, or 180 degrees.

Triangles are classified by either the lengths of their sides, or, more commonly, the measurement of their angles. All triangles have at least two acute angles, but the third angle, which can be used to classify the triangle, can be acute, right, or obtuse (for more about these angles, see above). The types of triangles based on angles are:

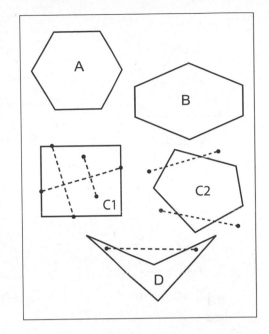

Types of polygons include regular hexagons (A), irregular hexagons (B), convex polygons (C1 and C2), and concave polygons (D).

Right triangle—There is one angle of 90 degrees.

Acute triangle—All three angles are less than 90 degrees, or the triangle has three acute angles.

Obtuse triangle—There is one angle greater than 90 degrees, or the triangle has one obtuse angle.

Equiangular triangle—An acute triangle in which all angles are congruent, or when all three angles are equal.

Triangles can be further classified by their sides, as in the following:

Scalene triangle—There are no sides—and therefore no angles—that are equal; in other words, no sides are congruent.

Isosceles triangle—Two of the sides are equal (congruent), and thus the base angles are equal.

Equilateral triangle—When all three sides are equal (congruent).

What are the **parts** of **right and isosceles triangles**?

There are special names for the parts of a right triangle. The *hypotenuse* is the side opposite the 90 degree angle—the side that will always be the triangle's longest. The shorter sides are called the *legs*.

Similar to the right triangle, the isosceles triangle has specific names for its angles and sides: Congruent (equal) sides are, as with the right triangle, called the *legs;* the angle formed by these two legs is called the *vertex angle;* and the *base* is the side opposite the vertex angle. The two angles that are formed by the base and the legs are called the triangle's *base angles.*

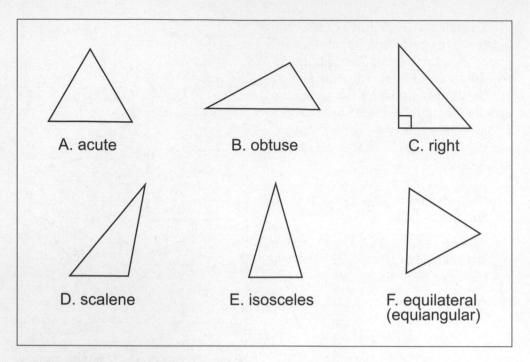

The basic types of triangles are acute (A), obtuse (B), right (C), scalene (D), isosceles (E), and equilateral (F).

How is the **Pythagorean theorem** connected to **right triangles**?

The Pythagorean theorem deals with right triangles: Simply stated, the sum of the squares of the legs equals the square of the hypotenuse (longest side). The converse of the Pythagorean theorem is also true: If the sum of the squares of a triangle's two sides equals the square of the longest side, then the triangle is a right triangle.

What are the various **types of quadrilaterals**?

There are several types of quadrilaterals: polygons with four sides. Interestingly enough, some definitions can be "combined"; for example, if a quadrilateral is both a rhombus and a rectangle, it is truly a square. The following lists the common quadrilaterals:

Square—The most obvious quadrilateral is the square. It is an equiangular quadrilateral with four right angles (it is also defined as having four congruent sides).

Rectangle—The second most well-known quadrilateral is the rectangle, a quadrilateral with four right angles, with the opposite sides parallel and congruent, and opposite angles congruent.

Parallelogram—A parallelogram is a quadrilateral with both pairs of opposite sides parallel; thus, opposite sides and angles are congruent.

Rhombus—A rhombus is a parallelogram with four equilateral (or congruent) sides.

Trapezoid—A trapezoid is a quadrilateral with exactly one pair of parallel sides. This is also seen in books as "a quadrilateral with at least one pair of parallel sides," but this latter definition is often debated among mathematicians, as the meaning is not the same as the first statement. With trapezoids, the parallel sides are called the *bases;* the nonparallel sides are called the *legs.*

Isosceles trapezoid—An isosceles trapezoid is one with nonparallel sides that are equal in length, or a trapezoid with a pair of equiangular base angles. The legs of an isosceles trapezoid are congruent. (For more about these figures, see elsewhere in this chapter.)

What is a **circle**?

A circle is one of the most fundamental shapes in geometry—and one shape we commonly see every day. For mathematicians, a circle is defined as a set of points on a plane at a certain distance from a center point. In reality, a circle is a polygon with an infinite number of sides.

The distance of a line segment from the center to the points on the circle is called the *radius* (or a line segment whose endpoints are on any point on the circle and its center). A line segment that travels from one endpoint on the circle, through the radius (center of the circle), and to another endpoint directly opposite is called the *diameter;* two times the radius of a circle is the diameter. The outer perimeter of the circle is called the *circumference*. The *chord of a circle* is a line segment whose two endpoints are on the circle. *Concentric circles* are two or more circles that lie in the same plane and have the same center, but with different radii. Circles with the same radius are called *congruent circles*. (For more about circle measurements, see elsewhere in this chapter.)

Why are **arcs** and **angles** important to **circles**?

Everything starts with the angle whose vertex is at the center of the circle (logically called the *central angle of a circle*). All the central angles of a circle add up to 360 degrees. Every central angle cuts the circle into two *arcs:* the *minor arc* (always less than 180 degrees) and the *major arc* (always more than 180 degrees). Thus, the measure of the minor

The parts of a circle include the center (o), radius (r), diameter (d), and circumference (c).

arc is actually the measurement of the central angle, while the measurement of the major arc is 360 degrees minus the measure of the central angle. An *arc length* is the distance between an arc's endpoints along the path of the circle. *Congruent arcs* are arcs with the same measurements. When the diameter of a circle separates the circle into two congruent arcs it is called a *semicircle*.

SOLID GEOMETRY

What is **solid geometry**?

Solid geometry is the study of objects in three-dimensional Euclidean space. It deals with solids, as opposed to plane geometry, which deals with two dimensions. This part of geometry is concerned with entities such as polyhedra, spheres, cones, cylinders, and so on. (For more about Euclidean space and dimensions, see elsewhere in this chapter.)

In geometry, solids are defined as closed three-dimensional figures, or any limited portion of space bounded by surfaces. They differ in subtle ways from what we perceive as solids: We see solids in terms of what surrounds us—three-dimensional figures with their surfaces the actual objects we perceive. Geometric solids are actually the union of the surface and regions of space; in a way, this adds another dimension to two-dimensional space.

What is a **polyhedron**?

The word polyhedron comes from the Greek *poly* (meaning "many") and the Indo-European word *hedron* (meaning "seat"). In geometry, a polyhedron is considered to be a three-dimensional solid that represents the union of polygonal regions, usually joined at their edges and having no gaps.

Polyhedrons are classified as *convex,* or if you extend any side, the figure lies on only one side of the plane (for example, a pyramid and cube); a *concave* polyhedron is one that can extend on both sides of such a plane (for example, a form that exhibits concavity on one or all sides of the polyhedron). The plural of polyhedron is often seen as "polyhedrons," but it is more correct to use "polyhedra."

What are the various **types of polyhedra**?

As with most forms, polyhedra are divided into many names, depending on the number of faces. The following lists some of them, based on their number of sides:

Types of Polyhedra

Sides	Polyhedra Name
4	tetrahedron
5	pentahedron
6	hexahedron
7	heptahedron
8	octahedron
9	nonahedron
10	decahedron
11	undecahedron
12	dodecahedron
14	tetradecahedron
20	icosahedron
24	icositetrahedron
30	triacontahedron

Sides	Polyhedra Name
32	icosidodecahedron
60	hexecontahedron
90	enneacontahedron

How are some **common solids** defined?

There are numerous objects defined in solid geometry. The following lists the most common (and some interesting) ones:

Cone—A cone can be both a surface and a solid. A solid cone is bounded by a region enclosed in a closed curve on a plane and a surface formed by segments joining each point of the closed curve to a point that is not in the plane. (Note: Two solid cones seen with their pointed ends together help define conic sections; for more about conic sections, see elsewhere in this chapter.)

Pyramid—A pyramid is a polyhedron (see above) with one face a polygon and all other faces as triangles with a common endpoint (vertex). They are named based on the polygon's base, such as the triangular pyramid, square pyramid, and so on. Some of the most famous "solid pyramids" are the sandstone pyramids of Egypt. These are actually called right square pyramids because the base of the polygon is a square and the vertical line from the vertex meets the center of the base.

Cylinder—A cylinder can be both a surface and a solid. A solid cylinder is one that forms by rotating a circle about an axis through the midpoints of the opposite side; it is also called a right circular cylinder. One of the most well-known cylinders is possibly sitting right next to you: A coffee cup, with its cylindrical shape, and the bases (in this case, the base and rim) considered to be congruent circles.

Prism—A prism is a polyhedron with two parallel, congruent faces that make up the bases of the shape; the other, lateral faces are considered to be parallelograms. If the lateral faces are rectangles, the prism is called a right prism.

Parallelepiped—This strange-sounding polyhedron is one that has all its faces as parallelograms, or a prism with parallelogram bases. The most familiar parallelepiped is a simple box—also called a rectangular parallelepiped—that has rectangles for all the six faces. (For more about these figures, including how to calculate their areas, see elsewhere in this chapter.)

What are the **Platonic solids**?

Platonic solids are also called regular solids, regular figures (a term also used in reference to polygons), regular polyhedra, or "cosmic figures." These solids are convex

polyhedra that have equal faces made up of congruent convex regular polygons. (To compare in terms of a two-dimensional polygon, a regular figure means that both the sides and the angles between them are equal.)

There are considered to only be five of these solids: the cube, dodecahedron, icosahedron, octahedron, and tetrahedron. These solids were described by Greek philosopher Plato (c. 428–348 B.C.E.) in his work *Timaeus*—thus the name Platonic solids. His definitions were certainly more whimsical than today's, as he believed the major "elements" were made up of atoms shaped like certain polyhedra. He associated the tetrahedron with the "element" fire, the cube with the earth, the icosahedron with water, the octahedron with air, and the dodecahedron with the material that makes up the constellations and heavens. The mathematical proofs of these solids were worked out long ago by Greek

The Greek philosopher Plato first described what are now called platonic solids, polyhedra with equal faces made up of congruent convex regular polygons.

mathematician and geometrician Euclid (c. 325–c. 270 B.C.E.) in the last part of his *Elements* (for more information about Euclid, see elsewhere in this chapter, as well as "Foundations of Mathematics").

How are **spheres described**?

A sphere in solid geometry is considered to be the set of points (or the "skin" of the sphere) in three-dimensional Euclidean space that are equidistant from the sphere's singular, central point. Or, more simply, a sphere is a perfectly round, three-dimensional object. The term "sphere" also extends into other dimensions; for example, a sphere in two dimensions is also called a circle.

What is **spherical geometry**?

Spherical geometry is the study of objects on the surface of a sphere; this differs from the type of geometry studied in plane or solid geometry. In spherical geometry, there are no parallel lines, and straight lines are actually great circles, so any two lines meet in two points. In addition, the angle between two lines is the angle between the planes of the corresponding great circles. There are also entities called *spherical triangles* (or

Euler triangles), when three planes pass through the surface of a sphere and through the sphere's center of volume; they have three surface angles and three central angles. There are also *spherical polygons,* in which a closed geometric object on the surface of a sphere is formed by arcs of great circles.

MEASUREMENTS AND TRANSFORMATIONS

What is the **perimeter** of a **two-dimensional geometric figure**?

The perimeter of a two-dimensional figure is what we perceive as the "outside" of the object. Mathematicians describe a perimeter more precisely as the sum of the lengths of a polygon's sides; the perimeter of a simple closed curve is measured as its length.

What is the **area** of a **two-dimensional geometric figure**?

The area of two-dimensional figures varies depending on the object. For the simpler two-dimensional figures (square, rectangle, parallelogram), the area can actually be found by calculating the number of square units in the interior of the object. Such a task can be difficult and time consuming, so mathematicians simply multiply the height (h) times the base (b), sometimes said as length times height or length times width (with rectangles).

How is the **area determined** for some common **two-dimensional polygons**?

Finding the areas of polygons is not as simple as determining the areas of a rectangle and square. In order to find the area of certain polygons, one essentially "breaks the shape down" into smaller shapes with simpler formulas; these types of shapes are called *composites*. The formulas for many of these polygons are all adaptations from the rectangle area formula—or height (h) times base (b). For example, a triangle is actually exactly half of a rectangle. Thus, the formula to find the area of a triangle is half the base times the height ($1/2bh$). In the case of the trapezoid, the figure can be divided into triangular sections, with the area equal to one half times the two bases times the height, or $1/2(B + b)h$.

The triangle formula also is used to find other regular polygon areas, but they are less obvious. For a regular polygon, a feature called the *apothem* is necessary for finding the area. This is the height of one of the congruent triangles inside the regular polygon. In general, to find the polygon's area, you need to find the area of one triangle and multiply it times the number of sides. For example, to find the area of a hexagon, divide the figure into six triangles, each with l equal to the height of each interior

How is the term "surface area" used in geometry?

Logically, the surface area is the area of a given surface. There are several ways to interpret this in geometry: Area can mean the extent of the surface region on a two-dimensional plane. Surface area (often called the lateral surface area, although there is a difference) formulas for three-dimensional objects are more complex—all the surface areas are added around the outside of the object, from a cube to a sphere.

Surface area is commonly denoted as S for a surface in three dimensions, and A for the surface area of a two-dimensional plane (commonly, it is simply called "the area"). But be careful: The surface area of a three-dimensional object should not be confused with "volume"—or the total amount of space an object occupies. (For more about volume, see below.)

triangle or apothem; l is also half of the smallest interior dimension of the hexagon, called w. Thus, the area of a hexagon is the square root of 3 divided by 2 times w squared (or $\sqrt{3}/2 \times w^2$).

There is still another way to determine the area of a polygon by using the Pythagorean theorem, a method that uses length and height, with the resulting formula for the area of a polygon looking much different. Both methods give the same results in numerical terms. For example, the area of a hexagon using the smallest interior dimension would be 0.866 times the square of the smallest width, w; the area of a regular hexagon using the Pythagorean theorem is 2.598 times the square of its side length. These may be different ways of presenting the solution, but both give the same correct area measurements.

What are the **measurements** of a **circle**?

There are many measurements of a circle. The perimeter of a circle is actually called the *circumference;* to calculate this, multiply pi (π) times the diameter, d (πd), or pi (π) times twice the radius, r ($2\pi r$). The area of a circle is calculated by multiplying pi (π) times the radius squared, or πr^2.

How was the **area of a circle** first determined?

When it comes to determining the area of a circle, there are many historical claims to this solution. One of the earliest techniques may have been the Chinese "comb" method, in which a circle is cut into n wedges, each $360/n$ degrees and each piece identical (with the same area). To see how this works, take the bottom half of a unit circle and cut it into wedges like slices of a pie; place all the wedges next to each other,

127

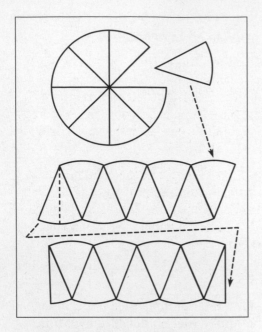

To calculate the area of a circle, the Chinese devised the Chinese comb method in which a circle is divided into pie slices and rearranged into a rectangle to greatly simplify the math involved.

with the points up (like the teeth of a comb or animal). Then split the top half of the circle in the same way, putting them next to each other above the other wedges, but this time point the tips of the wedges down. Close the "teeth"; as n goes to infinity, the shape of the combined wedges approaches a rectangle. Taking the formula for determining the area of a rectangle (width times height), the width is πr (or half the circumference) and the height is r. Thus, the area is πr^2.

What other way did **Archimedes** use to find the **area of a circle**?

The Greek mathematician Archimedes (c. 287–212 B.C.E.; Hellenic) also found a way to determine the area of a circle similar to the Chinese comb: a method he first recorded in his work, *Measurement of a Circle* (c. 225 B.C.E.). He also used a sequence of wedges to determine the area of a circle; as the number of wedges (or triangles) inside the circle increased toward infinity, they became infinitely thin. By giving each small triangle a base (b, a line connecting the points where the wedges touched the circle's circumference), he determined that the area was 1/2 times the radius (r) times the base, summed over all the infinitesimal triangles (or sum (1/2) rb). Because they all had the same height, that was factored out. Thus, the area became (1/2)r (sum (b)) = 1/2rc, with c being the circumference, or the sum of the bases (b) of all the triangles (since the bases make up what is perceived as the circle's circumference). This is interpreted as one half times the radius times the circumference ($c =$ $2\pi r$), which is the same as saying πr^2. (For more about Archimedes and his wedges, see "Mathematical Analysis.")

How are the **surface area** and **volume** of a **three-dimensional geometric figure** calculated?

The *surface area* (often abbreviated S.A.) of a three-dimensional geometric figure is the total surfaces of the solid; it actually has units of distance or length squared. For example, the surface area of a cube is $6a^2$, in which a is the length of the sides. To translate, a cube has sides of equal lengths (a); the area of a cube is the sum of the areas of the six squares (a^2) that cover it.

For more "diverse" figures, the surface area is actually equal to the *lateral area* plus the area of each base. For example, the surface area of a prism or cylinder is the lateral area plus the area of each base. (Because the bases for a prism or cylinder are congruent, this is often expressed as twice the area of the base.) The surface area of a pyramid or cone is the lateral area plus the area of the single base.

The *volume* of a three-dimensional geometric figure is the total amount of space the object occupies; volumes of such objects have units of length cubed. For example, the volume of a box (also called a rectangular parallelepiped) is length times width times height, or $l \times w \times h$; the volume of a cube is all the sides a cubed, or a^3.

What are **lateral surface areas**?

In many mathematical texts, the *lateral surface area* (L.A.) is given along with—or instead of—the surface area (S.A.). This type of area is the surface area of a three-dimensional figure, excluding the area of any bases. In other words, the lateral surfaces are the side faces (or surfaces) of a solid, or any face or surface that is not a base (or bottom of a figure).

What are the **surface area, lateral area,** and **volume** of a **sphere**?

A sphere is a set of points equidistant from a central point (a center); a sphere in two dimensions is a circle. In the case of a sphere, the lateral and surface areas are the same; therefore, a sphere with a radius r has a surface/lateral area of $4\pi r^2$; the volume of a sphere is $4/3 \pi r^3$.

What are **geometric transformations**?

Geometric transformations are rules that mean there is a one-to-one correspondence between two sets of points in two figures. A geometric transformation changes the plane or three-dimensional space. Each transformation can be defined by thinking about where each point is "taken," with a point said to be "taken to its image."

One way to visualize a transformation is to think of expanding, shrinking, or moving one figure to get a second figure. Depending on the transformation, the image will either be congruent (equal) to

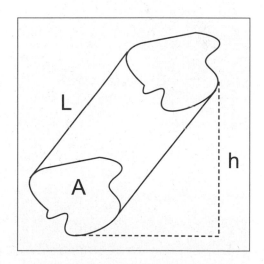

In this irregular prism shape, the lateral area equals the perimeter of shape A multiplied by L, and the surface area equals the lateral area plus two times the area of shape A.

the original image (called the *identity transformation*), similar but not necessarily equal, or will not resemble the original at all.

What are some **transformations** in geometry?

A transformation that keeps a figure's same shape and size, but moves it to a new location, is called *isometry*. There are several common types of these transformations. *Dilatation* is the only transformation that does not create equal figures. It means to take a shape and make it larger or smaller, but keep the same proportions. In terms of a circle, a dilatation creates another circle with the same center, also known as a concentric circle. *Reflection* is similar to what we called a "flip" in elementary school mathematics—like the flip side of an object. One easy way to see this is by noting one's reflection in a mirror—the "figure" is on one side of a line and the mirror image on the other. Reflection twice about two parallel lines is synonymous with translation; reflection twice about two intersecting lines is called rotation.

Another type of transformation is *rotation*. This is simple to understand: in elementary school mathematics it is sometimes called a "turn" or "spin." In this case, one point on a plane remains unchanged while keeping all the distances between the other points the same. Finally, a *translation* (or glide transformation) is similar to what is called a "slide" in elementary school mathematics. All the points in the plane move in the same direction and the same distance; or, the figure slides in a single direction. Translation is also considered to be reflection twice across two parallel lines.

René Descartes, who is more often remembered for developing the concept of Cartesian coordinates, also originated the idea of using letters when writing equations that include unknown values. *Library of Congress.*

ANALYTIC GEOMETRY

What is **analytic geometry**?

Analytic geometry is actually another name for coordinate (or Cartesian) geometry, a way to geometrically represent ordered pairs of numbers (or coordinates). The objects are described as n-tuples of points, in which $n = 2$ in a plane and $n = 3$ in a space (or two and three dimensions) in some coordinate system. Overall, analytic geometry allows mathematicians to determine the posi-

tion, configurations, and separations of objects using algebraic representation and manipulation of equations.

What is a **graph**?

The term graph has several different meanings in mathematics. It can mean the interpretations of numbers, including bar graphs, pie charts, and line graphs. For example, a pie chart (graph) is often used to represent percents, such as a breakdown of where a taxpayer's money is spent in the various government agencies for a certain year.

In analytic geometry, a graph is simply a way of plotting—thus, visually representing—points, lines, curves, and solids in order to understand and interpret certain geometric figures and to solve equations. For example, solving an equation with one to two variables (usually written as x and y, or two dimensions) results in a curve on a graph (note: a line is considered a curve in geometry). Equations that contain three variables (usually as x, y, and z, or three dimensions) result in a surface.

What is a **coordinate system**?

A coordinate system is one that uses *coordinates*—a number or numbers that identify a point on a number line, plane, or in space. These points are most often seen on a graph and can be a combination of two numbers for a two-dimensional figure or three numbers for three dimensions.

How are **two-dimensional Cartesian coordinates** determined?

With two-dimensional Cartesian coordinates (or rectangular coordinates), an *ordered pair* of two numbers is determined using two axes oriented perpendicular to each

other (for more about ordered pairs, see "Foundations of Mathematics"). The ordered pair coordinates are found by specifying points along the two axes: First, along the x-axis, the positive or negative amount on either side of the y, or vertical, axis; this is called the *abscissa* and indicated as x. The other number is the positive or negative amount on either side of the x, or horizontal, axis; this is called the *ordinate* and indicated as y. The coordinates are usually written in terms of x and y at the point as an ordered pair; for example, in the illustration of a two-dimensional coordinate system below, the ordered pair is (7, 8), in which x is 7 and y is 8.

What are **quadrants**?

Graphs used in the Cartesian coordinate system are broken down into quadrants, or four segments. For example, in a two-dimensional system, the x and y axis—with the origin as zero and the two axes perpendicular to each other—form the four quadrants. In the top left quadrant (quadrant II), the x is negative and the y is positive; in the top right quadrant (quadrant I), both coordinates are positive; in the bottom left quadrant (quadrant III), Cartesian coordinates are both negative; and in the bottom right quadrant (quadrant IV), the x is positive and the y is negative.

How are **three-dimensional Cartesian coordinates** determined?

The three-dimensional coordinates are those that describe a solid or three-dimensional object with three axes (or three planes): the usual two axes (as in the two-dimensional system), and an additional line. The coordinates are usually written in terms of x, y, and z, and are often called *ordered triples* or just triples.

What are some **terms** used in the **Cartesian coordinate system** and **graphs**?

There are numerous terms used in the Cartesian coordinate system. Besides the ones already mentioned, the following are some of the most common.

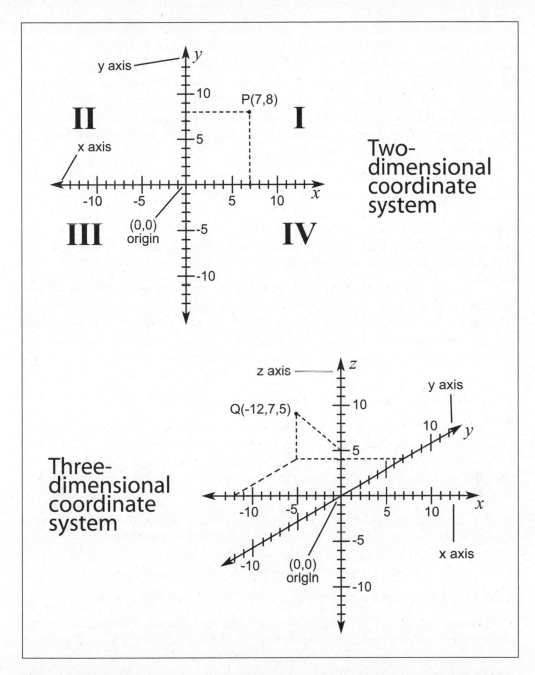

The four quadrants of a two-dimensional coordinate system are indicated above by the Roman numerals I, II, III, and IV. A three-dimensional coordinate system (bottom) adds a *z* axis so points can be indicated in real space, such as with point Q(–12, 7, 5) in this illustration.

An *intercept* is a point's distance on a coordinate system axis from the origin to where a curve or surface intersects the axis. On a graph, the x-intercept and y-intercept are two important features that show where a line cuts through the x and y axes, respectively. The *origin* is the fixed point from which measurements are taken. In most cases—especially in a standard, simple two-dimensional Cartesian coordinate system—this means the point that represents zero. This is often seen as (0, 0), or the point in which the x and y axes intersect on a graph. In a three-dimensional system, the coordinates are often seen as (0, 0, 0).

A *Cartesian plane* (or coordinate plane) is described as a two-dimensional space made up of points that are identified by their relation to the origin (zero), and the x and y axes. An *axis* (the plural is axes) is a reference line used in a graph or a coordinate system, such as the Cartesian system. For example, the x-axis and y-axis are perpendicular lines on a graph in a two-dimensional system; in a three-dimensional system, they are the x-axis, y-axis, and z-axis.

Collinear points are those that lie on a straight line. Any two points are considered collinear because a straight line passes through both. Many procedures in analytic geometry involve determining the collinear points that represent coordinates that solve an equation. Logically, those points that do not lie on the same line—or, in other words, that do not solve the equation—are called non-collinear points.

How is the **slope measure** and **y-intercept** of a line determined?

On a graph, the slope is the line in a plane completely specified by a point and a number. Mathematicians know that when an equation is written as $y = mx + b$, they can determine the slope measure and y-intercept (or slope intercept) of the line. In this case, the m (or x coefficient) is called the *slope measure* and the y-intercept are the coordinates that solve the equation.

For example, for $y = -2x + 4$, the slope measure is –2 and y-intercept is the coordinates (0, 4). To test this result, replace the x with the first coordinate (0); $-2 \times 0 = 0$; therefore, 4 is left, resulting in y (or the y-intercept) being 4.

What does **point-slope equation of a line** refer to in analytic geometry?

A point-slope equation of a line refers to Cartesian coordinates: If a point has coordinates (x_1, y_1) on a line and a slope equal to m, then the equation $y - y_1 = m(x - x_1)$ is the point-slope equation. Point-slope is most often used when finding an equation of a line.

Why are **functions** important to **analytic geometry**?

The intricacies of functions are important mainly because the function (and the graph of all the points in a function) is one of the basic foundations of analytic geometry.

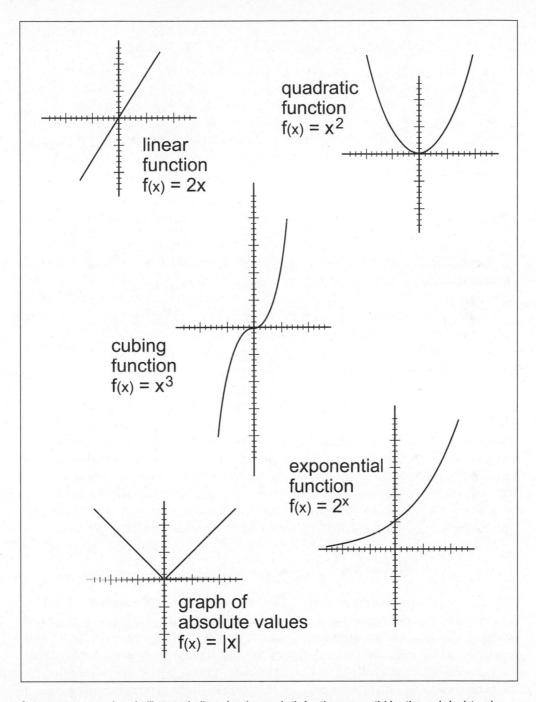

linear
function
f(x) = 2x

quadratic
function
f(x) = x^2

cubing
function
f(x) = x^3

exponential
function
f(x) = 2x

graph of
absolute values
f(x) = |x|

Some common types of graphs illustrate the linear function, quadratic function, exponential function, and absolute values.

Any figure represented by an equation in two variables is a curve in two dimensions. For example, the equation $3x + 4y = 8$ is also called a *linear function* because the solution represents a line (which is considered a "curve" in geometry) on a graph. There are also graphs of equations in three variables, with the solution as a surface—or the two-dimensional "outer layer" of a three-dimensional object.

This becomes even more evident when trying to solve complex equations or equations with more than one variable.

For example, when determining the solution to an equation, such as $3x + 4y = 8$, the two resulting numbers—called a *set of ordered pairs of numbers*—is called a *relation*. In turn, a function then becomes a relation in which each first element, such as *x,* is matched exactly with a second element, such as *y*. In other words, a function can take on a definite value (or values) when certain values are assigned to other quantities or independent variables of the function. (For more information about functions, see "Foundations of Mathematics" and "Algebra.")

What is a **one-to-one function**?

A one-to-one function is one in which each input (number that replaces the variable) has exactly one output (result of the equation). In such cases, the function needs to pass the "horizontal line test," showing that a horizontal line intersects the graph once and only once. For example, for the equation $f(x) = x^2$, if one restricts the answer to $x \geq 0$, the result is a one-to-one function; but the equation with no constraints is not a one-to-one function, as the output value of 4 has the two input values of 2 and –2.

What is the definition of a **conic section**?

This family of curves—first discovered (as far as we know) by the ancient Greeks—is generated by planes intersecting ("cutting into") a cone. The resulting feature depends on the angle between the plane and the axis of the cone, with none of the planes passing through the endpoint (vertex) of the cone. Each plane that cuts a cone creates a two dimensional figure called a *section,* thus the resulting figures are called *conic sections* or *conics*. In general, the possible resulting surfaces are a sphere (the cut perpendicular to the axis), ellipse (or the circle as a special case; a cut moderately inclined to the axis), parabola (a cut parallel to one of the straight lines that generate the cone), and hyperbola (using two cones tip to tip, the cut even more steeply inclined than all the others).

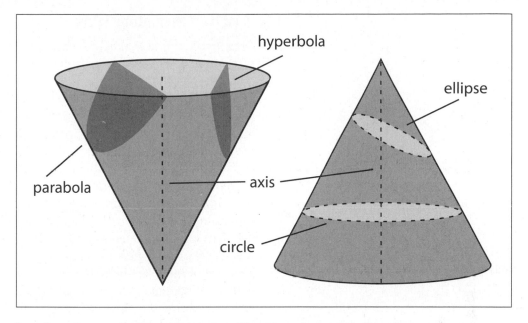

Depending on the way a plane intersects a cone shape, different types of curves will be the result.

What are **polar coordinates**?

Polar coordinates are actually an alternative system to the Cartesian coordinates. In two dimensions, they mark a point on a plane by its radial distance (r) from an "origin" and a polar angle (θ). This method also uses trigonometric functions such as sin and cos (sine and cosine; for more about such functions, see trigonometry in this chapter).

Polar coordinates in three-dimensional space—also called spherical coordinates—use r and two polar angles (θ, ϕ) to give the direction from the origin to the point. To compare, a three-dimensional polar coordinate system overlaps the Cartesian system in several ways: For example, θ is the angle between the line to the origin and the z-axis of the Cartesian (x, y, z) system; ϕ is the angle (counterclockwise when viewed from positive z) between the projection of that line onto the (x, y) plane and the x-axis.

What is an **Argand diagram**?

An Argand diagram is a graphical way of representing a function of a complex variable, often written as $z = x + iy$, in which x, y, and z are coordinates in three-dimensional space and i is an imaginary number. Its true discoverer is not actually known, but Swiss mathematician Jean Robert Argand (1768–1822) is given credit for the diagram. It is thought that this was also independently discovered by Danish mathematician Casper Wessel (1745–1818), and later by German mathematician and physicist Karl Friedrich Gauss (1777–1855) in 1832 (but he probably determined it much earlier); thus, its other name is the Gaussian plane.

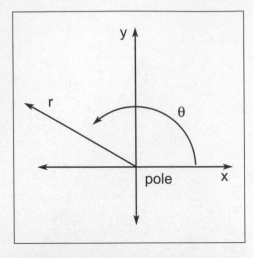

In the above illustration, x = r cos θ; y = r sin θ r² = x² + y²; and θ = arctan y/x (x=0).

What is an **asymptotic curve**?

On a graph, a line that approaches close to a curve (or even an axis) but never quite reaches it is an asymptotic curve. In an example similar to one of Zeno's paradoxes (see "Foundations of Mathematics"), if a kitten standing a yard from a box walks half the distance to the box each hour, it will technically never reach the box, because the distance it travels each hour is never more than half the remaining distance to the box. If this problem was illustrated as an equation, the answer would never quite reach its solution. A more mathematical example is the exponential function $y = 2^x$, which results in a line that approaches but will never quite reach the x-axis.

TRIGONOMETRY

What is **trigonometry**?

Trigonometry is the study of how the sides and angles of a triangle are related to each other. Interestingly, the angles are usually measured in terms of a circle around the x and y axes; from there, certain formulas are calculated, much as they are in algebra, to determine all the angles and units. Because trigonometry is such a mix of algebra and geometry, it is often considered "the art of doing algebra over a circle." Although "trig" (as it is nicknamed) is a small part of geometry, it has numerous applications in fields such as astronomy, surveying, maritime and aerial navigation, and engineering.

How are **angles measured** in trigonometry?

Angles in trigonometry are measured using a "circle" on x and y axes—often called circle trig definitions. The radian measure of an angle is any real number θ (theta; see illustration). Take an instance in which θ is greater than or equal to zero (θ ≥; 0): Picture taking a length of string and positioning one end at zero; then stretch the other end to 1 on the x axis, to point P(1, 0); this is also considered the radius of the circle. Then, in a counterclockwise direction, swing the string to another position, Q (x, y). This results in θ being an angle (associated with the central angle) with a vertex O or (0, 0) and passing through points P and Q; and because the string is "1 units" in length

all the way around, the point from Q to the vertex O will also be 1. The resulting angle θ is measured in degrees—and defined as a part of the circle's total number of degrees (a circle has 360 degrees); it can also be translated into radians.

How are **degrees and radians** translated?

When measuring the number of degrees in a circle, another unit called radians is often used in trigonometry. It is known that a circle is 360 degrees, with 1 degree equal to 60 minutes (60') and 1 minute equal to 60 seconds (60'); this is also called DMS (Degree-Minute-Second) notation. One revolution around the circle also measures 2π radians. Thus, $360° = 2\pi$ radians; or $180° = \pi$ radians. Simply put, to convert radians to degrees, multiply by $180/\pi$; to convert degrees to radians, multiply by $\pi/180$. The following are examples of how to convert degrees and radians:

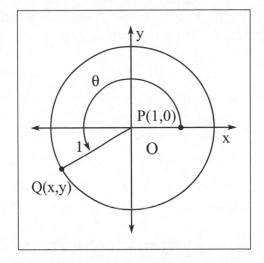

In this example of an angle measured using trigonometry, $x^2 + y^2 = 1$.

Convert the angle 236.345° to DMS notation (by breaking down the decimals into minutes and seconds):

236° + 0.345° × 60' /1°

236° + 20.7' = 236° + 20' + 0.7' × 60' /1'

= 236° 20' 42"

Convert the angle 236.345° to radians (convert the entire amount into radians by multiplying π radians by 180°, which is actually equal to "1" since, from above, 180° = π radians):

236.345° × π radians/180° = (236.345 × 3.141592) radians/180°

= 4.124998 radians

And, conversely, convert 4.124998 radians to degrees:

4.124998 radians × 180°/3.141592

= 236.345°

What are the **six trigonometric functions**?

There are six basic trigonometric functions that can be used to interpret the measurement of angles and triangles—most often defined as circle trig definitions. In terms of

the illustration below, the following lists the six trig functions of θ, all defined in terms of the coordinates of Q (x, y):

- cos θ = x
- sin θ = y
- tan θ = y/x if $x \neq 0$
- sec θ = $1/x$ if $x \neq 0$
- csc θ = $1/y$ if $y \neq 0$
- cot θ = x/y if $y \neq 0$

The full names for these functions are cos (cosine); sin (also seen as "sine"); tan (tangent); sec (secant); csc (cosecant); and cot (cotangent).

How are **trigonometric functions** used to **describe a right triangle**?

The trigonometric functions can be interpreted using the following illustration of a right triangle. If θ is the angle (see illustration), a is one leg (called the *adjacent* because it is adjacent to the angle), b is another leg (called the *opposite,* because it is opposite the angle), and c is the hypotenuse:

- cos θ = a/c = adjacent/hypotenuse
- sin θ = b/c = opposite/hypotenuse
- tan θ = b/a = opposite/adjacent
- sec θ = c/a = hypotenuse/adjacent
- csc θ = c/b = hypotenuse/opposite
- cot θ = a/b = adjacent/opposite

What are the same **functions using a circle**?

The following shows the same way of looking at the above triangle using a circle (also see illustration):

- cos θ = x/r
- sin θ = y/r
- tan θ = y/x
- sec θ = r/x
- csc θ = r/y
- cot θ = x/y

What is an **example** of finding a **trig function**?

One example of finding a trig function—including an illustration—follows: Find the trig functions of the angle θ = 60°. In this case, make a circle with a string extending

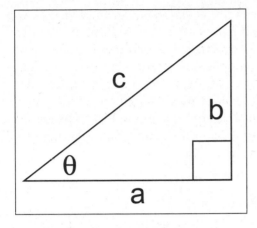

Trigonometric functions can be used to describe a right triangle.

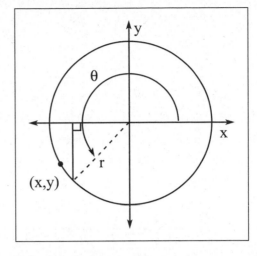

Trigonometric functions of a circle.

two units; then measure 60° from the vertex (O). Drop a line perpendicular from the point on the circle to the initial line, creating a 90° angle; that makes the last angle 30°. Because the result is a right triangle, with the values of the hypotenuse (2) and the adjacent leg (1), the Pythagorean theorem (see elsewhere in this chapter) is used to determine the length of the other leg, or $a^2 + b^2 = c^2$:

$$1^2 + b^2 = 2^2$$
$$1 + b^2 = 4$$
$$b^2 = 3$$
$$b = \sqrt{3}$$

Thus, by figuring out the cos (adjacent/hypotenuse) and sin (opposite/hypotenuse) for the angle 60°, Q is at point (1/2, $\sqrt{3}$/2) on the circle. The other trig functions can be determined using the methods in the questions above:

$$\cos \theta = 1/2 \ (x)$$
$$\sin \theta = \sqrt{3}/2 \ (y)$$
$$\tan \theta = \sqrt{3} \ (\sqrt{3}/1, \text{ or } y/x)$$
$$\sec \theta = 2 \ (1 / 1/2, \text{ or } 1/x)$$
$$\csc \theta = 2/\sqrt{3} \ (1/y)$$
$$\cot \theta = 1/\sqrt{3} \ (x/y)$$

What are some **identities in trigonometry**?

There are many fundamental identities—an equation that is true regardless of what values are substituted for any of the variables—based on trigonometric functions. Because there are relationships between the trig functions, identities can be used to

141

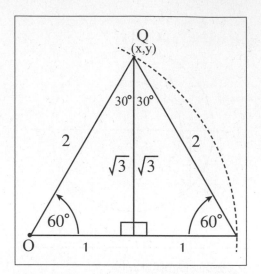

In this example, to find the trig functions of an angle of 60 degrees, draw a triangle with point O at the center of a circle with radius = 2; use the Pythagorean theorem to determine the length of the line dropping down at a right angle from point Q; and then calculate the trig functions using these measurements.

- $\csc\theta = 1/\sin\theta$
- $\cot\theta = 1/\tan\theta$

Ratio (or Quotient) Identities

- $\tan\theta = \sin\theta/\cos\theta$
- $\cos\theta = \cos\theta/\sin\theta$

rewrite equations, allowing the user to simplify or get more information out of an equation. The identities include reciprocal identities, ratio identities, periodicity identities, Pythagorean identities, odd-even identities, sum-difference identities, double angle identities, half angle identities, and several more. The following lists a few such identities:

Pythagorean Identities

- $\cos^2\theta + \sin^2\theta = 1$
- $\tan^2\theta + 1 = \sec^2\theta$
- $\cot^2\theta + 1 = \csc^2\theta$

Reciprocal Identities

- $\sin\theta = 1/\csc\theta$
- $\cos\theta = 1/\sec\theta$
- $\tan\theta = 1/\cot\theta$
- $\sec\theta = 1/\cos\theta$

What is a **periodic function**?

Periodic functions are those that repeat the same values at regular intervals. For trigonometric functions, the *period* (or the interval of repeated values) is 360 degrees or 2π for the sin, cosine, secant, and cosecant; and 180 degrees or π radians for the cotangent and tangent. (For example, this is often said as "the tangent function has period π.")

What are the **hyperbolic functions (or identities)**?

Similar to the other types of functions and identities above, hyperbolic functions (also called hyperbolic identities) are used to make it easier to find solutions to equations. In fact, there are corresponding trigonometric and hyperbolic identities. For example, the most commonly used trig identity, $\cos^2\theta + \sin^2\theta = 1$, has a corresponding hyperbolic identity:

$$\cosh^2 x - \sinh^2 x = 1$$

What is one of the most fundamental identities?

If one examines some of the above functions carefully, the sin and cosine functions are actually the coordinates of a point on the unit circle. This implies that the most important fundamental formula in trigonometry is as follows—one that some people call the "magic identity" but is more commonly known as one of the Pythagorean identities:

$\cos^2\theta + \sin^2\theta = 1$, in which θ is any real number.

This identity can be used in the following step-by-step example:

Show that:

$\sec^2\theta = \tan^2\theta + 1$

Because $\sec\theta = 1/\cos\theta$ (from the reciprocal identities), and $\tan\theta = \sin\theta/\cos\theta$ (from the ratio or quotient identities) then:

$\tan^2 + 1 - (\sin\theta/\cos\theta^2) + 1 =$

$(\sin^2\theta/\cos^2\theta) + 1 =$

$(\sin^2\theta + \cos^2\theta)/\cos^2\theta$ (where $\cos^2\theta$ divided by itself equals 1).

Then (using the Pythagorean identity):

$1/\cos^2\theta = \sec^2\theta$ (from the reciprocal identity).

In this case, the minus sign is used instead of a plus and the "cos" and "sin" changed to "cosh" and "sinh," respectively (also changed is the "θ" symbol to x; this is because many trig functions use the angle as the argument, while hyperbolic functions generally do not).

But these equations are not exactly the same. In particular, when one has a product of two sines it is replaced by minus a product of the two sinh's. For example, for the trig term \sin^2, the hyperbolic identity uses $-\sinh^2$ (this is called Osborn's rule). This is not always straightforward because the minus sign is often hidden.

OTHER GEOMETRIES

What is **projective geometry**?

Projective geometry is a branch of geometry that deals with the properties of geometric objects under projection; it was formerly called "higher" or "descriptive" geometry. Projection includes the transformation of points and lines in one plane onto another

plane. This is done by connecting the corresponding points on the planes using parallel lines—similar to shining a light on a person's profile and producing a silhouette on a nearby wall. Each point on the wall is a "projection" of the person's head.

What is **non-Euclidean geometry**?

Non-Euclidean geometry is a branch of geometry that deals with Euclid's fifth postulate—the "parallel postulate" that only one line is parallel to a given line through a given external point. This postulate is replaced by one of two alternative postulates. The results of these two alternative types of non-Euclidean geometry are similar to those in Euclidean geometry, except for those propositions involving explicit or implicit parallel lines.

What are **hyperbolic** and **elliptical geometry**?

Hyperbolic and elliptical geometry are the non-Euclidean alternative geometries mentioned above. The first alternative is to allow two parallels through any particular external point—or *hyperbolic geometry*. This studies two rays extending out in either direction from a point *P,* and not meeting a line *L;* thus, the rays are considered to be parallel to *L*. This also helps prove the theorem that the sum of the angles of a triangle is less than 180 degrees. It is called hyperbolic because a line in the hyperbolic plane has two points at infinity; this is similar to drawing a hyperbola that has two asymptotes.

The second alternative, called elliptical geometry, has no parallels to a given line *L* through an external point *P*. In addition, the sum of a triangle's angles is greater than 180 degrees. Sometimes called Riemann's geometry (who developed the idea even further; see below), it is called elliptic in general because a line in the plane of this geometry has no point at infinity (where parallels may intersect it), which is similar to an ellipse that has no asymptotes. (For more information about hyperbolas, ellipses, and asymptotes, see elsewhere in this chapter).

Who developed the **two alternatives** to **Euclidean geometry**?

Hyperbolic geometry was first announced by Russian mathematician Nikolai Ivanovich Lobachevski (1792–1856; also seen as Lobatchevsky) in 1826. He challenged Euclid's fifth postulate that one and only one line parallel to a given line can be drawn through a fixed point external to the line. Instead, he developed a self-consistent system of geometry in which the "flawed" postulate was replaced by one allowing more than one parallel through the fixed point.

This idea was already developed independently by Hungarian János (or Johann) Bolyai (1802–1860) in 1823 (after several attempts to prove the Euclidean parallel postulate, he developed his system by assuming that a geometry could be constructed without the parallel postulate) and German mathematician, physicist, and astronomer Karl Friedrich Gauss (1777–1855; also seen as Johann Carl [or Karl] Friedrich Gauss)

in 1816. But, as often happens in science and mathematics, the person who publishes an idea first gets most of the credit; this time, Lobachevski was the first to publish.

Who **further developed** the ideas in **non-Euclidean geometry**?

In 1854, German mathematician Georg Friedrich Bernhard Riemann (1826–1866) presented several new general geometric principles, laying the foundations of a non-Euclidean system of geometry called elliptical or Riemann geometry. In this, he represented elliptic space and generalized the work of German mathematician Karl Friedrich Gauss in differential geometry. Riemann's studies would eventually provide the basic tools for the general theory of relativity's mathematical expression. For example, the type of non-Euclidian geometry suggested by Riemann enabled Albert Einstein (1897–1955) to work on his general relativity theory (1916), showing that the true geometry of space may be non-Euclidian. (For more about Riemann, see "Math Basics.")

What is **topology**?

In general, topology is a branch of mathematics that examines patterns of geometric figures based on position and relative position without regard to size. It has also been called "rubber-sheet" geometry because objects examined in topology are under continuous transformation (also called topological transformation or homeomorphism). The shapes can be stretched, bent, and twisted in various ways, as long as they are not torn or cut as they are changed. For example, a circle is considered to be topologically equivalent to an ellipse (it can be deformed by stretching) and a sphere is equivalent to an ellipsoid. This includes changing an object based on a one-to-one correspondence. (For more about changing such shapes and one-to-one correspondence, see elsewhere in this chapter.)

What is a **good example** of a **topological structure**?

A good example of a topological structure is called the Möbius strip (also called the twisted cylinder). It was invented by German mathematician and astronomer August Ferdinand Möbius (1790–1868) in September 1858, although he did not publish his findings until 1865. The strip was also developed independently by German mathematician Johann Benedict Listing (1808– 1882), who discovered it in July 1858. Although Listing published his findings in 1861, Möbius's name is used for the strip.

This one-sided surface is easy to visualize: Take a long single strip of paper, give one of the two ends a twist (that gives the strip a half twist in its length, or

A Möbius strip is a one-sided topological structure.

a 180 degrees twist), then attach the two ends. Amazingly, you can verify that it has only one side—it is not possible to paint it with two colors. Even if you cut the strip in half (down the middle), you will still have a one sided-surface. In fact, ants would be able to walk on the Möbius strip's single surface indefinitely, since there is no true edge in the direction of their movement.

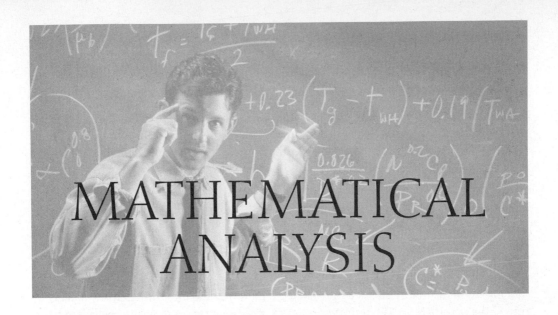

MATHEMATICAL ANALYSIS

ANALYSIS BASICS

What is **mathematical analysis**?

Mathematical analysis is a branch of mathematics that uses the concepts and methods common to the field of calculus. The key to mathematical analysis is the use of infinite processes; in turn, that involves passage to a limit, or, in other words, the basic branch of *calculus*. For example, a circle's area can be thought of as the limiting value of the areas of regular polygons within the circle, as the number of the polygons' sides increase indefinitely. The reason for calculus is simple: It is one of the most powerful and flexible tools not only in mathematics but in virtually every scientific field.

What culture took the first steps in the **development of mathematical analysis**?

Mathematical analysis—and, thus, the ideas of calculus—took centuries to develop. Probably the first to present some solid concepts in the field were the Greeks whose most important contribution was the method of exhaustion (expanding the measurements of an area to take in more and more of the required area).

For example, Zeno of Elea (c. 490–c. 425 B.C.E.) based many problems on the infinite; Leucippus of Miletus (fl. c. 435–c. 420 B.C.E.), Democritus of Abdera (460–370 B.C.E.; a student of Leucippus who also proposed an early theory about how the universe was formed), and Antiphon (c. 479–411 B.C.E.; who some historians believe tried to square the circle) would all contribute to the method of exhaustion. Eudoxus of Cnidus (c. 400–347 B.C.E.) would be the first to use the method on a scientific basis. Archimedes (c. 287–212 B.C.E.; Hellenic)—considered one of the greatest Greek mathematicians—took mathematical analysis one step further: He more fully developed the theory presented by Eudoxus that would eventually lead to integral calculus.

What is considered one of **Archimedes's** most **significant contributions** to mathematics?

Archimedes made many significant contributions to mathematics, though not all mathematicians would agree with the label "most significant." But one of his contributions *did* advance the field of calculus by showing that the area of a segment of a parabola is 4/3 the area of a triangle with the same base and vertex (endpoint), and 2/3 the area of the circumscribed parallelogram.

To figure this out, he constructed an "infinite" sequence of triangles (or wedges), finding the area of segments composing the parabola. He began with the first area, A, then added more triangles between the existing ones and the parabola to get areas of:

$$A, A + A/4, A + A/4 + A/16, A + A/4 + A/16 + A/64, \text{ and so on.}$$

Based on his iterations, he determined the following (the first time anyone had determined the summation of an infinite series; for more about infinite series, see below):

$$A(1 + 1/4 + 1/4^2 + 1/4^3 + \ldots) = A(4/3)$$

Archimedes also applied this *method of exhaustion* (not literally becoming tired, but close to it) to approximate the area of a circle, which, in turn, led to a better approximation of pi (π). Using such integrations, he also determined the volume and surface area of a sphere and cone, the surface area of an ellipse, and many others. His work is considered the first steps toward integration that would eventually lead to integral calculus. (For more information about Archimedes and his wedges, see "Geometry and Trigonometry.")

Astronomer and mathematician Johannes Kepler used sectors to calculate the shape of the elliptical paths of the planets.

What did **Isaac Newton** contribute to **mathematical analysis**?

English mathematician and natural philosopher (otherwise called a physicist) Isaac Newton (1642–1727) was one of the greatest scientists who ever lived. Overall, he contributed to physics (such as the discovery of his three famous laws of motion); fluid dynamics (fluid motion); the union of terrestrial and celestial mechanics using the principle of gravitation—thus explaining Kepler's laws of planetary motion; and he even explained the principle of universal gravitation.

By 1665 Newton had not only begun his work on differential calculus, but he

How did mathematical analysis develop after the 16th century?

Ideas about mathematical analysis took a long hiatus after the Greeks. It didn't begin to grow again until the 16th century, when the need to examine mechanics problems became important. For example, German astronomer and mathematician Johannes Kepler (1571–1630) needed to calculate the area of sectors in an ellipse in order to understand planetary motion. (Interestingly, Kepler thought of areas as the sums of lines—a kind of crude form of integration; even though he made two errors in his work, they canceled each other out and he was still able to determine the correct numbers.)

By the 17th century, many mathematicians had begun to contribute to the field of mathematical analysis. For example, French mathematician Pierre de Fermat (1601–1665) made contributions that eventually led to differential calculus. Bonaventura Cavalieri presented his *method of indivisibles*, one he developed after examining Kepler's integration work. English mathematician Isaac Barrow (1630–1677) worked on tangents that formed the foundation for Newton's work on calculus. Italian mathematician Evangelista Torricelli (1608–1647) added to differential calculus and many other facets of mathematical analysis. (In fact, collections of paradoxes that arose through the inappropriate use of the new calculus were found in his manuscripts. Unfortunately for mathematics, Torricelli died young of typhoid.) And, of course, the one name most associated with calculus—Isaac Newton—developed some of his most brilliant work during the 17th century.

also had published one of his greatest scientific works—*Philosophiae naturalis principia mathematica* (*The Mathematical Principles of Natural Philosophy*), often shortened to *The Principia* or just *Principia*. In it he presents his theories of motion, gravity, and mechanics, thus explaining the bizarre orbits of comets, tides and tidal variations, the movement of the Earth's axis (called precession), and motion of the Moon. And although he used calculus to find many of his scientific results, Newton also explained them using older geometric methods in the book. After all, calculus was very new. Perhaps he was the first scientist-writer to make sure everyone understood what he was proposing.

Why was **Gottfried Wilhelm Leibniz** important to calculus?

German philosopher and mathematician Baron Gottfried Wilhelm Leibniz (1646–1716) was a contemporary of Isaac Newton. He is considered by some to be a forgotten mathematician, being overshadowed by Newton, but his contributions to mathematics were just as important. In addition to many other contributions, he (independently of Newton) developed infinitesimal calculus and was first to describe it in print. Because

his work on calculus was published three years before Isaac Newton's, Leibniz's system of notation was universally adopted, including the notation for an integral. In 1684, he published *Nova methodus pro maximis et minimis, itemque tangentibus,* a work detailing differential calculus and containing the familiar d (or d/dx) notation, along with the rules for calculating the derivatives of powers, products, and quotients.

SEQUENCES AND SERIES

What is a **sequence**?

A sequence is defined as a set of real numbers with a natural order. A sequence is usually included in brackets ({}), with the *terms,* or parts of a sequence, separated by commas. For example, if a scientist collects weather data every day for many days, the first day of collecting can be written as x_1 data; then x_2 for the second day, and so on until x_n, in which n is the eventual number of days. This can be written as $\{x_1, x_2, \dots x_n\}_{n \geq 1}$. In general, the sequence of numbers in which x_n is the *nth* number is written using the following notation: $\{x_n\}_{n \geq 1}$.

A sequence can get larger or smaller. For example, in the sequence for $\{2^n\}_{n \geq 1}$, the solution is $2 \leq 4 \leq 8 \leq 16 \leq 32$, and so on, with the numbers getting larger. Whereas, for $\{1/n\}_{n \geq 1}$, the sequence becomes $1 \geq 1/2 \geq 1/3 \geq 1/4 \geq 1/5$, and so on, with the numbers getting progressively smaller. This does not mean that sequences only get progressively larger and smaller; certain solutions for sequences include a mix of the two.

What is the **range of a sequence**?

The range of a sequence is merely a set that defines the sequence. The range is usually represented by the set $\{x_1\}$, $\{x_2\}$, $\{x_3\}$, and so on; it is also written as $\{x_n; n = 1, 2, 3, \dots\}$. For example, in the question above, the data for each day that the scientist collects from his weather experiment is the range. Another example is the range of the sequence $\{(-1)^n\}_{n \geq 1}$: It is the two-element set $\{-1, 1\}$.

When is a **sequence monotonic**?

A sequence is called monotonic if one of the following properties hold: In the sequence $\{x_n\}_{n \geq 1}$, it is increasing if and only if $x_n < x_{n+1}$ for any $n \geq 1$, or it is decreasing if and only if $x_n > x_{n+1}$ for any $n \geq 1$.

For example, in order to check that the sequence $\{2^n\}_{n \geq 1}$ is increasing: Let $n \geq 1$; that gives $2^{n+1} = 2^n\,2$. Because 2 is greater than 1, which means that $1 \times 2^n < 2 \times 2^n$; thus $2^n < 2^{n+1}$, which shows the sequence is increasing.

How can a calculator determine the limit of a sequence?

There is an excellent way to understand the limit of a sequence by using a calculator. In scientific calculators that include geometric functions (such as cosine, sine, and tangent), a limit is easy to see: Find $x_1 = \cos(1)$, then $x_2 = \cos(x_1)$, and so on. Just put the calculator in the "radian" mode, enter "1," and then hit the "cosine" key repeatedly. The number will start at "0.540302305," then change to "0.857553215," and keep changing. As it approaches about the twentieth change, the amount gets closer and closer to a number that begins as "0.73 ...". This indicates the limit of the sequence is being reached.

What are the **bounds of a sequence**?

Once again, take the sequence $\{x_n\}_{n \geq 1}$. This sequence is *bounded above* if and only if there is a number M such that $x_n \leq M$ (the M is called an *upper-bound*). In addition, the sequence is *bounded below* if and only if there is a number m such that $x_n \geq m$ (the m is called a *lower-bound*). For example, the sequence $\{2^n\}_{n \geq 1}$, is bounded below by 0 because it is positive, but not bounded above.

The sequence is usually said to be merely *bounded* (or "bd" for short) if both of the properties (upper- and lower-bound) hold. For example, the harmonic sequence $\{1, 1/2, 1/3, 1/4 ...\}$ is considered bounded because no term is greater than 1 or less than 0; thus, the upper- and lower-bounds, respectively, apply.

What is a **limit of a sequence**?

The limit of a sequence is simply the number that represents a kind of equilibrium reached in the sequence. It is also phrased "approaches as closely as possible." (Limit is also a term used in calculus in relation to a function; see elsewhere in this chapter.)

What are the concepts of **convergent** and **divergent sequences**?

Convergent and divergent sequences are based on the limit of a sequence. A convergent sequence, the one most commonly worked on in calculus, means that one mathematical sequence gets close to another and eventually approaches a limit (convergence can also apply to curves, functions, or series). This is seen visually when a curve approaches the x or y axes but does not quite reach it. For example, take the sequence of numbers used above, or $\{x_n\}_{n \geq 1}$. Often the numbers come closer and closer to a number we'll call L; written in calculus, $x_n \approx L$. If the numbers do come closer, the sequence is said to be *convergent* and has a limit equal to L. Conversely, if the sequence is not convergent, it is called *divergent*.

Most mathematicians and scientists are not only interested in how a sequence converges (or diverges), but also how fast it converges, which is called the *speed of convergence*. There are several basic properties of the limits of a sequence, including that the limit of a convergent sequence is unique, every convergent sequence is bounded, and any bounded increasing or decreasing sequence is convergent.

How are **limits** written in terms of **convergent and divergent sequences**?

Limits of convergent and divergent sequences are written as follows (the figure eight on its side is the symbol for infinity):

$$\lim_{n \to \infty} x_n = L$$

$$\text{or } x_n \longrightarrow L \text{ when } n \longrightarrow \infty.$$

What is a **series**?

A series is closely related to the sum of numbers. It is actually used to help add numbers; therefore, in a sequence it can be the indicated sum of that sequence. In general, the idea is to start with a number, then do something to that number to get the next number, then do the same to that number to get the next number, and so on. For example, a *finite series* with six terms is $2 + 4 + 6 + 8 + 10 + 12$, in which 2 is added to each number to get the next number. An example of an *infinite series* is one with the notation $1/2^n$, with $n \geq 1$, or $1/2 + 1/4 + 1/8 + \dots$ (and so on).

To see a series written in notation, if set $\{x_n\}$ is a sequence of numbers being added, and set $s_1 = x_1$, then $s_2 = x_1 + x_2$; $s_3 = x_1 + x_2 + x_3$; and so on. And for $n \geq 1$, a new sequence is made, $\{s_n\}$, called the *sequence of partial sums,* or $s_n = x_1 + x_2 + \dots + x_n$.

What is the **notation** commonly used for **series and sequences**?

When looking at a sequence and series, we need to distinguish between the ones we want to add, and the ones we do not want to add. The common symbol used for addition with a sequence or a series is the summation symbol, seen as the symbol Σ. When discussing a series, this symbol is used to mean the sum of numbers. For example, for the series called x_n:

$$\sum_{n \geq 1} x_n$$

Also note that for any given series Σx_n, we have to also remember to associate it with the sequence of partial sums ($s_n = x_1 + x_2 + \dots + x_n$).

What are arithmetic series and sequences?

An arithmetic series—also called arithmetic progression—is one of the simpler types of series in mathematics. In such a series, each new term is the previous number plus a given number; it is usually seen in the form of $a + (a + d) + (a + 2d) + (a + 3d) +, ..., a + (n - 1)d$. An example of an arithmetic series would be $2 + 6 + 10 + 14 + ...$, and so on, in which d is equal to 4. The *initial term* is the first one in the series; the difference between each term (d, or 4 in this case) is called the *common difference*.

An arithmetic sequence is usually in the form of $a, a + d, a + 2d, a + 3d, ...$, and so on, in which a is the first term and d is the constant difference between the two successive terms throughout. An example of an arithmetic sequence is (1, 4, 7, 10, 13 ...), in which the difference is always a constant of 3. The notation for arithmetic sequences is:

$$a_{n+1} = a_n + d.$$

What does it mean if a **series is convergent**?

Convergence of a series is related to the convergence of a sequence, but don't confuse them. The convergence of the sequence of partial sums (usually written as $\{s_n\}$) differs greatly from the convergence of a sequence of numbers (usually written as $\{x_n\}$). For example, the series $\Sigma\, x_n$ (and its associated sequence of partial sums, or $\{s_n\}$), is convergent if and only if the sequence $\{s_n\}$ is convergent. Thus, the total sum of the series is the limit of the sequence $\{s_n\}$, seen as:

$$\lim_{n \to \infty} S_n = \sum_{n=1}^{n=\infty} x_n$$

What is a **geometric sequence**?

A geometric sequence—or geometric progression—is a finite or infinite sequence of real numbers with the ratio between two consecutive terms being constant (called the *common ratio* or r); in this case, each term is the previous term multiplied by a given number. In a geometric sequence, the formula for the nth term, in terms of the first number and the common ratio, becomes:

$$a_n = a_1 r^{n-1}$$

The first term is a_1, r is the common ratio, and the number of terms is n. For example, for the numbers 2, 6, 18, 54, 162, a_1 is 2, r is 3, and n is 5. The equation then becomes:

$$2 \times 3^{5-1} = 162.$$

What is a **geometric series**?

If we add the numbers in a geometric sequence, we end up with a geometric series. A geometric series is obtained when each term is determined from the preceding one by multiplying by a common ratio; there is a constant ratio between terms. For example, $1 + 1/2 + 1/4 + 1/8 + \ldots$, and so on, is a geometric series because each term is determined by multiplying the preceding term by $1/2$. To find the sum of a geometric series, the formula is: Sum $= a(r^n - 1) / (r - 1)$ or $a(1 - r^n) / (1 - r)$, in which a is the first term, r is the common ratio, and n is the number of terms.

For example, to find the sum of the first six terms of a series represented by $2 + 6 + 18 + 54 + 162 + 486$, define $a = 2$; $r = 3$; and $n = 6$. Substitute the numbers: Sum $= 2(3^6 - 1) / 3 - 1 = 729 - 1 = 728$. We could also have determined this number based on the first few numbers, such as $2 + 6 + 18 + 54$, as long as we knew the common ratio, the first number, and how many numbers in the series we wanted to add. This is something that can easily be determined based on just these four numbers.

CALCULUS BASICS

What are some **definitions of calculus**?

The definition of calculus is often confusing. Like many terms used over time in mathematics (and the sciences, for that matter), there is often an overlapping of names and terms. Thus, the term "calculus" is often a generic name for any area of mathematics dealing with calculation; arithmetic could be called the "calculus of numbers." It is also why there are such terms as *imaginary calculus* (a method of looking at the relationships between real or imaginary quantities using imaginary symbols and quantities in algebra) that *do not* mean the type of calculus discussed in this chapter.

Most mathematicians say that, in general, "a" calculus is an abstract theory developed in a purely formal way. "The" calculus is different, as it is a branch of mathematics that deals with functions; another name for the calculus is real analysis (a more archaic term is infinitesimal analysis). This type of calculus evaluates constantly changing quantities, such as velocity and acceleration; values interpreted as slopes of curves; and the area, volume, and length objects bounded by curves (remember, curves can also mean straight lines). It involves infinite processes that lead to *passage to a limit,* or the approaching of an ultimate, usually desired value. The tools of the calculus include differentiation (differential calculus, or finding a derivative) and integration (integral calculus, or finding the indefinite integral), both of which are foundations for mathematical analysis.

How is **modern calculus divided**?

Modern calculus is divided into many different types. The following lists just a few of the many divisions:

Basic calculus—Basic calculus is the branch of mathematics concerned with limits and with the differentiation and integration of functions. There is also *advanced calculus* that takes an even more complex view of calculus, with an emphasis on proofs.

Differential calculus—Differential calculus deals with the variation of a function with respect to changes in the independent variable(s). It does this by determining derivatives and differentials.

Integral calculus—Integral calculus (logically) deals with integration and its application to solve differential equations; it is also used to determine areas and volumes.

Predicate calculus—Predicate calculus, or functional calculus, is a branch of formal logic that involves logical connections between statements as well as the statements themselves.

Multivariable calculus—This is a branch of calculus that studies functions of more than one variable.

Functional calculus—Functional calculus is actually an older name for calculus of variations; it's sometimes used in place of predicate calculus.

Propositional calculus—This is the formal basis of logic dealing with the notion and usage of words such as "OR" or "AND."

Malliavin calculus—Malliavin calculus is one of the more esoteric studies; it is an infinite-dimensional differential calculus on the Wiener space, also called stochastic calculus of variations.

Other various analyses—Other parts of calculus entail various types of analyses, such as vector, tensor, and complex analyses, and differential geometry.

What is a **limit** in **calculus**?

A limit is a fundamental concept in calculus. Unlike a limit mentioned above (as in a series or sequence), a limit of a function in calculus takes on a somewhat different meaning. In particular, a limit of a function can be described as the following: If $f(x)$ is a function defined around a point c (but may not be at c itself), the formal limit equation becomes:

$$\lim_{x \to c} f(x) = L$$

Thus, the number L is called the limit of $f(x)$ when x goes to c.

What are **left-** and **right-limits**?

When a function is not defined around the point c (see the notation in the equation above), but only to the left or right of point c, then the limits are called the left-limit and right-limit at c. The formal left- and right-limit equations are the same as the usual limit equation, except below the "lim" sign, the $x \longrightarrow c$ is written as $x \longrightarrow c-$ for the left-limit and $x \longrightarrow c+$ for the right limit.

How is **infinity treated** when **discussing limits**?

Defining infinity is a definite part of calculus, especially when discussing limits and "negative" and "positive" infinity. Whenever the inverse of a small number is taken, a large number is generated, and vice versa. In calculus, this is written as:

$$1/0 = \pm\infty$$

But $\pm\infty$ are no ordinary numbers, because they do not obey the usual rules of arithmetic, such as $\infty + 1 = \infty$; $\infty - 1 = \infty$; $2 \times \infty = \infty$; and so on. Therefore, in calculus functions, and thus limits, infinity is treated much differently. For example, for the function $f(x) = 1/x - 3$, when $x \longrightarrow 3$, then $x - 3 \longrightarrow 0$. The limit function then becomes:

$$\lim_{x \to 3-} f(x) = \tfrac{1}{0-} = -\infty$$

$$\lim_{x \to 3+} f(x) = \tfrac{1}{0+} = +\infty$$

This example can be seen in the accompanying graph.

What is **infinitesimal calculus**?

Infinitesimal may mean infinitely small in most people's dictionaries, or bring up thoughts of subatomic particles. To those who study arithmetic, however, it may mean numbers greater in absolute value than zero, yet smaller than any positive real number.

But for those who study calculus, it is an area of mathematics pioneered by Gottfried Leibniz. His idea was based purely on the concept of infinitesimals; this was in opposition to the calculus of Isaac Newton, who based his calculus on the concept of the limit. Although historically the emphasis was placed on the minute, modern infinitesimal calculus actually has little to do with infinitely small quantities.

What are **vertical asymptotes** in association with limits?

Using the example above, as x gets closer to 3, the points on the graph get closer to the vertical line $x = 3$ (seen as a dashed line on the graph below). This line is called a *vertical asymptote*. The following charts shows four of the vertical asymptotes for the given function $f(x)$ and their notations.

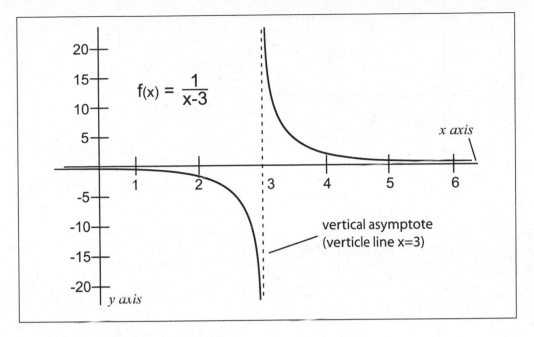

Graph of an equation with infinity limited by x = 3.

What are **horizontal asymptotes** in association with limits?

A *horizontal asymptote* is similar to a vertical asymptote, but it is associated with the y axis. For example, for the function

$$f(x) = \frac{2x + 1}{x - 1}$$

gives a solution of:

$$\frac{2 + \frac{1}{x}}{1 - \frac{1}{x}}$$

and, thus, the implied limit is:

$$\lim_{x \to \pm\infty} f(x) = \frac{2 + 0}{1 - 1} = 2$$

This is because we know that:

$$\lim_{x \to -\infty} \frac{1}{x} = 0 \text{ and } \lim_{x \to +\infty} \frac{1}{x} = 0$$

And as x gets larger (or closer to $\pm\infty$) the points on the graph come closer to the horizontal line $y = 2$ (seen as a dashed line on the graph on page 225), which is called the horizontal asymptote.

157

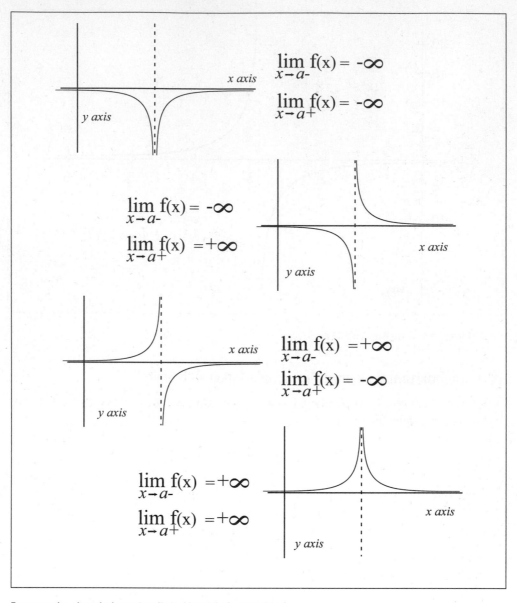

$$\lim_{x \to a-} f(x) = -\infty$$

$$\lim_{x \to a+} f(x) = -\infty$$

$$\lim_{x \to a-} f(x) = -\infty$$

$$\lim_{x \to a+} f(x) = +\infty$$

$$\lim_{x \to a-} f(x) = +\infty$$

$$\lim_{x \to a+} f(x) = -\infty$$

$$\lim_{x \to a-} f(x) = +\infty$$

$$\lim_{x \to a+} f(x) = +\infty$$

Four examples of graphed equations limited by vertical asymptotes.

What does **continuous** and **discontinuous** mean in calculus?

When talking about polynomial functions, we know that a polynomial function $P(x)$ satisfies the limit function:

$$\lim_{x \to a} P(x) = P(a)$$

in which a represents all real numbers. This is called continuity.

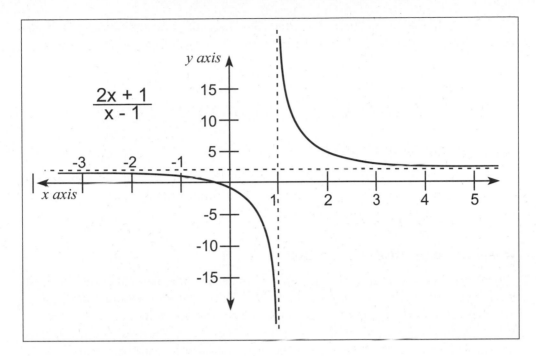

$$\frac{2x + 1}{x - 1}$$

A graphed equation limited by horizontal asymptote y = 2.

But if $f(x)$ is a function on an interval around a, then $f(x)$ is continuous at a iff (see below for the definition of "iff"):

$$\lim_{x \to a} f(x) = f(a)$$

if it is not, then $f(x)$ is called discontinuous at a.

What is the **concept of bound**?

Similar to sequences (see elsewhere in this chapter), in calculus bounds are divided into the upper (either greater than or equal to every other number in a set of numbers; or greater than or equal to all the partial sums of a sequence) or lower (less than or equal to every other number). The symbol for infinity (∞) is used to denote a set of numbers *without bound,* or that increase or decrease "to infinity." In calculus, the bounds can be divided even more into greatest or least. For example, the greatest lower bounds and least upper bounds are of special interest to calculus, as those numbers may or may not be found within a set.

What does the strange **symbol "iff" mean** in calculus?

The symbol (or "word") iff actually is shorthand for "if and only if." It is not only mathematics that depends on the iff, but also philosophy, logic, and many technical fields. It 159

is usually italicized; in addition, the phrase "P is necessary and sufficient for Q" is also seen as "Q iff P." The corresponding logical symbols for "if and only if" are \leftrightarrow and \equiv.

DIFFERENTIAL CALCULUS

What is the **differential calculus**?

Differential calculus is the part of "the" calculus that deals with derivatives. It deals with the study of the limit of a quotient, usually written as $\Delta y / \Delta x$, as the denominator (Δx) approaches zero, with x and y as variables.

What is the **derivative of a function**?

One of the most important, core concepts in modern mathematics and calculus is the derivative of a function—or a function derived from another function. A derivative is also expressed as the limit of $\Delta y / \Delta x$, also said as "the derivative of y with respect to x." It is actually the rate of change (or slope on a graph) of the original function; the derivative represents an infinitesimal change in the function with respect to the parameters contained within the function.

In particular, the process of finding the derivative of the function $y = f(x)$ is called differentiation. The derivative is most frequently written as dy / dx; it is also expressed in various other ways, including $f'(x)$ (said as the derivative of a function f with respect to x), y', $Df(x)$, $df(x)$, or $D_x y$. It is important to note that the differentials, written as dy and dx, represent singular symbols and not the products of the two symbols. Not all derivatives exist for all values of a function; the sharp corner of a graph, in which there is no definite slope—and thus no derivative—is an example.

What is the **standard notation** for the **derivative**?

The following represents the definition of the derivative of $f(x)$ (note: in order for the limit to exist, both $\lim_{h \to 0+}$ and $\lim_{h \to 0-}$ must exist and be equal; thus, the function must be continuous):

For $f(x)$'s derivative at point x_0:

$$\frac{df}{dx}(x_0) = f'(x_0) = \lim_{x \to x_0} \frac{f(x) - f(x_0)}{x - x_0} = \lim_{h \to 0} \frac{f(x_0 + h) - f(x_0)}{h}$$

For $f(x)$'s derivative at $x = a$:

$$f'(a) = \lim_{x \to a} \frac{f(x) - f(a)}{x - a} = \lim_{h \to 0} \frac{f(a + h) - f(a)}{h}$$

What is an example of the second derivative?

The second derivative is actually a function's derivative's derivative. In other words, the function's derivative may also have its own derivative, called the second derivative or second order derivative. If we let $y = f(x)$, the second derivative becomes $d/dx(dy/dx)$. This is equal to d^2y/dx^2, further represented by the symbols $f'(x)$ or y'. One good example of a second order derivative is acceleration—it is actually the second derivative of a change in distance. In other words, the first derivative gives instantaneous velocity (see above) while the second derivative gives acceleration.

Is there a **formula** for the **inverse of a derivative**?

Yes. In this case, the derivative of the inverse function represents the inverse of $y(x)$—or $x(y)$:

$$\frac{dy}{dx} = \frac{1}{\frac{dx}{dy}}$$

What are the **two ways** of **looking at the derivative**?

There are two major ways of looking at the derivative—the geometrical (or the slope of a curve) and the physical (the rate of change). The derivative was historically developed from finding the tangent line to a curve at a point (geometrically); it eventually became the study of the limit of a quotient usually seen as the change in x and y ($\Delta y/\Delta x$). Even today, mathematicians debate which is the best way to describe a derivative.

Geometrically, after determining the slope of a straight line through two points on a graph of a function, and the limit where the change in x approaches zero, the ratio becomes the derivative dy/dx. This represents the slope of a line that touches the curve at a single point—or the tangent line.

Physically, the derivative of y with respect to x describes the rate of change in y for a change in x. The independent variable, in this case x, is often expressed as time. For example, velocity is often expressed in terms of s, the distance traveled, and t, the elapsed time. In terms of average velocity, it can be expressed as $\Delta s/\Delta t$. But for instantaneous velocity, or as Δt gets smaller and smaller, we need to use limits—or the instantaneous velocity at a point B is equal to:

$$\lim_{\Delta t \to 0} \frac{\Delta s}{\Delta t}$$

What are some **examples** of **derivatives of "simple" functions**?

The following lists some derivatives of "simple" functions:

$$\frac{d}{dx}x^n = nx^{n-1}$$

$$\frac{d}{dx}\ln|x| = \frac{1}{x}$$

What are some **simple derivatives** as functions of the **variable x**?

There are simple derivatives as functions of the variable x. In this case, u and v are functions of the variable x, and n is a constant:

$$\frac{d}{dx}(c) = 0$$

$$\frac{d}{dx}(x) = 1$$

$$\frac{d}{dx}(x^n) = nx^{n-1}$$

$$\frac{d}{dx}(u \pm v) = \frac{du}{dx} \pm \frac{dv}{dx}$$

$$\frac{d}{dx}(cu) = c\frac{du}{dx}$$

$$\frac{d}{dx}(xu) = u\frac{dv}{dx} + v\frac{du}{dx}$$

$$\frac{d}{dx}\left(\frac{u}{v}\right) = \frac{v\frac{du}{dx} - u\frac{dv}{dx}}{v^2}$$

What is an **example** of **computing the derivative**?

The following solves the derivative at $x = a$ for the function $f(x) = x^2$, using the definition for a derivative (see above):

$$\frac{f(a+h) - f(a)}{h} = \frac{(a+h)^2 - a^2}{h} = \frac{2ah + h^2}{h} = 2a + h$$

$$\lim_{h \to 0} \frac{f(a+h) - f(a)}{h} = 2a$$

What is the Mean-Value Theorem?

The Mean-Value Theorem has nothing to do with crankiness, but it *is* one of the most important theoretical tools in the calculus. In written terms, it is defined as the following: If $f(x)$ is defined and continuous on the interval [a, b], and differentiable on (a, b), then there is at least one number on the interval (a, b)—or $a < c < b$—such that:

$$f'(c) = \frac{f(b) - f(a)}{b - a}$$

When $f(a) = f(b)$, this is a special case called *Rolle's Theorem,* when we know that $f(c)$ will equal zero. Interpreting this, we know that there is a point on (a, b) that has a horizontal tangent.

It is also true that the Mean-Value Theorem can be put in terms of slopes. Thus, the last part of the above equation (on the right of the equal sign) represents the slope of a line passing through $(a, f(a))$ and $(b, f(b))$. Thus, this theory states that there is a point $c \in (a, b)$, such that the tangent line is parallel to a line passing through the two points.

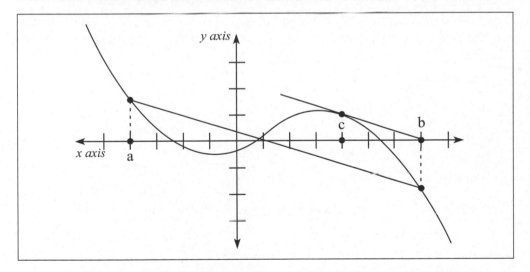

This graph illustrates the concept of the Mean-Value Theorem.

Are there **higher derivatives** of a **function**?

Yes, there are higher derivatives of a function, often referred to as higher order derivatives. The "initial" derivative is often written as $f'(x)$, but the " ' " is assumed in most cases. The next derivative is the second derivative (second order derivative), most often written as $f''(x)$; the next is the third derivative, or third order derivative, most

often written as $f'''(x)$; fourth derivative, or fourth order derivative, most often written as $f^{(4)}(x)$; and so on. The notation for the higher derivatives, or the nth derivative, is as follows:

$$d/dx\,(d^{n-1}y/dx^{n-1}) \;=\; d^{n}y/dx^{n} \;=\; f^{(n)}(x) \;=\; y^{(n)}$$

This equation is also seen written as $D^{n}(y) = d^{n}y/dx^{n}$.

What is a **partial derivative**?

Partial derivatives (seen written as the symbol ∂) are derivatives of a function containing multiple variables that have all but the variable of interest held fixed during the differentiation. Thus, when a function $f(x, y, \ldots)$ depends on more than one variable, the partial derivative can be used to specify the derivative with respect to one or more variables. There are other terms, too: Partial derivatives that involve more than one variable are called *mixed partial derivatives*. And a differential equation expressing one or more quantities in terms of partial derivatives is called, logically, a *partial differential equation*. These equations are well known in physics and engineering, and most are notoriously difficult to solve.

What are the **product, quotient, power,** and **chain rules** for derivatives?

There are numerous rules for derivatives of certain combinations of functions, including the product, quotient, power, and chain rules. The following lists their common notation:

For a product:

$$\frac{d}{dx}[f(x)g(x)] = f(x)g'(x) + f'(x)g(x)$$

where f' is the derivative of f with respect to x.

For a quotient:

$$\frac{d}{dx}\left[\frac{f(x)}{g(x)}\right] = \frac{g(x)f'(x) - f(x)g'(x)}{[g(x)]^2}$$

where, again, f' is the derivative of f with respect to x.

For a power:

$$\frac{d}{dx}(x^{n}) = nx^{n-1}$$

For a chain:

$$\frac{dy}{dx} = \frac{dy}{du}\cdot\frac{du}{dx}$$

Or:

$$\frac{dz}{dt} = \frac{\partial z}{\partial x}\frac{dx}{dt} + \frac{\partial z}{\partial y}\frac{dy}{dt}$$

where $\partial z/\partial x$ is a partial derivative.

What are the **derivatives** of **trigonometric functions**?

There are also derivatives of the six major trigonometric functions—sine, cosine, cotangent, cosecant, tangent, and secant (for more information on these trigonometric functions, see "Geometry and Trigonometry"). The following lists the formulas for those derivatives (in this case, the functions are written with respect to the variable u):

$$\frac{d}{dx}(\sin(u)) = \cos(u)\frac{du}{dx}$$

$$\frac{d}{dx}(\cos(u)) = -\sin(u)\frac{du}{dx}$$

$$\frac{d}{dx}(\tan(u)) = -\sec^2(u)\frac{du}{dx}$$

$$\frac{d}{dx}(\cot(u)) = -\csc^2(u)\frac{du}{dx}$$

$$\frac{d}{dx}(\sec(u)) = \sec(u)\tan(u)\frac{du}{dx}$$

$$\frac{d}{dx}(\csc(u)) = -\csc(u)\cot(u)\frac{du}{dx}$$

$$\frac{d}{dx}(\sin^{-1}(u)) = \frac{1}{\sqrt{1-u^2}}\frac{du}{dx}$$

$$\frac{d}{dx}(\cos^{-1}(u)) = \frac{1}{\sqrt{1-u^2}}\frac{du}{dx}$$

$$\frac{d}{dx}(\tan^{-1}(u)) = \frac{1}{1-u^2}\frac{du}{dx}$$

$$\frac{d}{dx}(\cot^{-1}(u)) = \frac{1}{1-u^2}\frac{du}{dx}$$

$$\frac{d}{dx}(\sec^{-1}(u)) = \frac{1}{|u|\sqrt{u^2-1}}\frac{du}{dx}$$

$$\frac{d}{dx}(\csc^{-1}(u)) = -\frac{1}{|u|\sqrt{u^2-1}}\frac{du}{dx}$$

INTEGRAL CALCULUS

What is the **integral calculus**?

The integral calculus is the part of "the" calculus that deals with integrals—both the integral as the limit of a sum and the integral as the antiderivative of a function (see below for more information). In general, the integral calculus is the limit of a sum of elements in which the number of the elements increase without bound, while the size of the elements diminishes. It is also considered the second most important kind of limit in the calculus (the first being limits in association with derivatives). It was originally developed by using polygons to approximate areas of geometrically shaped objects such as circles.

What are some **common integrals** in the calculus?

There are many standard integrals used in the calculus. The following lists only a few of those integrals in their common form:

$$\int adx = ax$$

$$\int af(x)\,dx = a\int f(x)\,dx$$

$$\int (u \pm v \pm w \pm \cdots)\,dx = \int udx \pm \int vdx \pm \int wdx \pm \cdots$$

$$\int udv = uv - \int vdu$$

$$\int f(ax)\,dx = \frac{1}{a}\int f(u)\,du$$

$$\int F\{f(x)\}\,dx = \int F(u)\frac{dx}{du}\,du = \int \frac{F(u)}{f'(x)}\,du$$

What is the **definite integral**?

In actuality, the area shown on page 233 is actually determined using limits. In the function $f(x)$, as n gets larger, the numbers determined by left (n) and right (n) will get closer and closer to the area Ω. This is seen as the following notation:

$$Area(\Omega) = \lim_{n\to\infty} LEFT(n) = \lim_{n\to\infty} RIGHT(n)$$

Thus, in the calculus terms, the area of the above graphic region is called the definite integral (also said as "the integral") of $f(x)$ from a to b, and is denoted by the following notation:

$$\int_a^b f(x)\,dx$$

The variable x can be replaced with any other variable. In other words, if the limits of integration (a and b) are specified, it is called a definite integral, and it can be interpreted as an area or a generalization of an area.

What is the **graphic representation** of the approximation of an **area under a curve** using integration?

It's easier to see the approximate area under a curve using integration by means of graphs—it all has to do with rectangles. The idea is to extend lines from the ends of the curve (here, $f(x)$) to the x-axis (or y-axis, depending on the curve); we'll call the total area under the curve Ω, then divide the entire area under the curve into equal-width sections ($x_1, x_2, x_3,$ and so on)

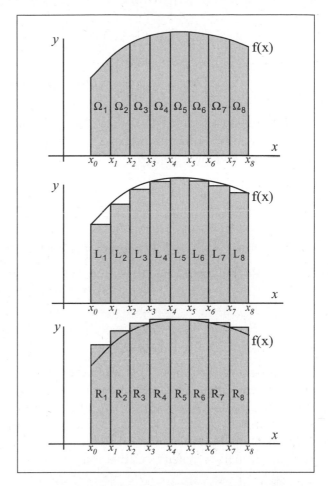

To calculate the area beneath a curve (top), you can first divide the area into equal parts with rectangles both beneath (middle) and above (bottom) the curve. Adjusting the width of the curves will result in an estimate that closely approximates the actual area.

that are equal to parts of Ω (the subregions Ω_1, Ω_2, and so on). The next step is to figure out the area of a rectangle if each section was "cut off" below the curve and then above the curve. This creates rectangles defined by left- and right-end points. From the left- and right-sums, and a few more calculations, we can approximate the area of Ω. This can be seen graphically on the accompanying charts.

What are some **properties** of the **definite integral**?

There are several useful properties of the definite integral. *Theorem one* is based on the idea that if $f(x)$ and $g(x)$ are defined and continuous on $[a, b]$, except perhaps at a finite number of points, then the following applies in which alpha is a constant:

$$\int_a^b (f(x) + g(x))\,dx = \int_a^b f(x)\,dx + \int_a^b g(x)\,dx$$

$$\int_a^b \alpha f(x)\,dx = \alpha \int_a^b f(x)\,dx$$

Theorem two is based on the idea that if $f(x)$ is defined and continuous on $[a, b]$, except at a finite number of points, then the following applies for any arbitrary numbers a and b, and any $c \in [a, b]$:

$$\int_c^c f(x)\,dx = 0$$

$$\int_a^b f(x)\,dx = \int_a^c f(x)\,dx + \int_c^b f(x)\,dx$$

$$\int_b^a f(x)\,dx = -\int_a^b f(x)\,dx$$

What is an **indefinite integral**?

From the above, we learned that when the limits of integration (in the case of a and b above) are specified, it is called a definite integral. Contrarily, if no limits are specified, it is called an *indefinite integral*. Thus, the indefinite integral is most often defined as a function that describes an area under the function's curve from some undefined point to another arbitrary point. This lack of a specified first point leads to an arbitrary constant (usually denoted as C) that is always part of the indefinite integral.

What are **antiderivatives** and **antidifferentiation**?

An antiderivative is often interpreted as the same as an indefinite integral, but they actually do differ in definition. Using the notations below describing the Fundamental Theorem of the Calculus (see boxed text for definition of the Fundamental Theorem of the Calculus), the function $F(x)$ is an *antiderivative* of $f(x)$, described as also equal to the integral of $f(x)$. The actual process of finding $F(x)$ from $f(x)$ is called *integration* or *antidifferentiation*.

What is an **improper integral**?

An integral as seen above means that the function $f(x)$ needs to be bounded on the interval $[a, b]$ (both real numbers), and the interval also must be bounded. But an improper integral is one in which the function $f(x)$ becomes unbounded (called a type I improper integral) or the interval $[a, b]$ becomes unbounded ($a = -\infty$ or $b = +\infty$, which is called a type II improper integral).

What is the Fundamental Theorem of the Calculus?

The Fundamental Theorem of the Calculus is the connection (or, more accurately, the bridge) between the integral and the derivative; in other words, it is another way of finding the area under a curve (see above) by evaluating the integral. In particular, if $F(x)$ is a function whose derivative is $f(x)$, then the area under the graph of $y = f(x)$ between the points a and b is equal to $F(b) - F(a)$. This is seen as the following notations:

$$\int_a^b f(x)\,dx = F(b) - F(a)$$

The number $F(b) - F(a)$ is also denoted by

$$\left[F(x)\right]_a^b \left(or\ F(x)\Big|_a^b \right)$$

Thus,

$$\int_a^b f(x)\,dx = \left[F(x)\right]_a^b$$

Are there **double** and **triple integrals**?

Yes, there are double and triple integrals—and even multiple integrals in equations (\iint, \iiint, and so on). For example, the integration of a function of three variables, $w = f(x, y, z)$, over a three-dimensional region R in xyz-space (three-dimensional space) is called a triple integral. The notation is as follows:

$$\iiint_R f(x,y,z)\,dV$$

To compute the iterated integral, we need to integrate with respect to z first, then y, then x. And when we integrate with respect to one variable, all the other variables are assumed to be constant.

DIFFERENTIAL EQUATIONS

What are **differential** and **ordinary differential equations**?

Logically, a *differential equation* is one that contains differentials of a function, with these equations defining the relationship between a function and one or more derivatives of that function. More specifically, differential equations involve dependent variables and their derivatives with respect to the independent variables. To solve such equations means to find a continuous function of the independent variable that, along

with its derivatives, satisfies the equation. An *ordinary differential equation* is one that involves only one independent variable.

What do the **order** and **degree** of a **differential equation** mean?

The *order* of a differential equation is simply the highest derivative that appears in the equation. The *degree* of a differential equation is the power of the highest derivative term. (For more information about power, see "Math Basics.")

What are **implicit** and **explicit differential equations**?

As seen above, an ordinary differential equation is one involving x, y, y', y'', and so on. Now add the idea that the order of the highest derivative is n. Thus, if a differential equation of order n has the form $F(x, y', y'', \ldots y^{(n)}) = 0$, then it is called an *implicit differential equation*. If it is of the form $F(x, y', y'', \ldots y^{(n-1)}) = y^{(n)}$, it is called an *explicit differential equation*.

What is an **example** of a **differential equation**?

An example of a differential equation involves letting y be some function of the independent variable t. Then a differential equation relating y to one or more of its derivatives is as follows:

$$\frac{\delta}{\delta t} y(t) = t^2 y(t)$$

In this equation, the first derivative of the function y is equal to the product of t^2 and the function y itself. This also implies that the stated relationship holds only for all t for which both the function and its first derivative are defined.

What are some **first-order differential equations**?

A first-order differential equation is one involving the unknown function y, its derivative y', and the variable x. As seen above, these types of equations are usually referred to as explicit differential equations.

There are several types of first-order differential equations, including separable, Bernoulli, linear, and homogeneous (for explanations of the last two, see below). A first-order differential equation takes the form:

$$\frac{dy}{dx} = f(x,y)$$

What is a **linear differential equation**?

A linear differential equation is a first-order differential equation that has no multiplications among the dependent variables and their derivatives, which means the coefficients are functions of independent variables. Other terms associated with such differential equations are *nonlinear differential equations,* which have multiplications among the dependent variables and their derivatives, and *quasi-linear differential equations,* in which a nonlinear differential equation has no multiplications among all the dependent variables and their derivatives in the highest derivative term.

What are the **"conditions"** in reference to **differential equations**?

In general, there are two "conditions" when discussing differential equations. The first are called *initial conditions,* in which constraints are specified at the initial point (usually in reference to time); such problems are called *initial value problems*. The other condition is the *boundary condition,* in which constraints are specified this time at the boundary points (usually in reference to space), with such problems called *boundary value problems*.

What are the **"solutions"** relative to **differential equations**?

There are three types of "solutions" when discussing differential equations:

General solution—This includes the solutions obtained from integration of the differential equations. In particular, the general solution of an nth order ordinary differential equation has n arbitrary constants from integrating n times.

171

Singular solution—Solutions that can't be expressed by the general solutions.

Particular solution—Solutions obtained from giving specific values to the arbitrary constants in the general solution.

What techniques are used to **solve first-order differential equations**?

There are usually three major ways to solve first-order differential equations: analytically, qualitatively, and numerically. The analytical way includes the examples mentioned above, such as the linear and separable equations. Qualitative methods include such methods as defining the slope of a field of a differential equation. Finally, numerical techniques can be thought of as something close to Euler's method, a way of finding the largest divisor of two numbers.

What is **Euler's method**?

Swiss mathematician Leonhard Euler (1707–1783) was one of the most prolific mathematicians who ever lived. He developed Euler's method, which is a way of determining the largest divisor of two numbers. For example, if we want to find the largest divisor of the numbers 6,975 and 525, we consider one to be the large number and the other the small number. We already know both numbers are divisible by 0 and 5 (as they both end in 5), but how do we determine if they have a larger divisor? And if so, what is that number?

The key is to take the remainders of long division until we arrive at a remainder of zero. In this instance, we would first divide 6,975 by 525; the answer comes out to 13 and a remainder:

$$
\begin{array}{r}
13 \\
525{\overline{\smash{\big)}\,6975}} \\
-\ 525 \\
\hline
1725 \\
-\ 1575 \\
\hline
150
\end{array}
$$

Take the remainder—in this case, 150—and then divide it into the 525. Take that remainder (which turns out to be 75) and divide it into the 150 remainder. The next iteration leads to no remainder (zero).

Large Number	Small Number	Remainder
6975	525	150
525	150	75
150	75	0

Thus, taking the number before we reached the zero—or 75—gives us the largest common divisor of both 6,975 and 525.

What are first-order homogeneous and non-homogeneous linear differential equations?

These differential equations may be long-winded phrases, but they are actually types of *first-order differential equations*. A first-order homogeneous linear differential equation can be written in the notation as follows:

$$\left(\frac{\delta}{\delta t}y(t)\right) + a(t)y(t) = 0$$

The first-order homogeneous linear differential equations are those that place all terms that include the unknown equation and its derivative on the left-hand side of the equation; on the right-hand side, it is set equal to zero for all t.

The non-homogeneous linear differential equations are those that, after isolating the linear terms containing $y(t)$ and the partial differentials inside the above large parentheses on the left side of the equation, do not set the right-hand side identically to zero. It is often represented by one function, such as the $b(t)$ (see below). The standard notation is as follows:

$$\left(\frac{\delta}{\delta t}y(t)\right) + a(t)y(t) - b(t)$$

What are **systems of differential equations**?

In real-life situations, quantities and their rate of change depend on more than one variable. For example, the rabbit population, though it may be represented by a single number, depends on the size of predator populations and the availability of food. In order to represent and study such complicated problems we need to use more than one dependent variable and more than one equation. Systems of differential equations are the tools to use. As with the first-order differential equations, the techniques for studying systems fall into the following three categories: analytic, qualitative, and numeric.

What is a **nonlinear differential equation**?

From above, we know that linear equations have specific rules; for example, the unknowns y, y', and so on, will never be raised to a power more than 1; they will not be in the denominator of a fraction; y times y' is never allowed (because two unknowns multiplied together is, in a sense, a power 2 of unknowns); and they won't be inside another function (such as a sine).

But a nonlinear equation is much different, allowing for powers of $2(y' = y^2)$, multiplying differences ($y \times y' = x$); and even being inside another function ($y' = x \sin y$). **173**

Rabbit populations are affected not only by birth rates, but also by factors such as predation, disease, and available food supplies. Systems of differential equations may be used to take all these elements into consideration and estimate actual population numbers.

Thus, the nonlinear equations are not as easy to solve as linear differential equations. But that does not mean they lack importance. In fact, because nonlinear equations are more realistic in describing real-life problems, they are much more interesting (and challenging) to mathematical and scientific researchers in many fields.

VECTOR AND OTHER ANALYSES

What is a **vector**?

A vector is considered to be an element of a linear or vector space. A vector is different than a point, as it represents the displacement between two points, not the physical location of a point in space. Vectors also define a direction; points do not. Vectors are usually represented by a line segment in a specific direction on a graph, with an arrow at one end of the segment. They can also be represented in several ways, including bold letters in an equation, for example, vectors **A** and **B**, and with arrows above the vector, such as \vec{x}.

What is the **component** of a **vector**?

A component of a vector is one with n numbers in a certain order. It is usually listed as $(x_1, x_2, ..., x_n)$, in which the numbers within the parentheses are called the components of the vector \vec{x}.

Logically, an infinite number of vectors can have the same components. For example, if the components are [3, 4], we know there are an infinite number of pairs of points in the plane with x and y coordinates whose respective differences are 3 and 4. All these vectors are parallel to each other, equal, and have the same magnitude and direction. Therefore, any vector with components of a and b can be said to be equal to the vector [a, b].

How is the **magnitude of a vector** determined?

The magnitude of a vector is equivalent to the length of a vector. Placing a pair of vertical lines (similar to the absolute value symbol) around a vector implies the magnitude of the vector. For example, if the variable V is used to represent a vector, then the expression ‖ indicates the magnitude of the vector.

What do **columns and rows** mean when discussing **vectors**?

Vectors can be described by columns and rows. For example, two-dimensional and three-dimensional vectors are usually represented as a single vertical column of numeric values. The following lists such columns in two and three dimensions:

$$V = \begin{vmatrix} x \\ y \end{vmatrix}$$

$$V = \begin{vmatrix} x \\ y \\ z \end{vmatrix}$$

A row vector is usually used for problem solving in which a vector is described as V = (x, y, z) during the specification of a problem. But note: Row vectors should not really be used with any mathematical descriptions.

How is the **length** of a **vector** calculated?

The length of a vector is calculated by taking the square root of the sum of the squares of each coordinate. For example, if the vector is defined by (x, y, z), then the length (L) of the vector is calculated this way:

$$L = \sqrt{x^2 + y^2 + z^2}$$

What is a **normalized vector**?

A normalized (or unit) vector is one in which the sum of the squares of all coordinates is equal to one. For example, the vector (2, 2, 0) is not normalized; the vectors (0.707, 0.707, 0.0) and (1.0, 0.0, 0.0) are normalized. (An *outward normal* is another name for a normalized vector; it represents the direction that a polygon surface or vertex [endpoint] is facing.) Normalized (or unit) vectors are often seen written as \vec{x}, but more usually as \hat{x} (the ^ is often referred to as a "hat").

A vector can be normalized by calculating the magnitude or length of the vector and dividing each coordinate by this value. For example, consider the following vector:

$$V = \begin{vmatrix} 3.0 \\ 4.0 \\ 0.0 \end{vmatrix}$$

The length of this vector is 5.0 (see above to determine how to solve for length of the vector); or |V| = 5.0. Thus, the value of the normalized vector is given by:

$$\frac{V}{|V|} = \begin{vmatrix} 3.0 \\ 4.0 \\ 0.0 \end{vmatrix} \cdot \frac{1}{5} = \begin{vmatrix} 0.6 \\ 0.8 \\ 0.0 \end{vmatrix}$$

In this case, 0.6 squared equals 0.36; 0.8 squared equals 0.64. Both added together with the zero equals 1. (If the vector is already normalized, then the value of |V| will be equal to one, and after division the vector will remain as it was before.)

How can **vectors** be **represented** in various **dimensional space**?

Vectors can be found in two-, three-, or multi-dimensional space. Two-dimensional vectors are seen visually on a graph as a line with an arrow connecting two points. A two dimensional vector is defined by length and direction measured by the angles that the arrow makes with the x and y coordinate system axes; a vector in such a coordinate system is written as two components, (x, y).

Vectors in a three-dimensional space are represented with three numbers, one along each coordinate axis. These are the coordinates of the arrow point, usually as (x, y, z) if the arrow starts at the origin. A more complex vector is one with multiple components, in which several different numbers in ordered n-tuples represent a vector. For example, $(4, 1, -2, 0)$ is an ordered 4-tuple representing a vector in four dimensions.

What is a **polar coordinate system**?

In effect, a polar coordinate system "wraps" a two-dimensional (Euclidean) coordinate system onto the surface of a sphere (for more information about coordinate systems, see "Geometry and Trigonometry"). A polar coordinate system examines a point in space defined in terms of its position and distance on a sphere with a unit radius. The center of the sphere is considered the origin; the first two coordinates are the longitude and latitude on the sphere; the third coordinate defines the distance of the point

from the center of the sphere—the values of latitude, longitude, and height. In polar coordinates—it's easy to see on a globe of our own planet—latitude ranges from +90 to –90, longitude ranges from –180 to +180, and height ranges from zero to infinity. Height can also be negative: The North Pole is at coordinates of (+90, —, +r) (the "—" means there is no longitude), the South Pole is at coordinates of (–90, —, –r), and a point on the equator is at coordinates (0, 0, r).

How are **vectors added**?

One way to combine vectors is through addition (or composition). This can be done algebraically or graphically. For example, to add the two vectors U [–3, 1] and V [5, 2], one can add their corresponding components to find the resultant vector R [2, 3]. One also can graph U and V on a set of coordinate axes, completing the parallelogram formed with U and V as adjacent sides, obtaining R as the diagonal from the common vertex of U and V.

How is the **product** of **two vectors** determined?

There are two distinct types of products of two vectors: scalar and vector products, sometimes called the inner and outer products (mostly in reference to tensor products; see below). The scalar (or dot) product of two vectors is not a vector because the product has a magnitude but not a direction. For example, if A and B are vectors (of magnitude A and B, respectively), their scalar product is: $A \bullet B = AB \cos \theta$, in which θ is the angle between the two vectors. This scalar quantity is also called the *dot product* of the vectors. These equations obey the commutative and distributive laws of algebra (for more information, see "Algebra"). Thus, $A \bullet B = B \bullet A; A \bullet (B + C) = A \bullet B + A \bullet C$. If A is perpendicular to B, then $A \bullet B = 0$.

The vector (or cross or skew) product of A and B is the length $C = AB \sin \theta$; its direction is perpendicular to the plane determined by A and B. In this case, this kind of multiplication does not follow the commutative law, as $A \bullet B = -B \bullet A$.

What is **vector analysis**?

Vector analysis is the calculus of functions with variables as vectors—a part of calculus also known for its derivative and integral equations. The components of a vector do not always have to be constants. They can also be variables and functions of vari-

ables, such as the position of a body moving through space represented by a vector whose x, y, and z components are all functions of time. In this case, the calculus can be used to solve such vector functions, which are also called vector analysis.

What are some **other types of analysis**?

There are numerous other analyses in mathematics and the sciences besides vector analysis. And each one has applications that sometimes intermingle but most often has specific uses in certain areas—from computer programming to electronics.

At one time, the study of tensors was known as the absolute differential calculus, but today it is simply called *tensor analysis*. Tensors were originally invented as the extensions of vectors. Tensor analysis is concerned with relations or laws that remain valid regardless of the coordinate system used to specify the quantities.

Complex analysis (or complex variable analysis) is the study of complex numbers and their derivatives, mathematical manipulations, and other properties. It is mostly used to find the solution to *holomorphic functions,* or those that are found in a complex plane, use complex values, and are differentiable as complex functions. Complex variables deal with the calculus of functions of a complex variable, incorporating differential equations and complex numbers; for example, one such variable of the form $z = x + iy$, in which x and y are real and the imaginary number $i = -1$. Complex-variable techniques have a great many uses in applied areas, such as electromagnetics.

Functional analysis is concerned with infinite-dimensional vector spaces and the mapping between them. It is also considered the study of spaces of functions.

There is also *differential geometry,* truly a branch of geometry, which includes the concepts of the calculus as applied to curves, surfaces, and other geometry entities. Originally, it included the use of coordinate geometry; more recently, it has been applied to other areas of geometry, such as projective geometry. In particular, differential geometry uses techniques of differential calculus to determine the geometric properties of manifolds (a topological space that resembles Euclidean space, but is not).

Another type of analysis is *nonstandard analysis,* developed in the 1960s, in which hyperreal numbers are used to define the existence of "genuine infinitesimals." (These are numbers less than one half, one third, one fourth, and so on, but greater than 0.) It is used in several fields, including probability theory and mathematical physics.

What is a **tensor**?

A tensor is a quantity that depends linearly on many vector variables. They are considered to be a set of n' components that are functions of the coordinates at any point in n dimensional space. Tensors are used in several fields of mathematics, such as the theory of elasticity (stress and strain) and mathematical physics, especially with regard to the theory of relativity.

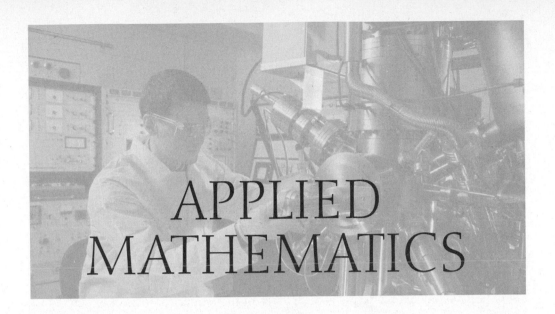

APPLIED MATHEMATICS

APPLIED MATHEMATICS BASICS

What is **applied mathematics**?

Applied mathematics is not only concerned with using rigorous mathematical methods, but also applications of those methods. It entails a wide range of research in the worlds of biology, computer science, sociology, engineering, physical science, and many other fields, especially in the experimental sciences. In each case, applied mathematics is used by a researcher to more thoroughly understand a particular application or physical phenomena. The many uses of applied mathematics include numerical analysis, linear programming, mathematical modeling and simulation, the mathematics of engineering, mathematical biology, game theory, probability theory, mathematical statistics, financial mathematics, and even cryptography.

How did **applied mathematics grow** over time?

Historically speaking, applied mathematics was always concerned with using mathematics to solve problems in physics, chemistry, medicine, engineering, the physical sciences, technology, and biology. In fact, applied mathematics is older than pure mathematics, as it was used in areas that formed the core of early physics research, such as mechanics, fluid dynamics, and optics. As mathematical tools became more powerful, these areas of physics became more mathematically based. This mathematical analysis tie to science and engineering has always had a great place in history and has led to some of its greatest discoveries.

How has **applied mathematics changed** over the past few decades?

In the past few decades, applied mathematics has made tremendous strides in explaining our world. In particular, with the advent of more powerful computers and their mathematically driven software—from linked computers over a network to supercomputers—many disciplines that use applied mathematics have greatly advanced. For example, the use of giant wind tunnels to examine wind flow over aircraft only a few decades ago has been replaced by computer simulation. Now the design and testing of aircraft is accomplished by these simulations, making the expense of building physical prototypes a thing of the past because it is now merely a matter of mathematically "drawing" the aircraft on the computer in order to test new designs.

How do various **disciplines use applied mathematics**?

Depending on the discipline, researchers use applied mathematics in various ways. For example, some disciplines rely heavily on pure mathematics. Numerical analysis—a form of applied mathematics—is a field that uses pure mathematics to decipher partial differential equations and variational methods (for more information about numerical analysis, see below; for partial differential equations, see "Mathematical Analysis"). There are also areas of applied mathematics that overlap other fields of study. For example, there are mathematicians who use applied mathematics to study the structure of matter—especially the behavior of subatomic particles—a field that also overlaps the same types of studies done by subatomic physicists.

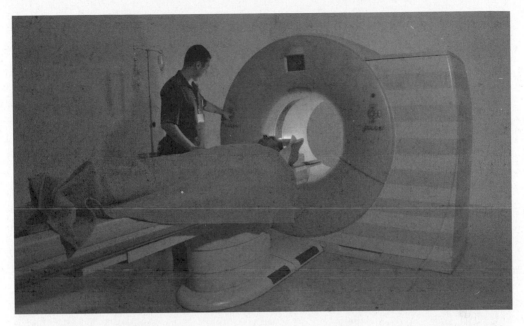

Applied mathematics is used in high-tech image processing, such as with this MRI (Magnetic Resonance Imaginge) machine used in hospitals to create scans of the inside of patients' bodies.

Why has the **combination** of **mathematical analysis** methods and **computers** been so important?

The combination of mathematical analysis and computers has been a strong alliance, especially with regard to engineering, technology, and the sciences. In the past few decades, researchers have used this combination to help predict the weather, describe in great detail nuclear fusion in the Sun, understand the movement of space bodies around the solar system (orbital mechanics), and the flow of water in underground aquifers (fluid dynamics). There are also the studies of chaos—the unpredictable behavior of nonlinear systems—and quantum mechanics, or the physics of very small particles, both of which entail the use of applied mathematics and computers.

In addition, in engineering (and almost all technology) the mathematical analysis–computer combination has helped create structures that surround us every day. This includes familiar modes of transportation and communication: from plans for airplanes and bridge construction to designing fiber optic cables and cell phone towers. It also includes how engineers design control systems, which are used in such diverse areas as robotics, aerospace engineering, and biomedical research.

Computers and mathematical analysis have also been a boon to such interdisciplinary fields at operations research (also called decision or management science). In this case, the mathematical science focuses on the effective use of the technology of an organization, such as forecasting, financial engineering, logistics, and industrial

183

One of many practical applications for mathematics includes processing images, which enhances the ability of electron microscopes like this one to produce more detailed visual information.

engineering. Applications may include, for example, scheduling airplanes and crews; signal processing, such as the transmission of radio signals or traffic light control signals; or managing the flow of water from a reservoir or dam site.

PROBABILITY THEORY

What are **events** and **probability**?

Probability is a branch of mathematics that assigns a number measuring the "chance" that some "event"—or any collection of outcomes of an experiment—will occur. It is a quantitative description of the likely occurrence of the event, conventionally expressed on a scale from 0 to 1. For example, a very common occurrence has a probability of close to 1; an event that is more rare will have a probability close to 0. In more common usage, the word "probability" means the chance that a particular event (or set of events) will occur—all on a linear scale expressed as a percentage between 0 and 100 percent (%). An even more detailed way of looking at probability includes the possible outcomes of a given event along with the outcomes' relative likelihoods and distributions.

What is a **sample space**?

In any experiment, there are certain possible outcomes; the set of all possible outcomes is called the *sample space* of the experiment. Each possible result is represented by one and only one point in the sample space, which is usually denoted by the letter S. To each element of the sample space (or to each possible outcome) a probability measure between 0 and 1 is assigned, with the sum of all the probability measures in the sample space equal to 1.

What are **ratios** and **proportions**?

A ratio is the comparison of two numbers; it is most often written as a fraction or with a ":", as in 3/4 or 3:4 to separate the two numbers. For example, if we want to know the ratio of dogs in a shelter that houses 24 animals to the total count, we first determine the number of dogs (say, 10); then the ratio of dogs to animals in the shelter becomes 10/24, or 10:24, which is also said as "10 to 24." But there are rules to ratios. For example, order matters when talking about ratios; therefore, the ratio 7:1 is not the same as 1:7.

A proportion is an equation with a ratio on each side, and is a statement that two ratios are equal. For example, 1/2 = 4/8, or 1/2 is proportional to 4/8. In order to "solve the proportion"—or when one of the four numbers in a proportion is unknown—we need to use cross products to find the unknown number. For example, to solve for x in the following: 1/4 = x/8; using cross product, $4x = 1 \times 8$; thus, $x = 2$.

What are some **simple probability events**?

The probability measure of an event is sometimes defined as the ratios between the number of outcomes. There are many simple illustrations of probability events, many of which we are all familiar with. One of the simplest examples of probability is tossing

a coin, with a sample space of two outcomes: heads or tails. If a coin were completely symmetrical, the outcome would more likely be 0.5 (ratio of 1/2) for heads and 0.5 for tails. As we all know, it never comes out that way, which may or may not mean our coins are not in perfect balance.

Another example is weather records. Many of us keep track of weather over the years. But if one were to gather all the records for the day of May 10 over 30 years from the weather service, one could do some simple probability event measurements. For example, take a (fictitious) sampling of the cloud-covered days in a certain area for the last 30 years on May 10. Say there were 10 cloud-covered May 10s in 30 years; thus, the probability measure would be a ratio of 10/30 to the event that the day will be cloudy on May 10.

Insurance tables are also figured out in a similar way. For example, if, out of a certain group of 1,000 persons who were 25 years old in 1900, 150 of them lived to be 65, then the ratio 150/1,000 is assigned as the probability that a 25-year-old person will live to be 65. On the other hand, the probability of such a person not living to be 65 is 850/1,000 (because the sum of the two measures must be equal to 1). It is true that such a probability statement is valid only for a set group of people, but insurance companies get around this by using a much larger population sample and constantly revising the figures as new data are obtained. Thus, even though many people question the validity of such "broadbrush" results, the insurance companies believe that, probability-wise, the values they use are valid for most large groups of people and under most conditions of life.

How are **probabilities of compound events** determined?

Besides the probability of simple events, probabilities of compound events can also be computed. For example, if x and y represent two independent events, the probability that both x and y will occur is given by the product of their separate probabilities; and

the probability that either of the two events will occur is given by the sum of their separate probabilities minus the probability that both will occur. For example, if the probability that a certain man will live to be 70 is 0.5, and the probability that his wife will live to be 70 is 0.6, the probability that they will both live to be 70 is $0.5 \times 0.6 = 0.3$; the probability that either the husband or wife will reach 70 is $0.5 + 0.6 - 0.3 = 0.8$.

What are the **definitions** of **chance**?

Chance is defined in many ways. For example, chance means opportunity to some, or the chance to do something. Chance can also mean luck or fortune, such as running into someone one has not seen in years by "pure chance." Chance also involves taking a risk, which may include some type of danger.

The probability of drawing a particular suit from a pack of cards is 25 percent.

Mathematically speaking, chance is a measure of how likely it is that an event will occur—in other words, a probability. For example, if a meteorologist says that a hurricane on a certain path has struck the coast of Florida, say, about 4 times out of 10, then the ratio becomes 4 to 10, with the chance of striking under the very same conditions being 40 percent. (In reality, this probability example is too simple; that's because there are so many variables that affect the movement of the hurricane, including the atmosphere and landmasses.)

What do the terms **random** and **stochastic** mean in probability?

When speaking about probability, the term *random* means the outcomes of an experiment have the same probability of occurring. Because of this, the outcome of the experiment produces a random sample.

Random also is commonly thought of as being synonymous with *stochastic*, which is from the Greek word meaning "pertaining to chance." It is usually used to indicate a particular subject seen from the point of view of randomness. Stochastic is often thought of as the "opposite" of *deterministic*, a term that means random phenomena are not involved. In the case of modeling, stochastic models are based on random trials, while deterministic models always produce the same output for a given starting condition.

Are **"random" numbers generated** by a **computer** truly random?

For most general purposes, random numbers generated by a computer can be considered "random." But in reality, because a computer follows a set of rules in any program, the numbers generated are not truly random. In order for a sequence or specific numbers to be truly random, they must not follow any sort of rules. That's something to think about the next time you purchase a computer-generated, "random-numbers" lottery ticket.

What is the concept of **relative frequency**?

Relative frequency is actually another term for proportion. It can be found by dividing the number of times an event occurs by the total number of times the experiment is done. In probability, this is often written in the notation $rfn(E) = r/n$, in which E is the event, n is the number of times the experiment is repeated, and r is the number of times E occurs. For example, a symmetrical coin can be tossed 50 times (n) in order to find out how many times tails will occur (E). If the result is 20 tails (r) and 30 heads, then the equation becomes 20/50, or 2/5 = 0.4; or, the relative frequency is 0.4 for tails. If this experiment is repeated over and over, the relative frequency will eventually get closer and closer to 0.5, which is the true value that should result when tossing a two-sided symmetrical coin.

How are the terms **outcome, sample space,** and **event** related?

These terms are definitely related: The *outcome* is the result of an experiment or other type of situation involving uncertainty; and the set of all possible outcomes is a sample space. Just as important are *events,* which are collections of the outcomes of an experiment, or any subset of the sample space. If there is only one single outcome in the sample space, it is called an elementary or simple event; events with more than one outcome are called compound events.

What are **independent events** in probability?

In probability theory, events are independent if the probability that they occur is equal to the product (multiply together) of the probabilities of either two or more individual events. (This is also often called statistical independence.) In addition, the occurrence of one of the events can give no information about whether or not the other event(s) will occur; that is, the events have no influence on each other.

For example, two events, A and B, are independent if the probability of both occurring equals the product of their probabilities, or P (A) | P(B) (the symbol "|" is often used to depict the product of the events in probability theory). One good example involves playing cards. If we wanted to know the probability of two people each drawing a king of diamonds (two independent events), it would be defined as $A = 1/52$

<div style="border:1px solid">

What is conditional probability?

Conditional probability is often phrased as "event A occurs given that event B has occurred." The common notation is a vertical line, or $A \mid B$ (said as "A given B"). Thus, P $(A \mid B)$ denotes the probability that event A will occur given that event B has occurred already.

Since there is always room for improvement—even in probability—conditional probability incorporates the idea that once more information becomes available, the probability of further outcomes can be revised. For example, if a person brings a car in for an oil change every 3,000 miles, it can be calculated that there is a probability of 0.9 that the service on the car will be completed within two hours. But if the car is brought in during a seatbelt recall, the probability of getting the car back in two hours might be reduced to 0.6. This is the conditional probability of getting the car back in two hours if there is a seatbelt recall taking place.

</div>

(the probability that one person will draw a king of diamonds) and $B = 1/52$ (the probability that the other person will draw a king of diamonds, assuming the first person puts the first drawn card back into the deck). Substituting the numbers into the equation, the result is: 1/52 | 1/52 = 0.00037, or a slight chance that both people will draw the king of diamonds from the deck.

What is **Bayes's theorem**?

Bayes's theorem is a result that lets new information be used to update the conditional probability of an event. The theorem was first derived by English mathematician Thomas Bayes (1702–1761), who developed the concept to use in situations in which probability can't be directly calculated. The theorem gives the probability that a certain event has caused an observed outcome by using estimates for all possible outcomes. Its simplest notation is as follows:

$$P(A \mid B) = \frac{P(A \cap B)}{P(B)} = \frac{P(B \mid A) \cdot P(A)}{P(B)}$$

What are **mutually exclusive events**?

Mutually exclusive events are those that are impossible to occur together. For example, a subject in a study of male and female humans can't be both male and female. Males are males; females are females. Thus, depending on what the study is about (such as a study of how many males versus females go to college from a certain high school), both "events" will be mutually exclusive.

189

What are the **addition rules** of probability?

In probability theory, the addition rule is used to determine the probability of events A or B occurring. The notation is most commonly seen in terms of sets: $P(A \cup B) = P(A) + P(B) - P(A \cap B)$, in which $P(A)$ represents the probability that event A will occur, $P(B)$ represents the probability that event B will occur, and $P(A \cup B)$ is translated as the probability that event A or event B will occur. For example, if we wanted to find the probability of drawing a queen (A) or a diamond (B) from a card deck in a single draw, and since we know there are 4 queens and 13 diamond cards in the deck of 52, the equation and resulting probability becomes: $4/52 + 13/52 - 1/52 = 16/52$ (the 1/52 is derived by multiplying $4/52 \times 13/52$).

But there are also rules of addition for mutually exclusive and independent events. For mutually exclusive events, or events that can't occur together, the addition rule reduces to $P(A \cup B) = P(A) + P(B)$. For independent events, or those that have no influence on each other, the addition rule reduces to $P(A \cup B) = P(A) + P(B) - P(A) \mid P(B)$.

What are the **multiplication rules** of probability?

In probability theory, the multiplication rule is used to determine the probability that two events, A and B, both occur. As with the addition rules, the notation for multiplication rules of probability are most commonly seen in terms of sets: $P(A \cap B) = P(A \mid B) \bullet P(B)$ or $P(A \cap B) = P(B \mid A) \bullet P(A)$, in which $P(A)$ represents the probability that event A will occur, $P(B)$ represents the probability that event B will occur, and $P(A \cap B)$ is translated as the probability that event A and event B will both occur. In addition, $P(A \mid B)$ is the conditional probability that event A occurs given that event B has already occurred, and $P(B \mid A)$ is the conditional probability that event B occurs given that event A has already occurred. Similar to the addition rules, if there are independent events (or those that have no influence on one another), the equation reduces to $P(A \cap B) = P(A) \bullet P(B)$.

What is the **law of total probability**?

The law of total probability can be written as follows: The probability that an event A will occur, $P(A)$, is equal to the probability that event A and event B both occur, plus the probability that event A and event B' occur (or A occurs and B does not). Using the multiplication rule, this is written as:

$$P(A) = P(A \mid B) \bullet P(B) + P(A \mid B') \bullet P(B')$$

What was the **"gambler's ruin"**?

The gambler's ruin is an application of the law of total probability that was first proposed by Dutch mathematician and astronomer Christiaan Huygens (1629–1695), although many people before him, including astronomer Galileo Galilei (1564–1642),

How is set theory used to represent the relationships among events?

Statisticians often use the set theory to represent relationships among events (collections of outcomes of an experiment). This is usually written in the following notation, in which A and B are two events in the sample space S:

- $A \cup B$, or "either A or B occurs, or both"; this is said as "A union B" in set theory;
- $A \cap B$, or "both A and B occur"; this is said as "A intersection B" in set theory;
- $A \subseteq B$, or "if A occurs, so does B occur"; this is said as "A is a subset of B" in set theory;
- A', or "A does not occur."

brought up the same probability problem, but phrased it differently. By 1656, Huygens wrote a draft version of *Van Rekeningh in Spelen van Geluck,* a treatise about fifteen pages long based on what he heard about the correspondence of French scientist and religious philosopher Blaise Pascal (1623–1662) and French mathematician Pierre de Fermat (1601–1665) the previous year. Of the fourteen problems he presents, the last five became known as the "gambler's ruin."

In particular, Huygens (and others) wanted to find the probability of a gambler's ruin. A common way of expressing the idea is by a game that has two players, with the game giving a probability q of winning one dollar and a probability $(1 - q)$ of losing one dollar. In the problem, if a player begins with 10 dollars and intends to play the game repeatedly until he either goes broke or increases his holdings to 20 dollars, the question asked is: "What is his probability of going broke?" The answer involves quite a bit of probability computation.

What are **permutations, combinations,** and **repeatables**?

In order to perform certain probability problems, specific counting techniques need to be used, including determining the number of permutations, combinations, or repeatables. The following explains each term; the examples are based on a set of five cats on a shelf—a, b, c, d, and e, for convenience. (Note: The cats can be arranged in 120 ways, expressed as $5 \times 4 \times 3 \times 2 \times 1 = 5!$ ["5 factorial"] $= 120$).

The number of *permutations* is the number of different ways specific entities within the cat group can be arranged, with the positions being important. For example, given five cats, how many unique ways can they be placed in three positions on the shelf if position is important? The answers include ade, aed, dea, dae, ead, eda, abc, acb, bca, bac, etc.—a total of 60 ways. The notation for this is 5 P3 =

Dutch mathematician and astronomer Christiaan Huygens devised the notion of the "gambler's ruin."

Galileo Galilei, best known for his work as an astronomer, had already discovered the ideas of probability later restated as the "gambler's ruin" by Christiaan Huygens.

$5!/(5 − 3)! = 5 \times 4 \times 3 \times 2 \times 1 / (2 \times 1) = 5 \times 4 \times 3 = 60$ (P in this case stands for permutations).

Combinations mean the number of different ways specific entities can be grouped; but in this case, position does not matter. For example, in the problem of the cats, how many can be grouped into threes if position does not matter? The answers include abc, abd, abe, acd, ace, ade; but groupings such as cba are not allowed since it is equal to another combination: abc. The notation for this is 5 C3 = $5!/((5–3)! \times 3!)$ = $5 \times 4 \times 3 \times 2 \times 1/(2 \times 1 \times 3 \times 2 \times 1) = 5 \times 2 = 10$ (C in this case stands for combinations).

With *repeatables,* position is important, too. But in this case, if one has five different cats, and many clones of each, how many unique ways can they be placed in three positions? This answer includes aaa, bbb, ccc, ddd, eee, eec, cee, etc.—a total of 125 ways. The notation for this is 5 R3 = $5^3 = 125$ (R in this case stands for repeatables).

What is the **Markov model**?

The Markov model was first developed by Russian mathematician Andrey (Andrei) Andreyevich Markov (1856–1922) about a century ago. It is a statistical method that estimates the likelihood of a future event based on patterns observed in the past. They are most useful when a decision problem involves risk that is continuous over time, when the timing of events is important, and when important events may happen more than once.

The Markov chain also has applications in statistical models, and is a mathematical system that undergoes transitions from one state to another in a chainlike manner.

Most often today, it is used in such fields as economics, genetics, and computer speech-recognition. It is often used extensively in clinical medical studies; for example, Markov models assume that a patient is always in one of a finite number of discrete health states, called Markov states. Such studies can be evaluated by matrix algebra or as a Monte Carlo simulation.

Games such as coin tossing and dice rolling are common examples of the rules of probability in action.

What are some **examples** in which **probability** is used?

There are thousands of examples in which probability is used, some are familiar, and some originate from the seamier side of life. For example, everyone has played at *coin tossing* at one time or another. Although there is no such thing as an idealized coin—a circular one of zero thickness—most coin tosses use the coins available, with either side face up ("heads" or "tails"; also phrased "heads up/down" or "tails up/down"). Thus, one can think of a coin as a two-sided die in lieu of the six-sided cubes we are all used to in a game of dice. If a coin is tossed with a good amount of spin, we can denote the two possible results as H for heads and T for tails. If we repeat the tosses N number of times, we obtain N(H) heads and N(T) tails. Thus, the fraction of N(H)/N and N(T)/N can be thought of as the chance (probability) to get a head or tail, respectively; P(H) and P(T) are the most common notations that represent the probability to get heads and tails, respectively. If we toss the coin many, many times, the result should be close to 0.5. Of course, this means that if we bet on the chances of heads and tails, we will not be much of a winner if we play too many games—and we will have to have really good luck to win if we play fewer games.

What is a **random walk**?

Although one might think of a random walk as one that a person takes on the spur of the moment in a part of town he has never walked before, it actually means something totally different in probability theory. A random walk is a random process made up of a discrete sequence of steps, all of a fixed length. For example, in physics, the collisions of molecules in a gas are considered a random walk responsible for diffusion; also in physics, random walks and some of the self-interacting walks are found in quantum field theory. In economics, the "random walk hypothesis" is used to understand and model stock share

prices, along with other factors. Biologists use random walks to understand individual animal movements; and geneticists who study population use a random walk to describe the statistical properties of genetic drift. One of the more understandable random walks is familiar to most of us—it is used to estimate the size of the World Wide Web.

STATISTICS

What is **statistics**?

The analysis of events governed by probability is called statistics. In statistics, a group of facts is collected and classified in a methodical manner, which is why such a study is important to the fields of science, finance, social research, insurance, engineering, and sundry other areas. In general, the data are grouped according to their relative number, then certain other values are determined based on the characteristics of the group. The most important part of statistical theory is sampling. This is because in most applications, the statistician is not only interested in the characteristic of the sample, but also the characteristics of some much larger population. (For information about samples and populations, see below.)

Why are **populations** important to statistics?

A population is the entire collection of items—from people, animals, and plants to street numbers and various other things of any size—from which the statistician collects data. These data are of particular concern because in most cases the statistician is interested in describing or drawing conclusions about the population (also called the *target population*). For example, take a population of 10 cats. None of them are identical, but certain common features between the cats can be measured, such as color, fur length, and weight. The data collected about one of the common features, such as the fur length of the 10 cats, would be defined as the population.

What is a **sample** in **statistics**?

A sample is a generalization about a population and is represented by a group of units selected from the population (also called a subset of the population). The sample is meant to be representative of the population; thus, in many studies, there are many possible samples. There are also types of samples, such as a matched sample, in which two of the members are paired; an example would be the IQ of twins. There is often a good reason for taking samples of a population: Most of the time, a population is too large to study as a whole.

For example, take the "smaller" example of the above population of 10 cats. Again, none of them are identical, but certain common features between the cats can be mea-

sured, including color, fur length, and weight. If data is collected about the fur length of the 10 cats (the population), then if we chose only to take the cats with long fur, that would be a sampling. Another example is the population for a study of physical condition of all children born in the United States in the 1970s; the sample could be all children born on July 5 in any of those years.

How does one **sample a population**?

Sampling is the term used when one obtains a sample of a population; the number of members in the sample is called the *sample size*. As with most mathematical concepts, there are several types of sampling.

Random sampling is a technique involving a group of subjects (the sample) from a larger group (population); it is a

A matched sample is a type of sampling method used in statistics. For example, in studying population IQs, identical twins could be paired up to measure and compare intelligence. *Photographer's Choice/Getty Images.*

method that reduces the likelihood of bias. In random sampling, each individual is chosen by chance, with each member of the population having a known (but often unequal) chance of being included in the sample.

Simple random sampling also involves a group of subjects (the sample) from a larger group (population), but in this case, each individual is chosen entirely by chance, with each member of the population having an equal chance of being included in the sample. In fact, each member of the population has an equal chance of being chosen at any stage of the sampling process.

Independent sampling comprises samples collected from the same (or different) populations that have no effect on one another. In other words, there is no correlation between the samples.

Stratified sampling includes random samples from various subgroups (also called subpopulation or stratum of the population) chosen to be representative of the whole population. It is often thought of as a better technique than simple random sampling. For example, if a sheep farmer wanted to determine the average weight (amount) of wool gathered from three types of sheep on his farm, he could divide his flock into the three subgroups and take samples from those groups.

In *cluster sampling* the entire population is divided into clusters (groups); then a random sampling is taken of the clusters. This technique is used when a complete list

of the population's members can't be studied, but a list of population clusters can be gathered.

What is a **statistic** and a **sample statistic**?

A statistic is the measure of the items in a random sample. A sample statistic is meant to give information about a specific population feature (or parameter). For example, if a sample mean is gathered for a set of data, that would provide information about the overall population mean.

What is the difference between **descriptive** and **inferential statistics**?

Descriptive statistics is a way to describe the characteristics of a given population by measuring each of its items, then taking a summary of the measurements in various ways. Inferential statistics, as the term implies, makes educated inferences (guesses) about the characteristics of a population by taking and analyzing data from a random sample.

What are **quantitative** and **qualitative variables** as used in statistics?

Variables are values used to come to conclusions in a statistical study. There are two main categories: *quantitative* and *qualitative* variables. Quantitative variables can be divided into three types. Ordinal variables are measured with an ordinal scale, in which higher numbers represent higher values, even though the intervals between numbers are not necessarily equal. For example, on a five-point rating scale measuring attitudes toward cutting back on air pollution, the difference between a rating of 2 and 3 may not be the same as the difference between a rating of 4 and 5. Interval variables are measured with an interval scale, in which one unit on the scale represents the same magnitude of the characteristic being measured across the whole range of the scale. For example, the Fahrenheit scale for temperature is an interval scale, in which equal differences on this scale represent equal differences in temperature, but a temperature of 30 degrees is not twice as warm as one of 15 degrees. The third type is the ratio scale variable. It is similar to the interval scale, but with true zero points. For example, the Kelvin temperature scale is a ratio scale because it has an absolute zero. Thus, a temperature of 300 Kelvin is twice as high as a temperature of 150 Kelvin.

How does opinion polling work?

We all know about opinion polls, especially during major elections. The statistical sampling method of most polling places is called *quota sampling,* a technique in which interviewers are given a quota of specific types of subjects to poll. For example, the sampling may involve asking 10 adult men, 10 adult women (both groups over 20 years of age) and 10 teenage (18- to 19-year-old) voters for their opinion on the presidential election. But often these types of polls are not as accurate as they should be, mainly because the sample is not random.

How do television ratings work? Most people associate such ratings with Neilsen Media Research, a group that measures the number of people watching television shows, making that data available to television and cable companies, marketing people, and the media. Overall, like political polling, they use statistical sampling to rate a show. To determine who is watching what shows, they have around 5,000 households that have agreed to be part of a representative sample—a group that is thought to represent the close to 100 million viewers in the United States. The data are collected from installed meters in the households; from there, each member of the household turns a button on and off to show when he or she begins and ends viewing. The data are collected each night and statistically analyzed to determine just what "everyone in America" is watching—or not watching—on television. This one statistical rating determines not only the placement of commercials, but can make or break a program. Such a small sampling of people is also why favorite viewer programs sometimes get cancelled.

Qualitative variables are measured on a nominal scale, or a measurement that has assigned items to groups or categories. With these variables, there is no quantitative information and no ordering of the items is conveyed—it is qualitative rather than quantitative. Religious preference, race, and gender are all examples of nominal scales.

What **other variables** are often used in **statistics**?

When an experiment is conducted, variables manipulated by the experimenter are called *independent variables* (also independent factors), while others measured from the subjects are called *dependent variables* (also dependent measures). For example, consider a hypothetical experiment on the effect of lack of sleep on reaction time: Subjects either stayed awake, slept for 2 hours for every 24, 5 hours for every 24, or 8 hours for every 24; they then had their reaction times tested. The independent variables would be the hours slept by each person and the dependent variables would be the reaction time.

197

Some variables can be measured on a continuous scale—a *continuous variable* being one that, within the limits the variable ranges, can take on any value possible. For example, we can make the time to eat a lunch at a certain restaurant be the continuous variable because it can take any number of minutes or hours to finish the meal. But other variables can only take on a limited number of values—or dependent variables. For example, if the variables were a test score from 1 to 10, then only those 10 possible values would be allowed; these are called *discrete variables*.

What are the **measures of central tendency**?

The measures of central tendency are statistics that describe the grouping of values in a data set around a common value that in some way represents a typical member. They are broken down into four types: median, mode, average (also called the arithmetic mean), and the geometric mean.

What are the **arithmetic mean** and **geometric mean**?

The average, in general, means the average value of a group of numerical observations—or the statistical measure of the arithmetic mean (or just the mean). On a scale of measurement, it is usually the place in which the population is centered. Numerically, it equals the sum of the scores divided by the number of scores. For example, the sum of 3, 7, 10, 15, and 25 is 60; thus, the mean is 60 divided by 5, or 12. The geometric mean is another type of mean: For two quantities, it is the square root of the quantities' product; the notation is for n quantities, and the geometric mean is the nth root of their product.

What are **median** and **mode**?

The median is considered half the sum of the two numbers nearest the middle. In other words, in an ordered data set, the median is the value at the halfway point, above and below which lie an equal number of data values. (But note: There is an actual middle number for a set with an odd number of members, but no middle number for an even number of members.)

The mode is considered a single value that occurs more often than any other in a set of data. It is not the frequency of the most numerous number, but the value of the number itself. Often there is more than one mode if two or more values are commonly found in the set—often called a multi-modal population.

What is the **range** of a set of numbers?

The range of a sample (or data set) is used to characterize the spread or dispersion among observations in a given population, as it is the distance between the highest and lowest numbers. In statistics, it is often (logically) referred to as the statistical range. Numerically, it is represented by the highest score minus the lowest score. For example, for the range of the numbers 34, 84, 48, 65, 92, and 22, the range is $92 - 22 = 70$.

What are chi-square tests?

The chi-square test is a way to determine the odds for or against a given deviation from the expected statistical distribution. This somewhat complex statistical test computes the probability that there is no major difference between the expected frequency of an event with the observed frequency of that event—and especially to determine if the set of responses is significantly different from an expected set of responses only because of chance.

There are even various ways to perform this type of test, such as the most common type, called the Pearson's chi-square test. Another is called the likelihood ratio chi-square test (or G test), in which a hypothesis is tested of no association of columns and rows in nominal-level tabular data. Yet another is the chi-square goodness-of-fit test, which is just a different use of the Pearson chi-square; it is used to test if an observed distribution conforms to any other distribution. Taking this test one step further (making it more powerful) is the Kolmogorov-Smirnov goodness-of-fit test, which is preferred for interval data.

What is the **average deviation**?

The average deviation is a way of characterizing the spread (dispersion) among the measures in a given population. To determine the average deviation, compute the mean, then specify the distance between each score and that mean without regard to whether the score is above or below the mean. The following is the notation for this calculation (the symbol Σ stands for "sum of"; the symbol $| \ |$ stands for absolute value):

$$\frac{\Sigma |x - \mu|}{N}$$

in which x is the various values of the samples, μ is the mean (or average) for the entire population, and N is the number of samples (the two vertical lines representing the absolute value means there are no negative numbers on top).

For example, if we have six people who weighed 166, 134, 189, 141, 178, and 150, the equation would read (μ is the average, or the total weight divided by the number of people, or $958/6 = 159.67$; $n = 6$, or the number of people; and x are the individual weights of the people):

$$\frac{\Sigma |166 - 159.67| + |134 - 159.67| + \cdots + |178 - 159.67| + |150 - 159.67|}{6}$$

The average deviation for this example is 18.

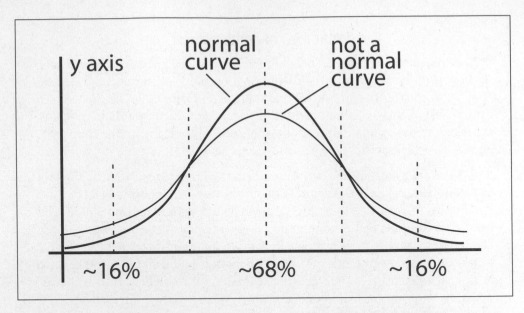

A "normal" curve has a bell shape to it into which the majority of a sampling of statistics falls within a certain average range.

What is the **variance**?

The variance is the average of the squares of a set's deviations. It is used to characterize the spread among the measures of a given population. First, calculate the mean of the scores; then measure the amount that each score deviates from the mean. Finally, square that deviation (in other words, multiply it by itself, add all of them together, then divide by the total number of scores). An even easier way is to square the numbers first. (Note: Taking the square root of the variance gives the standard deviation.)

For example, take the numbers 3, 5, 8, and 9, with a mean of 6.25 (the sum of the numbers divided by the total number of numbers). To calculate the variance, determine the deviation of each number from 6.25 (3.25, 1.25, 1.75, 2.75), square each deviation (10.5625, 1.5625, 3.0625, 7.5625), then take the average 22.75/4 = 5.6875, which is the variance. An easier way to calculate the variance is to square all the numbers first (9, 25, 64, 81) and determine the mean (9 + 25 + 64 + 81 divided by 4 = 44.75). Then subtract the square of the first mean (6.25^2 = 39.0625)—or 44.75 − 39.0625 = 5.6875.

What is the **standard deviation**?

The standard deviation is considered by some to be the second most important statistic (or statistical measure) in the field; it is the measure of how much the individual observations are scattered about the mean. In general, the more widely values are spread out, the larger the standard deviation. For example, if the test results for two different exams taken by 50 people in a geology class range from 30 to 98 percent for

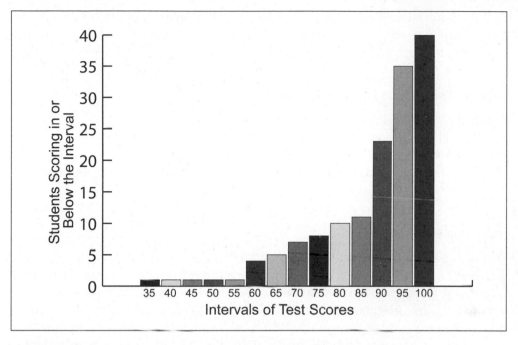

In this example of a cumulative distribution chart, all students (100 percent) fall within the maximum score of 100, while smaller numbers of students fall within each progressively lower score on a test.

the first exam and 78 to 95 percent for the second exam, the standard deviation is larger for the first list of exams. This spread (dispersion) of a data set is calculated by taking the square root of the variance; the notation for standard deviation is most commonly seen as follows: $\sqrt{V(x)}$ = s.d. (or simply s), in which $V(x)$ is the variance.

What is a **normal distribution**?

A normal distribution is an idealized view of the world, producing the familiar, symmetrically shaped "bell-shaped curve." It is usually based on a large set of measurements of one quantity—such as weights, test scores, or height—which are arranged by size. In a normal distribution, more than two-thirds of the measurements fall in the central region of the graph; about one-sixth of them are found on either side. Many of us are familiar with the normal distribution from standardized school test scores, as most result in a bell-shaped curve, with students hoping to at least fall in the middle of the curve.

What is a **cumulative distribution**?

A cumulative distribution is a plot of the number of observations that fall in or below an interval. For example, they are often used to determine where scores fall in a standardized test. For example, the x-axis (see bar graph illustration) shows the intervals of scores (such as the interval labeled 35 shows any score from 32.5 to 37.5, and so on)

and the y-axis shows the number of students scoring in or below each interval. This graphically illustrates for the students (and teachers) how well they did on the test compared to other students.

What are **skewness** and **symmetry**?

Skewness is when there is asymmetry in the distribution of the sample data values. In this case, the values on one side of the distribution seem to be further from the "middle" range than values on the other side. Symmetry essentially means balance: when the data values are distributed in the same way above and below (or on both sides of) the middle of the sample.

What is a **statistical test**?

A statistical test is a procedure used to decide if an assertion (often called a hypothesis) about a population's chosen quantitative feature is true or false. These tests usually entail drawing on a random sample (or simple random sample) from the chosen population, then calculating a statistic about the chosen feature. From the result, a statistician can usually determine if the hypothesis is true, false, rare, common, or something in between. Overall, for a statistical test to be valid, it is necessary to choose what statistic to use, what sample size, and what criteria to use for rejection or acceptance of the tested hypothesis.

What does the term **"statistically significant"** mean?

For most of us, "significant" means important; in statistics it means probably true (not due to chance) but not necessarily important. In particular, significance levels in statistics show how likely a result is due to chance. The most common level—one thought to make it good enough to believe—is 0.95, which means the finding has a 95 percent chance of being true.

This can also be misleading, however. No statistical report will indicate a 95 percent, or 0.95, in its answer, but it will show the number 0.05. Thus, statisticians say the results in a "backward" manner: they say that a finding has a 5 percent chance of not being true. To find the significance level, all one has to do is subtract the number shown from 1. For example, a value of 0.05 means that there is a 95 percent (1 – .05 5 0.95) chance of it being true; for a value of 0.01, there is a 99 percent chance (1 – 0.01 5 0.99) of it being true; and so on.

How is **statistical data presented**?

There are many ways to present statistical data, all of which involve graphical means to translate the results of statistical tests. A *histogram* is a graphical representation of a distribution function using rectangles. It is also most often constructed from a fre-

quency table (see below). The widths of the rectangles usually indicate the intervals into which the range of observed values are divided; the heights of the rectangles indicate the number of observations that occur in each interval. The shapes of histograms vary depending on the chosen size of the intervals.

Bar graphs are similar to histograms, but with the columns separated by each other by small distances. They are commonly used for qualitative variables. A *pie chart* is another way to represent data graphically. In this case, it is a circle divided into segments, or "pie" wedges. Each segment represents not only a certain category, but its proportion to the total set of data. Another type of graph is the *line graph,* which is similar to those seen in geometry: a representation of the data from connected point to connected point. They are one of the most common graphs seen for simple statistical data collection.

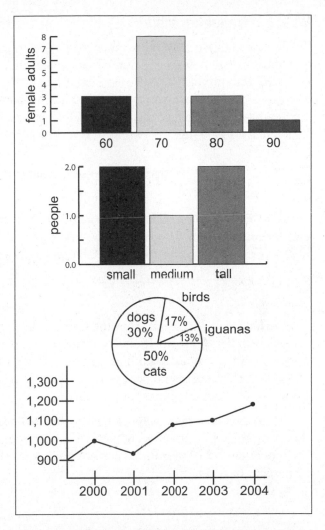

Here are four different types of charts used in statistics (from top to bottom): a histogram, a bar graph, a pie chart, and a line graph (statistics are not based on actual data here).

What is a **percent**?

A percent (using the symbol %) is the ratio of one number to another. Percents are quantitative terms in which n percent of a number is n one-hundredths of the number; they are usually expressed as the equivalent ratio of some number to the number 100. For example, the ratio of 25 to 50 means the number 25 is 50 percent of 50. They are not true numbers; thus, percents can't be used in calculations, such as addition or multiplication. But operations can be conducted with percents when they are translated into ratios and fractions, such as 25 percent is equal to 0.25 or 1/4.

203

What is a **frequency table**?

A frequency table is a way of summarizing data. In particular, it is a way of displaying how entities (such as scores, number of people, etc.) are divided into intervals, and of counting the number of entities in each interval. The result shows the actual number of entities, and even the percentage of entities in each interval. For example, if we survey the number of people working in the 10 offices in a building, the data set might look like the following:

Number of people working in each office:									
3	1	4	1	3	2	4	1	1	2

Another way to present this data is to note how many offices had 1, 2, 3, or 4 people working in them. This is known as finding the frequencies of each of the data values. An example of such a frequency table would be as follows:

number of people	0	1	2	3	4
frequency	0	4	2	2	2

This is a compact way of showing how the data values are distributed between the various number of people. It allows us to see, at a glance, the most "popular" number (also called the "modal class") of people working in an office for this building's 10 offices—in this case, a one-person office. Such data can further be visualized with the use of bar charts, histograms, or pie charts.

There are even more ways to see the data from this frequency table. We can also illustrate this chart in terms of percent. In particular, we can say that 40 percent of the offices contain 1 person, 20 percent have 2 people, 20 percent have 3 people, and 20 percent have 4 people.

MODELING AND SIMULATION

What is a **mathematical model**?

Mathematical models are a way of analyzing systems by using equations (mathematical language) to determine how the system changes from one state to the next (usually using differential equations) and/or how one variable depends on the value or state of other variables. Simply put (although working through the equations is not always simple), the process of mathematical modeling includes the input of data and information, a way of processing the information, and an output of results.

A mathematical model can describe the behavior of many systems, including systems in the fields of biology, economics, social science, electrical and mechanical

What are some types of mathematical models?

Mathematical models are commonly broken down into numerical or analytical models. Numerical models are those that use some type of numerical timing procedures to figure out a model's behavior over time. The solution is usually represented by a table or graph. An analytical model usually has a closed solution. In other words, the solution to the equations used to describe changes in the system can be expressed as a mathematical analytic function. Mathematical models can also be divided in other ways. For example, some models are considered deterministic (or a model that always performs the same way for a given set of initial conditions) or stochastic (or a model in which randomness is present).

engineering, and thermodynamics. For example, modeling is usually used in the sciences to better understand physical phenomena; each phenomenon is translated into a set of equations that describe it. But don't think that all the results of models are indicative of the real world. Because it is virtually impossible to describe a phenomenon totally, models are considered to be merely a human construct to help us better understand our surrounding real-world systems.

What are some **basic steps** to **building** a **mathematical model**?

Just like building a physical structure, there are basic steps to building a mathematical model. The first steps are to simplify the assumptions, or to clearly state those assumptions on which the model will be based, including an understandable account of the relationships among the quantities to be analyzed. Second is to describe all the variables and parameters to be used in the model, and identify the initial conditions of the model. Finally, use step one's assumptions and step two's parameters and variables to derive mathematical equations.

What is a common **example** of **mathematical modeling**?

One of the most common examples of a mathematical model has to do with the growth of populations—human, animal, or otherwise. In the sciences, this type of mathematical modeling often leads to intelligent hypotheses about the future and past of a population—from a possible population explosion to even extinctions. (For more information about the use of mathematical modeling in the sciences, see "Math in the Natural Sciences.")

What does *a priori* refer to in **mathematical modeling**?

The term *a priori* refers to the amount of information available in a system. Based on the amount of a priori information, mathematical modeling problems are often classi-

Many different types of data, including air pressure, temperature, humidity, and so on, must be taken into account when constructing computer models of hurricanes.

fied into white-box (a system in which all necessary information is available) or black-box (a system in which there is no a priori information available) models. Practically all systems are somewhere between the white-box and black-box models; thus, this concept only works as an intuitive guide on how to approach a mathematical problem.

Can a **mathematical model** be **too complex**?

Yes, mathematical models can be too complex for a number of reasons. For example, if we wanted to model the development of a hurricane, we would take data from a forming storm—water vapor, pressure, temperature, and so on—and incorporate it into our model. In this way, we would try to develop as close to a white-box model of the hurricane system as possible.

But in reality a collection of such a huge amount of data—not to mention the computational cost—would effectively inhibit the use of such a weather model. There is also uncertainty because the development of a hurricane is an overly complex system, mainly because each separate part of a hurricane and its development causes some amount of variance in the model. For example, not only would we have to know about the details of the hurricane's development, but other factors would come into play, such as the ocean-interaction variables that contribute to the hurricane, variability of solar radiation, and even how periodic events such as El Niño—a periodic warming of the waters off the South America coast—affect the hurricane. Thus, meteorolo-

How do simulators work?

Simulators use an interactive, physical device to simulate reality. For example, space shuttle simulators were used to help astronauts understand the intricacies and various scenarios associated with flying the shuttle; people can even improve their driving skills using driving simulators. But how do simulators work in terms of mathematics?

One way of seeing how this works is with an airplane flight simulator. Although there are different types—ranging from full cockpit to full motion simulators—they have the same purpose: to make the person "flying" the simulator feel as if he or she is really controlling an airplane. When a person sits in the cockpit, he or she sees a virtual world projected onto a screen—what it would look like outside a real plane's cockpit. As the pilot "flies" by moving the instruments, the actions get translated to a computer hooked to the simulator; from there, each component of the process is translated using physics-based equations that describe the relationship between the input and output of the actions. Not only do the instruments respond in kind, but often, if the simulator is hooked to hydraulic mounts, movements will also be fed by computer into the simulator. Thus, the pilot will truly feel as if he or she is flying—all thanks to mathematical equations translated by the computer and into the simulator.

gists usually use some approximations to make the mathematical model more manageable, which is also why we still can't predict where and how much rain, wind, and tornadoes will occur during a hurricane.

How can the **accuracy** of a **mathematical model** be determined?

There is usually one good way to determine the accuracy of a mathematical model: Once a set of equations has been built and solved, if the data generated by the equations agree (or come close to) the real data collected from the system, then we can determine its accuracy. In fact, the set of equations and models are only "valid" as long as the two sets of data are close. If a model result leads to conclusions that are not close to the real-world scenario, then the equations are further modified to correct for the discrepancies as much as possible.

For example, in weather prognostication, meteorologists use various numerical models to make long-term predictions of weather systems (for more information about models and weather prediction, see "Math in the Natural Sciences"). It is interesting to see how meteorologists use a combination of several of the weather models to forecast the weather in certain spots around the United States and the world—mainly because no weather forecasting model has all the right answers. Every day,

researchers are tweaking their respective weather models (based on more collected data) in hopes of eventually understanding our weather a bit better.

What is a **simulation**?

A simulation is an imitation of some real event or device. It is often used interchangeably with the word modeling (as in modeling of natural systems). A simulation tries to represent certain features (or behaviors) of a complex physical system based on the underlying computational models of the phenomenon, environment, or experience.

Simulations are used to understand the operation of real-world, practical systems; for instance, the modeling of natural systems such as the human body. They can be used to simulate a certain type of technology, such as a new type of airplane, or model an engineering concern, such as the stability of a building during an earthquake.

OTHER AREAS OF
APPLIED MATHEMATICS

What is **numerical analysis**?

Numerical analysis is a branch of applied mathematics that studies certain specialized techniques for solving mathematical problems; in particular, it is the study of algorithms that use numerical approximation for mathematical analysis problems. In general, it employs mathematical axioms, theorems, and proofs, and often uses empirical results to further analyze or examine new methods. Characteristics of numerical analysis methods include accuracy (the numerical approximation should be as accurate as possible); robustness (the algorithm should be able to solve many problems and should relate to the user when the results are inaccurate); and speed (the faster the computation, the better the method).

What are some **areas** that **numerical analysis addresses**?

Areas addressed by numerical analysis include computing the values of functions, solving equations, optimizing functions, evaluating integrals, and solving for differential equations. (For more about these areas, see "Mathematical Analysis.")

How does the **Monte Carlo method** work?

The Monte Carlo method has been used for centuries, but it was not truly thought of as a "viable" mathematical technique until around the first half of the 20th century. Some people say it was named after the city in the Monaco principality because of the

simple random number generator of roulette played in the Monaco casinos; others say the method's creator was honoring a relative having a propensity toward gambling.

It's known that Italian physicist Enrico Fermi (1901–1954) not only used the method to calculate neutron diffusion, but invented the Fermiac, a Monte Carlo mechanical device to determine the criticality in nuclear reactors. Further foundations of the method were laid down in the 1940s by Hungarian mathematician John von Neumann (1903–1957), along with Polish mathematician Stanislaw Ulam (1909–1984); and Nicholas Metropolis would go on to invent the computer chess program MANIAC I—the first to beat a human player—based on von Neumann's work. Simply put, the Monte Carlo method gives approximate numerical solutions to a number of problems that are too difficult to solve analytically by performing specific statistical sampling experiments. Although forms of the method have been known for a while, it was initially developed for numerical integrations in statistical physics problems during the early days of electronic computing.

But there is more to the Monte Carlo method than meets the computation. First, it's actually thought of now as a true numerical method that addresses some of the most complex mathematical applications. The list of applications seems endless, including cancer therapy, Dow-Jones forecasts, and stellar evolution. Second, there is more than one Monte Carlo method. For example, one method, called the *Markov chain Monte Carlo method,* has played a critical role in such diverse fields as physics, statistics, computer science, and structural biology. And the list of applications is long, especially in its usefulness and power for all types of prediction.

What is **operations research**?

Operations research, more commonly called optimization theory, is a form of applied mathematics designed to determine the most efficient way of doing something by using mathematical models, statistics, and algorithms in the decision-making process. It is a branch of mathematics that entails the many diverse areas of optimization and minimization, including the calculus of variations, control theory, decision theory, game theory, linear programming, and

Italian physicist Enrico Fermi used the Monte Carlo method to calculate neutron diffusion and to invent a device that determined criticality in nuclear reactors.

many others. Operations research is most often used to analyze complex, real-world systems, stressing the improvement in or optimization of performance.

What are some **applications** of **operations research**?

Applications of operations research span a wide variety of fields, especially with regard to reducing costs or increasing efficiency. The following lists just a few examples: constructing a telecommunications network at low cost and top efficiency, especially when under high demand or after being damaged; determining routes of school buses so fewer vehicles are needed; and designing a computer chip that will reduce manufacturing time.

What is **optimization**?

Optimization problems deal with the point at which a given function is maximized (or minimized). It is divided into several subfields, depending on the form of the objective function and the constraints that the maximized point often has to satisfy.

What is **information theory**?

Information theory is a branch of the mathematical theory of probability and statistics, allowing it to quantify concepts of information. It was formulated primarily by American scientist Claude E. Shannon (1916–2001; who was also called "the father of information theory") to explain the aspects and problems inherent in information and communication. In particular, it involves efficient and accurate storage, transmission, and representation of information, such as the engineering requirements—and limitations—of communication systems. (Note: Information theory has nothing to do with library and information science or with information technology.)

In information theory, the term "information" is not used in the traditional sense. Here it is used to mean a measure of the freedom of choice with which a message is selected from the set of all possible messages. Because it is possible for a string of non-

sense words and a meaningful sentence to be equivalent with respect to information content, "information" in this sense takes on a different meaning.

What is **game theory**?

As the words imply, game theory has to do with the mathematics and logic used in the analysis of games—or the situations that involve groups with conflicting interests. Another way to look at a game is as a conflict that involves gains and losses between two or more opponents who all follow a set of formal rules.

In particular, game theorists study the predicted and actual behavior of individuals in specific games, as well as the optimal strategies used in the games. Thus, the principles of game theory can be applied to games such as cards, checkers, and chess; or, they can be applied to real-world problems in economics, politics, psychology, and even warfare. For example, game theory is used to determine optimal policy choices of presidential candidates, or even to analyze major league baseball salary negotiations.

MATH IN THE PHYSICAL SCIENCES

PHYSICS AND MATHEMATICS

What **science fields use** an abundance of **mathematics**?

The sciences that are "heavy users" of mathematics are the so-called physical sciences, including physics, chemistry, geology, and astronomy. These scientific fields are often contrasted with the natural or biological sciences. The physical sciences analyze the nature and properties of energy and non-living matter, and they often need the help of mathematics to determine the complex relationships between their interactions.

What is **physics**?

Physics is often described as the science of the interactions between matter and energy. It includes the subfields of atomic structure, heat, electricity, magnetism, optics, and many other phenomena.

Traditionally speaking, physics is divided into classical and modern—although many subdivisions of the two overlap—and both are ruled by mathematics. Classical physics includes Newtonian mechanics, thermodynamics, acoustics, optics, electricity, and magnetism. Modern physics includes such fields as quantum field theory and relativistic mechanics.

Other common divisions of physics are experimental and theoretical physics. Theoretical physicists use mathematics to describe the physical world and predict how it will behave; they depend on experimental results to check, understand, change, or eliminate theories. Experimental physicists test their predictions with practical experiments, often using mathematics to conduct the experiments.

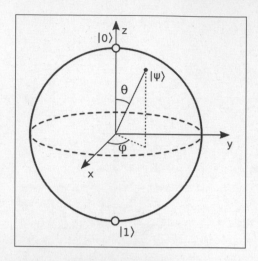

A diagram of a bloch sphere, or diagram of a qubit, which is the basic building block of quantum computers. Named after Swiss physicist Felix Bloch (1905–1983), the bloch sphere has two possible states, which can represent the 0s and 1s used in computing. It took highly advanced mathematics to develop this concept!

What is **mathematical physics**?

Mathematical physics uses the concepts of statistical mechanics and quantum field theory. But it is not the same as theoretical physics. Mathematical physics studies physics on a more abstract and meticulous level. Theoretical physics entails less mathematics than mathematical physics and has more to do with experimental physics. But like many fields of science, defining mathematical physics is not easy. For example, still another definition of modern mathematical physics states that it entails all areas of mathematics other than classical mathematical physics.

What are **some physics fields** that **rely** heavily on **mathematics**?

Almost every field of physics—especially modern physics—relies heavily on mathematics. For example, mathematics is needed to understand the concepts of acceleration, velocity, and gravitational forces. Statistical mechanics also uses an intense amount of mathematics. And it is impossible to comprehend quantum mechanics without a good knowledge of mathematics. In fact, the subject of quantum field theory is one of the most mathematically rigorous and abstract areas of the physical sciences.

CLASSICAL PHYSICS AND MATHEMATICS

How is **mathematics** used in physics **to describe motion**?

Everything in the universe is in motion, from the rotating Earth to subatomic particles. Motion in physics is described mainly through mathematics, including speed, velocity, acceleration, momentum, force (something that changes the state of rest or motion of an object), torque (when a force causes rotation or twisting around a pivot point), and inertia (a body at rest remains at rest, and a body in motion remains in motion, until acted upon by an outside force).

Unlike what most people think, speed and velocity are not the same. Speed is the rate at which something moves; velocity is speed in a certain direction. Speed is also called a scalar quantity, described by the following formula: speed = distance/time.

For example, if you drive 200 miles in 2 hours, and your speed is constant, your average speed is 200/2, or 100 miles per hour. On the other hand, velocity is known as a vector quantity (for more about vectors, see "Mathematical Analysis"). That gives velocity both speed and direction—and that leads directly to acceleration.

When an object's velocity changes, we say that it accelerates. Acceleration—also a vector like velocity—is represented as the change in velocity divided by the time it takes for the change to occur. We define the formula for acceleration—or the change in velocity per unit time—as $a = \Delta v/\Delta t$. In this equation, a is acceleration, Δv is change in velocity of an object (the delta symbol stands for change), and Δt is the change in time needed to reach the velocity. For example, if acceleration is constant, and a person drove from a standing point to 60 miles per hour in 5 seconds, the equation becomes: 60 miles per hour / 5 seconds (or final speed minus the initial speed, all divided by the elapsed time). This means that the acceleration is equal to 17.6 feet per second squared (you have to change the miles per hours to feet and seconds, respectively).

Momentum relates to the amount of energy maintained by a moving object; it is also defined as the force necessary to stop an object from moving. It depends on the mass and velocity of an object, and is represented as: $M = mv$, in which M is momentum, m is the mass of the object, and v is the object's velocity.

What is the **mathematical distinction** between **weight** and **mass**?

There is a definite difference between weight and mass, which is easily represented in the formula $W = mg$, in which W is weight (or the gravitational pull on an object), m is mass (or the quantity of matter in an object), and g is the gravitational pull. For example, if you wanted to lose weight, you could move further from the Earth or live on the Moon (in both cases, the gravitational pull would be less). But remember, no matter where you travel in the universe, you will always have the same mass—unless you diet!

Can **Newton's three laws** be expressed mathematically?

Yes, Newton's three laws are all based on mathematical formulas, but the equations would be too complex for this text. They are defined (some with applicable

Whether you are standing on the Moon or on Earth, your *mass* will always be the same; however, you will *weigh* less on the Moon because the gravitational pull on your body is less. *Taxi/Getty Images.*

Yes, mathematical equations can be used to describe work and energy. Energy comes in many forms, but its basic definition is in terms of work. Work is done when a force moves a body a certain distance. It is expressed in the simple equation: $W = Fd$, in which W is work, F is the force, and d is the distance. In this definition, only force in the direction of the object's motion counts.

mathematical notation) as follows: *Newton's First Law (Law of Inertia)* states that without any forces acting on an object, it will maintain a constant velocity. In other words, an object will stay still or keep moving in a straight line until something pushes it to change its speed or direction. The one force that stops almost everything from standing completely still or moving in a straight line is gravity. This is easily seen when you throw a baseball in the air: The ball does not move in one, continuous, straight direction because the Earth's gravity pulls it downward toward the surface.

Newton's Second Law (Law of Constant Acceleration) states that if a force acts on an object, the object accelerates in the direction of the force; the force creates an acceleration proportional to the force (and inversely proportional to the mass). This is written in the following notation: $F = ma$, in which F is the force, m is the mass, and a is the acceleration. Newton actually expressed this in terms of the calculus—a form of mathematics he created to explain these physical laws (for more about the calculus and Newton, see "Mathematical Analysis"). He wrote the equation as follows:

$$F = m\frac{\Delta v}{\Delta t}$$

in which m is mass, Δv is the change in velocity, and Δt is the change in time. This is because instantaneous acceleration is equal to the instantaneous change in velocity in an instance in time (or change in time).

Newton's Third Law (or Law of Conservation of Momentum) states that forces on an object are always mutual. To put it another way, if a force is exerted on an object, the object reacts with an equal and opposite force on the phenomenon that initially exerted the force. Simply stated, objects exert equal but opposite forces on each other. This is often phrased, "For every action, there is an equal and opposite reaction." The mathematical equations for these forces are complex and beyond the scope of this text.

What is **Newton's Law of Universal Gravitation**?

As hard as it is to comprehend, (almost) everything in the universe is attracted to everything else. This physical law is not only one of the most well-known but also one of the most important. Newton's law states that the gravitational force between two

masses, m and M, is proportional to the product of the masses and inversely proportional to the square of the distance (r) between them. In formula form, this is written as follows (note: in some texts, the masses of the two objects are written as m_1 and m_2):

$$F = G \times \frac{M \times m}{r^2}$$

G is a constant in nature (also called a universal constant), indicating how strong a gravitational force exists. In other words, the farther away the objects, the less the attraction between the objects.

What is **statistical mechanics**?

Statistical mechanics applies statistics to the field of mechanics—the motion of particles or objects when subjected to a force. It is used to understand the properties of single atoms and molecules of liquids, solids, gases—even the individual quanta of light that make up electromagnetic radiation—to the bulk properties of everyday materials. Because statistical mechanics mathematically helps to understand the interactions between a large number of microscopic elements, it is used in a wide range of fields. In a way, it is also the "opposite" of thermodynamics, which approaches the same types of systems from a macroscopic, or large-scale, point of view.

What is **Ohm's Law**?

Ohm's Law is important to the field of electrical studies. It states that direct current flowing in a conductor is directly proportional to the potential difference between its ends. First summarized by German physicist Georg Simon Ohm (1789–1854), it is usually seen in formula form as: $V = IR$ (or $I = V/R$), in which V is the potential difference (voltage), I is the current (also written in some texts as i), and R is the resistance of the conductor. This can also be written in terms of electric quantities (voltage = current \times resistance) and with units of measure (volts = amps \times ohms).

Who developed the **mathematical equations** that explain **electricity and magnetism**?

One of the major early works about electricity and magnetism was written by Scottish physicist James Clerk Maxwell

Georg Ohm discovered the law about how electrical currents flow through a conductor.

(1831–1879), who in 1873 published *A Treatise on Electricity and Magnetism*. It contained his mathematically based theory of the electromagnetic field. These equations, now known as *Maxwell's equations,* include four partial differential equations that provided a basis for the unification of electric and magnetic fields, the electromagnetic description of light, and, ultimately, Albert Einstein's theory of relativity. Although most people recognize Isaac Newton's work on mechanics, few remember Maxwell's electromagnetic theories (including the idea of the electromagnetic wave) when it comes to classical physics. But his theories eventually led to many things we take for granted today, including radio waves and microwaves.

MODERN PHYSICS AND MATHEMATICS

What is **modern physics** and how is **mathematics** used?

In contrast to classical physics—although there are overlapping topics—modern physics includes relativistic mechanics, atomic, nuclear and particle physics, and quantum physics. Mathematics is very relevant to all these topics, with physicists using mathematics as their toolbox to find out the physical answers to the universe. For example—and these are only generalizations—the study of quantum mechanics often means a person uses calculus, algebraic techniques, and to some extent, probability and statistics; general relativity uses differential geometry; and quantum field theory uses matrices and group theory. In fact, according to most physicists, you can never know enough mathematics when you study physics because it seems one type of math often leads to another in the natural, physical world.

How did **Albert Einstein** use **mathematics**?

German-born American theoretical physicist Albert Einstein (1879–1955) is recognized as one of the greatest physicists of all time, but he was also a notable mathematician. In 1905 he developed the special theory of relativity, mathematically demonstrating that two observers moving at great speeds with respect to one another will experience different time intervals and measure lengths differently, that the speed of light is the "speed limit" for all objects having mass, and that mass and energy are equivalent.

By around 1915, Einstein completed a mathematical formulation of a general theory of relativity, this time adding gravitational effects to determine curvature of a time-space continuum. He further tried to discover a unified field theory, which would combine gravity, electromagnetism, and subatomic phenomena under one set of rules, but he, and no one since, has ever found such a theory.

What does Einstein's famous equation $E = mc^2$ signify?

Among his other accomplishments, Albert Einstein showed mathematically that there was a connection between mass and energy: energy has mass, and mass represents energy. This equation, also called the energy-mass relation, is expressed as $E = mc^2$, in which E is energy, m is mass, and c is the speed of light. Because c is a very large number, even a very small amount of mass represents an enormous amount of energy.

What is **relativity**?

Relativity refers to the idea that the velocity of an object can be determined only relative to the observer. For example, if a fly moves around the inside of a car at about 1 mile per hour, inside the car's frame of reference, the fly is moving at 1 mile per hour. But if the car goes past you at 65 miles per hour, it will appear as if the fly is traveling at 66 miles per hour, not 1 mile per hour. In other words, it's all a matter of reference, and it's "relative" to your viewpoint.

What new ideas came out of Einstein's (and others') study of relativity? He showed that space and time could no longer be viewed as separate, independent entities, forming a four-dimensional continuum called *space-time* (also written as spacetime). It is not easy to verbally explain the intricacies of Einstein's theory. The best way to interpret his works is with the use of formulations from certain mathematical branches, such as tensor calculus (for more about tensors, see "Mathematical Analysis"). But such complex equations are beyond the scope of this book.

Did **Einstein's theories** change our concept of **dimensions**?

Yes, our ideas about dimensions changed dramatically thanks to Einstein's theories, not to mention the mathematics involved in producing those theories. In particular, one can't distinguish space and time as elements in the description of events. Instead, they are joined in what is called the *fourth dimension*—also called a four-dimensional manifold known as space-time (see above).

Although it sounds like something out of the television show *Star Trek,* space-time events in the universe are described in terms of the four-dimensional continuum. Simply put, each observer locates an event by three spacelike coordinates (positions) and one timelike coordinate. The choice of the timelike coordinate in space-time is not unique; hence, time is not absolute but is relative to the observer. The strange effects go on: In general, events at different locations that are simultaneous for one observer will not be simultaneous for another observer. (For more information about dimensions, see "Geometry and Trigonometry.")

Why was **Max Planck** important to **quantum theory**?

Quantum theory (or physics) entails the emission and absorption of energy by matter and the motion of material particles; it is a special situation in which very small quantities are involved. When added to the theory of relativity—in which great speeds are involved—both form the theoretical basis of modern physics.

One of the most important aspects of quantum theory is the quanta. In 1900 German physicist Max Karl Ernst Ludwig Planck (1858–1947) proposed that all forms of radiation—such as light and heat—come in bundles called quanta. These bundles are further emitted and absorbed in small, discrete amounts, thus behaving in some situations like particles of matter. For example, a bundle of light energy is known as light quanta or *photons*. Planck devised the equation: $E = hv$, in which E is the amount of energy in a single particle, v is the frequency of the wave, and h is the constant now known as *Planck's constant*.

It is interesting to note that some people divide physics using Planck's discovery: The term classical physics is often referred to as "before Planck"; while the term for modern physics is often referred to as "after Planck."

What is **quantum mechanics**?

Quantum mechanics is a branch of quantum theory that simply determines the probability of an event happening, although the mathematical calculations to prove such things are very rigorous and not simple. In fact, quantum mechanics is often called the "final mathematical formulation of the quantum theory." Developed during the 1920s, it accounts for matter at the atomic level, and is considered an extension of statistical mechanics, but based on quantum theory.

Physicist Max Planck was the first to propose the idea that energy existed in bundles called "quanta." His theories later led to the development of quantum mechanics and modern physics.

What is **Schrödinger's equation**?

Schrödinger's equation was, of course, developed by Austrian physicist Erwin Schrödinger (1887–1961) in 1926. Called a wave equation, it could be applied to any physical system. The actual equation has more than one solution, and each solution (also called a quantum state, matter waves, or probability waves) to the equation is a probability wave that describes

one of the possible outcomes, or behaviors, of that system. For example, looking at a hydrogen atom, each wave solution to the equations describes one of the allowed electron orbits of the atom.

What does **wave mechanics** mean in quantum studies?

One important part of quantum mechanics is *wave mechanics*, which is an extension of quantum mechanics based on Schrödinger's equation. This idea states that atomic events can be explained as interactions between particle waves.

What is the **Pauli's exclusion principle**?

Quantum theory also relies on the *Pauli exclusion principle*. This principle, developed by Austrian-born Swiss physicist Wolfgang Pauli (1900–1958) in 1925, states that two particles of a certain class— called femions, and otherwise known as

Austrian physicist Erwin Schrödinger developed the wave equation, the solution of which is a probability wave expressing the possible outcomes of a system.

electrons, neutrons, and protons—can never be in the same energy state. For example, two electrons with the same quantum number can't occupy the same atom.

How do **quantum physicists** regard **light waves**?

Added to the mix of the mathematically rich quantum theory was an idea developed by French physicist Prince Louis-Victor Pierre-Raymond de Broglie (1892–1987), who discovered the wave nature of electrons and of particles in general (and also devised a mathematical explanation of the kinetic theory of heat). He determined that not only do light waves often exhibit particle-like properties, but particles also often exhibit wave-like properties.

This opened a can of quantum worms. From there, two different formulations of quantum mechanics developed: first, the wave mechanics of Austrian physicist Erwin Schrödinger (1887–1961), who used a mathematical entity (the wave function) related to the probability of finding a particle in space at a given point. (Schrödinger also developed a model of the atom that differed from the traditional Niels Bohr model); second and mathematically equal to Schrödinger's theory was the matrix mechanics

German physicist Werner Karl Heisenberg developed the uncertainty principal, which states that it is impossible to note both the exact position and exact motion of an object at the same time.

of German physicist Werner Karl Heisenberg (1901–1976; for more about Heisenberg, see below).

What is the **Heisenberg uncertainty principle**?

German physicist Werner Karl Heisenberg (1901–1976) not only helped with quantum theory of light waves, he also developed the Heisenberg uncertainty principle, an idea used extensively in the modern electronics field. The principle states that it is impossible to determine, at the same time, both the energy and velocity of a particle. Or, in other words, it's impossible to predict, measure, or know both the exact position of an object and its exact motion at the same time. This principle made a huge dent in Newtonian physics, which relied on a deterministic, "predictable" view of the universe. In simple terms, it showed that the universe does what it wants.

How else is **mathematics** used in **physics**?

There are hundreds of other applications of mathematics in physics. The following lists only a few:

Fluid mechanics—This is the study of air, water, and other fluids in motion. It includes the mathematics of turbulence, wave propagation, and so on.

Geophysics—This is a geological study with a physics basis. Much of the field is dominated by the mathematics of large scale movement of materials, such as earthquakes, volcanic activity, and fluid mechanics (for example, underground molten volcanic material).

Optics—This is the mostly mathematical study of the propagation and evolution of electromagnetic waves, such as diffraction and the path of light rays. This requires a great knowledge of geometry and trigonometry, not to mention complex equations.

What are **superstrings**?

Amazing as it sounds, one of the most fascinating discoveries in our universe started with an instrument's vibrating strings. These structures are called superstrings and

are often compared to a string on a musical instrument, such as a violin. The musical notes made by the string are said to be excitation modes of the string under tension. In string theory, the observed elementary particles in a particle accelerator could be considered the excitation modes of elementary strings. But unlike the violin, superstrings are floating in space-time; they also have tension like the violin without being tied to anything.

Greek mathematician and philosopher Pythagoras of Samos (c. 582–c. 507 B.C.E.), an expert on the lyre, was probably the first "string theorist," as he figured out the (mathematical) harmonic relationship of the strings. He determined that vibrating lyre strings with equal tension but different lengths would produce harmonious notes (such as a middle C and a high C) if the ratio of the lengths of the two strings was a whole number. Eventually, mathematicians took Pythagoras's ideas to new heights, more precisely encoding the harmonics with complex mathematics.

And, of course, there are other mathematical calculations and measurements used when talking about superstrings. For example, the tension in string theory is denoted by the quantity $/(2 p a')$, in which a' is said to be "alpha prime" and equal to the square of the string length scale. There is also the size of the string (equal to the Planck length, or about 10^{-33} centimeters) and supersymmetry (for every particle that transmits a force, there is a corresponding particle that makes up matter).

CHEMISTRY AND MATH

What is **chemistry**?

Chemistry is the science of matter. It studies the composition, structure, and properties of substances (matter) and its reactions and changes. Because chemistry includes all materials in the universe, it is useful for studying many things—from the chemical composition of gases in galaxies to the chemical reactions within living cells. It also includes mathematics in many forms, such as when determining chemical compositions and understanding relationships between certain chemicals.

What are the **atomic number** and **mass** of an **element**?

The atomic number is the number of protons in an atomic nucleus. The atomic mass of an atom—usually measured in atomic mass units—is the total mass of the atom, or the combined mass of its protons and neutrons (the mass of the electrons is negligible). The importance of atomic numbers and mass is simple: The atoms of each element has a specific atomic number and mass—each determined by "adding" or "subtracting" protons and neutrons within the atom.

223

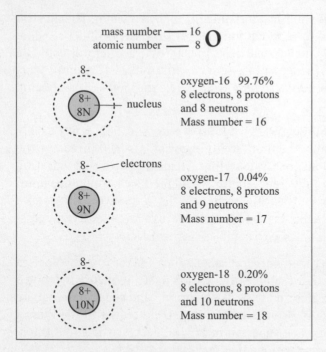

mass number —— 16 O
atomic number —— 8

oxygen-16 99.76%
8 electrons, 8 protons
and 8 neutrons
Mass number = 16

nucleus

electrons

oxygen-17 0.04%
8 electrons, 8 protons
and 9 neutrons
Mass number = 17

oxygen-18 0.20%
8 electrons, 8 protons
and 10 neutrons
Mass number = 18

Three naturally occurring isotopes of oxygen are oxygen-16, oxygen-17, and oxygen-18. They differ by the number of neutrons in their nuclei. Oxygen-16 is the most common form of oxygen in our atmosphere at 99.76% occurrence.

What is an **electron**?

Chemically speaking, matter is composed of minute particles called atoms; in turn, atoms contain elementary (or subatomic) particles: protons (positively charged particles), neutrons (particles with no charge), and electrons (negatively charged found around the nucleus of the atom). When an atom gains or loses electrons, it acquires a net electric charge.

There is a strange part of an electron's definition, especially in the field of physics: is an electron a particle or a wave? In reality, everything is a wave or particle; and the more mass an object has, the smaller the waves. Thus, electrons, which have less mass, have larger waves. In quantum mechanics, electron waves are actually thought of as probability waves (and so are matter waves in general). But again, there are some different characteristics of these waves. In particular, the wave does not indicate where the electron is found, only where it might be found—or the probability of the electron being in that place.

What is an **ion**?

Scientists know that atoms can gain or lose electrons, thus acquiring a negative or positive electrical charge (determined by the number of protons minus the number of electrons). For example, if there are 4 protons and 6 electrons, the net charge is –2 (often called the valence). An ion is an atom—or group of atoms—that takes on the net electric charge, and can be positive (cation) or negative (anion). Based on the "mathematics" of losing or gaining electrons, ions can be formed or destroyed. This is one example of where math comes in handy in chemistry.

What is an **angstrom**?

An angstrom (Å) is a unit of measurement often used in chemistry, most often in reference to molecules; for example, the average molecule diameter is between 0.5 to 2.5

angstroms. An angstrom is equal to about 3.937×10^{-9} inch or one hundredth of a millionth of a centimeter (10^{-8} centimeter).

What is **density**?

Density (usually abbreviated as d or r) is a mathematical concept used to describe the ratio between the mass of an object and its volume. The actual formula is the density times the volume is equal to an object's mass, or $d \times v = m$. In the standard (American) measurement system, density is measured in pounds per cubic foot. But in the sciences, the metric system is usually used and density is measured in grams per cubic centimeter (or grams per milliliter). For example, the density of water is 1 gram per cubic centimeter, lead is 11.3 grams per cubic centimeter, and gold is 19.32 grams per cubic centimeter. (Note: In the majority of cases, the higher the density, the "heavier" it feels to us on Earth.)

What are **formulas** and **equations** in **chemistry**?

Formulas and equations in chemistry don't always mean the same as in mathematics. *Formulas* in chemistry are representations of a chemical compound using symbols for the elements and subscripts for the number of atoms present. For example, the chemical formula for water is H_2O, in which there are two atoms of hydrogen (H) bonded to an atom of oxygen (O). The subscript 2 indicates that there are two atoms of hydrogen in the molecule; if there is no subscript number, as with the oxygen (O), a subscript of 1 is implied. (Remember, not all compounds are molecular; for example, NaCl, or sodium chloride [regular table salt], is called an ionic compound. In these cases, the formula shows the proportion of the atoms of each element making up the compound.) There are other types of formulas in chemistry, but this is the most familiar.

Equations in chemistry also differ from mathematics. Chemical equations represent the reaction relationship between two or more chemical compounds—along with the products of the chemical reaction. For example, the chemical equation $2H_2 + O_2 \rightarrow 2H_2O$ is the reaction of hydrogen with oxygen to form water. The arrow indicates the direction of the reaction toward the product; the reactants (or the substances that react) are hydrogen and oxygen. There is also a methodology in writing chemical equations. Simply put, first there is the process to determine the reactants and outcome; next, determine the formula for each substance; and finally, balance the equation.

What is the **pH scale**?

The "pH" scale stands for p(otential of) H(ydrogen) scale, or the logarithm of the reciprocal of hydrogen-ion concentration in gram atoms per liter. In simpler terms, the pH is merely the measure of the hydrogen ion concentration of a solution. The pH numbers are based on a scale from 0 to 14, in which numbers less than 7 represent acidic solutions and numbers greater than 7 represent alkaline (base) solutions. A reading of 7 is considered neutral.

Mathematically speaking, once the concentration of hydrogen ions is determined chemically (based on moles per liter), the pH value is established by taking the exponent used in expressing this concentration and reversing its sign. It is most often expressed as the notation $pH = -\log_{10}[H^+]$. For example, if the hydrogen ion concentration of a solution is determined to be 10^{-4} (or 0.0001) moles per liter, the pH is 4.

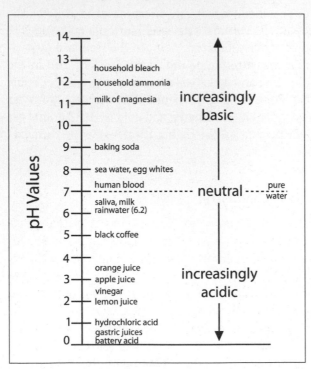

Many people are familiar with the pH scale from high school, especially the practice of using special whitish paper called litmus paper to check for pH. The paper contains a powder extracted from certain plants, allowing the user to determine acidity (the paper turns red), neutrality (the paper stays white), or alkalinity (the paper turns blue) of various solutions. The stronger the acid or base, the more intense the red or blue, respectively. And pH isn't just for use in

A pH scale indicating pH levels for common liquids and other substances.

What is radioactive decay?

Mathematics can also be applied to radioactive substances found within certain rocks. *Radioactive decay* is the disintegration of a radioactive substance and the emission of certain ionizing radiation (such as alpha or beta particles—or even gamma rays). Simply put, when rocks form, the minerals within the rock often contain certain radioactive atoms that decay at a specific rate.

Radioactive decay is especially important in radioactive dating, in which the original and decayed radioactive elements are used to determine the age of the rock. This is because certain radioactive elements will decay to a mixture of half the original element and half another element (or isotope) in a specific timeframe; this is also called the half-life of the original element. For example, "half" of the Uranium-238 in a rock will decay into Lead-207 in 704 million years (thus, the half-life of Uranium-238 is said to be 704 million years). Statistically, this change follows a specific decay function for each isotope of an element. And in each of these exponential functions, the time for the function's value to decrease to half is constant, making radioactive dating perfect in determining the age of certain rocks.

chemistry class. For example, it is also important to people who work the soil. All plants need a certain soil pH to grow and flourish, which is why most gardeners and farmers determine the acidity or alkalinity of their soil in order to grow better crops.

What is the **Universal Gas Law**?

The Universal Gas Law (also called the Universal Gas Constant or the Perfect Gas Law), is a chemical law that can also be looked at mathematically. It is represented by the equation $PV = nRT$, in which P is pressure, V is volume, n is the number of moles of gas, R is the gas constant, and T is the temperature in Kelvin.

What are **calories**?

To most people, calories are usually associated with a very large piece of chocolate cake. But in that case, they are called nutritionist's calories, or the unit of energy-producing potential equal to the amount of heat that is contained in food and released upon oxidation by the body. The body needs the calories in the foods we eat to use as energy. This is why nutrition and weight-control texts often contain such entries as "a 140 pound person walking for one hour at a moderate pace burns off 222 calories."

In chemistry, a calorie also refers to a unit of energy. But in terms of chemical experiments, a calorie is the amount of heat required to raise the temperature of 1

gram of water by 1 degree Celsius from a standard initial temperature at a pressure of 1 atmosphere (sea level). The unit measurement for energy is a joule, in which 1 calorie equals 4.184 joules; 1 joule is translated (most often in metric) as the energy needed to lift 2,000 grams a distance of 10 centimeters.

What is the **Boltzmann equation**?

In the late 1860s, British physicist James Clerk Maxwell (1831–1879) and Austrian theoretical physicist Ludwig Edward Boltzmann (1844–1906) developed the Boltzmann equation to predict how a gaseous material distributes itself in space, along with how it responds to various environmental factors, such as temperatures, pressure, or velocity—all combined into what is called the kinetic theory of gases.

For almost 140 years, the equation remained unsolved, but in 2010 researchers found solutions to the 7-dimensional equation using modern mathematical techniques. Overall, they used partial differential equations and harmonic analysis to prove that the equation does have solutions. This not only helps scientists understand the probability of where molecules exist, but also explains how molecules just glance off one another rather than collide head on, apparently a dominant way collisions work for the full equation.

What **other contributions** did Ludwig **Boltzmann** and James **Maxwell** make to science?

Boltzmann and Maxwell's contributions to science didn't stop at the Boltzmann equation. Boltzmann is considered the founder of statistical mechanics. He also developed a statistical interpretation of the second law of thermodynamics.

Maxwell contributed much more to the sciences. For example, he is well known for writing four equations that summarize the relationship between electricity and magnetism, collectively called Maxwell's equations. He also showed mathematically that an oscillating electric and magnetic field would propagate through space at the speed of light—meaning that light was a form of electromagnetic radiation.

ASTRONOMY AND MATH

What are **astronomy** and **astrophysics**?

Astronomy is the study of matter in outer space. It is usually considered a branch of physics. But because it encompasses (literally) an astronomical number of subjects—everything from the study of a star's surface to the end of the universe—it is often considered a field of its own. Astrophysics is a branch of astronomy dealing with the

physics of celestial bodies and the universe as a whole. It deals with problems that range from the structure, distribution, evolution, and interaction of stars and galaxies to the orbital mechanics of a near-Earth asteroid.

Who first **calculated** the **distance** from the **Earth** to the **Sun** and **Moon**?

Around 290 B.C.E., astronomer and mathematician Aristarchus of Samos (c. 310 B.C.E.–c. 230 B.C.E.) used geometric methods to calculate the distances to and sizes of the Moon and Sun. Based on his observations and calculations, he suggested that the Sun was about 20 times as distant from the Earth as the Moon (it is actually 390 times); he also determined that the Moon's radius was 0.5 times the radius of the Earth (it is actually 0.28 times). The numbers differ not because Aristarchus had no geometric knowledge, but because of the poor instruments used at that time.

These calculations were not the only contribution made by Aristarchus. He was also the first to propose that the Earth orbits the Sun—many centuries before Nicolaus Copernicus (see below). This concept was radical for his time, because it conflicted with geocentric religious beliefs and Aristotle's principle that all objects move toward the center of the Earth.

Who was **Hipparchus**?

Hipparchus of Rhodes (also seen as Hipparchus of Nicaea, as he was born there; c. 190–c. 120 B.C.E.) was one of the greatest Greek astronomers. A partial list of his discoveries includes: being the first to discover the precession of the equinoxes, compiling an extensive star catalogue, assigning "magnitudes" as a measure of stellar brightness, and calculating the length of the year to within 6.5 minutes of the correct value. His planetary models were mathematical, not mechanical. And although Hipparchus did not invent it, he was probably the first person to systematically use trigonometry, which was a necessity for most of his discoveries.

What was *De revolutionibus orbium coelestium*?

In the year of his death, astronomer Nicolaus Copernicus (1473–1543; in Polish,

The famous astronomer Nicolaus Copernicus (pictured here) is commonly thought of as the first person to propose a heliocentric (Sun-centered) model of the solar system, but actually Aristarchus surmised the truth centuries before him.

Mikołaj Kopérnik) published *De revolutionibus orbium coelestium* (*On the Revolutions of the Heavenly Spheres*). This manuscript gave a full account of his theory that the Sun, and not the Earth, was at the center of the solar system (or universe). Although this theory was not new, Copernicus offered the idea in all its mathematical detail. This heliocentric (versus geocentric) view of the heavens, now known as the Copernican system, is the foundation of modern astronomy.

What are **Kepler's Laws of Planetary Motion**?

A great deal of mathematics went into the formulation of Kepler's Laws of Planetary Motion. These laws were devised by German astronomer and mathematician (and Danish astronomer Tycho Brahe's [1546–1601] assistant) Johannes Kepler (1571–1630). He presented the first and second laws in his work *Astronomia nova* (*New Astronomy*) in 1609; the third law was published in 1619 in *Harmonice mundi*. The three laws are as follows:

Kepler's first law (or law of elliptic orbits)—Each planet moves about the Sun in an orbit that is an ellipse, with the Sun at one of the two foci of the ellipse.

Kepler's second law (or the law of areas)—An imaginary straight line joining a planet to the Sun will sweep out equal areas of the ellipse in equal periods of time.

Kepler's third law (or the harmonic law)—The square of the period of a planet's revolution is directly proportionate to the cube of the semi-major axis of its orbit.

Halley's Comet, named after Edmond Halley, last appeared near Earth in 1986 and will be seen again in the night sky in 2062.

How did **Pierre-Simon de Laplace** apply mathematics to **astronomy**?

French mathematician, astronomer, and physicist Marquis Pierre-Simon de Laplace (1749–1827) was one of the first to work out the gravitational mechanics of the solar system using mathematics. In his *Mécanique Céleste* (*Celestial Mechanics*), Laplace translated the geometrical study of mechanics used by Isaac Newton to one based on calculus (or physical mechanics). He also proved the stability of the solar system, but only on a short time scale. Laplace is also known for his theory about the formation of the planets. He believed they originated from the same primitive mass of material, a theory now known as Laplace's nebular hypothesis. His other studies included major contributions to differential equations and to the theory of probability.

What are **astronomical units** and **light-years**?

An astronomical unit is one of the more common measurements used in astronomy. It is a distance equal to the average distance from the Earth to the Sun, or 92,960,116 miles (149,597,870 kilometers); it is often seen rounded off to 93,000,000 miles (149,598,770 kilometers) and used in reference to great astronomical distances. For example, the Earth is 1 AU from the Sun; the planet Venus is 0.7 AU; Mars is 1.5 AU; and Saturn is 9.5 AU from the Sun.

A light-year is an even larger unit. As the name implies, it is the distance light travels in one year, or about 5.88 trillion miles (9.46 trillion kilometers). In most cases, light-year measurement is reserved for deep space objects.

What is the **Hubble constant**?

Astronomers have always been interested in the age of our universe and the speed of various objects in space. The Hubble constant was devised by American astronomer

231

Edwin Hubble (1889–1953). It is the ratio of the recessional speed of a galaxy—because the universe is expanding—to its distance from the observer. In other words, the velocity at which a typical galaxy is receding from Earth, divided by its distance from Earth.

The reciprocal of the Hubble constant is then thought to be the age of the universe, usually written in terms of kilometers per second per million light-years. If the number is high, the universe would be very young; if the number is low, the universe would be much more ancient. Although there have been numerous theories, the true age of the universe is usually considered to be somewhere between 12 and 20 billion years old.

The most recent agreed-upon rate at which the universe is expanding is approximately 20 kilometers per second per 106 light-years of distance. That makes the universe about 15 billion years old.

What is the **Titius-Bode Law**?

The Titius-Bode Law was developed by German astronomer Johann Daniel Titius (1729–1796); Titius's idea was brought to the forefront by German astronomer Johann Elert Bode (1747–1826). The law actually represents a simple mathematical rule that allows one to determine the distances (also called the semi-major axis) of the planets in astronomical units. It is determined using the equation $a = 0.4 + (0.3)2^n$, in which n is an integer and a is the astronomical unit. Interestingly enough, most of the planets—and even the asteroids in the Asteroid Belt—adhere to the law. The only exception is Neptune, the second-to-last planet in our solar system.

Distances of the Planets from the Sun in Astronomical Units

Planet	n	Titius-Bode Law*	Actual Semi-Major Axis**
Mercury	$-\infty$	0.4	0.39
Venus	0	0.7	0.72
Earth	1	1	1

Planet	n	Titius-Bode Law*	Actual Semi-Major Axis**
Mars	2	1.6	1.52
asteroid belt	3	2.8	2.8
Jupiter	4	5.2	5.2
Saturn	5	10	9.54
Uranus	6	19.6	19.2
Neptune	—	—	30.1
Pluto***	7	38.8	39.4

* The original formula was $a = (n + 4)/10$, in which $n = 0, 3, 6, 12, 24, 48 \ldots$; a is the mean distance of the planet to the sun.

** This is based on the formula $a = 0.4 + (0.3)2^n$, in which $n = -\infty, 0, 1, 2, 3, 4, 5, 6, 7$. The results can also be found using $a = 0.4 + 3 \times n$, in which $n = 0, 1, 2, 4, 8, 16, 32, 64, 128$. Both formulas are "modern versions" of the Titius-Bode Law.

*** Pluto is no longer considered a planet by modern astronomers, but many people still think of it as one.

How does **geometry** work in terms of **eclipses** of the Sun and Moon?

Eclipses of the Sun (called a solar eclipse, when the Moon is between the Earth and the Sun) and the Moon (called a lunar eclipse, when the Earth is between the Moon and the Sun) are all a matter of angles. For example, in a solar eclipse, the shadow of the Moon follows a narrow path on the Earth, creating a shadow only in certain regions—not the entire planet (the Moon isn't large enough to create a shadow that would cover the Earth). Depending on the angle and distance of the Moon from the Earth in its orbit, a solar eclipse can be an annular (the apparent size of the Moon is insufficient to cover the Sun completely, creating a ring of sunlight around the Moon); partial (the Moon only covers part of the Sun as seen from the Earth); or total (the Moon blocks out the entire face of the Sun in the eclipse path).

What type of **geometric path** does the **Sun** seem to take in the **Earth's sky**?

The Sun's apparent path in the Earth's sky is called an *analemma*, or the measurement of the Sun's declination over the year. In fact, if one recorded the position of the Sun in the sky at the same time every day, the Sun would appear to follow

Neptune is the only planet in our solar system that does not fit the model set by the Titius-Bode Law.

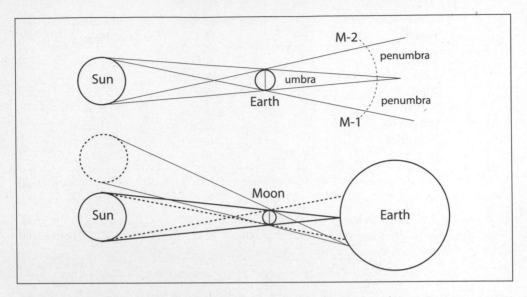

The illustration at the top shows what happens during a lunar eclipse, when the Moon passes through the shadow of the Earth (M-1 to M-2). Below that is what happens during a solar eclipse, when the Moon comes between the Sun and the Earth, casting a shadow on the Earth's surface. A and B points show where a total eclipse would be, and the region between the Cs would experience a partial eclipse.

a figure-eight path, the analemma—a feature often seen on globes of the Earth. Astronomers also use another way to note the path of the Sun: the difference in time between the clock and the position of the Sun (clock versus Sun times) is called the equation of time. For those living in the Northern Hemisphere, if one notes the Sun's position is to the east, the equation of time is negative; if the sun is to the west, the equation of time is positive.

Why does the Sun take such a different path across the sky each year? There are two main reasons: first the Earth's rotational axis (the Earth's rotation creates the day and night) is tilted 23.5 degrees in relation to the plane of its orbit around the Sun. Second, the Earth does not orbit the Sun in a circle, but orbits in an ellipse (oval-shape). Because of the tilt and the orbit, over a year the Sun's path seems to move in a figure-eight. (It's interesting to note here that because of the tilt and orbit of the other planets in the solar system, they, too, have analemmas all their own, which are different from the Earth's.)

What is the **Hertzsprung-Russell diagram**?

The Hertzsprung-Russell diagram is a "two-dimensional" graph of the mathematical relationship between the absolute magnitude, luminosity, stellar classification, and surface temperature of stars—all resulting in a diagram of the stellar life cycle. It was plotted by Danish astronomer Ejnar Hertzsprung (1873–1967) in 1911 and independently by American astronomer Henry Norris Russell (1877–1957) in 1913.

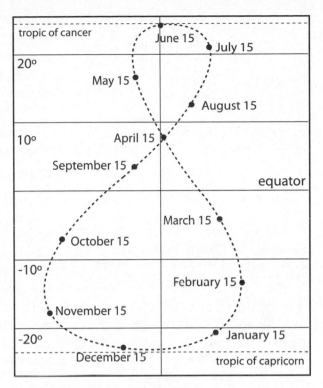

How do **astronomers determine** the **distances** to other **planets**?

Astronomers need mathematics, of course, to determine the distances to the planets and satellites of our solar system. One of the first astronomers to work this out was Nicolaus Copernicus (see above) using simple observations of planetary positions.

One of the earliest methods to determine such distances was to use the orbital period of a planet. This varies as the square root of the cube of the distance from the Sun: $T = k \times r^{(3/2)}$, in which T is the time for one revolution, r is the distance between the centers of the Sun and the planet, and k is a constant.

If you carefully chart the position of the Sun at the same time of day over the course of a year, at the mid-latitudes you will see that it appears to follow a figure eight pattern in the sky.

How do **astronomers** determine the **distances to the stars**?

Relatively nearby objects beyond the solar system appear to shift position relative to more distant objects as the Earth moves from one side of the Sun to the other—a phenomenon called *parallax*. You can use parallax to determine the distance to stars, as long as these stellar objects are within a few dozen light-years of Earth. (More distant objects in the sky do not change their position enough as the Earth orbits from one side of the Sun to the other.) First, measure the position of the star in the sky; then, measure it again in six months when the Earth is on the opposite side of its orbit. If the distance *a* and the angle *ac* are known (as seen in the diagram below), using trigonometry, *c* can be determined as *a* / cos (*ac*).

Is it easy to figure out the **size of a distant object**?

Yes, it is often possible to figure out the size of distant objects, as long as they aren't too small. The key is in knowing the distance to the object. For example, if someone holds a nickel at arm's length and then has someone hold the nickel 200 yards away, the coin may appear to be smaller, but its size really hasn't changed. If a person knows

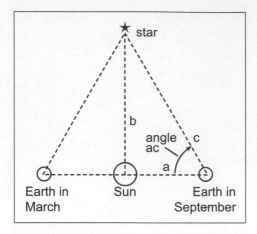

Using parallax to determine the distance to a star is done by calculating the apparent shift of a star as the Earth orbits the Sun.

how large an object appears to be, and how distant it is, they can work backward to determine the true size of the object. Simply put, this is also how astronomers work out the size of distant objects in outer space.

What "mathematical measurement" error once occurred when a spacecraft reached Mars?

The Mars Climate Orbiter spacecraft, a joint effort between Lockheed Martin and NASA's Jet Propulsion Laboratory (JPL), was supposed to go into orbit around the red planet on September 23, 1999. Instead, the Martian craft lost all contact with Earth. After much deliberation, a review panel for the incident came to a disconcerting conclusion: A thruster error developed when project teams used different measuring systems for the navigation commands—NASA used metric units; Lockheed Martin used English standard units, and no one caught the discrepancy.

To this day, scientists can only speculate as to what happened to the orbiter, a craft sent to study the climate and weather patterns of the Martian atmosphere. Some say that because the orbiter dropped down to within 36 miles (60 kilometers) of the planet—about 62 miles (100 kilometers) closer than planned—atmospheric friction probably overheated the propulsion system and tore the vehicle apart. Others believe the craft was propelled through the atmosphere (or bounced off) and out into space again and is now perhaps circling the Sun like an artificial asteroid or comet.

How was math used to discover extrasolar planets?

Astronomers have always dreamed about detecting other planets outside our solar system—extrasolar planets. In 1994, Polish astronomer Alekzander Wolszczan (1946–) announced the discovery of the first extrasolar planet—actually, two planets with masses 3.4 and 2.8 times that of Earth's mass—orbiting the pulsar PSR B1257+12. A pulsar star sends out a periodic pulse of light detected from Earth; Wolszczan found the planets by measuring the periodic variation in the pulse arrival time.

There are several major methods used to search for extrasolar planets, and all entail using mathematics. For example, the Doppler shift method measures the change in wavelength (color) of light coming from a star over the course of days, months, and years. The change in wavelength—or the Doppler shift of the light—is caused by the star orbiting a common center of mass with a companion planet. An example in our

own solar system is the gas giant Jupiter. Its massive gravitational pull causes the Sun to wobble around a circle with a velocity of 39.4 feet (12 meters) per second.

Another detection method is called astrometry, which measures the periodic wobble that a planet causes in the position of its parent star. In this case, the minimum detectable planet mass gets smaller in inverse proportion to the planet's distance from the star.

These methods work, and as of 2011 more than 700 such planets have been discovered. If you want to see an updated list of the extrasolar planets, try http://exoplanet .eu/catalog.php maintained by astronomers at the Paris Observatory in France.

MATH IN THE NATURAL SCIENCES

MATH IN GEOLOGY

What is **geology**?

The word "geology" comes from the Greek *geo,* meaning "the Earth," and the *ology* suffix comes from *logos,* meaning "discussion." Overall, geology is considered to be the study of the Earth. In modern times, thanks to space probes reaching into the solar system, geology also now entails the surface features on other planets and satellites.

Who first made some of the **first accurate measurements** of **Earth**?

Hellenic geographer, librarian, and astronomer Eratosthenes of Cyrene (276–194 B.C.E.) made several accurate measurements of the Earth, which is why he is often known as the "father of geodesy" (the science of Earth measurement). Although he was not the very first to deduce the Earth's circumference, Eratosthenes is thought by most historians to be the first to accurately measure it.

Eratosthenes knew the Sun's light at noon reached the bottom of a well in Syene (now Aswan on the Nile in Egypt) on the summer solstice (which meant the Sun was directly overhead). Thanks to a helper, he compared it to a well's shadow at the same time in Alexandria. He determined that the zenith distance—or the angle from the zenith (point directly overhead) to the point where the Sun was at noon—was 0 degrees at Syene, and at Alexandria it was about 7 degrees. By measuring these angles and the distance between the two cities, Eratosthenes used geometry to deduce that the Earth's circumference was 250,000 stadia. The number was later revised to 252,000 stadia, or 25,054 miles (40,320 kilometers).

The actual circumference of the planet is 24,857 miles (40,009 kilometers) around the poles and 24,900 miles (40,079 kilometers) around the equator, because the Earth

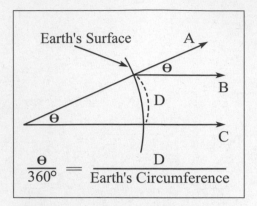

$$\frac{\theta}{360°} = \frac{D}{\text{Earth's Circumference}}$$

Eratosthenes brilliantly used his knowledge of angles and mathematics to be the first to determine the Earth's circumference accurately.

is not completely round. From his data Eratosthenes also determined another accurate measurement: the Earth's diameter. He deduced the Earth was 7,850 miles (12,631 kilometers) in diameter, which is close to the modern mean value of 7,918 miles (12,740 kilometers).

What is the difference between the Earth's sidereal and solar days?

The difference between the Earth's sidereal and solar days has to do with angles and the Earth's rotation. The mean solar day is equal to 24 hours, or the average of all the solar days in an orbital year. The mean sidereal day is 23 hours, 56 minutes, and 04.09053 seconds. It is not exactly equal to a solar day because by the time the Earth has rotated once, it has moved a little in its orbit around the Sun. Thus, it rotates for about another four minutes before the Sun is considered to be back in exactly the same place in the sky as it was the day before.

How do scientists measure the Earth's rotational speed?

The Earth's rotational speed is based on the sidereal period of the Earth's rotation, but it differs depending on where the observer is located. By dividing the distance traveled once around the Earth by the time it takes to travel that distance, the speed can be determined.

For example, a person on the Earth's equator will travel once around the Earth's circumference—or 24,900 miles (40,079 kilometers)—in one day. To get the speed, divide the miles by the time it takes to get back to the same place (around 24 hours), or just over 1,000 miles (1,609 kilometers) per hour. A person at one of the poles is hardly moving at any speed. This is because there is so little distance traveled in a day (a stick stuck vertically in the ice exactly at the North or South Pole will only travel about 0.394 inch [1 centimeter] per day.)

What about other places on Earth? Traveling north or south from the equator toward the poles decreases one's tangential rotational speed. Thus, the rotational speed at any point on the Earth can be calculated by multiplying the speed at the equator by the cosine of the point's latitude.

What is the geologic time scale?

The geologic time scale is a way of managing large amounts of time in a convenient chart. The scale is actually a measurement encompassing the entire history of the

What natural phenomena can change the Earth's rotational speed?

In general, the length of a normal Earth day is about 86,400 seconds; over the course of a year, the length varies by 1 millisecond, or 1,000 microseconds, because of a redistribution in the planet's mass. This is because Earth's rotation is not always consistent from year to year or even season to season. Scientists know there are other factors in the rotational equation, including the differences caused by widespread climatic conditions or natural events—and all of them are determined using geometry and mathematics.

For example, during El Niño years (the periodic upwelling of warmer waters around the equator in the Pacific Ocean off South America), the "drag" of the ocean water welling up can slow down the Earth's rotation. It happened between El Niño years 1982 and 1983, when Earth's rotation slowed by 1/5,000th of a second, prolonging the day.

Even a giant earthquake can speed up the planet's rotation by redistributing the Earth's mass. For example, on March 11, 2011, the 8.9-magnitude earthquake that struck northeast Japan shortened the length of Earth's day by 1.6 microseconds; the 2010 quake measuring magnitude 8.8 in Chile shortened it by 1.26 microseconds; and a 9.1-magnitude quake in 2004 that struck off Sumatra sped up the planet's rotation, shortening the day by 6.8 microseconds.

Earth—from its beginnings some 4.55 billion years ago to the present day. The largest divisions include eons, eras, and periods; the smaller time divisions include epochs, ages, and subages.

The actual divisions of geologic time are not arbitrary, or uniform. The larger divisions are based on major events that occurred sporadically over the Earth's long history. For example, the end of the Permian Period, about 240 million years ago, was marked by a major catastrophe. Some scientists estimate that close to 90 percent of all species on the Earth died at that time, resulting in a major extinction event that may have been caused by huge volcanic eruptions or even a space object striking the Earth. The smaller divisions are usually based on specific local structures or fossils found within the rock. Most often they are named after local towns, people, and sundry other nearby associations.

What is the **longest span of time** measured on the **geologic time scale**?

The longest span of time measured on the geologic time scale is the Precambrian Era (also called the Precambrian Eon). It represents the time between 4.55 billion years to about 544 million years ago, or about seven-eighths of the Earth's history. This time period includes the beginning of the Earth's formation, its cool-down, its crust's for-

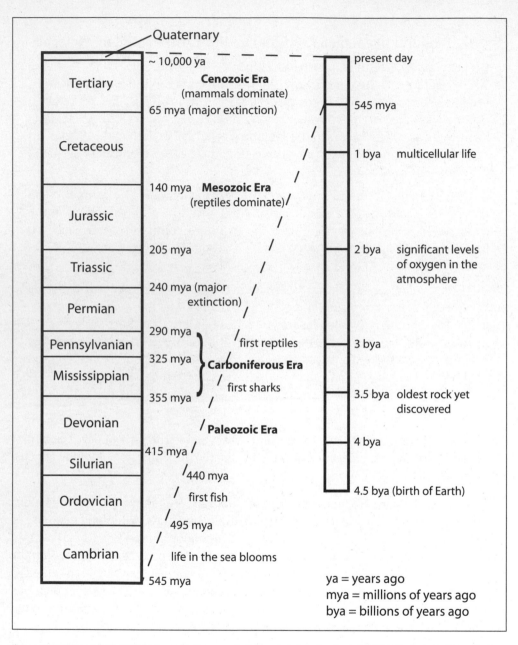

The geologic time scale is divided into epochs, ages, and other periods based on important historical events that radically changed life on Earth.

mation, and, within the last billion years of the time period, the evolution of the first single-celled to multi-celled organisms. The demarcation of 544 million years ago represents a burst in the evolution of multi-celled organisms, including the first plant and animal species.

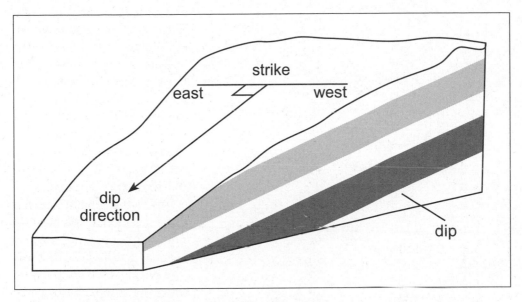

A "dip" is the angle at which a layer of rock or vein is inclined, while a "strike" is the angle made between the direction of true north and the direction of the planar feature, such as an incline or fault.

How do **geologists use angles** to understand **rock layers**?

Mathematics—especially geometry—is instrumental in understanding rock layers. In a branch of geology called stratigraphy, scientists measure angles and planes in rock in order to know the location of certain rock layers and the possible geologic events that affected the layers over time. In particular, geologists measure strike and dip. *Strike* is the angle between true north and a horizontal line contained in any planar feature, such as a fault (usually caused by an earthquake) or inclined bed (often caused by the uplift of hot molten rock around a volcano). *Dip* is the angle at which a bed or rock vein is inclined to the horizontal; it is measured perpendicular to the strike and in the vertical plane (as opposed to the strike's horizontal line).

How are the **shapes of crystals** classified?

Geometry plays an important part in the study of minerals. This is because certain minerals exhibit specific shapes called crystals, with specific crystalline forms occurring when a mineral's atoms join in a particular pattern or internal structure. This arrangement is determined by several factors, including the chemistry and structure of the mineral's atoms, or even the environment in which the crystal grew.

Overall, there are specific angles between corresponding faces of all crystals. Mineralogists (scientists who study minerals) divide these crystalline forms into 32 geometric

243

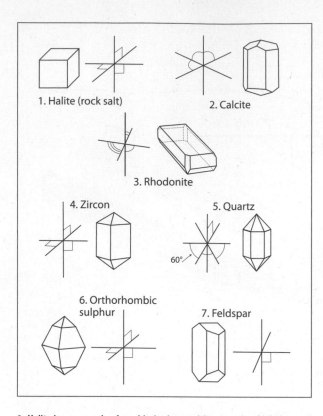

1. Halite (rock salt)
2. Calcite
3. Rhodonite
4. Zircon
5. Quartz
60°
6. Orthorhombic sulphur
7. Feldspar

1. Halite is an example of a cubic (or isometric) system in which three equal axes are all at right angles. 2. Calcite is formed with a trigonal (or hombohedral) crystal system in which the three axes are set obliquely at equal angles to each other. 3. Rhodonite is a crystal formed by a triclinic system in which the three axes are unequal and set obliquely at unequal angles. 4. In a tetragonal system minerals such as zircon are formed by crystals with three axes, all at right angles, in which one axis is longer than the other two. 5. Quartz is an example of a hexagonal system in which three axes at 60° angles to each other are positioned around a vertical axis that can be longer or shorter than the other three. 6. In an orthorhombic system (such as orthorhombic sulfur) the three axes are of unequal length and set at right angles to each other. 7. Finally, with a monoclinic system, two of three axes are at right angles with the third set obliquely, such as in the example of feldspar.

classes of symmetry; they use this information to identify and classify certain minerals. The crystals are also subdivided into seven systems on the basis of an imaginary straight line that passes through a crystal's center (or axis). The seven groups include cubic (or isometric), tetragonal, orthorhombic, monoclinic, triclinic, hexagonal, and trigonal (or rhombohedral). For example, a crystal in the cubic system has three axes that intersect at right angles; the axes are also of equal lengths. The best way to envision this crystal is to think of a box with equal sides—or a cube.

What is a **carat**?

A carat is a unit of measurement representing the weight of precious stones, pearls, and certain metals (such as gold). It was originally a unit of mass based on the carob seed or bean used by ancient merchants in the Middle East. In terms of weight measurement, a carat equals three and one-fifth grains troy, and it is also divided into four grains (sometimes referred to as carat grains). Diamonds and other precious stones are estimated by carats and fractions of carats; pearls are usually measured by carat grains.

Carats of gold are measured based on the number of twenty-fourths of pure gold. For example, 24-carat gold is pure gold (but for a goldsmith's standard, it is actually 22 parts gold, 1 part copper, and 1 part silver, as real gold is too malleable to hold its shape), 18-carat gold is 75 percent pure, 14-carat gold is 58.33 percent pure, and 10-carat gold is 41.67 percent pure gold.

What is Mohs' Scale of hardness?

Mohs' Scale of hardness (also seen as Mohs Hardness Scale, Mohs Scale, or even erroneously as Moh's Scale) was invented by German mineralogist Friedrich Mohs (1773–1839). This arbitrary scale measures hardness or the scratch resistance of minerals and is often used as a quick way to help identify minerals in the field and laboratory. But the numbers assigned to the various minerals are not proportional to their actual scratch resistance. Thus, the main reason for using the scale is to know that a mineral with a lower number can be scratched by a mineral with a higher number.

Mineral	Hardness
talc	1
gypsum	2
calcite	3
fluorite	4
apatite	5
orthoclase	6
quartz	7
topaz	8
corundum	9
diamond	10

How is **modeling and simulation** used in **geology**?

Like so many other fields of science, mathematical modeling and simulation is used in geology to understand the intricacies of physical events in the past, present, and future. For example, hydrologists (geologists who study water flow above and below the Earth's surface) often use models to simulate the effects of increased groundwater pumping of wells. They may also use a simulation to determine how much water can be presently pumped out of a well, or how much can be pumped out in the future without harm to the environment. Other hydrologists may use modeling to understand the flow of water in a river, bay, or estuary, for example, to determine how the water erodes a shoreline. Still other researchers may model how snow on a volcanic mountain melts, gathers debris, and potentially flows toward populated areas during an eruption event. (For more about modeling and simulation, see "Math in Computing.")

How do geologists **measure** the **intensity of earthquakes**?

Geologists measure the intensity of earthquakes in order to compare and judge potential damage. One of the first standard ways to measure intensity was developed in 1902

A devastating tsunami struck Indonesia in 2004. Scientists are using mathematics to study tsunamis and develop a more effective advance-warning system that could save lives.

by Italian seismologist Giuseppe Mercalli (1850–1914) and is called the Mercalli Intensity Scale (it was later modified and renamed the Modified Mercalli Intensity Scale). The numbers, in Roman numerals from I to XII, represent the subjective measurement of an earthquake's strength based on its effects on local populations and structures. For example, Roman numeral V on the scale represents a quake felt by nearly everyone, with some dishes and windows broken, unstable objects overturned, and disturbances of trees, poles, and other tall objects sometimes noticed.

But scientists wanted a more solid, less subjective scale. One of the first scales developed to measure the true magnitude was invented by American seismologist Charles Francis Richter (1900–1985) and German-born seismologist Beno Gutenberg (1889–1960). In 1935 these scientists borrowed the idea of magnitude from astronomers (stellar brightness is measured by magnitude), defining earthquake magnitude as how fast the ground moved as measured on a particular seismograph a specific distance from the quake's epicenter.

The Richter Scale is not a physical scale like a ruler, but rather a mathematical construct—it is not linear, but logarithmic. Thus, an increase in each whole number on the scale represents a ten-fold increase in power. Its numbers represent the maximum amplitude of seismic waves that occur 62 miles (100 kilometers) from the epicenter of an earthquake. Because seismographs are usually not located at this exact interval, the magnitudes are deduced using the arrival of specific waves of energy given off when an earthquake occurs.

How does mathematics help scientists understand tsunamis?

Depending on where it occurs, a powerful earthquake in the oceans can shift rock, displacing the water above and generating seismic oceanic waves called tsunamis. Erroneously called "tidal waves" (they do not form by tidal action), tsunamis are long surface waves—often expressed as "like dropping a pebble in a pond"—that can attain tens of feet in height once they reach a shoreline. They happen mostly in the Pacific and Indian Oceans, and more rarely in the Atlantic. Because of the Pacific's propensity toward tsunamis, there are several warning systems in effect; once an earthquake is detected, a network of early warning stations (with automatic sensors) send out signals that a tsunami may be imminent. If the warning is in time, coastal residents in the tsunami's path may be able to escape to higher ground.

Mathematicians are also trying to help understand the physics and processes of tsunamis, mainly because the landforms, coastlines, and depth of the ocean basins differ. For example, in one study to try and understand the mathematics of the deadly waves that occurred in the 2004 Indian Ocean tsunami, mathematical models have show that the waves were a "classic wave packet," or the wave behaved in a way that is close to that predicted by mathematical theory—waves traveling together as well as evolving in form as they cross the ocean. Mathematics also showed that, contrary to popular belief, the first tsunami to strike a shoreline is often not the largest; for example, in the Indian tsunami, the third and fourth waves were the larger than the first and second.

Another mathematical model developed in 2010 finds the best spots to install tsunami detection buoys and sea-level monitors in the Indian Ocean, and it can also be used for the less-tsunami-prone areas of the Atlantic Ocean, Mediterranean, Caribbean, and Black Seas. Yet another study used a mathematical model to show that the number and height of the waves hitting the shore depends on the shape of the initial surface wave in deep water.

Although the Richter Scale is mentioned most often in the media when a quake occurs, there is a more precise scale in use today that is based on the mathematics of motions caused by the earthquake. Called *moment magnitude,* this method uses a physical quantity related to the total energy released in the quake, which is called a moment. Seismologists can also deduce moment magnitude from a fault's geometry in the field or a seismogram reading. Scientists occasionally use moment magnitude when describing an earthquake event to the public, but because the concept is so difficult to explain the number is often translated into the Richter Scale.

247

What is **sea level**?

Sea level is the height of the ocean's surface at a certain spot and depends on changing conditions. It is also the basis for most Earth surface measurements, because sea levels are used as a reference point in determining land elevations and ocean depths.

Scientists have averaged out the highest and lowest altitudes and depths from sea level locations: The highest is Mount Everest (Nepal-Tibet), which has been measured at 29,022 feet, 7 inches (8,846 meters) above sea level, although China and Nepal have their own numbers, both agreeing on 29,029 feet (8,848 meters) above sea level. (The differences are because no one knows where to measure the height from—the ground or snow height; it may eventually be a moot point, since the ice melts and the ground is rising as the Indian continent is being pushed beneath China and Nepal.) The lowest point on land is the Dead Sea (Israel-Jordan), which measures 1,299 feet (396 meters) below sea level. The greatest depth *below* sea level is the Mariana Trench in the Pacific Ocean—a deep chasm measuring 36,201 feet (11,033 meters) below sea level.

What is **mean sea level**?

Mean sea level (MSL) is the average water level (height of the sea) for all stages of a tide. Locally, MSL is measured by tidal gages at one or more points over a given period of time. The resulting numbers average out wind waves and other periodic changes in sea level. The overall values of a MSL are measured with respect to level marks on land called benchmarks. Thus, scientists know a true change in MSL is either from a change in sea level from, for example, possible global warming effects, or changes in the gage's height on land, such as in the case of local uplift.

There is also a more mathematically intensive way to determine the MSL. To a geodesist (a person who studies the shape of the Earth), MSL is determined by comparing measured heights of the global Mean Sea Surface (MSS) above a level reference surface called a geoid—a mathematical model of an ellipsoid shape that approximates Earth's mean sea level. This comparison is done because the Earth does not have a geometrically perfect shape (for example, the Atlantic Ocean north of the Gulf Stream is about 3.3 feet (1 meter) lower than it is farther south). The MSS is not a "level" surface, thanks to such factors as currents created by wind, as well as atmospheric cooling and heating that cause differences in sea levels around the world. But interestingly enough, it never differs from the global geoid by more than about 6.56 feet (2 meters).

How do scientists use **mean sea level** in connection with **global climate change**?

Many scientists are interested in the long-term mean sea level change, especially in connection with global climate change. By taking such long-term measurements, these scientists are hoping to confirm the predictions of several climate models,

Mt. Everest (right peak, with Mt. Nuptse at left) in Nepal, rising to a height of 29,022 feet, is the tallest mountain on Earth when measuring height compared to sea level.

including the idea that global warming is a result of the "greenhouse" gases from either human or natural sources.

There are two major ways to determine such sea level variations. The first estimates sea level changes using tide gauge measurements, mathematically averaging the numbers. Graphs of the most recent estimates using this method show a 0.669 to 0.960 inch (1.7 to 2.44 millimeter) rise in sea level per year. The second method uses global positioning system (GPS) devices and satellite altimeter measurements, both of which accurately pinpoint global ocean heights quickly and more efficiently. For example, from 1994 to 2004, scientists mathematically constructed graphs from satellite altimeter measurements, showing that the global mean sea levels have risen anywhere between 1.10 and 1.18 inches (2.8 and 3.0 millimeters).

No matter what the method, scientists do know the global mean sea levels are slowly rising. Many believe that about one quarter of the rise is caused by thermal expansion as the oceans warm, and another one quarter by small glaciers melting around the world. Some rise may also be caused by such human activities as burning trees, pumping ground water, and draining wetlands. Currently, scientists are not quite certain about the true rate of sea level rise, mainly because of the intensity of working on the data: Ocean-tide gauge records must be averaged, over many decades, and corrected for variable ocean dynamics and distortions of Earth's crust.

MATH IN METEOROLOGY

What is **meteorology**?

Meteorology is the study of atmospheric phenomena, their interactions, and process-es. It is often considered part of the Earth sciences and is most commonly associated with weather and weather forecasting.

What is the **composition** of the **air**?

Meteorologists determine the composition of air by analyzing its various constituents; these are mainly displayed in terms of percent of the atmosphere. The first 40 to 50 miles (64 to 80 kilometers) above the surface contains 99 percent of the total mass of the Earth's atmosphere. It is generally uniform in composition, except for a high concentration of ozone, known as the ozone layer, at 12 to 30 miles (19 to 50 kilometers) in altitude.

In the lowest part of the atmosphere—the area in which humans, other animals, and plants live—the most common gases are nitrogen (78.09 percent), oxygen (20.95 percent), argon (0.93 percent), carbon dioxide (0.03 percent), and minute traces of such gases as neon, helium, methane, krypton, hydrogen, xenon, and ozone. Water vapor is also present in the lower atmosphere, although variable and at a very low per-cent. Higher in the atmosphere, the composition and percentages change as the atmosphere thins. (For more about percents, see "Math Basics.")

How is **air temperature measured**?

Simply put, there are two ways to look at air temperature: On the micro-scale, it is the small scale measure of gas molecules' average kinetic energy; on a larger scale, it is the action of the atmospheric gases as a whole. In physics, an entire branch is devoted to objects' temperatures and the transfer of heat between objects of differing temperatures. Called thermodynamics, it is a study that entails a great deal of mathematical knowledge.

No matter what the type of temperature discussed, the most common apparatus for measurement is the thermometer. The most familiar thermometers are thin, long, closed glass tubes containing some type of liquid—most often alcohol or mercury. When the temperature increases—or the air around the tube heats up—it causes the liquid to expand, moving it up the tube. Air temperature measurements are most commonly read in Celsius or Fahrenheit.

How are **snowflakes defined** using mathematics?

Thanks to some mathematical research in 2009, the symmetrical details of snowflakes has been revealed. Mathematicians have managed to build "snowflakes" using an elab-orate computer model designed to replicate the complex growth of the flakes in three

> ## Why do weather reports sometimes say the humidity is 100 percent when there is no rain or snow falling?
>
> A reading of 100 percent humidity usually means there is a high probability that rain will be or is occurring, but not always. It might be 100 percent RH because clouds are forming. If the RH near the ground is much less—for example, if a relatively dry air mass is in place—there will be no rain at the surface. This is why Doppler radar sometimes shows rain or snow in an area when none is actually reaching the ground.

dimensions. In reality, a snowflake begins when a piece of dust, pollution particles, or even bacteria are surrounded by water; the water freezes to form a small crystal of ice. Dictated by the temperature, local conditions, and humidity, the flakes form, each one containing around one million million million (quintillion) molecules. The results show the minute details seen in snowflakes, including long needles, dendritic-tendrils, and star-like features, based on theory and computations of the mathematical model. The researchers hope that this model will help meteorologists understand how the various snowflakes not only form in the clouds, but also how the flakes affect the amount of water reaching the Earth's surface.

How are **absolute** and **relative humidity** determined?

Like many other facets of meteorology, mathematics comes in handy when determining absolute and relative humidities. The absolute humidity is the mass of water vapor divided by the mass of dry air in a specific volume of air at a specific temperature. In this instance, the warmer the air, the more water vapor it contains.

On the other hand, relative humidity (RH) is the ratio of the absolute humidity to the highest possible absolute humidity, which in turn depends on the current air temperature. Mathematically, RH is often defined as the ratio of the water vapor density (mass per unit volume) to the saturation water vapor density, usually expressed as a percent. The equation for relative humidity is: RH = actual water vapor density / vapor saturation density × 100 percent.

More commonly, RH is thought of as the amount of water vapor in the air at a given temperature in comparison to the amount that the air *could* contain at the same temperature. For example, if an area is experiencing 100 percent relative humidity, that usually means the air is saturated with (can't hold anymore) water vapor.

What is the **heat index**?

Our bodies dissipate heat by varying the rate of blood circulation, losing water through the skin and sweat glands—and, as a last resort, by panting—when the blood

is heated above 98.6 degrees Fahrenheit (37 degrees Celsius), the average body temperature. Sweating cools the body through evaporation. You can get the same feeling when you put alcohol on your skin, because as the alcohol evaporates, the skin is cooled.

The Heat Index (HI) is an index that combines air temperature and relative humidity to estimate how hot it actually feels. It is based on a mathematical concept called the heat index equation, a long equation that includes the dry air temperature, relative humidity (in percent form), and many biometeorological factors too long to list here. The resulting heat index table represents the apparent, or "feels like," temperature. For example, if the air temperature is 90 degrees Fahrenheit, with the relative humidity at 60 percent, it will feel like 100 degrees Fahrenheit.

Why do meteorologists want people to pay attention to the heat index? The major reason involves how the body responds to high heat-value numbers: If the relative humidity is high, it curtails evaporation on the skin, and the body is unable to effectively cool itself (and a person will perceive that the air is warmer). When heat index values grow higher, conditions exceed the level a body can remove heat, causing the body temperature to rise. This can cause heat-related illnesses, such as sunstroke or heat exhaustion. For example, according to the United States National Weather Service, exposure to direct sunlight can increase the HI by up to 15 degrees Fahrenheit (9.4 degrees Celsius). And when a heat index between a mere 90 degrees Fahrenheit (32.2 degrees Celsius) to 105 degrees Fahrenheit (40.6 degrees Celsius) can cause possible sunstroke, heat exhaustion, and heat cramps, it is easy to see the meteorologists' concerns.

The following table shows how the heat we actually experience changes with temperature and humidity (humidity is expressed as a percentage; temperatures are in degrees Fahrenheit).

The Heat Index

Actual °F	90%	80%	70%	60%	50%	40%
80°F	85°F	84°F	82°F	81°F	80°F	79°F
85°F	101°F	96°F	92°F	90°F	86°F	84°F
90°F	121°F	113°F	105°F	99°F	94°F	90°F
95°F		133°F	122°F	113°F	105°F	98°F
100°F			142°F	129°F	118°F	109°F
105°F				148°F	133°F	121°F
110°F						135°F

According to the National Weather Service, sunstroke, heat cramps, and heat exhaustion are possible above 90 degrees Fahrenheit; temperatures above 105 degrees can also lead to heat stroke; and above 130 degrees heat stroke is likely if exposure to such temperatures is prolonged.

How is **barometric** (or air) **pressure measured**?

Barometric (or air) pressure, named after the instrument used to measure this pressure, is caused by the weight of the atmosphere pressing down on the land, ocean, and air below, with gravity creating the downward force. Because pressure is dependent on the amount of air above a certain point, pressures are greatest at the surface and less at higher altitudes. On the average, at sea level, the air has a pressure of 14.7 pounds per square inch (a one-inch square has 14.7 pounds of air pressure on each side).

The United States National Weather Service does not measure pressure in pounds per square inch, but in terms of inches of mercury—or how high the pressure pushes mercury in a sealed tube.

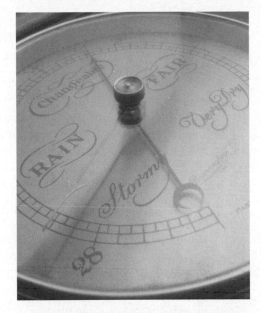

A barometer is a type of gauge that measures atmospheric pressure, which makes it useful in detecting high and low pressure systems that can predict changes in the weather.

Air pressure aloft is reported in millibars (or hectopascals [hPa], a term most often used by scientists to measure air pressure).

Most of us are very familiar with air pressure as it changes with the weather. For example, the use of the terms "high pressure system" and "low pressure system" are often indicators of the types of weather fronts traveling through a region. In general, falling air pressure (seen on a barometer) means that clouds and precipitation are more likely; rising air pressure means that clear weather is more likely. In addition, many people experience "personal" changes in air pressure. For example, the discomfort or even pain felt in a person's ears as they ascend or descend in an airplane, a large hill, or even in an elevator is evidence of changing air pressure.

How are **millibars converted** to **inches of mercury**?

Mathematically, the conversion is simple. The air pressure at sea level is 29.92 inches of mercury, or 1,013.2 millibars. For example, if you see air pressure of 1,016 millibars on a weather map, convert to inches of mercury by multiplying by 29.92, and then divide by 1,013.2. The result is 30.00 inches of mercury.

How much does **air pressure decrease** with **altitude**?

It takes mathematics to figure out how much air pressure decreases with altitude. Close to the surface, and due to the pull of gravity, the air pressure exerted by air mol-

ecules is greatest (around 1,000 millibars at sea level). From there, it declines quickly with altitude to 500 millibars at around 18,000 feet (5,500 meters). At 40 miles (64.37 kilometers), it will be 1/10,000th of the surface air pressure.

This can also be interpreted another way: For altitudes of less than about 3,000 feet (914.4 meters), the barometric air pressure decreases about 0.01 inches of mercury for each 10 feet (3 meters) of altitude (or a decrease of 1 inch of mercury for each 1,000 foot [304.8 meters] gain in altitude). If millibars are used, it is 1 millibar for every 26.25 foot (8 meter) altitude gain. That means if a person takes a ride in an elevator, hits the button for the 50th floor—and coincidentally has a barometer in his or her pocket—the pressure would fall by approximately 0.5 inch (1.27 centimeters) during the ascent. This also means that higher-altitude cities have major differences in barometric readings. For example, the air pressure in almost mile-high Denver, Colorado, is only 85 percent that of cities that reside at sea level.

How is **wind measured**?

Wind speed is the measurable motion of air with respect to the surface of the Earth. It is measured in terms of a unit distance over a unit time, such as miles per hour. The wind direction is also an indication of the wind's source. For example, a southerly wind means the wind is blowing toward north—it is coming from a southerly direction.

What is the **new formula** used for calculating **wind chill**?

Most people know about wind chill: the temperature your body feels when it is exposed to a certain air temperature combined with a particular wind speed. The higher the wind speed, the "colder" the wind chill temperature and the faster the exposed areas of a person's body will lose heat (a process known as transpo-evaporation; when moisture evaporates, the surface from which it evaporates loses some heat).

The newest wind chill chart—called the Wind Chill Temperature Index—took over from the old chart (developed in 1945) in the 2001–2002 winter season. The reason for the change was simple: The original wind chill index revolved around heat loss, with a standard set at the chill experienced while standing outside in air moving 4 miles (2 kilometers) per hour. Based purely on temperature and wind—and on how water freezes in plastic containers—the charts were developed in Antarctica by Paul Siple and his fellow explorer, P. F. Passel, back in 1939, partly with the intention of being used in World War II battlefield planning.

Not everyone was thrilled with this simplistic, two-factor interpretation, however. There were pieces missing from the wind chill puzzle, such as the fact that humans constantly generate heat to the lack of wind measurements above 40 and below 5 miles per hour (64 and 5 kilometers per hour). Passel and Siple's wind speeds were also taken about 33 feet (10 meters) above the ground, making the chart more valuable for a

How is air density related to air pressure?

The expression "thin air" is actually a reference to the atmosphere's density—or how "thick" the air molecules are near the Earth's surface. In chemistry terms, density is merely the mass of anything (including air) divided by the volume the mass occupies. For example, the density of dry air at sea level is high, mainly due to the pull of gravity. In metric system terms, sea level density is about 1.2929 kilograms/meter3, or about 1/800th the density of water. But as altitude increases, the density drops dramatically. Mathematically speaking, the density of air is proportional to the air pressure and inversely proportional to temperature. Thus, the higher up one is in the atmosphere, the lower the air pressure and the lower the air density.

There is somewhat of an athletic advantage to higher elevations—at least for players of such sports as football and baseball. Because the air density is lower, a ball thrown in high-elevation places like Denver, Colorado, will travel even farther than a ball thrown in a close-to-sea-level city, such as Miami, Florida. In fact, the air at the Denver stadium allows balls to travel almost 10 percent farther.

third-floor office than ground level. But the biggest problem overall was that the old wind chill chart could not accurately predict how humans perceive temperature.

Thus, the new wind chill index was created. This chart includes such changes as wind speeds calculated at the average height of a human head (about 5 feet [1.52 meters] above the ground); it is based on a human face model and sundry other more "modern" considerations. The actual general formula for the wind chill has now changed to the following: Wind chill in degrees Fahrenheit = 35.74 + 0.6215T − 35.75($V^{0.16}$) + 0.4275($V^{0.16}$), in which T is the air temperature (in degrees Fahrenheit), and V is the wind speed (in miles per hour).

The biggest difference between the old and new indexes is that the new index usually registers warmer temperatures than the old index. Still, no matter what the equation or chart, when temperatures are icy cold and winds are high, everyone should be careful and bundle up.

What are the **major scales** used in interpreting **hurricanes and tornadoes**?

There are two major scales used to interpret hurricane and tornado intensity—and thus potential damage. The *Saffir-Simpson Hurricane Damage-Potential Scale* is a hurricane force scale using the numbers 1 through 5 to rate a hurricane's intensity. The scale was developed by engineer Herbert Saffir (1917–2007) and pioneer hurricane expert Robert Simpson (1912–) in 1971. A number on the scale is assigned to a

Calculating the Wind Chill

Wind (mph)	Temperature (°F)																	
	40	35	30	25	20	15	10	5	0	−5	−10	−15	−20	−25	−30	−35	−40	−45
0	40	35	30	25	20	15	10	5	0	−5	−10	−15	−20	−25	−30	−35	−40	−45
5	36	31	25	19	13	7	1	−5	−11	−16	−22	−28	−34	−40	−46	−52	−57	−63
10	34	27	21	15	9	3	−4	−10	−16	−22	−28	−35	−41	−47	−53	−59	−66	−72
15	32	25	19	13	6	0	−7	−13	−19	−26	−32	−39	−45	−51	−58	−64	−71	−77
20	30	24	17	11	4	−2	−9	−15	−22	−29	−35	−42	−48	−55	−61	−68	−74	−81
25	29	23	16	9	3	−4	−11	−17	−24	−31	−37	−44	−51	−58	−64	−71	−78	−84
30	28	22	15	8	1	−5	−12	−19	−26	−33	−39	−46	−53	−60	−67	−73	−80	−87
35	28	21	14	7	0	−7	−14	−21	−27	−34	−41	−48	−55	−62	−69	−76	−82	−89
40	27	20	13	6	−1	−8	−15	−22	−29	−36	−43	−50	−57	−64	−71	−78	−84	−91
45	26	19	12	5	−2	−9	−16	−23	−30	−37	−44	−51	−58	−65	−72	−79	−86	−93
50	26	19	12	4	−3	−10	−17	−24	−31	−38	−45	−52	−60	−67	−74	−81	−88	−95
55	25	18	11	4	−3	−11	−18	−25	−32	−39	−46	−54	−61	−68	−75	−82	−89	−97
60	25	17	10	3	−4	−11	−19	−26	−33	−40	−48	−55	−62	−69	−76	−84	−91	−98

Wind (Kph)	Temperature (°C)													
	0	−1	−2	−3	−4	−5	−10	−15	−20	−25	−30	−35	−40	−45
0	0	−1	−2	−3	−4	−5	−10	−15	−20	−25	−30	−35	−40	−45
6	−2	−3	−4	−5	−7	−8	−14	−19	−25	−31	−37	−42	−48	−54
8	−3	−4	−5	−6	−7	−9	−14	−20	−26	−32	−38	−44	−50	−56
10	−3	−5	−6	−7	−8	−9	−15	−21	−27	−33	−39	−45	−51	−57
15	−4	−6	−7	−8	−9	−11	−17	−23	−29	−35	−41	−48	−54	−60
20	−5	−7	−8	−9	−10	−12	−18	−24	−30	−37	−43	−49	−56	−62
25	−6	−7	−8	−10	−11	−12	−19	−25	−32	−38	−44	−51	−57	−64
30	−6	−8	−9	−10	−12	−13	−20	−26	−33	−39	−46	−52	−59	−65
35	−7	−8	−10	−11	−12	−14	−20	−27	−33	−40	−47	−53	−60	−66
40	−7	−9	−10	−12	−13	−14	−21	−27	−34	−41	−48	−54	−61	−68
45	−8	−9	−11	−12	−13	−15	−21	−28	−35	−42	−48	−55	−62	−69
50	−8	−10	−11	−13	−14	−15	−22	−29	−35	−42	−49	−56	−63	−69
55	−8	−10	−12	−13	−14	−15	−22	−29	−36	−43	−50	−57	−63	−70
60	−9	−10	−12	−13	−15	−16	−23	−30	−36	−43	−50	−57	−64	−71
65	−9	−11	−12	−14	−15	−16	−23	−30	−37	−44	−51	−58	−65	−72
70	−9	−11	−13	−14	−15	−16	−24	−31	−37	−44	−51	−58	−65	−72
75	−10	−11	−12	−15	−17	−17	−24	−31	−38	−45	−52	−59	−66	−73

hurricane based on its peak wind speed; it is also used to give an estimate of the potential property damage and flooding expected along the coast from a hurricane landfall.

Saffir-Simpson Hurricane Scale

Category	Wind Strength	Pressure (mb)	Effects
1	74-95 mph (119-153 kph; 65-83 knots)	>980 mb	Oceans surge 4 to 5 feet above normal; minimal damage; some bushes and trees lightly damaged; unanchored mobile homes may shift; some coastal flooding and pier damage
2	96-110 mph (154-177 kph; 84-95 knots)	980-965 mb	Waters surge 6 to 8 feet above normal; considerable vegetation damage; some door, window, and roof damage; mobile homes and poorly built piers receive significant damage; coastal and low-lying areas flood from 2 to 4 hours before center hurricane reaches shore
3	111-130 mph (178-209 kph; 96-113 knots)	964-945 mb	Surges are 9 to 12 feet above normal; small homes and utility buildings receive structural damage; leaves blown off trees and some large trees blown over; mobile homes destroyed; coastal and low-lying areas flood 3 to 5 hours before center of hurricane reaches shore; evacuations of low-lying areas may be needed
4	131-155 mph (210-249 kph; 114-134 knots)	944-920 mb	Waters surge 13 to 18 feet above normal; small homes may lose roofs; trees and signs blown down; mobile homes destroyed; many doors and windows destroyed; low-lying and coastal areas flood 3 to 5 hours before center of hurricane reaches shore; all terrain lower than 10 feet above sea level should be evacuated before flooding; homes as far as 6 miles inland can be affected
5	>155 mph (>249 kph; >135 knots)	<920 mb	Waters surge more than 18 feet above normal levels; many house and commercial buildings lose their roofs; some small buildings and small utility structures completely destroyed; all vegetation leveled; major damage to lower levels of homes and other buildings that are less than 15 feet above sea level and within 500 yards of shoreline; massive evacuations required

The *Fujita-Pearson Tornado Intensity Scale* (or "F-Scale") is used to measure tornado wind speeds. It was developed in 1971 and named after Tetsuya Theodore Fujita (1920–1998) of the University of Chicago and Allan Pearson, who was then head of the National Severe Storms Forecast Center in Kansas City. It was Fujita who came up with

a system to rank tornadoes according to how much damage they cause. He developed his categories by connecting the twelve forces of the Beaufort wind scale (knots based on what the sea surface looks like—from smooth to waves over 45 feet) with the speed of sound (Mach 1). Then, for each category he estimated how strong the wind must be to cause certain observed damages. Fujita's scale was later combined with Pearson's scale, which measures the length and width of a tornado's path, or its contact with the ground.

Fujita Tornado Scale

F-Scale	Intensity	Wind Strength	Frequency	Damage Description
F0	Gale tornado	40-72 mph (64-116 kph; 35-62 knots)	29%	Some branches break off trees; some damage to buildings, such as to roof shingles and windows; billboards and other signs show damage
F1	Moderate tornado	73-112 mph (117-180 kph; 63-97 knots)	40%	Trees uprooted; cars overturned or pushed off roads; mobile homes shoved off foundations; roof surfaces torn off houses
F2	Significant tornado	113-157 mph (181-253 kph; 98-136 knots)	24%	Mobile homes destroyed; sheds and other small buildings destroyed; roofs on houses completely torn off; large trees broken and uprooted; train boxcars tilt over; some light objects become projectile missiles
F3	Severe tornado	158-206 mph (254-332 kph; 137-179 knots)	6%	Walls and roofs on houses blown down; metal buildings severely damaged or collapsed; forests and farmland destroyed; large cars lifted into the air and thrown; trains overturned
F4	Devastating tornado	207-260 mph (333-419 kph; 180-226 knots)	2%	Well-built homes nearly completely destroyed; cars thrown long distances; some structures with weaker foundations lifted and thrown; large pieces of concrete and steel become deadly projectiles
F5	Incredible tornado	261-318 mph (420-512 kph; 227-276 knots)	<1%	Homes destroyed, with even those with good foundations lifted and thrown long distances; large office and other buildings have considerable damage; trees debarked; cars and other car-sized objects become projectiles
F6	Inconceivable tornado	319-379 mph (513-610 kph; 277-329 knots)	<1%	Such tornadoes are highly unlikely; the areas they damage would not be recognizable and evidence for them would probably only be detected through engineering studies; such areas would likely be surrounded by areas damaged by F5 forces, with cars, large appliances, and other large objects causing additional damage

What is the **Enhanced Fujita Scale**?

Introduced by the National Weather Service in February 2006, and first put into use on February 1, 2007, the Enhanced Fujita Scale (EFS) was created to better reflect actual damages recorded since the original Fujita Scale was developed. Meteorologists have recently concluded that structures could be damaged by tornadic winds that were slower than previously thought. The original scale, which was felt to be too general, did not take into careful enough account the different types of construction, and it was hard to evaluate tornadoes that struck in low-populated areas where not many structures were present. The new scale also offers more detailed descriptions of potential damages by using 28 Damage Indicators that describe building types,

The strength of a tornado is rated on the Fujita-Pearson Tornado Intensity Scale, which takes into account wind speeds and damage created by the twister.

structures, and vegetation, accompanied by a Degrees of Damage scale. Otherwise, the EFS uses the same categories, ranking tornadoes from 0 up to 5.

Enhanced Fujita Scale

Scale	Wind Speed (mph/kph)	Damages
EF0	65–85/105–137	Tree branches break off, trees with shallow roots fall over; house siding and gutters damaged; some roof shingles peel off or other minor roof damage.
EF1	86–110/138–177	Mobile homes overturned; doors, windows, and glass broken; severe damage to roofs.
EF2	111–135/178–217	Large tree trunks split and big trees fall over; mobile homes destroyed, and homes on foundations are shifted; cars lifted off the ground; roofs torn off; some lighter objects thrown at the speed of missiles.
EF3	136–165/218–265	Trees broken and debarked; mobile homes completely destroyed and houses on foundations loose stories, and buildings with weaker foundations are lifted and blown distances; commerical buildings such as shopping malls are severely damaged; heavy cars are thrown and trains are tipped over.

When was mathematics first used to predict the weather?

One of the first people to use mathematics to predict the weather was English meteorologist Lewis Fry Richardson (1881–1953). In 1922 he proposed the use of differential equations to forecast the weather, an idea published in his book *Weather Prediction by Numerical Process*. He believed that observations from weather stations would provide data for the initial conditions; from that information, predictions of the weather could be made for several days ahead.

But Richardson's methods were extremely tedious and time consuming, mainly because they had to be done by hand in the pre-computer age. Thus, most of his calculations came too late to be of any predictive value. Richardson determined that 60,000 people would have to do the calculations in order to predict the next day's weather. But his ideas did lay the foundation for modern weather forecasting.

Scale	Wind Speed (mph/kph)	Damages
EF4	166–200/266–322	Frame houses leveled; cars thrown long distances; larger objects become dangerous projectiles.
EF5	>200/>323	Homes are completely destroyed and even steel-reinforced buildings are severely damaged; objects the size of cars are thrown distances of 300 feet (90 meters) or more. Total devastation.

What is **numerical weather prediction**?

Numerical weather prediction is forecasting the weather using numerical models. Because of the complexity of the mathematics involved—not to mention the number of variables needed to predict the weather—all numerical model studies are run on high-speed computers. The computer solves a set of equations, resulting in a computer model of the atmosphere showing how weather conditions will change over time.

How do **computer models** attempt to **predict the weather**?

In general, computer models used to predict weather use around seven equations that govern how the basic parameters—temperature, pressure, and so on—change over time in the atmosphere. Scientists call the study of how they can physically and mathematically represent all the processes in the atmosphere *dynamics*.

In reality, everyone knows computer models can't perfectly predict the weather at this time. This is because of several factors, including errors in the initial conditions (or the observations the model gets to begin making its forecast) and errors inherent in the model (a computer model can't take into consideration all the factors control-

ling the weather). Long-term forecasts are even more inaccurate because these two errors are compounded mathematically over time.

What are some examples of **weather prediction models**?

Because there is more than one group carrying out weather predictions, there are many computer models used by meteorologists around the world. For example, the United States National Weather Service's weather predictions are carried out at the National Centers for Environmental Prediction (NCEP). The NCEP runs several different computer models each day to determine the best weather forecasts. Some are used for short-term forecasting, others for the longer term; and some are used for global or hemispherical predictions, while others are only regional. They include the following mathematically intensive computer models (for more information about computer modeling, see , "Math in Computing"):

NGM—NGM, or the Nested Grid Model, is one in which observations are converted to values at various points that are evenly spaced, making it easy for computer programs to plug them into equations. This model is now considered to be obsolete.

WRF—The WRF (Weather Research and Forecasting) computer program is used for forecasting and research, created through the efforts of the National Oceanic and Atmospheric Administration (NOAA) and the National Center for Atmospheric Research (NCAR), along with more than 150 international organizations. A special version of the program is called the Hurricane Weather Research and Forecasting (HWRF) model.

AVN, MRF, and GSM—The AVN (Aviation Model), MRF (Medium Range Forecast), and the GSM (Global Spectral Model) convert data into a large number of mathematical waves; they then return the waves in a manner that will produce a forecast map.

GFS—The GFS (Global Forecast System) is a global numerical weather prediction computer model run by the National Oceanic and Atmospheric Administration (NOAA); it was upgraded in 2010 by the National Centers for Environmental Prediction (NCEP). It produces high resolution forecasts—the first part of the model representing up to 180 hours (seven days), the second part of the model up to 16 days in advance (beyond seven days is often thought to be the limit of weather prognostication). It depicts several types of weather phenomena, such as precipitation types, precipitation movements, temperature, and winds.

RR—The RR (Rapid Refresh) is the next generation of hourly updated replacement information for the RUC (Rapid Update Cycle) model. It was developed for users who needed frequently updated, short-range weather forecasts, especially those working in the aviation field and in severe weather forecasting facilities.

Ensemble forecasting is not all the meteorologists of the world getting together to predict the weather; it's a numerical prediction method used to generate a possible outcome of an event, in this case, weather events. This type of forecasting is actually a form of Monte Carlo analysis, in which the predictions are based on a different initial conditions that are relatively feasible—all based on observations and measurements that have happened in the past (for more about the Monte Carlo analysis, see "Applied Mathematics"). In fact, during hurricane season, many of us who watch the weather channels have seen the results of ensemble forecasting: notice some of the model simulations of the many possible tracks of a hurricane, for example, as it heads out of the Caribbean Ocean and towards the U.S. coastline.

ECMWF—The ECMWF (European Center for Medium-Range Weather Forecasts) is considered to be one of the most advanced weather forecast models in the world; it is mostly used for the Northern Hemisphere.

UKMET—The UKMET (United Kingdom meteorology offices) model also gives forecasts for the entire Northern Hemisphere.

MM5—The MM5 (Mesoscale Model #5) and WRF (Weather Research Forecast model) are actually the same models. The MM5 has long been a research computer model for smaller geographic forecast regions (such as Antarctica); the WRF is the name for MM5 as an operational model—not just for research.

What are some of the **mathematics** behind **global warming**?

There are plenty of mathematics and data behind the idea of global warming (or global climate change). In particular, forecasts of climate change are based on the mathematical interpretation of weather models—not just one, but many weather/climate models (more than 30 at this writing) that all seem to disagree with each other. In other words, in a way, mathematics has caused the global warming problem to become extremely controversial.

One mathematical field in particular that has caused an overall problem in the interpretation of global climate change—creating both the believers and deniers—is statistics. Some scientists claim that global warming advocates have skewed the data in their favor, and vice versa. The main problem is that the collection of sampled data has to be analyzed to show a real phenomena—not one inferred by a relatively small window of data collection or on very few data points. The real question many scientists ask is: do climate changes occur over the average lifetime of a human, or even every so many hundred years? Do changes in weather and climate come in cycles that are much longer than humans have collected data? For example, reliable weather data is

A growing number of scientists believe that our planet is experiencing global warming, which, among other effects, is causing ice at the poles to melt and lead to rising sea levels.

considered to have only started within the last century—and thus, scientists can't truly determine warming from human-related reasons versus a natural cycle.

Another fly in the ointment in determining global climate change is the use of computers and mathematics to determine changes (present and future) in the world's atmosphere. Even if the physical models are correct, computers and mathematicians can't solve the complex weather equations with the utmost confidence. This is because computers, no matter how advanced, cannot make enough computations that weather/climate predictions need. In addition, there are, at this time, too much data and variables involved in determining the weather and climate change. Thus, in a strange way, both camps—the global climate change believers and naysayers—are correct, at least until computers can take in more data and humans can collect enough data to make the predictions and definitive statements on global warming more accurate.

MATH IN BIOLOGY

What is **biology**?

Biology is the science of life. It includes the study of the characteristics and behaviors of organisms; how a population, species, or individual comes into existence and evolves; and the interaction of organisms with the environment and each other.

263

What is **mathematical biology**?

Mathematical biology is another word for biomathematics, the interdisciplinary field that includes the modeling of natural biological processes using mathematical techniques. Mathematical biology is carried out by mathematicians, physicists, and biologists from various disciplines within their fields. These scientists work on such problems as modeling blood vessel formation, with possible applications to drug therapies; modeling the electrophysiology of the heart; exploring enzyme reaction within the body; and even developing models that track the spread of disease.

What is **population dynamics**?

One major area of interest in mathematical biology is population dynamics. A population is the number of individuals of a particular species in a certain area; population dynamics deals with the study of short- and long-term changes in certain biological variables in one or several populations.

Population dynamic studies have actually been around for centuries. For example, weight or age comparisons of human or other animal populations—or even how such populations grow and shrink over time—have long been areas of study. With regard to human populations, the two simplest kinds of input in a population study are birth and immigration rates, and the two basic outputs are death and emigration rates. If the inputs are greater than the outputs, the population will grow; if the outputs are greater than the inputs, the population will shrink.

How does **population dynamics** use **mathematics**?

Gregor Mendel was an Austrian monk who, in the 19th century, developed matrices of characteristics in pea plants he was breeding, which led to his founding the science of genetics.

Population dynamics combines observations and mathematics, especially the use of differential equations (for more about differential equations, see "Mathematical Analysis"). For example, to determine what the population of a certain country will be in ten years, scientists use a mathematical model commonly called the exponential model, or the rate of change of a population as it is proportional to the existing population. (For more about population growth mathematics and the environment, see below.)

Who was **Gregor Mendel**?

Austrian monk Gregor Johann Mendel (1822–1884) performed experiments with

pea plants from 1857 to 1865 that eventually led to his discovery of the laws of heredity. Gathering 34 different kinds of peas of the genus *Pisum* (all tested for their purity), he attempted to determine the possibility of producing new variants by cross-breeding. By self-pollinating the plants—and covering them over so there was no unplanned cross-pollination—he determined the detailed characteristics of their offspring, such as height and color.

Prior to Mendel, scientists believed that heredity characteristics of a species were the result of a blending process, and that over time various parental characteristics were diluted. Mendel showed that

A simple Mendelian matrix.

characteristics actually followed a set of specific hereditary laws. He worked out what can be described as a mathematical matrix of the characteristics, thus determining what characteristics were dominant and recessive in the plants. (For more about matrices, see "Algebra.")

But Mendel had a hard time getting his results published. Even after publication by a local natural history society, his work was ignored. Mendel gave up both gardening and science when he was promoted to abbot. Coincidentally, and amazingly, by 1900 three different biologists working in three different countries—Hugo de Vries in the Netherlands, Erich Tschermak von Seysenegg in Austria, and Karl Correns in Germany—determined the hereditary laws independently. But they all knew about Mendel's work, graciously giving the credit for the findings to him. Mendel, rightfully, is now commonly considered the "father of genetics."

What is **Fisher's fundamental theorem** of natural selection?

Evolutionary biologist, geneticist, and statistician Sir Ronald Aylmer Fisher (1890–1962) first proposed Fisher's fundamental theorem of natural selection in 1930. A mathematical concept, it states that the rate of evolutionary change in a population is proportional to the amount of genetic diversity available. He is also often credited with creating the foundations for modern statistical science.

What were some contributions **John Haldane** made to **genetics**?

Scottish geneticist John Burdon Sanderson Haldane (1892–1964), along with Sir Ronald Aylmer Fisher (1890–1962) and Sewall Green Wright (1889–1988), developed population genetics. Among other contributions, Haldane's famous book *The Causes*

Charles Darwin took into account Mendel's ideas about genetics in forming his theory of evolution.

of Evolution (1932) was the first major work of what came to be known as the *modern evolutionary synthesis*. It made use of Charles Darwin's theory of the evolution of species by natural selection, presented in terms of the mathematical consequences of Gregor Mendel's theory of genetics, to form the basis for biological inheritance.

What is **computational biology**?

Computational biology refers to biological studies that include computation, mainly with computers. Many biologists study computational biology to develop algorithms and software to manipulate and analyze biological data; they also use computers to develop and apply certain mathematical methods to analyze and simulate molecular biological processes.

Another good reason for this marriage of biology and computers is obvious in today's world: the genome—human and otherwise. To take on the giant task of mapping genomes (the entire collection of genes in a species), scientists have turned to the computer, using it for such studies as genomic sequencing, computational genome analysis, and protein structure analysis.

Computational power is needed for a plethora of other tasks, too. For example, it is being used to develop methods to predict the structure and function of newly discovered proteins and structural RNA sequences in humans and other organisms, to group protein sequences into families of related sequences, and to generate phylogenetic trees (or lineage trees, such as the human relationship to apes) to examine evolutionary connections.

What is **bioinformatics**?

Bioinformatics is a field that evolved by joining biology and information science. In the past few decades, advances in molecular biology and the increase in computer power have allowed biologists to accomplish tasks such as mapping large portions of genomes of several species. For example, a baker's yeast called *Saccharomyces cerevisiae* has been sequenced in full.

Humans have not been exempt, either: The Human Genome Project was completed in 2003. It determined the complete sequence of the three billion DNA subunits

(bases) for humans, identified all human genes, and made all the associated information accessible for further biological study. Since that time, other universities and agencies have taken on the task of analyzing the results, such as determining the gene number, exact locations, and functions. Such a deluge of information has also made it necessary to store, organize, and index all the sequence data, which is where information science, or the method to store and work on such large amounts of data, comes in the form of bioinformatics. The computer experts who deal with such information are known as bioinformatics specialists.

How does the **adult brain** process **fractions**?

For those who found it challenging to work out fractions in elementary math class, researchers have discovered that the adult brain actually encodes fractions automatically without conscious thought. According to one study, the cells in the brain's prefrontal cortex and intraparietal sulcus seem to respond to particular fractions. And since these sections of the brain are responsible for processing whole numbers, it may mean that adults develop an intuitive understanding of fractions, whether they are presented as numbers (1/2) or words (one half). If this is true, can adults "speak in fractions"? Three-quarters, please.

How many **bases** are in a **human's genome sequence**?

There's a good reason why computers are so important to biologists working on the human genome. The amount of data is staggering, and would take scientists generations to analyze without the benefit of computers. For example, it would take about 9.5 years to read out loud (without stopping) the three billion bases in a person's genome sequence. This is calculated on a reading rate of 10 bases per second, equaling 600 bases per minute, 36,000 bases per hour, 864,000 bases per day, and 315,360,000 bases per year.

One million bases (called a megabase and abbreviated Mb) of DNA sequence data is roughly equivalent to one megabyte of computer data storage space. Because the human genome is three billion base pairs long, three gigabytes of

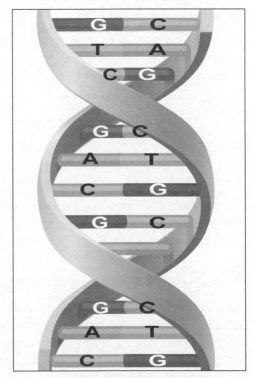

Human DNA contains about three million base pairs. Each base pair is made up of G–C (guanine-cytosine) and A–T (adenine-thymine) bonds.

computer data storage space are needed to store the entire genome. This includes something called nucleotide sequence data only and does not include other information that can be associated with sequence data. Because of such numbers, scientists working on the human genome are grateful they have computers on their side!

MATH AND THE ENVIRONMENT

What is **ecology**?

Ecology (also known as bionomics) is a branch of biology that deals with the abundance and distribution of organisms in nature, as well as the relations between organisms and their environment. It is an inherently quantitative science, with ecologists using sophisticated mathematics and statistics to describe and predict patterns and processes in nature.

How is **mathematics** used to **describe population growth** of organisms in a **certain environment**?

In general, a certain population of organisms—from rabbits to humans—will grow exponentially if it is left unchecked. That means that in a "perfect world" a population's rate of increase is constant. This can be seen in the following equations:

- after 1 year $\quad= P_0(1 + r)$
- after 2 years $\quad= P_0(1 + r)^2$
- after 3 years $\quad= P_0(1 + r)^3$
...
- after n years $\quad= P_0(1 + r)^n$

in which P_0 is the population today and r is the rate of increase. These equations are further modified for population growth statistics, but such intricate calculations are not within the scope of this book. (For more about population growth and biology, see above.)

Who were **John Graunt** and **Sir William Petty**?

English statistician John Graunt (1620–1674) is generally considered to be the founder of the science of demography, which is the statistical study of human populations. In 1661, after analyzing some major statistics of the London populace, he wrote what is considered the first book on statistics, *Natural and Political Observations upon the Bills of Mortality*.

The "Bills of Mortality" refers to the collections of mortality figures in London, a city that had suffered greatly from the outbreak of several plagues. Because the king wanted

an early warning system of new outbreaks, weekly mortality records were kept, along with the causes of death. Based on this information, Graunt made an estimate of London's population that is thought to be the first time anyone interpreted such data; it is therefore considered by some to mark the beginnings of population statistics.

Graunt's work influenced his friend, Sir William Petty (1737–1805). (He also influenced Edmond Halley, the astronomer and discoverer of Comet Halley; for more about Halley, see "Mathematics in the Physical Sciences.") Petty's work was a bit more practical (and political): he wanted to set up a central statistical office for the English crown in order to make estimates about the sum of England's overall wealth. His unusu-

Sir William Petty was a practical mathematician who wanted to establish a national statistics office in England that, among other studies, could calculate economic losses and benefits due to the plague.

al approach was to assume that the national income was the same as the total national consumption. He didn't forget about the plague, but added estimates of losses to the national economy due to the plague. From there, he suggested that modest investment by the state to prevent deaths from plague would produce abundant economic benefits.

What is a **logistic equation**?

A logistic equation (resulting in a curve on a graph) represents the exponential increase in numbers of a species until it reaches the carrying capacity in its specific environment. This carrying capacity, usually referred to by the letter K, is the maximum population size that can be regularly sustained by an environment. Change the environment and K changes, for example, by such events as adding a predator, removing a competitor, or adding a parasite. The notation that follows (in the form of a differential equation) represents a rate of population increase that is limited by interspecific competition (see above):

$$\frac{dN}{dt} = rN\frac{(K - N)}{K}$$

in which N is the population size, t is time, K is the carrying capacity, and r is the intrinsic rate of increase.

What are **survivorship curves**?

Survivorship curves record and plot the fate of the young, and their chances of survival in key age categories. Significant factors affecting all populations are birth rates,

The Lotka-Volterra Interspecific Competition Logistic Equations are concerned with the predator-prey relationships between species in the environment, and are based on differential equations (for more on differential equations, see "Mathematical Analysis"). Such predator-prey theories were developed independently by then-Austrian (now Ukrainian) chemist, demographer, ecologist, and mathematician Alfred James Lotka (1880–1949) and Italian mathematician Vito Volterra (1860–1940) in 1925. They refer to *interspecific competition,* or the competition between two or more species for some limiting resource, such as food, nutrients, space, mates, nesting sites, or anything in which the demand is greater than the supply.

death rates, and longevity. By recording the numbers of births and deaths over a period of time, researchers can determine the average longevity of organisms in each age class; these numbers tell a great deal about a population.

There are three basic survivorship curves. Type I curves represent species that have offspring with a high survival rate, with most living to a certain age and then dying; humans are an example. Type II curves represent organisms with a steady death rate from the time they are born or hatch until they die; their survivorship varies and includes such species as deer, large birds, and fish. Type III curves include those organisms that have a low survivorship shortly after being born, but with a high longevity for the individual organisms that survive; maple and oak trees can be included in this category.

What is the **air quality index**?

Mathematics plays an important part in the air quality index (AQI), a scale developed by the U.S. government to measure how much pollution is in the air. The AQI measures five specific pollutants: ozone, particulate matter, carbon monoxide, sulfur dioxide, and nitrogen dioxide. The levels range from 0 (good air quality) to 500 (hazardous air quality); the higher the index, the higher the level of pollutants and the greater the likelihood of detrimental health effects.

Most people think about the AQI in terms of being outdoors—and most weather broadcasts include air quality listings, especially in larger cities. When the readings are high, people are warned not to participate in strenuous activities like sports or hard work outside; people with asthma or other lung problems are urged to stay inside.

What is **environmental modeling**?

As with most of the sciences, mathematical modeling and computer simulations also come in handy for environmental applications on a local, regional, and global scale. For example, scientists model environmental landscape changes, global climate change and the impacts on ecosystems, watershed and reservoir interactions, and forest management and sustainability.

What is **computational ecology**?

Computational ecology can be considered a subset of environmental modeling, as it addresses practical questions arising from environmental problems using mathematics; in particular, researchers in computational ecology develop new ways to predict and mitigate the rapidly changing life support systems on Earth. For example, in the field of ecotoxicology, mathematical models are used to predict the effects of environmental pollutants on populations. Natural resource management uses mathematics to set quotas for fish and game. And conservation ecologists use mathematical models to determine the effects of various recovery plans for threatened species, and even to design nature preserves.

The most challenging efforts in computational ecology have to do with the current problems in global climate change. In particular, scientists who work on climate change are concentrating on such models as carbon-climate feedback models (to forecast future climates associated with various policy scenarios), forest VOC emissions (how forests release volatile organic compounds, or VOCs, and how they affect the global atmospheric chemistry), modeling tropical deforestation (the loss of trees means less carbon stores, not to mention the effects of the burning of vegetation involved in deforestation), and so on.

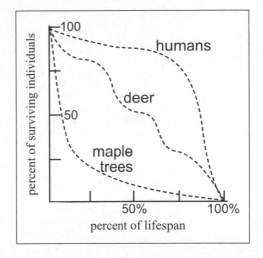

In this sample graph of a survivorship curve, it is easy to see how the survival rates of maple trees, deer, and people vary greatly over time.

MATH IN ENGINEERING

BASICS OF ENGINEERING

What is **engineering**?

Engineering is a discipline that deals with the "art" or science of applying scientific knowledge to solve practical problems, usually in the areas of commerce and industry. Scientists ask the "why" of a question, then research the answer; in contrast, engineers want to know how to solve the problem and then how to implement the solution. But it's not always easy to separate the two. Often a scientist has to use engineering basics (such as building special equipment for research), and engineers often have to do scientific research.

The word engineer (as well as engine) developed from the Latin root *ingeniosus* ("skilled"); in some languages, such as Arabic, the word for engineering also means "geometry." The various branches of engineering include aerospace, agriculture, architectural, biomedical, computer, civil, chemical, electrical, environmental, mechanical, petroleum, and material science.

What **types of mathematics** are used in **engineering**?

Mathematics is definitely a necessity in engineering, especially the fields of algebra, geometry, calculus, and statistics. Certain divisions of engineering rely on variations of mathematics, including combinations of arithmetic, algebra, geometry, calculus, differential equations, probability and statistics, complex analysis, and others. For example, civil and structural engineers use a great deal of linear algebra and work with matrices. Mechanical engineers use logs and exponents, calculus, differential equations, and probability and statistics. And a chemical engineer uses such mathematics as algebra and geometry, logs and exponents, integral calculus, and differential equations.

The accomplishments of French mathematician and physicist Baron Jean-Baptiste-Joseph Fourier (1768–1830) prove that not all famous mathematicians did just math. Fourier was a teacher, became involved in the messy French Revolution, and was arrested for his views and imprisoned in 1794. For a time, he even feared the guillotine, but political changes resulted in Fourier being freed. By 1798 Fourier joined Napoleon's army in its invasion of Egypt as a scientific adviser. After Napoleon lost the Battle of the Nile to Nelson and was confined to Malta, Fourier continued his work in Egypt, establishing educational facilities there and carrying out archeological explorations. Back in France with Napoleon in 1801, he supervised the draining of the swamps of Bourgoin and the construction of a highway from Grenoble to Turin. He also spent time writing *Description of Egypt,* a book that Napoleon edited, and included some historical rewrites (by the second edition of the book, Napoleon himself would be completely edited out of the text).

As if he wasn't busy enough, during this time Fourier wrote his now-famous 1807 paper, *On the Propagation of Heat in Solid Bodies,* a mathematical work on the theory of heat that presented one of his major contributions: the Fourier series. But it was an uphill battle to get approval from his peers. In 1811 he submitted his 1807 ideas for a mathematics prize, along with additional work on the cooling of infinite solids and on terrestrial and radiant heat. Only one other entry was received, making Fourier's work the obvious winner. Finally, by 1822, he published his 1811 essay, making the techniques of Fourier analysis available to everyone. To this day, the functions that he worked out have a multitude of applications in engineering, science, and mathematics.

What are **interpolation** and **extrapolation**?

Interpolation in mathematics involves finding a value (or outcome) of a function between already known values; in other words, it is a method of estimating the values in between sampled data points. Extrapolation in mathematics is estimating the value of a problem beyond the range covered by the existing data. Both methods are used a great deal in engineering.

What are the **Fourier series and Fourier transforms**?

The idea for the Fourier series and Fourier transforms was developed by French mathematician and physicist Baron Jean-Baptiste-Joseph Fourier (1768–1830). (For more about Fourier's life and times, see above.)

A Fourier series was developed as an alternate method of expressing a function by the expansion of the function. It is actually a specific type of infinite mathematical

series that involves trigonometric functions. More simply put, it is essentially an infinite sum of sine and cosine waves. The Fourier series is used in applied mathematics; the study of Fourier series is considered a branch of what is called Fourier analysis. In engineering and physics, it is used to split up periodic (or continuous) functions into a group of simpler terms; and in electronics, it is used to express the periodic functions seen in waveforms of communication signals.

The Fourier transform is a mathematical operation that essentially changes a signal into its constituent frequencies. For example, think of the Fourier transform as a "translator" that, as the name implies, "transforms" the signal. If one plots the electrical signal from a loudspeaker playing music, one sees a wavy (or sine) line, also referred to as the frequency. These waves can be big, small, close together, or

When Napoleon Bonaparte led his army into Egypt, French mathematician and physicist Baron Jean Baptiste Joseph Fourier joined him and was a scientific adviser. Fourier also worked for Napoleon when he was involved in draining the Bourgoin swamps and building a new highway.

farther apart. The collection of notes one hears from the speakers is the Fourier transform of the signal going into the loudspeaker. A type of Fourier transform is the fast Fourier transforms, or FFTs. They can be used for computer applications, with the speed and efficiency of the algorithm used to do the transform being "fast."

What is a **finite element analysis**?

A finite element analysis (also known as FEA or finite element method) is a powerful tool to solve problems in engineering, especially for heat transfer, fluid mechanics, and mechanical system problems. The FEA consists of a computer model of a material or design that is stressed; the outcome is then analyzed for specific results. In reality, the computer is conducting a numerical analysis technique used for solving differential equations, and relating it to stress in the engineering problem.

This technique was first developed in 1943 by Richard Courant (1888–1972), who used a form of FEA to find approximate solutions to vibrational systems. Early in the 1970s, only companies that owned expensive mainframe computers were using FEA, including the aeronautic, automotive, defense, and nuclear industries. Since the mid-1990s, however, use of FEA has grown with the advent of faster and cheaper computers with more memory. The results are more accurate, too, allowing various industries to analyze new product designs and refine existing products.

Why is finite element analysis important to many industries?

Finite element analysis (FEA) is important to various industries—especially those that need to predict failure of a structure, object, or material when under unknown stresses—because it allows designers to understand all of the theoretical stresses within the structure. This cuts manufacturing costs that would occur if a sample of the structure was actually built and tested.

FEA uses a complex system of points (nodes), making up a grid called a mesh. The mesh is programmed to contain all the material, properties, and other factors that constitute the structure and determine how it will react to certain load conditions, such as thermal, gravitational, pressure, or point loads. The nodes are then assigned a density throughout the material, all depending on the stress levels anticipated in a certain area. In general, points with more stress (such as corners of a building or contact points on a car frame) will usually have a higher node density than those with little or no stress. As researchers examine the results of the FEA, they learn how the structure responds to the various stresses. In this way, a prototype of the structure won't have to be built until the majority of the theoretical "kinks" are worked out of the system.

What **types of analyses** interest engineers?

There are several types of analyses that interest engineers, all of which involve mathematical modeling. *Structural analysis* deals with linear and nonlinear models and stresses on a material. The linear models assume the material does not plastically deform (the remaining deformation after the load causing it is removed); nonlinear models stress the material past its elastic capabilities. The stresses in the material then vary with the amount of deformation. *Vibrational analysis* deals with possible resonance and subsequent failure. It is used to test a material that may experience random vibrations, impacts, or shocks. *Fatigue analysis* is used to determine the life of a material or structure. It shows the effects of occasional (periodic) or cyclic loading on a structure or object, pointing out where cracks or fractures are most likely to occur. Engineers measure *heat transfer* to determine a material or structure's conductivity or thermal fluid dynamics. In this way, researchers understand how a material will respond to various hot and cold conditions—or even how it diffuses heat and cold—over time.

What is **dimensional analysis**?

Simply put, dimensional analysis is a way of manipulating unit measures using algebra to determine the proper units for a quantity that is being computed. For example, the units of length over time represent velocity in feet per second; acceleration is

velocity over time. Thus, acceleration will then have units of feet per second per second, or feet per second squared.

What is the **least squares method**?

This mathematical procedure, called either the least squares method or the method of least squares, finds the best-fitting curve for a given set of points by minimizing the sum of the squares of all deviations from the curve. It is often used in engineering for fluid flow, certain elasticity problems, and diffusion and convection in materials.

Why is **Laplace transform** important in engineering?

Laplace transform is a way to solve linear differential equations and translate them into simple algebraic problems that are easier to solve. It was developed by French mathematician and theoretician Marquis Pierre-Simon de Laplace (1749–1827). Although it carries his name, the Laplace transform seems to have been first used by Denis Poisson (1781–1840) in 1815. Today, it is used extensively in electrical engineering problems.

How are **modeling and simulation used in engineering**?

Modeling and simulation have become an essential part of engineering on both a small and large scale. Because building any sized structure takes time and money, engineers often develop a mathematical model, a set of equations that describe what may happen to a structure if it is built the way it is represented by the model. Using a computer (or graphic) representation gives the engineers a three-dimensional view.

For example, before the International Space Station was built, engineers used mathematical modeling to simulate what the entire station would eventually look like in three dimensions. In this way, the engineers learned how the ISS would orbit the Earth, how solar energy could be used to run the ISS, and even how to allow the various international spacecraft to dock with the station. The computer was the only way to solve such problems without real-life testing. It quickly and easily solved a plethora of mathematical equations, especially using such mathematics as calculus and differential equations.

Another more down-to-earth example is hydraulic modeling. Engineers need to know how the water will flow around and push on bridge pilings, how to control

One application for modeling is for engineers studying water flow to design stronger, more durable bridge pilings.

Who was Oliver Heaviside?

English electrical engineer Oliver Heaviside (1850–1925) was a self-taught genius who made several contributions to the field of electricity and even atmospheric studies. In 1902 Heaviside predicted that there was a conducting layer in the atmosphere that allowed radio waves to follow the Earth's curvature—a layer now named after him.

In electrical engineering, Heaviside was best known for *operational calculus,* a tool for solving linear differential equations with constant coefficients. It was usually applied to brief or fleeting (called transient) phenomena and was very similar to Laplace transform in its calculations. Although Laplace had developed his ideas almost a century before, Heaviside knew nothing of them, because they were not well-known during his time.

But Heaviside's operational calculus did have its problems, as well as its critics. It was severely limited because of its lack of mathematical theory. This not only limited its applications, but also created many uncertainties and ambiguities in the equations and solutions. Today, operational calculus has been replaced by Laplace transform, especially in fields such as electrical engineering.

drainage in cities and along coastline, and even how water flows through a city's culvert system. For example, the United States Geological Survey (USGS) often develops one-, two-, or three-dimensional computer models of bridges over certain major rivers. With such models they can understand such conditions as how the water surface elevations change (especially crucial for estuaries along the coast that are affected by the tides), the runoff from other creeks and drainage areas that flow into the river, and the velocity distribution of the river—for low and high flow events (flood conditions)—and how these conditions will affect the bridge. Such details can also help other engineers who deal with structures found around the river, such as dams, levees, and even how erosion and deposition of sediments affect the river's floodplain.

What is **fluid mechanics**?

Fluids are substances that flow, including gases and liquids. Fluid mechanics, or hydraulics, is the study of the physical behavior of these gases and liquids and their role in engineering systems. This includes the mathematics of the forces in and motion of substances, turbulence, wave propagation, and so on.

Most fluid mechanics problems in engineering are mathematically modeled using differential equations. These models can also be applied to other engineering areas, such as electromagnetism and the mechanics of solids (because solids still "move,"

albeit slowly). Other fluid mechanical studies include the compressibility of substances. In most cases, liquids are considered to be incompressible and gases are considered to be compressible. But there are exceptions in some everyday engineering applications, and they can easily be explored using mathematical modeling.

Engineers also use special mathematical equations to determine certain characteristics of fluid flow, such as whether the flow is slow and smooth (laminar) or turbulent. For example, the ratio of inertia forces to viscous forces within a fluid can be expressed by what is called the Reynold's number; laminar fluid flow can be described by the Navier-Stokes equations. For no viscosity (or an ideal flow called inviscid flow), the Bernoulli equation can be used. Finally, when the flow is zero (or static), the fluid is governed by the laws and equations of fluid statics.

How **old** is the study of **fluid mechanics**?

According to many historians, fluid mechanics may be the oldest subfield in physics and engineering. In particular, ancient civilizations needed to control water flow for agricultural development, drinking-water supplies, and transportation. Thus, the development of fluid mechanics, which is the study of the motion and behavior of fluids, led to even more (and complex) improvements. For example, agricultural requirements led to irrigation waterways, dams, weirs, pumps, and even crude forms of "sprinkler systems"; the need for a potable (drinkable) water supply led to better wells, fountains, and water storage systems; and water transportation innovations included improved sails and rigs, as well as methods to build and waterproof sailing vessels.

But early fluid mechanical studies did not end there. Over time, they extended into almost every realm of science and engineering. For example, mechanical engineering uses fluid mechanics because of the need to know about fluids used in combustion (ships and automobiles), lubrication (from the smaller inner workings of a wheel to larger mechanisms such as locks along a canal), and energy systems (hydroelectric power). Civil engineering utilizes fluid mechanical studies to interpret how fluid systems traveled over structures (aqueducts and pipes carrying drinking or waste water). Electrical engineers use fluid flow to analyze how to cool electronic devices with either air or water. Even early (and current) aeronautical engineers needed to know how air flowed over an airplane wing, providing the much-needed lift that allows a plane to become airborne.

To understand the way lava flows from a volcano, mathematicians apply their knowledge of fluid mechanics.

279

How are studies of **fluid mechanics** used **today**?

The list of engineering uses of fluid mechanics in the modern world seems endless—and no wonder, since it is one of the most widely applied areas of mathematics and engineering. Some of today's uses of fluid mechanics in various fields include: understanding the movement of molten (liquid) rock, or lava, in volcanic eruptions; studying the flow of air over objects to help design airplanes, the space shuttle, and even spacecraft that fly through the atmospheres of other planets; air flow studies in the automobile industry to design cars with more aerodynamic profiles; analyzing the ups and downs of the stock market; examining natural hazards, such as snow conditions that result in an avalanche; interpreting turbulent flow in sewer and water pipes, and in river channels; studying complicated flow of weather patterns in the atmosphere; researching the effects of gravity (and other) waves in space; and using fluid mechanics applications to study the deep oceans and coastal shorelines, including waves and currents.

CIVIL ENGINEERING
AND MATHEMATICS

How do **civil engineers** use mathematics?

Although most civil engineers actually spend only a small portion of their time doing calculations, mathematics is essential to this field. For example, civil engineers may use math to carry out the technical calculations in order to plan a construction project. They may use math to model and simulate the possible behavior of a structure before it is actually built. They also use math to understand the necessary chemistry (the strength of a material) and/or physical components (how strong parts need to be) of a construction project.

How do **surveyors** use mathematics?

Surveyors use mathematics—especially geometry and trigonometry—because they need to measure angles and distances on the ground. They then interpret the data, accurately plotting such information as boundaries and locations of structures on a map. These maps are then used for personal or legal means, such as a survey of a person's lot showing ownership boundaries in order to obtain a mortgage. The traditional method of surveying is called plane surveying, which does not take into consideration the curvature of the Earth because, for most small projects, this curvature doesn't really matter. When it does, especially for projects measuring greater distances, the method used is called geodetic surveying.

How do **surveyors** make **measurements**?

Most of a surveyor's measurements are gathered with a theodolite, an instrument that acts as a telescope, ruler, and protractor. The theodolite is set up over a known spot, such as a previously surveyed corner of a lot; its telescope then sights a specific spot, such as another corner of a lot, and the distance is measured (most modern theodolites use lasers to measure distance), supplemented by angular measurements in both the horizontal and vertical planes. The surveyor then uses trigonometry to analyze the data, converting it to a more usable form, usually in x, y, and z coordinates.

Geometry and trigonometry are essential mathematical disciplines that surveyors must understand to measure property boundaries accurately.

For example, depending on the desired outcome, the vertical angle and slope distances can be converted from polar measurements to show differences in elevations and horizontal distances. The horizontal distances and angles can also be converted from polar measurements to rectangular coordinates. (For more about coordinates, see "Geometry and Trigonometry.")

How is **linear algebra** used to determine the **stability of structures**?

Structural engineers use linear algebra a great deal, mainly because there are numerous equations with many unknowns associated with the analysis of a structure in equilibrium. Most of the time, these equations are linear, even when bending (material deformation) is involved. Linear algebra can also be used for other structural concerns, because it deals with the study of vectors, vector spaces, linear transformations, and systems of linear equations. Of course, linear algebra is not only used to understand structures; almost every subfield in engineering uses these types of mathematical calculations. (For more about linear algebra and linear equations, see "Algebra.")

How is math used to calculate the **pressure behind a dam**?

There are many engineering considerations and calculations needed when building a dam, the most important being the water pressure behind the structure. Engineers know that as the elevation of water behind a dam increases, the height and density of the water causes higher pressures at the bottom of the dam. Thinking in mathematical terms, the horizontal force acting on the dam is the integral of the water pressure over the area of the dam that is in contact with the water. The force exerted by the

Hoover Dam, an impressive structure on the Colorado River, could only have been made possible by engineers designing it in such a way that the walls were thick enough to withstand massive water pressure.

water pushes horizontally on the dam face, and this is resisted by the force of static friction between the dam and the bedrock foundation on which it rests. The water also tries to rotate the dam about a line running along the base of the dam; the torque resulting from the weight of the dam acts in the opposite sense.

For example, take the water pressure on a dam, such as the Hoover Dam on the Colorado River between Arizona and Nevada. Before building that dam, engineers needed to know the pressure not only along the entire structure, but also—and especially—at its base. In general, the pressure exerted by water equals the density times the depth, in which the density of water is 62.4 pounds per cubic foot. For Hoover Dam, this gives a pressure of 37,440 pounds per square foot, or 18.72 tons per square foot; the pressure calculated at half the height of the dam is 9.36 tons per square foot. This is why the base width of the dam is 1,660 feet (201.2 meters)—it is thicker to compensate for the increase in pressure at the bottom of the dam—while the width of the crest of the dam is only 45 feet (13.7 meters).

How is **mathematics** used to enable **buildings to withstand earthquakes**?

It is not usually the quake that kills people, but the collapse of structures. In particular, the horizontal shaking during a quake is mostly responsible for causing building or road damage and collapse. Most structures are designed to carry heavy loads, so they are strong in the vertical direction. Designing structures to withstand the horizontal earthquake shaking can save buildings and lives.

There may be other ways to mitigate the amount of structural collapse during quakes that include a healthy dose of simple and complex mathematics. One expensive way would be to design all buildings to withstand the largest ground shaking an area could expect. This could be done using mathematics familiar to designers and engineers; the math involved analyzes how large quake frequency waves travel through and area. Yet another, more practical, solution might be to design buildings to withstand the specific *types* of shaking expected in a region (this could be based on the rock underneath; earthquake waves travel differently in sand and rock). Again, mathematics could be used to determine the frequency at which each building vibrates (or the number of times a building sways per second) versus the potential type of quakes that roll through the area.

MATHEMATICS AND ARCHITECTURE

What is **architecture**?

Simply put, architecture is the design of structures, mainly buildings, by architects. But the definition does not end there. An architect not only builds the structures, he or she also takes into consideration the form, symmetry, spaces, and beauty of the building. In order to do this, mathematics is needed to work out such building factors as angles, distances, shapes, and sizes.

How has **math** been used **historically in architecture**?

Historically, there has been a great connection between architecture and mathematics. Ancient mathematicians were architects and vice versa, using their skills to build pyramids, temples, aqueducts, cathedrals, and a range of other architectural struc-

tures we find beautiful and awesome today. For example, in ancient Greece and Rome, architects were *required* to also be mathematicians. During medieval times, most buildings and structures carried some symbolic reference to the church; the mathematical end of architecture was almost forgotten during this time. By the European Renaissance around 1400, a new kind of architecture developed that emphasized mass and interior space to produce aesthetically pleasing "pictures" similar to those found in paintings and sculptures. This led to an entirely new way of looking at architecture and altered its connection to mathematics.

Who was **Vitruvius**?

Marcus Vitruvius Pollio (c. first century B.C.E.) was a Roman writer, architect, and engineer. He was the author of *De Architectura libri decem,* known today as *The Ten Books of Architecture*. This Latin treatise, dedicated to Octavian, the heir and adopted son of Julius Caesar, was written around 27 B.C.E.

The Akashi-Kaikyo Bridge in Japan is the world's longest suspension bridge, stretching almost 13,000 feet across the Akashi Strait near Kobe. Careful engineering was needed to make the bridge stable not only on routine days, but also in case of days when there are earthquakes in the geologically active region.

283

What is the world's longest suspension bridge?

Ten years after construction began, Japan's Akashi-Kaikyo Bridge—also known as the Pearl Bridge—was finally opened on April 5, 1998. At this writing, it still holds the title as the longest suspension bridge in the world, stretching 12,828 feet (3,910 meters) across the Akashi Strait to link the city of Kobe with Awaji-shima Island. Its main span length (or center section, which is the way "world's longest" status is determined) reaches 6,532 feet (1,991 meters) between support columns. The span length is almost a quarter mile longer than the previous record holder, the StoreBaelt (Great Belt East Bridge) in Denmark, which also opened in 1998.

But this bridge may eventually lose its longest status if the Italian government can keep on track with building the estimated 1.3 billion Euro bridge called the Strait of Messina Bridge, stretching between mainland Italy and Sicily. The idea for such a bridge has been around since Roman times. Fast-forward to modern times, and the idea for the bridge was backed by the government in 2001; with money tight, it was scrapped in 2006. As of this writing, it has been revived again; if it is built, it will be the longest suspension bridge in the world, spanning over the strait that connects the Ionian Sea in the south to the Tyrrhenian Sea to the north. It will be quite an engineering feat, with the main span reaching just over 10,827 feet (3,300 meters), which is almost double the main span of the Akashi-Kaikyo.

Interestingly enough, Japan and Italy are known to be tectonically active, with both receiving their fair share of volcanic eruptions and earthquakes, as well as, in Japan, tsunamis (seismic waves that form in the oceans and can be tens of feet high; for more about tsunamis, see "Math in the Natural Sciences").

Possibly the first works published about architecture, the books entailed a compilation of architectural ideas of Vitruvius's day and covered the following ten subjects: principles of architecture; history of architecture and architectural materials; Ionic temples; Doric and Corinthian temples; public buildings, theaters, music, baths, and harbors; town and country houses; interior decoration; water supply; dials and clocks; and mechanical engineering with military applications. Specifically, the topics included such forward-thinking ideas as the manufacture of building materials and dyes (material science), machines for heating water for public baths (chemical engineering), amplification in amphitheaters (acoustical engineering), and the design of roads and bridges (civil engineering).

De architectura was wildly successful, and Vitruvius's architectural advice was followed for centuries. But because Vitruvius's books were passed down through the ages, they were copied by various people, especially throughout the Middle Ages. Many

medieval engineers added information to the texts, treating the books as handbooks, not documents to be preserved. In the end, historians have had to winnow away the added sections to find the true writings of Vitruvius.

What is the **golden ratio**?

The golden ratio (also known as extreme and mean ratio, golden section, golden mean, or divine proportion) is a number that has many interesting properties; it is associated with the balance between symmetry and asymmetry used in art and design. Two quantities are said to be in the golden ratio if the "whole is to the larger as the larger is to the smaller." Euclid expressed it as, "A straight line is said to have been cut in extreme and mean ratio when, as the whole line is to the greater segment, so is the greater to the less." This is seen in the accompanying illustration, in which for two segments "a" and "b," the entire line is to the "a" segment as "a" is to the "b" segment.

The symbol for the golden ratio is ϕ (the Greek letter "phi," or a circle with a vertical slash through it); it is equal to about 1.6103398 and is considered an irrational number. The calculation to reach the golden ratio is as follows:

$\phi/1 = (1 + \phi)/\phi$

$\phi^1 = 1^2 + 1\phi$

This equals the quadratic equation:

$\phi^2 - \phi - 1 = 0$

which results in:

$\phi = 1/2 + \sqrt{5}/2 \approx 1.6103398$

What is the **historical significance** of the **golden ratio**?

It is thought that over the centuries many architects and painters used it in their works. Some historians believe that the Great Pyramid of Cheops contains the golden ratio. The ancient Greeks knew about the golden ratio from their works in geometry, but they never truly believed it was as important as numbers such as pi (π). Many works of art in the Renaissance are thought to have used the golden ratio within paintings and sculptures, although it may have been subconsciously incorporated into their compositions. In 1509

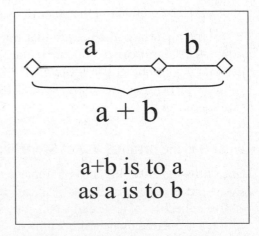

The idea of the golden ratio is illustrated here by the relationships between a, b, and a + b.

285

Cutting a nautilus shell in half reveals chambers that follow the rules of the golden ratio. It is a beautiful example of how math can be found all around us in nature.

Luca Pacioli published the work *Divina Proportione,* which explored the mathematics of the golden ratio, along with its use in architectural design.

Of course, humans aren't the only ones who "practice" the golden ratio. It is also seen in nature as the result of the dynamics of some systems. For example, the spacing of sunflower seeds—and even the shape of the chambered nautilus shell—are all often claimed to be related to the golden ratio.

In what way do some historians **link mathematics** to the **pyramids**?

The pyramids in Egypt were built as royal tombs for the pharaohs—first along the edges of cliffs as low rectangular structures called mastabas, then as tall, four-sided pyramids. The three structures most of us associate with pyramids were built at Giza, near Cairo, about 2500 B.C.E. The largest of these, the great pyramid of the pharaoh Cheops, measures 481 feet (147 meters) high. But there are no intricate pathways in this pyramid; it is merely a pile of limestone blocks weighing between 3 and 15 tons.

Why did the Egyptians choose the pyramid form? Historians know that the Egyptian Sun god, with its rays reaching for the Sun, was represented by pyramid-shaped stones, or ben-bens. And because the Egyptians worshipped the Sun as their chief god, the pyramids are thought to be huge renditions of the ben-bens. After a pharaoh died, the pyramids would be symbolic of the pharaoh ascending the Sun's rays to join his Sun god.

Some historians also believe that the pyramids may have had some (still hidden) numerical significance. In particular, some believe the ratio of the pyramid's perimeter to its height times two, or $P/(2 \times H)$, gives a close approximation to the value of pi (π); another claim is that the slopes of the pyramids' sides were also expressions of pi.

What was the **original use** of **Stonehenge**?

One of the most famous ancient stone complexes is England's Stonehenge, an impressive engineering and mathematical feat. Several groups of local inhabitants constructed this collection of large and small stones grouped in four concentric circles—two of which are created by paired upright stones bearing huge capstones—between 2950 and 1600 B.C.E. Based on how the stones line up with various astronomical events, historians believe the entire structure represents a huge (literally monumental) calendar.

The famous ancient structure of Stonehenge in England is now believed to have been designed to measure astronomical events as part of a religious tradition.

For example, various stones align with the Moon (the full moon's extreme positions on the horizon are marked at Stonehenge) and with the Sun (including the summer solstice). It is also thought that the complex served as a place in which ancient rites and rituals were performed on significant days of the year. And it was all built without the help of computers.

What are the **modern connections** between **architecture and mathematics**?

The foundations of modern architecture began with mathematics. Mathematical planning goes into creating almost every working, free-standing structure, from the smallest monument to the tallest buildings and bridges. For example, in order to build a structure, the area where the building will be erected must be measured to see if it will fit (measurements and surveys); then the building plans need to be drawn up in scale drawings made proportionally smaller to the structure's real size (for more information, see below); and the amount of building material must be estimated (mathematics to figure out the budget). Finally, the actual structure must be built to specifications so the building will stand without collapsing (geometry and measurement).

What **famous structures** were built using **mathematics**?

Actually, *all* famous structures needed mathematics, especially in the initial phases of design and construction. Some of the more famous—and exceptionally challenging—

287

Gustave Eiffel used mathematical concepts to design his famous Eiffel Tower in France between 1887 and 1889.

buildings include the Chrysler Building in New York (a steel frame skyscraper built around 1930 that was the tallest building in the world before the Empire State Building); the Empire State Building in New York (a steel-framed, stone-clad commercial office skyscraper built in 1931 that rises 1,252 feet [381 meters] high); the Eiffel Tower in Paris, France (designed by architect Gustave Eiffel and built between 1887 and 1889 as a 985-foot- [300-meter-] tall exposition iron observation tower); and the Willis Tower (formerly called the Sears Tower) in Chicago (built between 1974 to 1976, it is a steel-frame with glass structure standing at 1,450 feet [442 meters] tall and is, to date, the tallest building in the United States). Places such as the Monterey Aquarium (built around 1980 with reinforced concrete and made compatible with surrounding waterfront structures) also needed mathematics in order to be constructed. Of course, when one gets down to it, *all* types of construction require some math knowledge for them to be built, even a modest piece of cabinetry.

What are **scale drawings**?

Scale drawings are drawings or illustrations that are proportional in scale to the real structures they represent. In order for a new building to be designed, an architect must convert his or her ideas to drawings. But since the drawings can't be as large as the building, the architect uses scale drawings to depict the structure. These miniature versions of the actual structure show the sizes, shapes, and arrangements of rooms, along with structural parts, windows, doors, closets, and other important details of construction. The scale drawings of these buildings must be in exact proportion to the actual structure, with various scales used for this purpose. For example, 1/8 inch might be used to represent one foot; thus, an eight-foot-long building feature would be drawn as an inch long on paper. One of the most common scales used by architects is 1/4 inch = 1 foot. (These measurements can also be translated into the metric scale.)

Scale drawings are also used in other engineering fields, such as surveying. For example, distances measured in the field can be translated to a smaller scale (such as a drawing) in order to accurately depict what was measured. The ratio between the real

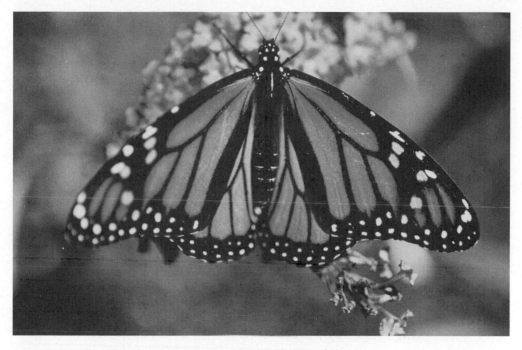

The patterns on a butterfly's wings demonstrate the concept of symmetry In nature.

distance and the drawn distance is called the drawing scale. If the measurement is 200 feet in the field, and on paper the desired line is 8 inches long, then 8 inches on the paper would equal 200 feet on the ground, and 1 inch would be equal to 25 feet on the ground. This is translated as a diagram with a scale of 1" = 25' (1 inch equals 25 feet), or 1:25. There is another way of approaching such an illustration: If the longest distance measured in the field was 300 feet and the desired drawing scale is 1 inch = 25 feet, then the minimum length of paper needed would be 12 inches, or 300/25.

How are the **principles of ratio, proportion,** and **symmetry** applied to architecture?

The definition of a *ratio* is a comparison by division of two quantities expressed as the same unit measurement. For example, a building that is 200 feet wide and 100 feet tall has a ratio of 2:1 (200:100) between its width and height; it is also seen as the fraction 1/2. Such a relationship was understood as far back as ancient Greece and Rome, when people used mathematics to give structure and aesthetics to buildings. This is especially important in architecture, in which building design is based on complex mathematical ratios.

Proportion is an equation stating that two ratios are equal. Every proportion has four terms, with the first and fourth terms being the extremes; the second and third terms are called the means. In each proportion, the product of the means equals the product of the extremes. The Greeks and Romans often used proportions in their

289

buildings and other structural designs. (The Roman architect Vitruvius was also instrumental in praising the virtues of proportion and symmetry in architecture; for more about Vitruvius, see above.) During the Renaissance, architects applied proportion (and other mathematical formulas) to produce aesthetically pleasing buildings—beauty that still holds true today.

Although there are other types of *symmetry,* the most common is line symmetry, in which a line divides an object, line, or other structure into two equal halves (an example in nature would be the wings of a butterfly). If a line of symmetry is drawn, each point on one side of the line has a corresponding point on the opposite side of the line. If you connect these two points, the line is perpendicular to the line of symmetry. There is a more mathematical way of defining symmetry: Two points are symmetric about a line if the line is the perpendicular bisector of the segment joining the two points. Symmetry was used by ancient (and modern) architects to maintain visual and sometimes structural balance of a building or structure.

ELECTRICAL ENGINEERING AND MATERIALS SCIENCE

How is mathematics important to **electrical engineering**?

There are many branches of mathematics that are important to electrical engineering. For example, abstract math is used in communication and signal processing. Complex differential equations—solving equations involving derivatives—are used in circuit theory and systems design; also in circuit theory, engineers need to know algebra and trigonometry. Engineers who deal with electromagnetism need to know calculus, especially Maxwell's equations. (For more about Maxwell, see "Math in the Physical Sciences.")

How are **imaginary numbers** used in **electrical engineering**?

Imaginary numbers are used in electrical engineering because complex numbers are an integral part of electrical problems. In fact, there are often more imaginary numbers in electrical engineering problems than there are real numbers. This is because a complex number is a pair of numbers in which one number is real, the other imaginary (or a real number multiplied by the value $i,$ defined as the square root of −1; for more information about imaginary numbers, see "Math Basics").

For instance, we know electricity flows through an electrical circuit component such as a light bulb. The bulb actually resists the flow of some electricity by doing work—or shining—thus, the current is real and measured by a current meter. But if the current can't flow through a device, the current becomes imaginary. For example,

How is mathematics used to determine resistor values in an electrical network?

Electrical engineers who deal with systems and circuit theory need to know the terms and functions of the basic circuit element—resistor, capacitor, and inductor—in terms of current-voltage associations determined by impedance (obstruction). Complex numbers, calculus, and Laplace transforms (see above) are all mathematical concepts used to understand circuit theory.

The best way to understand the basics are through the following simple equations:

Resistor—Voltage = current (I) times resistance (R), or V = IR.

Capacitor—Voltage = the square root of –1 (j, often called *i,* or an imaginary number) times frequency (w) times the capacitance (C)—all times the current (I), or V = (jwC)I;

Inductor—Voltage = the current divided by the square root of –1 (j), times frequency (w), times inductance (L), or V = I/(jwL).

a capacitor is two pieces of metal that do not touch; therefore, if one adds a voltage, no real current can flow through it.

Is math used to describe the **strength of materials**?

Materials science is also a major part of engineering, and includes a great deal of mathematics. For example, engineers need to know how materials stand up to stress and strain from the pressure of either a structure or overlying materials. A basic understanding of how structures respond to the action of forces and how these forces affect the performance of various building materials, such as wood, steel, concrete, and so on, is essential.

Are **advances in technology** fundamental to our **understanding of materials**?

Yes, advances in technology are truly fundamental to our understanding of materials, and vice versa. For example, transistors and superconductors were developed by understanding the mathematics of the materials that make up these objects. Math and materials science together have also advanced technology used in infrastructure (such as highways and overpasses), aerospace (such as satellites and shuttles), and micro-electronics (such as those found in automobiles). Today, the need to describe material behavior resulting from physical interactions is forcing scientists to develop new mathematics. In

fact, materials science has evolved to the point in which researchers from physics, engineering, and applied mathematics are working together on common problems.

CHEMICAL ENGINEERING

How is mathematics used in **chemical engineering**?

Mathematics is used a great deal in chemical engineering, especially since chemical engineers design materials and the processes by which those materials are made. To solve chemical problems, many types of mathematics are used, not least of which is calculus (including partial differential equations). Even simple calculations, such as working on chemical formulas and equations, involve mathematics. (For more information about chemical formulas and equations, see "Math in the Physical Sciences.")

Traditionally, chemical engineers worked in the petroleum and large-scale chemical industries. More recently, they have spread out to the pharmaceutical, foodstuff, polymer and material, microelectronics, and biotechnology industries. Using mathematics, they are involved in such studies as thermodynamics, chemical reaction processes, and process dynamics, design, and control. They help to develop new chemical products and processes, test processing equipment and instrumentation, gather data, and monitor quality.

Chemical engineers also build mathematical models and analyze the results, mostly to help understand the performance of a process. In fact, the "solution" to a math problem is often in the understanding of the behavior of the process described by the mathematics, rather than the specific numerical result.

What are some examples of **mathematical models** used by **chemical engineers**?

There are numerous examples of how mathematical models are used by chemical engineers—too many to mention them all here. One good example is modeling crystal growth: Liquids—from water to molten metals—become crystalline solids as they are cooled. Engineers can mathematically design software that helps in the manufacture of superior crystalline growth, especially for electronics and other industries. These improved crystal forms advance the quality of electronic hardware, including computers, and help engineers design better alloys for a wide range of applications.

How is math used to understand **chemical reactions**?

One of the simplest examples of mathematics used in understanding chemical reactions is based on two chemicals, A and B (they can be molecules or ions). If A and B

encounter one another, they can rearrange themselves into molecules or ions of two other substances: in this example, C and D. The reaction that takes place can give off or absorb energy, making the molecules move faster or slower. Although this is a simple example of what can happen in a chemical reaction, it can still be analyzed using mathematical modeling. For example, given starting amounts of A, B, C, and D molecules at time $t = 0$, what would the molecules be like at time t_1 (or after a specific amount of time)? These and more complex chemical engineering questions can be answered using mathematical modeling.

INDUSTRIAL AND AERONAUTICAL ENGINEERING

How are **statistics** used in **industrial engineering**?

Industrial engineers study the efficient use of personnel, materials, and machines in factories, stores, repair shops, and offices. They prepare layouts of machinery and equipment, plan the flow of work, make statistical studies, and analyze production costs. In particular, they rely heavily on a branch of mathematics called statistics and probability. (For more about statistics and probability, see "Applied Mathematics.")

How is math used in **statistical process control**?

Statistical process control (SPC) involves using statistical techniques to measure and analyze the variations within a process. With SPC, industrial engineers monitor, control, and, ideally, improve a process through statistical analysis. The four basic steps include measuring the process, eliminating variables within the process to make it consistent, monitoring the process, and, finally, improving the process to make the (usually better) intended product. But it is not the answer to everything. All the SPC does is ensure that the product is being manufactured and designed as intended. Thus, SPC does not tell whether the design is good or bad, just if it's made according to plan.

What is **reliability**?

Industrial engineers use another type of statistical technique called reliability, a system that always produces the same results and that hopefully meets or exceeds its specifications. A product is analyzed using the reliability function (or survivor function): the probability of a unit in a system that does not fail in a certain specified time interval. If the unit does fail in a system, it means the end of the unit's ability to perform the required function. This is determined by the failure distribution function, or the probability of an item failing in a specific time interval.

293

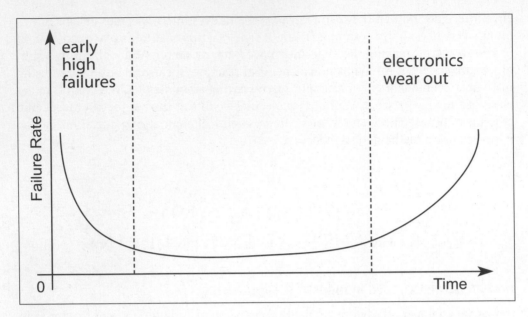

Calculations involving the common failure rates of various mechanical devices often results in a graph with a bathtub-shaped curve.

What is **statistical quality control**?

Quality control has been around for a while in a crude sense. When a certain product was manufactured, and consumers chose that product, the makers would try to improve the quality of the product or lower its price. The improvement of the quality did not stop with the product, but also included the process for making the product. But the use of mathematics was minor in early quality control. It was not until the 1920s that statistics was applied to industry and quality control, mainly because of the development of sampling theory. (For more about sampling, see "Applied Mathematics.")

Modern statistical quality control refers to using statistical techniques for measuring and improving the quality of processes; it is often broken down into statistical process control (SPC, see above) and statistical quality control (SQC). Both terms are usually used interchangeably, although SQC has a broader focus than SPC. To compare, SPC is the application of statistical techniques to control a process, reducing variation so that performance remains within specific limits; SQC is the application of statistical techniques to control quality and includes acceptance sampling (inspection of a sample from a lot to decide whether to accept that lot) as well as SPC.

What is the **bathtub curve**?

Industrial engineers usually know about the bathtub curve, especially in reference to an operating or failing unit. In other words, if enough units from a given population are observed operating and failing over time, it is relatively easy to compute week-by-

week (or month-by-month or year-by-year) estimates of the failure rate. The results of the calculated population failure rates over time produces a graph. Because the shape of this failure rate curve resembles the end-to-end section of an antique bathtub, it is widely known as the "bathtub curve." This type of analysis is usually used in industrial settings. For example, it can describe the expected failure rate of certain electronics over time: initially high; then dropping to 0 failures for most of the system's lifetime; then rising again to the other end of the "tub" as the electronics "tire out."

What is an **aerospace engineer**?

Aerospace engineers are directly involved with putting objects—from airplanes and the space shuttle to deep-space craft—into the sky and beyond. Using sundry mathematical models and techniques, they install, construct, maintain, and test systems used to launch, diagnose, or track aircraft and space vehicles. They may calibrate test equipment and determine causes of equipment malfunctions. Using computers and communications systems, aerospace engineers often record and interpret test data.

What is **orbital mechanics**?

Orbital mechanics, also called flight mechanics, is the study of the motions of artificial satellites and space vehicles moving under the influence of forces such as gravity, atmospheric drag, thrust, and so on. It is a modern spin-off of celestial mechanics, or the study of the motions of planetary and celestial bodies. One of the main scientists who built the foundations of orbital mechanics was mathematician Isaac Newton (1642–1727), who put forth his laws of motion and formulated the law of universal gravitation. (For more about Newton, see "Mathematical Analysis"; for more about Newton's laws, see "Mathematics in the Physical Sciences.") Today's aerospace engineers apply orbital mechanics to such problems as rocket and spacecraft trajectories, reentry and landing of space vehicles, rendezvous computations (such spacecraft to the International Space Station), and lunar and interplanetary trajectories for unmanned vehicles.

How do engineers determine the **escape velocity** of a **rocket**?

A ball thrown into the air will rise and then return, thanks to the Earth's gravity. If the ball is given a larger initial velocity, it will rise even higher and then return.

Without knowing the mathematics involved in orbital mechanics, the International Space Station would plunge back into the Earth instead of circling it in a stable orbit.

With even more velocity, the ball will reach a certain escape velocity, in which the ball "escapes" the gravitational pull of the planet. If the ball is launched with an initial velocity greater than the escape velocity, it will rise and not return. In this case, physicists say that the ball was given enough kinetic energy to overcome all of the negative gravitational potential energy—or, it launches into space. Thus, if m is the mass of the ball, M is the mass of the Earth, G is the gravitational constant, v is the velocity, and R is the radius of the Earth, then the potential energy is equal to GmM/R. The kinetic energy of the launched ball is equal to $mv^2/2$. That means the escape velocity is equal to:

$$\sqrt{\frac{2GM}{R}}$$

This is independent of the mass of the ball. To see how this works to an aerospace engineer, just replace the word "ball" with "space vehicle."

How is mathematics used in the **SETI program**?

Although as of this writing the SETI (Search for Extraterrestrial Intelligence) program has had funding problems, its use of mathematics in seeking intelligent life on other planets has always been fascinating. Large computers at several facilities, including the University of California at Berkeley, analyze data from various radio telescopes in real time (including at Arecibo in Puerto Rico), seeking out data that could be indicative of an alien civilization. Because of the large number of personal computers currently in use around the globe, SETI researchers have enlisted help from the public to seek out new civilizations. A program can be downloaded to private computers and used to run data in the background while the computer user works on other programs; the results are then automatically transmitted to SETI researchers.

Overall, a computer program looks at a large slice of the electromagnetic spectrum—a band 100 MHz (megahertz) centered around 1420 MHz. (It does this by performing a variety of digital signal processing operations on radio frequency data, translating the information using a special algorithm.) This part of the spectrum is where scientists predict an "advanced civilization" would most likely be sending out a signal, concentrating the message's power in one narrow frequency range, and if the signal strength gets higher that might be evidence of an extrasolar civilization.

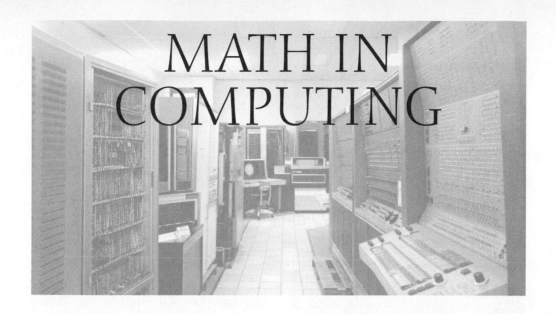

MATH IN COMPUTING

EARLY COUNTING AND CALCULATING DEVICES

Why were **counting devices developed**?

Early counting devices were developed for a logical reason: to allow people to count items in order to trade or to keep track of stock, such as cattle. They also used simple counting devices to keep track of the seasons (mostly for agriculture—in other words, to know when to plant), and for religious reasons, such as marking days for certain feasts.

What were some **early counting devices**?

The very earliest counting devices were human hands, with the fingers used as digits. There were limitations to this device, though, especially since each hand has only five fingers. To count more items, some cultures assigned even larger counts to other parts of the body. Such counting methods became tedious, so merchants and others who needed to keep track of assorted items turned to nature, using sticks, stones, and bones to count.

Eventually, devices called counting boards were developed. At first, the counting "boards" were simple, usually entailing drawing lines with fingers or a stylus in the sand or dirt. After all, merchants at outdoor markets needed to count items and calculate the cost of the goods in order to sell, and there was always plenty of sand and dirt at hand.

Portable boards made of wood, stone, or metal soon became more popular, with carved (or even painted) grooves or lines indicating units. These counting boards soon became more sophisticated, with beads, pebbles, or metal discs moved between the

297

The Salamis tablet, discovered in 1846, is the oldest surviving counting board. It was used by the Babylonians around 300 B.C.E.

grooves or lines, allowing for an even larger number of items to be counted. Over even more time, they grew into what is called an abacus, a device with a frame holding rods with free-moving beads attached.

What is an **abacus**?

An abacus (the plural being either abacuses or abaci) is one of the earliest counting devices. The term comes from a Latin word with origins in the Greek words *abax* or *abakon,* meaning "tablet" or "table"; these words probably originated with the Semitic word *abq,* or "sand." The devices—originally made from wood but now usually including plastic—perform arithmetic functions by manually sliding counters (usually beads or discs) on rods or wires.

Contrary to popular belief, abaci were not truly calculators in the sense of the word today. They were used only as mechanical aids for counting. The calculations were done inside the user's head, with the abacus helping the person keep track of sums, subtractions, and carrying and borrowing numbers. (For more about carrying and borrowing in arithmetic, see "Math Basics.")

Have there been **different types of abaci** over the centuries?

Yes, there have been many different types of abaci over the centuries, including the Roman abaci mentioned above. The first type of abacus came into use in China about 1300 and was called a suanpan. Historians do not agree as to whether it was a Chinese invention or not; some say it came from Japan via Korea. Although merchants used this type of abacus for standard addition and subtraction operations, it could also be used to determine square and cube roots of numbers.

The Japanese abacus, or soroban, was similar to the Chinese abacus, but it eliminated one bead each from the upper and lower deck in each column. Thus, it is more similar to the Roman abacus. The Russians also have their own version of an abacus; it uses ten beads on each wire, and a single deck. The separation in the wires is created by one wire with fewer beads.

What are the oldest surviving counting boards?

To date, the oldest surviving counting board is the Salamis tablet. Discovered in 1846 on the island of Salamis, it was once thought to be a gaming board, but historians have since determined that the white marble slab was actually used to count items. The tablet, which measures 59 inches (149 centimeters) in length, 30 inches (75 centimeters) in width, and is 1.8 inches (4.5 centimeters) thick, was used by the Babylonians around 300 B.C.E. It contains five groups of markings, with a set of five parallel lines equally divided by a vertical line in the center; below that is a group of 11 parallel lines, all divided by a perpendicular line.

But this was not the only counting board of that time. After the Salamis tablet was developed, the Romans brought out the Calculi and the hand-abacus around 300 B.C.E. to 500 C.E. These counting boards were made of stone and metal. One example of a Roman abacus had eight long and eight short grooves arranged in a row; beads would slide into the grooves, indicating the counted units. The longer grooves were marked I to indicate single units, X to indicate tens, and so on up to millions; the shorter grooves were used to indicate multiples of five (five units, five tens, and so on). There were also shorter grooves on the right side of the abacus, which were probably used to indicate Roman ounces and for certain weight measurements.

How are **modern abaci used**?

Today's standard abacus is typically constructed of wood or plastic and varies in size. Most are about the size of a small laptop computer. The frame of the device has a series of vertical rods or wires on which a number of wooden beads slide freely. A horizontal beam separates the frame into two sections called the lower and upper decks.

For example, in a Chinese abacus, the lower and upper decks each have 13 columns; the lower deck has five beads per column, while the upper deck has two beads. Each bead on the upper deck has a value of five, while each bead on the lower deck has a value of one (thus, it is called a 1/5 abacus). To use the abacus, users place the abacus flat on a table or their laps; they then push all the beads on the upper and lower decks away from the horizontal beam. From there, the beads are manipulated, usually with the index finger or thumb of one hand, to calculate a problem. For example, if you wanted to express the number 7, you would move two beads in the lower deck and one bead in the upper deck: $(1 + 1) + 5 = 7$.

This modern abacus is still used by shopkeepers in Asia and many so-called "Chinatowns" in North America. Students continue to be taught how to use the abacus in Asian schools, especially to teach children simple mathematics and multiplication. In fact, it is an excellent way to remember multiplication tables and is useful for teaching

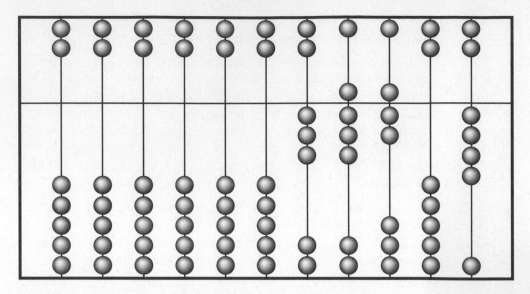

The beads are arranged in this illustration of an abacus to represent the number 38,704.

other base numbering systems, because it can adapt itself to any base. (For more about base numbers, see "Math Basics.")

What are the world's **smallest** and **largest abaci** to date?

In 1996 scientists in Zurich, Switzerland, built an abacus with individual molecules as beads that all had diameters of less than one nanometer, or one millionth of a millimeter. The beads of the world's smallest abacus were not moved by a mere finger, but by the ultrafine, conical shaped needle in a scanning tunneling microscope (STM). The scientists succeeded in forming stable rows of ten molecules along steps just one atom high on a copper surface. These steps acted like the earliest form of the abacus (grooves instead of rods to keep the beads in line). Individual molecules were then pushed back and forth in a controlled way by the STM tip, allowing the scientist to manipulate the molecules and "count" from 0 to 10.

There have also been contenders for the world's largest abacus. In 2001 the Science Museum in London, England, claimed to have the largest at 15.4 feet (4.7 meters) long by 7.2 feet (2.2 meters) wide. Also in 2001, a new contender from Thailand appeared: an 18-foot (5.5 meter) long abacus claiming to be both the world's biggest abacus and biggest non-electric calculator. It resides in the resort town of Rayong, southeast of Bangkok, and was made by a pharmacist who wanted to calculate drug bills faster than an electronic calculator; the latter claim has been shown to be true, at least by those who can work the abacus with high proficiency, though this was back in 2008, before today's many gigabyte personal computers and supercomputers (see below).

The people of the ancient Inca civilization of South America used knotted strings called khipus to make mathematical calculations.

What is a **khipu**?

Khipus (or quipu, in Spanish) were used by the Incas of South America. A khipu is a collection of knotted strings that record certain information. The approximately 600 surviving khipus use an arrangement of knotted strings hanging from horizontal cords. But these knots are nothing like those made by other cultures: They include long knots with four turns, single knots, figure-eight knots, and a whole host of other knot types. Historians believe these strings and knots represent numbers once used for accounting, inventory, and population census purposes.

There are also researchers who believe the khipus may contain certain messages in some sort of code—a kind of language used by the Incas—based on the strings, knots, and even a khipu string's type (usually alpaca wool or cotton) and color. But it may turn out that historians will never know the real story behind the khipus. When the Spanish conquered the Inca Empire starting in 1532, they destroyed most of the strings, believing they might be idolatrous items containing accounts of Incan history and religion.

What are **Napier's Bones**?

A tool called Napier's Bones (also called Napier's Rods) was invented by Scottish mathematician John Napier (1550–1617). These were multiplication tables inscribed on

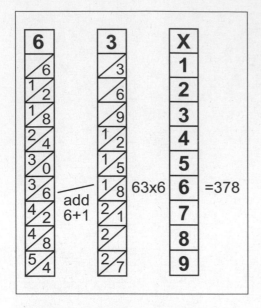

In this example of how to use Napier's Bones, 63 is multiplied by 6 to get the correct result of 378.

strips (also called rods) of bone (not Napier's, but animal bone), ivory, or wood. He published the idea in his book *Rabdologia,* which contained a description of the rods that aided in multiplication, division, and the extraction of square roots. (For more about Napier, see "Algebra.")

Each bone is a multiplication table for a single digit, with the digit appearing at the top of its bone. As seen below, consecutive, non-zero products of this digit are carved in the rod, with each product occupying a single cell. For example, to multiply 63 by 6, the two bones or rods corresponding to 6 and 3 would be put alongside each other and would look like the following illustration.

The first number would be the number in the diagonal at the sixth position (3); then the product (or solution) is evaluated diagonally, or by adding the two numbers diagonal from each other, or 7 (6 + 1); and the next number in the separate diagonal, or 8. In other words, 63 × 6 = 378.

Initially, the tables were used by merchants to speed up calculations. German astronomer and mathematician Wilhelm Schickard (1592–1635) would eventually build the first calculating machine based on Napier's Bones in 1623. His device could add, subtract, and, with help, multiply or divide. This is why he is often called the "father of the computing era" (see below).

MECHANICAL AND ELECTRONIC CALCULATING DEVICES

Who built the **first** known **adding machine**?

No one knows who built the first adding machine, although many historians believe it was German mathematician Wilhelm Schickard (1592–1635) who first invented a mechanical calculator in 1623 based on Napier's Bones (see above). Schickard and his family perished from the Bubonic plague. It was not until the mid-20th century that his notes and letters were discovered. They showed diagrams of how to construct his machine. Schickard apparently built two prototypes: One was destroyed in a fire and

**What did Blaise Pascal invent
that eventually caused his interest in math to wane?**

French mathematician and philosopher Blaise Pascal (1623–1662) devised the Pascaline in 1642, when he was only 18 years old; he had it built by 1643. This device was possibly the first mechanical adding machine used for a practical purpose. He built it with his father (a tax collector) in mind to help him with the tedious task of adding and subtracting large sequences of numbers.

But the device was not very helpful for a variety of reasons, especially since it used base 10 and did not match up with divisions of the French currency. Other reasons for its rejection are familiar to every century: The device was much too expensive and unreliable, along with being too difficult to use and manufacture. Eventually, Pascal's interest in science and mathematics waned. In 1655 he entered a Jansensist convent, studying philosophy until his death.

the other one's location is unknown, if it survived at all. His device, which he called the "calculating clock," was able to add and subtract up to six-digit numbers using a mechanism of gears and wheels.

But not all historians credit Schickard. Some believe that there was an even earlier attempt at mechanical computing by Leonardo da Vinci (1452–1519), who also apparently designed an adding machine. Some of his notes were found in the National Museum of Spain in 1967 and describe a machine bearing a certain resemblance to Pascal's machine (see below).

How did Gottfried Wilhelm von **Leibniz** advance **calculating devices**?

German mathematician and philosopher Gottfried Wilhelm von Leibniz (1646–1716) not only described the binary number system—a major concept of all modern computers—but also co-invented differential calculus and designed a machine that would perform the four basic arithmetic functions. By 1674 he had completed his design and commissioned the building of the Leibniz Stepped Drum, or the Stepped Reckoner, as he called his machine.

The device used a special type of gear named the Leibniz wheel (or stepped drum), a cylinder with nine bar-shaped teeth along a length parallel to the cylinder's axis. As the cylinder was rotated with a crank, a ten-toothed wheel would rotate from zero to nine positions, depending on its position from the drum. The movements of the various mechanisms would be translated into multiplication or division, depending on what direction the stepped drum was rotated.

Although there were apparently only two prototypes of the device (both still exist), Leibniz's design—along with Pascal's—were the basis for most mechanical calculators

in the 18th century. As with most such machines that could not be mass produced—much less understood by the masses—they were more curiosities for display than machines put to actual use.

How did **Joseph-Marie Jacquard's invention** benefit calculating devices?

In the late-18th century, French weaver and inventor Joseph-Marie Jacquard (1752–1834) developed a practical, automatic loom that wove patterns into fabric; it was controlled by a linked sequence of punched cards. This in itself was a major advance in the production of textiles, but it would also prove to be a boon to calculating devices. Borrowing Jacquard's idea, both Charles Babbage and Herman Hollerith (see below) would use such cards on their own computing machines. The company that Hollerith formed eventually became International Business Machines (IBM), a company that for 30 years promoted and benefited from mechanical punched card processing.

What was the **difference engine**?

Because of its automatic sequential approach, the difference engine is thought of by most mathematical historians to be the precursor to modern computers. Johann H. Müller, an engineer in the Hessian army, first developed the concept in 1786. His idea was to have a special machine that would evaluate and print mathematical tables by adding sequentially the difference between certain polynomial values. But he could not get the funds to build the machine.

Recognized for his connection to the famous difference engine, English mathematician Charles Babbage had to abandon his elaborate plans for a mechanical computer because the device was simply too expensive.

Müller's idea was soon lost before it was resurrected in 1822, when Charles Babbage obtained government funds to build a programmable, steam-powered prototype of Müller's device (for more information about Babbage, see below). Because of technical limitations, funding cuts, and Babbage's interest in a more advanced device of his own design, Müller's difference engine was only partially completed. Eventually, Swedish inventors George Scheutz (1785–1873) and his son Edvard (1821–1881) would in 1853 build the difference engine, the first calculator with the ability to print.

Who was **Charles Babbage**?

English inventor and mathematician Charles Babbage (1792–1871) is consid-

When was the calculating machine first mass produced?

Between the 1624 invention of Blaise Pascal's calculating machine and 1820, there were about 25 manufacturers of such devices. Because there were so many—most had little funding and only one person involved—very few machines were actually manufactured in any quantity.

By 1820 the first calculating machine to be commercially successful and produced in large numbers was the "Arithmometer." Invented by Frenchman Charles Xavier Thomas de Colmar (1785–1870) while he was serving in the French army, it was based on a Leibniz's "stepped drum" mechanism (see above). Colmar's machine used a simple system of counting gears and an automatic carry (automatically shifting a 1 to the left when the sum of a certain column was greater than 9). The technology of the times also helped catapult Colmar's success. Because it included springs and other machinery that offset the momentum of moving parts, the Arithmometer stopped at a specific, intended point, unlike what often happened with the older calculating machines.

ered by some historians to be the "father of computing." The main reason was his Analytical Engine, which is thought to be the true precursor of the modern computer.

One of his first ventures into calculating machines was the difference engine, which was based on Johann Müller's design and some of Thomas de Colmar's Arithmometer features (for more information about both, see above). The idea was sound, but the execution eventually lacked government funding, not to mention suffering from disputes with the artisan who was making the parts for the machine. Not only that, but Babbage's ambitions may have caused the difference engine prototype to come to a halt. Initially, he wanted the device to go to six decimal places and a second-order difference; then he began planning for 20 decimal places and a sixth-order difference. This much-larger machine was an overwhelming concept for its time.

The abandonment of the difference engine did not stop Babbage, however. Again approaching the government for funding, he promised to build what he called the Analytical Engine, an improved device capable of any mathematical operation, effectively making it a general purpose, programmable computer that used punch cards for input. This new device would use a steam engine for power, and its gears would function like the beads of an abacus, with the main tasks of calculating and printing mathematical tables. For eight years, he attempted to get more money from the government, but to no avail. He would never build his Analytical Engine.

Although the Analytical Engine was never completed in Babbage's lifetime, his son Henry Provost Babbage built the "mill" portion of the machine from his father's drawings, and in 1888 he computed multiples of pi (π) to prove the acceptability of the

305

One of the first "programmers"—in this case, of a calculating machine—was Ada Augusta Byron (1815–1852; also known as Ada King, Countess of Lovelace), the daughter of Lord George Gordon Noel Byron (1788–1824), the famous English poet. Inventor and mathematician Charles Babbage met Ada Byron around 1833, while still working on his difference engine. Her interest was reportedly more in his mathematical genius, not his machines.

Besides her admiration for him, Ada Byron also put Babbage's name on the computing map, writing up most of the information about his work, which was something Babbage supposedly could not do as well. For example, she translated an 1842 account of his Analytical Engine (written by French-born Italian engineer and mathematician Luigi Federico Menabrea [1809–1896]) from French into English. Babbage was so impressed that he suggested she add her own notes and interpretations of the machine. With his encouragement, she added copious notes, describing how the Analytical Engine could be programmed, and wrote what many consider to be the first-ever computer program. Her account was published in 1843. She was also responsible for the term "do loop" in computer language (a part of a program she called "a snake biting its tail") and for developing the "MNEMONIC" technique that eventually helped simplify assembler commands.

Ada Byron's life deteriorated after writing her notes because of family difficulties, gambling debts (though not her own), the lack of a scientific project to work on, and probably the fact that none of her friends were as deeply—and intuitively—involved in mathematics or the sciences as she was. Babbage was no help, either, having his own difficulties, including his ongoing attempts to obtain governmental funding for his Analytical Engine. In 1852, at only 37 years of age, Ada Byron died of cancer, but she was not forgotten. She was remembered and honored in 1980 when the ADA programming language was named after her.

design. This is often thought to represent the first successful test of a "modern" computer part.

What is a **troncet**?

The troncet (or addiator) is credited to J. L. Troncet of France, who invented the device in 1889. He called it his *Arithmographe*. (In actuality, his work was based on earlier designs that were first started by Claude Perrot [1613–1688].) It was used principally for addition and subtraction.

A troncet's flat, mechanical, palm-held calculator had three main components: the part for the calculation, a stylus, and a handle to reset the addiator. By inserting

the tip of the stylus into notches along a metal plate, numbers could be added by sliding either up or down strips of metal with numbers marked on them. No gears or inter-linked parts were involved. To "carry one" when the sum of two digits was greater than ten, the stylus was moved up to and around the top of the device.

What is a **slide rule**?

The slide rule is a ruler-like device with logarithmic scales that allows the user to do mathematical calculations. It is portable, with the most common slide rules using three interlocking calibrated strips; the central strip can be moved back and forth relative to the other two. Calculations are performed by aligning marks on the central strip with marks on the fixed strips, then reading marks on the strips. There is also a "see through" sliding cursor with a hairline mark perpendicular to the scales, allowing the user to line up numbers on all the scales.

Sadly for mathematical traditionalists, the use of the slide rule was eventually overtaken by the pocket calculator by the mid-1970s. But in other ways, this development was welcome. The slide rule had two major drawbacks, especially for calculations in mathematics, engineering, and the sciences: It was not easy to add with the device and it was only accurate to three digits.

How did the **slide rule evolve**?

In 1620 English astronomer Edmund Gunter (1581–1626) was responsible for constructing a scale rule that could be used to multiply. He divided his scale according to Napier's principle of logarithms, meaning that multiplication could be done by measuring and adding lengths on the scale. (It is also often considered the first analog computer.)

But there is disagreement as to the true inventor of the slide rule. Many historians give the credit to English reverend William Oughtred (c. 1574–1660), who improved upon Gunter's idea. About 1630 (although that date is highly debated), Oughtred placed two of Gunter's scales directly opposite each other and demonstrated that one could do calculations by simply sliding them back and forth.

The slide rule was not immediately embraced by scientists, mathematicians, or the public. It took until about 1850, when French artillery officer Victor Mayer Amédée Mannheim (1831–1906) standardized the modern version of the slide rule, adding the movable double-sided cursor that gives the slide rule its familiar appearance. Slide rules were used for many decades as the major calculator for the sciences and mathematics, and ranged in shapes from straight rules to rounded.

When was a **mechanical calculating device** first used for the **American census**?

When government officials estimated that the 1890 census would have to handle the data from more than 62 million Americans, there was a slight panic. After all, the

What is the Millionaire Calculator?

The Millionaire Calculator, invented in 1892 by Otto Steiger, saved many of the problems associated with other devices' multiplication. While earlier machines required several turns of their calculating handle to multiply, the Millionaire multiplied a number by a single digit with only one turn of its handle. Its mechanism included a series of brass rods varying in length; these rods executed functions based on the same concept as Napier's Bones (for more about Napier's Bones, see above). The calculator was a hit, and around 4,700 machines were manufactured between 1899 and 1935.

existing system was slow and expensive, using tally marks in small squares on rolls of paper, which were then added together by hand. One estimate determined that such an endeavor would take about a decade to complete, which would be just in time to start the process all over again for the 1900 census. In desperation, a competition was set up to invent a device that could easily count the 1890 U.S. census.

Thus, in the 1880s, American inventor Herman Hollerith (1860–1929), who is also known as the father of modern automatic computation, presented his competition-winning idea. He used Jacquard's punched cards to represent the population data, then read and collated the information with an automatic machine. With his Automatic Tabulating Machine—an automatic electrical tabulating device—Hollerith would put each individual's data on a card. With a large number of clocklike counters, he would then accumulate the results. From there, he would use switches so the operators could instruct the machine to examine each card based on a certain characteristic, such as marital status, number of children, profession, and so on. It became the first such machine to read, process, and store information.

The machine's usefulness did not end there, though. Eventually, Hollerith's device became useful for a wide variety of statistical applications. Certain techniques used in the Automatic Tabulating Machine were also significant, helping in the eventual development of the digital computer. Hollerith's company would also eventually become well-known, becoming International Business Machines, or IBM, in 1924.

What were some of the **first motor-driven calculating devices**?

Many historians believe that the first motor-driven calculating machine was the *Autarigh,* a device designed by Czechoslovakian inventor Alexander Rechnitzer (1879–1922) in 1902. The next step occurred in 1907, when Samuel Jacob Herzstark (1867–1937) produced a motor-driven version of his Thomas-based calculators in Vienna. In 1920 a prolific Spanish inventor named Leonardo Torres Quevedo (1852–1936) presented an electromechanical machine wired to a typewriter at the Paris Cal-

Has there ever been a competition between a calculator and an abacus?

Yes, there was once a competition between someone using a calculator and another person using an abacus. Although the abacus is often considered a "crude" device to do simple calculations, in expert hands it can work just about as fast as a calculator.

The contest took place in Tokyo, Japan, on November 12, 1946, between the Japanese abacus and an electric calculating machine. The event was sponsored by the U.S. Army newspaper *Stars and Stripes*. The American working the calculating machine was Private Thomas Nathan Wood of the 20th Finance Disbursing Section (from General MacArthur's headquarters), who was considered an expert calculator operator. The Japanese chose Kiyoshi Matsuzaki, himself an expert operator of the abacus, from the Savings Bureau of the Ministry of Postal Administration. In the end, the 2,000-year-old abacus beat the electric calculating machine in adding, subtracting, dividing, and a problem including all three with multiplication thrown in. The machine only won when it came to problems in multiplication.

culating Machine Exhibition. His invention performed addition, subtraction, multiplication, and division, and then used typewriters as input/output devices. Interestingly enough, even though the machine made a hit at the exhibition, it was never produced commercially.

More and more such calculating devices with electric motors were invented. By the 1940s, the electric-motor-driven mechanical calculator had become a common desktop tool in business, science, and engineering.

What is an **electronic calculator**?

Most people nowadays are familiar with electronic calculators: small, battery-powered digital electronic devices that perform simple arithmetic operations and are limited to handling numerical data. Data are entered using a small keypad on the face of the calculator; the output (or result) is most commonly a single number on an LCD (Liquid Crystal Display) or other display. It took a long time to go from the electronic motor-driven mechanical calculator to the electronic calculator. In 1961, the company Sumlock Comptometer of England introduced the *ANITA* (A New Inspiration To Arithmetic), the first electronic calculator.

MODERN COMPUTERS
AND MATHEMATICS

What is a **computer** in **today's sense** of the word?

In general, and simply put, a computer is a machine that performs a series of mathematical calculations or logic operations automatically. Computer specialists often divide computers into two types: An *analog computer* operates on continuously varying data; a *digital computer* performs operations on discrete data.

The majority of today's computers easily process information much faster than any human. The response (output) of a computer depends on the data (input) of the user, usually controlled by a computer program. A computer also can perform a large number of complex operations, and can process, store, and retrieve data without human interference.

There is a great deal of overlap for the word "computer." In a more archaic sense, a computer is called an electronic computer, or computing machine or device; the more common expressions include data processors or information processing systems. But remember, there is a definite difference between a computer and a calculating machine: a computer is able to store a computer program that allows the machine to repeat operations and make logic decisions.

What **problems** were computers originally **invented to solve**?

Originally, computers were invented to solve numerical problems. Now, very few mathematicians, scientists, computer scientists, and engineers—and even the general public—can imagine a world without computers. Advances in technology have led to an increase in accuracy, the number of problems that can be solved, data points that can be entered into the computers, and speed in solving problems. All this is a far cry from the earliest computers and computational devices.

What **type of number system** is used by **modern computers**?

Modern computers use the *binary system,* a system that represents information using sequences of 0s and 1s. It is based on powers of 2, unlike our decimal system based on powers of 10. This is because in the binary system, another number place is added every time another power of two is reached, for example, 2, 4, 8, and so on; in the decimal system, another place is added every time a power of 10 is reached, for example, 10, 100, 1000, and so on.

Computers use this simple number system primarily because binary information is easy to store. A computer's CPU (Central Processing Unit) and memory are made up of millions of "switches" that are either off or on—the symbols 0 and 1 represent

those switches, respectively—and are used in the calculations and programs. The two numbers are simple to work with mathematically within the computer. When a person enters a calculation in decimal form, the computer converts it to binary, solves it, and then translates that answer back to decimal form. This conversion is easy to see in the following table:

Decimal	Binary
0	0
1	1
2	10
3	11
4	100
5	101
6	110
7	111
8	1000
9	1001
10	1010
11	1011
12	1100
13	1101
14	1110
15	1111
16	10000
17	10001
18	10010
19	10011

What was the **Turing machine**?

In 1937, while working at Cambridge University, English mathematician Alan Mathison Turing (1912–1954) proposed the idea of a universal machine that could perform mathematical operations and solve equations. This machine would use a combination of symbolic logic, numerical analysis, electrical engineering, and a mechanical version of human thought processes.

His idea became known as the Turing machine, a simple computer that performed one small, deterministic step at a time. It is often thought of as the precursor to the modern electronic digital computer, and its principles have been used for application in the study of artificial intelligence, the structure of languages, and pattern recognition.

Who built the **first mechanical binary computer**?

German civil engineer Konrad Zuse (1910–1995) built the Z1—often thought of as the first mechanical binary computer—in his parent's living room around 1938. His goal was to build a machine that would perform the lengthy and tedious calculations needed to design building structures. His computer's design stored intermediate results in its memory and performed sequences of arithmetic operations that he programmed on punched paper tape (he initially used old movie film). This machine led to the Z3 in 1941. Since the machine used a binary number system, it is considered by some to be the first large-scale, fully functional, automatic digital computer.

What were some **highlights** in the **development** of **modern computers**?

The first general-purpose analog computer was designed in 1930 by American scientist Vannevar Bush (1890–1974), who built a mechanically operated device called a differential analyzer. The first semi-electronic digital computing device was built by mathematician and physicist John Vincent Atanassoff (1903–1995) and one of his graduate students, Clifford E. Berry (1918–1963), between 1937 and 1942. It was created primarily to solve large systems of simultaneous linear equations. It is interesting to note that Atanassoff's computer was overshadowed by the Electronic Numerical Integrator and Computer (ENIAC; see below), which was once credited as the first computer. In 1973, however, a federal judge recognized Atanassoff's work and voided Sperry Rand's patent on the ENIAC, saying it had been derived from Atanassoff's invention. Today, Atanassoff and Berry get the credit.

The Harvard Mark 1, or the Automatic Sequence Controlled Calculator, was built between 1939 and 1944 by American computer scientist Howard H. Aiken (1900–1973) and his team. It is thought of as the first large-scale automatic digital computer. But there are disagreements about this, with some historians believing that German

engineer Konrad Zuse's Z3 (see above) was the first such machine.

Other early computers were the ENIAC and UNIVAC. The ENIAC (Electronic Numerical Integrator And Calculator) was completed in 1946 at the University of Pennsylvania; it used thousands of vacuum tubes. Until 1973, it was thought of as the first semi-electronic digital computer. That credit was subsequently given to Atanassoff and Berry (see above). The UNIVAC (UNIVersal Automatic Computer) was built in 1951 and was the first computer to handle both numeric and alphabetic data. It also was the first commercially available computer.

Vannevar Bush was an American scientist who invented the differential analyzer, the first general-purpose analog computer.

The third-generation integrated-circuit machines were used primarily during the mid-1960s and 1970s, making the computers smaller, faster (close to a million operations per second), and far more reliable. The first commercial microprocessor was the Intel 4004, which appeared in 1971. It could only add and subtract, and it was used to power one of the first portable electronic calculators. The real push in microprocessors came during the late 1970s to 1990s, allowing for increasingly smaller and more powerful computers. For example, in 1974 the Intel 8080 processor had a clock speed of 2 megahertz (MHz); by 2004 the Pentium 4 ("Prescott") had a clock speed of 3.6 gigahertz (GHz).

What is a **microprocessor**?

A microprocessor is a silicon chip that contains a CPU, or central processing unit, which is normally located on the main circuit board in a computer. (In the world of personal computers, the terms microprocessor and CPU are often used interchangeably.) These chips, or integrated circuits, are small, thin pieces of silicon onto which the transistors making up the microprocessor have been etched. The computer industry has continued rapid growth, mainly thanks to the increased performance and speed of advanced microprocessors. The microprocessor is the heart of the "average" computer, from personal computers (desktops and laptop machines) and tablets to larger servers. They also have many uses; for example, they control the logic of almost all familiar digital devices—from microwaves and clock radios to fuel-injection systems for automobiles

How **fast** are some of the more **recent microprocessors**?

Most of us who own computers realize that microprocessors have increased the speed and performance of our machines in the last few decades, which is why many of us say

Mainframe computers like these can fill a room in a company's office, but smaller businesses that did not have the money or space for mainframes once used smaller mainframe units called minicomputers. By the late 1980s, microcomputers had become powerful enough to replace minicomputers.

that once we buy a machine it almost seems immediately obsolete. In other words, a computer we had a decade ago seems to most of us to be very, very slow compared to the processing speed of today's computers; it's all thanks to the development of better microprocessors.

The clock speed, also called the clock rate, is the speed at which the microprocessor of a computer executes instructions. In every computer, an internal clock is responsible for maintaining the rate of the instructions, even synchronizing the other computer components, such as the internal digital clock and date. Clock speed is measured in kilohertz (KHz, sometimes seen as KiloHertz), megahertz (MHz, sometimes seen as MegaHertz), or gigahertz (GHz, sometimes seen as GigaHertz). To understand this measurement, for example, 200 MHz is ten times the speed of 20 MHz; 1 GHz is simply equally to 1,000 MHz, and so on.

Overall, the faster the clock speed, the more instructions can be carried out by the computer's CPU, or the central processing unit. For example, in 1974, the Intel 8080 processor had a clock speed of 2 megahertz (MHz). The original IBM PC (International Business Machines Personal Computer) around 1981 had a clock rate of 4.77 MHz (that translates to 4,772,727 cycles per second). In 2004, the Pentium 4 ("Prescott") had a clock speed of 3.6 GHz (some say 3.4); and as of this writing, the highest clock speed microprocessor ever sold commercially is IBM's zEnterprise 196 mainframe, which, as of 2010, ran cores ("many-core" chips use an array of many processors) continuously at 5.2 GHz.

What is the **difference** between a **minicomputer** and a **microcomputer**?

The term minicomputer is not used much today. It is considered to be the type of computer built mainly from about 1963 to 1987, and refers to the "mini" mainframe computers that were not large enough to be called mainframes but were large enough to take up the space of a small closet. These computers were once popular in small businesses that could not afford the money or space for a mainframe computer. They were much less powerful than a mainframe and were limited in hardware and software, and they were built using what was called low-integration logic integrated circuits. Eventually, they were overtaken by microcomputers built around the microprocessor.

The microcomputer was a later development in computing. It was developed as a general-purpose computer designed to be operated by one person at a time. The single-chip microcomputer (complete with microprocessor) was, in many respects, a landmark development in computer technology, resulting in the commercialization of the personal computer. This is because computers became smaller and less expensive, and the design made parts easier to replace.

What are the **more common parts of a computer** in use today?

There are many basic parts of today's computers; the biggest differences between the various types of computers are the amount of memory and speed of the machines. The following lists the common parts of a computer:

Central Processing Unit (CPU) —The CPU is the heart of the computer. It is the component that executes the instructions contained in the computer software; in other words, it tells the entire computer what to do.

Memory—The memory of the computer allows the machine to temporarily (in most cases) store data, programs, and various results from using certain programs (such as remembering the words that are being typed right now).

Mass storage devices—These devices store the "long-term" memory, permanent data, and programs that one needs to retain. It includes the computer's disk drive.

Input devices—This is just as the words read, devices that allow you to input information into the computer, such as a keyboard, mouse, or other optional input devices such as a scanner.

Output devices—Output devices allow you to see the information processed by the computer, and include the computer screen, a printer, and audio speakers.

What is **computer science**?

Computer science is, of course, the science of studying computers. It is the study of computation and information processing, involving hardware, software, and even

315

mathematics. More specifically, it is the systematic study of computing systems and the computations that go behind making the computer function. Computer scientists need to know computing systems and methods; how to design computer programs, including the use of algorithms, programming languages, and other tools; and how software and hardware work together. They also need to understand the analysis and verification of the input and output.

What are **computer codes** and **programs**?

Mathematics is an important part of computers, because math is used to write computer codes and programs. The codes are the symbolic arrangement of data (or the instructions) in a computer program, a term often used interchangeably with "software." The code (also called the source code, or just source) is any series of statements written in some programming language understandable to the user. This source code within a software program is usually contained in several text files.

The program is the sequence of instructions (or computations) that a computer can interpret and execute. In other words, most programs consist of a loadable set of instructions that will determine how the computer reacts to user input when the program is running. The connection between codes and programs is often heard by students studying computer science or working professionals—and even in action movies and television programs, as in, "I need to add more lines of code to the program!"

What are the **definitions of computers** in use today?

It's easy to see why the word "computer" has so many connotations. They vary greatly, but include the following basic types, which are based mostly on the size and number of people who can simultaneously use the machines.

The first type of computers are called *mainframes*. These are considered the largest and most powerful general purpose computer systems. It is usually used to fill the needs of a large agency, company, or organization, because it uses hundreds of computer terminals at the same time. For example, it is used by statistical institutes and for meteorological surveys. *Supercomputers* are sophisticated machines designed to perform complex calculations at maximum speed. Because of their speed and the great amount of data they can process—they can perform hundreds of millions of instructions per second—they are most often used to model huge dynamic systems with many variables, such as complex weather patterns and groundwater flow.

Microcomputers are usually subdivided into personal computers (or desktop computers) and workstations. Oftentimes, microcomputers are linked together in a local area network (LAN) or by joining the microprocessors in a parallel-processing system. This allows smaller computers to work in tandem, giving them comparable power and computational abilities to mainframes.

What makes personal computers, laptops, cell phones, and even iPods and iPads so popular today?

When it comes to private use outside the business and scientific communities, computers and other high-tech devices are primarily used for communications—and most of that is for entertainment purposes. These devices have a variety of functions and activities to participate in, all of which, in an indirect way, are controlled by mathematics (in other words, they all need computer programs and codes to work). Although there are too many to list here, the following lists a few examples of some popular devices and their "output" to the user.

Modern personal computers and laptops often have enough processing power now to allow several functions never thought of before. For example, a user can partake in what is called a blog (a shortened version of web log) or a website or part of a site used to relay information about, for instance, the user's personal feelings about an issue or issues. Such blogs are updated whenever a person deems it is needed—daily, weekly, and even monthly or more—and are usually displayed in chronological order.

A personal computer or laptop user can participate in or listen to a *podcast*, or non-streamed webcast. Podcasts (once more commonly called a webcast until iPod became popular) are downloadable media content files, such as a concert, or an interview or lecture on a specific topic put together by someone (or a group) who is interested in offering such information. These series of audio or video digital media files can be released periodically over a special website, often through web syndication, or through a person's personal website.

There are also social networking venues. For example, Twitter is a website owned and operated by Twitter, Inc., which offers social networking (essentially "meeting and chatting" with others on the Internet); it also allows a person to partake in what is called microblogging, in which people are able to send short messages about, for example, what is happening in their lives at that moment in messages called "tweets." These text-based listings, which can contan no more than 140 characters per tweet, as of this writing, can be displayed not only on a person's cell phone (if it is capable), but also on a person's user profile page on Twitter.

Devices called iPods and iPads are some of the latest in technology, and are mostly used for entertainment. For example, iPods allow the user to pick and download favorite tunes or webcasts from various Internet sites (many times for a price). iPads are used mostly to browse the Internet and check email, but they also excel at gaming, video (especially through places such as Netflix, which offers downloadable, sometimes streaming movies over computers or iPads), and book reading.

Some of the more familiar, smaller microcomputers today are *notebooks* and *laptops*, which are very similar. Laptops are small enough to fit on a person's lap; notebooks are usually a bit smaller and lighter than a laptop. In recent years, the newest laptops (and sometimes notebooks) have the same capabilities as the "more powerful" desktop computers.

Still other, even smaller microcomputers are the hand-held computers, which fit in your hand, and the palmtops, which, literally, fit in your palm. These computers are limited in their capacity, but are good for such functions as phone books, calendars, and short notes.

Also considered a form of microcomputer is the tablet—a tablet computer developed by the company Apple (for more about the iPad, see below). It is easy to carry, and is a flat rectangle with a 9.7-inch touchscreen that allows the user to maneuver through phone numbers, drawings, word processing, and sundry other tasks with ease. It is only about a half inch thick and weighs a mere one and a half pounds. It is based on a phone (a device called an iPhone) operating system, and thus it can be connected to a wireless connection through what is called wireless fidelity, or Wi-Fi, which is why you can take your more recent laptop or other communication device with a Wi-Fi card inside to some popular bookstores and connect to the Internet.

What is an **"app"** in computer-terminology?

In January 2011, the American Dialect Society named "app" the word of the year for 2010, which shows how popular the word has become in the world of computers. In particular, the word app is a noun, and is short for "application"—in this case, to a software application program. According to computer scientists, such an app usually refers to software used on a mobile device such as the iPhone, BlackBerry, or iPad (see above), and is often specifically called a "mobile app" or "iPhone app." There are also "web apps" or "online apps," which are used mostly by businesses in which the user accesses the app via an online browser.

There are several reasons for using apps. For the general public, apps are found on the iPhone or other devices so you can access one online feature or another. They are also used to find out information concerning business offerings. For example, apps are now found in magazines: you can "scan" the app into your iPhone to take you to an extra feature the magazine is offering, such as a cooking magazine offering more recipes, or as a way to find out more information about an advertiser. For businesses, web or online apps are a more efficient way to share software among employees in a business; and a mobile app can be used by a company's workers to perform all sorts of business tasks while out on the road.

What are some **common** types of computer **software programs**?

There are many types of computer software—too many to mention here. Simply put, software is a set of programs, procedures, algorithms, and their documentation. The

What are some popular programming languages used to run today's computers and devices?

As stated above, programming languages are the software that keep your computer running smoothly. Some of the first programming languages included COBOL (COmmon Business-Oriented Language) and FORTRAN (derived from IBM's Mathematical Formula Translating System). More modern programming languages need to be written for newer applications and devices, and include JAVA, which is used to run many applications, including one of the more popular mobile operating systems, called Android; C #, developed by one of the largest computer companies, Microsoft; and C/C++ , used for a multitude of applications, such as systems software, device drivers, high-performance servers, and even video gaming software.

following lists the most common ones most of us are familiar with if we own any type of computer technology:

Application software—Application software includes what the user can use— mainly programs that help with word processing; it's also included in software important for video games.

Programming language—These software offerings keep your computer going and are the heart of all computer programs.

Testware—Testware is used to test hardware or other software programs.

Device drivers—These devices are controlled by computer software programs, such as your disk drive, printers, and CD/DVD drives.

Firmware—Firmware is considered "low-level" software stored on electrically programmable memory devices; it is usually treated like hardware, hence the name.

System software—This is the software that runs your computer operating system.

APPLICATIONS

How have computers been used to **factor large composite numbers**?

Computers have often been used to factor large numbers—and not just by number theorists having some fun. In fact, factoring such numbers has helped to test the world's most powerful computer systems, to promote designs of new algorithms, and

319

in cryptography used by people who need to protect sensitive information on their computers. For example, in 1978 several computer experts proposed using the reconstruction of the prime numbers from the product of two large prime numbers as an encryption technique. This method of encrypting sensitive data soon blossomed, especially because of the needs of the military and banking industry. The public also reaped the benefit of this idea as it eventually led to encryption methods such as the public-key encryption for banking and personal pages on the Internet.

Have **computers** been used to **solve mathematical proofs**?

Yes, there have been many mathematical proofs solved with the help of computers. One example is the *four color theorem,* which stated that it is possible to have a geographic map colored with only four colors so that no adjacent regions will have the same color. Another way of looking at the problem is: What is the smallest number of colors needed to color any flat map so that any two neighboring regions always have different colors? This idea was first presented in 1852, when Francis Guthrie (1831–1899) colored a map of English counties using only four colors. The idea of only four colors took on a mathematical bend and ended up being a theorem to be proved. It took until 1976, with the help of modern computers, before the four-color conjecture was finally proven to be true. Wolfgang Haker (1928–) and Kenneth Appel (1932–) of the University of Illinois took four years to write the computer program for the Cray computer, which took 1,200 hours to check 1,476 configurations. And in 2005, it was proven by Georges Gonthier with general purpose theorem-proving software.

Even though the theorem-proving software allows calculations to be checked along the way (by the computer), not all mathematicians are content with the result. They are troubled by the fact that the theorem was *still* proven by a computer, feeling that if it's so easy to understand it should have been proven by hand. Thus, anyone who can truly prove the theorem without using a computer may win the Fields Medal, the math equivalent of the Nobel Prize.

Another proof solved with computers is the *double bubble.* The double bubble refers to a pair of bubbles that intersect; they are also separated by a membrane bounded by

the intersection of the two bubbles. This is similar to two bubbles stuck together when a child blows bubbles using a water and soap mixture. Since the ancient Greeks, mathematicians have worked on the problem of finding a mathematical proof of the efficiency of a single round bubble. The problem became even more rigorous when considering enclosing two bubbles—or two separate volumes. The problem was solved around 1995 by mathematicians Joel Hass, Michael Hutchings, and Roger Schlafly. They used a computer to calculate the surface areas of the bubbles and found that the double bubble has

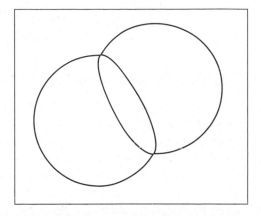

In the problem of the double bubble, ancient mathematicians worked on a proof that would demonstrate the efficient use of space created by two joined bubbles.

a smaller area than any other when the enclosed volumes are the same. But this isn't the last word: Scientists are currently working on triple bubbles.

How are **algorithms** connected to **computers**?

Algorithms are essentially the way computers process information. In particular, a computer program is actually an algorithm that tells the computer what particular steps to perform—and in what order—so a specific task is carried out. This can include anything from working out a company's payroll to determining the grades of students in a certain class. (For more about algorithms, see "Foundations of Mathematics.")

What is a **teraflop** and why is it important in computing?

A teraflop is a unit of measure of a computer's performance in which one teraflop is 10^{12} operations per second—in other words, it means a trillion floating point operations per second. It comes from the word "flop," or "Floating Point Operations Per Second." So far, teraflops are not found on your everyday desktop computer; such power is currently reserved for servers and desktop supercomputers, but probably not for long.

Teraflops are used whenever scientists and computer specialists need a great deal of power, such as in a server that needs to be fast and capable of doing many tasks at once in the foreground and background of an application. For example, they are used a great deal in video editing, especially with the advent of high-definition television. They are used in the music industry for editing and digital sound capturing. And they are used in servers that require a great deal of online storage.

But businesses and certain industries may not be the only ones that have teraflop capabilities in the future. They are currently being used in the video gaming industry, and because of the need for more power in more realistic gaming, the demand for ter-

aflops in the home computer is increasing. (There are currently some gaming consoles, such as the Xbox 360, that already have a combined computational power of 1 teraflop.)

What are some **modern computer games**?

There are a plethora of computer games out on the market. Two of the more popular ones are *video games* and *personal computer games*. Video games are electronic games that allow the user to interact with an interface—most often visual feedback on a video device (a computer screen). They are played on a platform, or your personal computer or a video game console. Most games have an input device, such as a hand-held joystick or button on a mouse. One of the most popular video game consoles is called PlayStation, a brand offered by Sony Computer Entertainment. It also has a PlayStation Network, an online service with over 69 million users around the globe, and includes a store and a social gaming network.

A personal computer game, or PC game, is a video game played on a single personal computer. Older personal computer games were slower and less visual. The more advanced personal computer games are offered on DVDs and CDs, through online downloads, or even streaming services. They are then downloaded into a person's computer. Because of their more powerful design and processing needs, they also typically require certain specialized hardware to play, such as a special graphics processing unit for 3-D games.

What is **cryptography**?

Because of the extensive connections between computers across the Internet, it has become necessary to find ways to protect data and messages from tampering or reading. This includes protecting people's personal information when they buy things over the Internet and those who need to keep banking data secure. One of the major techniques for ensuring such privacy of files and communications is called cryptography.

Cryptography is a mathematical science used to secure the confidentiality (and authentication) of data sent by a user to a certain site. It secures the data by replacing it with a transformed version that can then be reconverted to show the original data, but only by someone with the correct cryptographic algorithm and key. This is why, when ordering over the Internet, it is important to see the "lock" icon at the bottom of the screen. This is your way of knowing that cryptography is working and the data is secure, thus preventing the data's unauthorized use.

Have **computers** had an **effect** on the field of **statistics**?

Yes, computers have had a definite effect on the field of statistics. In particular, personal computers, software such as spreadsheets and professional statistical packages, and other information technologies are now an integral part of statistical data analy-

sis. These tools have enabled statisticians to perform realistic statistical data analysis on large amounts of data faster and cheaper than ever before.

Statistical software systems are most often used to determine examples, understand existing concepts in the statistics, and to find new trends in statistical data. Most of the packages allow the data to be entered into the computer program, but the emphasis then switches to the statistician's ability to interpret the data.

There are two well-known programs often used in statistics: the SAS and SPSS, both of which are commercial statistical packages. The SAS system is a statistics, graphics, and data management software package available for personal computers. It allows the desktop computer user to get the quality of results once reserved for users of mainframe computers. The SPSS (Statistical Package for the Social Sciences) is also a popular software package for performing statistical analyses. It enables the user to summarize data, determine if there are significant differences between groups, examine relationships among all the variables, and even graph the results.

To date, what **computer** has the **top speed** in operations per second?

The TOP500 project ranks and details the 500 most powerful known computer systems in the world, an idea that began in 1993. The results are published twice a year: the first coinciding with the International Supercomputing Conference in June, the second in November at the ACM/IEEE Supercomputing Conference. The following chart lists the top ten as of November 2011:

Fastest 10 Computer Systems as of November 2011

Computer	Maximum Speed in Petaflops*	Year Completed	Country
Fujitsu K computer	10.5	2011	Japan
NUDT Tianhe-1A	2.56	2010	China
Cray Jaguar	1.76	2009	United States
Dawning Nebulae	1.27	2010	China
NEC/HP Tsubame	1.19	2010	Japan
Cray Cielo	1.11	2010	United States
SGI Pleiades	1.09	2011	United States
Cray Hopper	1.05	2010	United States
Bull SA Tera	1.05	2010	France
IBM Roadrunner	1.04	2009	United States

*A petaflop is 10^{15} floating-point operations (flops) per second.

In actuality, the fastest computer in the world is the human brain, an amazing computing device with the best processor. To compare, the fastest computers measure speed in trillions of operations per second, but scientists speculate the brain can handle 10 quadrillion operations per second. The actual numbers are probably even higher than that.

Can robots help with daily household chores?

After decades of being promised that robots will one day take away those pesky household chores, researchers at Cornell University's Personal Robotics Lab may have just the right programming skills to develop that dream. The lab develops software for complex, high-level robotics, and one of the goals is to produce robots that can clean up a messy room, arrange books in a bookcase, or even pull out the dishes from your dishwasher and put them away.

And they are not the only ones. Researchers at the MIT Humanoid Robotics Group are developing Domo, the latest robot helper—or "human assistant"—in a series of robots. Domo comes with 29 motors, each complete with a computer chips running off a dozen computers that update the robot's information continuously. In this way, Domo is able to almost mimic the human response of adapting to "his" surroundings.

One of the most difficult tasks in developing such a mobile robot is to make the machine perceive information in a cluttered or unknown environment. Another challenge is to enable a robot to estimate depth. To do these tasks, the researchers have been developing a fast, efficient algorithms that allows the robots to "know" its location and orientation when, for example, picking up an object or locating where it is in a room. This not only involves detection algorithms, but also a knowledge of geometry and spatial orientation in three dimensions.

The list of robotics groups attempting to make better robots grows each year, but don't count on seeing any of these robots very soon. Researchers estimate that it will take a another decade or so before we see anything resembling the 1960s animated television program of the future—the Jetsons' Rosie, the robot maid—in our kitchens. You might want to start saving now, too—one researcher estimates that such a robot may cost you as much as a car.

How is **mathematics used by search engines** on the World Wide Web?

A search engine is a program that searches for World Wide Web (or WWW, which is why, when we write a URL to get to a certain website, we sometimes use www.) for documents using certain keywords. It then returns a list of documents in which those keywords are found. Search engines like Google are a general class of programs that use a proprietary search algorithm; they rely on probability, linear algebra, and graph theory to create a list that, ideally, produces the most relevant website results for the user.

EVERYDAY MATH

NUMBERS AND MATH IN EVERYDAY LIFE

(Note: Medical information contained in this chapter should not be a replacement for seeing your doctor. Please consult your doctor for any exercise programs you want to employ or any medical problems.)

What are the various **methods of keeping time**?

There are three basic methods of keeping time in common use today. They include time based on 12-hour intervals (a.m. and p.m.); a 24-hour clock; and Coordinated Universal Time clock (called UTC or Zulu time). All of these have to do with simple mathematics—mainly addition and subtraction.

A 12-hour clock (using the *12-hour interval* concept) is familiar to most of us. It represents half a day (24 hours divided by 2). The abbreviations "a.m." and "p.m."—terms that originated from the use of longitudinal meridians—are used to differentiate between the morning and afternoon hours. The term *meridian* (from the Latin *meri,* a variation of *medius,* or "middle," and *diem,* or "day") once meant noon. Thus, the time before noon was called "ante meridiem" and after noon was called "post meridiem." They were eventually shortened to "a.m." and "p.m.," respectively. Whether the terms are capitalized or not is not an issue either, as both are used in texts. The *24-hour clock* is, naturally, divided into 24 hour increments. It is commonly used by the U.S. military and other government agencies throughout many countries.

UTC (or Coordinated Universal Time; the letters are not a true abbreviation, but a variant of Universal Time) is equivalent to mean solar time at the prime meridian (0° longitude), formerly expressed as GMT, or Greenwich Mean Time. (The change was done to eliminate using the name of a specific location in an international standard.) Other names for UTC are World time, Zulu time, and Z time. UTC should not be confused with UT, or Universal Time, the basis for the coordinated broadcast of time signals, counted from 0000, or midnight.

A brass strip marks 0° longitude (the prime meridian) in Greenwich, England.

What are the ways to **convert** between **a.m and p.m.** and **24-hour time**?

When converting a.m./p.m. to 24-hour time for the hours between 12:00 a.m. and 12:59 a.m., just subtract 12 from the time. For instance, 12:45 a.m. minus 12 will equal 0045, and 12:59 a.m. minus 12 will equal 0059. Times between 1 a.m. and 12:59 p.m. are a straight conversion, such as 9:00 a.m. equals 0900 and 11:00 a.m. equals 1100. For the conversion between 1 p.m. and 11:59 p.m., add 12, such as 8:34 p.m. plus 12 equals 2034, and 11:59 p.m. plus 12 equals 2359 (also seen as 20:34 and 23:59).

To convert in the opposite direction from the above, add 12 for the hours between 0000 (midnight) and 0059, such as 0034 plus 12 equals 12:34 a.m., and 0059 plus 12 equals 12:59 a.m. To convert from 0100 to 11:59 and from 1200 to 12:29, there is a one-to-one conversion, the former to a.m. and the latter to p.m. For example, 0100 equals 1 a.m., 0345 equals 3:45 a.m., 1235 equals 12:35 p.m., and 1259 equals 12:59 p.m. To convert between 1300 and 2359, subtract 12, such as 1424 minus 12 equals 2:24 p.m., and 2359 minus 12 equals 11:59 p.m.

How are local **a.m./p.m.** and **24-hour times converted** to **Coordinated Universal Time** (UTC)?

When it comes to converting to specific times, Coordinated Universal Time (UTC) is a "standard." It is used for a variety of reasons, including certain scientific studies, such as weather forecasting and astronomical data. The following lists several examples of converting local standard time (a.m./p.m. and 24-hour) to UTC time, and local daylight savings time (a.m./p.m. and 24-hour) to UTC:

Converting 24-Hour Time to UTC

Local date	a.m./p.m.	24-hour clock	UTC
April 10	9:59 a.m. EST	0959	1459
April 10	5:00 p.m. EST	1700	2200
April 10	9:30 p.m. EST	2130	0200 April 11
May 10	9:59 a.m. EDT	0959	1359
May 10	5:00 p.m. EDT	1700	2100
May 10	9:30 p.m. EDT	2130	0100 May 11

Note: In the United States, for Eastern Standard Time (EST) add five hours to get UTC time, six hours to Central Standard Time, seven hours to Mountain Standard Time, and eight hours to Pacific Standard Time. For Daylight Savings Time, add four hours to Eastern Daylight Time to get UTC time, five hours to Central Daylight Time, six hours to Mountain Daylight Time, and seven hours to Pacific Daylight Time.

What is the **Dewey Decimal System**?

The Dewey Decimal System of Classification is a numerical method libraries use to classify nonfiction publications into groups based on subject. It was invented by American librarian Melville Louis Kossuth Dewey (1851–1931) as a system for small libraries. The subject of a book is classified by a three-digit numeral that represents ten classes of subjects (000–999). In order, these are Generalities, Philosophy and Psychology, Religion, Social Science, Language, Natural Science and Mathematics, Technology (Applied Sciences), Arts, Literature, and Geography and History. For example, *The Handy Math Answer Book* would be found in the Dewey Decimal System under the 500s for Natural Science and Mathematics.

A Dewey Decimal classification number is followed by the Cutter number, or Cutter. This method was invented by Charles Ammi Cutter (1837–1903) and is an alpha-numeric way to represent words or names by using one or more letters followed by one or more Arabic numerals used decimally. Both systems—the Dewey Decimal System and Cutter—are together called the "call numbers," a way of locating every book in a library.

What is a **ruler**?

Usually made of wood, metal, or plastic, a ruler is a measuring stick. Most rulers have a straight edge used for drawing straight lines and measuring lengths. The simplest and most well-known ruler has small scales, measured in terms of inches (and/or centimeters).

In order to read a ruler, the user needs to know the main divisions. For example, when looking at a foot ruler, the longest increments are represented by inches and are usually numbered 1 through 12; the measurement starts on the left end of the ruler, which may or may not be marked with a "0." The next divisions, from smallest to

What are some ways to measure when you don't have a ruler?

There are some pretty standard items that you can use if you don't have a ruler handy to measure something. Most of them are standard sizes, such as a sheet of paper measuring 8.5" × 11" so it will fit into most computer printers with ease. Here are a few of the best ways to do a quick measurement (remember, too—some of these are approximations):

- A sheet of standard letter paper is 8.5 by 11 inches long.
- U.S. paper currency measures 6 1/8 inches wide and 2 5/8 inches long.
- Most standard business cards measure 2 inches long by 3 1/2 inches wide.
- Most postcards measure 3 inches by 5 inches.
- The diameter of a quarter is about one inch; the diameter of a penny is approximately 3/4 of an inch.
- A credit card is about 3 3/8 inches by 2 1/8 inches.
- A standard AA battery is about 2 inches long.
- The average adult toothbrush is about 7 inches long.

largest, are: The distances between the smallest increments represent a sixteenth of an inch, the distances between the next largest increments represent an eighth of an inch, the next represent a fourth of an inch; and, finally, a half of an inch.

How can a person **calculate** the amount of **carpeting needed** to **redecorate a room** in a house?

Watching remodeling programs on television, visiting someone else's house, or even getting cabin fever in the winter often triggers the need to redecorate from floor to ceiling. But just how much new carpeting does a house need? The main way to discover how to cover up the floors is by using simple geometry, the branch of mathematics dealing with area, distance, volume, and the properties of shapes and lines. (For more about geometry, see "Geometry and Trigonometry.")

For example, if a person needs to buy new carpeting for a bedroom, just use the formula $A = L \times W$, or the area equals the length times the width. For a bedroom that measures 10 feet by 12 feet, the area would equal 120 square feet. Thus, the room would need 120 square feet of carpeting.

If a living room has a circular alcove, there is another measurement one can use: $A = pi (\pi) \times r^2$, or the area (A) equals pi times the radius squared. If the room measures 12 feet in width at the long end of the alcove (or the diameter of the alcove), the

radius of the alcove is 6 feet. Thus, A = 3.14159 × (6)2, or 113 square feet (rounded to the nearest square foot), would equal the area of an entire circle. Because an alcove is half of a circle, divide the 113 square feet in half, or about 56.5 square feet. Add this area to the rest of the room. For instance, if the rest of the room measures 10 by 12 feet, multiply 10 × 12 = 120, then add the alcove area of 56.6 to get the needed amount of carpeting: 176.5 square feet.

Measuring a room for a circular rug involves some basic knowledge of mathematics.

Are **ratio** and **proportion** important in cooking?

Yes, ratio and proportion—two major mathematical concepts—are important in cooking (as is addition, subtraction, multiplication, and division). For example, when a recipe calls for 1 cup of flour and 2 eggs, the relationship between these two quantities is called a ratio. In this case, the relationship of cups of flour to eggs is 1 to 2, or 1/2, or 1:2. Any change in this ratio and the recipe's result will not be the same—and the food might not be edible.

Another way of looking at cooking and mathematics is when changing the amount of ingredients in a recipe. For example, when a recipe calls for a certain amount of each ingredient, and the cook wants to make half a recipe, everything in the list is divided in half. Two cups of sugar becomes one cup, 1/2 teaspoon of vanilla becomes 1/4 teaspoon, and so on. The same logic applies if the cook wants to double the recipe, but in this case everything is multiplied by two. Two cups of sugar becomes 4 cups; 1/2 teaspoon of vanilla becomes 1 teaspoon; and so on.

What does it mean when a **test score** is marked **"on a curve"**?

A test score marked "on the curve" means that the marks will roughly follow what is often called a Gaussian Probability Distribution—or, more commonly, a bell curve. This symmetrically shaped curve is based on the test scores of the exam. In a perfect world, one-sixth of the scores would be on either end of the curve, with more than two-thirds falling in the middle, creating a normal distribution.

But most test results are not ideal. Thus, when a plot of the number of students versus the marks received are viewed, the relative difficulty of the test is known. It is then up to the teacher to decide how to distribute the grades (this is usually done by comparing each student's mark to the distribution curve). The teacher then decides where to cut off the passing and failing marks, which is often referred to as curving the grades. (For more about normal distribution, see "Applied Mathematics.")

What's the difference between wet and dry measurements when you're cooking?

Many cooks know there is a difference in the kitchen when it comes to dry and wet measurements. In particular, such differences are seen when one measures a cup of something as an ingredient in a recipe. For example, when measuring dry ingredients, cooks use a "dry measuring cup," in which the ingredient is easily scooped into the cup, filled to the brim, and leveled with a knife or other flat-edged utensil. Most of these cups are made so one cup of an ingredient will fill the cup.

A "wet measuring cup" usually has increments written on the side and a spout for easier pouring. A measured cup of liquid is below the outer rim of the cup, making it easier to see the meniscus (the concave upper surface of a still liquid caused by surface tension) that one lines up with the desired increment on the side of the cup. It would be rather messy to use a liquid in a "dry measuring cup," whereas, it's not as bad using a wet measuring cup with dry ingredients. Some cooking purists use a wet measuring cup for dry ingredients, then weigh the amount used. After making the desired recipe, the cook can judge just how much "dry" ingredients to use with a "wet" measuring cup.

For most of us who are not as picky in the kitchen, the dry or wet measuring cup is just fine for either type of foodstuff. The main reason for remembering that there is a difference may be for those who want to one day start their own cooking school; and it's also for chefs who make up recipes for publication or special uses. This is because measuring accurately is the most important cooking skill that can mean a good tasting meal versus a bad one. In particular, test kitchens need to know the differences between dry and wet measurements to test recipes. They vary the amounts of the ingredients—called "tolerance testing"—to make the best-tasting recipes, all helped by the knowledge of the basic rules of measuring.

What do the numbers on **gas and electric meters** measure?

Gas and electric meters measure the daily gas or power usage, usually of a house or other building. The standard electric meters are clocklike devices that record the amount of usage. As a house or business draws on the electric current, a set of small gears inside the meter move. The number of revolutions are recorded by dials in the meter, with the speed of revolutions determined by the amount of power consumed. Newer digital models record power usage digitally.

A gas meter measures the amount of gas used by a home or business. In this case, the meter measures the force of the moving gas in the pipeline. The dials on the meter

turn faster as the flow of gas increases, or slower as the gas flow decreases. To understand how the gas and electric companies charge a customer takes only an understanding of simple mathematics. In both cases, the difference between one month's reading and the next month's reading is the amount charged. For example, if the electric current reading is 3240 and the previous month's reading is 3201, the amount of electricity used is 39 kilowatts for one month. Then the company multiplies the number of kilowatts by the amount per kilowatt hour to arrive at the charge to the customer.

Electric meters like this one measure daily power usage.

What are some numbers associated with **tire pressure**?

Tire pressure is measured using a tire pressure gauge, with the most common measuring device being about the size of a pen. First, a bit about pressure: The atmosphere at the surface of our planet measures about 14.7 pounds (6.67 kilograms) per square inch, or a 1 inch (2.54 centimeters) square column of air weighs 14.7 pounds. This changes depending on the altitude. For example, at an altitude of 10,000 feet (3,048 meters), the air pressure decreases to 10.2 pounds (4.63 kilograms) per square inch.

But a car, truck, SUV, or bike tire needs more pressure in order to inflate. By increasing the number of atoms inside the tire, there are more collisions between the atoms and more pressure exerted on the sides of the tire. In other words, a pump stuffs more air into a constant volume (the confines of the tire), so the air pressure within the tire rises. A car tire's pressure is typically at about 30 pounds (13.61 kilograms) per square inch; a bicycle tire's pressure can be around 90 pounds (40.82 kilograms) per square inch.

How is **political polling** done?

Although polls seem to be magical, they are merely a matter of taking information and applying some simple statistics. Polling is a technique that uncovers the attitudes or opinions of a segment of the population, and is based on certain questions about politics, the economy, and even social conditions.

Polling as it is conducted today started in 1936, when George Gallup used statistical modeling to take the first political poll: the presidential election of Franklin D. Roosevelt over Alf Landon. FDR was successful, as we all know, and it was "predicted"

How often are political polls wrong?

Just because statistics are used does not make polling infallible or even reliable. For example, some questions may be misleading. The media is notorious for asking such polling questions as, Do you agree that keeping the environment clean is important? as if the majority of people would say no. Such questions often make the results of polling somewhat questionable, especially if the original questions asked are not presented with the results. Errors and questionable outcomes are caused by people lying, bad interview techniques, and even the sample of people interviewed. All too often, the results of polling create another consequence: swaying public opinion and creating a "jump on the bandwagon" effect. (For more information about statistics, see "Applied Mathematics.")

Finally, the average sample in a poll is around 1,500 people. This is said to reflect the entire population within around three percentage points (called the margin of error). In fact, this is also the reason why so many people don't pay too much attention to the media's political polls—too few "data points"—and why many politicians conduct their own polls before, during, and after the elections. Of course, others cite their own statistics, including one that says, since 1980, every presidential election has been accurately predicted by national polls.

by Gallup based on his model. After the further successes of his polling methods, he was quoted as saying that sampling public opinion was like sampling soup: "one spoonful can reflect the taste of the whole pot, if the pot is well stirred."

His words continue to be followed today in justifying political polling: sampling a small number of people to reflect a larger population. The sample population can be chosen randomly, stratified, or by other methods; people can be polled via a telephone interview, questionnaire in the mail, or personal interview, such as an exit poll during an election (polled as a person leaves a voting place). Statistics such as averaging and resulting percents are then used, mainly by the media, to determine the overall "pulse" of the public. Many commercial poll takers not only claim their results help in market research and advertising, but also get the peoples' concerns out in the open.

What is the purpose of the numbers found in a **mailing address**?

The Zone Improvement Plan (or ZIP) Code is a grouping of numbers assigned by the U.S. Postal Service to designate a local area or entity in order to speedily deliver and distribute mail. ZIP Codes most often refer to a street section, a collection of streets, a structure or building, or a group of post office boxes, but the numbers do not rigidly conform to boundaries of cities, counties, states, and other places.

Depending on the area, a ZIP Code includes 5, 7, 9, or 11 digits. In the most common codes—five-digit ZIP Codes—the first digits divide the country into ten large groups of states numbered from 0 in the Northeast to 9 in the far West. Each state is divided into geographic areas identified by the second and third digits of the ZIP Code. For example, New York and Pennsylvania have ZIP Codes starting with numbers between 090 and 199; Indiana, Kentucky, Michigan, and Ohio begin with numbers between 400 and 499. The fourth and fifth digits of a ZIP Code identify the local delivery area.

Why do we have certain **telephone (and cell phone) numbers**?

Telephone numbers have a long and numerical history. Starting around 1879 and before the 1920s, most telephone conversations started with cranking a crank, which would "connect" to an operator; from there, the caller would most often either give a person's name or company and/or address—mainly to other local telephone owners. At this time, too, each customer who had a phone was usually assigned a four digit code, which would be used by the operator to make the call.

After the late 1920s, this progressed to calling the operator and using an "exchange name" to get the party one was calling; in addition, telephones with automatic dialers were becoming vogue in homes, making it easier to dial a number yourself.

But in order to accommodate the many people using the telephone, and to stop the confusion caused by many people living in larger cities having the same names, telephone companies turned to an alternate system of calling another party on the phone. Whether using an operator (usually if a person was not home) or a home dial phone, telephone company AT&T used a combination system of numbers to reach a party, whereas Bell System used a name and number system: the first two letters and number was the switching office or exchange, while the last four numbers represented the customer's number. For example, the movie *Butterfield-8* was actually named after an early exchange name. And, for example, for the Bell System name and number listing, an older number the authors are familiar with began with the colorful "PIoneer 8-XXXX." No one really knows why the "letters and numbers" began, but it may have been that telephone companies believed that people would remember names better than the correct order of seven numbers.

By 1958 people began asking for their own telephone numbers, phasing out the exchange number/letter system. The first city to use all number calling was Wichita Falls, Texas. It took just over a dozen more years for the letter and numbers to be replaced all over the country. With this code, the first three digits are called the prefix (or exchange number); the last four digits represent the part of the town in which you live. Thus began the familiar area code numbers (to send the phone number to the right state) and seven-digit numbering system with which we're all familiar.

MATH AND THE OUTDOORS

How is the **amount of rainfall** measured?

The amount of rainfall—liquid precipitation that falls to the surface—is measured by a rain gauge. The most commonly used free-standing rain gauge is a cylinder with increments (most often in inches) inscribed on the outside of the tube. It is put in an area that is not obstructed by buildings, trees, or other tall structures than can impede the collection of rainfall.

The rain gauge can also measure snow, but added steps are needed to calculate the measurements. In this case, a rain gauge measures the liquid equivalent of snow. This is why meteorologists will often say that a snowstorm that produces 10 inches (25.4 centimeters) of snow will have a liquid equivalent of 1 inch (2.54 centimeters) of rain, or a ratio of 10:1. But this generalization can be tricky. If the weather system is super-cold, such as an Arctic air mass over Canada and the northern United States, the below-freezing temperatures might create more than 10 inches of snow. Meteorologists often call this the "fluff factor," because the snow seems "fluffier" due to the fact that there is more air between the snow crystals at much colder temperatures. In fact, in very cold air the snow-to-liquid equivalent ratio can be 15, 20, or even 30 to 1. (For more about weather and math, see "Math in the Natural Sciences.")

A weather station on top of the Alps, including a rain gauge and anemometer for measuring wind speed.

How is **wind speed measured**?

Wind speed is most often measured using an anemometer. The simplest ones are made with cup-shaped devices that spin and catch the winds. The number of spins translates into an approximate value for the wind speed. The more accurate electronic anemometer has a free-moving turbine suspended in the middle of the instrument that, when held correctly, measures the wind speed. The speed of the turbine sensed by an infrared light relays the signal to an electrical circuit. From there, the wind speed is digitally displayed.

How do you tell the **BTUs** of a certain **type of wood** for your woodburner?

There are numerous numbers involved in having a simple woodstove or fireplace.

What do the numbers on an aneroid barometer signify?

The non-liquid aneroid barometer measures air pressure. As the atmospheric pressure changes because of storm systems (or lack of storms), the instrument records the changes. (Because atmospheric pressure changes with distance above or below sea level, a barometer can also be used to measure altitude.) The aneroid barometer contains a small capsule that acts like a bellows, but with the air removed. When the air pressure increases, the sides of the capsule are pushed in and the connected needle rises (moves clockwise). When the air pressure decreases or falls, the capsule's sides puff out and the needle moves in a counterclockwise direction.

The numbers on a common barometer range from about 26 to 31, with divisions of 10 or more in between each number. A needle (actually a hand similar to a clock hand) points to the numbers on the barometer and moves in response to the changing air pressure. These numbers are based on the principle that atmospheric pressure supports 30 inches (76.2 centimeters) of liquid mercury in a tube with one end sealed; and this information is based on the mercury barometer, the first type ever made.

How is an aneroid barometer read? In general, a falling hand on a barometer indicates a low pressure system is on the way with poor weather (usually a storm with snow or rain); a steady barometer means there will be no changes with the ongoing pressure system; and a rising barometer means high pressure and fair weather; an even higher reading, around 31, means an extremely dry atmosphere. The timing of the barometric change is also telling: A change of a degree either way in a few hours means that the weather will change quickly; a slow change of 0.3 or so a day indicates weather arriving in 12 to 24 hours. A quick rise in the barometer also often indicates high winds and unsettled weather.

All barometers work because of our weather systems: Changes in air pressure are caused by differences in air temperature. And this, in turn, creates the wind and weather patterns that carry the high and low pressure systems around the Earth's lower atmosphere.

One of the most important is BTU, or the acronym for British Thermal Unit. In a physical sense, 1 BTU is equal to a unit of energy equal to the work done by a 1,000 watts working for 1 hour. When it comes to your fireplace or woodstove, the wood you put into the system has a certain amount of BTUs to keep you warm; some are higher, some lower, depending on the species of tree.

It's not cut and dry, so to speak. Each tree has not only a certain weight (some are denser than others), but BTUs per cord (a cord is equal to about 128 cubic feet of

stacked wood, or about 4 by 4 by 8 feet; it's interesting to note that only about 70 to 100 cubic feet of a cord is solid wood). A cord is different than a "face cord," or a pile 4 by 8 feet long and only one "log" (or "stick") deep.

The following lists some weights/cord and BTUs for some popular "burning woods" (note that the softer woods, such as pines, don't offer as much in terms of heat energy BTUs; in addition, they do not last as long burning-wise, or burn as hot, as woods with higher BTUs):

- White ash—3,689 pounds per cord, offers 23.4 BTUs
- Cherry—3,120 pounds per cord, offers 20 BTUs
- Norway Pine—2,669 pounds per cord, offers 17.1 BTUs
- Spruce—2,100 pounds per cord, offers 14.5 BTUs
- White oak—4,012 pounds per cord, offers 25.7 BTUs
- White cedar—1,913 pounds per cord, offers 12.2 BTUs
- Red maple—2,924 pounds per cord, offers 18.7 BTUs
- Sugar maple—3,757 pounds per cord, offers 24 BTUs

What do **plant hardiness zone numbers** mean?

Plant hardiness zones are another way numbers are used. In this case, they indicate the average annual minimum temperatures for landmasses around the world. For example, one common Plant Hardiness Zone Map is broken down into 20 different zones based on the average annual minimum temperatures. In zone 5a, for example, the average annual minimum temperature ranges from –20 to –15 degrees Fahrenheit (–26.2 to –28.8 degrees Celsius; for example, Des Moines, Iowa). In zone 11, such temperatures are above 40 degrees Fahrenheit (4.5 degrees Celsius; for example, Honolulu, Hawaii). And in zone 1, such temperatures are below –50 degrees Fahrenheit (–45.6 degrees Celsius; for example, Fairbanks, Alaska). There are other maps, too, that break down the zones into even more detail.

What **numbers** are important when people **fertilize** their **plants**?

Not only do you have to pay attention to the zone where you plant, but how and when to use the best and complete fertilizers. In many cases, your average soil will not have enough nutrients to support certain plants, especially if you decide to cultivate a vegetable garden.

All plants need oxygen, carbon, and hydrogen, which are collected by the plant from the air, sunlight, and water, respectively. But they also need a range of other chemical elements, such as nitrogen (N), phosphorus (P), and potassium (K). These are usually present in what are called the complete fertilizers (which means it contains all three elements). Most general fertilizers—liquid or dry—that you find in your local nursery, farm-based, or even hardware store have these three elements in varying amounts.

For example, if a bag of fertilizer reads "10-5-6" that means the ratio of these three elements is 10:5:6, or that the fertilizer contains mostly nitrogen and lesser (and almost equal) amounts of phosphorus and potassium. This does not mean the bag contains all three of these elements only; it means that the entire bag of fertilizer contains 10 percent total nitrogen, 5 percent phosphate, and 6 percent potassium (often called potash). If a bag reads 5-5-5, then all three elements are found in equal parts within the fertilizer.

When buying such fertilizer for your vegetable (or even flower or herb) gardens, you should pick the best fertilizer based on what your plant needs, such as nitrogen for better leaf growth, or phosphate for activating root growth. In most cases, the fertilizer is either added to the soil before you plant in the spring, or added as a side-dressing as the plant grows. Each bag usually tells you how much you should add to the garden per square foot. Liquid fertilizers can also be used as something called foliar feed, which is sprayed on the plants' foliage and absorbed quickly by the leaves. In the majority of cases, nitrogen is needed as a foliar feed, thus the container will have the first number (representing nitrogen, or N) as the largest number.

MATH, NUMBERS, AND THE BODY

Is a **human's normal body temperature** really 98.6 degrees Fahrenheit?

Although everyone seems to be taught that the normal human body temperature is 98.6 degrees Fahrenheit, in reality, "normal" has a range. In fact, a person's actual measured temperature is rarely exactly 98.6 degrees Fahrenheit. One reason for this has to do with how the old standard was calculated: using an oral mercury thermometer and basing the results on a small human sampling.

Gone are the days of putting a thermometer under one's tongue for five to ten minutes. Today's thermometers are more sophisticated, accurate, and faster. Thus researchers believe that, based on better data—and more people tested—normal body temperatures measured orally range from 97.5 to 98.8, with about 1 in 20 people having a bit higher or lower normal temperatures. These numbers change throughout the day, too, varying from 1 to 2 degrees (on the average, reaching a low at about 2 a.m. to 4 a.m., and a high twelve hours later). An even more accurate representation of a body's temperature is to measure the core temperature, or the actual temperature inside the body, usually by using a rectal or inner-ear (tympanic) thermometer.

What do **blood pressure numbers** mean?

Blood pressure is a measure of how much the blood presses against the walls of the arteries. This creates two forces: The first comes from when the heart pumps blood

into the arteries; the second is the force of the arteries to resist the blood flow. When a person "takes a blood pressure," he or she is taking a ratio: The higher number (called the systolic or top number) represents the pressure when the heart contracts to pump blood to the body; the lower number (called the diastolic or bottom number) represents the pressure when the heart relaxes between beats. For example, for a blood pressure of 120/76 (said, "120 over 76"), the systolic reading is 120 and the diastolic reading is 76.

When a nurse or doctor takes your blood pressure, the two numbers they read to you indicate systolic and diastolic pressures in your arteries.

In actuality, the numbers represent how high the blood's pressure would force a column of mercury to rise in a tube. For example, a systolic reading of 120 means the mercury would rise 120 millimeters (usually labeled mm Hg, with Hg the symbol for mercury) in a tube. Based on the most recent information (and it keeps changing), a blood pressure below 120/80 is considered optimal for adults; 120 to 139 over 80 to 89 is considered "prehypertension." Anything over 140/90 is considered hypertension, which includes three stages, with the highest hypertension reading, stage 3, being anything above 179/109.

How does one calculate **resting heart rate**?

Calculating resting heart rate (RHR) involves easy math. It is the number of heart beats per minute when the body is resting, with the beats per minute representing the number of times the heart contracts. To measure the RHR, just count the number of beats per minute via the pulse—usually taken either on the inside of the wrist or along either side of the neck—for 15 seconds. Then multiply this number by four ($15 \times 4 = 60$ seconds) to get the heart rate per minute. Or count for 10 seconds, then multiply this number times six ($6 \times 10 = 60$ seconds) to get the heart rate per minute. For example, if you count 12 beats in 10 seconds, multiply 12 by 6 to get a resting heart rate of 72.

How does one calculate **heart rate** during **exercise**?

One reason to calculate heart rate during exercise is to know if a person is getting beneficial exercise to keep the heart and body healthy. In order to determine the safe and effective range of exercise to get cardiovascular benefits, two measurements are often taken. The first is the *maximal heart rate,* a number related to a person's age (the heart beats slower with age). To estimate the maximal heart rate, subtract a person's age from the number 220. For example, if someone is 40 years old, his or her maximal heart rate is 180.

The next measurement is the *target heart-rate zone*. This number uses the maximal heart rate and represents the number of times per minute at which a heart should be beating during aerobic exercise. For most healthy people, the range is 50 percent at the lower limit to 80 (some charts say 75) percent at the upper limit of their maximal heart rate. When a person's heart rate reaches a value within this zone during exercise, it means he or she has achieved a level of activity that contributes to his or her cardiovascular fitness. For instance, from the above example of a maximal heart rate of 180, the beats per minute for the lower range would be 180 multiplied by 50 percent (0.50), or 90 beats per minute; the upper range would be 180 multiplied by 80 percent (0.80), or 144 beats per minute.

If you work out and maintain a lower-than-50- or higher-than-80-percent limit, there are few beneficial effects from the exercise. In terms of the lower limit, the heart is not working hard enough for any cardiovascular benefit; in terms of the upper limit (besides the strain and injuries that can result), the heart is working too fast for any benefit and the body can't replenish oxygen that quickly.

What do **cholesterol numbers** mean?

Cholesterol numbers indicate the amount of cholesterol in the bloodstream (cholesterol is a waxy, fat-like substance manufactured in the liver and found in all tissues). For humans, a total cholesterol number above 200 means there is an increase in the risk of heart disease (between 200 and 239 is considered borderline high cholesterol); for anything below 200, there is less of a risk for heart disease.

But total cholesterol is not the only number to know. There is also Low Density Lipoprotein (LDL), or "bad" cholesterol. LDL is the main source of the buildup and blockage in the arteries (risk levels are above 130, measured in milligrams per decaliter). There is also High Density Lipoprotein (HDL), the "good" cholesterol that helps keep the plaque from building up (risk levels are below 40, measured in milligrams per decaliter).

When there is too much cholesterol in the blood, it can build up on the walls of the arteries. Over time, the buildup (often called plaque) causes "hardening of the arteries," or a narrowing of the arteries that restricts or stops blood flow to the heart. Blood carries oxygen to the heart, and if there is less blood (and thus, less oxygen) reaching the heart, chest pain can result. If there is a near-complete or complete blockage that cuts off the blood supply to a portion of the heart, a heart attack (myocardial infarction) is often the result. This is why most doctors recommend watching your numbers for total cholesterol, HDL, and LDL for signs of any change.

Why is **measuring medications** so **difficult**?

There are many ways that medications are measured, which often leads to confusion when someone asks what kind, amount, and dosage of medications you consume (and

How much is a "teaspoon" of medicine? Because people often measure medicines in different ways at home, it is common that people do not administer correct dosages for themselves or their children.

why doctors recommend you to carry a list of your medications, along with the amount of each pill and dosage).

Pills come in a wide variety of types, of course, ranging from tiny and round to what was once referred to as very large "horse pills." Most pills have the needed ingredient—usually 5 to 10 percent of the tablet—along with other substances that either make them palatable or easier to swallow, and allow the pill to dissolve in your system. Dosage is the most confusing topic when taking a medication. Many times, a label will read, "one teaspoon before bedtime." But the problem comes in when you realize that not everyone has the same teaspoon, or measures the same way. In fact, in one study, people were asked to pick out a spoon size that would measure 5 milliliters, the proper measurement meant by "a teaspoon" when using medications. Most people chose spoons (they ranged from 4.4 to 10 milliliters) that were higher in dosage, sometimes choosing a spoon that would give them double the dose. This is why doctors recommend a medicine spoon or dosing syringe.

The following is a list of numbers that you may see in your medicine cabinet. Many medicines (seen with pills mostly) are measured using metric weights:

- 1 kilogram (kg, Kg) = 1,000 grams (1000 g)

- 1 gram = 1,000 milligrams (1000 mg)

- 1 milligram = 1,000 micrograms (1000 mcg)

- 1 microgram = 0.001 milligrams (0.001 mg)

- 1 milligram = 0.001 gram (0.001 g)

- 1 microgram = 0.000001 gram (0.000001 g)

And in terms of measuring out dosages, the following lists some of the more common measurements:

- 1 cubic centimeter (cc) = 1 milliliter (ml)

- 1 teaspoon = 5 cc = 5 ml

- 1 tablespoon = 15 cc = 15 ml = 3 teaspoons

- 1 ounce (oz) = 30 cc = 30 ml = 2 tablespoons = 6 teaspoons

How do the **body's natural rhythms** and mathematics seem to fit together?

The body has several natural cycles it experiences, including one called circadian rhythm (CR). In general, CR refers to the many body clocks that regulate our daily rhythms, natural cycles that control our appetite, energy, body temperature, sleep, and moods. The reason for such rhythms is mainly because your body's cells don't have enough energy to perform their many tasks at a constant rate and at the same time; thus, biological processes are rhythmic, giving cells time to alternately rest and be active. In its simplest form, this is why animals (and plants) have a dormant (sleep) cycle.

One of the more interesting interpretations of rhythms—albeit somewhat controversial, as most people believe it's more "trendy" than scientific—are your biorhythms, or how your life is affected by biological cycles that cause oscillations (think of an up and down sine wave). It's divided into cycles that show how you are doing intellectually (a 33-day cycle; peak days you're at your best memory-, logically-, and alertness-wise), physically (a 23-day cycle; peak days you're at your best strength-wise and well-being-wise), and emotionally (a 28-day cycle; peak days you're at your best creativity-, sensitivity-, perception-, and mood-wise).

Each biorhythm varies throughout the days, affecting you depending on where on the sine wave you fall that day. To determine each part of the cycle, use the following: For physical $= \sin(2\pi t/23)$; emotional $= \sin(2\pi t/28)$; intellectual $= \sin(2\pi t/33)$; and an extra cycle, the intuitive $= \sin(2\pi t/38)$, with t being the number of days since you were born. Plot them each day to see how you're doing through the week or year. Or just do it the easy way and go to a "biorhythm calculator" on the Internet.

What is a **dog's** and **cat's age equivalent** compared to a human?

All animals "age" at different rates, and our domestic dogs and cats are no exception. Unlike humans, these pets seem to age more rapidly in terms of human years, with both animals being of an age equivalent to about 15 human years by the time they are one year old. There are, however, some differences for dogs. Some people have determined an age range depending on the size of the animal. For example, a dog over 90 pounds may only be equivalent to 12 human years by the time it is one year old; a dog 51 to 90 pounds is about 14 human years old when it is one year old; and dogs under 50 pounds are the equivalent of 15 human years by their first year. These age differences are reflected for the entire life of the dog. Below is a simplified table illustrating dog and cat years and their human age equivalents.

Human Years versus Cat/Dog Equivalents

Human Age Equivalent	Cat Age	Dog Age
10 years		5 months
13 years		8 months

Human Age Equivalent	Cat Age	Dog Age
14 years		10 months
15 years	1 year	1 year
24 years	2 years	2 years
28 years		3 years
32 years	3 years	4 years
36 years	5 years	5 years
40 years	6 years	6 years
44 years	7 years	7 years
48 years	8 years	8 years
52 years	9 years	9 years
56 years	10 years	10 years
60 years	11 years	11 years
64 years	12 years	12 years
68 years	13 years	13 years
72 years	14 years	14 years
76 years	15 years	15 years
80 years	16 years	16 years
84 years	17 years	17 years
88 years	18 years	18 years
89 years		19 years
92 years	19 years	
93 years		20 years
96 years	20 years	21 years
99 years		22 years
103 years	23 years	
106 years	24 years	

MATH AND THE CONSUMER'S MONEY

How do I **make change**?

"Making change" is an important monetary endeavor no matter where a person travels or lives. It is defined as the change (in coins and/or bills) a customer receives after making a purchase, especially when the customer gives the merchant more money than the amount due. For example, say a person visiting a farmer's market in the United States buys a half pound of garlic for $2.60 and gives the merchant a $20.00 bill. To

make change, the merchant would first subtract $20.00 – $2.60 = $17.40; or the customer is to receive $17.40 in change.

The resulting change would start with the highest denomination and work down: a $10 bill, a $5.00 bill, two $1.00 bills, a quarter ($0.25), a dime ($0.10), and a nickel ($0.05). The merchant would then count the change out to the customer, stating each amount in the "opposite" fashion: "That's a total of $2.60 out of $20.00; your change is two sixty-five [$2.65 as the nickel is given], two seventy-five [$2.75 as the dime is given], three dollars [as the quarter is given], four dollars [as the first dollar bill is given], five dollars [as the second dollar bill is given], ten dollars [as the five-dollar bill is given], and twenty [as the ten-dollar bill is given]."

What is a **store discount**?

Many stores—from apparel shops to bookstores—offer a discount on the retail price or, less often, on the sale price. For example, say a sweater that originally costs $50.00 is discounted by 25 percent during a sale at a department store. The customer will actually pay 75 percent (or 75/100 or 0.75) of $50.00. To determine the sale price, multiply $50.00 by 25 percent ($50 \times 0.25 = 12.50$); then subtract the discount from the original price to find the sale price, or $50.00 – $12.50 = $37.50.

How does a person calculate **sales tax** on purchases?

Most states and cities charge sales tax on retail purchases made by customers—from clothes to certain foods. This sales tax is based on a percent of the purchase price, with the percentage of tax called the tax rate. In turn, each state's tax rates vary greatly, often with the counties charging additional taxes: For example, in Vermont, the state and local sales tax rate stands at 5 percent; Florida has a state sales tax rate of 6 percent. And in various counties of New York, the sales tax rates start as low as 7.25 percent to as high as 8.75 percent.

How is the sales tax calculated at the checkout? Take, for instance, a purchase of a $100.00 ring in New York City, a place with a sales tax rate of 8.265 percent. Multiply $100 times 8.265 percent, or $100 \times 0.08265 = $8.265, which rounds up to $8.27 for sales tax. The merchant would then charge the customer a total of $100.00 + $8.27 = $108.27. If the same $100.00 ring was purchased in Florida, the sales tax would be $100.00 \times 6 percent, or $100 \times 0.06 = $6.00, with a total purchase price of $106.00. Of course, not every purchase will be as straightforward as this, since some cities can also add local taxes and/or surcharges and fees to the bill.

How do you determine the **interest** rate on **savings bonds**?

U.S. savings bonds have been around for decades. During World War II, they were used to not only invest in the country, but to help pay for the war effort. Since then, buying

How is the price of gold determined?

The price of gold on the market has had a long and lustrous past. It's been used as money for centuries because of its rarity and, no doubt, luster, heft, and malleability. Gold pricing is thought to have begun in London in the late 17th century; by 1717, then Master of the Mint, scientist Sir Isaac Newton (the same Newton of "laws of gravity" fame) declared that the gold price would be 4.25 pounds per troy ounce, an amount that was held mostly the same for close to two hundreds years.

Although the first gold standard was established by the Bank of England in 1696, it took until around the late 1800s for most other European countries to adopt a gold standard. Many of these countries halted the standards during the financially troubled times of World War I; then began again in earnest after World War II. The U.S. dollar represented a gold rate of $35 per troy ounce after the war; by 1971, the U.S. stopped the convertibility of the dollar to gold (yes, at one time, although difficult to do, you could "trade" a dollar bill for gold). One can see evidence of this on the older "silver certificate" one dollar bills printed before 1971. Other countries also dropped the currency-into-gold standards, with Switzerland being the last country to do so in 2000.

Today, gold is still sold most often as gold coins, with each coin having a certain amount of the metal, usually one troy ounce. The daily price of gold is determined by the trading on several exchanges, with the price of gold based on the London gold fix. The gold fix, or price, is set twice a day: at 10 a.m. and again at 3 p.m. in London, the latter time originally chosen to coincide with the opening of U.S. markets. The gold fix is determined by several banks (or bullion trading firms), a system that has not changed in decades, but the member banks have changed. Gold is also traded based on a "spot price"—the price paid for immediate delivery (versus "futures prices" in which delivery and payment is made at a future date)—and is derived from global over-the-counter gold trading markets.

bonds is still thought of as a patriotic way of "lending" money to the government to finance the country's borrowing needs (for more information about bonds, visit the official savings bond site at Treasury Direct, www.treasurydirect.gov).

There are several features to know when buying bonds and all of them have to do with a certain degree of mathematics. Bonds are backed by the government, and if you buy one for $500, your cashed-in value will never fall below the $500 you initially paid. That's why they are considered safe, conservative investments. They have competitive interest rates, even between the different types of saving bonds. Although there are several rules concerning cashing certain bonds (including not cashing one in for over a year in some cases), no state or local taxes are charged, and the federal tax is deferred

until the bond is cashed in. Depending on the bond, it can be for face value or half the face value. For example, people who bought Series I bonds bought them for $100 with a face value of $100; and people who bought Series EE bonds bought them for $50 with a face value of $100.

The interest rates also represent mathematics. Some bonds have a fixed rate—especially older bonds—never changing in interest over the life of the bond. But there are several types of bonds that are affected by changes in the economy, including some that have fixed rates. And although it seems as if "fixed" means never moving, in this case, it is not. The government can still change the rates in certain situations, such as in "deflationary situations." Thus, every May and November, based on the changes in the Consumer Price Index for all Urban Consumer (CPI-U) and combined with the fixed rate, the earning rate of this type of bond is determined. This means that if you have one of these types of bonds, and it started with a rate of 4 percent, under certain economic conditions it can change to, for example, 2 percent (at this writing, I-bonds were in this category).

Gold, surprisingly, is not as rare an element as many people believe, and, despite some industrial uses such as in circuitry, is not as useful as other, stronger metals. What gives it its worth is that peopler *perceive* it to have great value, as well as the fact that it is a very pretty substance.

What are some interesting **gold and numbers facts**?

Gold and numbers go together for many reasons. The following lists some interesting gold and number facts from the World Gold Council:

- The 40,000 miners who joined the California Gold Rush in 1849 were called "49-ers"; only a very few ever "struck it rich."

- One ounce of gold can be stretched to a length of 50 miles, with the resulting wire just five microns wide.

- One ounce of pure gold could be hammered into a single sheet covering 9 square meters (96 square feet).

- Gold melts at 1,064 degrees Celsius (1,947 degrees Fahrenheit) and only boils at 2,808 degrees Celsius (5,086 degrees Fahrenheit).

- Over 90 percent of the world's gold has been mined since the California Gold Rush.

- The number of grams in a troy ounce of gold: 31.103.

How does a person calculate the amount of a tip?

A tip, or gratuity, is the money given to a person who performs a service for a customer, such as a waiter or waitress at a restaurant. Depending on the service, in the United States a 10 percent to 20 percent tip is usually left, with the most common being 15 percent, although many people have stories about the 0 percent tip they left after a bad experience. The tip is based on the total bill—the meal and the tax—although some people base the gratuity on just the meal. For example, if a meal at a restaurant costs a total of $10.00 (meal and taxes), a 15 percent tip would be $10 \times 0.15 = $1.50. The tip is usually left at the table (or given to the waiter or waitress), or taken out by the establishment and added to a "tip pot" shared by all the wait staff.

There are some mathematical tricks to remember when leaving a tip at a restaurant, to a hairdresser, doorman, or in other appropriate circumstances. A good way to estimate a tip is to round the total bill to the most significant place value. For example, an $18.50 meal would round to $20. Next, move the decimal point of the rounded amount one place to the left ($20 to $2.00), or 10 percent of the total cost. Then divide this amount in half to determine 5 percent (or $2.00/2 = $1.00). Add the two resulting amounts to estimate 15 percent of the total—in this instance, $2.00 + $1.00 = $3.00 tip. (In reality, 15 percent of $18.50 is $2.78, which is close enough to $3.00.)

But remember, not ever country tips the same. Tipping is a way of life in Egypt, but taxi drivers don't accept tips. French restaurants must add the tip to the bill by law, usually at 15 percent. Tipping in Australia is almost nonexistent; no one tips in mainland China (mainly because the government tacks on enough charges to visitors); there is no tipping in New Zealand, either, as the price usually includes services; and don't even think about tipping in Japan (it's almost an insult)!

- Fort Knox holds 4,600 tonnes of gold (10,141,264.06 pounds); the U.S. Federal Reserve holds 6,200 (13,668,660.25 pounds).

- There was a 394 percent increase in the price of gold from December 2000 to October 2010.

- There are 750 parts per thousand of pure gold in 18-carat gold.

- The largest ever true gold nugget weighed 2,316 troy ounces (158.8 pounds) when found at Moliagul in Australia in 1969; it is called the "Welcome Stranger."

- Even at only 10 parts of gold per quadrillion, the world's oceans are estimated to hold up to 15,000 tonnes (33,069,339.33 pounds) of gold.

How is **unit price** used to **determine total price**?

The unit price is simply the cost for each item (or unit). The term is often used to compare the cost of the same quantity of items that come in different sizes, or it is used to determine total costs for services. For example, if a person was having a birthday party at a local restaurant for 100 guests, and each meal (unit) cost $7.50, the total cost of the celebration would be $7.50 \times 100 = $750.00. Add a tip to the total (see above), and it's easy to see why most people celebrate at home or only invite a few friends.

How do some **businesses price their products** to sell?

Did you ever wonder why some businesses price their products with a 99-cent cost at the end of the price? In this case, it appears that how we view numbers in association with money—or interpret our change—can affect the way we buy, especially when it comes to our impulse purchases. According to researchers, consumers are actually more likely to buy a product with the ".99" included in the cost.

To see what numbers most affected the consumer, researchers set up three catalogues, one with traditional prices, one with prices ending in .00, and one with prices ending in .99. They found that the 99-cent catalogues did much better than the .00 one, or the traditional catalogue, even though it only meant a one-penny difference. They believe the reason for reaching for the 99 cent article versus the $1.00 one is the 99-cent ending makes the consumer feel the price is less.

The researchers called the perception of 99-cents the "left and right digit effects." The study showed that the biggest impact in pricing items at 99 cents comes when it changes the left-most digit in the price; for example, $29.99 instead of $30.00 would be thought of as a "better value" than $2.49 versus $2.50. Other research found that 99-cent pricing in the opposite directions also had an affect on the consumer. For example, with the prices $29.99 versus $29, one out of four consumers would not even notice the .99 after the $29.99—or the right hand digits are ignored, yielding one penny short of an extra dollar for the business.

To further prove that money perceptions of consumers are often skewed, in one college experiment students who compared the prices of $99.99 with $150.00, then compared the prices of $100.00 with $150.00 concluded that the gap between the $99.99 and $150.00 to be significantly larger—even though there was only a cent difference between the two.

What is the lesson? Pay attention to what you're really paying for, and don't ignore the 99 cents at the end.

What is **balancing a checkbook**?

Balancing a checkbook is often a challenge. For some people, forgetting to enter checks written against or deposits made into the account creates the biggest balancing prob-

lems. For others, it is not depositing enough money to cover written checks. There really is no "art" to keeping a checkbook. It is just a matter of checks and balances—or debits and credits—and a little bit of simple mathematics.

To keep a healthy checkbook, there are several things a person can do. For example, keep a running balance of distributed checks in a check ledger. Whenever you write a check, write the amount in the ledger booklet most banks give with the checks. In the proper column, list the check number, who the check is made out to (and any other important information), the amount in the negative (–, or debit) column, and subtract the check amount from the last balance.

Balancing a checkbook involves reconciling one's bank statement with the record that you yourself have kept track of in expenses and deposits. By keeping tabs on deposits and withdrawals, you will hopefully not become overdrawn on your account.

Along with making out checks (taking out money), keep a record of deposits made in the checkbook register. Deposits are usually written in the positive column (+, or credit). Don't let the money get low—if the account balance goes into negative numbers, the account does not have enough money to cover the checks. If more money is not put into the checking account at this point, the checks will "bounce," or not clear with sufficient funds. (This is *not* good!) Most banks charge substantial fees to the account owner for bounced checks, not the person to whom the check is made out.

Whenever you receive your bank statement, check to see if the balance agrees with your checkbook. This is called "balancing the checkbook." As you compare the checks that have cleared with the listing in the register, check each off with an "X" or check mark. Also subtract any bank charges, such as ATM (Automated Teller Machine) fees. If all of the checks have cleared, and all charges have been accounted for, the balance of the checkbook and statement should agree (unless the bank gives interest on checking accounts; if so, add the interest to the checkbook under the "+" or "credit" column). If not all the items have cleared, check the bank statement and note the ones not marked; total all these outstanding transactions. Subtract the total of the outstanding transactions from the end balance on the bank statement; then add any deposits that are not on the bank statement to this new balance. The numbers should match the balance in the check register. If they don't, go back over the addition and

subtraction in the checkbook register to catch any inaccuracies, which is often the reason why a checkbook doesn't balance.

How do **modern cash registers** automatically know how much an item costs?

Modern cash registers are actually computers that are able to read a code consisting of a series of vertical bars varying in width. These are called bar codes (or barcode) and represent numbers and other symbols. The bar code is scanned by a laser beam that is sensitive to the reflections from the line along with space thickness and variation. The reader trans-

Many store items these days are labeled with bar codes, which use lines of varying widths to indicate numbers that can be read by laser scanners.

lates the reflected light into digital data that is transferred to a computer for immediate action or storage—usually both—resulting in the addition of items purchased and an immediate inventory for the store. (For more information about computers, see "Math in Computing.")

But bar codes aren't only for stores. They are also used to check out books from the library, identify hospital patients, and track manufacturing and shipping movements. There are even very small bar codes used in scientific research, for example, to tag and keep track of honey bees.

What is the **Annual Percentage Rate,** or APR?

The Annual Percentage Rate (APR) is an expression of the yearly interest rate that will be paid on a loan (which includes credit cards). It differs from the advertised interest rate, as it includes one-time fees in an attempt to calculate the "total cost" of borrowing the money. Therefore, it is wise to always look for a low APR. Because lenders are required to disclose the APR before a loan or credit application is finalized, it makes it easier to compare lenders. For example, if a person borrows $100 for one year at 5 percent simple interest (they will owe $105 at the end of the year), and the lender charges a $5.00 fee, the total cost to borrow the money will actually be $10, meaning the APR is 10 percent.

What are some **terms** to know when getting a **credit card**?

There are several terms—many that include a bit of mathematics—one should know when getting a credit card. An important one is the *annual fee,* which is often charged

by the credit card company and is a flat, yearly charge similar to a membership fee. A *finance charge* is the dollar amount you pay to use credit; it should be listed on your credit card statement. It usually includes the interest on the borrowed money and other charges associated with transactions, such as cash advance fees or exchange rate calculation fees when paying for an item in a foreign country.

As stated in the question above, the *annual percentage rate* (APR) is a measure of the cost (or relative cost) of credit on a yearly basis. With credit cards, APR commonly includes interest and other charges, such as a yearly rate. Credit cards often offer two types of *interest rates,* too. In the variable-rate plan, as the name implies, the interest is variable; it is usually tied to other interest rates, such as the Treasury Bill or prime rates. A fixed-rate plan is a rate not tied to changes in other interest rates; it remains steady, unless the credit company raises or lowers rates for everyone, which they can periodically do.

What are the ways **credit card companies** calculate **finance charges**?

When the credit card issuer calculates the finance charge on a card, it applies a periodic rate to a balance. In order to calculate that balance, the company uses various methods. The most common is the average daily balance method, in which the balance is calculated by taking the amount of debt in the account each day during a specific period and averaging it. The previous balance method uses the outstanding balance at the end of the period to compute the finance charges. The adjusted balance method derives the balance by subtracting any payments made during the cycle from the previous balance, with new purchases not being counted.

What is a **mortgage**?

A mortgage is a method of using property as security for the repayment of a loan. It is based on a 14th-century coinage of a Latin word meaning "dead pledge." The interpretation was that the property was "dead" to the borrower if he defaulted on the debt, and the pledge was "dead" to the lender after the loan was repaid. For centuries, it's been figured out using mathematics.

What **mathematical concept** is used to calculate **mortgage payments**?

In most cases, a mortgage is based on amortization, which is the gradual elimination of a liability (a financial obligation or debt, such as a mortgage) in regular, fixed, systematic payments (such as monthly) over a specific period of time. These payments must be enough to cover both the principal borrowed and the interest. Although it is usually written in a complex set of mathematical calculations, simply put amortization means a part of the payment goes toward the interest cost and the remainder goes toward the principal (or the amount borrowed). The interest is then recomputed

How are "points" determined in a real estate transaction?

When buying a home through a real estate group or bank, "points" may be paid by the borrower at the time a loan is made. This is usually to get a lower interest rate, because the lender often offers certain rate/point combinations that may help the homeowner save money. Actually, points usually refer to the commission charged by the mortgage broker or the loan fee charged by the lender when the loan is made. Points can be also negative, in which case they are called "rebates" from the lender to the borrower and are often used by borrowers to defray other settlement costs.

In general, each point is 1 percent of the loan amount. For instance, three points would be equal to 3 percent of the total loan amount. There is no set number of points offered by a lender, as it is not controlled by any laws. For example, on a $100,000 loan, one point is equal to $1,000; 10 points is equal to $10,000. A homeowner looking for a loan should try to find a mortgage broker or lender that charges fewer points. Some financial institutions might even be willing to negotiate for lower points. But beware of lenders offering no or zero points, because they usually charge much higher interest rates than those offering loans with points.

Although it is a matter of mathematics and a person's budget, there are some very general guidelines when choosing a mortgage. Low-rate, high-point loans are usually used by borrowers who can meet the down-payment cash requirement and either want to stay in a house a long time or want to reduce their monthly mortgage payments. High-rate, low-point combinations are for borrowers who don't expect to be in their houses very long, or who are short on cash.

on the amount owed, and therefore it gets smaller and smaller as the ending balance of the loan becomes less and less. That is why the homeowner pays a great deal toward interest and not the principal for the first several years of a home mortgage.

For example, if a mortgage is taken out for $100,000 at 6.5 percent for 30 years, the fixed monthly principal and interest payment is $632.07. For the first month, the homeowner pays interest on the $100,000 (or $541.67), with the remainder of the payment ($90.40) going toward principal. In other words, the debt on the principal is reduced by $90.40. By the next month, the homeowner owes interest on a lesser amount of money—on $99,909.60 (or $100,000 – $90.40), not the $100,000, with $541.18 going toward interest and $90.89 going toward principal. As payments are made month after month, the interest decreases and the principal reduction increases. By the 360th payment (or 30 years later), the payment contributes $3.41 to interest and $628.66 to principal.

351

MATH AND TRAVELING

How are **positions on Earth** determined?

Positions on Earth are determined using two numbers that represent latitude and longitude. These numbers are actually two angles, measured in degrees (°), minutes of arc ('), and seconds of arc ("). On a globe of the Earth, latitude lines circle parallel to the equator, and differ in length depending on their location. The longest line is at the equator (latitude 0 degrees); the shortest lines—actually pinpoints—are at the poles (90 degrees north at the North Pole; 90 degrees [or –90 degrees] south at the South Pole). In the Northern Hemisphere, latitude degrees increase as you move north away from the equator; in the Southern Hemisphere, latitude degrees increase as you move south away from the equator.

Longitude lines, or meridians (once called "meridian lines" and eventually shortened to "meridians"), are those that extend from pole to pole, slicing the Earth like segments of an orange, with each meridian crossing the equator. In the Western Hemisphere, longitude increases as you move west from Greenwich, England (0 to 180 degrees). In the Eastern Hemisphere, longitude also increases as you move east from Greenwich, England (again, 0 to 180 degrees). All points on the same line of longitude experience true noon (and any other hour) at the same time. But note: Longitude lines are not to be confused with time zones, most of which follow a more erratic demarcation. (For more information on time zones, see below; for more information about latitude and longitude with regard to polar coordinates, see "Geometry and Trigonometry.")

How does a **GPS work**?

What is often called a GPS, or Global Positioning System, is actually a receiver that locks on to the signals from satellites in a constellation of 27 Earth-orbiting crafts (only 24 are used, with three as backup). The GPS-receiving device allows people on Earth to determine their positions on the globe—and that's all about mathematics.

Solar-powered satellites (with backup batteries in case of a solar eclipse) travel about 7,000 miles per hour and circle the globe twice in just less than 24 hours. As they orbit about 12,000 miles above the Earth, they send signals to the ground that can be received by a GPS. When the GPS locates four or more of the satellites, the data can be used to pinpoint the user's location through trilateration, or the use

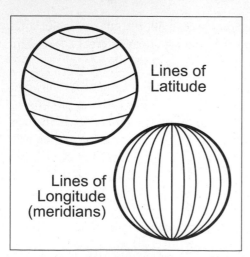

Lines of Latitude

Lines of Longitude (meridians)

Why is Greenwich, England, called the Prime Meridian?

The reason for Greenwich, England, being the Prime Meridian is historical. An imaginary line passes through the old Royal Astronomical Observatory, which was chosen by astronomers of the day as zero longitude. The observatory is now a public museum located at the eastern edge of London. It is a great spot for tourists, who can find there a long strip of brass that stretches across the yard marking the "prime meridian." Here it is possible to straddle the line with one foot in the Earth's Eastern Hemisphere and the other in the Western Hemisphere.

of geometric techniques that determine the location in three-dimensional space, which is actually the user's location in terms of latitude, longitude, and altitude.

Simply put, the receiver compares the time a signal was transmitted by a satellite and compares it to the time it was received, a way of telling the distance to the satellite. From there, it contacts the other satellites, gathering the same information, thus pinpointing the receiver's location. The reason it works is that any time, anywhere on Earth, there are at least four accessible satellites in orbit, which is why you can determine your location even on such remote places as Mt. McKinley or even Mt. Everest. (In fact, in 1999, the U.S. Expedition Team used a GPS to measure the elevation of Mt. Everest at 29,035 feet [8,850 meters], although this result is still debated.)

How does one **convert latitude and longitude** to degrees from readings containing degrees, minutes, and seconds?

It takes simple mathematics to convert the degrees, minutes, and seconds of latitudes and longitudes into degrees only. It helps to know that there are 60 seconds in one minute, and 60 minutes in one degree. Therefore, to translate 65° 45' 36" (also written as 65:45:36) south latitude into degrees you would do the following calculation: –65 degrees (south makes the number "negative") + 45 minutes × (1° /60') + 36 seconds × (1'/60") × (1°/60") = –65.76° latitude.

What are **time zones**?

Time zones are any of the 24 regions on the globe (loosely divided by longitude but more erratic in their demarcations), which is divided according to the number of hours in a day. Within each zone, all clocks are set to the same time. Time zones include the international date line, an imaginary line of longitude generally 180 degrees east or west of the prime meridian; the date becomes one day earlier to the east of this line.

Time zones are truly a product of mathematics. Initially, people used local solar time, resulting in slightly different times between towns. With technology—especially

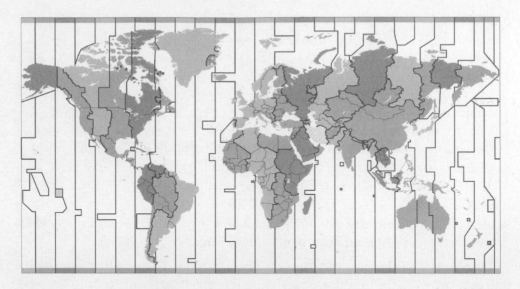

The world is divided up into time zones, sometimes rather irregularly; and not all time zones are separated by a full hour—some only have a half hour difference from adjacent zones.

trains and telecommunications—more accurate timekeeping became a necessity. Thus, time zones helped solve many of the problems by setting the clocks of a region to the same mean solar time. The time zones made it easy for neighboring time zones to be labeled "one hour apart." Not that the system is perfect. The hour separation is not universal, and because they often follow political boundaries, the shapes of the time zones can be extremely irregular.

How does one determine the **distance** and **amount of time** a **trip** will take?

There are several ways to determine the distance and amount of time a trip will take. For example, if the traveler knows that his or her car travels 20 miles for every gallon of gas in the tank, he or she could represent the total number of miles it is possible to drive based on how much gas is put into the tank. This can be expressed as $20g$, in which g stands for the number of gallons in the tank. For example, if someone bought 10 gallons of gas to reach a destination (10 gallons \times 20 miles/gallon), the traveler can go about 200 miles (the gallons in the top and bottom of the equation cancel each other out, leaving miles).

Another example involves cars and mileage. If the traveler drives down a highway at a steady rate of 65 miles per hour, the driver can determine how long it will take to get to a destination, especially if he or she knows how many miles it is to that destination. The equation is mileage divided by 65 miles per hour ($m/65$). For example, if the traveler is going 650 miles, the (650 miles)/(65 miles per hour) equals 10 hours (the miles in the top and bottom of the equation cancel each other out, leaving hours).

354

What is the **scale of a map**?

Most travel, street, or highway maps show a measurement scale, usually in terms of miles and kilometers. To determine a straight line (horizontal) distance on a map, take a piece of paper and mark the origin and destination as tick marks on the paper. Then measure the "distance" between the tick marks based on the map scale to find the distance in miles or kilometers.

Topological maps also have scales, but in this case the scale is a ratio representing the measure on a map to some number of the actual units of measure on the Earth's surface. For example, a map with a scale of 1:25,000 means that one inch on the map is equal to 25,000 inches on the ground. Because both numbers have the same units, it can also be interpreted as any unit measure. For example, the same map could also be interpreted as 1 centimeter equals 25,000 centimeters on the ground, or 1 meter equals 25,000 meters, and so on. For those who prefer to measure in miles and kilometers, most topographic maps also offer a graphic scale in the legend. (For more about scales, see "Math in Engineering.")

What is a **currency exchange rate**?

When traveling to another country, it is important to know the currency exchange rate, which is the value of a traveler's home currency compared to the currency of the country being visited. Like all currency, the U.S. dollar fluctuates daily when compared to other countries' currencies. For example, if you travel to Canada, and the U.S. dollar can buy 1.02 Canadian dollars, then the exchange rate is 1.02 to 1. If you go to New Zealand, and the U.S. dollar exchange rate is 0.5477, then 1 New Zealand dollar is worth 54.77 U.S. cents. The daily change in rates is based on many global economic factors, including the economic stability and health of the various countries, the price of commodities such as oil, gas, and gold, and the ups-and-downs of the various stock markets around the world. So before you travel, it's best to check the Internet for the latest currency exchange calculator to compare your money to the currency rate in the place you intend to travel.

What are some **non-Hindu-Arabic numerals** encountered around the world?

Although Hindu-Arabic numerals are the dominant numerals used around the world, there are some places in which other number symbols are used. For example, there are Chinese, Japanese (kanji), Greek, Thai, and Hebrew numerals. The following lists some of the ones encountered by world travelers (for more information about numbers, see "Math Basics").

Hindu-Arabic	Greek	Hebrew	Japanese
1	α′	א	一
2	β′	ב	二
3	γ′	ג	三
4	δ′	ד	四
5	ε′	ה	五
6	ϛ′	ו	六
7	ζ′	ז	七
8	η′	ח	八
9	θ′	ט	九
10	ι′	י	十

Besides our familiar Hindu-Arabic system, numbers are expressed using different characters in such languages as Greek, Hebrew, and Japanese. (For Chinese characters, see table in the chapter "Math Basics.")

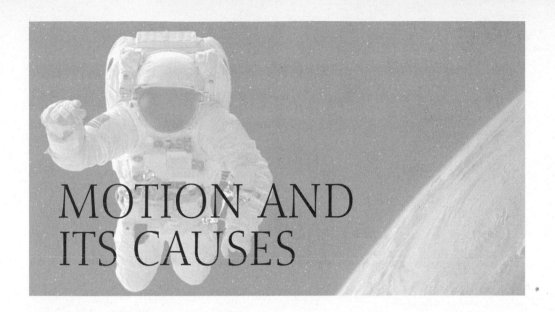

MOTION AND ITS CAUSES

What is my **position**?

Physicists define an object's location as position. How would you define your present position? Are you reading in a chair 10 feet from the door of your room? Perhaps your room is 20 feet from the front door of the house? Or, your house is on Main Street 160 feet from the corner of 1st Avenue? Notice that each of these descriptions requires a reference location. The separation between your position and the reference is called the distance.

What is **displacement** and how does it **differ** from **distance**?

The examples above involved only distance, not direction from the reference location. Distance has only a magnitude, or size. In the example of a house, the magnitude of the distance of the house with respect to 1st Avenue is 160 feet. Displacement has both a magnitude and direction, so the displacement of the house from 1st Avenue is 160 feet west. Or, you define west as the positive direction (because house numbers are increasing when you go west). Then the house's displacement from the reference location, 1st Avenue and Main Street, could be written as +160 feet. A quantity like this that has both a magnitude and a direction is called a vector.

How can you **represent** a **vector quantity** such as displacement?

A convenient way to represent a vector is to draw an arrow. The length of the arrow represents the magnitude of the vector; its direction represents the direction of the arrow. For example, you might create a drawing where 1 inch on the drawing represents 100 feet, and west points toward the left edge of the paper. Then the displacement of the house from 1st Avenue would be represented as an arrow 1.6" long pointing toward the left.

This diagram is similar to what navigators once used to calculate sea and air travel motion.

Can **displacement** be defined in **more than one dimension**?

More often than not you have to define a displacement in two or three dimensions. As an example, suppose you want to locate a house that is 160 feet west of 1st Avenue and 200 feet north of Main Street. The displacement is a combination of 160 feet west and 200 feet north. But how are they combined? You can't simply add them, because they have different directions. Go back to the drawing with the arrow. Define north as the direction toward the top of the page. Then add a second arrow 2.0" long in the upward direction. The tails of the two arrows are at the same place, representing the intersection of Main Street and 1st Avenue.

The two arrows are half of a rectangle 1.6" wide and 2.0" high. Draw lines completing the rectangle. The location of the house would be at the upper right-hand corner of the rectangle. Draw a third arrow, with the tail at the intersection of the other two vectors and the heat at the upper right-hand corner. The length of the arrow can be measured on your drawing, or calculated using the Pythagorean Theorem: the square of the length (the hypotenuse of a right triangle) is equal to the sum of the squares of the other two sides. In this case: $1.6^2 + 2.0^2 = 6.56$. Then length is the square root of that, or 2.56". So in real life the displacement would have a magnitude of 256 feet.

How is **GPS used**?

One very important use of GPS is to send time signals that allow clocks to be calibrated to within 200 ns (200 billionth of a second). Why would you need to know the time this accurately? Businesses that use computers in many parts of the world can synchronize their computers so that the precise time that transactions occurred are known.

GPS also provides navigation information. Hikers use GPS to replace maps, which are often outdated, compasses, and lists of landmarks. Automobile and truck drivers use GPS to replace paper maps and to find local businesses, such as banks, restaurants, and gas stations. Farmers use GPS to map precise locations in their fields. Not only does this information improve planting, it can be used to mark the locations of areas that need additional insect control chemicals or fertilizers.

Engineers are now working on GPS systems to improve the flow of automobile traffic and reduce crashes. Each car would have a GPS receiver that would then broadcast its position. This information could be used to change red traffic lights to green if

How can you use GPS to find your location?

GPS, or the Global Positioning System, was developed by the Department of Defense and was made operational in 1993. It consists of three parts. The first part is 24 satellites in 12-hour orbits that broadcast their location and the time the signal was sent. The second part is the control system that keeps the satellites in their correct orbits, sends correction signals for their clocks as well as updates to their navigation systems. The third component is the receiver. Some receivers are designed to be mounted in autos or trucks and display a map of the region around the receiver. Some are used by boaters to monitor their locations either in rivers or lakes or the open sea. Some are hand-held and can be used in the field by hikers and campers. Others are so small that they can be built into cell phones.

there were no opposing traffic. If two cars were equipped this way, the system could determine the distance between them and their relative speeds. If they were on a collision course the system would apply the brakes to avoid a crash.

How could you define your **position on Earth**?

If you use a GPS device, you might find that your location is given as a latitude and longitude. For example it might give you latitude: 40° 26' 28.43"N and longitude 80° 00' 34.49"W. Note that these are angles, not distances. The reference for latitude is Earth's equator. The reference for longitude is the "Prime Meridian" that runs through Greenwich, England (a suburb of London).

How can you **convert latitude** and **longitude** to a **distance** measurement?

A precise conversion is difficult because Earth is not a perfect sphere. Latitude is easier to convert. The circumference of Earth taken over the poles is 24,859.82 miles, which is equivalent to 360° of latitude. Therefore one degree is equal to 69 miles. So, the north-south distance between two cities 5° of latitude apart would be 345 miles.

Longitude is more complicated. At the equator 360° is Earth's circumference, 24,901.55 miles. But at the poles it is zero! So the conversion of longitude to distances depends on the latitude. If you use trigonometry to find the distance, you will find that the circumference at a latitude of θ degrees is the circumference at the equator times the cosine of the angle θ. So, at the latitude 40°, the circumference is 19,076 miles, and one degree of longitude is 53 miles. This result is only approximate because Earth is not a perfect sphere. For more accurate conversions consult a website such as http://www.nhc.noaa.gov/gccalc.shtml.

What is **speed**?

If something moves from position to position then speed is a measure of how fast it moved. Speed is defined as the distance moved divided by the time needed to move. Both change in position or distance and time are measured quantities. Frequently speed is called the time rate of change of distance. For example, if you drive 240 miles in 4 hours then your speed is 60 miles per hour (abbreviated mph). It is unlikely that you drove the whole trip at a constant 60 mph; this example calculated your *average speed*. If you were pulled over for speeding and were told you were going 80 mph, you wouldn't be able to avoid a ticket by saying "But officer, my average speed is only 60!"

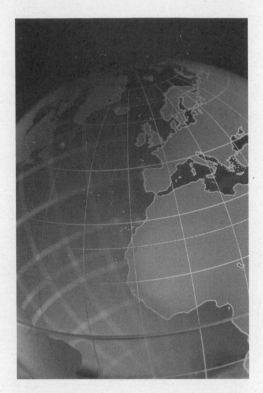

The vertical lines you see on a map or globe are lines of longitude and the horizontal lines are lines of latitude.

What **units** are used to **describe speed**?

In the English units used in the United States, speeds are usually given in feet per second or miles per hour. In the metric system meters per second or kilometers per hour are more common. Here are some typical speeds in the four systems of measurement.

Description	feet/sec	miles/hour	meters/sec	kilometers/hour
Walking	5.9	4.0	1.8	6.4
Sprinting	33	22	10	36
Car speed limit	103	70	31	113
Pitched baseball	139	95	42	153
Speed of sound	1,100	750	335	1,207
Speed of space shuttle orbit	25,667	17,500	7,823	28,164
Speed of light	98,425,197	67,108,089	30,000,000	108,000,000

What is **instantaneous speed** and how is it measured?

If you reduce the time interval between measurements of position both the distance moved and the time required are reduced. If the speed is constant, then the ratio of the two does not change. Instantaneous speed is defined as the limit of distance divided by time

How was motion perceived in the ancient world?

To the ancient Greeks motion was either natural or violent. The four elements sought their natural locations. Earth (including metals) fell down because it had a property called gravity. Fire (including smoke) went up because it had a property called levity. Water was between Earth and air. Heavenly objects, made of aether, moved in circles.

Arrows or other objects that were thrown were said to move because they were given violent motion. What was violent motion? The bow transferred force to the arrow; the thrower transferred force to the rock. Once in air (or water) the medium pushed the object along. When the force ran out the medium now opposed the motion and the object fell to Earth.

In the sixth century, the commentator Philoponus doubted Aristotle's view of the role of the medium in motion. Avempace, whose Arabic name was Ibn Bajja, was a Spanish Arab who died in 1138. He also discussed the role of the medium. While Aristotle claimed that motion in a vacuum would be impossible Avempace stated that motion in a vacuum would continue forever because nothing opposed it.

It wasn't until 1330 that the possibility that motion could vary was suggested. In that period philosophers at Merton College, part of Oxford University, developed their ideas of instantaneous speed and acceleration. Scholars at the University of Paris contributed greatly to these definitions that made the modern measurements of motion possible.

interval when the time interval is reduced to zero. In practice you can't reach the limit, but it is possible to measure positions every thousandths of a second. There are indirect methods of measuring instantaneous speed. For example, police use the Doppler shift (that will be discussed later in this book). That is, the change in frequency that occurs when the radio or light wave is reflected from a moving object. Automobile speedometers often use the turning force (torque) on an aluminum disk produced by a magnet that is rotated by the turning car axle. This force will also be discussed later in the book.

What is the **difference** between **speed** and **velocity**?

Just as you can add direction to a change in position and end up with displacement, you can also specify the direction of motion. The combination of speed with direction is called velocity. Velocity is the displacement divided by the time required to make the change, or the time rate of change of displacement. Velocity is a vector quantity, like displacement.

You might walk at 4 mph north, or a balloon might move at 5 feet per second up. If you assign the variable x to represent north/south, y to east/west, and z to up/down

If you can find a place free of light polution, on a clear night you can see the stunning view of our Milky Way galaxy. The earth not only rotates around the sun, but also around the entire Milky Way. A Cosmic Year is one rotation of the Milky Way, which takes about 225 million years.

position, then both the change in position and speed would be positive for movement to the north, east, or up. Your walking velocity would be $+4x$ mph. The balloon's would be $+5z$ ft/s.

Average speed is almost always more useful than average velocity. For example, in a NASCAR race the starting and finish lines are in the same position. So, no matter how fast the cars go, their average velocity is zero because the beginning and ending positions are the same. Instantaneous velocity, however, is more useful than instantaneous speed, as will be shown shortly.

Does **velocity affect distance** and **time**?

Einstein's Special Theory of Relativity shows that both distance and time change with velocity. Einstein reached this conclusion by noting that one must define methods of measuring both distance and time. The result is that as objects move near the speed of light their length (in the direction of motion) shrinks and their internal clocks that measure time run slower. The amount of change is described by a factor called γ (gamma), which is always larger than one. Thus the time given by a moving clock is γt, where t is the time shown by a fixed clock, and length is given by $l\gamma$, where l is the length of the fixed object. The table below shows γ for a variety of velocities (note that c is the speed of light):

How can you be standing still and yet moving?

Suppose you are reading *The Handy Physics Answer Book* while sitting on a moving bus? To another bus passenger your velocity would be zero, but to a person watching you while standing on a sidewalk your velocity would be equal to that of the bus. If you were walking forward on the bus, then the standing observer could show that your velocity was the sum of that of the bus plus your walking speed. Similarly, if you were walking toward the back of the bus, your velocity would be the velocity of the bus less your walking velocity.

Earth itself is in motion. It is rotating on its axis, revolving around the sun, and moving with the entire solar system around the center of the Milky Way galaxy. If is therefore important that the frame of reference for motion be specified. Usually Earth's surface is used as the frame of reference, which means that its velocity is zero.

Velocity	γ
550 mph	$1 + 3 \times 10^{-11}$
17,500 mph	$1 + 3 \times 10^{-8}$
0.5 c	1.2
0.9 c	2.3
0.99 c	7.1
0.995 c	10.0

How much does a **moving clock** slow down?

A clock on a jet plane (v = 550 mph) would lose 0.9 milliseconds per year, while one in the space shuttle (v = 17,500 mph) would lose 0.9 s/yr. In 1971 atomic clocks were placed on planes, one of which flew around the world eastbound, the other westbound. The changes in time were measured and agreed with relativity theory. Clocks on GPS satellites must be adjusted for the loss of time. More conclusive tests have been done with very fast moving (0.995c) muons. Muons, when at rest, decay in 2.2 μs (microseconds). The number of muons, produced high in Earth's atmosphere by cosmic rays, were measured at the peak and base of a high mountain. The ratio of numbers at the two heights showed that the muons lived 22 μs, which agreed with their measured speed of 0.995c. From the viewpoint of the muons, they decayed in 2.2 μs, but the height of the mountain was 10 times shorter than that measured by observers on Earth. Thus the predictions of slower clocks and shorter distances have been tested and agree with Einstein's predictions.

363

Do **all** relative **velocities add**?

Suppose you were riding on a spaceship moving at half the speed of light. If you were to point a laser in the direction the ship was moving, the person on the spaceship would be able to determine that the speed of the laser light was the speed of light, 300,000,000 meters per second. What speed would a stationary observer measure? Surprisingly, she would find that the light was traveling at the speed of light, not the sum of the speed of the spaceship and the speed of the laser light as measured by the traveling person. That is, the speed of light is the same in all frames of reference. This is another of the results of Einstein's Special Theory of Relativity. It has been tested, not with spaceships, but with gamma rays emitted by subatomic particles moving near the speed of light.

What is **acceleration**?

Speed and velocity are seldom constant. Usually they vary, and acceleration is a description of how that variation occurs. Acceleration is called the time rate of change of velocity. That is, it is the change in velocity divided by the time over which the change occurs. For example, a car might accelerate from 0 to 60 miles per hour. A sports car might do this in five seconds, while an economy car might require nine seconds. Which car has the larger acceleration? Both have the same change in speed, but the sports car requires less time to make the change, so it has the larger acceleration.

Like velocity, acceleration is a vector. That is, it includes both magnitude and direction. In speeding up, in which the change in velocity is positive, acceleration is a positive quantity. If the object is slowing down then the acceleration is negative. If, however, the object is going in the negative direction—for example, a car going in reverse—then speeding up is a negative quantity because the final velocity is more negative than the initial velocity.

Physicists do not use the term deceleration. Whether positive or negative, speeding up or slowing down, the term acceleration is always used.

The table below shows some typical accelerations in a variety of units. The rightmost column, labeled "g," compares the acceleration to that of an object falling in Earth's gravitational field. This ratio is frequently used in both everyday and scientific writing.

Description	feet/sec²	Miles per hour/sec	Meters/sec²	Kilometers per hour/sec	g
Auto from 0 to 10 mph	29.3	20.0	8.9	32.2	0.9
Sprinter first 1 s of 100m dash	18	12	5	19	0.5
Boeing 757 (takeoff)	10	7	3	11	0.3
Auto stopping from 60 mph	−30	−20	−10	−33	−0.9
Auto crash from 35 mph	−1,585	−1,080	−483	−1,739	−49
Object falling due to gravity	32.2	21.9	9.8	35.3	1.0

FORCE AND NEWTON'S LAWS OF MOTION

What **causes motion**?

Between 500 B.C.E. and 1600 C.E. there were many other ideas developed about the causes of motion. Some said a stone fell because of the "weight of a stone," supposing that weight is a property of the stone. Others, saying "the apple is attracted to Earth" supposed, like Aristotle (384–322 B.C.E.), that there is a desire of an object to move toward Earth. Others suggested that force is something that is transferred from one object to another, as discussed above. Still others, starting with Leonardo da Vinci (1452–1519), wrote that force was an external agent that exerted a push or a pull on a body.

What can **exert a force**?

The first answer that might come to mind is that a person can exert a force. He or she can throw a ball, pull the string on a bow to shoot an arrow, push a chair across the floor, or pull a wagon up a hill. Many animals can do the same thing, so one might say that living organisms can exert forces.

What if you place a rock on a table? Does the table exert a force on the rock, or does it just block the rock's natural motion toward the floor? If you put a heavy rock in your hand, it would sag downward because you would have trouble exerting the upward force on the rock. The same happens with a table. If the table is made of thin wood, it will also sag. What would happen if the table were replaced with a sheet of paper? The paper might hold small stones, but with a heavy rock it would tear because it could not exert a strong enough force. The heavier the rock, the greater the force the table or floor exerts. In summary, inanimate objects can also exert forces.

Forces like these, exerted by humans or tables that touch the object, are called contact forces. What are other contact forces? You might think of rubber bands on sling shots, roads on the wheels of your car, or ropes pulling carts. Water and air can also exert a force. Think of a stick moving down a stream, or what you feel when you stick your hand out the window of a fast-moving car.

In what **units** is **force measured**?

In *SI* (the metric system) force is measured in newtons, abbreviated N. In the English system, force is measured in pounds, abbreviated lbs.

How are **acceleration** and **force related**?

If you have a miniature toy car or even a smooth hard ball that can roll on a smooth level surface you can explore the effects of force on motion. When the toy car or ball is

motionless, give it a gentle tap with your finger. Note how it moves. Now, while it is moving give it a second, then a third or even a fourth gentle tap. What happened?

You saw that when the toy car was at rest and a force was exerted on it, it started to move in the direction of the force. When a force was applied in the direction of its motion, it sped up. Each additional tap caused it to speed up more. What do you think would happen if you were able to exert a constant force on it while it was moving? It's difficult to do, but try it.

You can conclude from this exercise that a force applied in the direction of motion causes it to speed up, or accelerate in the direction of the force. If the direction of motion is called the positive direction, then both the force and acceleration would also be positive.

Now start the toy car moving and give it a gentle tap in the direction opposite its motion. Don't tap it so hard that it stops or changes direction. See if you can tap it two or three times, again without stopping the car. What did you observe?

You should be able to conclude that a force applied in the direction opposite its motion causes it to slow down, or accelerate in the direction of the force. If you had defined the direction of motion as positive, then the force and acceleration would both be negative.

What happens when no force is applied? You saw in the beginning that when the toy car started at rest it remained at rest until you exerted a force on it. What happened while it was moving? It probably slowed down some, with the amount depending on the condition of the toy car and the hardness of the surface. But, the amount it slowed was certainly much less than it was when you exerted a force in the opposite direction.

How does **force affect acceleration**?

From your explorations you could draw the conclusion that when there is only one force exerted on an object, the larger the force, the larger the acceleration.

How does **mass affect acceleration**?

The best way to find out is to have two toy cars. Then add some mass to one of them. For example, you could tape coins to the car. Then line them up side-by-side and use a pencil or ruler to apply the same force to both of them. Again, just give them a tap. Which one goes faster? You probably found that the one without the added mass sped up more.

That is, for the same force, the greater the mass, the less the acceleration.

What is **inertia**?

Inertia is the property of matter by which it resists acceleration. That is, an object that has inertia will remain at rest or will move in a uniform motion in a straight line unless acted on by an external force.

In this simple pendulum game called Newton's Cradle, lifting one hanging ball and allowing it to drop and hit the second ball exerts a force on the next ball. The force on the ball at the other end causes it to swing out and back, according to Newton's laws.

What are **Newton's Laws of Motion**?

You have just explored how force and mass affect acceleration. Sir Isaac Newton (1642–1727) summarized these results in what is called *Newton's Second Law of Motion*. For a single force, like you used, it can be written as: Acceleration is equal to the force applied divided by the mass, or $a = F/m$.

That is, the acceleration (a) varies directly with the force applied (F). The stronger the force, the greater the acceleration. And it varies inversely with the mass (m). The larger the mass, the smaller the acceleration.

What happens in there is no force? The equation says that there is no acceleration. That is, if the velocity was zero it remains zero. If the object was moving, it continues to move with the same velocity. These statements are called *Newton's First Law of Motion*.

What happens if **more than one force acts** on an **object**?

You can explore this question with your toy car or ball. Try exerting two forces, like two finger taps in the same direction. You can see that the car or ball moves faster. The forces add. What happens if the two forces are in opposite directions? You can try pushing each end of a motionless toy car. What happens if both forces are equal? If one is stronger than the other? If they're both equal, the car will remain motionless. That is, it will act as if there is no force on it. If one is stronger than the other, then it will move in the direction of the smaller force, but it will accelerate less. That is, the

results will be the difference between the two forces. We'll explore forces that act in different directions later.

Physicists say that the combination, addition, or subtraction of forces produces a *net force* and it is the net force that affects the acceleration. Thus Newton's laws should be written as follows.

Newton's First Law: If there is no net force on an object, then if it was at rest it will remain at rest. If it was moving, it will continue to move at the same speed and in the same direction.

Newton's Second Law: If a net force acts on an object, it will accelerate in the direction of the force. The acceleration will be directly proportional to the net force and inversely proportional to the mass.

That is, $a = F_{net}/m$. Or, $F_{net} = ma$.

What are the **properties** of **friction**?

If you push a couch across a room, it will feel like someone is on the other end pushing back. If you pull on the couch, it will feel like someone on the other end is also pulling. If the couch is heavier, the opposing force will be larger. The amount of force opposing you will depend on the surface the couch is on. A carpet will have a stronger opposing force than a smooth surface, like wood or tile. These observations summarize the properties of friction between two objects that are in contact. Friction is always in the direction opposite the motion. Friction is greater if the moving object is heavier. Friction is greater if the surface is rougher. But, friction does not increase if the speed of motion increases.

How is the **friction between two surfaces** characterized?

In most cases the frictional force is proportional to the force pushing the surfaces together (N). This proportionality is usually written as $F_{friction} = \mu N$. The Greek letter μ (mu) is called the coefficient of friction. It is important to remember that the two forces, $F_{friction}$ and N are not in the same direction.

Do smoother surfaces always have less friction?

Surprisingly, if two metal surfaces are polished until they are extremely smooth, the coefficient of friction will actually increase. Recent experiments show that friction doesn't depend on surface roughness at the atomic scale! Friction is usually caused by chemical bonds between atoms on the two surfaces, but the fundamental causes of surface friction are still a problem that is not totally solved.

You probably noticed that it took more force to start the couch moving than it was to keep it moving. Physicists say that the coefficient of static friction is larger than the coefficient of kinetic (moving) friction.

Surfaces	Static friction	Kinetic friction
Teflon on teflon	0.04	0.04
Oak on oak (parallel to grain)	0.62	0.48
Steel on steel	0.78	0.42
Glass on glass	0.94	0.4

How can you **reduce** the **coefficient** of **friction**?

One method is to use surfaces that have less ability to form chemical bonds. Teflon is one such surface. Another is to have a thin film of oil between the surfaces. The oil will prevent bonding of the atoms in one surface with those of the other. Oil or other lubricants can reduce the coefficient of friction to about 0.1 to 0.2.

Do **rolling objects** experience contact **friction**?

Whether it is a bowling ball rolling down the alley or a wheel rolling on the road, there is no sliding between the ball or wheel and the flat surface, so there can be no contact friction. What is the cause of rolling friction? Rolling friction is the result of deformations of either the rolling object or the surface. Think about how much faster a rolling ball stops on grass or sand than on a hard surface. In those cases the ball has to push down the surface in front of it, which acts the same as contact friction. Or, remember when you rode a bicycle with soft tires. In this case the tire is squeezed when it contacts the street, which also acts like friction.

Does a gas or a **liquid** exert a **friction-like force**?

If you stick your hand out of the window of a moving car you can explore the properties of "air drag." The faster you go, the stronger the force. If your palm is facing up or

down the drag is much smaller than when your palm faces forward or backward, showing that the shape of the object matters. A smaller hand experiences less drag than a larger one. So, drag depends on velocity, area, shape, and the density of the air. These properties are different from other contact friction forces, but the force is still exerted in the direction opposite motion, so it slows down the object. Liquids exert similar, but stronger, drag forces.

Aren't there three Laws of Motion? What is **Newton's Third Law**?

Forces are interactions between objects. You need more than one object to have a force. Therefore, if two objects interact, each exerts a force on the other. If you push on a friend's hand, his or her hand pushes back on you. If you stand on a floor, you exert a force on the floor and the floor exerts a force on you.

Newton's Third Law of Motion states that these two forces are equal in magnitude but opposite in direction. If you exert an 800-newton force downward on the floor, the floor exerts an 800-newton force upward on you.

Note that Newton's Second and Third Laws are different. The Third Law describes forces on two different objects. Those forces can then be used with the Second Law to find out how the motions of the objects are changed.

What are some **applications** of the **Third Law**?

How do you accelerate your car? You press on a pedal called the accelerator. Does that cause the car to speed up? It cannot because the net force that causes the acceleration must be exerted on the car from outside it.

What does the car interact with? When it is not moving, it is touching the road, and thus interacting with it. When you press on the accelerator the engine causes the wheels to rotate in a direction that, because of friction between the tires and the road, pushes backward on the road. By Newton's Third Law, then, the road pushes forward on the tires and the car accelerates in its forward direction. What happens if you car is on ice? Often then the friction between the tires and the ice is so small that the wheels can's exert enough backward force on the ice for the ice to exert the force needed to accelerate the car.

Note that friction, instead of being a bad thing, as suggested earlier, is needed in this case. How else is friction useful in accelerating things? How do you walk or run? Your feet are also interacting with the ground. As long as there is sufficient friction, when you push your feet backwards, the ground pushes you forward.

How does **gravity act** on **us**? Is it a contact force?

Newton recognized that the gravitational force of Earth acts not only on objects close to Earth, like the famous apple, but also on objects as far away as the moon. But, how

exactly does a celestial object such as the sun reach out the approximately 93 million miles and hold Earth in its orbit? An early idea was that it was an "action at a distance" force, for example, that the Sun attracted all objects, like Earth, without anything between the two.

In the middle of the nineteenth century, physicist Michael Faraday (1791–1867) proposed that one magnet creates a field of force around it, and another magnet interacts with the field at its location. Based on the field idea, Earth then creates a gravitational field. The apple and the moon have a force exerted on them, not directly by Earth, but by the gravitational field that exists at the location of the apple and the moon.

Many scientists now believe that gravity is the result of mass warping space-time. While the effects of gravity have long been studied and its laws defined, what the force of gravity actually is still is a matter of debate.

What would happen to Earth if the sun suddenly disappeared? How soon would Earth recognize that the sun's gravitational field was gone? It couldn't happen instantaneously, because Einstein's Special Theory of Relativity says that no information can travel faster than the speed of light. So, it would take about eight minutes before Earth would both experience the lack of sunlight and the lack of gravitational force.

On what does the **gravitational field**, like that of Earth, **depend**?

Newton demonstrated that the gravitational force on one object caused by another is proportional to the product of the masses of the two objects divided by the square of the distance between them. The gravitational field of an object would then be the force divided by the mass of the object on which the force is exerted. The symbol used for the gravitational field is g, and G is the so called universal gravitational constant. It is called universal because it is the same for objects made of any material and of any mass—from a 1-kg apple to a galaxy.

The equation that describes the gravitational field at a specific location is $g = GM/r^2$ where M is the mass of the attracting object and r is the distance from the center of this mass to the location in space. The gravitational field is a vector quantity. Its direction is toward the center of the attracting object. We'll consider its magnitude shortly.

What's the **strength** of the **gravitational field** of **Earth**?

Earth's mass is 5.9736×10^{24} kg and the gravitational constant is 6.673×10^{-11} N m^2 kg^{-2}. At the surface of Earth, 6.4×10^6 m from the center, then $g = 9.8$ N/kg. Thus a

kilogram of meat, for example, experiences a gravitational force of 9.8 N toward Earth's center.

The International Space Station orbits at about 320 km above Earth's surface. How large is the gravitational field at that altitude? Its distance from Earth's center is about 6.7×10^6 m, so $g = 8.9$ N/kg. That's not much different than at Earth's surface.

The moon is 384×10^6 m from the center of Earth. At that distance $g = 0.0027$ N/kg. So the force of Earth's gravity on the same kilogram of meat would be only three thousandths of a Newton! How does this very small gravitational field keep the moon in its orbit? The answer, of course, is that the moon has a large mass, 7.2×10^{22} kg, and so the force on it is 2.0×10^{20} N. When we explore orbits later we'll use this result.

How is the **gravitational field** related to **force**?

As was described above, the force of gravity on an object is equal to the object's mass times the gravitational field strength, expressed as $F = mg$. Thus if you have a mass of 70 kilograms (154 pounds), the force of gravity on you is 686 newtons.

Mass has been **defined** both in terms of **acceleration** and **gravitational force**. Are these the **same**?

Mass defined as $m = F_{net}/a$ is called inertial mass. Mass defined as $m = F_{gravitation}/g$ is called *gravitational mass*. Many physicists, starting with the Hungarian Baron von Eötvös, have done experiments to determine if the two kinds of mass are equal and if they are the same for all materials. Recent experiments have shown that if they are dif-

ferent, the difference is only one part in 10^{15}! Furthermore, Einstein's General Theory of Relativity explains that they are identical, and calls this fact the "Principle of Equivalence" between gravitation and acceleration. In other words, the laws of physics in an accelerating reference frame or a gravitating frame are indistinguishable. You can't tell the difference between falling or being acted on by gravity.

Jupiter, the largest planet in our solar system, also has the strongest gravitational pull.

What's the **strength** of **gravitational fields** of other **astronomical objects**?

This table shows the properties of the sun, planets, and Earth's moon. It also shows the strength of the sun's gravitational field at each planet and the strength of the planets' gravitational fields at their surfaces. The sun and Jupiter, Saturn, Uranus, and Neptune are gaseous and have no solid surfaces.

Which planet has the strongest gravitational field? Is it also the planet with the largest mass? Why do you think that the sun, which has a mass 1,000 times that of Jupiter, has a surface gravitational field only about 10 times that of Jupiter? As a hint, look at the equation that defines g and see what properties other than mass are involved.

Name	Distance from Sun (10^3 km)	Radius (km)	Mass (kg)	g (Sun) (N/kg)	g (surface) (N/kg)
Sun	0	695,000	1.99×10^{30}		274.66
Mercury	57,910	2,439.7	3.30×10^{23}	3.96×10^{-2}	3.70
Venus	108,200	6,051.8	4.87×10^{24}	1.13×10^{-2}	8.87
Earth	149,600	6,378.14	5.98×10^{24}	5.93×10^{-3}	9.80
Moon	384.4 (from Earth)	1,737.4	7.35×10^{22}		1.62
Mars	227,940	3,397.2	6.42×10^{23}	2.55×10^{-3}	3.71
Jupiter	778,330	71,492	1.90×10^{27}	2.19×10^{-4}	24.80
Saturday	1,429,400	60,268	5.69×10^{26}	6.49×10^{-5}	10.45
Uranus	2,870,990	25,559	8.69×10^{25}	1.61×10^{-5}	8.87
Neptune	4,504,300	24,746	1.02×10^{26}	6.54×10^{-6}	11.15

Does the **gravitational force** also **obey Newton's Third Law**? How?

All objects have gravitational fields surrounding them. So, just as the moon has a force exerted on it due to Earth's gravitational field, Earth has a force on it due to the

moon's field. As a result, the moon does not orbit around Earth's center, but the moon and Earth orbit around a point roughly 2,900 kilometers from Earth's center. The sun and other planets also exert gravitational forces on Earth, and Earth does on them.

The gravitational fields of the planets, in particular Jupiter, cause the sun to orbit around a point near its surface. Thus, if an observer on another planetary system studied the motion of the sun carefully he or she could determine that planets were orbiting the sun. This method has been used to detect well over 200 planets (called exoplanets) or planetary systems and other stars.

How did **Einstein describe** the **gravitational field**?

Einstein in his General Theory of Relativity showed that the gravitational field was actually a distortion of space-time caused by the mass of the object. Because space-time has four dimensions that are very difficult to visualize, the distortion is best seen with a two-dimensional model. Often the model consists of a rubber sheet in which a bowling ball is placed. The sheet is pulled down by the ball, which represents the sun. Earth is a tiny ball that is placed on the sheet and given a push perpendicular to the direction of the sun. This ball "orbits" the sun a few times until friction causes it to speed up and spiral into the sun. In the words of physicist John Wheeler:

> Spacetime grips mass, telling it how to move.
> Mass grips spacetime, telling it how to curve.

Has **Einstein's theory** been **tested**?

It has been tested in many ways. It is being used every day in adjusting the clocks in GPS satellites. They run faster because they are at high altitudes where the distortion of space-time is smaller. Both the effects of special relativity (clocks running slower) and general relativity (clocks running faster) must be used to keep the clocks running accurately.

How does **gravity cause tides**?

As someone who lives near an ocean will know, there are two high tides and two low tides each day. They're not at the same time each day, but depend on the phase of the moon. The heights of the tides vary over the seasons as well. What causes the tides?

The moon's gravitational field exerts a force on the water. Because the field and force depend on distance, the force on the water closest to the moon is strongest. The force on Earth is weaker, and the force on the water on the far side of Earth is smallest. So the water nearest the moon is pulled toward it, and Earth is pulled toward the moon more strongly than the water farthest from the moon. For that reason there is a tidal bulge in the water near the moon, and another on the far side. The bulges, which are the high tides, are not directly under the moon because Earth's rotation drags the water along with it. Because the day is shorter than the lunar month, the high tides actually come about two hours before the moon is overhead.

Tides also vary greatly with location. The largest tidal variations occur in the Bay of Fundy between the Canadian provinces of Nova Scotia and New Brunswick, where the largest recorded range was 17 meters, or almost 56 feet. There have been many proposals to put a dam across the bay and use the tides to generate electricity, but environmental concerns have blocked construction in that bay.

The sun also affects the tides, but much less than the moon. When the sun, Earth, and the moon are aligned, which happens at both full and new moons, the tides are especially high.

How can you **describe the motion** of an object in a **gravitational field**?

As long as the force exerted by a gravitational field, such as Earth's, is the only force on an object, then Newton's Second Law can be used in the form $a = F/m_{inertial}$. But the force due to the field is given by $F = m_{gravitational}g$. And, as has been tested by experiment and explained by Einstein's theory, $m_{inertial} = m_{gravitational}$, so $a = g$.

There is one more thing to question. The acceleration a is measured in meters per second squared, while the gravitational field strength is measured in newtons per kilogram. How can these two quantities be equal? The answer can be found by looking at Newton's Second Law again. In the form $F_{net} = ma$, you can see that the units of force, newtons, must be equal to the units in which m times a are measured. The mass, m, is measured in kilograms and the acceleration in meters per second squared. Therefore a newton must be a kilogram times a meter per second squared. Thus a newton per kilogram (N/kg) is a meter per second squared (m/s^2).

How do the **speed** and **position** of a **dropped object vary** with **time**?

As long as the only force is the gravitational force, then the acceleration is the acceleration due to gravity, g. At Earth's surface the value is 9.8 m/s^2. (In the English system $g = 32.2$ ft/s^2.) If the object is dropped from rest at time $t = 0$, then the velocity at a future time t is simply $v = gt$. That is, the velocity increases by 9.8 m/s each second. If we measure the distance fallen from the position where it was dropped, then at time t

it has fallen a distance $d = 1/2\ gt^2$. The following table shows velocity and distance fallen for some selected times.

Time	Velocity	Distance	Velocity	Distance
0.10 s	0.98 m/s	4.9 cm	3.2 ft/s	1.9 in.
0.15 s	1.42 m/s	11 cm	4.8 ft/s	4.3 in.
0.20 s	1.96 m/s	20 cm	6.4 ft/s	7.7 in.
0.50 s	4.90 m/s	1.2 m	16.1 ft/s	4.0 ft.
1.0 s	9.8 m/s	4.9 m	32.2 ft/s	16.1 ft.
2.0 s	19.6 m/s	19.6 m	64.4 ft/s (44 mph)	64.4 ft.

Why are those times chosen to calculate velocity and distance fallen?

The first three times are chosen so that you can explore your reaction time. Have another person hold a ruler vertically by one end. Place your finger and thumb at the lower end of the ruler, but don't let them touch the ruler. Have the other person drop the ruler and you use your finger and thumb to grab it. Note the distance the ruler has dropped in the time it takes you to react to it being dropped. Compare the distance with the first three distances to see if your reaction time is between 0.1 and 0.2 seconds.

What happens if an object is not dropped, but is thrown up or down?

Physicists would say that the ball has been given an initial velocity. But this initial velocity doesn't affect the force of gravity on the ball, so the ball would still gain a downward velocity of 9.8 m/s each second it is in flight.

Suppose the ball is thrown down with a velocity of 2.0 m/s. Then at time $t = 0$, the time it was thrown down, it would already have a velocity of 2.0 m/s downward. If you use the table above you see that 0.10 s later it would have a velocity of 2 + 0.98 m/s = 2.98 m/s. Half a second after launch its downward velocity would be 2 + 4.9 m/s = 6.9 m/s. That is, the initial velocity is just added to the increasing velocity caused by the gravitational force.

Now suppose the ball is thrown upward with the same 2.0 m/s speed. Now we have to be very careful with the sign of the velocity. We have chosen the downward direction as positive. So the initial velocity of the ball is actually –2.0 m/s.

The gravitational force acts in the downward direction. By Newton's Second Law that means that the ball will slow down at a rate of 9.8 m/s each second. After 0.1 s it would be going –2.0 + 0.98 = –1.02 m/s. After 0.20 s it would be going –2.0 + 1.96 = –0.04 m/s. It is almost at rest! But the gravitational force is still acting on it, so it continues to accelerate downward. After 0.30 s it would be going –2.0 + 2.94 = +0.94 m/s. That is, it would now be moving downward.

How can the acceleration be independent of mass?
Doesn't a bowling ball fall faster than a soccer ball?

Which weighs more, the bowling ball or soccer ball? You can use your hands to hold first one ball and then the other. You'll notice that you have to exert a much larger upward force to hold the bowling ball at rest. From Newton's First Law, if an object is at rest then the net force on it is zero. That is, the downward force of gravity has the same strength as the upward force of your hands. So, you can conclude that the force of gravity, the weight, of the bowling ball is greater than that of the soccer ball.

Galileo was said to have dropped a pressing iron and a wooden ball from the Tower of Pisa and found that they arrived at the bottom at the same time. He also argued that if you tied two wooden balls together, thus doubling the mass, they would obviously fall at the same rate as they would have not tied together.

How can we understand this result? When you drop the ball, the force of gravity is the only force on it, so $a = F_{\text{gravity}}/m$. An object with a larger force on it will accelerate faster than one with a smaller force, but only as long as the masses are equal. If the forces are equal but the masses different, then the object with greater mass will accelerate more slowly. As described above, because the force of gravity is proportional to the mass, the two effects cancel, and $a = g$ for all masses.

When it is at its maximum height does it stop? At an instant in time it is indeed at rest, but it doesn't stay motionless for any time interval because the gravitational force keeps acting on it.

How does **air drag affect** the **motion** of dropped objects?

Air drag adds a second force exerted on the object that is in the direction opposite its motion. The net force is the difference between the downward force of gravity and the upward force of air. As was discussed above, the force of the air increases as the speed increases. Therefore, as the object falls and gains speed, the upward force increases. At some time it will equal the downward force and there will be no net force on the object. So, according to Newton's First Law, the object's speed will now become constant. This constant velocity is called the terminal velocity.

On what does the **terminal velocity depend**?

Air drag depends on the density of the air, the size, velocity, and the shape of the object. Therefore the terminal velocity will depend on all of these, plus the mass. You can test to see if the air drag depends on the velocity or the velocity squared by doing a

The force of the air on this person's parachute—the air drag—increases as speed increases, and eventually the force of gravity and the upward force of the air equalize, resulting in a constant speed called the terminal velocity.

simple experiment. You'll need only five filters for a drip coffee maker. The filters must be cup-shaped. If the drag depends on velocity, then the terminal velocity will be given by $kv = mg$, where k is some constant. Thus v will be proportional to m. On the other hand, if the drag depends on the square of the velocity then the terminal velocity will be given by $kv^2 = mg$, so v will be proportional to the square root of the mass.

The experiment depends on the fact that you can compare two velocities by dropping two objects at the same time, allowing them to fall different distances, and observing whether they hit the ground at the same time. If the drag depends on velocity, then doubling the mass will double the velocity. Stack two filters and hold them above your head. Hold a single filter in the other hand half that distance above the ground. Drop them at the same time and see if they hit the ground together, as they should if two filters fall twice as far in the same time. What did you observe? You probably found that they didn't hit the ground at the same time. Now add two more filters so you have a total of four. The square root of four is two, so if the drag depends on the square of the velocity, the four filters will now fall twice as fast as the single filter. Try it. Do they hit the ground at the same time?

Air drag is more complicated than this simple experiment suggests. At slow speeds the drag constant, k, is larger than at higher speeds. Many studies have been done on the air drag of tennis balls, baseballs, and soccer balls. The fuzz, stitches, and panels have a strong effect on air drag, as anyone who has tried to hit a knuckle ball will testify.

How do sky divers and **parachutists** use **air drag** to control their speed?

Sky divers can change their body shape, and thus their terminal velocity, by extending their arms, or separating their legs. Parachutists can tilt the chutes to control the direction in which they're falling.

What is **weightlessness**?

Weight is defined as the force of gravity. Strictly, then the only way one can be weightless is to be so far from any massive object, like a planet or star, that the gravitational field is zero! No human has achieved this state. In a satellite the gravitational field is about 80% as large as it is on Earth's surface, so the force of gravity on an astronaut in the satellite is not much smaller than it is on the astronaut on Earth.

An astronaut orbiting Earth actually experiences a gravitational force almost as large as on Earth's surface!

How do you measure weight? If you stand on a scale, the scale measures the upward force of the scale on your feet. According to Newton's Third Law, that force is equal to the downward force of your feet on the scale. (Actually, there is a slight difference because of the rotation of Earth.) If you stand on a scale in an elevator, you'll see that your "weight" changes as the elevator accelerates. When it is going up and increases its speed, the scale will record a larger weight. The same will happen when you are going down and come to a stop. When it slows while going up or speeds up while going down the scale will show a smaller weight. Newton's Second Law can explain these changes using the fact that a net force is needed to accelerate you along with the elevator. (Note that you don't really need a scale to sense these accelerations. You can feel them in your stomach!)

What would happen if the cable holding the elevator would break? You and the elevator would both be in free-fall, accelerating at g. There would be no weight shown on the scale. You and the elevator would both be in the state of "apparent weightlessness." We'll meet this term again when we explore the motion of satellites. The apparent weightlessness of astronauts will be explained there.

Are there **non-contact field-type forces** other than gravity?

Both the electric force between charged objects and the magnetic force between magnetized objects can be described as the force caused by an electric or magnetic field caused by one object on the charge or magnetic moment of the second object.

379

What is the **difference** between **force** and **pressure**?

Why does the stiletto heel of a woman's shoe sink deep into the ground while if she wears a running shoe the heel does not? The force on the two heels is the same. What is different is the force divided by the area of the heel. The quotient of force divided by area is much larger on the stiletto heel. That quantity is called the pressure.

As an example, consider the case of a 110-lb (50-kg or 490-N) woman who first wears shoes with heels 1.5 cm by 1.5 cm. The area of each heel is about 2.2 cm². Assuming that she puts all her weight on the two heels the pressure will be 500 N / 4.4 cm² or 4.5 N/cm². Pressure is usually expressed in pascals (Pa) or N/m². In this case the pressure would be 1.1 million pascals or 1100 kPa. If she were to wear running shoes with heels about 7.5 by 7.5 cm then the pressure would be only 45 kPa.

The pressure of air is about 101 kPa. Why don't we feel this atmospheric pressure? First, it is exerted uniformly on all parts of our bodies. Second, it is balanced by pressure from the insides of our bodies. We can feel the pressure if you try to breathe in but close your mouth and pinch your nose closed. You can tell that the external pressure on your lungs exceeds the internal pressure.

What about **pins, needles,** and **beds of nails**?

A pin or needle has a very small area at its sharpened tip, so even a small force on it will create a large pressure at the tip, enough to penetrate cloth or your skin.

Have you ever seen the bed of nails demonstration? A large number of nails are pounded into a board that is about the size of a person's back. The person very carefully lies on the bed. Sometimes a second bed is placed on his chest. A concrete block is put on this bed and a sledgehammer is used to shatter the block.

The person is not harmed. How can that be? Even though the nails have very tiny tips and would certainly penetrate the skin if there were only one, because there are dozens of nails in the bed, the person's weight is distributed over many nails, and the force of each nail is quite small. The pressure is not enough to penetrate the skin.

Anyone doing this demonstration has to take precautions. The parts of the body not on the lower bed have to be supported at the height of the nails. If the concrete block is broken the person must wear safety goggles, and a sheet of wood should be held to keep any concrete from flying into the person's face.

How can you **describe** the **path** of a **thrown ball**?

You know what happens when a ball is dropped. It accelerates downward, gaining speed at a rate of 9.8 m/s each second. What would happen if the same ball rolled off a table?

To answer this question you should define a coordinate system. One axis points down, the other, perpendicular to the first, points in the horizontal direction of the

How can atmospheric pressure collapse a steel drum?

Aspectacular demonstration is often used to show the effect of atmospheric pressure. A 55-gallon steel drum is placed on a stand over a propane burner. A quart of water is poured into the drum. The burner will eventually boil the water, filling the drum with steam. When steam has displaced the air, the cap on the drum is tightened and the burner turns off. As the drum cools the steam condenses back to water. The volume of steam is about 1,000 times the volume of water, so when it has condensed it no longer exerts an outward pressure on the drum. But, the atmospheric pressure of 101,000 newtons on each square meter of the drum's surface is still there. The drum collapses with a thunderous noise.

This demonstration can be done on a much smaller scale with an empty soda can and a bowl of water. Put about 1/4" of water in the bottom of the soda can and heat the can on a stove or hot plate. When steam has come out of the hole of the can for several minutes, using a protective glove, quickly turn the can over and put the top into the water. Once again, the steam will condense into water, but because of the small opening, only a small amount of water from the bowl will be able to get into the can. What do you think will happen?

rolling ball. The force of gravity acts in the downward direction, causing the ball to accelerate downward, but there is no force in the horizontal direction, so the ball's horizontal speed would not change. Because only the downward acceleration affects its fall, it would hit the ground at the same time that a dropped ball would. The path the ball takes is a parabola.

Galileo's Principle of Relativity, not Einstein's, can help you understand this result. Galileo imagined a sailor dropping a ball from a high mast on a moving sailboat. The sailor would see the ball drop straight down, but an observer on the shore would see the ball having a horizontal velocity equal to the velocity of the boat. Therefore this observer would see the ball's parabolic path. But both would agree when the ball hit the deck of the boat at the same time. Galileo said that the laws of physics are independent of relative motion. This statement is called the principle of relativity.

What happens if the **ball** is **launched at an angle**?

The ball would now have both an initial horizontal velocity and an initial vertical velocity. Again, the horizontal velocity would be constant because there is no force in that direction. Its vertical velocity would be the same as it was when the ball was thrown either down or up. An initial upward velocity is much more interesting, so let's consider that.

We can specify the initial velocity two ways. First, the way we did before by choosing the horizontal and vertical velocities separately. The second, and more useful way,

381

is to specify the velocity and direction. Suppose a batter hit a baseball at a speed of 90 mph. This speed is 132 ft/s or 40 m/s. The angle could be anything from 90°, a vertical pop-up, down to an angle between 10° and 30° that might be called a line drive to 0° or even a negative angle that would be a ground ball.

The distance the ball travels before hitting the ground depends on both the speed and the angle. If air drag is very small, then the distance is maximum for an angle of 45°. Air drag causes the angle for maximum distance to drop to around 35°. During World War II extensive tables were calculated so that gunners could find the angle for the gun to achieve the desired distance.

How can you get **circular motion**?

If an object moves in a circle, either a planet, a satellite, or even a ball on a string twirled around, then there is no change in speed as it moves around the circle, so there can be no force in direction of motion. There must be a force, because the direction of the ball is changing, so its velocity is changing. The force must be perpendicular to the motion.

Try to make a ball move in a circle. This works best with a ball the size of a soccer ball or basketball on a smooth (wood or tile) floor. Start the ball moving, then kick it gently in the direction perpendicular to its motion. Try another kick or two. Note that its direction changes in the direction of the kick—the momentary force you placed on the ball. If you could exert a constant force that is always perpendicular to the motion the ball would move in a circle. Note that the direction of the force is always toward the center of the circle. Such a force is called "centripetal," or center seeking.

The force required to keep an object moving in a circle depends on three quantities: the mass of the object, the speed of the object, and radius of the circle. The force must be larger for larger mass, greater speed, and smaller radius of the circle.

What supplies this **centripetal force**?

Centripetal force must be supplied by something or someone exerting the force on the object. In a rotating drum ride at a carnival you stand with your back on the drum. As the drum speeds up you can feel the force of the drum pushing on your back, toward the center of the circle. Often the floor drops down and only the force of friction between your back and the drum keeps you from dropping down with the floor.

When a car makes a turn what supplies the centripetal force on it? The road supplies this force. The road is in contact with the tires, and friction between the tire and road is necessary for the force of the road to be exerted on the car. If the road is covered with ice, the friction often isn't large enough and the car goes straight, rather than along the curve. A racetrack is often banked so the tilt of the track can supply at least part of this inward force, reducing the need for friction.

If you're sitting in the car there must be a sidewise force on you so that you stay with the car as it makes the turn. Usually the friction between you and the seat is sufficient, but sometimes you have to hold onto the door handle to exert more force.

Why do you feel an **outward force** on you when you are in **circular motion**?

When we introduced Newton's Laws we neglected to state an important warning. These laws work only in an "inertial reference frame," that is a reference frame where there is no acceleration. A car when it is speeding up, slowing down, or changing direction is accelerating. Therefore, a person in the car experiences other "forces." When the car is speeding up, you feel pushed back into the seat. When the car is slowing down you feel yourself being pushed forward. When rounding a curve, you feel pushed outward. These are not real forces, but are often called "inertial," "fictitious," or "pseudo" forces. For objects in circular motion there are two such forces, the centrifugal and Coriolis forces. The centrifugal force is the fictitious outward force you feel when your car is rounding a curve.

What are the effects of the **Coriolis force** on Earth?

A reference frame, or coordinate system fixed on Earth, is not an inertial frame. The Coriolis force affects the rotation of winds around high and low pressure areas in Earth's atmosphere. Air flows into a low pressure center. The Coriolis force in the northern hemisphere causes all flows to be deflected to the right, creating a counterclockwise flow around the center. In the southern hemisphere the deflection and rotation are in the opposite direction. On the other hand, air flows away from a high-pressure center, and so the deflection causes a clockwise rotation in the northern hemisphere and the opposite in the southern.

How does the **gravitational force cause** the **motion** of **planets**?

In antiquity the planets (the name comes from the fact that they seem to wander across the sky) were assumed to have circular orbits. In order to account for the observations, their motion was thought to involve circles attached to other circles. In between 1600 and 1605 Johannes Kepler (1571–1630) made careful studies of the observations of Mars made by Tycho Brahe (1546–1601). He found that

Johannes Kepler studied the orbit of Mars using the measurements made by Tycho Brahe. He concluded that Mars's orbit is actually an ellipse and not a circle. The elliptical shape of the orbits of the planets in our solar system is called Kepler's First Law.

a circular path required Tycho's observations to be wrong by 2 minutes of arc (four times the apparent size of the moon), but he knew that Tycho's work was better than that. After some 40 failed attempts he finally discovered that the orbit could be described as an ellipse. We now know an ellipse fits the orbits of all planets, comets, and other bodies about the sun, as well as satellites about planets. The shape of the orbit is called Kepler's First Law.

An ellipse is not a circle, so the gravitational force of the sun is not always perpendicular to the motion. Therefore the planet's speed changes as it moves around its orbit. Kepler's Second Law says that in equal times planets sweep out equal areas. Thus if the planet is closer to the sun, it will move faster than it does when it is farther away.

Kepler's Third Law was actually obtained in 1595 and was based primarily on philosophical and theological arguments. It stated that the relative sizes of the orbits of planets around the sun could be obtained by nesting the five Platonic solids: the cube, tetrahedron, dodecahedron, icosahedron, and octahedron. The planets' orbits were in the spheres that circumscribed each solid. Today we state this law as the square of the period of the planet is proportional to the cube of the radius of the orbit. The proportionality constant depends on the mass of the object about which the orbit occurs and the universal gravitational constant. The law summarizes two of the properties of orbits of planets or satellites about a central star or planet.

What is meant by a **law** as opposed to a **theory**?

Laws summarize observations. They describe phenomena. A theory explains a large number of observations. Einstein's theory of gravity explains Newton's law of gravitation, which can be used to derive Kepler's three laws. A theory cannot become a law because they are essentially different things.

What does **Kepler's Third Law** tell us about the motion of **satellites around Earth**?

Kepler's Third Law relates the period of a satellite to its distance to the center of Earth. The table below shows the mean radius of the orbit, the altitude above Earth's surface, and the period for some typical satellites.

Satellite	Type of Orbit	Altitude (km)	Mean Radius of Orbit (km)	Period
International Space Station	Equatorial	278–460	6,723	91.4 min
Hubble Space Telescope	Equatorial	570	6,942	95.9 min
Weather Satellite (NOAA 19)	Polar	860	7,234	102 min
GPS Satellite	Equatorial	20,200	25,561	718 min
Communications Satellite	Equatorial	36,000	42,105	1,436 min
Moon	Ecliptic	364,397–406,731	384,748	27.3 days

Weather satellites have polar orbits so that the view of their cameras sweeps across the entire surface of Earth many times each day. The moon's orbit is aligned with Earth's orbit around the sun, not Earth's equator.

Kepler's Third Law holds for satellites about other planets and for planets revolving around the sun, but you need either Newton's laws or Einstein's relativity theory to explain these results.

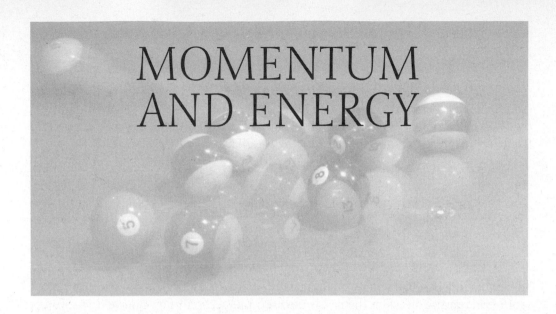

MOMENTUM AND ENERGY

MOMENTUM

Why do we need to introduce momentum and energy? Aren't Newton's Laws good enough?

Newton's laws could be used, but when you analyze the motion of more than a few interacting objects, Newton's laws are just too complicated. When you use momentum and energy you concentrate on the beginning and end of an interaction, not on the details of the interaction.

A sports team can be said to have momentum. What does momentum mean in physics?

Momentum is defined as the product of mass and velocity. Momentum is a vector quantity—it has both magnitude and direction. Consider a football player—a lineman. Linemen are massive. If they can run fast, then the product of their mass and velocity is their momentum (mv). The momentum is in the direction the player is moving.

How are modern cars designed to decrease the chance of injury in a car crash?

If your car hits a barrier or another car, it will slow or even stop. Modern cars are designed so that the front end collapses, extending the time that the forces of the barrier or other car act, thus reducing the force needed to stop the car.

Cars also have airbags that don't act on the car, but on the passenger. When a sudden very large acceleration of the car is detected the airbags are deployed. A chemical

reaction within the bag rapidly fills the bag with gas. The front surface of the airbag speeds toward the passenger at speeds up to 180 mph! But the momentum of the passenger is decreased slowly because he or she compresses the airbag. In addition, because the airbag has a large area, the force isn't concentrated, but spread out. This reduces the pressure on the body, reducing the chance of injury.

Most recent cars also have side airbags to protect passengers from side collisions. But, airbags have caused injuries to smaller persons. Safer airbags inflate less, reducing the force on the passengers, who, because they have less mass, require less impulse to be stopped.

What are other examples of **impulse and change** of momentum?

If you catch a baseball or softball, especially without a mitt, you know that you move your hand in the direction the ball is moving. You certainly don't move it toward the moving ball. In stopping the ball its change in momentum is the same, no matter how you catch it. Thus the impulse your hand gives the ball is also the same. What changes? When you move your hand in the direction of the ball you increase the time the force of your hand acts on the ball. That means that the force is less.

If two **objects interact** what happens to the **momentum** of the other object?

According to Newton's Third Law if your hand exerts a force on the ball, the ball exerts a force on your hand. Thus there must be an impulse on your hand. Does the momentum of your hand change? Of course your hand is just a part of your body, and if you are standing firmly on the ground, your body is unlikely to move. Let's pick a simpler situation. Suppose you are sitting in a desk chair with wheels on a smooth floor and you catch a heavy ball thrown by someone. In this case you and the chair will roll backward. In other words, the momentum of you and the chair will increase as the momentum of the ball decreases.

What happens to the **momentum** of the ball and you and the chair **all together**?

As long as external forces are zero or small, then in any interaction the momentum of the system, in this case the ball, you, and the chair will be constant. This result is called the conservation of momentum. The sum of the decrease in momentum of the ball and the increase in momentum of you and the chair will be zero.

What are other **examples** of the **conservation of momentum**?

If there is only one object in the system, then with no external forces Newton's Second Law says that its velocity will not change. Conservation of momentum also says that its momentum won't change. If the momentum was zero, it will remain zero.

If you shoot a rifle or shotgun you are often told to hold the gun tightly against your shoulder. What's the physics explanation for this admonition? When the gun is

> ## How do you change the momentum of a lineman?
>
> **I**f you're trying to stop a lineman, you need to exert a force in the direction opposite the direction of his motion. The greater the force and the longer you exert it, the greater the momentum change. The product of force and the time the force is applied is called the impulse. Because force is a vector, so is impulse. Thus the direction of the impulse that stops the lineman is opposite his motion. The larger the impulse the greater the change in momentum.

fired the bullet's momentum changes. Its new momentum is in the forward direction. So, according to the law of conservation of momentum the gun must gain momentum in the opposite direction. It will recoil. If the gun isn't held tightly to your shoulder its mass is relatively small, and so its recoil velocity will be large. When it hits your shoulder it could cause injury. If, on the other hand, the rifle is tight against your shoulder, then the mass is the mass of the rifle and your body. The recoil velocity will be much smaller.

How do **rockets accelerate** in space?

When a rocket's motor is fired it expels gas at a high velocity backward. Thus the gas, originally at rest in the rocket, is given a large momentum backward. With no external forces on the rocket-gas system, the rocket's momentum must increase in the forward direction. It will speed up.

When the rocket is on the launch pad there is an external force on it, the force of gravity. How can the rocket take off? Now the momentum of the gas and rocket isn't conserved, but still the impulse the rocket gives the gas in pushing it backward is equal and opposite to the impulse the gas gives the rocket. Thus the rocket rises, just more slowly than it would if there were no gravity.

How does Einstein's **Special Theory of Relativity** affect **momentum**?

The same factor, γ, that affected distance and time, affects momentum in the same way, that is relativistic momentum is γmv. Gamma is 1 at slow speeds and becomes large only when the velocity is near the speed of light.

Does **momentum** apply to objects that **rotate**?

Quantities that describe rotation are similar to, but different than, those that describe straight-line motion. Position is replaced by angle, velocity by angular rotation, accel-

eration by angular acceleration. Force is replaced by torque.

What plays the role of **force** in **rotation**?

You have had experiences that illustrate how torque works. Suppose you want to push open a door that rotates about its hinges. You know that the speed with which the door opens depends on how hard you push. It also depends on how far from the hinges you push—the farther the faster. It also depends on the angle at which you push. Pushing at a right angle to the door is much more effective than pushing at a smaller or larger angle. If you push at a right angle, then torque equals the force times the distance from the axis of rotation.

With nothing to technically "push against" in space, it seems odd that rockets could accelerate in space. The explanation is that the force of the combusting rocket fuel itself pushes the rocket, accelerating it forward.

What plays the role of **mass** in **rotation**?

Mass is defined as the net force on an object divided by its acceleration. By analogy, then, the property that takes the place of mass should be the torque divided by angular acceleration. The property is called rotational inertia or the moment of inertia. It depends not only on mass, but on how far the mass is from the axis of rotation. The further the mass is from the axis, the larger the moment of inertia. If you sit on a swiveling stool or chair while holding heavy weights, the further you extend your arms, the more difficult it is for someone to start you rotating. That is, it will require more torque to achieve the same angular acceleration.

What plays the **role of momentum** in **rotational motion**?

The angular momentum of a rotating object is proportional to the product of its moment of inertia and its angular velocity. If there are no external torques on the object, then its angular momentum does not change.

An object with linear momentum that has no external forces on it cannot change its mass, so its velocity is constant. But a rotating object can change its moment of inertia, so, even without external torques, its rotational speed can be changed.

390

How can **athletes** use **angular momentum**?

Let's explore two different sports. In platform diving a person pushes off the tower, and thus the platform exerts a force on her (Newton's Third Law). But, if she isn't standing straight up, the force also exerts a torque on her, and starts her rotating. If she pulls her arms and legs in, then her mass is closer to her axis of rotation, and her speed of rotation increases. To slow this rotation, she can extend her arms and legs. With good timing, she can hit the water with a bare minimum of rotation.

Put a toy gyroscope on a stand and spin the wheel. Gravity pulls down on the center of gravity of the gyroscope, creating a torque on the axis of rotation, causing it to rotate downward.

Consider a figure skater. She can start spinning on the point of one skate by pushing on the ice with the second skate. Again, the force of the ice exerts a torque, and so her rotational speed increases. She can extend her arms to slow the rotation, or pull them in as close as possible to attain the highest spin rate.

Can the **axis of rotation change**?

A toy gyroscope contains a rotating wheel. If you put it on a stand the axis moves in a circle. Why? The gravitational force pulls down on the center of mass of the wheel. Thus the gyroscope begins to rotate downward. The effect of this new torque is to cause the axis to change direction; to precess.

Precession is also important for bicycles and motorcycles. If the cycle starts to tip to the right, then the rotating front wheel's axis will rotate, and the wheel will turn to the right, helping to keep the cycle from tipping over.

ENERGY

What is **energy**?

An object with energy can change itself or its environment. That's a pretty abstract definition. Let's explore some of the many ways an object can have energy and what changes it can cause.

A speeding car has energy—think what damage it can do if it hits a wall or another car. The energy of motion is called kinetic energy. A rotating wheel also has ener-

gy—if you try to stop a spinning bicycle wheel with your hand, it may hurt you. This kind of energy is called rotational kinetic energy.

A compressed spring or a stretched rubber band can cause a stone to move. The energy in the squeezed spring or stretched band is called elastic energy. There are a variety of other forms of energy that are stored in a material. The random motion of the atoms that make up the material means that the atoms have kinetic energy. A measure of the amount of the kinetic energy in the random motion of the atoms is called temperature; the more energy, the higher the temperature. Kinetic energy in the random motion of atoms in a material is called thermal energy. If you charge or discharge a battery, like the one in your cell phone, you change the chemical composition of the battery materials. When you charge it you increase its chemical energy. You can also increase the chemical energy of your body by eating. Even mass has stored energy—splitting the nucleus of a uranium atom results in elements that have smaller mass but a large amount of kinetic energy.

How can **energy** be **transferred**?

Any energy transfer involves a source, whose energy is reduced; a means of transferring the energy; and an energy receiver, whose energy is increased. It's convenient to use a diagram to keep track of the source, the transfer, and the receiver.

For example, if a moving pool ball collides with another ball it can transfer all or part of its kinetic energy to the other ball. Transfer of energy by this kind of mechanical interaction is called *work*. The moving ball does work on the stationary ball and its kinetic energy is reduced. The kinetic energy of the stationary ball is increased by the work done on it.

When a slingshot does work on the stone, its stored elastic energy decreases and the kinetic energy of the stone increases.

When you throw a ball your stored chemical energy is reduced, work is done on the ball, and the ball's kinetic energy is increased.

Other methods of transferring energy that do not involve work will be discussed later.

What **energy transfers** are involved when a **ball is tossed**?

If you lift an object like a ball you increase the energy in Earth's gravitational field. Energy is transferred from you to the field, resulting in a decrease in your stored chemical energy. Suppose you toss the ball up. When you toss it you do work on the ball, transferring energy from your body to the ball, increasing its kinetic energy as well as the gravitational field energy. Once you let go of the ball it continues to rise, but its velocity decreases as the gravitational field energy increases and the ball's kinetic energy decreases. It reaches its maximum height; at that instant the kinetic energy is zero—all energy is in the field. On its way back down it speeds up, so its kinetic energy

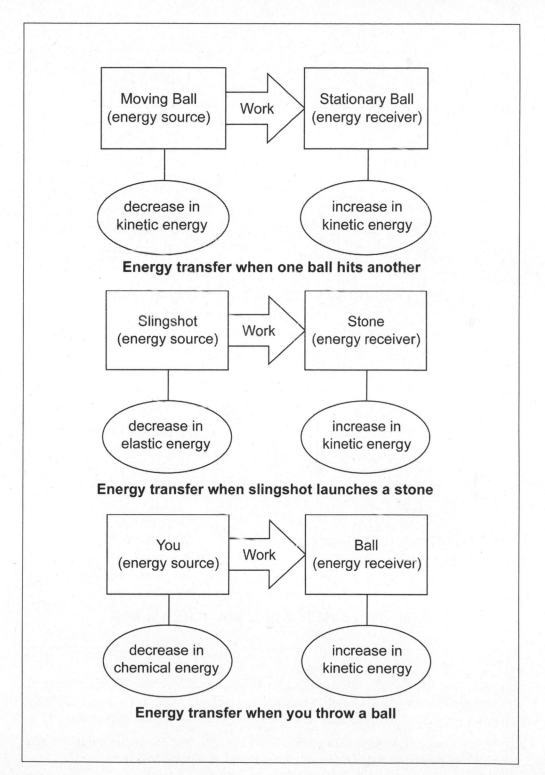

Energy transfer when one ball hits another

Energy transfer when slingshot launches a stone

Energy transfer when you throw a ball

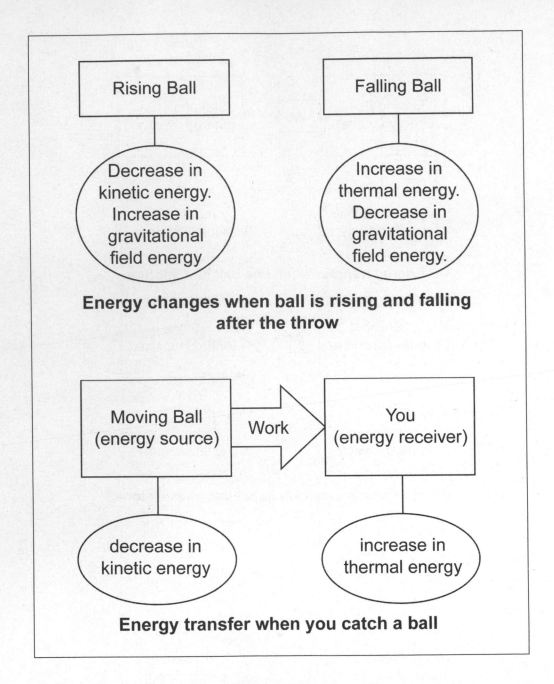

**Energy changes when ball is rising and falling
after the throw**

Energy transfer when you catch a ball

increases but the energy stored in the gravitational field decreases. While you are not touching it the sum of the kinetic energy of the ball and the gravitational field acting on it is a constant. Energy changes from one form to the other and back again.

As you catch it, stopping its motion and thus reducing its kinetic energy to zero. The ball does work on you. But, your stored chemical energy does not increase.

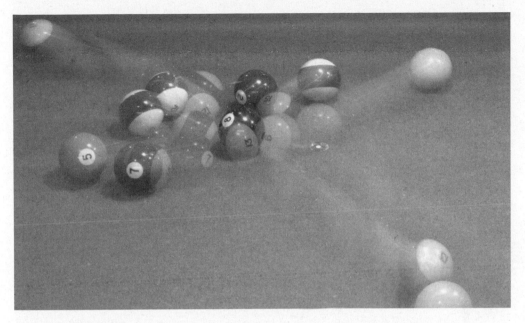

When a moving pool ball collides with another one, all or part of its kinetic energy will be transferred to that ball, which is what makes this fun game possible.

Does the **total energy** of a system ever **change**?

No. Think about a block of wood on a table. You push it, doing work on the block and transferring energy from your body to the block. The block starts moving, but quickly slows and comes to a stop. Where did its kinetic energy go? What was the effect of the friction between the block and table?

To explore friction, rub a pencil eraser on the palm of your hand. Then quickly put the eraser against your cheek. You probably found that both the eraser and your hand became warmer. The friction between the block and table had the same effect, but the temperature change was probably too small to detect. If the temperature increases, then the thermal energy in the object has increased. Thus the decrease in kinetic energy of the block was accompanied by increased thermal energy in both the block and the table. The energy just changed forms.

Scientists have made careful measurements of energy in a variety of forms and have always found that energy is neither created nor destroyed. In other words, the energy put into a system always equals the energy change in the system plus the energy leaving the system.

These measurements have led to a law: the Conservation of Energy. As long as no objects are added to or removed from a system, and as long as there are no interactions between the system and the rest of the world, then the energy of the system does not change.

energy in = energy change + energy out

Energy In ⟹ | **System** | **Energy Out** ⟹

Energy changes in system

How are **conservation of momentum** and **conservation of energy** used in **everyday life**?

These two laws are most often used when two objects collide. Momentum is conserved if there are no external forces, and it changes very little if the forces during the collision are much greater than the external forces. For example, if two cars collide, the two cars are the system. The forces between them are much larger than the forces on the wheels that come from outside the system, so momentum is conserved. Is energy conserved? While total energy is conserved, the kinetic energy before the collision is much greater than the energy afterward. Much of the energy goes into bending metal and breaking glass and plastic. Automobile crash reconstruction is a way of using conservation of momentum to figure out the speeds of one or both of the cars before the collision.

Kinetic energy is not always converted to other forms of energy in collisions. The toy "Newton's Cradle" has a set of steel balls that swing on strings. In these collisions kinetic energy is almost totally conserved. The incoming ball stops when it hits a second ball, and the second ball moves away with the same speed, and thus kinetic energy, as the incoming ball had. Collisions of pool or billiard balls is another case where kinetic energy is conserved. This kind of collision is called "elastic" while the case of cars colliding is called "inelastic."

A hot object has **thermal energy**. How can it **transfer** this **energy**?

What happened to the increased thermal energy of the eraser and your hand, or to the block and the table? A short time later all will have cooled. They have transferred their

Energy transfer from a hot object

thermal energy to the cooler surroundings. Energy transfer that results from a difference in temperature is called *heat*. Heat always flows from the hotter (energy sources) to the cooler objects (energy receivers).

Thermal energy can be transferred in three ways: conduction, convection, and radiation. Conduction occurs when two objects are in contact, like when you put your hand in hot water. Convection is the motion of a fluid, usually air or water. The fluid is heated by the hotter object, then moves until it contacts a colder object where it heats that object. You can think of convection as two instances of conduction. Radiation is infrared waves that are emitted by hotter objects and absorbed by colder ones. You can feel radiation if you bring your hands near a hot electric burner on a stove. The sun heats Earth by radiation.

What happens to the thermal energy in the surroundings? They get warmer, so their thermal energy increases. Then they transfer this energy to a colder object. Earth is warmer than the space around it, and so it radiates energy into space. When that energy reaches another planet or star, those objects are warmed, and so on through the entire universe.

Is there a **difference** between **work and energy**? Between **heat and thermal energy**?

Energy, whether kinetic, stored, or thermal, is a property of an object. Gravitational field energy is a property of the gravitational field. Work and heat are means of energy transfer. Work is transfer by mechanical means. Heat is transfer between two objects

with different temperatures. Examples of work are you throwing a ball, a slingshot launching a stone, a ball being caught in a mitt. Examples of heat are your hand being warmed by putting it in hot water, a bottle of soda being cooled in a refrigerator, and Earth's surface being warmed by sunlight.

Who developed the ideas of conservation of momentum and conservation of energy?

Isaac Newton (1642–1727), considering collisions, first described momentum as the product of mass and velocity, but he called it "the quantity of motion." Energy took 150 years from the first statement of principles until the terminology was worked out. Collisions also inspired the Dutch physicist Christiaan Huygens (1629–1695), who wrote that in the collision of two perfectly elastic spheres the sum of what we today call kinetic energy would not be changed by the collision. The German scientist Gottfried Wilhelm Leibniz (1646–1716) gave the name *vis viva* in 1695 to kinetic energy. But how could the conservation of *vis viva* be extended beyond elastic collisions? Finding the answer to this question took over 150 years!

An important contribution was made by Benjamin Thompson (1753–1814). Thompson was born in Massachusetts, but because he opposed the American Revolution he left for England and was knighted by King George III and given the title Count Rumford. While in America he spied for the British. While in England he spied for the French and was a counter spy for the British. He moved to Bavaria, now part of Germany, and became Minister of War, among other duties. Because he ran an orphanage and wanted to save money he studied heat and invented many items, like an efficient stove and a coffee percolator. A long series of experiments led him to conclude in 1798 that thermal energy was nothing more than the vibratory motion of what we know today as the atoms that make up the material.

About twenty years before Rumford's work the French scientists Antoine-Laurent de Lavoisier (1743–1794) and Pierre-Simon Laplace (1749–1827) showed that heat produced by a guinea pig after eating was very close to the heat produced when the food was burned. The development of steam engines by James Watt and others stimulated studies of the relationship between work done and heat produced and how to make engines more efficient. Around 1807 the word "energy" was used with its modern meaning.

In 1842 a German physician, Julius Robert von Mayer (1814–1878), proposed that all forms of energy are equivalent and that the sum of all forms is conserved. He wrote in general, qualitative terms, although in later essays he included quantitative evidence based on the work done when a gas was heated. But his work resulted in little recognition until the end of his life.

About the same time, a British amateur of science, James Prescott Joule (1818–1889), began a series of experiments designed to determine the relationship between

work done and thermal energy increase that resulted in heat transmitted to the outside. He explored electric generators, the compression of gasses, and stirring water. His experiments lasted eighteen years. As he continued to publish his results they were taken more and more seriously.

The German physicist and physiologist Hermann von Helmholtz (1821–1894) developed a mathematical description published in 1847 that showed precisely how energy was conserved in many fields including mechanics, thermal energy and heat, electricity and magnetism, chemistry, and astronomy. With his results the scientific community recognized the great achievement of Rumford, Mayer, Joule, and others and fully accepted energy conservation.

What does **energy efficiency** mean?

In most cases thermal energy is not a useful form of energy for a system. You want the energy content in the gasoline in your auto to give it kinetic energy, not to make it hotter. The cooling system uses a water-antifreeze mixture to cool the engine and warm the radiator, where air flowing through it is heated, thus cooling the fluid. The thermal energy in the heated air is often called rejected or waste energy. An auto is about 20% efficient. That is, only 1/5 of the energy in the gasoline is converted into the kinetic energy of the auto. In addition to the hot air from the engine, tires get warm from flexing, and the brakes get hot when they are applied. All this thermal energy is rejected or waste energy.

Your home furnace converts the chemical energy in oil or gas or electrical energy into thermal energy, either of air or water, depending on whether you have forced-air heat or hot water radiators. But not all the energy goes into heating the house; some leaves through the chimney as rejected or waste energy. Heating systems used to be about 60% efficient. Newer systems can be as much as 95% efficient.

Means of increasing the efficiency of auto and home appliances is an active area of research as nations try to conserve as much of the produced energy as they can.

Your body also uses only a fraction, again about 20%, of the food energy to move your limbs when you walk or run. Your body is cooled by contact with the air, or by evaporating liquid—either perspiration or the humid air expelled by your lungs.

How is **energy measured**?

The SI unit for energy is the joule (J), but energy is often measured in other units. The calorie (cal) and the kilo-calorie (kcal) or food calorie are used both for chemical energy stored in foods and to measure heat. The British Thermal Unit (BTU) is most often used to measure heat in homes and industries. The kilowatt-hour (kWh) is used to measure electrical energy. A completely unofficial, but useful unit is the jelly doughnut (JD), the energy in a medium-sized jelly-filled doughnut. It helps relate all these

units to a tasty treat. The table below illustrates conversions among the units. To use it read across. For example, 1 J = 0.239 cal, 1 cal = 4.186 J, 1 JD = 239 kcal.

	joule (J)	calorie (cal)	food calorie (kcal)	British thermal unit (BTU)	kilowatt-hour (kWh)	jelly doughnut (JD)
J	1	0.239	0.000239	0.000949	0.000000278	0.0000001
cal	4.186	1	0.001	0.00396	0.00000116	0.00418
kcal	4,186	1,000	1	3.96	0.00116	4.18
BTU	1,055	253	0.253	1	0.293	0.001055
kWh	3,600,000	859,000	859	3.41	1	3.6
JD	1,000,000	239,000	239	949	0.278	1

How much **energy** is there in **commonly used fuels**?

In comparing fuels used to heat a home (natural gas, electricity, fuel oil, and wood) more has to be considered than just the cost of the fuel per MJ of energy. The furnaces that distribute the heated air or water have quite varied efficiencies themselves.

Fuel	MJ/liter	MJ/kg	Common Units	Cost (2009)	$/MJ	MJ/$
Gasoline	35	47	121 MJ/gal	$2.60/gal	0.021	47
E85 (ethanol)	22	38	76 MJ/gal	$2.50/gal	0.033	30
Diesel	39	48	135 MJ/gal	$2.70/gal	0.020	50
Natural gas	0.039		11,000 MJ/mcf (1,000 ft^3)	$11/mcf	0.001	1,000
Electricity			0.278 MJ/kWh	$0.12/kWh	0.43	2.3
Fuel oil	38		148 MJ/gal	$2.75/gal	0.019	54
Wood		18	36,000 MJ/cord	$250/cord	0.007	144
Coal		27	12,000 MJ/ton	$40/ton	0.003	300
Uranium (not enriched)		54,000	240,000 MJ/ton			
Candy bar		2.1	0.12 MJ/1 oz. bar	$1/bar	8.4	0.12

What's a **watt**?

Suppose you climb the stairs to the second floor. Whether you run or walk, because you have gone up the same distance the increase in the gravitational field energy will be the same. The difference is the rate at which the energy has changed. The rate, the change in energy divided by the time taken is called *power*. Power is measured in the

Scottish inventor James Watt came up with the term "horsepower," which is equal to 746 watts, the amount of energy it takes an average horse to pull 33,000 pounds of coal one foot in one minute.

unit called the watt. One watt (W) is one joule (J) per second (s). A kilowatt is 1,000 watts or 1,000 joules per second.

Automobiles can accelerate from 0 to 60 miles per hour, but the more powerful ones can do it in six seconds or less while ones with less powerful engines may take more than 10 seconds.

Where did the **term horsepower** originate?

The term horsepower came from Scottish inventor James Watt. The value for a unit of horsepower was determined after Watt made an extensive study of horses pulling coal. He originally determined that the average horse was able to lift 33,000 pounds of coal one foot in one minute. The conversion between watts and horsepower (hp) is that 1 hp = 746 W = 0.746 kW.

In the United States automobile engines are rated in horsepower while in the rest of the world kilowatts are used. In a hybrid car the power of the gasoline engine is usually measured in hp while the electric motor is measured in kW.

What are the **sources** and **uses of energy** in the **United States**?

The tables below explain how much energy the United States uses per source and where the energy is used. The United States used 99.2 quads of energy in 2009, where

each quad equals one thousand billion BTUs. Electrical generation (39.97 quads) is very inefficient. Only 31.5 percent of the energy from the source (coal, natural gas, oil, nuclear) is transformed into electrical energy. The transportation industry is also wasteful in terms of energy, with 75 percent of the energy (mostly petroleum) it uses being wasted as heat.

Energy Source	Percentage of Use in U.S.
Petroleum	37.13%
Natural Gas	23.84%
Coal	22.42%
Nuclear	8.45%
Biomass	3.88%
Hydroelectric	2.45%
Solar	0.9%
Wind	0.51%
Geothermal	0.35%

Energy Used By	Quads Used	Quads Wasted	Percentage Wasted
Transportation	27.86	20.90	75%
Industry	23.94	4.78	20%
Residential	11.48	2.29	20%
Commercial	8.57	1.71	20%

What are some typical power outputs?

The following table was adapted from Wikipedia's entry on "Orders of magnitude (power)" retrieved on November 13, 2009.

Unit	Example*
femtowatt (10^{-15} watt)	

 10 fW — approximate lower limit of power reception of digital cell phones

picowatt (10^{-12} watt)

 1 pW — average power consumption of a human cell

microwatt (10^{-6} watt)

 1 µW — approximate consumption of a quartz wristwatch

milliwatt (10^{-3} watt)

 5–10 mW — laser in a DVD player

watt

 20–40 W — approximate power consumption of the human brain

What might be the consequences of automobiles powered by electricity rather than gasoline?

The need for petroleum would be reduced, but unless the fuels for electrical generation are changed, the need for coal would increase.

70–100 W — approximate basal metabolic rate used by the human body

5–253 W — per capita average power use of the world in 2001

500 W — power output of a person working hard physically

909 W — peak output power of a healthy human (non-athlete) during a 30-second cycle sprint

kilowatt (10^3 watts)

1.366 kW — power received from the sun at Earth's orbit by one square meter

up to 2 kW — approximate short-time power output of sprinting professional cyclists

1 kW to 2 kW — rate of heat output of a domestic electric tea kettle

11.4 kW — average power consumption per person in the United States as of 2009

40 kW to 200 kW — approximate range of power output of typical automobiles

megawatt (10^6 watts)

1.5 MW — peak power output of a wind turbine

2.5 MW — peak power output of a blue whale

3 MW — mechanical power output of a diesel locomotive

16 MW — rate at which a typical gasoline pump transfers chemical energy to a vehicle

140 MW — average power consumption of a Boeing 747 jumbo jet

200–500 MW — electrical power output of a typical nuclear power plant

gigawatt (10^9 watts)

2.074 GW — peak power generation of Hoover Dam

4.116 GW — installed capacity the world's largest coal-fired power plant

18.3 GW — current electrical power generation of China's Three Gorges Dam, the world's largest hydroelectric power plant

terawatt (10^{12} watts)

3.34 TW — average total power consumption of the United States in 2005

50 to 200 TW — rate of heat energy release by a hurricane

petawatt (10^{15} watts)

> 4 PW — estimated total heat flux transported by Earth's atmosphere and ocean away from the equator towards the poles
>
> 174.0 PW — total power received by Earth from the sun

yottawatt (10^{24} watts)

> 384.6 YW — luminosity of the sun

Higher

> 5×10^{36}W — approximate luminosity of the Milky Way galaxy
>
> 1×10^{40}W — approximate luminosity of a quasar
>
> 1×10^{45}W — approximate luminosity of a gamma-ray burst

What does **sustainable energy** mean?

The amount of fossil fuels is limited. There have been major advances in discovering oil and extracting more from existing reservoirs, as well as recent advances in obtaining natural gas and oil from shale. But these sources, as well as coal and uranium, are not being replaced. Sustainable energy sources, primarily wind, water, and solar energy, ultimately receive their energy from the sun, and therefore will be available for billions of years. The present use of these sources is minimal. There are many difficulties in increasing their use. Wind power is highly variable. Water energy from traditional dams and reservoirs causes environmental problems. Energy from waves and tides has yet to be developed widely. Solar energy can be directly converted to electricity using photovoltaic cells. But these cells, at least at present, are inefficient and costly. Large solar "farms" exist, at which solar energy heats a fluid so it can boil water to use with steam turbines driving electrical generators. An additional problem in increasing the use of many of these sources is that they require the use of very rare materials, which are both costly and not easily obtained. Nevertheless, recent analyses suggest that a combination of nuclear, wind, water, and solar energy could replace most of the use of coal and oil for electric energy production.

Because we will eventually run out of fossil fuels, we need to explore other, more sustainable forms of energy, such as solar power.

What are **simple machines**?

Simple machines are devices that match human capabilities to do work to tasks that need to be done. They can reduce the force required or reduce the distance or direction an object must be moved.

Suppose you want to lift a heavy object. If you use a machine you will use your stored chemical energy to do work on the machine. The machine, in turn, does work on the object, which increases its energy. If the force is constant and in the direction of motion, then work is the product of force and distance moved ($W = Fd$). The mechanical advantage (MA) of a simple machine is the output force divided by the input force ($F_{output} / F_{input} = MA$). To make the output force larger than the input force you must choose a machine that has a mechanical advantage larger than one. The drawing below illustrates the process. Note that you exert a small input force over a large distance. The machine exerts a larger output force over a smaller distance.

What are the **limitations** on **simple machines**?

Simple machines must, like everything else, obey the law of conservation of energy. That means that the work done on the machine equals the work the machine does plus the heat the machine puts out because friction has increased its thermal energy. Some machines are highly efficient, meaning input and output work are almost the same, while others put out only a fraction of the work put in.

The drawing on page 74 shows a simple machine where the machine has warmed up. That means its thermal energy has increased. It is now hotter than its surroundings, so it transmits heat to its surroundings (which are not shown on this diagram). The output work of the machine is smaller than the work put into it. That means that for the same input force, the output force is reduced by an inefficient machine.

How can a **machine** with a **mechanical advantage less than or equal to one** be useful?

If a simple machine has a mechanical advantage less than one then you exert a larger force on it than it puts on whatever object it contacts. The output force is less than the

405

Energy transfer in an inefficient simple machine

input force. How can that be useful? It's because the distance moved (output distance) is larger than what you move (input distance). And, therefore, the output speed is also greater. A baseball bat, tennis racket, and golf club can be considered simple machines in which high speed of the end of the implement is desired.

Are machines with mechanical advantage equal to one useful? They are because they change the direction the force is exerted, which often makes it easier for the person to exert that force.

What are the **types** of **simple machines**?

There are four major groups of simple machines: levers (including wheels and axles), pulleys (including gears), and the inclined plane (including wedges and screws).

What is an **inclined plane**?

A ramp is an example of an inclined plane. Instead of lifting an object to the height at the end of the ramp, you move it a much longer distance on the surface of the ramp, but it requires much less force. So, the ramp has a larger output force than an input force; it has a mechanical advantage greater than one. That is, $MA = F_{output} / F_{input} =$ (length of ramp) / (height of ramp).

According to the Americans with Disabilities Act a wheelchair ramp should have a maximum increase in height of 1' for every 12" length of the ramp. The Act says that the maximum rise should be 2–1/2', so the ramp must be 30' long. The input work is $F_{input} \times L$, where L is the length of the ramp. The output work is $F_{output} \times d$, where d is the rise and F_{output} is the weight of the person plus wheelchair. If there is no sliding or

rolling friction, then $F_{input} \times L = F_{output} \times d$. The mechanical advantage is L/d. So $F_{input} = F_{output}/MA$ and the force needed to push a wheelchair up the ramp is given by $F_{input} = F_{output} / (L/d)$. If the weight of the person plus the wheelchair is 200 lbs., then the force needed to push the person up the ramp is $F_{input} = 200\text{lbs} / (30'/2.5') = 17$ lbs.

Look at the cutting edge of a scissors. It's an inclined plane where the input is the force and motion of the closing blades and the output is the outward movement of the paper after it is cut.

Why is a **wedge** like an **inclined plane**?

A knife is one example of a wedge. Look carefully at the sharp edge of a kitchen knife. It looks like two inclined planes put back-to-back. As the knife blade moves down through food, the wedge pushes the pieces apart. A hatchet or axe is another example of a wedge. Wedges are also used to split wood. In this case the flat end of an axe is often used to drive the wedge into the end of a log, which is then forced apart. Wedges are inefficient machines because there is usually a large amount of friction between the wedge and the material, which leads to increased temperature of both the material and wedge, and thus heat transfer.

What type of simple machine is a **screw**?

You can think of a screw as an inclined plane wrapped around an axle. The ancient Greeks used a screw to lift water. Screws and bolts are also used to fasten two pieces of wood, plastic, or metal together.

Screws have a large mechanical advantage, and thus the distance the screw thread moves in its circular motion is much larger than the distance the screw moves into the material. Therefore the force the screw or bolt exerts to hold the material together is large in comparison to the torque used to turn the screw. Screws and bolts are also inefficient machines because of the friction between the screw and material, or between the metal of the bolt and nut.

What is a **lever**?

A lever is a bar that rotates around a fulcrum or pivot. The locations where the input and output forces are exerted relative to the location of the pivot determines the class of the lever, as shown on page 76.

The width of the arrows illustrates the force while the length shows the distance moved.

How **efficient** are **levers**?

The only place where friction can occur with a lever is at the pivot point. So, as long as friction is minimal there, the lever can approach 100% efficiency!

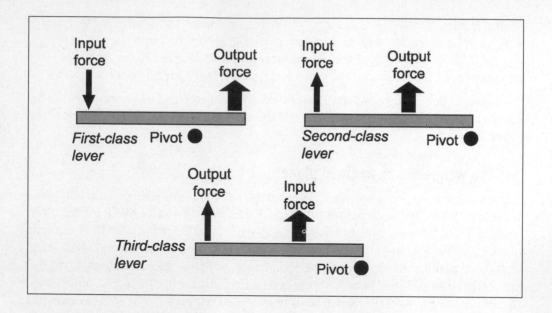

What are **examples of levers**?

The first-class lever shown above has a mechanical advantage greater than one. How could you arrange the location of the pivot to make the mechanical advantage less than one? Look closely at a pair of scissors. Note that you can adjust the mechanical advantage by moving the region of the scissors you are using to cut. Where would you put the material to be cut if more force is needed to make the cut? You would put it, nearer the pivot. On the other hand, if the material is easily cut, cutting near the tip of the blades provides enough force and speeds up the cutting. What class lever is a can or bottle opener? Locate the pivot point and compare to the three drawings above.

Your forearm is a lever, with the elbow joint being the pivot. Where does the bicep muscle attach? The attachment is close to the elbow, so the forearm is a third-class lever. Are other muscles and bones in your body so easily characterized? Most are not because tendons that transmit the force from the muscle to the bone are long and go through several bends.

Consider sports equipment like baseball bats, tennis racquets, and golf clubs. They are often used as extensions of your arms, so the person plus the bat or club has to be examined together. But note that in every case the system is a third-class lever, where a large distance moved (and therefore greater speed) is favored over an increased force.

How is a **wheel** and **axle similar** to a **lever**?

What is a wheel and axle? It consists of a disk (the wheel) attached to a thin rod (the axle) so that the two rotate together. Typically the input force is applied to the outer

What Earth-moving statement did Archimedes make about the lever?

Archimedes (c. 287–c. 212 B.C.E.) had first described the lever in 260 B.C.E. While conducting his research on levers, he stated, "Give me a firm spot on which to stand, and I will move the Earth." Archimedes was referring to the use of levers; theoretically, with a long enough lever and a non-Earthbound place to rest a fulcrum, one could move the Earth. Which class of lever would you use?

edge of the wheel, and the output force is exerted on something, like a rope, attached to the outer edge of the axle. If the two forces are exerted in the same direction, then it is like a third-class lever. If the two are in the opposite direction (for example, a person pushing down on one side of the wheel while a rope is pulled up on the other side), then it is like a first-class lever. One may also have the input force exerted on the axle, in which case it is like a second-class lever.

Both the lever and the wheel and axle are really torque, not force, multipliers. Recall that if the force is at right angles to the line from the axis of rotation to the point where the force is applied, then the torque is given by Fr. Therefore, if the radius of the axel is a and the radius of the wheel is w, then if the input force is applied to the wheel, the output force is given by $F_{output} = F_{input}$ *(w/a)*.

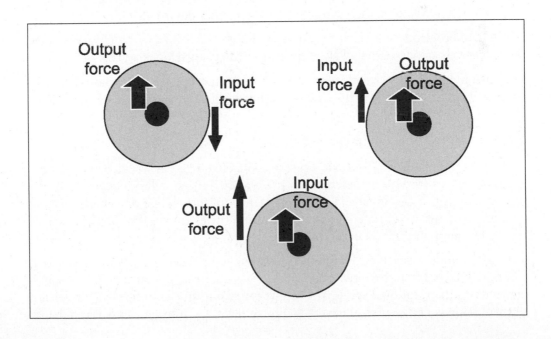

What are **examples** of **wheels and axles**?

The screwdriver is one example The larger the diameter of the handle the greater the torque that can be applied to the screw. Many examples have a rope or chain wrapped around the axle. A sailing ship's steering wheel could be represented by either the left-hand or the center drawing, depending on whether the helmsman pushed down or pulled up on the edge of the wheel. The rope around the axle is connected to the rudder, which is then turned to the right or left.

A similar device would be a device to lift a bucket from a well. The wheel is then replaced by a crank, but the operation of the device is exactly the same. Again, the crank can either be pulled up or pushed down to exert a force on the rope to pull the bucket up.

The rear wheel of a bicycle can be thought of as two wheels on an axle. The large wheel has a rubber tire and exerts a backward force on the road while the smaller wheel is the sprocket that the chain turns. The right-hand drawing above shows that the force of the chain is larger than the wheel's force on the road.

Are **pulleys** really simple machines?

A fixed, or unmovable, single pulley can be considered a wheel and axle where both have the same radius. The mechanical advantage is one, but the pulley changes the direction of the force.

If the pulley is allowed to move and the output force is exerted by the axle of the pulley, then the input force is shared by the two ends of the rope. If you fasten one end and pull up on the other, then you achieve a mechanical advantage of two.

A combination of fixed and movable pulleys is called a block and tackle. Archimedes is said to have pulled a fully loaded ship using a block and tackle.

Energy loss in a block and tackle comes from friction between the axle and its holder as well as the stretching of the rope and rolling friction between the rope and pulley.

Are there **other ways pulleys** can be **used**?

Two or more pulleys, on fixed axles, can be connected together with a belt. If the two pulleys are of different diameters, then the one with the smaller diameter will turn faster, and thus it can exert a larger torque. In your automobile one or more pulley and belt systems are used to deliver torques from the engine to the valve crankshaft, the water pump, the air conditioning compressor, and the alternator.

Continuously variable automobile transmissions are used in a few modern cars to connect the engine to the drive shaft. The torque that can be delivered by an engine depends on the rotational speed. The torque is maximum at an intermediate speed. A transmission is designed to allow the engine to revolve at a speed where it can deliver

Fixed pulley

Movable pulley

Block and
tackle

411

How did gears play a role in an ancient astronomical computer?

In the first century B.C.E. a Roman merchant ship carrying Greek treasures to Rome sank. In 1900 C.E. a storm caused a party of Greek sponge divers to seek shelter on the island of Antikythera. After the storm passed the divers, seeking sponges, found the wreck of the Roman ship. Over the next nine months they recovered much of the treasure, including a badly corroded block the size of a telephone book. A few months later it fell apart, showing remains of bronze gears, plates covered with scales, and inscriptions in Greek. The German scientist Albert Rehm (1871–1949) understood in 1905 that the device was an astronomical calculator. In 1959 the American historian of science Derek de Solla Price (1922–1983) wrote a *Scientific American* article describing some of the details of the device and the calculations it could do. By 1974 he had described 27 gears, including the number of teeth on most. By analyzing the teeth he discovered that the ratio could describe lunar cycles known by the ancient Babylonians.

In 2005 Hewlett Packard and X-Tek Laboratories teamed up to produce astonishing images of the device. HP contributed a camera system that used computer enhanced techniques to show inscriptions that were otherwise invisible. X-Tek brought an eight-ton X-ray machine that could produce extremely high resolution 2-D and 3-D images of the internal mechanisms. The X-ray machine also discovered thousands of Greek letters that described details of the mechanisms. They found thirty gears, but analysis suggests that there must have been at least five more to perform the calculations that move dials on the front and back of the box.

The Antikythera device can predict solar and lunar eclipses, the dates of future Olympic games, and can show the complicated motion of the moon. The precision with which the gears were made was greater than any made in the world for the next thousand years. But who made it and where? It is uncertain, but likely to have been made in one of the colonies of Corinth on the island of Sicily, perhaps by a student of Archimedes decades after he was killed in 212 B.C.E.. (See *Scientific American*, December 2009, and http://www.antikythera-mechanism.gr).

torque to the drive shaft, the axle, and the wheels that are revolving at a variety of speeds. When the auto is accelerating from a stop the wheel rotation speed is slow, and so the transmission needs to match a large-diameter pulley attached to the engine to a smaller one connected to the driveshaft. On the other hand, when the auto is traveling at a high speed, the engine can revolve at the same or even a smaller rate than the driveshaft.

One method of creating a pulley with a variable diameter is to use a v-shaped belt and a pulley with a groove that can be adjusted in width. This kind of transmission is often used with hybrid cars and is being developed as a means of decreasing fuel use.

Who developed **gears**?

As early as 2600 B.C.E. in India and other parts of southern Asia gears were used to open and close doors in temples and to lift water. Around 400 B.C.E. Aristotle (384–322 B.C.E.) described how gears were used. Archimedes described worm gears around 240 B.C.E., and in 40 B.C.E. Vitruvius showed how gears could convert motion from a horizontal axle to a vertical one. In the 1300s C.E. gears were used in clocks in bell towers and on churches.

What are **gears** and why are they **simple machines**?

Gears are toothed wheels which transmit torque between two shafts. The teeth prevent them from slipping, so they are called positive drives. The smaller gear in a pair is called a pinion and the larger one a gear.

Because the teeth mesh, in a given amount of time, the number of teeth engaged on the pinion equals the number on the gear. The number of teeth is proportional to the circumference of the gear that, in turn, is proportional to the radius of the wheel. Therefore if the pinion makes 1 turn, the gear will make (r_{pinion} / r_{gear}) turns. Because energy is conserved, the torque exerted by the gear equals the torque applied to the pinion (r_{gear} / r_{pinion}).

Gears are often used in an automatic transmission, converting the high-speed, small torque output of the engine to the low-speed, large torque output needed to turn the wheels. This kind of gear drive is called a step-down drive. On the other hand, in a windmill, the blades turn at a low speed but provide a large amount of torque. The gear drive in a windmill is a step-up drive. The electric generator, on the other hand, requires high speed, but can work with a smaller amount of torque. Gears also allow a bicyclist to match the speed with which she can rotate the pedal sprocket with the speed needed to drive the wheels.

How are **clocks important** to the **development** of **gears**?

As clocks have improved, so have the gears used within them. The pendulum

Windmill blades may move slowly, but they can produce a lot of torque. Gears increase the rotational speed but reduce the torque, driving an electric generator. Almost all the energy from the wind is delivered to the generator.

413

clock uses a type of a gear called an escapement to drive the pendulum, which regulates the time marked out by the clock. Precision gears allow clocks to use less power and have greater accuracy.

How are **gears used today**?

In addition to automobiles and clocks, gears are used in washing machines, electric mixers and can openers, and electric drills, as well as hard drives and CD/DVD drives in computers. Today much of the development of gears is associated with improvements in the materials used. New metal alloys increase the lifetime of gears used in automobiles and industries. Consumer electronics uses plastic gears that require no lubricant and are quiet.

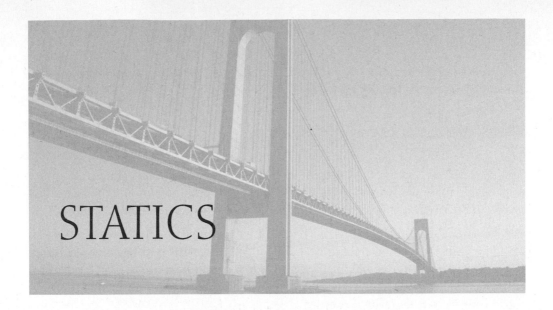

STATICS

CENTER OF GRAVITY

When tossed in the air, why do hammers wobble end over end?

In earlier chapters we considered only "point objects." That is, an object so small that it could be thought of as the tiniest ball. Now we want to expand our considerations to large objects.

First think of a baseball. If a baseball is tossed into the air, the ball follows a smooth parabolic path as described earlier in this book. If, however, a hammer is tossed its path appears much more complex. Why?

All objects are made of atoms. The mass of the object is the sum of the masses of all the atoms. And, the force of gravity on each atom is proportional to the mass of that atom. In a baseball the center may be made of different materials than the surface, but, if you ignore the laces, the ball is made up of the same materials regardless what the direction is. That is, the ball is spherically symmetric. The center of gravity in any object is defined as the average location of its weight. Because the mass is distributed evenly throughout a baseball, the center of gravity is located in the center of the ball. However, for an object such as a hammer, with a metal head and a wooden handle, the center of gravity is not directly in the middle. Since more mass is located in the metal head of the hammer, the center of gravity is closer to that point.

The laws of physics state that the center of gravity follows a parabolic curve when tossed in the air. Indeed, although the ball and the hammer do not appear to have similar motions, their centers of gravity do. If you watch closely both the center of a baseball and the center of gravity of a hammer, you will see that they both follow parabolic paths when thrown.

415

Because the force of gravity is proportional to the mass, the center of mass is at the same location as the center of gravity.

Where is the **center of gravity** of a **person**?

The center of gravity of a person depends on how that person's weight is distributed. The distribution is typically different in adult males and females. Males have more upper-body mass while females have more mass in the hip region. A male's center of gravity is about 65% of his height while that for a female is about 55%.

Try this. Stand facing a wall with your toes against the wall. Now try to rise to stand on your toes. Can you do it? Standing on your toes moves your point of support in front of your center of gravity, so you will tip backwards. If not against a wall, how can you stand on your toes? You naturally move your arms forward or bend forward to move your center of gravity forward.

If you stand with your back against a wall, can you bend forward so the trunk of your body is horizontal? Most likely if you're male you will tend to fall forward, while if you're female you are more likely to be successful. Again, the question is whether or not the center of gravity of your body is above your point of support—in this case your toes, or in front of it.

Why is it **easy to tip over** some objects?

If you want to tip something over you'll have to rotate it. As you have seen, rotation means you need to apply a torque. An object sitting on a surface has several forces on it. First, is the gravitational force that acts on its center of gravity. Second, is the upward force of the surface. Third, is friction between the object and the surface that exists only if the surface is on a slant.

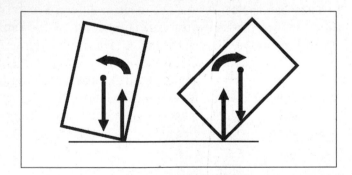

Now suppose you exert a sideways force near the top of a box. That creates a torque and the box begins to rotate. If you now let go will the box continue to roll or will it go backwards? It depends on the relative locations of the center of gravity and the force of the surface as seen in the illustration above.

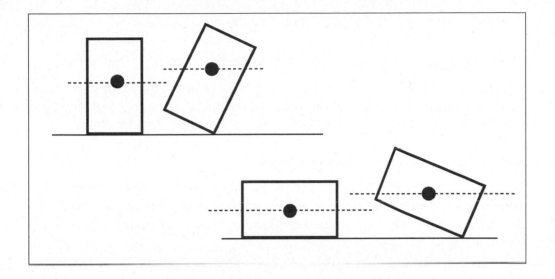

If the center of gravity is above the bottom of the box then the box will return to its upright position. If the center is directly above the corner of the box, then the box won't rotate at all. If the center is outside the bottom of the box, then it will tip over.

Why do **some things tip easily** while others are stable?

As you can see from the example above, when the center of gravity is outside the base of the object it will tip. That suggests the general rule: it will be stable if it is low and wide. That is, keep the center of gravity low and the base wide!

Not only is a larger torque needed to tip an object that is wide and low, but the center of gravity has to be lifted higher for the low and wide object. As a result the work needed to tilt the object is larger.

Left: a "tall and narrow" object can be more easily tipped over.

Right: a "low and wide" object is more difficult to tip.

You can see from the dashed lines the amount the center of gravity must be lifted to tip over the object.

What are applications of this rule? Autos and trucks that are narrower and have high center of gravities are less stable against rollover. Football players and wrestlers are taught to get down low and spread your feet apart. This stance follows the "low and wide" rule making your body more stable and difficult to knock over. Your opponent, in order to knock you over, would have to exert a force to lift up your center of gravity and then push you over. If you simply stood upright, with your feet close together, you would be "tall and narrow" and your opponent would have less difficulty pushing you and your center of gravity.

417

STATICS

What does it mean to say that an object is **static**?

Static means "not moving." In the fields of engineering and physics to be static means that the object does not move. When static, all the forces acting on a body must sum to zero. That is, the net force on the body is zero so the object does not move.

Why are we **static** when **sitting in a chair**?

As long as you are sitting in a chair and not moving (relative to Earth), you are static. That means that the chair is supporting you with an upward force that is equal to your weight. You would remain static until some external force was exerted on you to start you in motion.

What is the name of the **supporting force** from the chair?

Another term for a supporting force is "normal force." The normal force is always directed perpendicularly out of the surface. The normal force of a chair is straight up if the chair is on a level surface, while the normal force of an incline would be perpendicular to the surface of the incline, and not perfectly vertical. The term "normal" was derived from the geometrical name for a 90° angle and is not the opposite of "abnormal."

What **kind of forces** can you **exert** on an object?

Hold a book in your two hands. What kind of forces can you exert on it? You could pull on the book to try to make it longer or you push it to try to make it shorter. The name for the force on the book that pulls on it is a tension force, while the name for the force that pushes on it is a compressive force.

You could also try to twist it, applying what is called a torsional force. Finally, place one hand on the front cover and the other hand on the back cover. Now push one hand to the right and the other to the left. This places a shear force on the book.

Tension forces are common. If you hang from a chin-up bar, your arms experience a tension force. Pulling on a rope, wire, or cable also exerts tension on them. Materials experiencing tension will stretch, some more and some less. Materials that stretch easily are called pliant; those that do not are called rigid.

Scientists have measured the response of materials to tension and compression. The ratio of the applied pressure (called stress) to the change in length divided by the original length (called strain) is called Young's modulus. Its value varies from 10 GN/m² (10 billion newtons per square meter) in wood to 200 GN/m² in steel and cast iron. That means that for an equal force on it steel will stretch (or compress) 1/20 as much as wood. If you would hang a 120-kilogram (264 pound) ball from a 6-meter (19.7 feet) long steel cable 2.5 millimeters (0.9 inches) in diameter it would stretch 7 millimeters (0.3 inches).

In the case of the cable above when you remove the weight the cable will return to its original length. It is called an elastic material. If you exert a much larger force the cable won't return to its original length. This is called the plastic region. At some point it will break. The force that breaks it is called the tensile strength. For steel the tensile strength is 1 GN/m². Thus for cable in the example above it would take a hanging mass of 500 kilograms (1,100 pounds) to break the cable.

Young's modulus also describes the change in length of an object when a compressive force is exerted on it. When you stand you exert a compressive force on your leg bones and they will shrink somewhat in length. But a 70-kilogram (154 pound) person standing on one leg will compress it by only 0.01% of its length! The Young's modulus for cartilage, the material between the bones in all parts of your body, is one ten-thousands as large as that of bone. So putting the weight of a 70-kilogram (154 pound) mass on a piece of cartilage with same area as the femur in your leg would compress it by 10% of its original thickness.

For compressive forces there is a compressive strength. But, many materials will buckle if too great a compressive force is placed on it. Brittle materials will, on the other hand, break. The compressive and tensile strength of bones is almost exactly the same.

What determines **how much** a **material** will **bend**?

Try to bend a ruler. Hold one end tightly on your desk and push down on the other end. You are exerting a tension force on one surface and a compressive force on the other. The amount the ruler bends depends again on the Young's modulus (Y) of the material as well as its length (L), width (w), and thickness (t). The bending (x) is proportional to the force applied (F) and the length cubed and inversely proportional to its thickness cubed. Or, in the form of an equation, $x = FL^3/(t^3 wY)$ That is why the joists supporting a floor are much thicker than they are wide. Typically wood 1–1/2" wide but 10" or 12" thick is used. The larger thicknesses are used if the span between supporting walls is longer.

An "I" beam is often used to support weight. The beam is in the shape of the letter I. The vertical member, tall and narrow, keeps it from bending while the top and bottom members keep the vertical member from twisting. While I beams are most often made of steel, wood beams are now used in houses because they are stronger, lighter, and cheaper than steel.

What materials are used for **static structures**?

The first materials used were made of stone, especially stones like flint that could be chipped to make sharp edges and points. Ancient peoples discovered metals, either in pure form, or in ore, that is mixed with non-metals. Copper, tin, gold, and iron were known before 2000 B.C.E. Copper, tin, and gold are very soft and not very useful as tools or weapons.

A method of hardening metals is to mix two or more different metals forming what is called an alloy. Bronze is made by adding tin to copper and was known by about 4000 B.C.E. in what is now Iran and Iraq. The tin came from southern England. Bronze is a hard metal that can be melted and cast in various shapes, including statues. Today bronze is used for bells and cymbals.

Not much later methods were found to convert iron ore, which is iron mixed with either oxygen or sulfur, to pure iron using a charcoal fire. Iron replaced bronze as a material for tools and weapons because it was cheaper and didn't require long trade routes to obtain the tin. To keep iron from being brittle the carbon must be removed. If the iron is heated to red-heat and then hammered the carbon is forced to the surface where it can be removed. The result is steel that contains less than about 1% carbon.

Steel is a versatile alloy of iron and carbon because additional materials can be added to change its properties. Very hard steel, called tool steel, contains tungsten, molybdenum, and chromium, among other minor additions. Its hardness can be changed by heating it and then cooling it very quickly by quenching it in water or other liquids. Stainless steel used in knives, forks, and spoons has 18% chromium and 10% nickel. Other stainless steels use different amounts of these two metals as well as molybdenum and magnesium. Stainless steel does not rust, but isn't as hard as tool steel.

Pewter is a tin alloy that was developed in England for plates and cups. It adds copper, bismuth, and antimony to tin. Originally lead was used, but because it is poisonous, it is no longer found in pewter.

Brass is typically 80% to 90% copper with zinc added. Actually, brass was made before metallic zinc was isolated! The zinc ore calamine was melted with copper. Brass is used as a decorative metal as well as in bullet casings. If aluminum and tin are added it is resistant to corrosion by sea water.

Gold is another very soft metal. It can be made harder by adding copper and silver in equal quantities. Gold alloys are measured in karets. 24-karat gold is pure gold while 18-karet gold has 18 parts gold and 6 parts other metals. 10-karet gold has 10 parts gold and 14 parts other metals.

Titanium is used in many alloys today because it is lightweight and corrosion resistant. Many alloys of both metals and non-metals are used in electronics. Some LED lamps contain the metals gallium and aluminum and the non-metal arsenic.

What are **composite materials**?

As was mentioned above, brittle materials like concrete have larger compressive strength than tensile strength. For that reason reinforcing bars (rebars) made of steel are embedded in concrete. The steel supports the concrete when it is under tension, reducing its tendency to crack and thus keeping it from failing.

Composite materials have been used since ancient times when straw was added to clay to make bricks.

The most recent composite materials use carbon fibres (less than 0.01 mm in diameter) that are light in weight (they're made of pure carbon) with very high tensile strength but low compressive strength. They are added to plastics to make them more rigid (increase their Young's modulus) without adding weight. Golf club shafts are often made of a plastic filled with carbon fibres, giving the shaft great strength with low weight. By varying the amount of carbon fibres the flexibility of the shaft can be changed.

Reinforcing concrete blocks with rebar (steel bars) helps support the concrete and keep it from cracking. Composite materials such as these blocks are an example of how combining materials that have compressive strength with those that have tensile strength is an effective strategy in construction.

Although it isn't really a composite, glass can be made to be less brittle. The key idea is to keep the surface under compression at all times so it won't crack. Glass sheets are made from the fluid state by cooling. If the surfaces are cooled quickly with strong blasts of air it produces a form of glass called case-hardened that was used for shatterproof lenses in eyeglasses. In the 1970s a chemical method was invented that could be used on cold glass. It involves putting the glass into a bath of potassium salts. The potassium replaces sodium in the surface layers of the glass. The larger potassium atoms expand the surface layers so that the interior portion of the glass compresses the surface, keeping it from developing cracks.

What is **shear**?

Scissors, also known as shears, use each of their blades to move the object it is attempting to cut in opposite directions. Thus they exert a shearing force on the object to be cut. Earthquakes often cause land and roads to experience significant shearing forces. Pictures of torn-up roads after earthquakes show how one side of a street moved one way while the other side of the street moved in the opposite direction, tearing up the pavement as the parts moved past one another.

What **other major force** can be experienced by **structures**?

A torsion force, usually from winds, is responsible for twisting structures. Buildings, bridges, and towers use cross-supports to prevent such forces from damaging the structures. For example, the John Hancock building in Chicago has visible cross-supports.

421

BRIDGES AND OTHER "STATIC" STRUCTURES

What was the **first type** of **bridge**?

The first type of bridge ever used was a beam bridge. This bridge was probably just a fallen tree that was used to cross a ravine or a small stream; the tree was probably supported by the river bed or by a group of rocks. Beam bridges consist of a horizontal roadbed supported by vertical piers on the shores that are planted in the ground. Beam bridges are limited by the resistance of the roadbed to bending.

How can you **reduce the bending** of a **beam bridge**?

The simplest way to keep the roadbed from bending is to use a king post. In the illustration below, the downward force of the center of the bridge pulls down on the vertical post. This places the diagonal braces under compression. They transmit the force to the piers. The upward force on the post makes the net force on the post zero. It is under tension.

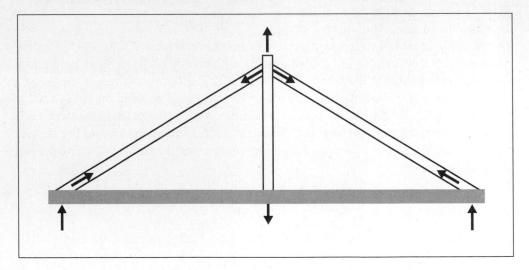

While the king-post bridge can reduce the bending in the center of the bridge, it can do nothing about bending between the pier and the bridge center. One solution is to add a second vertical post and connect the two by a horizontal member, creating a queen-post bridge. But a method that allows much more support on a longer bridge is the truss.

Similar methods of translating downward forces to compression forces exerted on the piers on the ends of the bridge were known to the Romans who worked in stone and concrete. They were famous for the arches used in their massive aqueducts. One such aqueduct, the Pont du Gard, was completed in 18 B.C.E. and was used to carry water a length of 270 meters (886 feet) over the Gardon river valley in southern France.

How does the **suspension bridge** support the roadway?

The twenty longest bridges in the world are all suspension bridges. Suspension bridges are able to span huge distances because the long cables suspending or holding up the roadbed are draped over a set of tall vertical towers called pylons. The pylons support the suspension cables from which vertical cables are attached that lift the deck. The ends of the suspension cables must be anchored into the ground at each end of the bridge to exert the tension forces on the cables.

The first known suspension bridge was constructed in the seventh century C.E. by Mayans at their capital Yaxchilan, Mexico. It spanned 100 meters.

Where is the **longest bridge** in the **United States**?

The longest bridge in the United States, a suspension bridge, ranks as the sixth longest bridge in the world. The Verrazano Narrows Bridge is between Staten Island and Brooklyn, New York. This bridge, completed in 1964, spans 1,298 meters (4,260 feet).

The span between the towers of the Mackinac Bridge that links the upper and lower peninsulas of Michigan at 1,158 meters (3,800 feet) is shorter than that of the Verrazano Narrows Bridge, but when measured by the distance between the cable anchorages it is the longest bridge in the western hemisphere The length of the entire bridge, shore to shore, is 5 miles.

What is the **newest hybrid** of **bridges**?

One of the newest, prettiest, and most economical bridges is the cable-stayed suspension bridge. With its sleek lines and thin roadways, it is the perfect bridge for most

423

mid-span designs. The Tatara Bridge, in Onomichi, Japan, completed in 1999 is the longest cable-stayed bridge in the world, with a span of 890 meters (2,919 feet). Cable-stayed bridges suspend the roadbed by attaching multiple cables directly to the deck supporting the roadbed. These cables are then passed through a set of tall vertical towers and attached to abutments on the ground. Such engineering methods reduce the need for heavy, expensive steel and the massive anchorages that are needed to support suspension bridges.

At 4,260 feet, the Verrazano Narrows Bridge in New York is the longest suspension bridge in the United States.

What **challenges** are there in **building skyscrapers**?

The first challenge is to design a foundation that can support the tremendous weight of a large building. The best way is to dig down to the bedrock. This can be as close as about 21 meters (70 feet) in New York City to almost 61 meters (200 feet) in Chicago. If the distance is short holes can be bored and concrete piers can be formed in the holes. More frequently a caisson is required. This is a large hollow waterproof structure that is sunk through the mud, pulling it into and then out of the top of the caisson. A third method is go build a large steel and concrete underground pad that "floats" on the top of a hard clay layer.

The load that the foundation must support includes the weight of the building, its furnishings and equipment, and the changing load of occupants. In addition to the loads, strong winds must also be considered.

The walls of early tall buildings were constructed of masonry that supported the weight of the building. The 16-story 65.5-meter (215-foot) high Monadnock Building in Chicago, built from 1889 to 1891, required 1.8-meter (6-foot) thick walls at the base. It was so heavy that it sank, requiring steps to be constructed between the sidewalk and the ground floor. The second half of the building used a steel frame on which masonry was attached, allowing much wider windows to be used.

The steel frames can be bolted, riveted, or welded together. When the 59-story, 279-meter (915-foot) tall Citigroup building was constructed in New York City from 1974 to 1977 the frame was bolted together, but later computer models showed that if hurricane-strength winds struck the building it would be in danger of collapse. As a hurricane moved up the eastern seaboard in 1978 workers hurriedly welded plates over the bolted joints. Luckily the hurricane moved out to sea, sparing New York.

What makes a building a skyscraper?

The name "skyscraper" is an informal term. The first skyscraper had load-bearing outer walls made of stone and concrete. Today a skyscraper is supported by an internal iron or steel skeleton. Skyscrapers are economical in crowded cities because they take advantage of the more abundant vertical space that is available.

Another effect of winds on tall buildings is to make them sway back and forth. While a variety of braces can reduce the sway, they add weight to the building. Another method is now used. The Citigroup building has a 400-ton concrete damper at the top. The damper moves back and forth, opposing the wind-driven motion of the building and reducing sway. Dampers, both liquid and solid, are used in tall buildings, towers, off-shore oil drilling platforms, bridges, and skywalks. The 210 meter (690 foot) Burj al-Arab hotel in Dubai has 11 mass dampers. The dampers can also mitigate the effect of earthquakes.

Transporting large numbers of people into and out of upper floors is a challenge to those who design the elevator systems. As was demonstrated in the collapse of the World Trade Center buildings on September 11, 2001, stairways can be used in emergency situations, but the simultaneous movement of occupants down and firefighters up the stairways caused severe problems.

Another consideration is the safety of occupants in case of fire. Some buildings have entire floors designed to be especially fire-resistant so that people could gather there and be safer than on other floors.

What is the **tallest building** in the world?

The tallest building, until recently, was the Sears Tower (now the Willis Tower) in Chicago, Illinois, which was built in 1974 and is 443 meters (1,453 feet) high. Three new skyscrapers in Asia now surpass this height. The Petronas Towers in Malaysia, completed in 1996, are 452 meters (1,483 feet) high. The Shanghai World Finance Centre in China, completed in 2008, stands 492 meters (1,614 feet) high—almost half a kilometer into the sky. The Burj Dubai (Dubai Tower), 818 meters (2,684 feet) high, the world's highest, opened in January 2010.

What is the **tallest structure** ever built?

Structures and towers are listed separately from skyscrapers. The Warszawa Radio Tower on the outskirts of Warsaw, Poland, was the tallest structure ever built. Although it needed to be supported by long cables to keep it up, the tower reached 646

meters (2,119 feet) into the sky. Unfortunately, in August 1991, the tower came crashing down during repair work.

The tallest structure ever built that is still in existence is the KTHI-TV tower in North Dakota, which stands—with the help of cables—629 meters (2,063 feet) tall. The tallest self-supporting tower in the world is the Canadian CN Tower, whose tip is 553 meters (1,815 feet) above the city of Toronto.

What is the difference between a **dead load** and a **live load**?

In order to remain static, bridges (and all structures, for that matter) must be able to withstand loads placed on them. A load is simply the engineering term for force. Dead load is the weight of the bridge or structure itself. The live load, on the other hand, is the weight and forces applied to the bridge as a result of the vehicles and people that move across the bridge at any one time. Of course, in order to be safe, engineers account for much higher live loads than would normally occur.

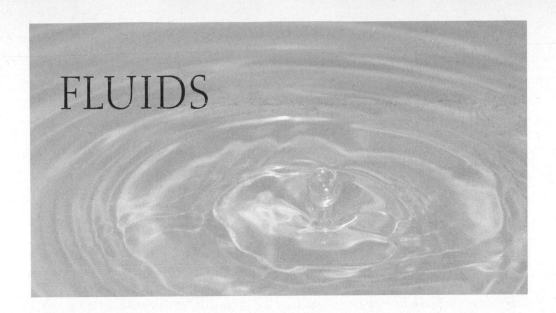

FLUIDS

What is a **fluid**?

Solids retain their shape because strong forces hold the atoms in their places. In a liquid the forces keep the atoms close together, but they are free to move. In a gas the atoms are about ten times further apart than in either solids or liquids and forces between them are very weak. As a result of weaker forces, a liquid or gas can flow freely and assume the shape of their container. They are called fluids.

There are two main areas of fluid study. The field that studies fluids in a state of rest is called static fluids, and the field that analyzes the movement of fluids is called fluid dynamics. We will first explore static fluids.

WATER PRESSURE

What is **water pressure**?

Pressure is the force divided by the area over which it is exerted. In 1647 the French scientist Blaise Pascal (1623–1662) recognized that water exerts the same pressure in all directions. This statement is known as Pascal's Principle.

To understand Pascal's Principle, think of a small cube of water as shown on page 96. The grey arrow in the middle is the force of gravity on the cube. As a result the total downward force of the cube is larger than the upward force.

Now, by Newton's Third Law, the outward force of the water is equal to the inward force on the water. What exerts this force? If the cube is at the edge of the container, then the container exerts the force. You can check that for yourself. Use an empty fluid container—say a juice box or milk carton. Punch a hole in one side. Pour water

427

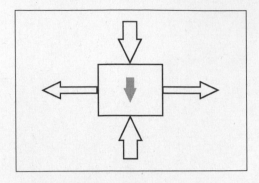

into the container. To keep the water from leaving through the hole you have to exert a force with your thumb. The same would be true if the hole were in the bottom. What exerts the downward force on the top of the cube? If the cube is not at the top surface, then the force is exerted by water above it. If it is on the top, then air pressure, which we will discuss shortly, exerts this force.

Because the downward force exerted by the fluid is greater than the upward force, the force, and hence the pressure, increases as the depth of the fluid increases. So the pressure at the bottom of a container of fluid is greater than at the top. The amount of increase in pressure is given by the product of the density, ρ, the gravitation field strength, g, and the depth, h, or ρgh. That is, the pressure on the bottom, $P_{\text{bottom}} = P_{\text{top}} + \rho gh$.

What does it mean to say that **water seeks its own level**?

The surface of water placed in a single container (a glass or a bathtub or a lake) will remain at the same level relative to Earth on both sides of the container. Adding water to one side will only make the entire level uniformly rise; there can never be one section of the glass or tub or lake that is at a higher elevation than another section. To understand this fact, consider adding the small cube of water on top of the surface at one location. It would exert a downward force on the water under it. But, because water can flow, water under it would flow outward, raising the level elsewhere in the container until the pressure is equal everywhere.

Water also seeks its own level in other containers. If you fill a hose or tube with water and hold the tube in a "U" shape, the water level will be at the same locations in the two ends. You can use the "U" tube to make a device to show you equal heights at two different locations. You may have a coffeemaker that has a water height indicator on the side. This is a small tube that connects to the water reservoir at the bottom. The water level in the narrow tube and the wide reservoir is the same.

What are the **units** used to **measure pressure**?

Pressure is force divided by area, so in the metric system pressure is measured in newtons per square meter, called a pascal (Pa). One pascal is a very small pressure, so usually the kPa, or 1,000 Pa, is used. In the English system, pounds per square inch (psi) is often used. Another unit used is a measurement of the height of mercury in a glass tube that would create a pressure that balances the pressure of the fluid. That unit that used to be called millimeters of mercury is now called the torr. Here is how these units compare: 760 torr = 14.7 psi = 101.3 kPa.

Why are **water towers** needed on **tall buildings**?

A typical home requires water pressures of 50 to 100 psi. City water systems use pumps to maintain that pressure in the pipes. Vertical pipes are needed to supply the upper floors with water. Each foot of height reduces the pressure by 0.443 psi. Auxiliary pumps at various floors can provide the needed increase in pressure. An alternative is to put a large storage tank on the roof and use pumps to fill it. It then supplies the building with water under pressure due to the height of the tank. It also allows the pumps to be run to fill it at night when electricity rates may be cheaper. In addition, it provides a backup source of water in case of fire.

Water towers such as these in New York City are often placed on top of tall buildings. This way, the force of gravity supplies the water pressure needed to deliver water throughout the building.

Small towns, which often use wells as a water source, use water towers to store water in case there is an interruption in electrical service. It also allows the town to use smaller pumps because the tower can supply the pressure during peak water demands. A typical daily water use is 500 gallons per minute, but this can rise to 2,000 gallons a minute in peak times. A tower typically stores one day's worth of water.

Why are many **water towers placed** on **high towers**?

The height of the water determines the pressure. Since a holding tank is up high, it places a lot of pressure on the water in the rest of the water network. The tank should be as large across as possible so that for the same amount of water the vertical dimension of the tank can be as small as practicable. This design limits the variation in pressure as the tank empties or is filled.

Why do your **ears hurt** when you dive to the **bottom** of a **swimming pool**?

Just as the weight of the air above us creates atmospheric pressure, the weight of water creates liquid pressure. Close to the surface of a pool there is very little water that can push down and increase water pressure. The further a person dives below the surface, however, the greater the water pressure. The eardrums are especially sensitive to the increased pressure, for they do not have the reinforcement that the diver's skin has. In fact, your eardrums can usually feel pressure when diving just 1.5 to 3 meters (5 to 10 feet) below the surface of the water.

429

> ## Where is the water pressure greater, in a lake 20 meters (65.6 feet) deep or in the ocean at a depth of 10 meters (32.8 feet)?
>
> **A**lthough the ocean contains a lot more water than a lake, it is the depth that determines the weight of water directly over a diver that defines the amount of pressure the diver experiences. Therefore, a diver who is 20 meters below the surface of a lake will experience more pressure, in fact, twice the pressure, than the ocean diver experiences at 10 meters. Saltwater is denser than freshwater, but the increase in pressure caused by the increased density is small in comparison to that caused by the difference in depth.

Why are **dams thicker** at the **bottom** than at the top?

Dams hold back bodies of water, and water pressure increases with the depth of the body of water, so the pressure from the water pushing horizontally on the dam is greater at the bottom than at the top. If holes were bored near the bottom, middle, and top of a dam, the longest horizontal stream of water would fire out through the bottom hole because the water pressure is greatest there.

BLOOD PRESSURE

What does it mean to **measure** your **blood pressure**?

Blood pressure is the pressure your blood exerts on the walls of your arteries. The fluid dynamics of blood play a major role in blood pressure. The heart is the pump that moves the blood throughout the body, with vessels carrying the blood to different sections of the body.

The device used to measure blood pressure is the sphygmomanometer. It is placed around the upper arm, inflated, and then deflated, while a meter measures the pressure passing through that section of the arm and either a person using a stethoscope or an electronic sensor detects the pulse.

Why is your **blood pressure** taken from your **upper arm**?

Liquid pressure is dependent on the depth of the fluid. Since blood pressure can't be measured around the heart, and the depth of the fluid must be the same as the heart, doctors and nurses need to find a location at the same depth as the heart. A convenient location at that level is your upper arm. When lying down, however, your blood

pressure can be taken just about anywhere, since most of the blood is at the same vertical level as the heart.

The cuff is inflated until no pulse can be heard. It is then slowly lowered. As the pressure falls below the systolic pressure the pulse can be heard. When it's below the diastolic pressure the pulse gets weaker. The report "120 over 70" means that the systolic pressure is 120 torr, the diastolic pressure 70 torr.

ATMOSPHERIC PRESSURE

How is the **pressure** of a **gas similar** to **liquid pressure**?

The pressure from a gas, acts the same way liquid pressure does. One difference between gaseous and liquid pressure is that gases are about 1/1000 as dense as liquids and therefore apply less pressure. The second difference is that gases can be easily compressed while the compressibility of liquid is very small.

What is the **atmospheric pressure**?

Earth's atmosphere extends approximately 100 kilometers (328,000 feet) above the ground, but it gets less and less dense as the altitude increases. If the density were constant, then the atmosphere would be about 8-kilometers high (26,246 feet; close to the height of Mt. Everest). Some 63% of the atmosphere is below that height. The amount of force on an area of one square meter is about 101,300 newtons. That is, the pressure is 101.3 kPa. Atmospheric pressure varies with temperature and other conditions. Our weather is mostly influenced by high and low pressure regions, which can deviate by about 5% from normal.

The pressure decreases as your altitude increases because the amount of air above you creating the pressure is smaller. At an altitude of 3 kilometers (10,000 feet) above sea level the atmospheric pressure is about 70% of what it is at sea level. At 100 kilometers it is 3 millionths of the sea level pressure!

What are the **bends**?

Nitrogen under normal atmospheric pressure is nearly insoluble in blood. Under pressure, the solubility increases. Thus, as a diver goes deeper the blood holds more and more nitrogen, which dissolves in the blood during gas exchange in the lungs. As the diver ascends, the pressure decreases, and hence the blood is now supersaturated with nitrogen. The supersaturated nitrogen forms bubbles as it comes out of solution in the blood, or cells. These bubbles collect in veins and arteries. They cause pain, and can rupture cell walls and block the flow of blood to cells, causing injury or even death.

A barometer is an instrument used for measuring gas pressures. They are also used to help predict weather, as low pressure systems tend to bring inclement weather while high pressure systems bring fair skies.

The best way to avoid the bends is to rise to the water surface slowly, allowing the liquid pressure from the water to gradually decrease and prevent any physical damage. Most scuba divers use "nitrox" that contains 35% oxygen and 65% nitrogen (rather than normal air that contains 20% oxygen and 80% nitrogen) to reduce, but not eliminate the possibility of getting the bends.

How is **atmospheric pressure measured**?

A device to measure gas pressure is called a barometer. There are two major types of barometers, the mercury barometer and the aneroid barometer. Galileo's secretary, Evangelista Torricelli (1606–1647; the unit of pressure, the torr, was named after him), developed the mercury barometer in 1643. It consists of a thin glass tube about 80 centimeters (31 inches) long, which is closed at the top, filled with liquid mercury and placed upside down in another mercury-filled dish. Depending upon the atmospheric pressure pushing on the mercury in the dish, the level of mercury in the tube will rise or fall because there is no air above it. By measuring the height of the mercury, which would usually be between 737 and 775 millimeters (29 to 30.5 inches) high, atmospheric pressure of the atmosphere can be measured.

The most common household barometer is the aneroid barometer, in which atmospheric pressure bends the elastic top of an extremely low-pressure drum; by measuring the amount the top bends, a measurement of atmospheric pressure can be determined. The aneroid barometer is often used in airplane altimeters to measure altitude. Since atmospheric pressure decreases as altitude increases, the aneroid barometer is an ideal instrument to use. It is much safer than the mercury barometer, because mercury vapor is poisonous and the mercury must be exposed to the atmosphere.

What happens to a **balloon** when it is **submerged in water**?

When an air-filled balloon is placed underwater, the water (which has higher pressure than the air) exerts a force on all sides of the balloon. The pressure from the water causes the air to compress inside the balloon. The deeper the balloon is taken into the water, the greater the pressure, and therefore, the smaller the balloon will become. The pressure from the water will compress the balloon until the air pressure within the balloon can supply an equal amount of force against the water.

If the air pressure is 101,300 newtons per square meter, why don't we get crushed?

Since our bodies have air inside them, the air inside our bodies is at the same atmospheric pressure as the air outside our bodies. Therefore, the pressures are equal and we can move quite freely in our atmospheric environment. The remainder of our body is mostly liquid water and cannot be compressed.

The same cannot be said for divers. As the divers go deeper and deeper, the water pressure increases. At a depth of 10 meters (32 feet) it is about twice atmospheric pressure. A diver can breathe in compressed gas to balance this pressure. If a diver goes to extreme depths and then ascends too rapidly the diver can suffer the "bends."

Why do **closed containers** sometimes **dent** or even **collapse** on **cool days**?

Just as a balloon can become smaller when placed under water, a sealed container can change its shape and even collapse under certain atmospheric conditions. For example, a container that stores gasoline for a lawnmower is usually sealed when it's not being used. If the container were sealed on a warm day, when there was little atmospheric pressure, subsequently on a cool, high-pressure day, the gasoline container could be crushed. A second reason is that gasoline vapor exists in the tank, and at low temperatures more of the vapor condenses to liquid, reducing the pressure of the gases in the tank.

Why do some **athletes** go to **high elevations** to **train**?

Runners have always trekked to the mountains of Colorado to train in higher elevations because of the lower atmospheric pressure that the mountains provide. Since the air is not as dense as it is at lower elevations, the lungs need to work harder to supply the body with a sufficient amount of oxygen. Many athletes feel that training in such conditions gets their bodies used to lower amounts of oxygen. Therefore, when running in a competition at lower elevations, they can compete quite well because their bodies are used to working hard to get a great deal of oxygen.

SINKING AND FLOATING: BUOYANCY

What **distinguishes** objects that **sink** from those that **float**?

An object will sink if the downward forces on it are larger than the upward forces. There are two downward forces: the force of the liquid above the object and its weight

433

(the force of gravity). The upward force is the force of the liquid below it. Let's think of a cubic object of height h and area of the top and bottom A. Its volume, V, is then given by $V = hA$. Density is the mass divided by the volume, or $\rho = m/V$.

Let's start by considering the difference in water pressure between the bottom and top of this cube. Pressure is force divided by area, so, using $P_{bottom} = P_{top} + \rho_{water}gh$, we can write $F_{bottom}/A = F_{top}/A + \rho_{water}gh$ so $F_{bottom} = F_{top} + \rho_{water}ghA$. Now we recall that hA is the volume of the cube and $\rho_{water}hA$ is therefore the mass of the water, m_{water}, whose place is taken by the cube of matter.

The net downward force on the object in the water is then the force on the top plus the object's weight less the force on the bottom. That means

$$F_{net} = F_{top} + m_{object}g - F_{bottom}$$

From the results of the paragraph above, $F_{net} = m_{object}g - m_{water}g$. Therefore, if the object's mass is larger than the mass of the water whose place it takes, it sinks. If the mass is smaller, then it will rise. Weight is the mass times the gravitational field strength, g, so the net force is $F_{net} = W_{object} - W_{water}$. The water whose place the object takes is normally referred to as the "water displaced" by the object.

What is the **buoyant force**?

From the equation obtained in the answer to the last question, you can see that when you place an object in water, its weight is reduced by the weight of the water displaced. The reduction in weight, $W_{object} - W_{water}$, that is the net upward force of the water, is called the buoyant force.

Why does a **stone sink** but **wood float**?

A stone is more dense than water. That is, if you compare the mass of a stone to the mass of the same volume of water, the stone's mass will be greater. Therefore its weight will also be greater, so $W_{stone} - W_{water}$ will be positive, and there will be a downward net force. Therefore the stone will move downward through the water until it rests on the bottom.

Wood, on the other hand, is less dense than water. If the wood is pushed under water $W_{wood} - W_{water}$ will be negative. There will be an upward force on the wood and it will rise. How far will it rise? As some of the wood rises above the level of the water the volume and the mass, and therefore the weight, of the water displaced will be reduced. When the weight of the wood and the weight of the water displaced are equal, the net force on the wood will be zero and it will no longer move.

Why is a **stone easier** to **lift** when it is **in water**?

Even though the stone sinks because it is denser than water, there is still a buoyant force on it given by $W_{stone} - W_{water}$, so the stone's weight is reduced.

Hot air balloons work by expanding the gas within the balloon so that the air within is at a lower pressure than the surrounding atmosphere.

Floating usually refers to a liquid such as water, but **can anything float** in a **gas**?

Remember that there is a difference in pressure of any fluid between the bottom and top of an object in it given by $P_{bottom} = P_{top} + \rho g h$. Even though the density of a gas, ρ, is much smaller than that of a liquid, there is still a pressure difference, and therefore a buoyancy. There is another difference between a liquid and a gas. A gas can be compressed, and so the density of the atmosphere decreases as you rise. When a hot air balloon is launched the air within it is heated and it will rise. As it rises the density of the air decreases, and so the buoyant force decreases. At some height the weight of the balloon and basket equals the weight of the air displaced and the balloon stops rising. The operator of the balloon can go higher by making the gas in the balloon hotter, and thus less dense.

What **major discovery** did **Archimedes make** in the third century B.C.E. and how did he apply it?

Archimedes (c. 287–c. 212 B.C.E.) lived in the city of Syracuse on the island of Sicily, then part of Greece. He was charged by the king of Sicily to find out if his crown was made out of pure gold, or an alloy of gold and silver. Archimedes had to do this without destroying the crown. One day, when bathing in the public baths he noticed that when he stepped into the bath the water rose! He had seen this many times before, but this time he recognized that this common occurrence could help him solve his prob-

A huge steel ship like an aircraft carrier can float instead of sink like a stone because it can displace enough water to compensate for its weight and because the air inside of the ship makes its density actually less than the water around it.

lem. Legend has it that he was so excited that he ran naked through the streets of Syracuse shouting "Eureka!" or "I have found the answer!"

He then did experiments where he hung the crown on one end of a balance and a piece of first gold and then silver from on the other end. When the weight of the crown and that of the metal were equal the balance was horizontal. He then immersed the balance in water. If the crown and the metal had different volumes, the water they displaced would be different and the balance would tip. He found that the balance tipped when both the silver and gold pieces were on the balance. Archimedes had found that the crown was not pure gold, but a mixture of silver and gold. The king had been cheated!

Archimedes had discovered a principle of hydrostatics (liquids at rest) that would one day carry his name: Archimedes' Principle states that an object immersed in a fluid will experience a buoyant force equal to the weight of the displaced fluid.

Why does a **small clump** of **steel sink**, while a **50,000-ton steel ship** can **float**?

In order to remain afloat, a ship needs to displace an amount of fluid equal to its own weight. Therefore, if a clump of steel is placed in water, it will sink because it is much denser than water and its volume isn't large enough to displace a weight of water equal to its own weight. A 50,000-ton steel ship can easily stay afloat because it can

How do hippopotamuses sink to the bottom of a riverbed?

Hippopotamuses spend over half their day in the water. In order to eat, the hippo, which can reach almost 3 meters (10 feet) in length and weigh 10,000 pounds, must sink to feed off the vegetation that grows on the bottom of rivers. The hippo, however, has one major problem: his low density forces him to float at the surface, and he is not agile enough to quickly dive down to the bottom and come back up again. In order to reach the bottom, he needs to increase his density, so the buoyant force cannot supply a large enough force to keep the animal afloat. To do this, the hippo exhales, reducing the air in his body to increase his density.

displace 50,000 tons of water. That is because its hull isn't all steel, but contains a large amount of air. Therefore its density, its mass divided by its volume, is less than that of water.

What happens to the **buoyancy** of the **ship** when **cargo and passengers** are **added**?

When cargo and passengers are added to a ship its weight increases. As the ship's weight increases is sinks further into the water, displacing a greater weight of water. If it sinks so far that water can spill into the ship, increasing its weight even more, the ship sinks to the bottom of the water.

The amount the ship sinks in the water as a result of cargo and passengers can be critical for navigation and maneuverability. Large cargo and cruise ships have numbers on the bow of the ship that indicate how far the distance is between the water line and the bottom of the ship. This distance is called the ship's draft. If the ship has a 6-kilometer (20-foot) draft and the water is only 5.5 kilometer (18 feet) deep, cargo and passengers must be unloaded to allow the ship to rise.

How much **water** does a **ship need** in order **to float**?

Not a lot of water is needed to keep a ship afloat, just enough so that it can displace enough water to equal its weight. Therefore, if a ship were to enter a canal that was just a bit larger than the size of the ship's hull, it would float as long as there was a small film of water around the entire hull of the ship.

How do **blimps** remain at a chosen **altitude**?

A blimp is a non-rigid airship that floats in the air solely due to the buoyant gas within the giant balloon-like bag. It typically carries over 5,000 cubic meters of helium at a

Because helium is a safer gas than hydrogen, it is what is used in today's blimps.

density about seven times less than air. An airship floats in the air in the same manner as a ship floating in water. The weight of the airship must equal the buoyant force of the gas inside the bag. In order to increase the altitude of the blimp, the pilot increases its buoyancy by adding gas from pressurized tanks to the blimp, which expands the flotation bladders, displacing the heavier air and increasing the buoyant force until the reduced weight of the blimp equals the reduced weight of the air. To lower the airship, the buoyancy is decreased by releasing gas from the flotation bladders, which then decrease in size, displacing less of the heavier air.

Why is **helium** used inside **airships** instead of **hydrogen**? Isn't hydrogen more buoyant?

Although hydrogen is twice as buoyant as helium, and would be more effective in lifting an airship off the ground, hydrogen gas is extremely dangerous. The German airship, or zeppelin, the *Hindenburg*, the world's largest airship at the time, was destroyed on May 6, 1937, in Lakehurst, New Jersey, when it exploded into a huge fireball while attempting to land. Thirty-six people died in the explosion.

In 1937, the United States was about the only source of helium in the world, mostly from one gas well in Texas. The Nazis wanted to buy helium for their zeppelins, but the United States refused to sell it to them—as it was considered a strategic resource. Helium is formed from the radioactive decay of uranium and thorium in

438

rocks. It is used today to cool devices and make them superconductive. As a result, the amount of helium available is rapidly decreasing.

What are **airships used** for?

Since the first airship flight in 1852, by Henry Giffard in France, the dirigible, or airship, was used predominantly for military purposes. In the first and second World Wars airships were used for bombing and surveillance on both sides of the Atlantic. Commercial passenger transportation on airships was conducted for only a few years, while today's blimps are used for advertising and for televising sporting events from high elevations.

What happens to the **helium balloon** that a **child releases**?

If the balloon is tied tightly, the balloon will expand as its altitude increases. This expansion is caused by the lower atmospheric pressure at higher altitudes. Eventually, the helium's volume increases so much that the rubber balloon breaks, releasing the helium.

FLUID DYNAMICS:
HYDRAULICS AND PNEUMATICS

What is **fluid dynamics**?

Fluid dynamics is the study of fluids in motion.

What is **hydraulics**?

Hydraulics deals with the use of liquid in motion, usually in a device such as a machine. Oil is the most common liquid used in pumps, lifts, and shock absorbers.

How does a **hydraulic lift** work?

Pascal's Principle states that pressure in a liquid is independent of direction. Pressure is force divided by area, so force exerted by a liquid is equal to the pressure times the area. A hydraulic lift has a small piston in a cylinder. If you exert a force on the piston, it will create a pressure in the fluid. The lift also has a second, large area cylinder and piston. The fluid creates a pressure in this cylinder that exerts a much larger force on the piston because of its larger area. Therefore the lift has a mechanical advantage. Of course, energy is still conserved, so the small piston must move much farther than the large piston.

An automobile lift, used in many automotive repair shops, allows the operator to use very little force to lift an automobile off the ground, by pushing liquid from a

This heavy crane boom uses hydraulics to lift the boom.

small-diameter cylinder and piston through a thin tube that expands into a larger-diameter cylinder and piston, which is located beneath the vehicle to be lifted. Since the liquid cannot be compressed like air, the liquid from the small cylinder is pushed into the large cylinder, forcing the large piston to move upward.

What are some other places where hydraulic lifts are used?

Besides their valuable use in auto-repair shops, hydraulic lifts are used in elevating crane and backhoe arms, adjusting flaps on airplanes, and applying brakes in automobiles. It is the non-compressible characteristics of liquids that make hydraulic devices so useful. Oil is used rather than water because it does not freeze.

What is pneumatics?

Whereas hydraulics uses liquids to achieve mechanical advantage, pneumatics uses compressed gas. Since gases can be compressed and stored under pressure, releasing compressed air can provide large forces and torque for machines such as pneumatic drills, hammers, wrenches, and jackhammers.

In what ways do fluids move?

When fluids move slowly they exhibit steady or laminar flow. When the speed increases the flow becomes turbulent. In some cases laminar flow is desired, in others turbulent flow is better.

What is the difference between laminar and turbulent flow?

The film of fluid that touches the container does not move because of friction with the container's surface. But the fluid in the middle of the stream does. In laminar flow the transition from not moving to moving at full speed is continuous. Each thin film of water moves slightly faster than the one closer to the surface. In turbulent flow this transition from not moving to full-speed motion occurs suddenly, and the water moves in tiny circles in this region. Laminar flow has more friction than turbulent. A baseball, for example, has more drag in the laminar flow region.

> ### Why does a river's current run faster when the river is narrower?
>
> When water flows down a river, the current is measured by the volume of water that passes by a cross-section of the river divided by the time taken for the water to pass. For example, if the current of a river is 2,000 m³/min (cubic meters per minute), this means that in every minute 2,000 cubic meters pass by every part of the river. We can write this as (2,000 m²) × (1 m/min). If the river narrows, the 2,000 cubic meters of water still must pass in one minute because the water from behind continues to flow downriver. Since the river is narrower, the area (measured in meters squared, m²) is smaller, so the speed (measured in meters per minute) must increase. This fact is called the principle of continuity.

What makes a **fluid flow**?

As in all of physics, objects move as a result of a net force. In a fluid the net force comes about because there is a difference in pressure between two points. The fluid flows in the direction of decreasing pressure.

AERODYNAMICS

What is **aerodynamics**?

Aerodynamics is an aspect of fluid dynamics dealing specifically with the movement of air and other gases. Engineers studying aerodynamics analyze the flow of gases over and through automobiles, airplanes, golf balls, and other objects that move through air. They also study the effect of moving air on buildings, bridges, and other static objects.

What is **Bernoulli's Principle**?

In 1738, a Swiss physicist and mathematician named Daniel Bernoulli (1700–1782) discovered that when the speed of a moving fluid increases, such as the wind blowing through the corridors of a city, the pressure of that fluid decreases. Bernoulli discovered this while measuring the pressure of water as it flowed through pipes of different diameters. He found that the speed of the water increased as the diameter of the tube decreased (the continuity principle), and that the pressure exerted by the water on the walls of the pipes was less as well. This discovery would prove to be one of the most important discoveries in fluid mechanics.

441

The explanation behind this question is not meteorological, but physical. In major cities, there are skyscrapers and other tall buildings that obstruct the flow of wind. In order to flow past these large obstacles, the wind speed increases in the narrow corridors of the streets and avenues. The same effect can also be found in tunnels and outdoor "breezeways." It is the continuity of the fluid that increases its speed through the narrow corridors of streets and avenues that makes the city such a windy place.

How does an **airplane wing** create **"lift"**?

The upward force on an airplane wing caused by the air moving past it is called lift. According to Newton's Third Law, if the air exerts an upward force on the wing, then the wing must exert a downward force on the air. There are three causes of this downward force. The first is the tilt, or angle of attack of the wing. The tilt deflects the airflow downward. The second is the Bernoulli Principle. Because of the shape of the wing, the speed of the air on the top surface of the wing is faster than at the lower surface, and so the pressure is lower. Thus the downward force on the wing is reduced. The third reason is the fact that air "sticks" to the surface of the wing. The air coming off the upper surface is moving downward. This exerts an additional downward force on the air. The downward forces produce the lift needed to keep the plane airborne.

What is **drag**?

Drag is a force that opposes the motion of an object through a fluid. An object is often said to be "aerodynamic" when its drag forces are kept to a minimum.

There are two types of drag on an airplane: parasitic and induced. Parasitic drag is the force when an airplane wing, automobile, or any other object moves through a fluid. The amount of drag depends on the density of the fluid, the square of the speed of the object, the cross-sectional area of the object, and its shape. A large fuselage, like that of a 747, has more drag than a small fighter airplane. A tear-drop shaped object has less drag than a rectangular block. A parachute is designed to have a high drag.

Induced drag is a consequence of the lift generated by the wing. It is a function of the angle of attack of the wing—the lower the angle of attack, the smaller the induced drag. It occurs at the outer edge of the wing where the downward motion of the air caused by the wing meets the undisturbed air next to it. Induced drag causes vortices, the spiral motion of air that can be extremely dangerous to planes flying behind or below. Induced drag can be reduced by putting small, tilted surfaces on the wing tips.

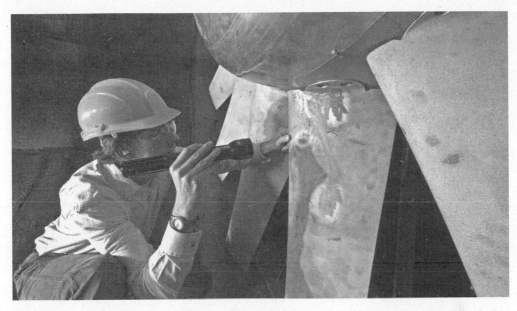

An engineer checks the fan in a wind tunnel. Smoke introduced into wind tunnels makes streamlines visible, which in turn help with the analysis of the efficiency of airfoils and automobiles.

What are **streamlines**?

Streamlines are lines that represent the flow of a fluid around an object or through another fluid. Streamlines are often made visible by putting thin films of smoke in the air. They are used in wind tunnel testing of airfoils (wings) and automobiles. A wind tunnel is a closed chamber with vents in the front and rear of the tunnel that allow wind and the streams of smoke that make streamlines visible to pass around an object. If the streamline smoke appears to be flowing in a gentle pattern without breaking up, then the object is considered aerodynamic. If the smoke breaks up upon encountering sections of an object, the flow has become turbulent. If the flow is turbulent the drag may be increased.

How does a **curve ball curve**?

The curve ball experiences the Magnus Force like the golf ball. The pitcher can give the ball a backward spin, creating lift, or a sideways spin, causing the ball to curve sideways. When a pitcher throws a knuckle ball the ball spins very slowly. The laces on the ball create small forces that make the ball move erratically through the air.

Why is it **better** for a **discus** to be **thrown into the wind** instead of with the wind?

In most sports, throwing or traveling with the wind at your back (called tail wind) is a lot easier than working against the wind (called a head wind). In football, teams flip a

443

Golfing has been played for several centuries, but dimpled golf balls have existed for only a hundred years. The dimples in golf balls, first introduced by the Spalding Company in 1908, can double the distance a golf ball can fly. Without the dimples the flow of air is laminar and the ball drags a thin layer of air completely around the golf ball. The dimples break up this air layer, creating turbulence that reduces drag. Golf balls can also experience lift. When hit with a slight backspin, the air passing over the top section of the ball flows in the direction opposite the motion of the ball. This creates low pressure above the ball. On the bottom of the ball the ball's motion in the same direction as the air and the pressure is higher. According to Bernoulli's Principle, such a pressure difference provides a lifting force, called the Magnus Force on the ball, giving the ball a few more seconds in flight.

coin to determine who will be kicking with the wind. In sailing, it is easier and faster to travel perpendicular to or with the wind and takes more skill to travel against the wind. In track, the world record in the 100-meter dash could more easily be broken if running with a strong tail wind. In most sports, having the wind at your back can be a major advantage.

In the field event of discus throwing, however, the advantage comes when there is a head wind. In fact, it has been documented that a discus can travel up to 8 meters (26 feet) further while experiencing a head wind of only 10 m/s (meters per second). Although the discus still experiences a drag force from the head wind, the lift that the discus gets from pressure differences over and under the disc is substantially more significant than the drag force. Because the discus will remain in the air longer, it will travel farther.

What is the **most aerodynamic shape**?

Some think the narrower and more needle-like an object is, the lower its drag force will be. Although a needle-head cuts easily through the wind, the problem emerges at the tail end, where the wind becomes turbulent and forms small eddy currents that hinder the streamline flow of air. The optimum shape depends on the velocity of the object.

For speeds lower than the speed of sound, the most aerodynamically efficient shape is the teardrop. The teardrop has a rounded nose that tapers as it moves backward, forming a narrow, yet rounded tail, which gradually brings the air around the object back together instead of creating eddy currents.

At high velocities, such as a jet airplane or a bullet may travel, other shapes are better. For turbulent flow, the least drag comes from having a blunt end, which inten-

tionally causes turbulence. The rest of the air then flows smoothly over the region of turbulence behind the object.

How are **airplane controls** different from the controls in an automobile?

Automobiles travel on two-dimensional surfaces, and therefore only need two separate controls, the accelerator and brake to control the forward movement, and the steering wheel to control side-to-side movements. Airplanes, on the other hand, travel in three-dimensional space. The forward thrust on an airplane is controlled by the throttle, and the "braking" is achieved by closing the throttle and increasing the drag, usually by deploying the plane's flaps. Yaw, which is responsible for the side-to-side movement of a plane, is controlled by the plane's rudder.

To control the pitch, or up-and-down orientation of the nose, the pilot uses elevators or horizontal control surfaces near the plane's rudder. To roll the plane (the rotation of the plane about an axis that goes from the nose to the tail), the pilot uses control surfaces on the back end of the wings called ailerons. The Wright Brothers recognized that roll control was crucial to successful flight. They invented a method of warping the wings, creating a primitive but useful aileron.

THE SOUND BARRIER

What is a **shock wave**?

Just as a boat moving through the water forms a series of V-shaped waves, airplanes create conical (cone-shaped) waves as they fly through the air. The waves that the airplane produces are waves of compressed air. When an aircraft reaches the speed of

sound, Mach 1, the plane's pressure waves that move at the speed of sound overlap each other, creating a shock wave. The shock wave creates one single, loud sonic boom heard by observers on the ground. When the plane travels slower than the speed of sound, the sound waves do not overlap and instead of hearing a sonic boom, observers simply hear the delayed sound of the plane.

If **Mach 1** is the speed of sound, what is **Mach 2**?

Mach is the ratio of a velocity to the speed of sound, so Mach 2 is two times the speed of sound, Mach 3.5 is three and a half times the speed of sound, etc. Any velocity greater than Mach 1 is referred to as "supersonic."

You can think of sound waves as being similar to water waves, emanating from a central source and spreading out in a regular pattern unless they are interfered with.

Who was the **first pilot** to **break the sound barrier**?

On October 14, 1947, Chuck Yeager (1923–) broke the sound barrier in his Bell X-1 test plane, "Glamorous Glennis." In order to reach the sound barrier, the X-1 was carried in the belly of a B-29 bomber to an altitude of 3,658 meters (12,000 feet) where it was dropped. The X-1's rocket engine ignited and Yeager took the plane to an altitude of 13,106 meters (43,000 feet). At this altitude, Yeager was able to break the sound barrier by traveling 660 miles per hour. The X-1 experienced a turbulent set of compression waves just before he broke past the barrier at Mach 1.05. Yeager kept the plane at this supersonic speed for a few moments before he cut off the rocket engine and headed back toward Earth.

Why did **Chuck Yeager** go to such a **high altitude** to break the **sound barrier**?

Sound travels approximately 760 miles per hour in the warm, dense air found close to sea level. The cooler and less-dense air is, however, the lower the speed of sound. Since air is less dense at higher elevations, physicists and engineers felt it would be easier to break the sound barrier at those elevations. Knowing the temperature and density of the air at 12,192 meters (40,000 feet) above sea level, scientists determined that the speed of sound would be reduced to only 660 miles per hour. As an added bonus engineers found that not only was the speed of sound slower at such elevations, but when the air has such low density, the parasitic drag (the drag due to friction), is very low as well. There-

fore, to break the sound barrier, Yeager traveled as far up as 13,106 meters (43,000 feet) above sea level to both reduce the sound barrier and decrease the parasitic drag.

What **concerns** did pilots and engineers have about **breaking the sound barrier**?

To reach the sound barrier in an airplane was a major goal for many in the aeronautical field, a goal that carried some uncertainties. Pilots and engineers alike wondered and feared what would happen to a plane's maneuverability when it broke through the shock wave as well as what would happen to the plane itself, structurally.

Near the end of the Second World War there were fighter planes that were very strong and had powerful engines and experienced pilots. A number of pilots died when their planes broke apart in mid-air, often when in dives. There were two problems with these aircraft: first, the wings were not swept back, and second, they were driven by propellers. As the shock wave forms near Mach 1, it bends backward from the nose of the plane, like a bow wave on a boat. If the shock wave encounters the wings (that is, the wing extends through the shock front), there are tremendous forces on the wings. In a supersonic plane the wing is always designed to be fully behind the shock front, because the shock front can tear the wing off the plane. The propeller causes a pulsation in the pressure on the wing: every time one of the blades goes by, it produces a region of slightly higher pressure behind it, followed by a region of low pressure. All of these things came together and helped cause mid-air structural failures of the WWII fighter planes.

SUPERSONIC FLIGHT

Why are the **angles of wings** important for **supersonic flight**?

When a plane breaks the sound barrier, the shock wave in front of the plane has a difficult time moving out of the plane's way. In order to break the sound barrier with less difficulty, aeronautical engineers have designed more aerodynamic fuselages and efficient wing designs. As mentioned above, wings on supersonic planes must remain behind the shock front to prevent structural failure and allow the plane to maneuver safely. The swept-back wing design, as found on both military and commercial airplanes, allows the airplane to accelerate easily and faster before major pressure builds up around the wings. The delta wings, as found on many jet fighters, are large and extremely thin, to keep the wings behind the shock front while increasing lift and reducing drag.

Problems can also occur when using swept-back wings. As a plane moves faster, the center of lift on the wings can move too far backward, causing unbalanced forces on the plane, which can affect the maneuverability and safety of the plane.

Why are there no commercial supersonic planes?

From 1973 to 2000, the Concorde was a symbol of fast and expensive air travel for business people. The plane was a fast but inefficient plane that could carry 78 passengers. The sleek, delta wing design and pinpoint nose, which tilts down during liftoff and landings, could achieve speeds of up to Mach 2.2 at 15,240 meters (50,000 feet) above sea level. But an accident involving a landing wheel, which killed all 109 passengers and crew, grounded the Concorde. Over the next sixteen months the plane was extensively renewed and tested. Unfortunately, the terrorist attacks on September 11, 2001, reduced the demand for fast flights. Both British Airways and Air France suspended commercial flights. The remaining twelve aircraft are in museums around the world.

What is the **fastest aircraft**?

Just like Chuck Yeager's Bell X-1, which was the first plane to break the sound barrier, the X-15A-2, the fastest aircraft ever built, was dropped from the belly of a B-52 bomber. When released, the X-15A-2's rockets ignited, taking it to a maximum speed of 4,534 miles per hour. That speed, which is equivalent to 7,297 kilometers per hour, is Mach 6. The X-15 series flew 199 flights before being retired in 1969. The SR-71 (blackbird) was the fastest known aircraft that can take off under its own power. It was retired in 1998.

THERMAL PHYSICS

What is **thermal physics**?

Thermal physics is the study of objects warm and cold, and how they interact with each other. It is difficult because most of the vocabulary dates from the time before scientists understood what makes an object hot. Terms like "heat," "heat capacity," and "latent heat" suggest that warm objects contain some material that depends on their temperature. As was discussed in the chapter on Energy, it wasn't until the early 1800s that our present understanding was developed. Yet, almost 200 years later, our common usage is based on earlier ideas.

THERMAL ENERGY

Who discovered what **makes** an object **hot**?

Benjamin Thompson, Count Rumford (1753–1814), who was born in the Massachusetts Bay Colony, but did most of his scientific work in the Kingdom of Bavaria, now part of Germany, deserves most of the credit. Before his experiments, most scientists thought that hot objects contained an invisible fluid called caloric. Experiments done before Rumford showed that when you heated an object it didn't gain weight, so caloric must be weightless as well as invisible. This result made many scientists suspicious of the caloric explanation, or theory.

In 1789 Rumford drilled holes in bronze cannons through which a cannon ball would be shot. He found that both the cannon and the metal chips that resulted from the drilling became hot. He determined the amount of water that could be raised to the boiling point by both the cannon bodies and the chips and showed that the caloric theory did not agree with his results. He finally concluded that in hot objects the par-

ticles that made up the material moved faster than they moved in cold objects. Using our present terminology, they had more kinetic energy. In their motion they vibrate back and forth; they do not move together like a thrown ball.

What is **thermal energy**?

Thermal energy is the random kinetic energy of the moving atoms and molecules that make up matter. But objects expand when heated, so the bonds holding the atoms together stretch. That means they have more elastic energy. So thermal energy is the sum of the kinetic and elastic energy of the atoms and molecules, and the bonds that hold them together. It is energy that is inside the object, and so it is called a form of internal energy.

TEMPERATURE AND ITS MEASUREMENT

What is **temperature**?

Temperature is a quantitative measure of hotness. In many substances, temperature is proportional to the thermal energy in the object, but the relationship between temperature and energy depends on many factors.

How is **temperature measured**?

Temperature is measured by a device called a thermometer. There are many different kinds of thermometers, but they all have a property that depends on temperature.

The most common type of thermometer contains a thin column of liquid in a glass tube. When the temperature goes up, the liquid expands, and the height of the column increases. Earlier thermometers used mercury, a metal that is a liquid at room temperature. Because mercury is poisonous, all thermometers sold today contain red-colored alcohol. The glass tube has markings on it from which the temperature can be read.

Many thermometers today are electronic. Most contain a tiny bead of a semiconducting material whose resistance varies with temperature. The bead is called a thermistor, or thermal resistor. Others contain a tiny semiconducting diode. The voltage across this diode varies with temperature. To measure very high temperatures, a wire made of the metal platinum is used because its resistance also varies with temperature and platinum is not affected by high temperatures. Another electronic thermometer uses two wires made of different materials that are welded together. Typically the wires are made of copper and a nickel-containing alloy. This kind of thermometer is called a thermocouple and is often used in gas furnaces or water heaters to make sure that the pilot flame is burning when the gas to the main burn-

ers is turned on. Voltage and resistance will be discussed later in this book.

A less accurate, but convenient thermometer is a strip of plastic whose color changes with temperature. The plastic contains liquid crystals. The geometric arrangement of molecules in the crystals depends on temperature, and so does their color.

If two different metals are bonded together in a strip when the temperature changes the strip will bend. Because there are two metals, often brass and steel, the device is called a bimetallic strip. This kind of thermometer is often used in household thermostats.

Who **invented** the **first thermometer**?

Although Galileo (1564–1642) is credited with developing the first thermometer in 1592, his thermometer was open to the atmosphere, so it measured a combination of temperature and atmospheric

This thermometer is similar to one developed by Galileo. The objects inside the tube have varying densities that rise or fall, depending on the temperature.

pressure. It was not until 1713 that Daniel Gabriel Fahrenheit (1686–1736) developed the first closed-tube mercury thermometer. Combined with the temperature scale he defined the following year, Fahrenheit made a significant contribution to science.

What is the **Fahrenheit temperature scale**?

Temperature scales are artificial in the sense that they are related to temperatures important to humans. The German physicist Daniel Gabriel Fahrenheit developed the first well-known temperature scale in 1714. Equipped with the first mercury thermometer, Fahrenheit defined a scale in which the freezing point of water was 32°F and the boiling point was 212°F.

Why did Gabriel **Fahrenheit define** the **freezing point** of water to be **32°F** instead of 0?

Fahrenheit did not define 32° as the freezing point of water. Instead, he defined 0° as the freezing point of a water and salt mixture. Since salt lowers the freezing point of

water, the freezing point for this mixture was lower than it would have been for plain water. Upon defining the degree intervals between the freezing and boiling points of the water and salt mixture, and he found that water itself freezes at 32°F.

Who developed the Celsius scale?

On the Celsius scale the freezing point of water is 0° and the boiling point is 100°. The Celsius scale is named after a person whose life work was dedicated to astronomy. Anders Celsius (1701–1744), a Swedish astronomer, spent most of his life studying the heavens. Before developing the Celsius temperature scale in 1742, he published a book in 1733 documenting the details of hundreds of observations he had made of the aurora borealis, or northern lights. Celsius died in 1744 at the age of forty-three.

What do Celsius temperatures feel like?

If you live in the United States you learn what various temperatures feel like. You recognize that 86°F is typical of a hot summer day and that –4°F is a very cold winter day. But what does 10°C feel like? Here is a handy guide:

Temperature	Celsius	Fahrenheit
Extremely hot day	40	104
Hot summer day	30	86
Room temperature	20	68
Jacket weather	10	50
Water freezes	0	32
Cold winter day	–10	14
Very cold winter day	–20	–4

What is the **Kelvin scale**?

The Kelvin temperature scale, developed by William Thomson, Lord Kelvin (1824–1907), in 1848, is widely used by scientists throughout the world. Absolute zero is the temperature at which thermal energy is at a minimum. Each division in the Kelvin scale, called a kelvin (K) is equal to a degree on the Celsius scale, but the difference is where zero is. In the Celsius scale, 0° is the freezing point of water while in the Kelvin scale, the zero point is at absolute zero. Therefore, 0°K is equal to –273.15°C; 0°C is equal to 273.15 kelvins. The Kelvin scale is used for very low or very high temperatures when water is not involved.

How do the three **temperature scales compare**?

The following table provides some examples for the three commonly used temperature scales:

Temperature	Celsius	Kelvin	Fahrenheit
Absolute zero	–273.15	0	–459
Water freezes	0	273.15	32
Normal human body temperature	37	310.15	98.6
Water boils	100	373.15	212

How do you **convert** from **one scale** to **another**?

Use the conversion chart below to convert between Celsius, Fahrenheit, and Kelvin.

From	To	Formula
Fahrenheit	Celsius	°F = 9/5°C + 32
Celsius	Fahrenheit	°C = 5/9°F – 32
Kelvin	Celsius	K = °C – 273.15
Celsius	Kelvin	°C = K + 273.15

Can a **temperature** be **measured without contacting** the object?

As was described in the chapter on energy, when an object is hot it transfers energy to colder objects. If it is in contact with the other object the transfer is by means of conduction. But all objects at temperatures above absolute zero radiate electromagnetic waves in the infrared part of the spectrum (see the chapter on waves for a description of the spectrum). A hotter object radiates more energy this way, and so there will be a net transfer of energy from the hot object to cold objects around it. An electronic sensor can detect the infrared radiation and convert the amount and wavelength of radiation it receives to a temperature. The sensors can be built into cameras that create a picture that shows the temperature of every location in the picture. Such a picture is known as a thermograph.

An electronic thermometer within the thermostat in your home or office triggers a switch that turns your furnace on or off, according to the temperature.

How can **temperature** be **controlled**?

A device that maintains a constant temperature is called a thermostat. A traditional home thermostat contains a coiled bimetallic strip. When the temperature drops below a set point, the strip trips a switch that turns on the furnace. More modern home thermostats use an electronic thermometer and electronic circuits that turn the furnace and air conditioning system on and off.

How are **thermographs** used?

Thermographs, which detect the amount of infrared radiation emanating from objects or regions, use colors to display the temperature on an image. Typically, red indicates the warmest temperatures, while blue indicates cooler temperatures. Thermographs are used throughout science, but are well noted for their use in detecting humans in wilderness areas, identifying areas of homes that need more insulation, and in measuring the temperature over regions of Earth.

How do **astronomers determine** the **temperature** of the **sun**?

When iron is hot, you can feel the energy radiating from it. That radiation is in the form of infrared waves leaving the iron. When iron gets extremely hot, it produces a red glow—and when it gets even warmer, it can take on a whitish glow. The tempera-

ture of iron and other objects can be measured by the amount of radiation flowing from it as well as by the light it emits.

Scientists measure the temperature of stars and the sun by analyzing the color and brightness of the stars. From such measurements, astronomers have determined that the surface of the sun is approximately 5,500°C (9,900°F).

ABSOLUTE ZERO

What is the **lowest possible temperature**?

The lowest possible temperature is called absolute zero (0 K). It is the temperature at which molecular motion is at a minimum and cannot be further reduced. While absolute zero can never be reached (see the Third Law of Thermodynamics later in this chapter), the present record low temperature is 4.5 nK (4.5 billionths of a kelvin).

Is there a **highest temperature** that can be achieved?

Although there is an absolute zero temperature, there is no highest temperature. The highest temperatures achieved to date have been from nuclear explosions, where the temperature can reach as high as one hundred million kelvins.

What are the average **surface temperatures** of the **planets** in our solar system?

For the planets that have atmospheres (mixtures of gases surrounding the surface of a planet), the average temperature stays relatively constant because the atmosphere acts as a type of insulator. These planets have only small variations in the temperature when a section of the planet faces away from the sun. Mercury, on the other hand, with no atmosphere and an elliptical orbit has very large differences. In the table below the temperatures of Mercury, Venus, Earth, and Mars are taken on the planetary surface, while those of Jupiter, Saturn, Uranus, and Neptune are taken at the tops of the clouds, there being no solid surface on these planets.

Planet	Temperature Range (°C)
Mercury	−184 to 420
Venus	427
Earth	−55 to 55
Mars	−152 to 20
Jupiter	−163 to −123
Saturn	−178
Uranus	−215
Neptune	−217

This plasma lamp—an apparatus you often see at science fairs and novelty shops—emits streams of plasma, electrically charged particles that are found in everything from stars to television displays and fluorescent lights.

STATES OF MATTER

What are the different **states of matter**?

The four phases of matter are the solid, liquid, gaseous, and plasma states. Solid phases are found at lower temperatures; as the amount of internal energy increases, the material changes from the solid to the liquid and then to the gaseous phase and finally, under extreme conditions, to the plasma state. Water, for example, changes from ice, its solid state, to liquid water, and finally to steam, its gaseous state. The temperatures at which the phase changes occur depend on the properties of the material.

In the solid phase the atoms or molecules are held in rigid positions by the chemical bonds between them. They can vibrate, but not change positions.

When the temperature is at the freezing point the solid melts into a liquid. In the liquid phase molecules, or small groups of molecules can move easily past one another. In most liquids the spacings between the molecules is slightly larger than in solids, giving them a lower density. In water, however, the spaces are larger in ice than in liquid, meaning that ice has a lower density than water, so it floats.

When the temperature reaches the boiling point the liquid becomes a gas. In the gaseous phase the atoms or molecules have essentially no forces between them, so

> ## Do all substances go from a solid to a liquid to a gas as the temperature increases?
>
> **N**o. Carbon dioxide (CO_2) goes from the solid state called dry ice directly to its gaseous state. This process is called sublimation.

they are free to move independently. They are about 10 times further apart than in a liquid or solid, meaning that the density of a typical gas is 1/1,000 that of the solid.

To enter the plasma state one or more electrons must be removed from the atom. Plasmas consist of electrically charged particles. Plasmas are found in fluorescent lamps, in some television displays, in the upper atmosphere, in the sun and other stars, and in interstellar space.

What determines the amount of energy required to increase the temperature of a substance?

The amount of energy needed to increase the temperature of a substance with a mass of one kilogram by one degree Celsius is called the specific heat capacity. For example, to raise one kilogram of water (one liter) by a degree Celsius requires 4,186 joules of energy. The following table lists specific heat capacities of common solids, liquids, and gases:

Substance	Specific Heat Capacity (J/kg °C)
Aluminum	897
Copper	387
Iron	445
Lead	129
Gold	129
Silver	235
Mercury	140
Wood	1,700
Glass	837
Water	4,186
Ice	2,090
Steam	2,010
Nitrogen	1,040
Oxygen	912
Carbon Dioxide	833
Ammonia	2,190

How do you **use specific heat capacity information**?

Specific heat capacity is the energy per kilogram per change in temperature. So, to find the amount of energy needed to heat something you need to know the material, its mass, and the change in temperature desired. For example, if you wanted to increase the temperature of 2 liters (2 kilograms) of water from room temperature (20°C) to the boiling point (100°C) you need to multiply the specific heat capacity of water (4,186 J/kg°C) by 2 kg and by 80°C to obtain 669,760 J, or about 670 kJ.

Suppose that the water is placed in an aluminum pan with a mass of 300 g (0.3 kg). How much extra energy is needed to heat the pan? The answer is found by multiplying the specific heat capacity of aluminum (897 J/kg°C) by the mass (0.3 kg) and by the temperature change (80°C) to obtain 144,000 J or 144 kJ. So the total energy needed to heat both the water and the pan is 814 kJ. Note how much more energy is needed to heat the water than the pan. Look through the list of specific heat capacities on page 125 to find other metals from which you could make a pan that would need less energy to heat it.

The high specific heat capacity of water makes it a good material to use, for example, in cooling an automobile engine by circulating the water through the engine where the water is heated and then through the radiator where flowing air can cool the water.

How much energy is needed to **change** the state of water from **ice to water to steam**?

The amount of energy needed to change phase is called latent heat. The latent heat involved in the transition from solid to liquid is called the latent heat of fusion while the energy involved in the transition from liquid to gas is called the latent heat of vaporization. For water the latent heat of fusion is 334 kJ/kg. The latent heat of vaporization is 2,265 kJ/kg.

Energy must be added to go from ice to water and water to steam, but if steam condenses to water it produces 2,265 kJ for each kilogram of steam condensed. That's the reason that steam burns are so dangerous. Almost all of that energy is transferred to your skin. If water freezes it releases 334 kJ for each kilogram of water frozen. In a freezer that amount of energy must be removed by the freezing mechanism.

On a warm day, why do **water droplets** accumulate on the **outside** of **glasses** and **soda bottles**?

The water does not seep through the container, but instead comes from the air surrounding it. Water vapor is the gaseous form of water that is in air below the boiling point of water. As discussed above, it takes a larger amount of energy to vaporize water, so the

What is a calorie?

Heat, like work (processes that transfer energy), is measured in the joule, a unit named after James Prescott Joule. Although the joule is the international standard for measuring energy, heat flow is often measured in calories. A calorie defines the amount of energy needed to increase one gram of water by one degree Celsius. The energy required for one calorie is 4.186 joules, which is a relatively small amount of energy. Nutritionists also use the term "calorie" to describe the amount of energy a particular food can provide a person. A nutritional calorie is really a kilocalorie (1,000 calories), which is also written as the capitalized "Calorie."

Another unit used to measure heat flow is the British Thermal Unit, or Btu. The Btu is the amount of energy needed to increase the temperature of one pound of water by one degree Fahrenheit. This unit, which is used only by countries such as the United States that still employ the English standard method of measurements, is equal to 252 calories.

molecules of water in the air have more thermal energy than do the molecules in the colder glass. So when the water molecules strike the glass they transfer much of their thermal energy to the glass. The colder water molecules join together to form water droplets on the glass. The process is called condensation. Condensation also occurs on window panes when the outside is cold and the interior air is warm and humid.

How do **liquids evaporate**?

A substance does not have to boil to change from liquid to gas state. The boiling point is where the pressure of the water vapor equals the atmospheric pressure. At all temperatures there is a great variation in the kinetic energy of the molecules that make up the substance. When the molecules with high energy reach the surface they have the possibility of escaping into the air. The process of changing from liquid to gas at a temperature below the boiling point is called evaporation.

When the molecules with higher energy leave the liquid the remaining molecules have a lower average energy, and thus a lower temperature. It is cooled by evaporation.

How do **clouds form**?

As warm air rises into the atmosphere through convection currents, the air expands as it experiences less atmospheric pressure. During the expansion, the warm water vapor quickly cools and condenses, forming water droplets in the air. When the droplets begin to accumulate, they attach themselves to dust particles in the air and form clouds.

How can **evaporation** be a **cooling process**?

Because evaporation leaves a cooler liquid, the material on which the liquid rests is cooled. Evaporation is an effective way to cool our bodies. Perspiration leaves a coating of water on our skin that evaporates, cooling the skin. Alcohol evaporates more quickly than water and has an even greater cooling effect. For that reasons parents are advised to rub alcohol on the skin of babies who are running dangerously high temperatures. It can reduce the fever and keep the baby out of danger.

HEAT

What are some ways of **transferring thermal energy**?

Heat is the transfer of energy from a warmer to a cooler object. The transfer can occur by two different processes. If the hot object is in contact with a cooler one, the process is called conduction. The faster molecules in the hotter object strike the slower ones in the cooler one, transferring their thermal energy. The average speed, and thus kinetic energy of the molecules in the warmer object are reduced, while those in the cooler object are increased.

If the warm object is in contact with air or water, it heats the fluid. Hotter fluid has a lower density, and so it rises. Its place is taken by colder fluid, creating moving currents of the fluid, called convection currents. Convection is a very efficient way of transferring energy from hot to cold objects.

The thermal energy can also be transferred even if the warmer object isn't in contact with any other object. The vibrations of the molecules create infrared electromagnetic waves that carry energy. These waves are called radiation. The warmer the object, the more energy in the waves. More energy goes from the warmer to the cooler object than in the reverse direction, so radiation cools the warmer object and warms the cooler one.

What are common **methods** of **heating a home**?

Homes using forced air heat have a furnace that heats the air in it and a fan that blows the hot air into heating ducts that allow the hot air into the rooms. It rises and forces the colder air out of the room through return ducts, the entrance to which are usually near the floor. Hot water heat has pipes carrying hot water that have fins on them. The fins promote convection of air past the hot water pipe. This warmed air then circulates through the room. Electrical baseboard heat works in the same way. Electric resistance wiring in the floor or ceiling can warm the air in contact with these surfaces, again creating convection currents. Convection is the movement of thermal energy through a fluid (such as liquid or gas).

How do **convection currents** create **sea breezes**?

During a day at the shore, the sun warms the ground and the water. The ground has a lower specific heat and so its temperature increases more than the temperature of the water. The ground heats the air above it, which rises in convection currents and cooler air from over the ocean flows toward the shore to "fill in the gap" left by the rising warm air. This flow of cooler air from the ocean toward the shore creates what is known as a sea breeze.

In the evening, when the sun dips below the horizon, the ground cools faster than the water. Therefore the air over the ocean is warmer than the air over the shore, and the reverse takes place. The warmer ocean air rises while a breeze flows from the shore to the water.

How does **heat flow** by **conduction**?

When part of a substance is heated its thermal energy is increased. The fast-moving atoms or molecules strike the slower-moving cooler atoms. They begin to move faster, and so gain thermal energy. Their temperature increases. The ease of conduction depends on the material. Most metals are good conductors—even a small difference in temperature produces heat flow. Other materials are poor conductors. There can be large temperature differences without significant heat flow. In that case one part of the substance is hot, another cold.

Heat conductivity is higher in metals that have freely moving electrons. So copper, silver, gold, and aluminum are good conductors. Stainless steel is a poor conductor.

In non-metals conductivity depends on their ability to transfer vibrations of the atoms. The conductivity of ice, concrete, stone, glass, wood, and rubber is less than 1/100 that of metals. Conductivity depends on the material, its thickness, the area it covers, and temperature difference.

Light gases have better conductivity than heavier gases. For example the heavy gas argon is used to fill the space between dual-pane windows because of its lower heat conductivity.

How does **clothing** keep us **warm**?

Our skin is cooled primarily by convection currents in the air. Clothing, especially wool, traps air in small pockets, which reduces or eliminates convection. There can still be conductive cooling through the cloth, but cloth is a good insulator.

Home insulation, like styrofoam panels, fibreglass or blown-in cellulose act like clothing in reducing heat transmission by convection. Home insulation is rated by its R value of resistance to energy transfer. R is the inverse of conduction: $R = 1/U$.

Air pockets within snow and ice function as excellent insulators. Many small mammals build snow dens to keep themselves warm, thereby taking advantage of the

461

insulating properties of the snow. Natives of the Arctic build igloos that also keep the inhabitants warm by reducing loss by convection.

Many farmers protect their crops during sub-zero temperatures by spraying water on the crops, and when the water freezes, the plants are insulated by the poor conductive properties of the ice.

Why is it often **cooler** to wear **white clothes**, rather than black clothes?

White surfaces reflect all the colors of the rainbow, whereas black absorbs all the colors in the light spectrum. The absorption of this energy heats the black material, increasing its temperature. This, in turn, increases the temperature of the air between the clothing and the person. So white, which absorbs much less radiative energy from the sun, is cooler in hot climates.

THERMODYNAMICS

What is **thermodynamics**?

Thermodynamics is the field of physics that studies changes in thermal energy and the relationship between energy, heat, and work. The field of thermodynamics was developed when people sought to increase the efficiency of early steam engines. There are four laws of thermodynamics, which for reasons of history, are numbered 0 through 3 rather than 1 through 4.

What is the **zeroth law** of thermodynamics?

The zeroth law is so obvious that it wasn't added as a law until after laws one through three were developed. It is based on thermal equilibrium between two bodies. As has been stated, if two objects have different temperatures, heat will flow from the hotter to the colder. If there is no temperature difference, there is no net heat flow. They will be in thermal equilibrium. The zeroth law states that if objects A and B are in equilibrium and B and C are in equilibrium, then A and C are also in equilibrium. Suppose object B is a thermometer. You put it in contact with object A. Heat flows until they are at the same temperature. You then move the temperature to object C. If the thermometer shows no change, then B and C are in equilibrium and we can conclude that objects A and C are at the same temperature.

What is the **first law of thermodynamics**?

The first law of thermodynamics is a restatement of the conservation of energy. It says that the energy loss must equal the energy gain of a system. It relates the heat input and output, the work done on the system and the work the system does, and the change in internal energy, or temperature change.

For example, the cylinder and moving piston of an automobile engine is heated by the burning of gasoline in the cylinder. The piston moves out, doing work, and heat is transferred to the coolant because of the higher temperature of the cylinder and piston. As long as the temperature of the cylinder and piston does not change, the heat input equals the work output plus the heat output. Energy isn't gained or lost, it just changes form.

Another way to state the first law is that net heat input equals net work plus change in thermal energy. Note that heat can be either positive (heat input) or negative (heat output). Work can also be positive (work done by the system) or negative (work done on the system). Thermal energy can also go up or down.

What is the second law of thermodynamics?

In the early 1800s many scientists and engineers worked to improve the efficiency of steam engines. The French military engineer and physicist Sadi Carnot (1796–1832) tried to answer two questions: Is there any limit to the amount of work available from a heat source, and can you increase the efficiency by replacing steam with another fluid or gas? Carnot wrote a book in 1824 called *Reflections on the Motive Power of Fire* that was aimed at a popular audience, using a minimum of mathematics.

The most important part of the book was the presentation of an idealized engine. This engine could be used to understand the ideas that can be applied to all heat engines. A heat engine is a device that converts heat into work in a cyclical process. That is, the engine periodically returns to its starting point. A steam engine, gasoline or diesel power automobile engine are all heat engines where the pistons return to their starting positions. A rocket is not a cyclic heat engine. A diagram of Carnot's simplified model allowed him to give answers to his two questions. He found that the efficiency, that is, the work output divided by the heat input, depended only on the temperatures at which heat enters and leaves the system, or efficiency $= (T_{hot} - T_{cold})/T_{hot}$. It doesn't depend on the fluid or gas used in the engine. Real engines would have lower efficiencies, but no engine could have a higher efficiency.

A simplified version of the Second Law according to Carnot is that it is impossible to convert heat completely into work in a cyclic heat engine; there is always some heat output. Note that the First Law would allow a heat engine to have no heat output, the heat input would equal the work done. The Second Law can be shown in the diagram below where the input heat is taken from a "reservoir" that maintains a constant high temperature and the output goes to a second reservoir at a constant low temperature.

This turbine plant in California uses natural gas to heat water into steam that then produces energy in the turbines that generate electricity. Not all the energy from the natural gas can be converted to electricity, and lost energy escapes as heat.

For example, a steam turbine gets its heat from high temperature steam and puts its output heat into a much colder lake or river.

Carnot's model engine is reversible. That is, it can be run backwards, which is impossible for a real engine. Thus all real engines are less efficient than the ideal one. Friction also lowers the efficiency of real engines.

The Second Law, according to Carnot, means that there is no such thing as a perpetual motion machine. Although such a machine could obey the law of conservation of energy, the heat it puts out means that the machine would eventually stop.

Carnot died in a cholera epidemic at age 36. Because people were concerned with the transmission of this deadly disease, all his papers and books were buried with him after his death. Thus only a few of his works have survived.

Despite the limitations of Carnot's model, his work inspired Rudolf Diesel (1858–1913) to design the engine named after him to achieve higher efficiencies than steam engines. So, Carnot's book was important to the design of practical engines.

A second version of the Second Law can be stated as "Heat doesn't flow from cold to hot without work input." For example, a refrigerator removes heat from the food at a low temperature and outputs heat from the coils in the bottom or back of the refrigerator. It will not move the heat from cold to hot, however, without a motor doing work on the circulating gas.

How do **refrigerators** and **air conditioners** work?

As you know, when a liquid evaporates into a gas, it is cooled. Heat flows into the system. The opposite process, the condensation of a gas into a liquid results in an increase in thermal energy and an output of heat. A refrigerator circulates a refrigerant, a liquid that evaporates at a low temperature, through tubing, The gas is compressed by an electrically-driven compressor. The pressure and temperature of the gas increases. Coils of the tubing outside the refrigerator cool the liquid and heat the air around them. As it cools the refrigerant condenses back to a liquid that goes through a tiny hole, called the expansion valve. The pressure drops, evaporating the liquid, making the gas cold. The tubing containing the cold gas is in the inside of the refrigerator, making it cold, and cooling the food.

An air conditioner works in a similar way. The evaporator is in the unit inside the house and the compressor is outside. Because of the work put into the compressor heat is removed from the air inside the house and transferred to the outside air. The diagram below shows work and heat flows in a refrigerator or air conditioner.

The first home refrigerators used ammonia as a refrigerant, but ammonia is toxic. In the 1930s Freon was first developed by the DuPont Company of Wilmington, Delaware. Freon is a chlorofluorocarbon (CFC). If Freon escapes it carries chlorine atoms to the upper atmosphere. There ultraviolet radiation from the sun separates one of the chlorine atoms from the CFC. That atom converts ozone back to oxygen, contributing to the destruction of the ozone layer, an essential barrier against harmful ultraviolet sunlight.

Freon's destructive nature has been known since the 1970s, but it was not until the early 1990s that legislation was implemented banning the use of Freon in new air conditioners and refrigerators. It has been estimated that in 2002 there was six million tons of Freon in existing products. Unfortunately, when the chlorine destroys an ozone molecule, the chlorine is not destroyed, but instead continues to live for a while destroying more ozone. In fact, more Freon is still headed toward the upper limits of the atmosphere, for it can take several years for Freon to reach such elevations.

DuPont and other corporations have developed replacements for Freon that replace the chlorine atoms with hydrogen atoms. These substances do not harm the ozone layer and are in use in refrigerators, air conditioners, and aerosol cans.

How **efficient** are **electrical generators** and **vehicles**?

In the United States, electrical generators are only 31% efficient, while 75% of energy used for transportation is wasted.

Engineers are working on both improving efficiency and in making use of the "rejected" energy. For example, the warm water that carries away the waste heat in an electrical generating plant can be used to heat homes close to the generator.

What is the **third law of thermodynamics**?

The third law of thermodynamics states that absolute zero, the lowest possible temperature, can never be reached. The entropy of a system is zero at absolute zero. A procedure can remove a portion of the entropy, but not all of it. Thus it would take an infinite number of repetitions of the procedure to reach absolute zero. It's been possible to achieve temperatures as low as a few billionth of a kelvin, but it has never been able to reach absolute zero.

What is **entropy**?

The German physicist Rudolf Clausius (1822–1888) was concerned about Carnot's use of the term waste heat. He developed another version of the Second Law that involves the concept of entropy. Entropy can be defined as the dispersal of energy. The greater the dispersal or spreading the larger the entropy. For example, when salt and pepper are in separate piles the two substances are in distinct locations. If you mix them together they are no longer in separate regions of pure salt and pure pepper, but dispersed throughout the combined pile. Further, it is not possible for the salt and pepper grains to separate themselves. Thus the mixing of salt and pepper increases the entropy of the system. If the salt and pepper could be shaken in such a way that they would separate, then entropy would be decreased, but such an event has never been observed.

Suppose you place ice in water. Ice and water are separate. The water has higher thermal energy, the ice lower, and so the system has low entropy. When the ice melts the two can no longer be separated. The thermal energy is dispersed throughout the system, so the entropy has increased. But wait, you might say, the ice water (the system) has cooled the air around it (the environment), decreasing its entropy because hot gas has greater entropy than cold gas. Calculations, however, show that the increase in the ice/water mixture is greater than the decrease in the air. So a statement of the Second Law is that the entropy of the system and the environment can never decrease.

The increase in entropy suggests a direction of time, sometimes called the "Arrow of Time." The "forward" direction of time is the one in which entropy increases or remains the same.

Clausius had given Carnot's work a firmer foundation. Later work by Ludwig Boltzmann, Josiah Willard Gibbs, and James Clerk Maxwell developed the statistical basis for entropy.

467

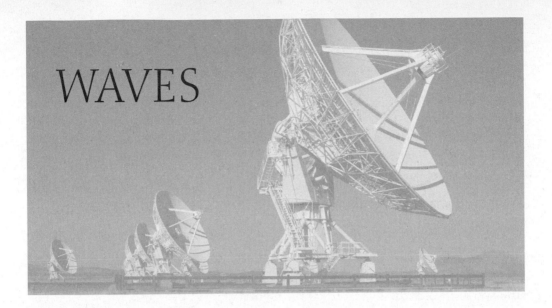

WAVES

What is a **wave**?

A wave is a traveling disturbance that moves energy from one location to another without transferring matter. Oscillations in a medium or material create mechanical waves that propagate away from the location of the oscillation. For example, a pebble dropped into a pool of water creates vertical oscillations in the water, while the wave propagates outward horizontally along the surface of the water.

What are the **types of waves**?

Transverse and longitudinal waves are two major forms of waves. A transverse wave can be created by shaking a string or rope up and down. Although the string moves up and down, the wave itself and its energy moves away from the source, perpendicular to the direction of the oscillations.

The oscillations in longitudinal waves move in the same direction that the wave is moving. The medium in longitudinal waves alternately pushes close together (compression) and separates from each other (rarefaction). The best example of longitudinal waves are sound waves, which are a series of back and forth longitudinal oscillations of atoms or molecules that form alternate regions of high and low pressure in a medium such as air.

Water waves are a combination of transverse and longitudinal waves that move in circles. Just as in the case of transverse and longitudinal waves, energy is transferred but matter is not moved.

What **determines** the **velocity** of a **wave**?

The velocity of a wave depends upon the material or medium in which it is traveling. Typically, the stronger the coupling between the atoms or molecules that make up the medium, and the less massive they are, the faster the wave will travel. All waves of the

same type (transverse or longitudinal) travel at the same speed. For example, a sound wave in air at 0°C will travel at 331 meters per second, regardless of the sound's frequency or amplitude. Electromagnetic waves can travel either through empty space or through material. Their velocity depends on the electric and magnetic properties of space or the material but not on frequency or amplitude. The velocity of water waves depend both on the properties of the water and on the frequency of the wave.

What are some of the **terms used** to define the **properties of waves**?

The table below summarizes the different properties of waves.

Type of Wave	Term	Definition
Transverse	Crest	The highest point of the wave.
	Trough	The lowest point of the wave.
Longitudinal	Compression	An area where the material or medium is condensed and at higher pressure.
	Rarefaction	An area that follows a compression where the material or medium is spread out and at lower pressure.
Transverse & Longitudinal	Amplitude	The distance from the midpoint to the point of maximum displacement (crest or compression).
	Frequency	The number of vibrations that occur in one second; the inverse of the period.
	Period	The time it takes for a wave to complete one full vibration; the inverse of the frequency.
	Wavelength	The distance from one point on the wave to the next identical point; the length of the wave.

What is the **relationship** among **frequency, wavelength,** and **velocity**?

Suppose you shake a rope up and down at a constant rate. The rate or frequency is the number of times your hand is at the top of its motion per second. As the waves move along the rope, the distance between the crests of the rope, the wavelength, will remain the same. The wavelength depends both on the frequency of oscillation and on the velocity of the wave along the rope. The relationship is velocity = frequency \times wavelength ($v = f\lambda$) or wavelength = velocity/frequency ($\lambda = v/f$). Therefore, if the frequency of a wave increased, the wavelength decreases while the velocity, being a property of the medium (rope) doesn't change. The frequency and wavelength are inversely proportional to each other.

The following table shows the relationship between frequency and wavelength for a sound wave in 0°C air:

Velocity of Sound	Frequency (Hz)	Wavelength (m)
331	128	2.59
331	256	1.29
331	512	0.65
331	768	0.43

What is the **relationship** between **frequency** and **period**?

Frequency, f, is how many cycles of an oscillation occur per second and is measured in cycles per second or hertz (Hz). The period of a wave, T, is the amount of time it takes a wave to vibrate one full cycle. These two terms are inversely proportional to each other: $f = 1/T$ and $T = 1/f$.

For example, if a wave takes 1 second to oscillate up and down, the period of the wave is 1 second. The frequency is the reciprocal of that, 1 cycle/sec, because only one cycle occurred in a second. If, however, a wave took half a second to oscillate up and down, the period of that wave would be 0.5 seconds, and the frequency would be the reciprocal, or 2 cycles per second. So, you see that a wave with a long period has a low frequency, while a wave with a short period has a high frequency.

On what does the **amplitude** of a **wave depend**?

The amplitude of a rope wave depends on how hard you shake it. For a sound wave it depends on how much compression the loud speaker or musical instrument creates. In other words, it depends on the energy the source put into the wave. It does not depend on frequency, wavelength, or velocity.

Does the **amplitude** of a **wave depend** on **distance** from the source?

The energy carried in a wave depends on the wave's amplitude and its velocity. Waves can be put into two categories: those that spread, like water waves on a pond, sound waves, or electromagnetic waves; and those that are confined to a narrow region, like waves on a rope or electrical oscillations on a wire. A water wave spreads on the surface of a pond, lake, wide river, or ocean. As it spreads its energy is spread over a larger area, so the energy transmitted to a particular location is reduced when the source is farther away. Therefore the amplitude of the water wave is also reduced in proportion to the distance from the source. Sound and electromagnetic waves usually spread in two dimensions. Again, as they spread the energy carried is also spread, so as the distance from the source is increased, the amplitude is decreased, but this time as the square of the distance.

On a rope or wire, the wave doesn't spread, but often a different mechanism reduces the amplitude. In a rope there is friction between the fibers, which changes

471

some of its kinetic energy to thermal energy. If a signal is sent through a wire as an oscillating voltage the resistance of the wire will convert some of the electric energy to thermal energy, reducing the voltage and thus the amplitude of the wave. This loss is reversed by putting amplifiers along the wire, putting more energy into the wave and increasing its amplitude.

WATER WAVES

What type of wave is a **water wave**?

Ocean or water waves look like transverse waves, yet are actually a combination of both transverse and longitudinal waves. The water molecules in a water wave vibrate up and down in tiny circular paths. The circular path of the water wave creates an undulating appearance in the wave.

How **fast** does the **wind** need to blow in order to **produce different types** of **waves**?

Wind rubbing against the water surface is a major cause of waves. Since the water cannot keep up with the wind velocity, the water rises and then falls, creating the familiar wave-like motion. Depending upon the wind velocity and the distance the wind has been able to travel over the water, different size waves are generated.

Type of Wave	Wind Velocity	Effect
Capillary waves	Less than 3 knots	Tiny ripples. The longer they are generated, the larger their amplitude
Chop or regular	3–12 knots	Combined capillary waves that have traveled far and formed larger waves
Whitecaps	11–15 knots	Amplitude of wave must be over 1/7th the wavelength in order to break into a whitecap
Ocean swells	No specific speed	Form over long distances from a combination of different waves

How do **speeds** of **ocean waves** vary?

The speed of an ocean wave depends on the distance between two successive crests, its wavelength. The longer the wavelength, the faster the wave travels. A small surface wave, such as a ripple created by the wind, travels quite slowly because it has such a short wavelength. A swell, the larger, longer wavelength waves created by constant

Waves break as they approach a shoreline because the lower part of the wave moves more slowly than the top part of the wave due to increasing friction with the shallower ocean bottom.

winds, have longer wavelengths and travel at higher velocities. The energy that the wave carries depends on the square of the height of the wave, which explains why high waves can cause so much damage to shorelines.

Why do water **waves break** as they **approach** the **beach**?

Water waves rarely break, or form whitecaps, when they come in contact with a cliff or mountainside shoreline. Waves only break as they approach a gradual decrease in depths, such as a beach. A shoreline with a gradual decrease in depth will produce more spectacular whitecaps than a wave that encounters a steep decrease in depth.

The reason waves break is the result of the way the wave velocity depends on the depth of the water. Consider a water wave with a large amplitude. As the wave moves toward the beach, at first it travels at a constant velocity. As the ocean depth begins to decrease, the bottom of the wave gradually encounters more and more friction with the beach, causing the lower part of the wave to travel slower than the upper part. As the lower part slows down, the crest, moving faster, moves over the trough. When there is not enough water to support the crest, the wave breaks or forms a whitecap.

Where are the **best surfing beaches**?

The best surfing beaches are located along the edges of oceans when wind conditions have produced waves with large wavelengths. Another requirement of a good surfing beach is a gradual decrease in water depth.

How can they be similar? Surfing is done on water; skiing on snow. The main similarity is that in both cases the athlete and board travel down a hill. In skiing, the hill is a mountain covered with snow, while in surfing the hill is the rising water of a breaking ocean wave. An ideal surfing wave has a large amplitude as it reaches an extremely gradual decrease in ocean depth. While the surfer moves down the wave, the water on the front edge of a crest continually rises underneath the surfer, allowing the surfer to ride down the wave without actually moving downward.

Some of the best surfing is done on Waikiki beach on Oahu in the summer and the north shores of Oahu and Kaua'i in Hawaii in the winter. In the continental United States the best surfing is in southern California. The Pacific Ocean, famous for its long wavelengths and gradual decreasing depth beaches, has some of the best surfing in the world.

What is a **tidal wave**?

A tidal wave, or tsunami, is not caused by windy conditions or tides, but instead by underwater earthquakes and volcanic eruptions. The seismic disturbances create huge upward forces on the water, the opposite of dropping rocks into water. A tsunami is a series of several waves with a period of more than 30 minutes between each crest. The ocean first recedes from the beach, then water rushes inland at a very high speed. Large tsunamis can be quite destructive upon reaching the shoreline due to their amplitudes.

The most deadly recorded tsunami occurred December 26, 2004, in the Indian Ocean. The earthquake that caused it was off the west coast of Sumatra, Indonesia. That quake released an amount of energy equivalent to 550 million times the energy released in the Hiroshima nuclear bomb. One part of the ocean bottom was lifted by 4 to 5 meters (13 to 16 feet) and moved horizontally 10 meters (33 feet). The tsunami, traveling at a speed of 500 to 1,000 kilometers per hour, had a low amplitude (60 centimeters) in mid-ocean, but when it crashed into the coasts from Thailand to India and as far as South Africa it had an amplitude as high as 24 meters (79 feet). Some 230,000 people were killed and more than a million made homeless.

ELECTROMAGNETIC WAVES

What is an **electromagnetic wave**?

Electromagnetic waves consist of two transverse waves: one an oscillating electric field, the other a corresponding magnetic field perpendicular to it. Light, infrared, ultraviolet, radio, and X rays are all examples of electromagnetic waves.

All electromagnetic waves travel at the speed of light when they are in a vacuum. Electromagnetic waves are characterized by their frequency or wavelength and amplitude. Electromagnetic waves differ from other waves in that they do not need a medium such as air, water, or steel through which to travel.

How is an **electromagnetic wave created** and **detected**?

Electromagnetic waves are created by accelerating electrons that create an oscillating electric field. This field in turn creates an oscillating magnetic field, which creates another oscillating electric field, and so on. The energy carried by the waves radiates into the area around the moving charges. When it strikes a material whose electrons can move freely, it causes these particles to oscillate.

What is the **electromagnetic spectrum**?

The electromagnetic spectrum is the wide range of electromagnetic (EM) waves from low to high frequency. The spectrum ranges from low-frequency radio waves, all the way to gamma rays, which have a very high frequency. In the middle of the spectrum is a small region containing the frequencies of light.

Who **predicted electromagnetic waves**?

In 1861, James Clerk Maxwell (1831–1879) demonstrated the mathematical relationship between oscillating electric and magnetic fields. In his *Treatise on Electricity and Magnetism*, written in 1873, Maxwell described the nature of electric and magnetic fields using four differential equations, known to physicists today as "Maxwell's Equations." Putting the four equations together predicted the existence of the electromagnetic wave.

Maxwell was a professor at Cambridge University in England from 1871 until his death in 1879. He published other works on thermodynamics and the motion of matter as well. He also developed the kinetic theory of gases, and performed research in the field of color vision. Although Maxwell is not widely known to the lay audience, he is revered in the scientific community, and rates in the pantheon of physics greats with Newton and Einstein.

Who **demonstrated** that **electromagnetic waves exist**?

Heinrich Hertz (1857–1894) was a German physicist who was the first person to demonstrate that electromagnetic waves existed. He designed a transmitter and receiver that produced waves with a 4-meter wavelength. He used standing waves to measure their wavelength. He showed that they could be reflected, refracted, polarized, and could produce interference. It was Hertz's breakthroughs in electromagnetic waves that paved the way for the development of radio. In 1930 Hertz was honored by having the unit of frequency, which was cycles per second, replaced by the hertz (Hz).

475

COMMUNICATING WITH ELECTROMAGNETIC WAVES

How did **radio communications** develop?

An electromagnetic wave with no changes in amplitude or frequency carries no information—it cannot be used for communication. The first method of using these waves to communicate was to switch them on and off in regular patterns. Letters were represented by a combination of long and short pulses using what is called Morse Code after Samuel S.B. Morse, who developed the code to transmit information over wires (the telegraph).

In 1895 Guglielmo Marconi (1874–1937), a twenty-year-old Italian inventor, created a device that transmitted and received electromagnetic waves over a 1-kilometer (3,280 foot) distance. Later improvements to his antenna and the development of a crude amplifier enabled him to receive a British patent for his wireless telegraph. In 1897, he transmitted signals to ships 29 kilometers (18 miles) from shore and in 1901 he was able to send wireless messages across the Atlantic Ocean. As a result of Marconi's work on radio transmitters and receivers, he was the co-winner of the 1909 Nobel Prize in physics. Over the next decade transmitters and receivers were improved enough that they could be installed in ocean-going ships.

Voice communication over the telephone had existed since 1876, but if the distance was to be extended, the voices had to be amplified to be heard. In 1906 Lee De Forest invented a vacuum tube amplifier he called the Audion. It took until 1915 for a radio receiver to be sold using Audions. In 1916 De Forest had developed an Audion-based transmitter that allowed dance music to be transmitted 40 miles. A number of other experimental stations demonstrated music by radio—then called wireless. A large number of radio amateurs made significant advances. When the United States entered World War I in 1917 all stations not owned by the government were shut down and it became illegal for people to listen to any radio transmission.

During the war, radio was used to communicate between ships and between land and the ships. After the war, amateurs were forced to use only one wavelength, 200 meters (1,500 hertz). Wavelengths shorter than that were thought to

Samuel S.B. Morse was famous for inventing the Morse Code that allowed people to first transmit messages over telegraph wires.

be useless for government use. One amateur was able to send signals 3,000 miles. In 1921 transatlantic voice transmissions were made. Companies began to use radio for specialized needs, like to send time information to jewelers to allow them to set their clocks. From 1919 through 1921 radio was mostly used to transmit musical concerts. The first transmission of a football game occurred in November 1919. By 1922 newspapers had developed radio stations transmitting news, weather reports, crop reports, and lectures. Large companies such as General Electric, Westinghouse, AT&T, and RCA. began to be involved in developing commercial broadcasting.

From 1922 to 1923, as the number of stations grew without regulation, chaos reigned. In 1928 the government announced new assignments in the frequency band 550 to 1,600 kHz. Many more assignments were added after World War II, but these regulations are still in use today.

How do **antennas transmit** and **receive signals**?

Antennas for radio and television signals are used to either transmit or receive electromagnetic radio waves. Oscillating voltages produced by the transmitter cause the electrons in a metal wire or rod, the transmitting antenna, to oscillate, creating an oscillating electric field that in turn creates an oscillating magnetic field that creates another oscillating electric field. The combined electric and magnetic wave moves away from the antenna at the speed of light. A receiving antenna is a metal rod, wire, or a loop. When an electromagnetic wave strikes the antenna it causes the electrons in the metal to oscillate at the same frequency as that of the wave. The oscillating electrons produce a voltage in the receiver that eventually results in the sounds and/or pictures produced by a radio or television.

Does the **dimension** of an **antenna** play a significant **role** in the **reception** of an electromagnetic wave?

The length of an antenna determines the frequency that it best receives. The most efficient antennas have a length equal to half the wavelength of the wave it is receiving. This allows the induced electrical current in the receiving antenna to resonate at that particular frequency. If the antenna is a simple rod it is most sensitive when its length is one quarter the wavelength.

A loop or coil antenna are used for the low-frequency, long-wavelength signals in the AM band. A half-wavelength straight wire antenna would be over one hundred of meters long. Shorter wires or rods can be used and are more efficient if coils of wire are used to "load" the antenna.

Home FM radio and television antennas are designed to receive a broad range of frequencies, but with less sensitivity. Antennas for the ultra-high frequencies used in

digital high definition televisions are very short and can be easily mounted outside on rooftops or on top of television sets.

What are the different **frequencies** of **radio waves** and **microwaves** that allow for **communication**?

The table below shows the regions of the electromagnetic spectrum and their uses. The unit for frequency is hertz (Hz). Hertz is the name for the number of oscillations or cycles per second of a wave. The letters kHz mean one thousand hertz, Mhz a million hertz, and Ghz a thousand million or a billion hertz or cycles per second.

Frequency Range	Wavelength Range	Name & Abbreviation	Use
Less than 30 kHz	More than 10 km	Extremely low frequency (ELF)	Submarine communication
30 kHz to 300 kHz	10 km to 1 km	Low frequency (LF)	Maritime mobile, navigational
300 kHz to 3 Mhz	1 km to 100 m	Medium frequency (MF)	Radio broadcasts, land and maritime mobile radio
3 Mhz to 300 Mhz	10 m to 1 m	Very high frequency (VHF)	Television broadcasts, maritime and aeronautical mobile, amateur radio, meteorological communication
300 Mhz to 3 Ghz	1 m to 10 cm	Ultrahigh frequency (UHF)	Television, radar, cell phones, military, amateur radio
3 Ghz to 30 Ghz	10 cm to 1 cm	Superhigh frequency (SHF)	Radar, space and satellite microwave communication, wireless home telephones, wireless computer networks
30 Ghz to 300 Ghz	1 cm to 1 mm	Extremely high frequency (EHF)	Radio astronomy, radar

478

PUTTING INFORMATION ON ELECTROMAGNETIC WAVES

What is the difference between **analog** and **digital signals**?

All transmitters create what is called a carrier wave at a specific frequency. For licensed commercial broadcasters, the Federal Communications Commission (FCC) assigns the frequency. The carrier wave transmits no information. For information to be carried, some property of the carrier wave must be changed. The earliest methods of radio broadcasting used analog signals from a source like a microphone. Sound striking a microphone produces a varying voltage output. That is, the output of a microphone has the same shape of the amplitude of the sound wave that strikes it. The smooth graph below represents an analog signal from a microphone.

Time	Voltage
0	3
0.5	4
1.0	1
1.5	1
2.0	2
2.5	7
3.0	0
3.5	4

To create a digital signal the analog output of the microphone is converted into a series of numbers. For example, consider the graph above. Suppose the signal is "sampled" every 2,000 times each second. That is, the voltage is recorded each 0.5 millisecond. The dots show the results of the sampling. Voltage can be in only whole numbers. The series of numbers representing the waveform would then be those shown in the table.

Next the voltages are converted into binary digits, a series of 0s and 1s. The table on the right shows the conversion to binary for numbers 0 through 7. The binary digits reading left to right represent the numbers 4, 2, and 1. Thus 5 = 4 + 1 or 101.

Now the binary numbers are converted into a series of voltages to be sent to the transmitter. One method is called *Pulse Width Modulation* or PWM. A narrow pulse 479

represents a 0, a wider pulse represents 1. For example, the first four samples would produce the following wave train:

The receiver knows that three bits should be converted into a number. If the receiver is to convert the signal back to analog, then that number determines the amplitude of the analog wave.

Does this look like the original analog signal? No way! Note that there are two problems. First, the "wiggles" in the wave are missing. Second, with only 8 choices of voltages, the vertical resolution is too small. To make a more accurate conversion you need to sample the wave more often, at least every 0.1 millisecond and to allow more than 8 voltage choices; 32 or more would be better. To obtain the quality of sound in a CD the sampling interval is 22 μs (22 microseconds) and there are at least 4,096 voltage choices.

What do **AM** and **FM** mean?

Traditional radio broadcasting uses analog, not digital, methods. AM, or amplitude modulation, and FM, or frequency modulation are methods of transmitting informa-

tion on a radio. In each case a property of the "carrier" wave is changed, or modulated. These variations carry the transmitted information.

AM was the first method invented and the simplest to transmit and receive. Edwin Howard Armstrong demonstrated transmission and reception of Frequency Modulation in 1935. Listeners were amazed the way that FM eliminated "static" because noise, like that due to thunderstorms, changes the amplitude, but not the frequency of signals. The FM receiver's output does not depend on the amplitude of the signal. Due to opposition from the radio networks and receiver manufacturers, commercial FM broadcasts were delayed and did not become widely available until after World War II.

Radios once only had AM (Amplitude Modulated) frequencies available; then came FM (Frequency Modulated) in 1939. Today, there is talk among radio professionals that AM stations might become a thing of the past.

Where are **AM and FM broadcasts** found in the **electromagnetic spectrum**?

In the United States commercial AM stations broadcast between 550 kHz and 1600 kHz. Commercial FM stations broadcast between 88 MHz and 108 MHz. In the AM band the frequencies of stations are spaced by only 10 kHz. As a result, the broadcasts are limited to sound frequencies up to only 4kHz, while the ear can detect frequencies as high as 15 kHz. Why are broadcast frequencies so limited? Suppose the analog signal is a 440 Hz tone, the A above middle C on a piano. A typical AM transmitter would have a carrier wave frequency of 1 megahertz (MHz). The result is a signal with three different frequencies: 1 MHz, 1MHz + 440 Hz and 1MHz – 440 Hz. Thus the total signal requires a set of frequencies 880 Hz wide. Sounds with a frequency of 4kHz require a range of frequencies, called the bandwidth, 8 kHz wide, just about the spacing between adjacent stations.

FM stations, on the other hand, were developed to transmit sounds more faithfully, which means that sounds up to 15kHz must be accommodated. That means that the bandwidth of the broadcasts is 30kHz wide. At the very high frequencies used by FM stations there is more bandwidth available and stations are spaced by 200kHz.

The electromagnetic spectrum has many other users. Police and firefighters usually use AM while aircraft, where noise reduction is important, use FM. Television stations used to use AM for the picture and FM for the sound, but as of June 12, 2009, they now all use digital signals. Other users are the military, marine ship-to-shore ser-

The "G" stands for generation. Early cell phones that could only make analog voice phone calls are called first generation devices, or 1G. Networks that use digital methods that allow many more simultaneous users are called second generation, or 2G systems. The increased capacity of 2G systems allows emails and short text messages to be exchanged between cell phones. In the year 2000 standards were released for 3G networks stating that these devices should be able to download television-like video and exchange video images. By 2009 "smart" phones were in common use. They include many of the features of computers, GPS location detection, video cameras, and telephones. The high-speed transfer of data to and from the phone offered by a 3G network is important for proper operation of the smart phones. Standards for 4G networks include transmission rates of 100 M bits/s, in comparison to 14 M bits/s for 3G networks. The technology, which requires new base stations, antennas, and phones, is still evolving.

vices, weather broadcasts, commercial mobile phones, the citizen band, and amateur radio operators. They all share the HF, VHF, UHF, and SHF bands.

What **alternative analog methods** are used?

As was described above, modulating a carrier wave produces additional frequencies above and below the frequency of the carrier. These frequencies are called sidebands. There is identical information in the two sidebands, so many radio services filter out one of the two sidebands, resulting in a single-sideband broadcast, or SSB. SSB can work with either AM or FM radios. It has half the bandwidth of a double-sideband broadcast, so more radios can use the same part of the spectrum.

How does an **FM band station transmit stereo** sound?

Stereo sound means that two separate sounds, the left (L) and right (R), are produced from a pair of speakers. Because stereo broadcasts must also be usable by receivers that cannot reproduce stereo the signal that all receivers can detect consists of the sum of the left and right channels ($R + L$). The difference of the two channels ($R - L$) is broadcast 38 kHz above the $R + L$ signals. Mono receivers can't detect these very high frequencies. The stereo receiver, though, can and from the $R + L$ and $R - L$ signals creates separate R and L signals to be amplified and sent to the corresponding speaker.

FM stations have enough bandwidth to accommodate a third signal. This signal can be sold to users to provide background music for stores or elevators. Education stations can deliver lessons to schools, or broadcasts in a second language.

How **far away** can **FM** and **AM** stations be **received**?

All electromagnetic waves travel in a straight line while in a uniform medium such as the lower atmosphere. Therefore, most radio waves only have what is called a line-of-sight range. That means that if a mountain range or the curvature of Earth were in the way of the radio signal, the receiver would be out of range and would not receive the signal. This is why most broadcasting antennae are placed on tall buildings or mountains to help increase the line-of-sight range.

Waves with frequencies below about 30 Mhz are able to reflect off the charged particles in Earth's ionosphere; this is referred to as "skip." Instead of passing through the ionosphere and entering space as higher-frequency electromagnetic waves do, the lower frequencies on the AM band can be reflected back toward Earth to increase their range dramatically. After sunset the ionosphere's altitude permits stations to be heard thousands of kilometers from a transmitting tower. A handful of AM stations are "clear channel" stations. That is, there is only one station in the continental United States broadcasting on that frequency. Those stations can be heard across almost the entire country without interference from other stations. Broadcast FM stations, with frequencies 88–108 megahertz penetrate the ionosphere, and so can only be heard 80–160 kilometers from the transmitter.

How do **cell phones** work?

Cell phones use the UHF part of the electromagnetic spectrum, 800 to 900 MHz, 1,700 to 1,800 MHz, and 2,100 to 2,200 MHz. The service area for a cell phone provider is divided up into hexagonally shaped cells, each one served by base stations with antenna towers at three corners of the cell. The stations can both receive and transmit information to cell phones. The stations are connected to a network that uses fiber optic cables. When a cell phone is turned on it searches for available services according to a list stored in the phone. It selects the correct frequencies to transmit and receive data, then sends its serial and phone numbers to the system, registering itself in that cell. The network makes sure that the phone number is part of its system and that there is money in the account to pay for a call. After registration is complete and a call is made to that phone, the network can direct the call to the correct cell. The cell

The technology behind the cell phones we take for granted today is amazing. Transmitting and receiving messages in the electromagnetic spectrum, cell phones automatically select and correct appropriate frequencies, send serial numbers to servers, and register themselves in the cell in which they are located at the time.

phone always searches for the strongest signal from a tower. If the phone moves during the conversation, then the signal strengths will change and the phone will "hand off" the call to a different base station.

Cell phones digitize the voice signals. Special circuits, called digital signal processors, then compress the voice signals and insert codes that can detect errors in transmission. Compression is achieved by sending only the changes in the digital signals, not what stays the same. Cell phone systems also send many different conversations at the same time. One method, called TDMA (time division multiple access), splits up three compressed calls and sends them together. CDMA (code division multiple access) uses TDMA to pack three calls together, and then puts six more calls at two other frequencies. Each of the nine (or more) calls is assigned a unique code so that it can be directed to the correct recipient. Spread CDMA systems use a wide band of frequencies that permit more simultaneous calls.

MICROWAVES

How are **microwaves** used for **communication**?

Microwaves are electromagnetic waves with frequencies above about 3 Ghz. They are used in homes equipped with wireless internet devices, wireless telephones, Bluetooth devices, for satellite radio and television. In addition, industries, governments, and the military use microwaves for communicating from one installation to another.

Microwaves can be transmitted one of two ways. The first is the line-of-sight approach, where the microwave transmitter is pointed at a microwave receiver (these must be no more than 30 kilometers apart). The second method of transmission is to send the signal up to a satellite that receives it and retransmits it back down to a receiving dish.

What are **other uses** for **microwaves** besides communication?

In addition to having a great range of frequencies to transmit information, microwaves are used every day in kitchens around the world. Microwave ovens generate 2.4 GHz waves and scatter them throughout the oven. The microwaves excite water and fat molecules into resonance and cause them to rotate, increasing their thermal energy. Different kinds of molecules absorb the energy at different rates, so some foods are heated more than others. Microwave-safe containers are made of materials that do not absorb microwave energy and so remain cool.

What is the function of the **grating** on the **door** of a **microwave oven**?

People using microwave ovens want to see the food cooking inside the oven, yet not be bombarded by potentially harmful microwaves. In order to prevent the escape of

Can a microwave oven be used to dry things?

Since water molecules are warmed and eventually boil off by microwaves, anything that is wet can be dried in the microwave. However, there is one very important consideration that must be made before placing the object inside a microwave—the object being dried must not contain a great deal of water itself. Microwaves are wonderful at drying wet books, papers, and magazines, but must never be used to dry things like plants or small animals. Living things would be killed by the resonance of water molecules inside their bodies.

microwaves through the plastic or glass door, a grating consisting of small holes is used to reflect the microwaves back into the oven. The microwaves (which have a wavelength of about 12 centimeters [4.7 inches]) are too big to pass through the holes, but visible light, whose wavelength is smaller than the opening, can easily pass though the grating. Although the grating protects people from the microwaves, some microwaves can still leak out through the door seal, however, if it's not cleaned occasionally.

Why **shouldn't metal** objects be placed **inside microwave ovens**?

Manufacturers caution consumers about placing metal containers and aluminum foil inside microwave ovens for two main reasons. The first reason is that metal and aluminum may impede cooking. Microwaves warm food by transmitting energy to water and fat molecules within the food. If food is placed under aluminum foil or in a metal container, the microwaves will be reflected from the metal and won't be able to reach the water molecules and cook the food.

The second reason for not placing metal objects inside a microwave oven is for the safety of the microwave oven itself. Metal acts as a mirror to microwaves. If too much metal is placed in the oven, the microwaves will bounce around the oven in waves that can damage the magnetron that produces the microwaves. If the metal is the correct size it can act as a microwave receiver and the induced voltages can produce sparks that can ignite the food.

THE PRINCIPLE OF SUPERPOSITION

What is the **Principle of Superposition**?

When two waves overlap they don't crash and destroy one another; instead, they pass through each other without interaction. The graphs below show two waves approach-

485

ing, overlapping, and moving away. They continue to move at the same velocity throughout. The arrows show their motions. The dotted drawings show the individual waves while the solid drawings show the resultants.

The amplitudes of the two waves add together, producing either a larger wave if they are both positive or both negative. They produce a smaller wave if one is positive and the other negative. In fact, as shown (4), they can produce no amplitude at all. The large amplitudes are called constructive interference. The reduced amplitudes are called destructive interference.

What are **dead spots** in **auditoriums**?

Poorly designed auditoriums can have dead spots. Dead spots are places where destructive interference occurs from the interaction of two or more sound waves. For example, a soloist on stage sends sound waves into the audience. Some of the waves hit the walls of the auditorium, while other waves travel directly to the listeners. In some situations, a direct wave can destructively interfere with a reflected wave so they cancel each other out at that particular location. As a result, the listeners seated in those particular seats would hear nothing from that soloist. Someone sitting a few seats over from the dead spot, however, might not experience the destructive interference and would hear the soloist just fine. (Refer to the chapter on Sound for handy answers dealing with acoustical engineering.)

What is a **standing wave**?

The example used above showed what happened when two single waves going in opposite directions met. A continuous wave is a set of single waves, one after another. You can produce such a wave by shaking one end of a rope up and down at a constant frequency. Now, if the other end of the rope is tied to something that doesn't move, the wave will be reflected back toward you. If you shake the rope at the correct frequencies the two waves will overlap each other and will seem to stand still, producing a standing wave. Two distinct regions on a standing wave can be seen. At certain points the rope won't be moving. That point is called a node. The point where the motion of the rope is largest is called the anti-node.

The nodes are locations of destructive interference where the two waves moving in opposite directions have opposite amplitudes; the crest of one wave and the trough of the other are at the same location. The anti-nodes are at locations of constructive interference where the two waves have both positive or negative amplitudes; that is, both are either crests or troughs.

The frequencies that produce standing waves depend on the length of the rope and the velocity of the wave on the rope. The lowest frequency will have nodes at the two ends and an anti-node in the center. The next higher frequency will have a node in the center and ends and two anti-nodes. At each higher frequency the number of nodes and anti-nodes increases by one.

How are **standing sound waves** generated in **musical instruments**?

Many instruments depend on standing waves to produce their sound. Standing waves are created on the strings of a guitar, piano, or violin, and in the air columns of a trumpet, flute, or organ pipe. The string is caused to oscillate either by plucking it (pulling it aside and then letting go), or by bowing it, where the stickiness of the horsehair on the bow also pulls the string aside and then releases it. In a piano a felt-covered hammer strikes the string, starting it vibrating. In a trumpet or other brass instrument the player's vibrating lips create the traveling sound wave that is reflected when it reaches the open end of the instrument. In a flute or organ pipe that mimics a flute, the player blows air over a hole. The moving air interacting with the hole produces a periodic change in the pressure of the air inside the tube, which creates the travel-

Many musical instruments, such as clarinets and violins, depend on standing waves to produce sound.

ing sound wave. In a clarinet or saxophone the player blows through a narrow gap between a flexible piece of bamboo called the reed and the mouthpiece. Oboes and bassoons have two reeds separated by a thin gap. The stream of air causes the reed to vibrate, periodically stopping the air flow and causing the sound wave.

In order to change the pitch produced by an instrument the standing wave inside the instrument must be altered. By changing the length of a wind instrument, or the tension and length of the strings for a string instrument, a different frequency standing wave is produced, which creates a different musical pitch. Pressing a key on a trumpet inserts an additional length of tubing into the instrument. On a flute, clarinet, or saxophone a hole on the instrument is covered or uncovered, changing the effective length of the instrument. On a piano each note uses a string of a particular length. On a violin or guitar the player's finger is used to change the length. Thicker strings have lower pitches than thinner strings of the same length. Increasing the tension on a string increases the frequency of the standing waves, and thus the pitch.

RESONANCE

What is **resonance** and how can it be achieved?

All objects that can vibrate have a natural frequency of oscillation. If you hold one end of a ruler on a desk and push down and then suddenly release the other end you will see it vibrate. The natural frequency depends on the material and its width, thickness, and length.

Resonance occurs when an external oscillating force is exerted on an object that can vibrate. When the frequency of the external force equals the natural frequency then the amplitude of the oscillation reaches a maximum. This condition is called resonance. A very small external force is needed to create a large oscillation amplitude.

You can explore resonance with a mass, like a yo-yo or a heavy metal washer on a string. Hold the top of the string still and pull the object to one side and watch it oscillate at its natural frequency. Then shake the top of the string at the same frequency and watch the amplitude of the oscillation increase. You will have found the resonance frequency. If you raise or lower the shaking frequency you'll find that the amplitude of the oscillation is smaller.

Where can **resonance** be found on the **playground**?

Children discover resonance early in life. When playing on swings, they use their arms and legs to pump themselves back and forth on the swing. They recognize that if they pull back on the chains every time the swing is at its largest backward displacement they will achieve the largest amplitude. If, however, the pull back at other times, or if a parent

pushes at the wrong time, the amplitude will be decreased because the external frequency isn't at the natural frequency.

How can **resonance** cause crystal **glasses** to **break**?

Many years ago Ella Fitzgerald performed a physics experiment in an advertisement for Memorex® audio tape cassettes. The company claimed that the famous singer could create a pure tone at just the right frequency to cause a crystal wine glass to break and that the Memorex® tapes recorded and played back sounds so accurately that the glass would break both when Ms. Fitzgerald sang and when the recorded sound was played. "Is it live or is it Memorex®?" was the advertising question.

Although it is hard to think that glass is something that can bend, if you tap the rim of a thin wine glass you can hear it "ping." The shape of the rim of the glass oscillates. When the amplified sound waves pushed on the glass it distorted its shape. Some of the kinetic energy in the sound wave was transferred into the kinetic energy of the oscillating glass. When the frequency of the sound wave matched the natural frequency of the glass the amplitude of oscillation was large enough to shatter the glass.

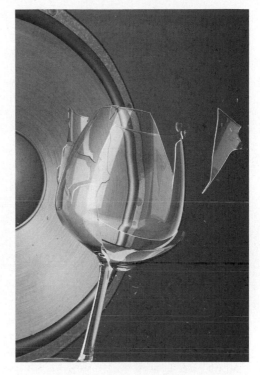

Sound can make glass break when amplified because the sound waves can cause the glass to oscillate and bend. When enough kinetic energy is used, the sound waves can distort the glass to the point where it cracks or shatters.

How did **resonance destroy** the **Tacoma Narrows Bridge** in Washington State?

The Tacoma Narrows Bridge, or "Galloping Gertie" as it was often called, was built in 1940 and was known for its unusual, undulating movement. All bridges vibrate to some extent, but to many motorists, the suspension bridge in Tacoma felt more like an amusement park ride than a bridge.

On the morning of November 7, 1940, four months after the bridge opened, the wind was blowing at approximately 42 miles per hour. This moderate wind hit the solid bridge deck and caused the deck to vibrate back and forth as it did almost every day since the bridge had opened. But the bridge began to vibrate more dramatically than ever before. It appeared as though a standing wave had formed between the two

If the energy of a resonant standing wave is large enough, a crystal wine glass can shatter quite easily, but when the amplitude is smaller, the wine glass can produce a sound instead. Take, for example, a person rubbing his finger around the moist lip of a crystal wine glass. The glass seems to sing or hum. The humming is caused by the rubbing of the wet finger on the glass that causes it to have a standing wave pattern. The resonating glass generates enough energy to vibrate the surrounding air and create a steady humming sound. In 1761 Benjamin Franklin (1706–1790) invented the glass harmonica (that he called the armonica) in which wine glasses of various sizes were fastened to a rotating shaft. The musician rubbed his fingers on the appropriate glass to play music. Wolfgang Amadeus Mozart and almost 100 other composers wrote music for the glass harmonica.

towers of the bridge. There was one distinct node in the center of the bridge and an anti-node on each side of the node. After several hours of dramatic vibrations, the bridge deck collapsed into the river below, along with its only casualty, a dog named "Tubby," left in a car by its owner, who narrowly escaped death himself.

There is still an active controversy about the exact cause of the collapse of the bridge. Was it the steady wind, or variable winds? What factor did the solid deck and the solid, high sides to the deck play? Was the deck just not stiff enough? Suffice it to say that more recently built bridges use perforated decks and lower, open sides.

What is a **torsional wave**?

A torsional wave, such as the wave that the Tacoma Narrows Bridge created, is a wave that is not only displaced vertically, but twists in a wave-like fashion as well. The torsional wave on the Tacoma Narrows Bridge achieved resonance in two orientations. The first resonance was seen as the undulating movement that took place over the length of the bridge, while the second resonance, seen as the twisting motion, occurred from side to side on the bridge.

IMPEDANCE

What is **impedance matching**?

Impedance is the opposition to wave motion exerted by a medium. When a wave travels from one medium into another, the impedance changes, causing some of the energy of the wave to be reflected back into the original medium. Therefore not all of the

wave's energy travels into the new medium. An impedance matching device between the two media allows for a smooth transition in impedance and reduces reflections.

What are **transformers**?

An impedance matching device is called a transformer. Instead of an abrupt change between the two media, a transformer provides a smoother, gradual transition from the old to the new medium. Depending upon the wave and the medium, different transformers, such as quarter-wavelength and tapered transformers, can be used to help minimize reflection.

An example of a tapered transformer can be found in soundproof rooms or sound studios. Any sound that is produced is supposed to be absorbed by the impedance matching material on the walls. Special foam, tapered in a V-like shape, is used as a transformer to gradually absorb all the sound into the walls. The gradual changeover from the air medium to the wall medium prevents sound from reflecting back into the air.

An example of a quarter-wavelength transformer can be found on many camera lenses and eyeglasses. The quarter-wavelength thick coating on a lens is used to reduce reflections off the lens surface, allowing more light into the lens.

Electrical transformers are also used to match impedances by changing the varying voltages and currents in an electronic circuit. Modern electronic circuits make very minimal use of transformers because of their weight and size.

THE DOPPLER EFFECT

What is the **Doppler Effect**?

The Doppler Effect is the change in frequency of a wave that results from an object's changing position relative to an observer. A well-known example of the Doppler Effect is when an ambulance zooms by you and makes a "wheee-yow" sound. The high-pitched "whee" is caused by sound waves that are bunched together because the ambulance is moving in the same direction as the emitting sound waves. The bunching together of sound waves creates an increase in the frequency and results in a higher-pitch sound. The low-pitched "yow" sound occurs when the vehicle moves away from the propagation of the sound wave. Since the ambulance moves away from the sound wave, the spacing between successive waves becomes greater. This decrease in the frequency of the sound wave results in a lower pitch.

Who was the **Doppler Effect** named after?

Johann Christian Doppler (1803–1853), the Austrian mathematician for whom the Doppler Effect is named, proposed in 1842 that the color of double stars rotating about each other would depend on whether the star was approaching or receding from Earth.

The effect was too small to be measured. But in 1845 Christophorus Henricus Diedericus Buys Ballot (1817–1890) set up an experiment using had two sets of trumpeters. One set remained at rest while the other was on an open railway car traveling at the then fantastic speed of 40 miles per hour. Although both sets of trumpeters played the same note, the change in tone was clearly heard. Doppler later extended his theory to the case when both sound source and observer were moving. French physicist Hippolyte Fizeau (1819–1896) later extended Doppler's theory to light.

What is the difference between a **red shift** and a **blue shift**?

The visible color spectrum ranges from the low-frequency red, orange, and yellow, to the higher-frequency green, blue, indigo, and violet. Astronomers observing the planets, stars, and galaxies use the Doppler Effect to measure the velocity at which objects are moving, rotating, or revolving. The faster the object is moving, the more the frequency is shifted. Most galaxies are moving away from us and their light is red-shifted. In general, the further away, the greater the red shift. Recently astronomers have detected more than 400 planets revolving about other stars using the Doppler Effect. The gravitational force of the planet on the star causes the planet and star each to circle around a common point, usually close to, but not in the center of, the star. As a result the star "wobbles" with the same period as the orbital period of the planet.

The effect is truly tiny. Jupiter causes the sun to wobble in a circle with a speed of 12 meters per second. By measuring the Doppler Effect in the light from the star they can find its velocity and how it changes over time. With that information they can determine the period, distance from the star, and mass of the planet. Most discoveries have been of extremely massive planets, but recently a planet with a mass only a few times that of Earth was detected. It is close to a dim reddish star and the temperature of its surface is estimated to be tens of degrees below the freezing point of water. If the planet has greenhouse warming it might be able to sustain life.

What does the fact that most **galaxies** are seen with a **red shift** mean to **astronomers**?

The fact that astronomers observe most of the galaxies in the universe as having a red shift means that overall, galaxies are moving away from our galaxy, the Milky Way. This can only be happening if the universe as a whole is expanding. The expansion of the universe led to the development of the big bang theory of the universe's creation.

How do the **police** use the **Doppler Effect** in **radar guns**?

The police use the Doppler Effect when checking for speeding vehicles. A radar gun sends out radar waves at a particular frequency. As the radar wave hits a vehicle, the

wave reflects back toward the radar gun at a different frequency. The frequency of the reflected wave depends upon the direction and speed of the vehicle. The faster the speed, the greater the frequency change. The radar gun determines the speed of the vehicle by measuring the difference between the emitted frequency and the reflected frequency and computing the speed from that measurement.

Radar guns used by police to monitor traffic speeds work by taking advantage of the Doppler Effect.

RADAR

What is **radar**?

Radar is an acronym for "RAdio Detection And Ranging." A radar installation emits electromagnetic waves and detects the waves reflected from an object. It measures the time for the "echo" to return to find the distance of the object. The radar dish is constantly rotating, permitting it to find the direction of the object as well. Radar is used in many different arenas, but was first used in World War II to detect the approach of enemy bombers.

Who developed **radar**?

Radar was developed independently in many countries in the 1930s. But, in 1935, Robert Watson-Watt (1892–1973), a Scottish physicist, was the leader of a group that created the first radar defense system for the British military. Although a large number of nations, from the United States and Canada, to Britain, France, and Germany, to the Soviet Union and Japan, worked to develop radar systems during the 1930s, the British system of ground-based radar stations were the first to use radar effectively in warfare. By the early 1940s radar systems were miniaturized enough to be installed in aircraft so that they could engage other aircraft in fights at night.

Ironically, Watson-Watt became a deserving victim of his own technology nineteen years later. According to Canadian police, Watson-Watt had been speeding on a stretch of Canadian road, and was detected by a police radar gun. Watson-Watt willingly paid the fine and drove away.

What is a **stealth plane**?

Stealth aircraft are planes that are able to avoid radar detection. The materials on the plane's surfaces and their peculiar shapes and angles deflect radar waves away from

493

the plane, or in some instances, the plane's outer fuselage can actually absorb the radar waves without reflecting it back to the enemy radar transmitter. (Refer to the Fluids chapter for more information about aerodynamics and aviation.)

How has **radar** been used in **astronomy**?

In radar astronomy electromagnetic waves are aimed at planets. By analyzing the reflected signals, the position, velocity, and shape of objects in our solar system can be determined. In the early 1960s, radar was used to determine the exact distance between Earth and Venus and Earth and Jupiter. Later, radar was installed on the space probe *Magellan* to map the surface of Venus. Radar astronomy has been beneficial in determining distances in our own solar system, but the reflected signals would be much too weak from objects outside our solar system.

NEXRAD DOPPLER RADAR

What is **NEXRAD** Doppler radar?

NEXRAD, or next-generation weather radar, is one of the most recent technological breakthroughs for weather forecasting. NEXRAD relies on the Doppler Effect to calculate the position and the velocity of precipitation. The spherical NEXRAD radar tower emits radar waves 360° around and calculates the frequency shift of the reflected radar waves off rain, sleet, and snow. The NEXRAD computers then translate the information and represent the possible weather problems on a color-coded map for analysis. The maps are readily available in real time over the Web.

The goal and main function of NEXRAD precision radar is to save American money and lives by predicting threatening weather problems and warning the public

before tragedy strikes. Meteorologists estimate that this new tool for weather forecasting has saved millions of dollars and many lives through its early warning systems. One of the most impressive advancements has been in pinpointing tornadoes and hurricanes more accurately than what was possible before NEXRAD.

Each NEXRAD station scans a radius of 125 miles with excellent accuracy, and less accurately up to 200 miles. A new system, developed since 1994, is Terminal Doppler Weather Radar, or TDWR. This system, installed at 45 airports, uses radar waves with 5-centimeter wavelength rather than the 10 centimeters (3.9 inches) used in standard weather radar. As a result it can resolve objects with twice as much detail, permitting it to detect wind shear and microbursts. Its range, however, is half that of NEXRAD and it can't see through heavy rain. Radar images are available to the public at www.radar.weather.gov.

RADIO ASTRONOMY

How is **radio astronomy different** from **radar astronomy**?

Radar astronomy measures the reflections of transmitted radio waves to determine an object's size, position, velocity, and surface characteristics. Radio astronomy is like optical astronomy but it uses the VHF, UHF, and microwave portions of the electromagnetic spectrum rather than the infrared and visible portions. Radio waves penetrate the dust that hides the centers of galaxies and obscures regions where stars are forming. They can also detect hydrogen gas that constitutes 85% of the known mass of the universe.

What do **radio astronomers hear**?

Radio astronomers detect what sounds like noise, but is actually signals from atoms, molecules, and ions in stars, galaxies, and particles in interstellar and intergalactic space. In order to detect these signals, radio telescopes are used. These are shaped like large satellite dishes, and are able to detect wavelengths between 1 millimeter and 1 kilometer.

Where is the **largest radio telescope**?

The largest single radio telescope is the 305-meter (1,000-foot) diameter Arecibo Telescope, located in Puerto Rico. The reflecting dish, made of 40,000 perforated aluminum panels, is located in a mountain valley. The actual antennas are in a 900-ton platform, suspended on cables 137 meters (450 feet) above the dish. The antennas, sensitive to frequencies from 50 MHz to 10 GHz, detect signals collected by and reflected from the dish, and can be moved to determine the direction from which the signals are coming. Arecibo also performs radar astronomy using a 1 megawatt radar transmitter to send signals to the other planets. The telescope then detects the faint echos.

Highly sensitive telescope arrays like this one are used by radio astronomers to detect signals created by atoms, molecules, and ions from space.

How are **radio telescope arrays** used?

A group of 27 radio telescopes, each 25 meters (82 feet) in diameter, spaced as much as 13 miles apart from each other in Socorro, New Mexico, is known as the Very Large Array (VLA). The signals from this group of radio telescopes are combined by a computer. Constructive and destructive interference between the signals allows the array to make very accurate measurements of the location and size of objects.

Larger still are Very Long Baseline Interferometry radio telescopes. These radio telescopes are located around the world. Cables can't be used to combine the signals, so each telescope needs a very precise clock to determine the arrival time of the signals. Hydrogen masers, whose frequency is stable one part in a million billion, are used. Again, although the signal strength is small, the wide spacing increases the effectiveness of using interference to measure very fine details of the shape, size, and location of stars and galaxies.

SOUND

What is the **source** of every **sound**?

Sound waves are created by some type of mechanical vibration or oscillation that forces the surrounding medium to vibrate. A tuning fork is an excellent example of a vibrating sound source. When struck by a rubber mallet, the tines of the tuning fork vibrate, causing the air molecules around them to move back and forth at the same frequency, creating areas of compressions (where the molecules are close together and air pressure is slightly increased) and rarefactions (where the molecules are spread apart and thus the air pressure is reduced). These pressure changes then move away from the tines creating the longitudinal sound wave.

What **type of wave** is a **sound** wave?

A wave that consists of compressions and rarefactions—such as a sound wave—is called a longitudinal wave. The medium, the material through which the wave is traveling, does not get transferred from sender to receiver; the molecules only vibrate back and forth about a fixed position. The wave does, however, carry energy from its source to the receiver.

SPEED OF SOUND

How **fast** does **sound** travel?

Light travels almost one million times faster than sound—specifically, 880,000 times the speed of sound. Light and all electromagnetic waves travel at a speed of 3×10^8 meters per second, while the speed of sound is only about 340 meters per second or 760 miles per hour on a typical spring day.

Can sound take the ocean's temperature?

Between 1995 and 1999 the ATOC, or Acoustical Thermometry of Ocean Climate, experiments measured the speed of sound in the Pacific Ocean. Sound sources at 75 hertz were located off the California coast and near the island of Kuaui in Hawaii. Detectors were positioned at various depths off the coast of Alaska, near the Big Island of Hawaii, near Kamchatka, Russia, and New Zealand. The waves took up to an hour to travel these large distances and the system was able to find the time of travel to under 0.02 seconds, so extremely accurate measurements of the speed of sound could be made. The speed of sound in saltwater depends only slightly on the degree of salinity, but increases 6.4 meters per second for every degree Celsius increase in temperature. They were able to measure the water temperature to within 0.01°F.

The speed of sound compared to the speed of light can be observed at a baseball game. A spectator sitting in the outfield bleachers sees the batter hit a ball before she hears the crack of the bat.

Who determined that **sound needs** a **medium** through which to travel?

In the 1660s, English scientist Robert Boyle (1627–1691) proved that sound waves need to travel through a medium in order to transmit sound. Boyle placed a bell inside a vacuum and showed that as the air was evacuated from the chamber, the sound of the bell became softer and softer, until there was no sound.

What did **Newton** add to the knowledge of **sound media**?

Although he mainly concentrated on classical mechanics and the principles of geometric optics, Isaac Newton (1642–1727) did make several important discoveries in the field of sound. His major contribution was his work on sound wave propagation. He showed that the velocity of sound through any medium depended upon the characteristics of that particular medium. Specifically, Newton demonstrated that the elasticity and the density of the medium determined how fast a sound wave would travel. Because Newton worked before the field of thermal physics was developed, his theory has errors, but they are not significant to the calculation of sound speed.

How **fast** does **sound travel** in **different media**?

A simple model that explains the main factors affecting the speed of sound is a collection of balls (molecules) connected to each other by springs (bonds between molecules). Vibration from one ball will be transferred by the springs to neighboring balls,

and in succession throughout the collection. The stiffer the springs and the lighter the balls, the faster the vibrations will be transferred. The springs are a model of the *bulk elasticity* (how the volume changes when the pressure on it changes) of the material, the balls and their spacing model the density of the material. In general, the speed is slowest in gases, fastest in solids. Even though liquids and solids are about 1,000 times denser than gases, the greater elasticity of liquids and solids more than compensates for the larger density. In gases the speed depends on the kind of molecule and temperature. For air, the speed depends only on temperature. The following table illustrates some examples of the speed of sound in different media.

Medium	Speed (m/s)
Air (0°C)	331
Air (20°C)	343
Air (100°C)	366
Helium (0°C)	965
Mercury	1,452
Water (20°C)	1,482
Lead	1,960
Wood (oak)	3,850
Iron	5,000
Copper	5,010
Glass	5,640
Steel	5,960

What is the **sound barrier**?

The sound barrier is the speed that an object must travel to exceed the speed of sound. The speed of sound is often used as a reference with which to measure the velocity of an aircraft. The speed of sound, 331 meters per second at 0°C, is Mach 1. Twice the speed of sound is Mach 2, three times the speed of sound is Mach 3, and so on.

What is a **sonic boom**?

A sonic boom occurs when an object travels faster than the speed of sound. The boom itself is caused by an object, such as a supersonic airplane, traveling faster than the sound waves themselves can travel. The sound waves pile up on one another, creating a shock wave that travels through the atmosphere, resulting in a "boom" when it strikes a person's ears. A sonic boom is not a momentary event that occurs as the plane breaks the sound barrier; rather, it is a continuous sound caused by a plane as it travels at such a speed, but the shock wave travels with the plane, so we hear it only when the plane is in one location.

Supersonic planes, such as this F-15 fighter jet, can go beyond Mach 1. When they do, they generate a "sonic boom" caused by sound waves piling up and creating a shock wave.

All objects that exceed the speed of sound create sonic booms. For example, missiles and bullets, which travel faster than the sound barrier, produce sonic booms as they move through the atmosphere. The shockwave created by an F-15 fighter plane, for instance, is visible.

Does **sound travel faster** on a **hot** or **cold day**?

Air molecules move faster in hot and humid environments due to their increased thermal energy. Since sound relies on molecules bumping into one another to create compressions and rarefactions, increased speed of molecules makes the sound waves move faster. The speed of sound increases by 0.6 meters per second for every degree Celsius increase in temperature. Water vapor in the air also increases the speed of sound because water molecules are lighter than oxygen and nitrogen molecules. Therefore, on hot and humid days, sound travels faster than on cool, dry days.

The following formula gives the speed of sound in air: Speed of Sound = (331 m/s) (1 + 0.6 T) where temperature, T, is measured in Celsius.

How **far away** was that **lightning**?

When a lightning bolt goes from cloud-to-cloud or cloud-to-ground it suddenly heats the air through which it passes. This sudden increase in temperature causes thunder that occurs at the same time as the lightning. Although it takes virtually no time to see the lightning, depending upon the observer's distance from the lightning, it can take quite a while to hear the thunder.

The speed of sound at room temperature is about 1,100 feet per second. A mile is 5,280 feet, so it takes about five seconds for sound to travel one mile. So, to determine how far away lightning has struck, when you see the lightning, count the number of seconds it takes before hearing thunder. Divide the number of seconds between the lightning and thunder by five to determine how many miles away the thunder and lightning occurred. For example, if you see a flash of lightning and approximately 10 seconds later you hear the thunder, divide the 10 seconds by the 5 seconds per mile to find that the lightning occurred 2 miles away.

HEARING

How does a person **hear sound**?

The ear is the organ used to detect sound in humans and some animals. The ear consists of three major sections: the outer ear, middle ear, and inner ear. The outer ear, the external section of the ear, consists of a cartilage flap called the pinna. The pinna's size and shape forms a transformer to match the impedance of the sound wave in air to that at the end of the ear canal by gradually funneling the wave's sound energy into the ear. To hear more sound, people can increase the size of the pinna by cupping their hand around the back of the pinna—in effect, increasing its size and funneling capabilities.

Once the sound has entered the ear canal, it moves toward the eardrum, where the longitudinal waves cause the eardrum to move in and out depending upon the frequency and amplitude of the wave. The middle ear includes the eardrum, the hammer, anvil, and stirrup, the three smallest bones in the human body, and the oval window on the inner ear. The eardrum is 17 times larger than the oval window, and this difference in area makes the inner ear act like a hydraulic machine, increasing the changes in pressure on the eardrum to that on the oval window at least seventeen-fold. The three bones link the eardrum to the oval window. They act like a lever system to further increase pressure on the oval window. The mechanical advantage of the lever system varies with frequency, peaking at about 5 in the 1 to 2 kilohertz frequency range. Thus the middle ear is like a complex machine that can amplify the pressure on the eardrum by a factor approaching 100 as it transfers the energy of the sound wave to the inner ear. Muscles connected to the eardrum and the three bones can react to very loud sounds and reduce the sensitivity of the ear, thus protecting it from damage.

The inner ear is a series of tubes and passageways in the bony skull. It consists of the cochlea, a spiral-shaped tube that changes the longitudinal sound wave into an electrical signal on the nerves connecting the ear to the brain. The inner ear also has three semicircular canals that sense the body's motions and give rise to a sense of balance. The oval window is at one end of the cochlea. Sound waves transmitted through the middle ear to the oval window cause a traveling wave in the fluid of the cochlea. This wave in one of the three tubes within the cochlea, the Organ of Corti, causes hair cells, called cilia, to tilt back and forth. The tilting causes chemicals to pass through channels in the nerve, creating electrical impulses that travel along the auditory nerve to the brain for analysis. The further the hair cells are from the oval window, the lower the sound frequency to which they are sensitive. Thus different nerves are excited by different frequencies, allowing the ear to distinguish the sounds' frequencies.

What are the **frequency limits** of the **human ear**?

The ear allows humans to hear frequency ranges between 20 hertz and 20,000 hertz, but it is most sensitive to frequencies between 200 hertz and 2,000 hertz.

501

The lower and upper fringes of this bandwidth can be difficult to hear, but many people—especially younger people—can hear these frequencies quite well. As people age their sensitivity to high frequencies diminishes. Damage to the hair cells caused by exposure to loud sounds also reduces the ear's sensitivity to high frequencies.

What are the **bandwidths** of hearing for **other animals**?

Animal	Lowest Frequency	Highest Frequency
Human	20 Hz	20,000 Hz
Dog	20 Hz	40,000 Hz
Cat	80 Hz	60,000 Hz
Bat	10 Hz	110,000 Hz
Dolphin	110 Hz	130,000 Hz

ULTRASONICS AND INFRASONICS

What are **ultrasonic sounds**?

Ultrasonic sounds are those frequencies above human hearing. Frequencies above 20,000 Hz are not heard by people, but are heard by those animals whose hearing is sensitive to ultrasonic frequencies. For example, dolphins use ultrasonic frequencies to communicate and bats use ultrasonic sounds as a tool for navigation and hunting.

What is **ultrasound**?

Ultrasound is a method of looking inside a person's body to examine tissue-based and liquid-based organs and systems without physically entering the body. Ultrasound sys-

Dolphins can detect frequencies of between 110 and 130,000 Hertz. Their hearing is over six times more sensitive than that of a human being.

tems direct high-frequency sound (usually between 5 and 7 megahertz) into particular regions of the body, and measure the time it takes for the sound wave to reflect back to the machine. By analyzing the pattern of reflections received, a computer can create a visual representation of the interior of the body.

Ultrasound is sometimes used instead of X rays because it does not use ionizing radiation and thus is safer for the person being examined. Obstetricians use ultrasound to examine the progress and/or problems that a fetus might be experiencing. Ultrasound is also used to observe different fluid-like organs and systems in the body such as the nervous, circulatory, urinary, and reproductive systems.

Ultrasound can also be used to pulverize kidney "stones." In this application very intense, tightly focused beams of high-frequency sound are directed at the stone. The stones are shattered and the small pieces can be passed through the urinary track with little or no pain.

What is **sonar**?

Sonar, an acronym for "SOund NAvigation Ranging," is a method of using sound waves to determine the distance an object is from a transmitter of sound. The sonar contains a transducer that converts an electrical impulse to sound when it transmits and a sound wave to an electrical impulse when it receives. Sound waves, usually brief pulses of ultrasound, are emitted from the transducer, reflected off an object, and

503

Tornadoes generate subsonic sounds that cannot be heard by humans but *can* be detected by instruments that can then be used to warn people up to a hundred miles away of approaching danger.

reflected back to the transducer. Electronic circuits measuree the length of time it took for the sound waves' round trip, and use the speed of sound to calculate the distance the object is from the transducer.

Sonar is used predominantly as a navigational tool by humans and animals. Dolphins and bats, among other animals, use sonar for navigation, hunting, and communicating. Machines such as depth-finders on boats, distance meters used in real estate and construction, and motion detectors for security devices all employ sonar.

What is **infrasound**?

Whereas ultrasonic sounds are frequencies above the human bandwidth of hearing, infrasonic (or "subsonic") sounds are those frequencies below the human bandwidth of hearing, or 20 hertz. Infrasounds as low in frequency as 0.001 hertz are produced by a variety of natural sources like earthquakes and volcanoes, as well as man-made structures and nuclear explosions. Elephants are known to make sounds as low as 12 hertz, and can communicate in this way over large distances.

How can **infrasonic sounds** provide **early warning** of **tornadoes**?

Using sound sensors that detect infrasound, scientists discovered quite by accident that the spinning core or vortex of a tornado produces sounds that are a few hertz

below the human bandwidth of hearing. The tornado, much like an organ pipe, produces low frequencies when the vortices are large, and higher frequencies when the vortices are small. Since the infrasound waves from tornadoes can be detected for up to 100 miles away, they could help increase the warning time for tornado strikes.

INTENSITY OF SOUND

What is **sound intensity**?

Sound intensity is the power in the sound wave divided by the area it covers. Power is energy per unit time, so the intensity is the wave energy passing through a surface point divided by the time taken. The energy transferred by the wave is proportional to the square of the amplitude of the wave. In the case of sound the amplitude is the amount the peak pressure in compression is greater than the average pressure.

Why does **sound diminish** as you move **farther** from the source?

Sound waves do not travel in a narrow path, but spread out into the surrounding medium as spherical waves. As long as the energy in the sound doesn't change, the power per unit area decreases as the area increases. In some cases, there is some transfer of the sound's energy into thermal energy of the medium. Thus, there can be some loss of sound energy with distance, but this loss is usually small.

How much does a **sound's intensity diminish** as you move away?

When the total energy in the sound wave remains the same as the sound spreads over a sphere the intensity decreases as the area of the sphere increases. The area of a sphere is proportional to the square of its radius, so the intensity is inversely proportional to the square of the distance. That is, sound intensity diminishes according to the inverse square law. For example, if a person stands 1 meter (3.3 feet) away from a source, the sound intensity might be an arbitrary unit of 1. If that same person moved so she was 2 meters (6.6 feet) away from the source, the intensity would be 1 over the square of the distance, or one fourth the intensity. Again, if the listener moved 3 meters (9.8 feet) away, the intensity would be one ninth it was at the 1-meter mark.

Does **sound's intensity** always follow the **inverse-square law**?

Sound doesn't always spread uniformly. You may have experienced this if you shout while you walk through a tunnel. You hear echoes and a person at another part of the tunnel will hear you much more clearly than he or she would in an open area. Whis-

pering chambers are often found in science museums. They are rooms with walls in an elliptical shape. If you stand at one focus of the ellipse and another person stands at the other focus you can hear each other speak even if you whisper while other people in the chamber are talking loudly. Sound can also be transported through the ocean with less spreading using an acoustic waveguide, similar to the way light can travel in an optical fiber (see the chapter on Light). The ocean water can separate into layers at different temperatures. The speed of sound depends on water temperature, and if there is a layer of cold water where sound speed is lower under a layer of warmer water where the speed is higher, then some of the sound moving through the cold layer will be reflected at the boundary back into the cold layer, keeping it from spreading. The name of this channel is SOund Frequency And Ranging (SOFAR) Channel. It is 100 to 200 meters below the surface in the cold waters off Alaska but 750 to 1,000 meters deep in the warmer Hawaiian waters.

What is a **decibel**?

A decibel (dB) is the internationally adopted unit for the relative intensity of sound. The sound intensity of 0 decibel is the threshold of human hearing, 10^{-16} watts/cm^2. This corresponds to a pressure of 2×10^{-5} newtons/m^2 or 2 billionths of atmospheric pressure. The ear is extremely sensitive! The decibel scale is a logarithmic scale, meaning for every 10 decibels, the intensity is increased by a factor of ten. For example, a change from 30 decibels to 40 decibels means the sound will be ten times more intense. A change from 30 decibels to 50 decibels would mean the new sound would be one hundred times more intense.

The following chart shows a typical sound environment, how many times louder those levels are than the threshold of human hearing, and the relative intensity of that sound compared to the threshold of hearing.

Sound	Times More Intencse	Relative Intensity (dB)
Loss of hearing	1×10^{15}	150
Rocket launch	1×10^{14}	140
Jet engine 50 meters away	1×10^{13}	130
Threshold of pain	1×10^{12}	120
Rock concert	1×10^{11}	110
Lawnmower	1×10^{10}	100
Factory	1×10^9	90
Motorcycle	1×10^8	80
Automobiles driving by	1×10^7	70
Vacuum cleaner	1,000,000	60
Normal speech	100,000	50
Library	10,000	40

Why do people hear ringing after leaving a loud rock concert?

After leaving loud rock concerts, many concert-goers often complain of ringing in their ears. The ringing sound is a result of the damage to the cilia by the intense sounds. Usually the ringing is gone the day after the concert, but permanent damage has already been done, because those hair cells will not recover. Although the effects of such hearing loss may take many years and repeated exposure to loud sounds to become apparent, they can nonetheless become very devastating.

Sound	Times More Intense	Relative Intensity (dB)
Close whisper	1,000	30
Leaves rustling in the wind	100	20
Breathing/whisper 5 meters away	10	10
Threshold of hearing	0	0

Are there **federal standards** for using **hearing protection**?

Federal regulations mandating the use of hearing protection in the workplace state that if an employee works for eight hours in an environment in which the average noise level is above 90 decibels, the employer is required to provide free hearing protection to those employees. For example, many high school and college students work for landscapers in the summer. Since the average decibel level for a lawnmower is about 100 decibels, and if the employees are working for eight or more hours per day, free ear plugs or ear muffs must be provided to the employees.

What is the **maximum decibel level** that a person can experience **without pain**?

The threshold of pain for humans depends on the person in question, but typically ranges between 120 decibels and 130 decibels. Such pain can be experienced at extremely loud rock concerts and next to jet engines and jackhammers, for example.

What are the best ways to **protect** one's hearing at **loud rock concerts**?

The first protection against damage to the cilia is to increase the distance from your ears to the speakers. In plain English, the farther away one is from the speakers, the lower the intensity of the sound. By simply doubling the distance, the intensity becomes one fourth of what it was originally. That can work in open areas where the

Loud music from live concerts can cause hearing loss over time by damaging the cilia within the ear. Standing or sitting farther back from speakers can help prevent harm, while musicians themselves often wear earplugs.

sound can spread, but in arenas or halls the sound can reflect off the ceilings and walls and does not decrease with distance.

The second method of protecting one's ears is to dampen the sound waves as they enter the ear. Many musicians, both rock and classical, to avoid gradual hearing loss, now use earplugs to decrease the amplitude of the wave entering the ear. The fluid in the cochlea transfers less energy to the cilia than if the listener were wearing no hearing protection.

What is the **difference** between **loudness** and **sound intensity**?

Sound intensity is a physical property that depends on energy. Loudness describes how a listener responds to sounds and is subjective. The ear doesn't respond equally to all frequencies, even between 20 hertz and 20 kilohertz. So, a sound with an intensity of 60 decibels will sound louder at some frequencies than others. The ear is most sensitive to frequencies between 1 kilohertz and 3 kilohertz and its sensitivity is much less for both low (20-100 hertz) and high (10-20 kilohertz). As people age their ears respond less to all frequencies, but especially frequencies above 5 kilohertz. Loudness also depends on the type of tone, whether a very pure tone, a more complex tone, or noise.

Loudness doubles for each 10-dB increase in sound intensity. It is measured in sones. Normal talking, which is between 40 and 60 dB has a loudness of 1 to 4 sones. Hearing damage from sustained sound, 90 dB, is 32 sones.

ACOUSTICS

What is **acoustics**?

Acoustics is the branch of physics that deals with the science of sound. Although sound has been studied since Galileo (1564–1642) made some predictions in the early 1600s, the ability to study sound has grown tremendously in the past few decades because of the advent of electronic sound generators and measuring devices. In addition to the study of sound itself, the field of acoustics has several applied sub-fields, the most important being speech and hearing, architectural acoustics, and musical acoustics.

What is **architectural acoustics**?

Theaters, concert halls, churches, classrooms, and sound-proof rooms have to be designed and constructed so that their acoustic properties match their uses. In some spaces it is important that the speaker, singer, or musician or group be heard clearly in all parts of the room. A good concert hall has intimacy— music should sound as if it were being played in a small hall. It should have liveness and warmth—fullness of bass tones. The sound should be clear, and the audience should be able to locate the source of the sound. The sound should be uniform over the entire hall, and sounds from the stage should be blended by the time they are heard by the audience. Finally, the hall should be free of noise, from air handling systems as well as outside sounds.

In order to achieve these goals an acoustical engineer must consider not only the size and shape of the hall, but also the acoustic properties of materials used on the floors, ceilings, and walls of the room, as well as chairs and other objects in the room. Even the audience and air humidity affect the acoustic properties of the room! In general hard surfaces such as concrete, plaster, wood, and tile reflect sound while soft materials like carpet, heavy drapes, and plush upholstered chairs absorb sound. Room shapes and sizes that create standing waves should be avoided because sound at frequencies at which the standing waves occur will not be uniform. They will be loud in some places, soft in others.

What is **reverberation time**?

The reverberation time for a sound is the time it takes for the echoing sound to diminish by a factor of 60 decibels, that is, to 1/1,000,000th of its original intensity. The longer the reverberation time, the more echoing is heard because the sound has reflected off walls and other surfaces. The shorter the reverberation time, the less echo is heard.

What **role** does **reverberation time** play in **acoustics**?

Reverberation time plays a major role in the quality of sound heard in a concert hall. Acoustical engineers carefully design concert halls to achieve a typical reverberation time between one and two seconds. Rooms designed for speech should have reverbera-

Sound-absorbing foam panels with bumpy surfaces are commonly used in recording studios to reduce echo.

tion times less than one second, movie theaters a little over one second, and rooms designed for organ music have as much as two seconds. If the reverberation time for middle and high notes is too short, the sound will diminish almost instantaneously and the room will sound "dry." A "full" bass tone requires a longer reverberation time for low notes. If the reverberation time is too long, however, as it is in many gymnasiums, the echoing effects will interfere with the new sounds, making music sound "mushy" and words of a speaker difficult to understand.

What determines the **amount** of **reflection** or **absorption**?

A good absorber of sound matches the impedance of sound waves between air and the new medium, while a poor absorber has a very different impedance and reflects the sound back into the environment. Typical absorbers have an open structure with holes of various sizes into which the sound waves can penetrate and transfer their energy to thermal energy of the material.

What **materials** are **effective absorbers** of **sound**?

Different materials will absorb certain frequencies of sound better than other frequencies, but some of the best absorbers of sound are soft objects. Materials such as felt, carpeting, drapes, foam, and cork are good at matching the impedance of a sound wave and reflecting back very little sound. Materials such as concrete, brick, ceramic tile, and metals, on the other hand, are effective reflecting materials of sound. That is why gymnasiums (with hardwood floors, concrete walls, and metal ceilings) have relatively long reverberation times, while concert halls furnished with upholstered seats, carpeted floors, and long drapes have relatively short reverberation times. People are also effective sound absorbers, so a full concert hall has different acoustic properties than an empty one.

What is the **optimal shape** of a **concert hall**?

Building a concert hall is a mixture of science, engineering, art, and politics. Politics is important because the people who provide the funds have goals for the use of the

What was the first concert hall to be designed by an acoustical physicist?

Boston Symphony Hall, designed by physicist Wallace Clement Sabine (1868–1919), is the first concert hall designed specifically to enhance the sound of an orchestra. Sabine, who designed the hall in the late 1890s, discovered the relationship between sound intensity, absorption, and reverberation time. Sound reflections can either enhance or ruin a sound. Sabine discovered that having strong reflections immediately after a sound was produced would enhance the acoustics, but if sound was reflected midway between the source and the listener it would detract from the acoustics because the time of travel would be significantly different.

Sabine's Boston Symphony Hall, built in 1900, established an excellent reputation for sound quality, mostly due to the choices of sound absorption materials as well as the strategic placement of reflecting material. The goal was to use the sound reflecting materials (high percent reflection ratios) to create strong initial reflections, while using sound absorbing materials (low percent reflection ratios) to absorb most of the energy from sound that would ordinarily reflect off of the high ceiling and the side walls in the rear of the hall.

hall. Consider, for example, the history of Philharmonic Hall in Lincoln Center, New York City. It was originally designed to be similar to the Boston Symphony Hall—long and narrow. But, a campaign led by one of the major newspapers in the city argued that the hall should seat more than 2,400 people, and so the architects made the hall wider. But when it was completed in 1962 critics were very unhappy with the sound. The wider hall did not have enough initial reflections and sounded dry. It was equipped with "clouds," reflectors hung from the ceiling, but reflections from them were too delayed to be effective. Another problem was that performers on the stage couldn't hear each other.

In 1973 Mr. Avery Fischer contributed over $10 million to support a complete reconstruction of the hall, and the hall is now named after him. The changes improved the acoustics, but the large stage reduced the loudness of bass sounds and the initial reflections were still too strong. Curved surfaces on the stage made of extremely tight-grain maple wood have improved bass problem, and reflectors consisting of 30,000 dowel rods were installed on the side walls.

Except for classical music concerts and opera, most performances use electronic amplification. Loud speakers can be located throughout the hall, and their response to different frequencies can be adjusted to compensate for shortcomings in the hall. The signal to speakers far from the stage can be delayed so sound from all speakers arrives

at the same time. Further, these changes can be adjusted so that the hall has the best acoustics for any type of use.

MUSICAL ACOUSTICS

What is the **difference** between **pitch** and **frequency**?

Frequency, like sound intensity, is a physical property. Pitch, like loudness, is a description of how the ear and brain interpret the sound. Pitch is primarily dependent on frequency, but depends somewhat on loudness, timbre, and envelope, which will be discussed below. Humans hear pitch in terms of the ratio of two tones. The ear perceives two notes to be equally spaced if the they are related by a multiplicative factor. For example, the frequency of corresponding notes of adjacent octaves differ by a factor of 2. Notes in common chords are related by ratios of 3:2, 4:3, 5:4, etc. In the same way, the perceived difference in pitch between 100 hertz and 150 hertz is the same as between 1,000 hertz and 1,500 hertz.

Does a **musical tone** have a **single frequency**?

It does not have a single frequency, but many. To understand why, consider a stringed instrument like a guitar, piano, or violin. The string can oscillate in response to it being plucked, hit, or bowed. Standing waves will be formed as they would be if you shook a rope back and forth. By shaking it at different frequencies you can make it oscillate in several different modes. The lowest frequency results in nodes only at the ends. Twice this frequency produces nodes at the ends plus one in the middle. Three times the lowest frequency give nodes at the ends plus two nodes at 1/3 and 2/3 its length.

If you pluck, hit, or bow the string of a stringed instrument you cause it to vibrate in many of those nodes at the same time, depending on the location you plucked it. The lowest frequency of oscillation is called the fundamental frequency. Plucking the string 1/4 from one end results in oscillations at 2, 3, 4, 6, and 7 times the fundamental frequency. The higher frequencies are called harmonics. For example, if the fundamental frequency were middle C, 256 hertz, then the second harmonic would have a frequency of 512 hertz, the third 728 hertz, the fourth 1,024 hertz, etc.

The sound made by the vibrating string is very weak. On acoustic stringed instruments the strings pass over the bridge that transmits the oscillations to the top plate of the body of the instrument. Low frequency sounds also excite oscillations in the air and in the bottom plate of the guitar's body. Sounds from the oscillations of the air pass through the sound holes in the top plate into the surrounding air. The amplitude of the fundamental frequency is the largest. The relative amplitudes of the higher harmonics depend not only on the string, but the shape and size of the body of the instrument. Electric guitars will be discussed in the chapter on Magnetism.

The relative intensities of the higher harmonics depend on the instrument. The sound spectrum produced by the instrument is characterized by these relative amplitudes. The spectrum is also called the quality of sound, or the timbre. The sound quality also depends on how the sound starts and stops.

How do **wind instruments** like flutes, saxophones, and trumpets **produce sounds**?

In wind instruments the column of air is the oscillating object. The musician must create the oscillation. Perhaps you have blown over the top of a soda bottle and created a tone. When you blow some of the air goes into the bottle. That increased air pressure is reflected off the bottom of the bottle and returns to the top where it deflects the blown air upward. This process repeats, resulting in a tone whose frequency depends on the length of the bottle. The energy in your breath is converted into the energy of oscillation of the air in the bottle.

A flute works in a similar way, where the player blows over a hole in the side of the flute. The other end of the flute is open. The sound wave is reflected because the impedance in the tube is different from that of the room air. The spectrum of a flute contains all harmonics. If the player blows harder and changes the location of her top lip she can make the flute play one or two octaves higher. In other words, the fundamental frequency of the flute is increased by a factor of two or four.

The frequency of a flute or other woodwind instrument can be changed by opening holes along the side of the instrument. This shortens the length of the oscillating air column, increasing the frequency.

In a saxophone or clarinet the vibrations are caused by a thin piece of wood called the reed. The player blows through a gap between the reed and the instrument's mouthpiece. The pulse of air is reflected off the end of the instrument and returns to the reed, pushing it open to admit another pulse of air. Double-reed instruments like the oboe and bassoon work in the same way. The clarinet is shaped like a cylinder. Its spectrum consists of only the odd harmonics: 1, 3, 5, and 7, etc. A clarinet can be played in a higher register by opening a small hole near the mouthpiece that strongly reduces the amplitude of the fundamental tone. The new pitch is an octave and a fourth higher than the lower register. Saxophones are not shaped like cylinders, but like cones. As a result all harmonics are included in its spectrum, and opening the register key raises the instrument's pitch by one octave.

In a bugle, trumpet, trombone, French horn, or other brass instrument the oscillations are caused by the player's lips. The lips act as a valve, causing pulses of air into the instrument, which causes the oscillations in the air column. In a brass instrument the fundamental tone is absent. By adjusting the tightness of the lips the player can cause the instrument to play at the 2nd, 3rd, 4th harmonic, etc. The valves on a brass instrument add small lengths of tubing, lowering the pitch. In a trombone the length

of the tube can be varied continuously, allowing any frequency to be played. The spectrum of a brass instrument depends strongly on its pitch and loudness. The louder it is played, the more energy there is in the higher harmonics.

How does a **synthesizer imitate** any **musical instrument**?

A synthesizer is an electronic device that generates, alters, and combines a variety of waveforms to produce complex sounds. Often a piano-type keyboard allows the musician to select the notes to be constructed. Synthesizers may use electronic circuits to create the tones or use software that controls a circuit that converts a digital number to a voltage. Some synthesizers use a computer rather than a keyboard to select the notes. The computer can then control electronic circuits through the MIDI interface. The most common method of creating the synthesized sounds is to use a frequency modulated synthesis that creates higher harmonics that match

Some synthesizers like this one use keyboards to select the sound to be generated, while others use computers. The ability of a synthesizer to immitate various instruments is accomplished using frequency modulated synthesis to create "voices."

those of the musical instrument being imitated, or create an entirely new musical sound. Instruments also have characteristic attacks, sustain times, and decays. Attack describes how fast the amplitude rises from zero to its full value. Sustain times describe how long the tone amplitude remains the same, and decay describes how the amplitude decreases at the end of the played note. Synthesizers can create hundreds of different sounds, typically called voices.

How is the **human voice similar** to a **wind instrument**?

The vibrating source of the human voice are the vocal cords in the throat. Their vibration, at a relatively low frequency of 125 hertz, creates oscillations in the air that fills the throat and mouth. By varying the size and shape of your mouth and position of the tongue you can change the frequency of the sound as well as the relative amplitude of the harmonics. Try it yourself! Sing a constant pitch, while you vocalize the vowel sounds—"a," "e," "i," "o," and "u." Note how you change the shape of your mouth and position of the tongue when you go from one vowel sound to another.

> ## Why does a singing duet sometimes sound as if there were a third voice contributing to the music?
>
> When two people sing loudly at slightly different pitches, the frequencies can mix, causing a difference tone, or third pitch. You may also experience this phenomenon with fire whistles blaring through a town, or even the beeps or tones emitted by a clock radio. In fact, many difference tones are intentionally created to enhance the sound.

What is the **difference** between an **overtone** and a **harmonic**?

A harmonic is a mode of vibration that is a whole-number multiple of the fundamental mode. The first harmonic is the fundamental frequency. The second harmonic is twice its frequency, etc. Many instruments, especially bells, oscillate in modes that are not whole-number multiples of the fundamental frequency. These higher modes are called overtones. Overtones include harmonics, but harmonics do not include overtones. Another confusing point is that the first overtone is not the fundamental. The second harmonic is the first overtone.

How does the **spectrum of a sound** relate to its **waveform**?

Jean-Baptist-Joseph Fourier (1768–1830), a French mathematician and physicist, made discoveries in a number of fields, including the greenhouse effect. He developed mathematical tools known as Fourier series and transforms that are used in a wide variety of applications. The Fourier Theorem states that any repetitive waveform can be constructed from a series of waves of specific frequencies, a fundamental and higher harmonics. The reverse is also true—if you add together waves of frequencies f, $2f$, $3f$, etc., specifying their amplitudes, you can construct a complex waveform. Using Fourier analysis, then you can record the waveform of a musical instrument and determine the amplitudes of the harmonics of which it is made, that is, its spectrum.

Today Fourier analysis is very easy to do. Most computers either have built in microphones or can use an external microphone. Free software can be downloaded from the web that will display the spectrum.

What are **difference tones**?

Difference tones are frequencies that are produced as a result of two different frequencies mixing with each other. This mixing can only occur if a device is non-linear. That is, if the output is not a multiple of the input. You can create difference tones with two toy slide whistles. Place both in your mouth and blow hard. Adjust their lengths so

that the two tones are the same pitch. Then adjust one. As you move its pitch away from the other you will hear a low-pitched sound whose pitch increases as the two whistles' pitches get further apart. For example, if the high-frequency sound was 812 hertz, while the lower frequency was 756 hertz, the difference tone from the interfering sound waves would be 144 hertz. The non-linear device in this case is your ear!

NOISE POLLUTION

Why is **noise pollution dangerous**?

In the past, noise pollution was only thought to create health effects if the intensity was large enough to cause hearing damage. Studies over the past several decades, however, have found that long-term exposure to noise can cause potentially severe health problems—in addition to hearing loss—especially for young children. Constant levels of noise (even at low levels) can be enough to cause stress, which can lead to high blood pressure, insomnia, psychiatric problems, and can even impact memory and thinking skills in children. In a German study, scientists found that children living near the Munich Airport had higher levels of stress, which impaired their ability to learn, while children living further from the airport did not seem to experience the same problem.

What **limits** have been **established** to **reduce exposure** to **noise pollution**?

The World Health Organization has recommended that noise during sleep be limited to a level of 35 decibels, and governments are beginning to place restrictions on noise levels in both residential and business environments. In the Netherlands, for example, regulations specify that new homes may not be built in areas of high noise levels—those that exceed average noise levels of 50 decibels. In the United States, employers must provide hearing protection for those who endure noise levels of 90 decibels for more than eight hours a day.

Does my neighbor's motorcycle have to be that loud?

At times, engineers try to achieve just the right sound or noise for a particular product. The product, whether it's a vacuum cleaner, lawnmower, or motorcycle, needs to be quiet enough so as not to cause stress, yet has to have enough sound to seem powerful. For example, muffler technology has the ability to greatly reduce the noise a motorcycle produces, yet many engineers and manufacturers feel that consumers would not purchase the product if it does not sound "powerful" enough. Hybrid automobiles are so quiet that people with limited sight have difficulties knowing that they are approaching. Engineers are developing noise generating devices for these cars to let sightless people know the location of the cars.

What **methods** are being **used** to **reduce noise pollution**?

Since noise creates stress and can lead to other health problems, industries and governments around the world are working to reduce noise levels, especially around populated regions. One method of reducing noise pollution around airports has been rerouting airline traffic so that it passes over less-populated areas. Sound barriers have been installed along many highways to absorb and/or reflect sound away from houses built alongside the roads. In countries such as Austria and Belgium, roadways are being constructed with a material called whisper concrete that engineers claim reduces noise by 5 decibels. Finally, Swedish engineers have developed a road surface made of pulverized rubber that can reduce the noise level by as much as 10 decibels.

What is **active noise cancellation**?

Active noise cancellation, or ANC, creates a waveform that is the opposite of the noise so that the noise is cancelled. An ANC headset consists of a one or two microphones that detect the noise, electronic circuits that invert the waveform, and a headphone driver. Low-frequency noise is more successfully cancelled than noise at higher frequencies, so passive noise reduction is used to reduce high-frequency noise. As a result, low-frequency noises found in helicopter, jet engine, and muffler noise can be controlled using ANC while the high squealing sounds of jet engine noise are more difficult to cancel out.

If **anti-noise** is produced by the **headphones** can a person hear other people, music, etc.—sounds that aren't "noise"?

The objective of active noise cancellation is to cancel out the noise waveform by producing anti-noise to interfere with the original noise pattern. Since the result is less

noise, other sounds are easier to hear. ANC technology is now available for consumers in headsets that reduce noise and allows for easier communication in loud environments. As a result of this new technology, factory workers and helicopter pilots can communicate more easily, and their amount of stress due to noise pollution should be reduced. Airline passengers can listen to music through ANC headphones while noise from the airplane is cancelled or reduced.

What is **psychoacoustics**?

Psychoacoustics, which connects acoustics with psychology, is the study of how the mind reacts to different sounds. This field of study is especially important to consumer product manufacturing, because a consumer associates particular sounds with certain products or sensations. For example, people associate low-frequency rumbling sounds with power and torque, while higher-frequency sounds often represent high speeds and out-of-control occurrences. Psychoacoustics can play a major role in the development and commercial success of many products.

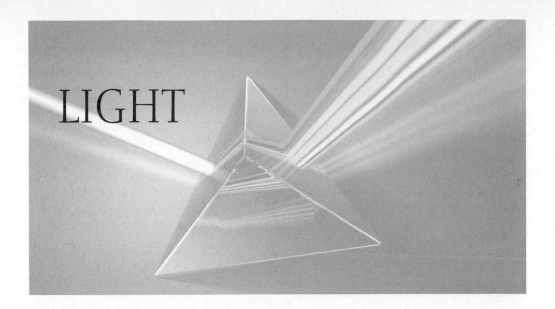

LIGHT

What is **optics**?

Optics is an area of study within physics that deals with the properties of and applications of light. Optics can be used not only with light, but with other parts of the electromagnetic spectrum, including microwaves, infrared, visible, ultraviolet, and X rays.

What were some **early ideas** about **light**?

Does light travel at a finite speed or is it infinite? Is light emitted by the eye or does it travel to the eye? These questions were debated for centuries. In ancient Greece, Aristotle (384–322 B.C.E.) argued that light is not a movement. Hero of Alexandria (10–70 C.E.) said it moves at infinite speed because you can see the stars and sun immediately after you open your eyes. Empedocles (490–430 B.C.E.) said it was something in motion, so it must move at a finite speed. Euclid (325–265 B.C.E.) and Ptolemy (90–168 C.E.) said that if we are to see something light must be emitted by the eye. In 1021 Alhazen (Ibn al-Haitham) did experiments that led him to support the argument that light moves from an object into the eye and thus it must travel at a finite speed. At the same time al-Biruni noted that the speed of light is much faster than the speed of sound. The Turkic astronomer Taqi al-Din (1521–1585) also argued that the speed of light was finite, and that its slower speed in denser objects explained refraction. He also developed a theory of color and correctly explained reflection.

In the 1600s the German astronomer Johannes Kepler (1571–1630) and the French philosopher, mathematician, and physicist René Descartes (1596–1650) argued that if the speed of light was not infinite, then the sun, moon, and Earth wouldn't be in alignment in a lunar eclipse. Despite this misconception, Kepler, in his 1604 book, *The Optical Part of Astronomy*, essentially invented the field of optics. He described the inverse-square law, the workings of a pinhole camera, and reflection by flat and concave mirrors. He also recognized the influence of the atmosphere on both eclipses and the

Isaac Newton used a prism to separate white light into a spectrum, leading to the publication of his findings in his *Theory of Colors* (1672).

apparent locations of stars. Willibrord Snellius (1580–1626) discovered the law of refraction (Snell's Law) in 1621. Descartes used Snell's Law to explain the formation of rainbows shortly thereafter. Christiaan Huygens (1629–1695) wrote important books on optics and proposed the idea that light was a wave. Isaac Newton's (1642–1727) celebrated experiments using a prism to separate white light into its colors led to Newton's Theory of Colors published in 1672. He recognized that telescope lenses would cause colored images and invented the reflecting telescope using a concave mirror that would not have this fault. Newton believed that light was made up of very lightweight particles, or corpuscles.

In 1665, a publication by Francesco Grimaldi (1618–1663) described how light could be diffracted when passing through thin holes or slits or around boundaries. In 1803, Thomas Young's (1773–1829) experiments with one and two slits demonstrated the diffraction and interference of light. Augustin-Jean Fresnel (1788–1827) and Siméaon Poisson (1781–1827) did both theoretical and experimental work that firmly established the wave theory of light in 1815 and 1818.

What is the **modern conception** of **light**?

As demonstrated by the work of Young, Poisson, and Fresnel, and later by James Clerk Maxwell (1831–1879), and Heinrich Hertz (1857–1894), light is an electromagnetic wave to which human eyes respond. It is located on the electromagnetic spectrum between infrared and ultraviolet. The limits of human vision define the lower and upper boundaries of light. The lowest frequency is 4×10^{14} Hz, which has a wavelength of 700 nanometers (700×10^{-9} m). Its upper boundary is 7.9×10^{14} Hz, a wavelength of 400 nanometers. Wavelength rather than frequency is commonly used when describing light because until the past three decades only wavelength measurements were possible—light frequencies were too high to measure directly.

Light has all the properties of a transverse wave. That is, it can transfer energy and momentum. It obeys the principle of superposition and can be diffracted and interfere with itself. On the other hand, it also has the properties of a massless particle. While in a medium it moves in a straight line at a constant velocity. It can transfer energy and momentum. A full description of the true nature of light—wave, particle, or both—will be discussed in the "What Is the World Made Of?"

How is **light emitted**?

You undoubtedly have seen the light emitted by hot objects. Whether it is the dull red glow of the heating coil on an electric range or the orange glow of the element in an electric oven or the bright yellow-white of the glowing filament of an incandescent lamp, you have seen light emitted by hot objects. Even the yellow glow of a fire comes from light emitted by hot carbon particles. Energy, usually from stored chemical energy, is converted into thermal energy. That energy is transferred to the surroundings by radiation, including light. Unfortunately, producing light in this way is very inefficient because about 97% of the energy goes into infrared radiation that warms the environment rather than light that can be seen. Because of their large energy use, many countries will be banning incandescent lamps in the next few years.

A close-up shot of a transparent LED. LED's use the same materials as laser pointers and operate more efficiently than incandescent lights.

Light can also be emitted by gases and solids. Neon signs are one example of a gas that glows because electrical energy is converted into light energy. High-intensity lamps use either sodium or mercury vapor to produce intense light. Fluorescent tubes and compact fluorescent lamps (CFLs) use electrical energy to excite mercury atoms. The ultraviolet emitted by these atoms causes compounds deposited on the inside surfaces of the lamps to glow. The colors can be chosen to emulate incandescent lamps or daylight. CFLs convert up to 15% of the electrical energy into light.

Lasers, mostly used today in CD and DVD players and supermarket bar-code scanners and pointers, usually consist of a small crystal composed of a mixture of elements like gallium, arsenic, and aluminum. The lasers produce single-color, intense light that is emitted as a compact ray. The LED lights that are often used as on/off indicators, traffic lights, car taillights, stop, and turning lights also use electrical energy and the same kind of materials used in laser pointers to produce light that is radiated into many directions. White LEDs that are beginning to be used in home lighting are costly to produce, but are much more efficient and last much longer than incandescent lamps.

How is **light detected**?

Light carries energy, so a light detector must convert light energy to another form of energy. In most cases light is converted into electrical energy. In the eye, which will be discussed more thoroughly later in this chapter, light strikes a molecule called an

opsin. The absorption of light changes the shape of the molecule, which results in an electrical signal sent on the optic nerve. In detectors used in digital cameras when light is absorbed in a semiconductor one or more electrons are released. The charge they carry produces a voltage that is then converted into a digital signal. In photographic film molecules consisting of silver and chlorine, bromine, or iodine are used. When light strikes these molecules it transfers its energy to electrons. The molecules are broken apart and a tiny crystal of metallic silver remains.

THE SPEED OF LIGHT

What is the **history of measurements** of the **speed of light**?

In 1638 Galileo (1564–1642) proposed a method of measuring the speed of light. Galileo would have one lamp and an assistant a great distance away would have a second lamp. The assistant was to uncover his lamp immediately when he saw Galileo uncover his own lamp. The speed could then be determined by measuring the time it would take the light to travel from Galileo to the assistant and back again. Galileo claimed to have done the experiment several years before 1638 but there was no record of his results. In 1667 the academy of sciences in Florence, Italy, carried it out between two observers a mile apart. They reported there was no measurable delay, showing that the speed of light must be extremely rapid.

The first measurement of the speed of light in a laboratory was by Hippolyte Armand Fizeau (1819–1896) in 1849. He used a beam of light that passed through the gaps between teeth of a rapidly rotating wheel, was reflected from a mirror 8 kilometers away, and returned to the wheel. The speed of the wheel was increased until the returning light passed through the next gap and could be seen. The speed was calculated to be 315,000 kilometers per second. Leon Foucault (1819–1868) improved on this a year later by using a rotating mirror in place of the wheel and found the speed to be 298,000 kilometers per second. He also used this technique to determine that light travels slower in water than in air.

The American physicist Albert Michelson (1852–1931) greatly improved Foucault's measurement using an eight-sided rotating mirror and a plane mirror located on Mount San Antonio, 35 kilometers (114,800 feet) away from the source on Mount Wilson in California. By measuring the speed of the rotating mirror and the distance between the mirrors, Michelson made the most accurate measurement of the speed of light to that date. In 1907, he was honored by being the first American to win the Nobel Prize in physics. In 1926 he made a new measurement that yielded 299,796 kilometers per second with an uncertainty of 4 kilometers per second.

After Maxwell published his theory of electromagnetism it became possible to calculate the speed of light indirectly from the relationships between an electric charge

and its electric field and an electric current and the magnetic field it produces. In 1907 Rosa and Dorsey obtained 299,788 kilometers per second in this way. The uncertainty of 30 kilometers per second made it the most precise measurement to that date.

Research on microwaves used in radar during World War II led to a new method of measuring the speed of light. By 1950 Louis Essen reported a result of 299,792 kilometers per second, slightly more precise than Michelson's result. In the 1970s scientists at the National Institute of Standards and Technology in Boulder Colorado succeeded in directly measuring simultaneously the wavelength and the frequency of an infrared laser. From these two measurements they could calculate the speed of light: 299,792.4562 kilometers per second with an uncertainty of only 1.1 meters per second!

This new technique prompted an investigation of the length standard, the wavelength of light from the gas krypton. The new techniques discovered that the standard was "fuzzy" and had to be replaced. In 1983 the Conférence Générale des Poids et Mesures decided to fix the speed of light in a vacuum at 299,792.458 kilometers per second and define the meter as the distance light travels in 1/299792458 of a second.

Here is a summary of the history of measurements of the speed of light.

Date	Author	Method	Result (km/s)	Uncertainty (km/s)
1676	Ole Rømer	Jupiter's satellites	220,000	
1726	James Bradley	Stellar aberration	301,000	
1849	Hippolyte Fizeau	Toothed wheel	315,000	
1862	Leon Foucault	Rotating mirror	298,000	±500
1879	Albert Michelson	Rotating 8-sided mirror	299,910	±50
1907	E.B. Rosa and N.E. Dorsey	Electromagnetic constants	299,788	±30
1926	Albert Michelson	Rotating 8-sided mirror	299,796	±4
1947	Louis Essen and A.C. Gordon-Smith	Cavity resonator	299,792	±3
1958	K.D. Froome	Radio interferometer	299,792.5	±0.1
1973	Evanson et al.	Lasers	299,792.4562	±0.0011
1983		Adopted value	299,792.458	

Source: K.D. Froome and L. Essen, *The Velocity of Light and Radio Waves*, Academic Press (London, New York) 1969.

What **astronomical methods** have been used to **measure** the **speed of light**?

The Danish astronomer Ole Rømer (1644–1710) measured the orbital period of Jupiter's innermost moon, Io. He found the period was shorter when Earth was

approaching Jupiter than when it was moving away from it. He concluded that light travels at a finite speed and estimated that it would take light 22 minutes to travel the diameter of Earth's orbit. Christiaan Huygens combined this estimate with an estimate for the diameter of Earth's orbit. He concluded that the speed of light is 220,000 kilometers per second.

In 1725 the English astronomer James Bradley noted that the location of a star changed with the seasons. He proposed that the shift was due to the addition of the speed of light and the speed of Earth in its orbit. Bradley observed the shift in several stars and determined that light travelled 10,210 times faster than Earth in its orbit. The modern result is 10,066 times faster.

How **long** does it take **light** to **travel** certain distances?

The table below lists some travel times for light.

Distance	Time
1 foot	1 nanosecond
1 mile	5.3 microseconds
From New York City to Los Angeles	0.016 seconds
Around Earth's equator	0.133 seconds
From the Moon to Earth	1.29 seconds
From the Sun to Earth	8 minutes
From Alpha Centauri to Earth	4 years

Some of the destinations above would require light to travel in a circular or curved path, which it does not do.

What is a **light-year**?

A year is a unit of time, but a light-year is a unit of distance. Specifically, it is the distance that light travels in one year. Since light travels at 299,792 km/s and a year consists of 31.557×10^6 s, a light-year is 9.4605×10^{12} km or about 6 trillion miles.

The light-year is used to express distances to stars and galaxies.

Does the **speed of light** depend on the **medium**?

Waves travel at different speeds when traveling in different materials. In the vacuum of space, light travels at 299,792 km/s. When light encounters a denser medium, however, like Earth's atmosphere, it slows down ever so slightly to 298,895 km/s. Upon striking water it slows down rather dramatically, to 225,408 km/s, three quarters of its original speed. Finally, when light passes through the dense medium of glass, it slows to only 194,670 km/s. The ratio of the speed of light in a vacuum to that in a medium

is called the *refractive index*, represented by the symbol n. The refractive index will be discussed in further detail in the section on lenses.

How is the **brightness** of light **measured**?

There are two separate systems to measure the intensity of light. The first is a physical system that measures energy or power transferred. The second system measures the effect of light on the eye—in other words, how bright we see the light. You are familiar with the watt. It's the rate at which energy is transferred. The equivalent unit for light, the luminous power, is the lumen. If you look at the box a lamp comes in you'll find both the electric power it dissipates in watts (W), and the luminous power in lumens (lm). For example, a 25-W clear bulb emits 200 lm. A 100-W lamp emits 1,720 lm. A 60-W halogen lamp emits 1,080 lm. Compact fluorescent lamps produce more light for the same power: a 25-W lamp is rated at 1,600 lm.

Light travels at slower speeds through mediums denser than a vacuum, such as air or water or glass. Light travels at about 225,400 km/s through water versus 299,792 km/s in a vacuum.

The intensity of light depends on the degree to which the lamp spreads or focuses the luminous power. If the light goes into all directions it won't be as intense as it would be from a reflector spot lamp that reflects light to form a narrow beam. The unit in which light intensity is measured is the candela (cd). If a 100-W, 1,720-lm lamp could spread the light into all directions it would have an intensity of 137 cd. But, if the same lamp were a spotlight, concentrating all the light into a 30° angle, then the intensity would be about 640 cd.

As the distance between the lamp and the surface illuminated increases, the illuminance provided by the lamp decreases according to the inverse square law. Suppose you have a light luminous power of 1,000 lm 1 meter (3.2 feet) away from the surface. If you now moved the lamp to 2 meters (6.5 feet) away, the illuminance would be 1,000 lm divided by the distance squared, or $1/2^2$. That is, 1/4 of the illumination at 1 meter. If you moved the lamp to 3 meters (9.8 feet) away, the illuminance would decrease to one-ninth the original illuminance.

POLARIZATION OF LIGHT

What is **polarized light**?

Light is an electromagnetic wave that consists of an oscillating electric field and an oscillating magnetic field. The two fields are perpendicular to each other. In most cases the direction of the electric field has no preferred direction because different parts of the source produce light with electric fields in different directions. Such light is unpolarized. Some sources, however, like laser pointers, emit light whose electric field is always in one direction. Such light is called polarized.

How does **light become polarized**?

Light can be polarized in two ways. If a shiny surface such as water or an automobile window reflects light, it can be partially polarized. Or, you can use a polarizing filter that passes only the light that has the electric field in one orientation. A Polaroid® filter has long, thin molecules, all oriented in the same direction, embedded in plastic. The molecules absorb light that has an electric field parallel to the long dimension of the molecules. Therefore the light passing through the Polaroid® has an electric field perpendicular to the long dimension of the molecules.

Why are **polarized glasses** useful?

Polarized glasses are useful when driving, sailing, skiing, or in any situation where unwanted glare is present. Glare is caused by light reflecting off a surface, such as water, a road, or snow. Such light is polarized. Navigating your way through some situations could be difficult without polarized sunglasses.

Take, for example, light reflecting off the surface of a lake. The light polarized parallel to the water's surface is reflected with a greater intensity than that polarized perpendicular to the surface. So, sunglasses that pass vertically polarized light will reduce the glare from the water.

How can you **check** to make sure a pair of **sunglasses** is **polarized**?

Polarized lenses are transparent only to light that has its electric field oriented in one direction. Therefore, if a pair of sunglasses is polarized, two pairs of the same sunglasses, when aligned perpendicular to each other, should not allow any light to pass through the lenses.

Light from the sky is also partially polarized due to the scattering of light off gas molecules in the atmosphere, so if you put on a pair of polarized sunglasses and tilt your head so that your ear were near your shoulder, you should see a change in the intensity of the sky on a clear, sunny day. If you see no such change, then the sunglasses are not polarized.

How do **LCD devices** use polarized light?

LCD stands for Liquid Crystal Display. A liquid crystal is composed of long, thin molecules that are free to move like a liquid but organize themselves in a regular array like a crystal. In an LCD display the liquid crystal material is in a thin layer between two glass sheets. The bottom sheet is rubbed in one direction so that the molecules in the liquid crystal touching the surface align themselves with the rubbing. The top sheet is rubbed in the perpendicular direction, aligning the molecules touching it in that direction. As a result, over the thickness of the liquid crystal material the direction of the long axis of the molecules rotate through 90°. Polarizers are placed on the outsides of the glass sheets in the same direction as the rubbing. When light enters the back of the display it is polarized. As it passes through the crystal its polarization direction is rotated through 90° so that it passes through the second polarizer. Thus light passes through the display; it appears bright.

Each glass sheet is coated with a thin, electrically conductive layer. If a voltage is placed across the sheets the molecules align themselves with the electric field. The molecules no longer rotate the direction of polarization of the light, so no light passes through the display. It appears dark. By varying the voltage different degrees of darkness can be produced.

An LCD television screen uses liquid crystals composed of long, thin molecules between two glass sheets. An electrical field rotates the molecules in the prixels so that polarized light either passes through or is blocked. Color filters are added to the pixels to achieve color.

527

The entire display is composed of tiny pixels, each connected to a source of the control voltage. Thus each pixel can be switched between light and dark. Color filters can be placed over each pixel to produce a full color display. In a 1,080 pixel high-definition television display there are 1,920 pixels in the horizontal direction and 1,080 in the vertical, for a total of 2,073,600 pixels.

OPAQUE, TRANSPARENT, AND TRANSLUCENT MATERIALS

What is an **opaque material**?

An opaque object is something that allows no light through it. Concrete, wood, and metal are some examples of opaque materials. Some materials can be opaque to light, but not to other types of electromagnetic waves. For example, wood does not allow visible light to pass through it, but will allow other types of electromagnetic waves, such as microwaves and radio waves to pass. The physical characteristics of the material determine what type of electromagnetic waves will and will not pass through it.

What is the **difference** between **transparent** and **translucent**?

Transparent media such as air, water, glass, and clear plastic allow light to pass through the material. Rays of light are either not bent or closely spaced rays are bent together. Translucent materials, on the other hand, allow light to pass through, but bend closely-spaced rays into different directions. For example, frosted glass and thin paper are translucent because they let light through, but are not transparent because you cannot see clearly through them.

Is **Earth's atmosphere transparent** to **infrared** and **ultraviolet radiation** as well as to light?

Oxygen and nitrogen, the two principal components of our atmosphere, are transparent to light and to most infrared (IR) and ultraviolet (UV) wavelengths. Infrared from the sun helps warm Earth and long-wavelength ultraviolet is necessary for our bodies to produce vitamin D. Too much UV, however, harms the skin, and may damage our DNA. A high-altitude layer of ozone in our atmosphere protects Earth from all but a small fraction of the UV radiated by the sun. Ozone molecules have three oxygen atoms as opposed to the two in oxygen gas. In recent years large and growing holes in this protective layer have developed due to the emission of chlorofluorocarbon (CFC) molecules from things such as escaped gases from refrigerants and aerosol propellants. Because these gases are no longer being manufactured and existing stocks are gradually being replaced, the the growth of the holes should eventually stop.

Carbon dioxide, methane, and water vapor are transparent to light and short-wavelength infrared radiation, but are opaque to the long-wavelength infrared emitted by warm objects. They are called greenhouse gases. These gases pass the IR rays that warm Earth but reflect the IR rays emitted by the warm Earth back to the ground. Thus they act as an insulating blanket for Earth. Over the past decades the amount of carbon dioxide in the atmosphere has increased dramatically. Much of the increase is due to human activity. This increase is likely to lead to a warmer Earth that could shift weather patterns, disrupting food production, causing shifts in locations of forests and animals, and, by melting polar ice, increasing sea levels. The degree of warming and its impact on Earth and humans is under intensive investigation.

SHADOWS

What are **shadows**?

Shadows are areas of darkness created by an opaque object blocking light. Whether created when someone puts their hand in the light from a movie projector, stands outside in the sunshine, or sees the moon move between Earth and the sun during an eclipse, shadows have always intrigued us.

How is an **eclipse** a **shadow**?

An eclipse is created just as any other shadow, by the presence of an object in the path of light. In a lunar eclipse, Earth blocks the sun's light illuminating the moon. In a solar eclipse the moon keeps the sun's light from reaching Earth. Thus the shadow of the moon on Earth is what we call a solar eclipse.

What is a **lunar eclipse**?

A lunar eclipse occurs when Earth is directly between the sun and the moon. Earth blocks the sun's light rays from hitting the moon, leaving it in complete darkness. For an observer on Earth, a shadow appears on the moon, causing it to become dark. As Earth moves out from between the sun and the moon, the moon is gradually illuminated until the entire full moon is seen again.

What is a **solar eclipse**?

An eclipse of the sun occurs when the moon casts its shadow on Earth. As the moon moves between Earth and the sun, darkness falls upon the small part of Earth where the moon blocks the light.

Since the moon has monthly cycles, why don't solar eclipses occur each month?

The moon has a monthly orbital cycle around Earth. If the moon had a circular orbit that was in the same plane as Earth's orbit around the sun, there would be monthly solar and lunar eclipses. But the moon's orbit is tilted with respect to Earth's orbit, so the sun–Earth–moon alignment is only very infrequently perfect enough to create an eclipse. The moon's elliptical orbit causes its distance from Earth to vary. When it is closer, the path of totality is wider and eclipses last longer. When it is farther from Earth the moon can't cover the entire sun and an annular eclipse is seen. In an annular eclipse the moon covers all but a thin circular ring of the sun.

How dark can it get on Earth during a solar eclipse?

Some observers reported that they saw Venus and some of the brighter stars during a total solar eclipse. It is not entirely dark, however, because light comes from the sun's corona, the extremely faint glow surrounding the sun that is produced by ionized gases emitted by the sun. More light may come from reflection of light by the atmosphere in nearby areas not in the path of totality. The complete eclipse of the sun lasts for an average of about 2.5 minutes, but can last over 7 minutes.

What is the difference between the umbra and penumbra of a shadow?

A shadow produced by a large light source has two distinct regions. The umbra is the area of the shadow where all the light from the source has been blocked, preventing any light from falling on the surface. The penumbra, or partial shadow, is a section where light from only part of the source is blocked, resulting in an area where the light is dimmed, but not totally absent.

During an eclipse, the region of total darkness is the umbra; no direct sunlight can reach this area, resulting in a total eclipse. As Earth rotates, the moon's shadow races across Earth, producing the path of totality. Regions on either side of the path of totality experience the penumbra shadow and see the sun only partially covered by the moon.

Can the size of umbras and penumbras change?

An umbra and penumbra exist wherever there are shadows produced by a large light source. When an opaque object casts a shadow on a surface close to it the shadow will be clear and distinct, because it has a large umbra section and small penumbra. If, however, the object casting the shadow is closer to the light source, there will be

A lunar eclipse occurs when the earth is directly between the moon and the sun.

regions on the surface where light from some of the source is not blocked by the object, producing a smaller umbra and a larger penumbra.

How often do solar and lunar eclipses occur?

Solar eclipses (including partial eclipses) occur more frequently than lunar eclipses; over the entire Earth there are two to five solar eclipses per year, while the average number of lunar eclipses per year is between one and two. A solar eclipse can only be observed by a narrow path on Earth's surface while a lunar eclipse can be seen over a much larger area.

When a solar eclipse occurs, is the entire Earth in the moon's shadow?

The shadow of the moon only covers an area of about 300 kilometers in diameter. This shadow, the umbra, moves along a path of Earth's surface at about 1,000 miles per hour. In the penumbra a partial eclipse is seen, but even this path is quite narrow.

When and where will there be total solar eclipses over the next few decades?

The following map shows the date and location of total solar eclipses that took place from 2001 to 2010, as well as those that will take place into the year 2020:

The last total solar eclipse in the United States was seen on February 26, 1979.

531

Total and Annular Solar Eclipse Paths: 2001 — 2020

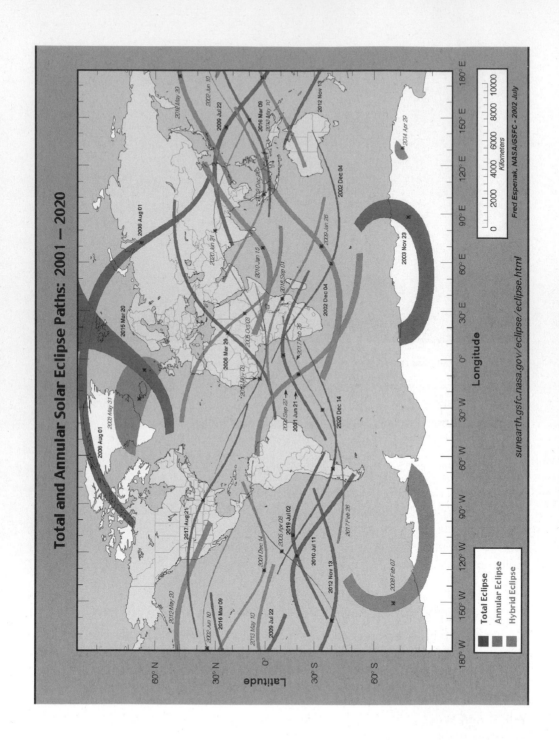

Latitude

Longitude

Total Eclipse
Annular Eclipse
Hybrid Eclipse

Kilometers

0 2000 4000 6000 8000 10000

sunearth.gsfc.nasa.gov/eclipse/eclipse.html

Fred Espenak, NASA/GSFC - 2002 July

When will the **United States** see its **next total solar eclipse**?

Although the entire United States will not see the eclipse, it will sweep across the country from Oregon to South Carolina on August 21, 2017. Mark your calendars!

When and where will there be total lunar eclipses for the next few decades?

The following table shows the date and location of future lunar eclipses.

Date	Where Eclipse Will Be Visible
June 15, 2011	South America, Europe, Africa, Asia, Australia
December 10, 2011	Europe, East Africa, Asia, Australia, Pacific, North America
April 15, 2014	Australia, Pacific, Americas
October 8, 2014	Asia, Australia, Pacific, Americas
April 4, 2015	Asia, Australia, Pacific, Americas
September 28, 2015	Eastern Pacific, Americas, Europe, Africa, Western Asia
January 31, 2018	Europe, Africa, Asia, Australia
July 27, 2018	Asia, Australia, Pacific, Western North America
January 21, 2019	South America, Europe, Africa, Asia, Australia
May 26, 2021	Asia, Australia, Pacific, Americas
May 16, 2022	Americas, Europe, East Asia, Australia, Pacific
November 8, 2022	Americas, Europe, Africa
March 14, 2025	Americas, Europe, Africa
September 7, 2025	Pacific, Americas, West Europe, West Africa
March 3, 2026	Europe, Africa, Asia, Australia
December 31, 2028	Europe, Africa, Asia, Australia
June 26, 2029	Europe, Africa, Asia, Australia, Pacific
December 20, 2029	Americas, Europe, Africa, Middle East

Why is it **dangerous** to **look** at a **solar eclipse**?

Looking directly at the photosphere of the sun (the bright disk of the sun itself), even for just a few seconds, can cause permanent damage to the retina of the eye, because of the intense visible and ultraviolet rays that the photosphere emits. This damage can result in permanent impairment of vision, up to and including blindness. The retina has no sensitivity to pain, and the effects of retinal damage may not appear for hours, so there is no warning that injury is occurring.

Under normal conditions, the sun is so bright that it is difficult to stare at it directly, so there is no tendency to look at it in a way that might damage the eye. During a total eclipse, however, with the sun covered, it is easier and more tempting to

Many ancient cultures that worshiped the sun believed that the sudden eclipse of the sun was a terrible occurrence. These events did not happen very often, but when solar eclipses did occur and darkness set in on the area, worshipers would gather and pray, often for days, to the sun gods. During the Zulu War in South Africa Zulu warriors massacred a British battalion. During the afternoon of the battle there was a solar eclipse. The Zulus named the day of the battle, January 22, 1879, the day of the dead moon.

Because eclipses were often either recorded or suggested in ancient myths or documents, solar eclipses can be used to find the date and place of events recorded in these documents. For example, in the sixth century B.C.E., the Medes and Lydian armies were in a war when a solar eclipse occurred. The eclipse halted the battle and helped bring about a peace between the two armies because they thought that the disappearance of the sun was an omen. A candidate eclipse was on May 28, 585 B.C.E., near the Halys River in modern Turkey.

In an Indian epic story, Arjun vowed to kill Jayadrath to avenge Jayadrath's killing of Abhimanyu. During a solar eclipse Jayadrath came out of hiding to celebrate his survival, but when the sun reappeared Arjun killed him. Eclipses occurred in this region in 3129 B.C.E. and 2559 B.C.E., thus providing two possible dates for the event.

stare at it. Unfortunately, looking at the sun during an eclipse is dangerous even if totality occurs only briefly. Viewing the sun's disk through sunglasses or any kind of optical aid (binoculars, a telescope, or even an optical camera viewfinder) is extremely hazardous. The best methods are to use special solar filters, welder's glasses, or a pinhole camera.

REFLECTION

What is the **difference** between **physical** and **geometrical optics**?

Geometrical optics deals specifically with the path that light takes when it encounters mirrors and lenses. Geometrical optics uses the ray model of light in which an arrow represents the direction light travels. The ray model does not consider the wave nature of light. Ray diagrams trace the path that light takes when it reflects and refracts in different media.

Reflection occurs when light bounces off a surface, whether it is a piece of paper or a mirror. Shiny metals and very still water make good reflectors, creating images that resemble objects from which the light is coming.

Physical optics, on the other hand, is the division of optics that depends on the wave nature of light. It involves polarization, diffraction, interference, and the spectral analysis of light waves.

What is **reflection**?

When light strikes an object it can either be absorbed, transmitted, or reflected. Opaque objects absorb or reflect light. Transparent and translucent materials transmit light, but can also reflect it. The energy carried by the light must be conserved. The sum of the energy reflected, transmitted, and absorbed must equal the energy that strikes the material. Light energy that is absorbed increases the thermal energy of the material so the material becomes warmer.

Reflection occurs when light "bounces" off of a surface, such as a mirror or a sheet of paper. A smooth surface, like that of a mirror, reflects light according to the rule that the angle of incidence equals the angle of reflection. Light that strikes the surface at, for example, 30° above the surface is reflected at 30° above the surface. You can test this for yourself with a small flashlight, a mirror, a sheet of paper, and a helper. Hold the piece of paper. Have the helper hold the flashlight, aim it at the mirror, and move it around until the reflected light ray hits your piece of paper. Change the angle with which the light from the flashlight strikes the mirror and see that you have to move the paper closer to the mirror to have the light hit it.

535

What happens when light hits a sheet of paper? Replace the mirror with a sheet of paper. Darken the room. Aim the flashlight at the paper and use a second sheet to catch the reflection. You'll see that the second sheet is illuminated in many different locations. The light is reflected from the paper, but into many directions. This kind of reflection is called diffuse reflection.

Polished, smooth surfaces that do not absorb light are the best reflectors; examples of reflective materials are shiny metals, whereas non-reflective materials are dull metals, wood, and stone.

MIRRORS

How were the **first mirrors** made?

People have seen their reflections in water for hundreds of centuries, but some of the earliest signs of human-made brass and bronze mirrors have been mentioned in the Bible and in ancient Egyptian, Greek, and Roman literature. The earliest glass mirrors, backed with shiny metal, appeared in Italy during the fourteenth century. The original process for creating a glass mirror was to coat one side of glass with mercury and polished tinfoil.

The German chemist Justus von Liebig (1803–1873) in 1835 developed a method for silvering a mirror. His process consisted of pouring a compound containing ammonia and silver onto the back of the glass. Formaldehyde removed the ammonia, leaving a shiny metallic silver surface that reflected the light. Today, most mirrors are made by evaporating metallic aluminum directly on the glass.

How do **one-way mirrors**, the ones used in interrogation rooms, work?

A one-way mirror seems to be a mirror when seen from one side, but as a window when seen from the opposite side. Thus the window is disguised as a mirror to allow secret surveillance. Physically, there is no such thing as a one-way mirror. That is, the amount of light reflected from one side is the same as that reflected from the other. The light transmitted in one direction is equal that transmitted in the opposite direction. How then does a one-way mirror work? First, the mirror isn't totally reflecting. It transmits half the light and reflects the other half. The second requirement has to do with lighting. It is imperative that the observation room remain dark, because if a lamp were turned on, some of that light would pass through into the interrogation room as well.

What does a **mirror reverse**?

If you look in a mirror you seem to see yourself reversed left-to-right. Your left eye appears to be your right eye in the mirror. Yet the vertical direction is not reversed.

Why can't you always see yourself in a mirror?

The answer is a matter of angles. The law of reflection states that the angle of light incident on a mirror must be equal to the angle of the reflected light. If you are standing directly in front of a mirror, the angle of incidence (that is, the angle between the direction the incoming light is traveling and the mirror surface) might be 90° and as a result reflects directly back to your eyes at an angle of 90°. If, however, you stand off to one side of the mirror, then the angle of reflectance is much smaller, and so the incident light won't come from your face, but from another part of the room.

Your chin is still at the bottom of your face. What happens if you look at a mirror while lying down? Now left and right are not reversed—your chin is on the same side of both you and your image. But if your right eye was higher than your left, then in the image the left eye will be higher. What indeed is reversed?

What makes a glove right-handed or left handed? If you examine a vinyl or latex glove you'll notice that it can fit on either hand. How does such a glove differ from an ordinary glove? The thumb is in line with the fingers. In other words, there is no front or back! A mirror reverses not left and right or up and down, but front and back. When you look at yourself you are facing the opposite direction. It's just like facing another person—his or her left and right sides are also reversed.

On the front of many **ambulances**, why is the word **"ambulance" printed backwards**?

The word "ambulance" is printed backwards (left and right reversed) so that when viewed in a mirror—specifically, the rearview mirror of a car—it will appear correctly (that is, forwards), ensuring that the driver can read it and respond as quickly as possible.

How do **day/night rearview mirrors** function in vehicles?

When drivers traveling at night encounter a bright light from the vehicle behind them shining in their eyes, many will flip a tab on the underside of the rearview mirror to deflect the light up toward the ceiling of the car. The silvered surface of the mirror reflects approximately 85–90% of the incident light on the mirror, which is now directed toward the ceiling. The remaining 10–15% of the light is reflected by the front of the glass on the mirror. The mirror is wedge-shaped, thicker at the top than at the bottom. Thus the front surface is angled downward to allow the much smaller amount of light to be reflected into the driver's eyes.

537

What is an **image**?

Suppose light falls on your face. Light is reflected diffusely from this surface. That is, it is reflected into a wide variety of directions. Consider a very tiny object, like the end of an eyelash. Light from that point will leave in many directions. That point is called an object. An optical device can cause the light rays from the object to converge again to a single point. That point is called the image.

The word "AMBULANCE" is printed backwards on these emergency vehicles so that drivers will see the word correctly in their rearview mirrors.

Does a **mirror** produce an **image**?

The light reflected from an object by a flat, or plane, mirror is not redirected so it will converge again. What you see when you look in a mirror is a virtual image. It is located behind the mirror. Some of the rays from the object are reflected by the mirror and enter your eye. Your eye believes that all these rays came from a single point, and that point is behind the mirror. The image isn't real, it is virtual. Virtual images can also be formed by lenses. They cannot be focused on a screen.

What is a **real image**?

A concave mirror or a convex lens can redirect light from an object so that it does converge to a single point. That point is a real image. It is in front of a concave mirror and on the other side of a convex lens from the object. If you place a screen, piece of paper, or wall at the location of the image you'll see it on that surface.

What is a **concave mirror** and what is it used for?

A concave mirror is curved inward so that the incident rays of light are reflected and can be brought together. If the rays striking the mirror were parallel to each other, as they would be from a distant source, then the reflected rays converge at the focal point. Concave mirrors are typically used to focus waves, whether it is a microwave signal to a receiver, or light to an observer. They can produce real images.

If, however, the object is closer to the mirror than the focal point, as is often the case with a concave bathroom mirror, the image is virtual and upright. If you look at the reflection of a more distant object, like the bathroom wall, you'll notice that it is upside down, or inverted. The wall is farther away from the mirror than the focal point, and its image is real.

**Why do side-view mirrors in vehicles state:
"Objects viewed in mirror may be closer than they appear"?**

This statement, seen on most side-view mirrors, is a very important safety message—the message warns the driver that the mirror is deceiving. Why would an automobile manufacturer put a deceiving mirror on a car? A flat, plane mirror would only show the driver a small, narrow section of the road behind the car; if, however, a convex mirror is used, the driver can not only see behind the car, but to the side as well, reducing his or her blind spot. In the process, however, convex mirrors make objects appear smaller and therefore farther away, so the message is there to serve as a reminder that the image is not exactly as it appears.

What is a **convex mirror** and what is it used for?

A convex mirror is the opposite of a concave mirror in that it is curved outward. The reflected light spreads out rather than converging at a point. Therefore convex mirrors form virtual images. Convex mirrors are used for security purposes in stores because they broaden the reflected field of vision, allowing clerks to see a large section of the store. The images are smaller than the objects, but the mirrors help to see a wide area.

REFRACTION

What is **refraction**?

Refraction is the bending of light as it goes from one medium to another. The most common use of refraction is in lenses. Eyeglass lenses refract light so that the wearer's eyes can focus the light properly. A magnifying glass is used to see enlarged images. Lenses in cameras produce an image on the film or CCD sensor. Refraction also occurs when sunlight strikes Earth's atmosphere and when it goes through water.

How can the **refraction** of light be **determined**?

The extent to which a beam of light bends when it hits a different medium depends on the indices of refraction of the medium as well as the medium from which it came and the angle at which the light strikes the boundary between the two media.

All materials have an index of refraction that depends on the speed of light in the material. The index of refraction is the speed of light in a vacuum divided by the speed of light in the material. A vacuum has a refractive index of 1, water is 1.33, and glass is

Magnifying glasses make images larger by bending light through a glass medium.

around 1.5. The higher the index of refraction, the more slowly light travels through the medium.

Snell's Law of Refraction, named after Dutch physicist Willebrord Snellius (1580–1626), tells us how light behaves at a boundary between two different media. Consider the interface between two media where the refractive index of the top medium is lower than that of the bottom medium. According to Snell's Law, when light hits the boundary between two materials it is bent from its original path to a smaller angle with respect to the line perpendicular to the surface of the interface. As the incoming, or incident angle increases, so does the refracted angle. When light goes from a medium with a higher refractive index into one with a lower index then it is bent away from the line perpendicular to the surface.

What is the **index of refraction** for light traveling through different media?

The following are some sample indices of refraction. The index of refraction, represented by n, is the ratio of the speed of light in a vacuum divided by the speed of light in the material. The larger the index of refraction, the greater the bending that takes place.

Medium	Index of Refraction (n)
Vacuum	1.00
Air (usually rounded to 1.0)	1.003
Water	1.33
Crown glass	1.52
Quartz	1.54
Flint glass	1.61
Diamond	2.42

How does **Earth's atmosphere affect** the apparent locations at which we see stars?

The light from stars refracts slightly as it enters Earth's atmosphere. Refraction is largest nearest the horizon. As a result the true position of the stars is a bit off from where we observe them. Refraction of light from the sun results in sunrise being slightly earlier than it would be without the atmospheric refraction, and sunset is

> ## Why does a person standing in a pool of water often appear short and stocky?
>
> The portion of a person's body that is above water does not appear out of proportion because the light entering your eye is not going through a different medium and refracting. The part of the body that is underwater, the person's legs, appears to be short because the light reflecting off their legs is traveling through water and then into the air. Due to this change in medium, refraction occurs. Since the index of refraction for water is larger than the index of refraction for air, the legs of the person appear compressed and stocky.

slightly later. Refraction also distorts our view of the sun and moon when they are very close to the horizon.

What is a **mirage**?

Mirages typically occur on hot summer days when surfaces such as sand, concrete, or asphalt are warm. Mirages look like pools of water on the ground, along with an upside-down image of a building, vehicle, or tree in the distance. As one approaches a mirage, the puddle of water and the reflection seem to disappear.

A mirage occurs because of a temperature difference between the air directly above the surface, which is hot and thus less dense, and the cooler, denser air a few meters above the surface. The denser air has a higher refractive index and that causes the light from an object to bend up toward the observer. As a result, the object is right side up while the refracted image is inverted and underneath the original object. The illusion of water is also a refracted image, the image of the sky. Mirages can only occur on hot surfaces and objects that are at relatively small angles in relation to the observer. Therefore, a person cannot see a mirage from an object that is just a few meters away. A mirage is not a hallucination, but instead a true and well-documented optical phenomenon.

LENSES

When were **lenses first made**?

The word "lens" comes from the name of the lentil bean because of the similarity in shape of the bean and a converging lens. Lenses have been used for over three thousand years. It's possible that ancient Assyrians used them as a burning glass to start fires. A burning glass is mentioned in a play by Aristophanes written in 424 B.C.E.

Roman emperors used corrective lenses and knew that glass globes filled with water were able to produce magnified images. Al-Haitham (Alhazen; 965–1038 C.E.) wrote the first major textbook on optics that was translated into Latin in the twelfth century and influenced European scientists. Shortly thereafter, in the 1280s, eyeglasses were used in Italy. The use of diverging lenses to correct nearsightedness (myopia) was documented in 1451.

Today, lenses used in eyeglasses and cameras are usually made of lightweight plastics that are cheaper and more durable than traditional glass lenses.

What is a **converging lens**?

A converging lens has at least one convex side. Its shape causes the entering light rays to converge, that is, come closer together. A converging lens can create a real, inverted image that may be projected on a screen. When used as a magnifying glass it creates a virtual, upright image.

What is a **diverging lens**?

A diverging lens has at least one concave side. The shape of the lens causes the entering light rays to spread apart when they leave the lens. A diverging lens is often used in combination with converging lenses. Eyeglasses to correct nearsightedness use diverging lenses.

What is the **focal length** of a lens?

The focal length measures the strength of a lens. Consider a converging lens. Rays from a very distant object come together at the focal point. The focal length is the distance from the lens to the focal point. Lenses with very convex surfaces have shorter focal lengths, while flatter lenses have longer focal lengths. For diverging lenses the focal point is virtual. That is, it is the point from which the diverging rays leaving the lens would have come from if a point object were placed there.

How does a **pinhole camera** work?

A pinhole camera is typically made from a box with a small "pinhole" in one side of the box and a screen on the other side. The pinhole is so small that only a very small number of light rays can go through it. The diagram on page 211 shows how a pinhole creates a reproduction of the object on the screen. Note that it is not an image because light rays do not converge on the screen.

Pinhole cameras are easy to make and are often used during solar eclipses because it is very dangerous to look directly at the sun (during an eclipse or otherwise). With the sun at your back, point the hole up toward the sun and view the image of the moon passing in front of the sun on the screen.

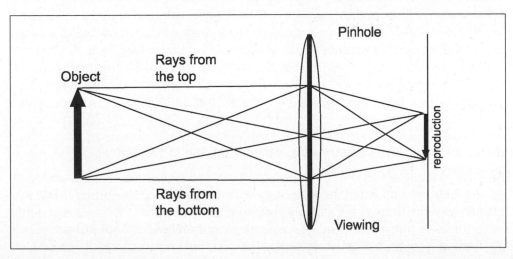

Why do diamonds sparkle so much?

Diamond has a very large index of refraction and therefore a small critical angle of only 25°. If the diamond is cut correctly light striking the top of the diamond will be internally reflected and will emerge again from the top rather than the sides of the diamond

How does a **camera lens create** an **image** on the sensor?

The diagram below shows what would happen if there were three pinholes, each creating an inverted reproduction of the object.

Now, if a converging lens is placed just behind the pinholes it will bend the rays going through it. If the focal length of the lens and the distance between the lens and screen are chosen correctly, then the three reproductions from the pinholes will all be at the same location. Light rays from the top of the object will converge on the appropriate point on the image. Note that the image is inverted and the same size as the reproductions. What would happen if you had a multitude of pinholes at the location of the lens? The reproductions from all the pinholes would be at the same location, and many more rays from the object would end up at the same place on the image. The image would be much brighter. So, you can model the formation of an image by a lens as a collection of reproductions of pinholes. The larger the lens, the brighter the image.

What are **total internal reflection** and **critical angle**?

Total internal reflection occurs when a ray of light in a medium with a higher index of refraction strikes the interface between that medium and one with a lower index of refraction. When the incident rays are at a small angle with respect to the perpendicular to the interface the rays pass through the interface being refracted to a larger angle. As the angle of incidence increases so does the refracted angle. At the "critical" angle the refracted angle is 90°, that is, the ray's direction is along the interface. If the angle of incidence is increased any more there is only a reflected ray, the refracted ray no longer exists. Because all the light is reflected it is called total internal reflection.

If you open your **eyes underwater**, can you **see out** of the **water**?

Another example of total internal reflection can be seen when you are underwater. If you look straight up out of the water, you will see the sky and any other visible surroundings directly above the water. If, however, you look out of the water at an angle of 48° or more from the vertical, you will not see out of the water, but instead will see a reflection from the bottom of the water. The next time you are in a pool or a lake, try

looking up out of the water and you will see a point on the surface where you no longer can see out of the pool, for the light has reached its critical angle.

FIBER OPTICS

How do **optical fibers** use **total internal reflection** to transmit information?

Strands of glass fiber, commonly known as optical fibers, use the principle of total internal reflection to transmit information near the speed of light. The fiber has an inner core of glass with a high refractive index surrounded by a cladding of glass with a lower index. A laser sends light into the end of a strand of fiber. When the light strikes the interface between the core and the cladding, the light is reflected back into the cable, continuing to move down the length of the fiber.

Light or near-infrared radiation can travel kilometers through fibers without significant energy loss. One reason is the total internal reflection. The second reason is that the are made from materials designed to absorb as little as possible of the infrared radiation. A second advantage of optical fibers is that information sent through the fibers is more secure because it doesn't escape the fiber and thus be accessible to those trying to intercept the information.

How did **fiber optics originate**?

The idea that light could travel through glass strands originated as far back as the 1840s, when physicists Daniel Collodon and Jacques Babinet (1794–1872) demonstrated that light could travel through bending water jets in fountains. The first person to display an image through a bundle of optical fibers was a medical student in

Germany by the name of Heinrich Lamm, who, in 1930, used a bundle of fibers to project the image of a light bulb. In his research, Lamm ultimately used optical fibers to observe and probe areas of the human body without making large incisions. From that point on, serious research in optical fibers ensued, expanding later with the development of the laser.

Where are **fiber optics used** today?

The transmission of light information through optical fibers has had a huge

Fiber optics are glass fibers that transmit laser light that can contain digital information more quickly and efficiently than metal cables.

545

impact on the technological world. The medical field has benefited greatly from the use of flexible fiber optic bundles that enable the viewing of areas of the body that would otherwise be inaccessible.

Communications is probably the field that is benefitting the most from the advent of fiber optic technology. Long-distance telephone, computer, and television signals use fiber optic cables. Some systems even use fiber optics to transmit information directly to the home or business. Fiber optics can transmit large amounts of data at high speeds permitting hundreds of television channels, very high speed internet connections, and telephone conversations to be sent and received at the same time.

DIFFRACTION AND INTERFERENCE

What is the **diffraction** of light?

Reflection and refraction use the ray model of light. But, when light goes through a very small opening the ray model is no longer sufficient. The wave properties of light become important. Suppose you pass light through a round aperture whose diameter you can change. Let the light fall on a screen. As you first begin reducing the size of the hole you'll find the size of the bright spot shrinking. But, when the hole becomes very small a strange thing happens. The spot no longer shrinks, but its outer edge becomes fuzzy. Light begins to bend around the edge of the hole. Diffraction also occurs when light is sent through narrow slits or if there are small objects that cast shadows in a broader beam of light. Diffraction occurs with all types of waves. You can often see it in water waves and it is one reason that sound waves spread when they come through a door or window.

What is the **interference** of light?

We've explored wave interference before in the Waves chapter. The key to the interference of light is that the two (or more) waves interfering must have the same wavelength and phase. While interference can be seen with ordinary light, interference is most easily seen using laser light. If light from a laser passes through two slits that are a small distance apart the diffraction patterns from the two slits will overlap. When they do a pattern of light and dark bands will be seen. The bright bands are where waves from the two slits are constructively interfering. The distance the light has traveled from the two slits will be equal or they will differ by an integer number of wavelengths. The dark bands occur when the waves destructively interfere. In this case the difference in distance light from the two slits will have traveled will be an odd number of half wavelengths. That is, one-half, three-halves, five-halves, etc. Light can also interfere if it is reflected off two closely spaced interfaces, like the two surfaces of a soap bubble or oil film.

Why do **soap bubbles** and **gasoline spills** create different **color reflections**?

Iridescence is the spectrum of colors that are produced when light hits a thin film such as a soap bubble or gasoline layer. The interference of light waves resulting from reflections of light off the two surfaces of the thin film causes iridescence. A soap bubble displays an iridescent pattern because light reflects off the front and back surfaces of the soap bubbles. As the thickness of the layer varies, the interference between the two reflections will vary, causing the color to vary.

Soap bubbles have an iridescent shine when light hits them because light waves reflect off the two surfaces of their thin film.

Gasoline spills are easily seen on wet roads; this is not because people spill more gas when it has rained, but is instead due to the iridescent patterns that result from light reflecting off of the top of the gasoline, and the boundary between the gasoline and water. The resulting pattern appears as the colors of the visible light spectrum in the thin film of gasoline.

COLOR

What is **white light**?

White light is the combination of all the colors in the visible light spectrum. When separated from each other, the different wavelengths have different colors. The longest wavelength light is the color red, and decreasing wavelengths result in orange, yellow, green, blue, indigo, and finally, the shortest wavelength visible color, violet.

Who is **Roy G. Biv**?

The colors of the visible light spectrum, in order from long wavelength to short, can be remembered using the fictitious name "Roy G. Biv," which is an acronym for Red, Orange, Yellow, Green, Blue, Indigo, and Violet. Each individual color has a particular wavelength, and as the wavelength changes, the color changes to the next color on the spectrum. When combined with the appropriate intensities these colors form white light.

What is **indigo**?

Indigo is the color between blue and violet in the spectrum, but almost no one can distinguish that color. Why, then are there seven colors rather than six? It's because

Isaac Newton was drawing an analogy between color and musical tones. There are seven notes in the familiar European scale—A, B, C, D, E, F, and G. So, Newton decided there should be seven colors in the spectrum, and he identified indigo as the seventh. So don't be too disappointed if you can't see it.

How do we see objects?

In order to see an object, light from the object must enter our eyes. We can see stars, lightning, and light bulbs because they are emitting or giving off light. We depend on the light emitted from these sources in order to see objects that don't emit light—we see those objects because they reflect light into our eyes. The paper on which this book is printed, for example, does not emit light. We see it because the paper reflects light into our eyes.

Why do we see specific colors?

When we "see" colors, we are seeing only part of the spectrum of colors that make up white light. The rest of the spectrum is missing. Selecting the color seen can be done in three ways. You can view the object through a transparent material that transmits only some part of the spectrum while absorbing the rest. The object may be colored itself. That is, it reflects part of the spectrum while absorbing the rest. Finally, the spectrum can be physically separated, as it is by interference or by refraction by a prism or rainbow. For example, theatrical "gels" on spotlights produce colored effects for a stage show. Snow reflects all of the spectrum so it appears white, but green paper reflects only the green part of the spectrum. A black cloth absorbs all light, and so it appears black.

Who discovered that white light could be separated into the colors of the rainbow?

By the seventeenth century glass makers had learned to make gem-shaped pieces that were used in chandeliers. Candlelight was refracted in these pieces. When viewing the candlelight different colors were seen, depending on the angles made by the light, the glass, and the viewer's eye. Newton, who was intrigued by the colors that were produced by those chandeliers, decided to examine how a piece of glass shaped as a rectangular prism could create a spectrum of colors. In his own words: "In a darkened Room make a hole in the [windowshade] of a window, whose diameter may conveniently be about [one-third] of an inch, to admit a convenient quantity of the Sun's light: And there place a clear and colourless Prisme, to refract the entering light towards the further part of the Room, which, as I said, will thereby be diffused into an oblong [spectrum]."

To prove that the colors did not come from the prism, Newton expanded the experiment by reversing the procedure and forming white light from the spectrum of colors. He accomplished this by placing a lens in the middle of the spectrum to con-

verge the colors on a second prism in the path of the colors. Sure enough, a beam of white light emerged out of the second prism.

Why does a **prism** separate light into a spectrum of colors?

If all wavelengths of light were refracted by the same amount when entering and leaving a prism then there would be no separation of colors. The refractive index of all materials depends on the wavelength of light. In diamond the refractive index for blue is 1.594, for red 1.571. In flint glass the index varies from 1.528 to 1.514. In crown glass the variation is from 1.528 to 1.514, while in water it is only 1.340 to 1.331. In all cases the refractive index of blue is larger than that of red, so the blue light is refracted through a larger angle than the red. The large difference in diamonds accounts for their "flash."

If white is the combination of the colors of the rainbow, **what is black**?

Black, the exact opposite of white light, is the absence of light or the absorption of all light. It may seem obvious to us, but Newton was the first to recognize this fact. A black piece of paper appears black because all the light is being absorbed in the paper—none is reflected back out to our eyes.

What are the **primary colors** from a light source?

When mixing light (or "additive color mixing") the three primary colors are blue, green, and red. Computer monitors and both cathode ray tube (CRT) and flat-panel television sets use these colors. The combination of these primary colors results in other colors, and when all three colors are combined with equal intensity, white is formed.

What are the **secondary colors**?

When any two of the three primary colors are mixed, secondary colors are formed; they are called secondary because they are by-products of the primary red, green, and blue colors. Red light mixed with green creates yellow light. Red and blue produces magenta. Finally, cyan is formed when blue light and green light are added together.

What are **complementary colors**?

Complementary colors are pairs of one secondary and one primary color that, when mixed, form what is close to white light. For example, yellow and blue light are complementary because when combined, they form white light, as will magenta and green, and cyan and red.

What is **subtractive color mixing**?

As opposed to the mixing of light ("additive color mixing"), subtractive color mixing occurs only when combining dyes, pigments, or other objects that absorb and reflect

light. For example, you could shine white light through two colored filters or gels. Or, you can reflect light from colored surfaces. If you shine white light on a blue wall, the wall absorbs red and green but not blue. So if we know what colors are reflected we know the color of the object.

The primary pigments or dyes are magenta, which reflects blue and red light but absorbs green; cyan, which reflects blue and green but absorbs red; and yellow, which reflects red and green but absorbs blue. These are the same colors as the secondary colors obtained when mixing light. Note that if we combine magenta, cyan, and yellow, the red, green, and blue are all removed, leaving nothing; that is, black.

Blue is light in the range of 400 to 500 nanometers. Green is roughly 500 to 560 nanometers. Yellow is 560 to 590 nanometers, orange 590 to 620 nanometers, and red beyond 620 nanometers. It may seem surprising that yellow filter transmits green, yellow, and red. But the eye is not very sensitive to red in comparison to green and yellow. That's the same reason that the transmission of the blue and indigo filters beyond 660 nanometers does not impact what the eye sees. Finally, note that purple is a mixture of blue and red.

What are the **secondary colors** in **subtractive color mixing**?

The secondary colors for dyes and pigments are the same as the primary colors in additive color mixing. Red, green, and blue dyes or pigments reflect their own color while absorbing the other two colors. For example, red would reflect red but absorb the green and blue light.

Color inkjet printers use black, along with yellow, cyan, and magenta, because the colored pigments do not cover the full spectrum. Therefore, they cannot produce a dark black but only a muddy dark brown.

Why do most **color inkjet printers** use **four colors** to print, instead of the three primary colors for subtractive color mixing?

It would seem that a color inkjet printer mixing the three primary pigments of yellow, magenta, and cyan should be able to produce all the other colors, including black. When all three primary colors are combined, however, the mix looks more like a muddy brown color than black. Although these are the primary colors of which other shades can be created, they do not represent all the colors of the spectrum needed to form black. That is, there are gaps in the wavelengths that

What is colorimetry?

Because the perception of color is mostly a neurophysiological function between the eyes and the brain, it can vary slightly from person to person. Further, the subtractive color seen depends on the light source. If you plan to paint a room you should examine the color when illuminated by several different lights sources: sunlight, light from incandescent lamps, and light from fluorescent lamps. The colors may look very different. They will even look different in the sunlight at noon versus that near sunset. Scientists, artists, advertisers, and printers need an objective method of specifying color as it relates to the frequency of light. This technique for measuring the intensity of particular wavelengths of light is known as colorimetry.

these pigments absorb. Therefore, most color inkjet printers have a cartridge with yellow, cyan, and magenta ink, and another separate ink cartridge of just black.

What is the **difference** between **hue** and **saturation**?

Hue is related to the wavelength of a color. Saturation is the extent to which other wavelengths of light are present in a particular color. For example for the hue red, deep red is saturated, but pink is a mixture of red and white.

On **humid summer days**, why does the **sky** take on a **white** or **grayish** appearance?

When high amounts of humidity are in the air, water molecules are more prevalent than on a cool, dry day. Water molecules, which have two hydrogen and one oxygen atom, are larger than oxygen and nitrogen found in the air, and the size of a molecule plays a significant role in what frequencies of light are scattered. When white light encounters a larger molecule or dust particle, larger wavelength light will be scattered, whereas if a smaller molecule is struck by white light, smaller wavelength light will be scattered. Snow, beaten egg whites, and beer foam look white for the same reason.

If the water or smoke is dense enough, then all light waves are scattered many times, and the cloud looks grey.

Why are **sunrises** and **sunsets** often **orange** or **red**?

During the evening and early morning, when the sun is lower in the horizon, the light that the sun emits has to travel through more of the atmosphere to reach us than it does during midday, when the path through the atmosphere is shorter. Since the dis-

tance through the atmosphere is much larger for sunlight in the morning and evening than during midday, more of the shorter wavelengths of light are scattered out of the direct light from the sun. Thus the sun's color goes from yellow to orange and finally to red. Dust and water vapor in the atmosphere enhance this effect, making sunsets even redder.

Why is the **ocean blue**?

There are two major reasons why the ocean and most bodies of water appear blue. The first can be observed by looking at the water on a cloudy day and then on a sunny day. There is a rather large difference in how blue the water appears to be on the two different days, because the water acts as a mirror for the sky. So on a sunny day with a blue sky, the water will have a richer blue color than on a cloudy day.

The second reason why bodies of water have a blue appearance is that water scatters short wavelength light more than the longer. In fact, water absorbs some orange, red, and the very long-wavelength infrared. As a result it absorbs more energy in the sunlight, increasing its temperature. The much larger amounts of reflected, short-wavelength light results in a crisp blue-colored body of water.

Some bodies of water may take on a more greenish or at times a brownish or black color. Usually this is due to other elements in the water such as algae, silt, and sand. Runoff water from glaciers is very white due to the tiny grains of silt in the water. Still, in the majority of cases, water looks blue.

RAINBOWS

How do **rainbows occur**?

A rainbow is a spectrum of light formed when sunlight interacts with droplets. Upon entering a water droplet, the white light is refracted, and dispersed, that is, spread apart into its individual wavelengths, just as in a prism. The light inside the droplet then reflects against the back of the water droplet before it refracts and disperses as it exits the droplet. The angle between entering and leaving is 40° for blue light, 42° for red.

What **conditions** must be met in order to see a **rainbow**?

There are two main conditions for witnessing a rainbow. The first is that the observer must be between the sun and the water droplets. The water droplets can either be rain, mist from a waterfall, or the spray of a garden hose. The second condition is that the angle between the sun, the water droplets, and the observer's eyes must be between 40° and 42°. Therefore, rainbows are most easily seen when the sun is close to the horizon so the rays striking the droplets are close to horizontal.

Is there such a thing as a **completely circular rainbow**?

All rainbows would be completely round except that the ground gets in the way of completing the circle. However, if viewed from a high altitude, such as an airplane, circular rainbows can been seen when the angle between the sun, the water droplets, and the plane is between the 40° and 42°. In this case, the rainbow is horizontal, meaning that it is parallel to the ground and therefore not blocked by the ground. This is quite a sight!

What is the **order of colors** in a **ralnbow**?

The order of colors in a rainbow goes from longest-wavelength red on the outer arc to shortest-wavelength blue on the inside of the arc. The full order from outer to inner is: red, orange, yellow, green, blue, indigo, and violet.

Who was the **first person** to **explain** how **rainbows** are formed?

Newton was not the first person to understand the optical characteristics of a rainbow. In fact, it was a German monk in the early fourteenth century who first discovered that light refracted and reflected inside a water droplet. To demonstrate his hypothesis, the monk filled a sphere with water, sent a ray of sunlight through the sphere, and observed the separation of the white light into colors along with the reflection on the back of the water droplet.

What is a **secondary rainbow**?

The secondary rainbow has its color spectrum reversed, is outside of the original rainbow, and is significantly dimmer than the primary rainbow. A secondary rainbow occurs because an additional reflection of the light takes place inside the water droplets. Instead of reflecting once in the water droplet, the light reflects twice inside the water, reversing the order of the colors. The secondary rainbow appears between the angles 50° and 54°.

EYESIGHT

How does the human **eye see**?

The eye is really an extension of the brain. It consists of a lens to focus the image, an iris to regulate the amount of light entering the eye, and a screen called the retina. The cells of the retina do some preliminary processing of the information they receive then send signals along the optic nerve to the brain.

The cornea is a transparent membrane on the outer surface of the eye. Between the cornea and lens is a fluid. Light refracts when going through the convex surface of the cornea into the fluid. In fact most of the focusing of light in the eye occurs at the cornea. Light passes through the iris that opens and closes in response to the amount of light entering the eye. The iris can only change the amount of light to a going through it by a factor of twenty, while our eye can respond to differences in light level of ten trillion! The major task of the iris then can't be to control light intensity. In addition, when the opening in the iris shrinks the eye can keep objects in focus from a wider range of distances. After passing through the iris the light goes through the lens.

The lens consists of layers of transparent fibers covered by a clear membrane. In order to focus in on objects that we want to see, our eye changes the shape, and thus the focal length of the lens and cornea by contracting or relaxing the ciliary muscle around the eye. Light then passes through a liquid called the vitreous humor that fills the major volume of the eye and falls on the retina. The cornea and lens have created an inverted image on the surface of the retina.

The retina is composed of a layer of light-sensitive cells, a matrix of nerve cells, and a dark backing. There are two kinds of light-sensitive cells: cones and rods. The 7 million cones are sensitive to high light levels and are concentrated around the fovea, the part of the retina directly behind the lens. Surrounding it are some 120 million rods that are sensitive to low light levels. The entire retina covers about five square centimeters. There aren't 127 million nerves in the optic nerve that goes to the brain, so a system of nerves in the retina do some preliminary processing of the electrical signals produced by the rods and cones before sending the results to the brain.

What is the difference between **cones** and **rods**?

Cones are cone-shaped nerve cells on the retina that can distinguish fine details in images. They are located predominantly around the center of the retina called the fovea. The cones are also responsible for color vision. Some cones respond to blue light, being most sensitive to 440-nanometer wavelengths. A second kind has peak sensitivity in the green: 530-nanometer light. The third is sensitive to a wide band of wavelengths from cyan through red. Its sensitivity peaks in the yellow, 560 nanometers.

As the distance grows from the fovea, rod-shaped nerve cells replace the cones. The rods are responsible for a general image over a large area, but not fine details. This explains why we look at objects straight on when examining something carefully. The image will be focused around the fovea, where the majority of cones pick up the fine details of the image. The rods, being much more sensitive in low light levels, are used a lot for night vision.

What **wavelengths of light** are our **eyes most sensitive** to?

Our eyes are most sensitive to the wavelengths corresponding to the yellow and green colors of the spectrum. Flashy signs and some fire engines are painted in a yellowish-green color to attract our attention. Even simple objects such as highlighters, used to emphasize words or phrases while taking notes, are typically bright yellow and green. When we glance over something or see an object out of the corner of our eyes, we are more likely to notice bright yellowish green objects than red or blue objects, because the eye is less sensitive to these wavelengths.

What is the **shape** of a **lens** when **focusing on objects** far away and objects up close?

The ciliary muscle, responsible for changing the shape of the lens, adjusts its tension to focus on different distances. When focusing on objects far away, the lens needs a large focal length, so the muscle is relaxed in order to make the lens relatively flat. When an object is closer to the eye, however, a shorter focal length is needed. The ciliary muscle contracts, reducing the focal length of the lens by making it more spherical. The process of adjusting the shape of the lens to focus in on objects is called "accommodation."

What is color blindness?

Some people are unable to see some colors due to an inherited condition known as color blindness. John Dalton (1766–1844), a British chemist and physicist, described color blindness in 1794. He was color blind himself, and could not distinguish red from green. Many color-blind people do not realize that they cannot distinguish colors. This is potentially dangerous, particularly if they cannot distinguish between the colors of traffic lights or other safety signals. Those people who perceive red as green and green as red are known, appropriately, as "red-green color blind." Other color-blind people are only able to see black, gray, and white. It is estimated that 7% of men and 1% of women are born color blind.

When **swimming underwater**, why is **vision blurred** when you open your eyes, but clear when wearing swimming goggles?

Although the eye's lens changes shape to focus images on the retina, most of the refraction of light takes place during light's transition from air to the cornea. When water is substituted for air, the angles through which light is refracted is reduced, producing a blurred image on the retina.

How **close** can an **object** be before it **appears blurry**?

There is a limit as to how close an object can be to the eye before the lens can no longer adjust its focus. Up to about thirty years of age, the closest an object can be focused is approximately 10 to 20 centimeters (4 to 8 inches). As one grows older, the lens tends to stiffen and it becomes more difficult for the person to focus on close objects. In fact, by the time a person reaches the age of seventy, their eyes cannot focus on objects within several meters of their eyes. As a result, most aging adults need reading glasses to focus on close objects.

What is **nearsightedness** and what can be done to correct it?

Nearsighted vision means that a person can only clearly see objects that are relatively near the eye. Images from distant objects are focused in front of the retina. Nearsightedness, or myopia, is most often caused by a cornea that bulges out too much. The lens cannot be flattened enough to compensate, and so distant objects appear fuzzy.

To correct for the short focal length of the lens, a concave lens is used to make the light rays diverge just enough so that the image will fall on the retina. So contact lenses to correct for myopia are thicker at the edges than at the center.

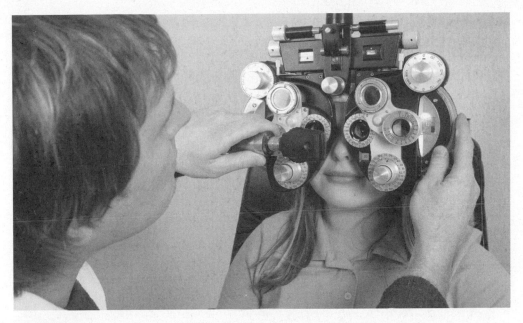

Farsightedness and nearsightedness are common eyesight problems. The former occurs when images entering the eye are focused behind the retina, and in the latter images focus in front of the retina.

What is **farsightedness** and what can be done to correct it?

Farsightedness, or hyperopia, occurs when the lens of the eye can see objects far away, but cannot focus in on objects at closer range. The cornea and lens of the person with farsightedness cause the image to focus behind the retina, resulting in the images from objects close to the eye to be blurred. In order to correct for farsightedness, a convex lens is used to converge the light rays closer together, permitting the image to fall on the retina. The rigidity in the eyelens that affects older people, making them unable to focus on close objects, is called presbyopia.

What allows **nocturnal animals** to **see better** in the **dark** than humans can?

There are three main reasons why some animals can see better than humans can at night. The first reason is that their eyes, relative to body size, are larger and can gather more light than human eyes can. More light results in a brighter image.

The next reason has to do with the rods and cones in the nocturnal animal's eyes. Cones are used for detail and work best in bright light. A nocturnal animal has little need for the color vision provided by the cones and therefore has more room for the rods that detect general information such as motion and shapes.

The third reason why nocturnal eyes excel in the absence of light is due to the *tapetum lucidum*, a membrane on the back of the retina that reflects light back to

557

How do 3-D movies and television work?

When a three-dimensional movie is filmed, two cameras film the movie from slightly different positions. When the film is projected on the screen, each projector uses a separate polarizing filter. The left projector might use a horizontally polarized filter, while the right projector uses a vertically polarized filter. The viewer wears polarized glasses. The glasses allow the left eye to see only the image produced from the horizontally polarized image of the left projector, while the right eye sees the image produced by the vertically polarized right projector. This arrangement simulates the different perspectives that each eye sees when looking at a real-life 3-D scene, allowing the brain to interpret the difference as depth (the third dimension).

The newest methods of producing three-dimensional views use digital methods rather than film. In the method best suited to 3-D television the images from the left and right camera lenses alternate at a rapid rate. The viewer wears glasses in which each lens can be switched from transparent to opaque on command from an infrared signal sent from the television set. Thus each eye sees only the frames captured by the appropriate camera lens. Another method that is more suited to movies, again uses digital images that alternate between those captured by the right camera lens with those captured by the left. A device placed in front of the projector lens switches the polarization of the light coming from the projector so that left images are polarized one way, right images are polarized the other way. The movie viewer wears polarized glasses so that each eye sees only the appropriate frames.

the retina to double the retina's exposure to light. The reflective tapetum can be seen in the light reflected back out of animals' eyes at night when you shine a flashlight on them.

What is **three-dimensional** (3-D) **vision**?

Seeing in three dimensions, which is how a person with normal eyes sees, means that in addition to perceiving the dimensions of height and width (such as seen on a piece of paper, a poster, or a TV or movie screen), one can see the third dimension of depth. We see real objects in 3-D because we have two eyes that see slightly different perspectives of the same view. The combination of these views, when interpreted by our brain, gives us the ability to perceive depth, the third dimension.

If you close one eye, your ability to perceive depth is eliminated. With only one eye, the world won't look very different to you, but you'll experience difficulty in judging distances.

CAMERAS

How is a **camera similar** to, and different from, the **eye**?

A camera performs many of the functions of the eye. It has a lens to form an image on a photosensitive surface. The lens must be able to form sharp images of objects both close and far away. The amount of light reaching the photo detector must be controlled to make the exposure correct. In older cameras the photosensitive surface was film. Today cameras use a digital sensor. These sensors are small—most are between 3/8" and 1" in size—but contain as many as 10 million separate light detectors called pixels. Each pixel is covered by a red, green, or blue color filter so the camera can produce full-color images.

A camera's lens isn't flexible like the one in the eye, but the distance between the lens and the sensor can be varied. Bringing a distant object into focus requires that the lens be closer to the sensor. A close object requires that the lens be moved further away. The amount of light is controlled two ways. One is to have an aperture that can be opened to admit more light or closed down to reduce the amount of light. The second is a shutter that controls the amount of time light is allowed to reach the sensor. While leaving the sensor exposed for a longer amount of time is needed when the light is dim, it also will cause a blurred image if the object is moving. Thus it is important to select the correct combination of aperture and shutter speed to take good pictures.

What causes **red-eye** in **photographs**?

Red-eye occurs when a flash is used because there is not enough light for a good exposure. Under normal conditions, in order for enough light to enter the eye, the pupil dilates. But when a flash is fired, the pupils are not expecting the bright light and do not have a chance to constrict. As a result, a large amount of light enters the eye and reflects off the blood vessels that supply the retina in the back of the eye. The redness on the pupil is actually the reflection off these blood vessels captured by the camera.

Camera lenses are similar to human eyes in that both have lenses that focus images onto a surface, but camera lenses are not flexible like an eye lens.

What is used to **reduce red-eye**?

Red-eye reduction is a feature found on many modern cameras. It simply attempts to constrict a person's pupil so that not as much light can be reflected back from the

retina. There are several methods of accomplishing this. One method is to have a smaller light that illuminates before the real flash; another method is to have a quick burst of five or six mini-flashes that cause the pupil to contract before the picture is taken.

TELESCOPES

Who invented the first telescope?

There are a number of conflicting claims for the first person to combine two lenses to "see things far away as if they were nearby." The Dutch eyeglass makers Hans Lippershey, Sacharias Jansen, and Jacob Metius were some of the first. Lippershey described the design and applied for a patent on October 8, 1608, but was turned down. Copies of Lippershey's device, which was constructed from a convex and a concave lens and had a magnifying power of 3, were common in the Netherlands that year. Galileo (1564–1642) heard about the invention in June 1609, in Venice. By the next day he had figured out how it worked and as soon as he returned home to Padua he constructed one. A few days later he demonstrated it to the leaders in Venice, who, in return awarded him a lifetime position at the University in Padua. Over the next year Galileo improved his instruments, and in 1610, using a telescope with a magnifying power of 33, he discovered the moons of Jupiter, the rotation of the sun, phases of Venus, spots on the sun, and mountains on the moon. The Galilean telescope with convex and concave lenses produces an upright image.

Based on the ideas of astronomers Johannes Kepler (1571–1630) and Christoph Scheiner, the telescope was improved by using two convex lenses separated by a distance equal to the sum of their focal lengths. Such a telescope inverts the image. To achieve high magnifications one of the focal lengths had to be very large. Refracting telescopes proved to be cumbersome and difficult to use. The prism-like shape of the lenses introduced colors into the images that weren't there. This defect, called chromatic aberration, was eliminated 120 years later using a lens made of a combination of two glasses. But this invention did not stop the weight of the large lens from causing it to sag, creating distorted images.

Reflecting telescopes that use mirrors to focus light, were invented by Isaac Newton (1642–1727) in 1668. Today, telescopes, both refractors and reflectors, are relatively cheap; the average person can set one up in his or her backyard and gaze up at the heavens with much better equipment than Galileo or Newton ever dreamed possible.

What is a refractor telescope?

The refractor telescope was the first telescope ever created. It employs one lens to gather, refract, and focus light toward an eyepiece. The eyepiece contains one or more

> ## What was wrong with the Hubble Space Telescope when it was first put into orbit?
>
> An error (1/50th the thickness of a human hair) in the curvature of the main mirror caused major focusing problems for the Hubble Space Telescope. The 2.4 meter (94.5 inch) diameter mirror, was not able to focus all the light it collected to the correct point in the telescope. NASA suffered great embarrassment for this multi-million dollar mistake.

lenses that create an image that they eye can see. The larger the diameter of the lens, the more light the telescope can gather. The weight of the lenses then limits the practical size of refractor telescopes.

What is a **reflecting telescope**?

A reflecting telescope uses a mirror to gather light and focus the light toward the eyepiece. It usually consists of two mirrors: one large curved mirror at the end of the telescope to gather light and a smaller mirror used to direct the light to the eyepiece

What are some of the **largest reflecting telescopes**?

The larger a reflecting telescope, the more light it can gather. The following is a list of some of the largest reflecting telescopes in the world.

Name	Effective diameter	Type	Location	Date Completed
Large Binocular Telescope (LBT)	11.8 m (464.6 ft.)	Multiple mirror	Arizona	2004
Gran Telescopio Canarias (GTC)	10.4 m (410 ft.)	Segmented	Canary Islands	2006–9
Keck 1	10 m (400 ft.)	Segmented	Hawaii	1993
Southern African Large Telescope (SALT)	9.2 m (362 ft.)	Segmented	South African Astronomical Observatory	2005
Hobby-Eberly Telescope (HET)	9.2 m (362 ft.)	Segmented	Texas	1997
Subaru (JNLT)	8.2 m (323 ft.)	Single	Hawaii	1999

What is a **segmented mirror telescope**?

When mirrors exceed 8 meters (26 feet) in diameter, they are no longer rigid enough to maintain the same shape when they are tilted. The Keck I telescope was the first to

be built of 36 hexagonal mirrors. The tilt of each mirror is controlled electronically so that they all focus their light rays at a single point. The electronics can position each corner of the mirror to an accuracy 4 nanometers to create the final image. Constructing the telescope of multiple smaller mirrors greatly reduced the cost of the telescope. The Large Binocular Telescope consists of the Keck I and Keck II 10-meter (33-foot) telescopes. When they are used together they can detect the interference of light from a star and thus determine its size and location much more precisely.

The Hubble Space Telescope can see deeper into space than earthbound telescopes because there is no atmospheric distortion to interfere with how it sees images.

What are the advantages of the **Hubble Space Telescope**?

The Hubble doesn't have a mirror as large as the new Earth-based telescopes, but being in space it is not limited by the distortions caused by variations in the refractive index of air above the telescope. In addition, a space telescope can detect the infrared and ultraviolet rays blocked by Earth's atmosphere. Other space-based telescopes are designed to detect X rays and gamma rays from extremely energetic stars and galaxies.

What was done to **correct** the **Hubble's vision problems**?

Three years after the Hubble was placed in orbit around Earth, a team of astronauts from the space shuttle Endeavor installed two tiny mirrors that would correct the focusing problems that the Hubble was experiencing. The telescope has since had several servicing calls, the most recent in 2009. Upgraded detectors and spectrometers have been installed, faulty positioning gyroscopes replaced, and its batteries replaced. The batteries are used when Earth's shadow blocks the sunlight on the solar panels.

Since its repairs, the Hubble Space Telescope has aided research into the age of the universe and the rate at which it is expanding, and has enabled observation of other stars and galaxies that previously were never seen by earthbound telescopes. More than 8,000 scientific papers have been published using Hubble data. Equally important, the beautiful photos taken by Hubble have fascinated the public and broadened its understanding of the incredible range of objects in our universe.

ELECTRICITY

What is **electrostatics**?

Electrostatics is the study of the causes of the attractive and repulsive forces that result when objects made of two different materials are rubbed together. Electrostatics is the study of what is often called static electricity.

What can you **discover** about **static electricity**?

How about exploring the basic ideas of electrostatics? All you'll need is a roll of cellophane tape. Any brand will do—the cheaper the better. Pull off a strip about 5 inches long, then fold over about 1/4 inch at one end to serve as a handle. Press the tape on your desk or a table. Mark the strip with the letter "B." Make a second identical tape and press it down next to the first.

Holding the two tapes by their handles, quickly pull them off your desk. They'll probably be attracted to your hands, so shake them until they hang free. Then bring them closer together. What do you see? You should see them bending, evidence that there is a force between them. If they don't bend, stick them on the desk again and again pull them off. Do they provide evidence that there is an attractive or repulsive force between them?

We'll say that pulling them off the table caused them to be "charged," although we have no evidence with what they are "charged." They were obviously charged in the same way, so we can conclude that objects with like charges repel each other. By the way, we'll work toward an explanation why they're attracted to your hands.

Press the two strips back on your desk. Now make two more strips the same length and press them on top of the first two strips. Mark these strips "T" to identify them as the top tapes, as opposed to the "B" or bottom tapes.

Electrostatics—or static electricity—involves the attractive and repulsive forces that result when objects made of two different materials are rubbed together.

Slowly pull the T + B pair of tapes off the desk together. If they are attracted to your hand then use the other hand to gently pat both sides of them over their entire length. That should remove any residual charge from the pair of tapes. If not, pat them down again.

You have a pair of objects with no charge. Holding the two handles of the pair rapidly pull them apart. Again, if they are attracted to your hands, shake them until they hang freely. Bring them closer together. Is there evidence of a force between them? Is it attractive or repulsive?

You started with a pair of objects with no charge. Pulling them apart caused them to be charged, but not in the same way, because they didn't repel each other, but attracted. Thus you can conclude that they must be charged differently, and objects with different charges attract.

To keep your charged tapes you can hang them from the edge of your desk or a desk light. Make a second T+B pair and see if the two T (top) tapes are charged alike or differently. If the tapes stop interacting you can repeat the charging procedure as often as you like.

Hang a T and a B tape so you can bring objects near them to see if there are forces between them. Make a list of the objects you tried and whether they attracted or repelled the T tape and the B tape. Try your finger. Then try rubbing a plastic pen on a piece of wool. Try plastic rubbed by silk or polyester. Try glass and metal.

Do some objects attract both tapes? Repel both tapes? Attract one and repel the other? If they do the latter, you can characterize them as being charged like the T tape or like the B tape.

We'll come back to understand why some objects can attract both kinds of charge, but no objects can repel both.

What is the **history** of **electricity**?

Pre-historic people valued and traded amber, a gem-like material that is petrified tree sap. Surely more than once a person would have rubbed amber on his or her fur clothing and noticed that fur was attracted to the stone. Perhaps she rubbed it hard enough to produce sparks. The Greek philosopher Thales of Miletus wrote about these effects around 600 B.C.E.

But it wasn't until 1600 C.E., some 2,200 years later, that William Gilbert (1544–1603), an English physician, named this effect "electricity" after the Greek name for amber: "elektron." Gilbert showed that sulfur, wax, glass, and other materials behaved the same way as amber. He invented the first instrument to detect what we now call the electrical charge on objects called a versorium, a pointer that was attracted to charged object. Gilbert also discovered that a heated body lost its charge and that moisture prevented the charging of all bodies.

In 1729, the English scientist Stephen Gray (1666–1736) determined that charge, or what he called the "electric virtue," could be transmitted over long distances by metals, objects that couldn't be charged.

How was **electricity used** as a form of **entertainment**?

In the mid-1700s demonstrations of electrostatics were extremely popular, especially in Parisian salons, where wealthy men and women gathered to discuss events of the day. Benjamin Franklin (1706–1790) was a popular guest. In Stephen Gray's most famous demonstration, called the Flying Boy experiment, a boy was suspended horizontally using two silk threads hung from hooks placed on the ceiling. When a charged tube was held near his foot, pieces of metal foil were attracted to his face and to his outstretched hands.

Louis-Guillaume le Monnier discharged a Leyden jar through a chain of 140 courtiers in the presence of the King of France. Jean-Antoine Nollet (1700–1770) attempted to measure the speed of electricity by having a line of monks 1 kilometer (3,280 feet) long hold hands. The monks at the ends of the line touched a machine that produced charge. They all jumped simultaneously when they felt the painful shock, so he concluded that electricity moved instantaneously.

How do **fluids** model **electric charges**?

How could these results be explained? Charles-François Dufay (1698–1739) concluded that there were two types of electricity. He named them "vitreous" (meaning glass, precious stones) and "resinous" (amber, sealing wax, silk). Friction separates the two types. When they are combined they neutralize each other. Jean-Antoine Nollet modeled these types as two fluids, each composed of particles that repelled each other. Charging amber gave it an excess of resinous fluid. Charging glass with silk gave it an excess of vitreous fluid. When the two were touched together the fluids combined with each other leaving the objects uncharged.

Benjamin Franklin believed there was only one fluid. When glass was rubbed the fluid filled the glass. When amber was rubbed the fluid left the amber. He called an object with an excess of fluid "positive" and one with too little fluid "negative." When they were touched the fluid flowed from the glass to the amber, leaving each with its

proper amount of fluid. The flow was likened to water in a river. The "electrical tension" (difference in potential) and "electrical current" were analogous to the difference of water levels between two points and of the amount of water transferred.

What makes an object positively charged, negatively charged, or neutral?

The massive nucleus of an atom consists of positively charged protons and uncharged neutrons. It is surrounded by a cloud of negatively charged electrons. Normally atoms are neutral: the number of electrons equals the number of protons in the nucleus. A negatively charged object is an object that has an excess of electrons. A positively charged object has fewer electrons than protons in the nucleus.

What combination of charges causes attractive and repulsive forces?

As you observed, unlike gravitational forces, which only attract masses to each other, electrostatic forces can either attract or repel charges. Like charges (positive–positive or negative–negative) repel each other. Unlike charges (positive–negative) attract each other. A common phrase describing many human social relationships, "opposites attract," holds true for electrostatic forces.

What are the two ways to charge an object?

When a rubber rod is rubbed with fur, the fur transfers electrons to the rubber rod. The rod and fur, originally neutral, are now charged. If an object touches the rod some of the excess electrons on the rod can move to the object, charging it. The rod, which is now negatively charged because it has excess electrons, can attract positive charges. This method is called charging by contact.

But, as you observed with the cellophane tapes, your hand and other neutral objects attract both positively and negatively charged objects. How does this happen? The rod attracts positive charges and repels negative charges. Neutral objects contain equal numbers of positive and negative charges. In a conductor the charges are free to move and so the electrons can be pushed to the far end of the object making it negatively charged and leaving the close end positively charged. An object that is neutral but has separated charges is polarized. Is there a net force on a polarized object? And can it exert a net force on the charged object, like the cellophane tape? Yes, because the electrostatic force is stronger at closer distances. Thus the attractive force between the unlike charges is stronger than the repulsive force between the like charges, and there is a net attractive force.

In non-conducting materials the charges cannot be widely separated, but they can move within the atoms or molecules. So insulators, like pieces of paper, dust, or hair, can also be attracted, even though they are neutral.

Did you ever see a piece of paper attracted to a charged rod, touch it, and then jump away? How would that happen? If it touched the rod, it became charged with a charge like that of the rod, and so it would now be repelled. A conductor can also be charged after being polarized, but without touching the charged object. If you bring a large metal object, like a pie plate, near a charged rod, the positive charges will move to the far end of the plate. If you now touch this end briefly with your finger the positive charges will be pushed even further away into your finger. When you remove your finger the pie plate is negatively charged. This process is called charging by induction.

Rubbing a glass rod with silk will achieve the same effect. The glass rod is positively charged, while the silk receives the excess negative electrons. The glass rod can still pick up small objects, but attracts the negative charges in those objects instead of the positive charges. When the pie plate is charged by induction it will be positively charged.

Why does a rubber **balloon** that has been **rubbed** in your hair **stick** to a **wall**?

The attraction between a charged balloon and a wall is the result of electrostatic forces. When rubber is rubbed on human hair or a wool sweater, electrons transfer easily to the rubber balloon. The balloon is charged by rubbing. The hair or sweater fuzz may stand up as a result of the excess positive charges repelling each other. When the balloon is brought near the wall, it polarizes the wall, moving the positive sources toward it and repelling the negative charges away. The negatively charged balloon is attracted to the many positive charges in the wall. As long as the electrostatic force and frictional force between the balloon and the wall are stronger than the gravitational force pulling the balloon down, the balloon will remain on the wall.

Why do you sometimes get a **shock** when **touching a doorknob**?

This annoyance happens usually on dry days after walking on carpeted floors. The friction between the carpet and your shoes or socks causes charges to be moved between

Circuit boards are sensitive to electrostatic buildup, and can be damaged if such a charge accumulates on sections of the circuit.

your body and the carpet. Usually your body becomes negatively charged. When your hand approaches a doorknob the negative charges in your hand are attracted to the positive charges in the doorknob (created by polarization), causing an electrical spark when the two charges meet.

What are some **good conductors** of electricity?

In order to be an effective conductor, a material must allow the electrons to move easily throughout it. The atoms in good conductors, such as most metals, have one or two electrons that can be easily freed from the nucleus to move through the material. Water is a fair conductor, but when salt is added it becomes a better electrical conductor.

What is a **good insulator** of electrical charge?

In an insulator the electrons are strongly bound to their nuclei and thus cannot move through the material. Good insulators are non-metals, such as plastic, wood, stone, and glass. Your skin is a good insulator, unless it is wet.

How is the strength of an **electrical force measured**?

British philosopher, theologian, and scientist Joseph Priestley (1733–1804) suggested that the force caused by static electricity might depend on distance the same way gravity does. Using Priestley's idea, the French physicist Charles Coulomb (1736–1806) made quantitative measurements of the force of attraction and repulsion between charged objects using an apparatus shown in the accompanying illustration. He found that the force depended on the charge of the two objects and the distance between them. The relationship he found is called Coulomb's Law and the unit of measurement of charge as the coulomb (C).

What is **Coulomb's Law**?

Coulomb's Law describes the strength of the electrical force between two charged objects. The formula is $F = k \, (q_1 \, q_2/r^2)$, where k is a constant equal to 9.0×10^9 Nm^2/C^2 (newton-meters squared per coulombs squared). The charges q_1 and q_2, measured in coulombs, represent the charges on the objects that cause the force F, mea-

sured in newtons. Finally, r is the distance between the centers of the two charged objects. A negative force is an attractive force, while a positive force is repulsive.

What is a **coulomb** of charge?

A coulomb of charge is equal to the charge of 6.24×10^{18} electrons (negative) or protons (positive). A coulomb is a very large charge. Objects that are charged by rubbing or induction have typically a microcoulomb (10^{-6} C) of charge.

What is an **electroscope**?

An electroscope is a device used to measured the charge on an object. It consists of two metal leaves (either thin aluminum foil or gold leaf) attached to a metal rod. If you touch a charged object to the metal rod the two leaves will be charged with like charges, and so they will repel each other. The larger the charge, the greater the angle will be between the leaves.

What is an **electric field**?

As discussed before, a gravitational field surrounds Earth or any object with mass. Another object with mass that is placed in this field will experience a gravitational force on it. In the same manner, an electric field surrounds a charged object. Another charged object placed in that field will experience a force. If a positive force creates the field then the force caused by the field on a negative force will be toward the source of the field. A positive charge will experience a force away from the source. The English physicist Michael Faraday (1791–1867) was the first to use the concept of a field to describe the electrostatic force.

LEYDEN JARS AND CAPACITORS

What is the **Leyden jar**?

Water can be stored in a jar. In what can charge be stored? In November 1745 Ewald Jürgen von Kleist (1700–1748), dean of a cathedral in Pomerania, put a nail into a small medicine bottle and charged it with an electrical machine. When he touched the nail he received a strong shock. In March 1746 Pieter van Musschenbroek (1692–1761), a professor at the University of Leyden in Holland, performed a similar experiment with the device, now called the Leyden jar.

How does a **Leyden jar work**?

A Leyden jar is an insulating container with conductors on the inner and outer surfaces. When charging the Leyden jar the source of charge is connected to a rod touching the

The modern capacitor is an updated version of the Leyden jar, consisting of two conductors and an insulator.

inner conductor while the outer conductor is connected to ground. The inner and outer conductors become oppositely charged. It takes energy to move additional charges to the jar as the charges overcome the repulsive forces of the charges already on the conductors. The jar stores this electrical energy. If the inner and outer conductors are connected by a wire the charges flow and make the two conductors neutral again.

What were **uses** of the **Leyden jar**?

In the late eighteenth and nineteenth centuries, people attempted to use the Leyden jar in a variety of ways. Some felt that it could cure medical ailments, and many doctors used the jar as primitive electroshock therapy. Others used it as a demonstration device and for entertainment purposes. Still more people felt that it could be used in cooking. Try cooking a turkey with an electrical spark!

What is the **modern-day version** of a **Leyden jar**?

The capacitor is the modern version of the Leyden jar. Like the jar, it consists of two conductors separated by an insulator. The insulators used can be air, a thin plastic film, or a coating of oxide on the metallic surface. One use of a capacitor is to store the energy needed to fire a flash lamp on a camera. A battery-powered circuit slowly charges the capacitor. When the flash lamp is triggered the capacitor's energy is quickly transferred to the lamp, creating a brief, intense flash of light. Capacitors are also used in electronic devices from telephones to televisions to store energy and reduce changes in voltage.

What did **Benjamin Franklin's** famous **kite experiment** prove?

Benjamin Franklin is probably most famous for flying kites in thunderstorms. In the mid-1700s there were three different phenomenon that had similar effects. You could draw sparks with frictional or static electricity. Lightning appeared to be a giant spark, and electric eels could cause shocks like static electricity. But no one knew if these three had the same or different causes. Franklin touched a Leyden jar to a key tied to the string of his kite. When sparks jumped from the cloud to the kite, the charges went down the string and charged the Leyden jar. Thus Franklin showed that lightning and frictional electricity were the same.

Does Benjamin **Franklin's definition** of **positive** and **negative** agree with today's understanding of **charge**?

Franklin decided that sparks given off by an object charged by a glass rod (vitreous electricity) looked more like fluid leaking out than did the sparks from an object charged by a rubber rod (resinous electricity). Thus he decided that glass had an excess of electrical fluid.

Today we know that electric charge is mostly carried by electrons. Electrons are charged the same way that rubber or plastic is (negatively). Thus we say that they have a negative charge. Because they are transferred much more easily than are the more massive positively charged nuclei, when there is an excess of electrons the object is negatively charged; when there is a lack of electrons it is positively charged. So even though Franklin made the wrong choice, we still follow his convention.

Benjamin Franklin did not discover electricity, but he did show that lightning and frictional electricity were the same thing with his famous kite experiment involving a key and a Leyden jar.

How can you **construct** your **own Leyden Jar**?

You can use either a glass or plastic container that has a tight-fitting cap. Use a small nail to make a hole in the center of the cap. Straighten a paper clip and push it through the hole. Make sure the end of the clip reaches the bottom of the jar. Cover the outside of the jar with aluminum foil and fill the jar about 2/3 full of water. Make sure that the jar cap is dry. Now rub a plastic pen with wool and touch the pen to the paper clip. Repeat the rubbing and touching several times. Then touch the clip with your finger. You should feel a very tiny shock. The jar has stored the charge that you gave the pen when you rubbed it.

VAN DE GRAAFF GENERATORS

What is the **Van de Graaff generator**?

Named after its American creator, Robert Jemison Van de Graaff (1901–1967), the Van de Graaff generator has been the highlight of many electric demonstrations in both physics classrooms and museums around the world. The device, created in 1931, con-

sists of a hollow metal sphere that stands on an insulated plastic tube. Inside the tube is a rubber belt that moves vertically from the base of the generator to the metal sphere. A metal comb attached to the base almost touches the belt. The rubber belt carries negative charges from the comb up the tube and into the metal sphere. There, a second metal comb captures the charges. They repel each other and spread over the exterior surface of the metal sphere. As more and more charge is carried upward, it takes more and more energy from the motor to move them up because of the repulsive force of the charges already there. The energy of the charges can reach up to a million joules per coulomb of charge. That is, up to one million volts.

What happens if you **touch** the **Van de Graaff generator**?

If you place your hands on the upper sphere while the generator is charging it the electric charges accumulating on the sphere move onto your body as they are repelled by the other charges. When your body has enough charge your hair may stand up on end because the electric charges on the hair repel each other. You won't be hurt because the current through your body is very small. Just don't touch anything or anyone else!

What happens if you get **close** to a **charged Van de Graaff**?

The sphere on the Van de Graaff is a conductor surrounded by an insulator (the air). While there are strong forces on the negative charges on the sphere, they're not strong enough to break down the insulating properties of the air. If, however, you bring another object with less negative charge close to the generator the forces on the air molecules can become strong enough to rip them apart, separating their negative electrons from the positive nuclei. A spark will jump. If that object is your finger, you'll feel a shock when the charges carried through the spark move through your body. While the shock can be painful, one produced by the kind of Van de Graaff in physics classrooms is not harmful.

An old, damaged photograph of British physicist Michael Faraday, who was the first to describe an electric force in terms of a field. He also invented the Faraday Cage, which permits electric charges on the outer shell but not within the cage itself.

How much **charge** is **inside** the **sphere** of a **Van de Graaff generator**?

Zero. When negative charges leave the rubber belt, they move immediately to the outer surface of the sphere. Negative charges like to be as far away from each other as possible, so they move to the outer surface of the Van de Graaff generator's sphere.

What is a **Faraday Cage**?

A Faraday Cage, named after British physicist Michael Faraday, is a cage, metal grating, or metallic box that can shield electrical charge. Charges gather on the outer shell of the cage because they are repelled by one another and can be further from each other if they are on the outside of the cage. This results in no charge within the Faraday Cage. The metal sphere of a Van de Graaff generator is a Faraday Cage. Cars and airplanes can be Faraday Cages as well, and may provide some protection from lightning during an electrical storm.

LIGHTNING

What Is **lightning** and how is it created?

Lightning is an electrical discharge in the atmosphere, like a giant spark. There is still debate about the cause of the separation of charges needed to create the discharge. Atmospheric scientists believe that strong updrafts in the clouds sweep droplets of water upward, cooling them far below the freezing point. When the droplets collide with ice crystals the droplets become a soft mixture of water and ice. As a result of these collisions the ice crystals become slightly positively charged and the water/ice mixture becomes negatively charged. The updrafts push the ice crystals up higher, creating a positively-charged cloud top. The heavier water/ice mixture falls, making the lower part of the clouds negatively charged.

The ground under the cloud is charged by induction. The build-up of negative charges on the underside of a thundercloud attracts the positive charges in the ground. The negative charges are repelled further into the ground, leaving a positively charged surface.

How do the **charged regions** of **clouds** and the **ground** act as a **giant capacitor**?

A capacitor consists of two conducting plates with opposite charge separated by an insulator. When a wire is connected between the two plates, a large electric current flows the charges rapidly from one plate to the other, neutralizing the capacitor.

The charged regions of the clouds act as conducting plates while the air between them acts as the insulator. The same thing occurs between the lower section of the cloud and the ground. The air between these sections acts as the insulator, but when the forces exerted by the charges on the air molecules are large enough, they can rip the electrons from the molecules. The result is a positively charged molecule, called an ion, and a free electron. The air is changed from an insulator to a conductor. The mobile electrons gain more energy, creating more and more ions and additional free

electrons. When the electrons and ions combine again light is emitted. The tremendous amount of energy released rapidly heats the surrounding air, producing thunder.

Does lightning always strike the ground?

Although most people think of lightning when it goes between Earth and clouds, the most common type of lightning occurs inside and between thunderclouds. It is usually easier for lightning to jump between the clouds than it is for it to jump from the clouds to Earth. As a result, only one quarter of all lightning strikes actually strike the ground.

How does the air become a conductor?

When the charges have enough energy to begin to ionize the air a the free electrons will form a negatively charged "stepped leader" that will go from the cloud and make its zigzagged and often branched trip toward the ground. This process is slow, taking a few tenths of a second. The leaders are also weak and usually invisible. The atoms in the air near the ground, feeling the attractive force from the electrons in the stepped leader, separate into ions and free electrons. The positively-charged air ions from tall objects, such as trees, buildings, and towers leave in streamers. When a stepped leader and streamer meet, a channel of ionized air is created, allowing large amounts of charge to move between the cloud and the ground. The return stroke of charge back to the cloud is the brightest part of the process.

How much energy is contained in a lightning flash?

An average lightning bolt transfers about five coulombs of charge and about half a billion joules of energy. The transfer takes about 30 millionth of a second and the electrical power in a bolt can be as large as 1,000 billion watts.

Where in the world does lightning occur most frequently?

Satellite lightning detectors show that over the entire Earth lightning strikes about 45 times each second, or 1.5 billion strikes each year. In the eastern region of the Democ-

How many people are killed or injured by lightning?

Of the 40 million lightning strikes per year in the United States, 400 of those strikes hit people. Half die as a result of the strike, while many of the others sustain serious injuries.

ratic Republic of the Congo in Africa every year each square mile, on average, has some 200 lightning strikes. A section of Florida known as "lightning alley" is a 60-mile wide hot-spot of lightning activity in the United States. On average there are 50 lightning strikes in each square mile per year.

SAFETY PRECAUTIONS

Is it true that **lightning never strikes** the same place **twice**?

This is absolutely false. The Empire State Building in New York City is just one example of where lightning has struck more than once. In some thunderstorms, the tower on the Empire State Building has been hit several dozen times.

Why is a **car** often the **best place to be** when lightning strikes?

It is not because of the rubber tires! Many people think the rubber tires of a car provide insulation from the lightning striking the ground. If this were the case, wouldn't riding a bicycle do the same thing? The real reason why a car is a safe place to be when struck by lightning is because most cars have metal bodies, which act as Faraday Cages, keeping all the electrical charge on the outside of the car. Since the charge is kept on the outside of the vehicle, the person sitting inside the car is kept perfectly neutral and safe. It is the shielding of the metal car body, and not the rubber tires, that protects people in automobiles.

What happens to an **airplane** when it is **struck by lightning**?

Airline pilots tend to avoid thunderstorms, but when a plane is struck by lightning, the passengers inside the plane are kept perfectly safe, for they are inside a Faraday Cage, which shields them from the massive electrical charge. The lightning can, however, disturb and even destroy some of the sensitive electronics used to fly the plane.

Studies were performed by NASA in the 1980s in which they flew fighter planes into thunderstorms to see how the planes would react to lightning. The scientists quickly found that the planes actually encouraged lighting, because the planes caused

Studies in the 1980s showed that airplanes actually attract lightning. While lightning storms can still be dangerous, passengers inside airplanes are safe from electric shock because they are actually inside a Faraday Cage.

increases in the electric field of the cloud, which in turn caused the lightning to hit the plane's metal body.

What are some **things you should do** if caught in a **lightning storm**?

The safest place to be during an electrical storm is inside a building (where you should stay away from electrical appliances such as the phone and television, as well as all plumbing and radiators) or car, but if you are unable to shield yourself in this way, the following precautions should be taken:

- Crouch down on the lowest section of the ground, but do not let your hands touch the ground. If lightning strikes the ground, the charges spread out sideways and can still reach you. If only your feet are on the ground (especially if you're wearing rubber-soled shoes), this might limit the amount of charge that passes through your body. If you must lie down because of an injury, try to roll up into a tight ball.
- Take off and move away from all metal objects unless they act as Faraday Cages (refer to the question about Faraday Cages).
- Move away from isolated and tall trees.
- Avoid the tops of hills or mountains and open areas such as water and fields.
- If out on a lake or on the ocean, get back to shore as quickly as possible. If that is not practical, get down low in the boat and move away from any tall metal masts or antennas.

Why shouldn't you stand under a large tree during a thunderstorm?

During thunderstorms, many people stand under trees in an effort to stay dry. However, this can have dire consequences. In the spring of 1991, a lacrosse game at a Washington, D.C., high school was postponed after lightning was observed in the sky. Over a dozen spectators ran for shelter under a tall tree to protect themselves from the rain. A few seconds later, lightning struck the tree, injuring twenty-two people and killing a fifteen-year-old student.

Trees are tall points where positive streamers can originate and attract the stepped leader, starting a lightning bolt. By standing under a tree, holding an umbrella, swinging a golf club, or batting with an aluminum bat, people are making themselves part of a lightning rod.

Why are **lightning rods effective** in keeping tall trees and homes safe from lightning?

Lightning rods are pointed metal rods that are installed above a tree or rooftop to protect the object. The rod, connected to the ground by a metal wire, both encourages and discourages a lightning strike. The rod discourages the lightning strike by "leaking" positive charges out of its pointed top to satisfy the need for positive charge in the clouds. If the rod cannot leak out enough charge to satisfy demand the stepped leader from the cloud is instead attracted to the rod, and a flash of lightning occurs. Therefore, the rod attempts to discourage lightning, but if it cannot satisfy the negative charge, it attracts the lightning to the rod instead of the tree or house.

If the lightning rod doesn't have a good connection to the ground through the wire it can increase the danger to the building. Often these heavy grounding wires come loose from the lightning rods, and if the rod is then hit by lightning, the charges will flow along the surface of the building to the ground and could cause a fire. The rods can become disconnected from lack of routine maintenance; it is wise to check these connections on a regular basis.

Who invented the lightning rod?

Although a Russian tower built in 1725 had what would now be called a lightning rod, credit is usually given to American inventor Benjamin Franklin (1706–1790). He invented the lightning rod in 1749 to protect houses and tall trees from being destroyed by lighting bolts.

CURRENT ELECTRICITY

When was it thought that there were **different kinds** of **electricity**?

As you have seen, Benjamin Franklin's kite experiment showed that lightning and static electricity were the same. Since ancient times humans knew that certain fish, such as the electric eel, could shock a person. Was this "animal electricity" the same as static electricity? According to legend the Italian physician Luigi Galvani (1737–1798) was making frog-leg soup for his sick wife. Whenever a nearby static electricity machine created a spark the legs jerked. After completing several experiments, in a 1791 paper Galvani reported that when one metal touched the muscle of a frog's leg while another metal touched the nerve, the muscle contracted. Thus Galvani helped to show that there was a connection between static electricity and electric effects in animals.

How did **Luigi Galvani's experiments** lead to the **development** of **current electricity**?

Galvani believed that the flow of charge from the nerve into the muscle caused the contractions. His fellow scientist at the University of Bologna, Alessandro Volta

(1745–1807), recognized that Galvani's frog leg was both a conductor and a detector of electricity. In 1791 he replaced the leg with paper soaked in salt water, a conductor, and used another means of detecting the electricity. He found that charges flowed only if the two metals touching the paper were different. The combination of two different metals separated by a conducting solution is called a galvanic cell after Galvani.

Volta went further. He found that the two metals that produced the greatest electrical effect were zinc and silver. In 1800 he stacked alternating disks of zinc and silver, separated by a card wetted with salt water. He found that this device, called the voltaic pile, was a continuous source of charge flow. Sir Humphry Davy showed that the charge flow was due to a chemical reaction between the metals and the conductive solution in the cards.

You can use the acidic juice within a lemon—or a potato, if you're short on lemons—to create a simple battery. Insert two different metals (zinc and copper) and electrons will flow from the zinc to the copper to create a current weak current. Connecting multiple lemons gives you a stronger current.

> ## How can water be used to model voltage and current?
>
> Think of a river flowing downhill from one lake into another. The water flows from a higher to lower altitude. Electrical potential difference is like the change in height of the water on the two ends of the river. Electric current, the flow of charge, is like the water current, the flow of water over the falls. If there is no difference in altitude of the two lakes, then there will be no flow of water. If there is no difference in voltage, there will be no flow of charges.

What **causes** the **flow** of charges in a **voltaic pile**?

Volta invented the term "electromotive force" (*emf*) to describe what causes the separation of charges. The more disks there were in the voltaic pile, the greater the *emf*. Unfortunately, the word "force" is an incorrect use of that term, because there is no mechanical push, measured in newtons, on the charge. The correct term is potential difference or voltage, the energy change per unit charge separated. Both the term *voltage* and the unit in which it is measured, the *volt* (V), are named after Volta.

What is **potential difference** or **voltage**?

In a voltaic pile, today more commonly called a battery, chemical energy is converted into increased energy of electric charges. Positive charges at the positive terminal of the battery have a greater energy than those at the negative terminal. The quantity that is important is not the total energy difference of charges at the two terminals of the battery, but the energy difference divided by the charge. This quantity is called the electric potential difference, or more commonly, the voltage.

What is **current**?

Current is the flow of charge. It is measured in amperes (or "amps"), named after the French mathematician and physicist André-Marie Ampère (1775–1836). One ampere is equal to one coulomb of charge passing through a wire divided by one second. The greater the voltage difference across the wire, the larger the current.

RESISTANCE

What is **resistance** to current flow?

All objects encounter friction when moving. Electrons are no different, but we refer to the friction that electrons encounter as resistance. The electrons collide with the atoms in a wire and are deflected from their paths. For the same voltage difference,

the greater the resistance the smaller the current. Resistance causes the electric charges to lose energy. The energy goes into the thermal energy of the wire or other conductor. That is, they get hot! The thermal energy can produce heat in a toaster and heat and light in an incandescent lamp.

What **factors** determine the **amount of resistance** of a conductor?

The resistance of a wire or other conductor depends upon the following:

- The length of the conductor (the longer the wire, the more resistance).
- The cross-sectional area of the conductor (the thinner, the more resistance).
- The properties of the material (for metals, the fewer the number of free electrons, the more resistance).
- The temperature of the conductor (for metals, the warmer, the more resistance; for carbon the cooler, the more resistance).

What are **resistors**?

Resistors are devices used in electrical circuits to put a definite resistance in a circuit. Normally they are made of graphite or a thin carbon film coated on glass. Larger resistors are cylindrical and have four color bands that encode the value of the resistance. On computer boards they are tiny, rectangular devices barely a millimeter on a side with conductive ends that are soldered to the board. If they are designed to dissipate a large amount of power, they are made of high-resistance wire.

SUPERCONDUCTORS

What is a **superconductor**?

Superconductors allow electrical current to travel without resistance, and therefore no voltage drop across them or energy loss within them. Superconductors must be cooled below their critical temperatures to have no electrical resistance. Some elements, compounds, and alloys that are superconductors are lead and niobium nitride, and a niobium-titanium alloy. All these require liquid helium to cool them to their critical temperatures. In the 1980s some ceramics were found to have much higher transition temperatures that could be reached using much cheaper liquid nitrogen. The first found was yttrium barium copper oxide. As of 2008 a family of materials including iron, such as lanthanum oxygen fluorine iron arsenide, was developed.

Who discovered **superconductivity**?

The creation of materials without resistance was thought to be impossible, but a Dutch physicist by the name of Heike Kamerlingh Onnes (1853–1926) proved it was

Who won the Nobel Prize for their work in superconductivity?

Three American physicists, John Bardeen, Leon N. Cooper, and John R. Schrieffer, explained why superconductivity occurs in metals and alloys. Their development of the BCS theory for superconductivity was cited when they won the Nobel Prize in 1972.

Fifteen years later, two other physicists won the Nobel Prize for discovering superconductive materials that achieved zero resistance at temperatures thought to be too high for superconductors. Physicists Georg Bednorz and Alex Müller of IBM found that a ceramic substance called lanthanum barium copper oxide became a superconductor at 35 kelvins. This was a much higher temperature than anyone thought possible at the time.

possible in 1911. Onnes lowered the temperature of different metals, including mercury, close to absolute zero. He then measured the electrical resistance of the materials at such low temperatures and found that mercury, at only 4.2 kelvin (−277.2°C), had zero resistance to electrical current.

What **technologies** have developed as a result of **superconductivity**?

Superconductors are most commonly used in large electromagnets. With no resistance, once the current is started, it will continue forever without change. Therefore the magnets dissipate no power and do not heat up. These magnets are most often used in magnetic resonance imaging (MRI) machines. An MRI allows a doctor to view the inside of the human body without using harmful radiation. They are also used in particle accelerators that reveal the fundamental structure of matter by smashing the nuclei of atoms together. The most powerful accelerator is the Large Hadron Collider (LHC) in Switzerland. Another application of superconductivity is the SQUID (Superconducting QUantum Interference Device) that is an extremely sensitive detector of magnetic fields used in geological sensors for locating underground oil.

OHM'S LAW

What is **Ohm's Law**?

In the early 1800s, Georg Simon Ohm (1789–1854), a German physicist, developed the law that bears his name: the resistance of an object is independent of current through it. Many materials do not obey Ohm's Law. For example, when the current through

the tungsten filament wire in a lamp is increased the temperature of the wire increases and so does its resistance.

What are the **units** and **symbols** used for current, voltage, and resistance?

Quantity	Unit	Symbol
Current (I)	Ampere (amp)	A
Voltage (V)	Volt	V
Resistance (R)	Ohm	Ω

What is the **relationship** between **current, voltage**, and **resistance**?

Voltage = Current \times Resistance, or $V = IR$. That is, the voltage difference across a resistor is equal to the current through it multiplied by its resistance.

What levels of **current** are **dangerous**?

Approximately 1 mA (0.001 A) is enough to produce a tingling sensation. 10 mA is painful. 12-20 mA is enough to paralyze muscles, making it impossible to let go. 60-100 mA causes ventricular fibrillation of the heart. That is, the heart is beating in such a way that it cannot pump blood through the circulatory system. Greater than 200 mA causes the heart to clamp down and stop beating.

How much **resistance** do **our bodies** have to **electrical current**?

On average, the human body has an electrical resistance between 50,000 and 150,000 ohms. Most of this resistance is across the skin. If the skin is wet the resistance drops to about 1,000 ohms. If the skin is broken, then resistance across organs in the body is on the order of a few hundred ohms. In this condition 10 volts is sufficient to cause serious, if not fatal damage.

Do **electric eels** really use electric fields to capture their prey?

Electric eels do indeed set off electrical pulses to stun and even kill their prey. These eels have special nerve endings bundled together in their tails that can produce 30 volts in small electric eels to 600 volts in larger eels. Besides using the electrical shocks for hunting, the eels produce a constant electrical field for use in navigation and self-defense. Most people do not have to worry about encountering electric eels, however. This variety of eel is native only to the rivers of South America.

Birds can perch safely on electric wires, as long as they don't come into contact with objects that have two different voltages.

Why don't **birds** or **squirrels** on **power lines** get electrocuted?

In order to get electrocuted on a bare wire, a bird would have to be in contact with objects that had two different voltages. The difference in voltage along the wire over the distance between the animal's feet is very small. The animal would be in danger only if it made contact with both a high-voltage wire and the ground or a wire connected to ground (low voltage). Then there could be a large current through its body.

Why do **electricians** work with **"one hand behind their back"**?

When working on high-voltage circuitry, many electricians like to place one hand behind their back because this way there is little chance for each hand to touch objects of different electrical potentials and cause a shock.

Does **voltage shock** you?

Signs around power plants and breaker boxes often state, "CAUTION: High Voltage Area." It is not voltage that can hurt you; it is the electrical current that flows through your body that can produce serious and sometimes fatal consequences. The Van de Graaff generator creates hundreds of thousands of volts, but produces such a low amount of current that the sparks it emits only cause muscles to tingle.

ELECTRIC POWER AND ITS USES

What is a **watt**?

A watt is the unit of power, or the rate of energy transfer. Light bulbs, toasters, hair dryers, televisions, and other electrical appliances are rated by the power they use. In the context of electricity, the watt is the unit for electrical power and is often found on light bulbs and other devices used in electrical circuits. The formula to find the power used is $P = I \times V$ (power equals current times voltage).

Who **invented** the electric **light bulb**?

The first person to generate light from a wire filament was the British Sir Humphry Davy. Davy was known for his work on electric arc lamps in the early 1800s, and his breakthrough discovery was the first electric light. His lamp used a very thin piece of platinum wire that had high resistance and emitted a soft glow. The lamp didn't last long, and so it was not practical, but it did pave the way for others.

What contribution did **Thomas Edison** make to the electric light?

The American inventor Thomas Alva Edison (1847–1931) tried literally hundreds of different materials as filaments for the lamp. He found that heating a cotton thread in the air left a thin length of almost pure carbon. The carbon filament was connected to wires sealed in a glass bulb from which the air was removed. In 1878 this first practical electric lamp lasted for hours more than any other lamp.

What is the difference between a **kilowatt** and a **kilowatt-hour**?

A kilowatt, 1,000 watts, is the unit used to describe the power, the rate at which the energy is being converted. Energy is the power multiplied by the time it is used, in this case hours. Therefore a kilowatt-hour, the product of power and time, is a unit of energy. The utility company charges you for the number of kilowatt-hours of electricity you use in a month.

For example, a 100-watt light bulb uses 100 watts (or 0.1 kilowatt) of power. If that light bulb were left on for an entire month, the energy that the bulb consumed would be 0.1 kilowatts \times 24 hour/days \times 30 days/month, which equals 72 kilowatt-hours/month. If the energy cost is $0.12 per kilowatt-hour, the bill for that one light bulb would be $8.64 per month. Replacing the 100-watt incandescent lamp with a 23-watt compact fluorescent lamp that is equally bright would cost only $1.98 per month. An LED lamp equally bright has a power rating of only 13 watts, and therefore would cost $1.12 to light.

Why is a 100-watt bulb brighter than a 25-watt bulb?

A light bulb transforms electric energy first into the thermal energy of the heated filament and then into light and heat. The rate at which these energy changes occur is determined by the way the bulb is constructed. The 100-watt bulb has a lower resistance filament—the thin wire in the bulb that gets hot. Assuming that both bulbs are connected to a 120-volt outlet, there will be more current through the 100-watt bulb than the 25-watt bulb. Lower resistance is created by making the filament out of thicker wire. The lower resistance means higher current, which in turn means higher power and more light and heat output.

CIRCUITS

What is needed to **create a circuit**?

A circuit is a circular path through which charge can flow. So, the first requirement is a complete, unbroken conducting path. Second, there must be a source of potential difference—most often a battery. The battery provides the voltage that will produce the current in the circuit. With only a battery and wire connecting the two ends of the battery the resistance in the circuit will be almost zero, and the amount of current will be very high. This situation is called a short circuit. The wire will become hot enough to burn you. So, for a useful circuit there must be a third element—a device with resistance. This may be a resistor, lamp, motor, etc.

In terms of energy, the energy input to the circuit is the chemical energy stored in the battery. When the circuit is complete, the chemical energy becomes electrical energy in the wires. That energy is then converted to thermal energy in the resistor or lamp, or kinetic energy in the motor. The hot resistor or lamp then radiates heat and light into the environment.

In our households the battery is replaced by the electric generating station operated by the utility company. It may use the chemical energy in fossil fuels such as coal, oil, or natural gas to boil water (i.e. produce thermal energy). The steam from the boiling water then turns the generator, converting the energy to rotational kinetic energy. The generator then converts this energy of rotation into the electrical energy that is transmitted to the home. A nuclear power plant uses the nuclear energy in the nucleus of the uranium atoms to heat the water and produce steam. From that point on the nuclear and fossil fuel power plants are essentially the same.

What is an **open circuit**?

A circuit is a closed loop through which electric charges can flow. If the loop is opened, then it is called an open circuit and charges no longer flow. A switch is com-

The Indian Point Energy Center on the Hudson River in New York state uses nuclear fission to heat water and produce steam. Except for the fuel source, nuclear power plants operate just like any other type of power plant.

monly used to open and close a circuit. If a wire breaks, the connection between the wire and another part of the circuit fails, or if a lamp burns out (its filament breaks) then the circuit is opened and there is no current.

What is the danger of **short circuits** in a home?

As described above, if there is only a tiny amount of resistance in a circuit the current is very large and the wires get extremely hot. If, for example, the insulation on the wires in an appliance fails and the wires touch each other, the resistance drops and current rises. The wires, including those in the walls, can get hot enough to cause a fire. Household circuits are protected by fuses or circuit breakers. They are designed to open when current exceeds a predetermined limit. With the circuit now open, current stops and the wires will cool.

AC/DC

What is a **DC circuit**?

In a DC, or direct-current, circuit charges travel only in one direction. The voltage source, a battery or direct current power supply, has one positive and one negative terminal, so there is current in only one direction.

> ## Did Thomas Edison use AC or DC when he used his incandescent lamps to light a neighborhood?
>
> **E**dison invented the first practical incandescent lamp in 1878. In 1882 he connected 59 customers in the neighborhood around his New York City laboratory to a DC generator that supplied 100 volts. The customers used the electrical power for lamps and motors. The relatively low voltage matched the resistance of the lamps and was not believed to be very dangerous. Unfortunately, in order to carry much power, at low voltage the current must be high, and this heated the wires. Customers had to be within two miles of the generating system to avoid serious loss of energy in the wires.

What is an **AC circuit**?

In an AC, or alternating-current circuit, the polarity of the voltage source changes back and forth at a regular rate. In the United States one terminal of the source changes from positive to negative and back to positive 60 times each second. Therefore the flow of charge also alternates in direction 60 times a second as the electrons in the circuit vibrate back and forth. An alternating current is usually found in wall outlets in buildings. Most of our electrical appliances run on alternating current.

What important contributions did **Nikola Tesla** and **George Westinghouse** make in the late nineteenth century?

Nikola Tesla (1856–1943) worked for Edison's company in Europe. Edison offered Tesla a large sum of money if he would invent an improved generator. When Tesla did, Edison refused to pay, saying he had been joking. Tesla quit.

In 1884 George Westinghouse (1846–1914), a prolific American inventor and businessman, formed the Westinghouse Electric Company in 1884. Four years later he persuaded Tesla to join his company and purchased his patents from him. Westinghouse had improved a transformer invented in France, but Tesla's AC induction motor, invented in 1883, and three-phase generator were essential for Westinghouse's dream of transmitting electric energy efficiently over long distances.

Why is **AC preferred** over DC?

In the late 1880s Edison and Westinghouse battled over the relative merits of DC and AC power distribution systems. After the electric chair had been developed Edison attempted to name electrocution "Westinghousing" because it used AC, but he failed. The AC system was victorious because transformers could raise the voltage to thou-

587

Are holiday lights in series or parallel circuits?

Many years ago holiday lights used large bulbs designed to work on 120 volts. Those strings were wired in parallel. Today holiday lights are wired in series so that the tiny bulbs have only low voltages across them. If a lamp burns out because the filament fails, there will be no current through the string. But, there will be 120 volts across the failed bulb. The bulb has a wire touching the two thick wires that deliver current to the filament. The wire is covered with a thin insulating film. The film remains insulating when the voltage difference across the bulb is small, but when it becomes 120 volts, sparks break the insulating film and weld the wire to the thick wires. This short-circuits the bulb, completing the circuit through the remaining lamps.

sands of volts for transmission, then lower it for use in homes and businesses. At the high voltages the current needed to transmit large amounts of power is reduced, and so is the energy lost to thermal energy because the heating of transmission wires depends on current and resistance.

SERIES/PARALLEL CIRCUITS

What is a **series circuit**?

A series circuit consists of electrical devices such as resistors, batteries, and switches arranged in a single line. There is only one path for the charges to flow through, and if there is a break anywhere in the circuit, the current will drop to zero.

What is a **parallel circuit**?

A parallel circuit allows the charges to flow through different branches. For example, the wire from the battery would be connected to one terminal of each of three bulbs. The other terminals are connected together and to the negative terminal of the battery. The charges now have three separate paths through which they can flow. If one bulb burns out or is removed from the socket, that bulb would no longer light, but the current through the other two lamps would not change. They would continue to glow.

What happens to a **series circuit** if more **bulbs** are **added**?

If more light bulbs or other resistors are placed in a series circuit, there is more resistance in the circuit, and so the current, and the brightness of the lamps would be reduced.

What happens in a **parallel circuit** if **more bulbs** are added?

In a parallel circuit the current goes through separate branches. If another branch is added with another bulb, the current has an additional path to take. But, the battery (or generator) produces a constant voltage, so the current through the original bulbs does not change, and neither does their brightness.

Are **series** or **parallel circuits** used in our **homes**?

Each circuit, by itself, contains a series connection of a switch and lamp or appliance. The circuits themselves are connected in parallel so that they can be used independently.

ELECTRICAL OUTLETS

Many outlets have **three holes**—what is the **purpose** of each hole?

Outlets have two slots, one longer than the other, and a "D"-shaped hole. The contacts in the shorter slot are connected to a black wire. This is the "hot" connection that carries the 120 volts. The contacts in the longer slot are connected to a white wire, called the neutral wire. The white wire is connected to ground in the electric distribution box. Thus there is a potential difference of 120 volts across the two contacts. The third hole is attached to a green wire that is at ground potential. Why do you need two connections at the ground potential? Because when the appliance plugged in draws current, there is current through both the black and white wires. Each wire has resistance, so there will be a voltage drop across the white wire, and it will be above ground potential at the outlet. While this voltage will be small, it could be dangerous. The green wire, which carries no current, will remain at ground. It can be connected to the metal case of the appliance, assuring that the case will remain at ground potential.

What if the tool or appliance has a **three-prong plug** but you have only **two-slot outlets**?

Do not use the appliance if you do not have the proper outlet for the device. Cutting off the grounding prong will defeat the safety feature of the separate ground wire.

When installing an electrical outlet, note that the green wire (okay, you can't tell in this black and white photo, but it is there!) is the grounding wire, which must be attached to the grounding contact on the outlet.

The United States uses a 120-volt system, while European countries use a 220-volt system. Why?

The United States was the first country to establish widespread use of electricity for the public. At the time it was implemented, a 120-volt system seemed to provide enough voltage for users, yet was not enough to cause arcs in small motors. When electrical wiring was installed in European countries some years later, technological advancements allowed those devices to run safely at higher voltages. Therefore, the standard became 220 volts for Europe, while the United States remained at 120 volts. The advantage of 220-volt systems is that the current is almost half as much used by the same appliance on a 120-volt system, and so power losses due to resistance in the house wiring are smaller.

What is the little **green wire** or plate on the three-to-two adapter?

The green wire or metal tab attached to adapters is the grounding wire. Since the adapter is circumventing the ground prong, an alternate means of grounding is needed. If the screw on the outlet plate is grounded, the green wire on the adapter should be attached to it. This way, if there is an electrical short, the current can still flow through the grounding wire. If the screw is not grounded, then the adapter should not be used. An outlet tester that is available at most hardware stores can be used to make sure the screw is grounded.

What is a GFI, or **Ground Fault Interrupter**?

A ground fault interrupt outlet is now required by building codes for outlets within six feet of a sink or in any other environment where water could be close to the outlet. Normally the currents in the black and white wires will be equal, but if the water provides an alternative current path, then the two currents will no longer be the same. The GFI detects this difference and shuts off the circuit within milliseconds. GFIs should be tested periodically to make sure the electronic circuit is still working.

Why is it dangerous to operate **electrical devices** in **bathtubs, showers,** and over full **sinks**?

Although water reduces the resistance of the human body and thus makes it more susceptible to electrical shock, it is the plumbing that is the main hazard. Take, for example, a person who likes to watch a plugged-in TV while sitting in the bathtub. If the TV is not connected to a GFI-protected circuit and fell into the tub, the water would come in contact with the 120-volt wires in the TV. With the metal plumbing of the tub connected to ground, the grounding path would cause a current through the water.

Unfortunately, this translates into a bad day for the bather; an mp-3 player or battery-powered smart phone is much safer.

When was **magnetism discovered**?

The discovery of rocks that attracted certain metals is lost to history. As was the case with electrostatics, Aristotle (384–322 B.C.E.) credited Thales of Miletus (625–545 B.C.E.) with the first scientific discussion of the attractive power of the rock later called lodestone. The word "magnet" comes from the region of Greece where lodestone is found. But the power of lodestone was found by other people around the same time. At the time of Thales' life an Indian surgeon, Sushrata, used magnets to aid surgery. In the fourth century B.C.E. the Chinese *Book of the Devil Valley Master* says "Lodestone makes iron come."

In the eleventh century C.E. the Chinese scientist Shen Kuo wrote about the use of a magnetized needle as a compass in navigation. By the next century the Chinese were known to use a lodestone as a shipboard compass. One hundred years later the British theologian, Alexander Neckham, described the compass and how it could be used to aid navigation. Some people thought that the Pole Star attracted the compass, while others thought that the source was a magnetic island near the north pole. In 1269 the Frenchman Petrus Peregrinus wrote a detailed paper on the properties of magnets. But the most comprehensive and famous work was written by William Gilbert in 1600. Gilbert concluded that Earth was a giant magnet.

What are the **properties** of **magnets**?

You've probably played with magnets since you were a child. It is likely that you found that magnets attract some materials but not others. You may have found that you can use a magnet to magnetize items like paper clips, nails, and screws. If you played with two magnets you found that they could either attract or repel each other.

Whether you played with metal bar-shaped magnets, rectangular or circular ceramic magnets, you found that the magnet exerted stronger forces at the ends or faces of the 593

magnets. Those regions are called "poles." If you hang the magnet from a string so it can rotate freely you'll find the magnet orienting itself north-to-south. The end facing north is called the north pole, the other the south. Like poles repel each other while unlike poles attract, but either end can attract other materials.

Magnetic poles always come in north-south pairs called dipoles (two poles). Some theories predict the existence of isolated north or south poles, called monopoles. But, there have been extensive searches for monopoles over the past decades and none has ever been found.

Children often discover some of the properties of magnetism by playing with bar magnets and metal shavings. In this way, you can easily discover that magnets have opposite poles and create magnetic fields.

What is a **magnetic field**?

Just as the gravitational field is the region around a massive object that causes the attractive force on another object with mass, a magnetic field is the region around a magnet that causes forces on magnetic materials or other magnets.

What **materials** are **attracted** to magnets?

Iron, nickel, and cobalt and most of their alloys are attracted to magnets. Other metals, like silver and gold, copper, tin, stainless steel, zinc, brass and bronze are not attracted. Non-metals are not attracted.

Iron, nickel, and cobalt are called ferromagnetic. All materials respond to magnetic fields, but most respond so weakly that the forces are hardly felt. Those that are repelled are called diamagnetic; those attracted are paramagnetic.

What **causes materials** to be **attracted** to magnets?

The ultimate cause of magnetism is electrons. When electrons are in a magnetic field the forces they experience cause them to move in tiny circles. The circling electrons create their own magnetic fields that give rise to diamagnetism. Electrons are tiny magnets themselves, with north and south poles. In most atoms these magnets are paired so their fields cancel. But, if there are an odd number of electrons, the unpaired electron produces a paramagnet. Oxygen, for example, is paramagnetic.

In ferromagnets the unpaired electrons in large groups of atoms interact with each other so that they point in the same direction. This group is called a domain. When a ferromagnet is put in a magnetic field the domains can line up with their

poles facing the same direction, making the material a magnet. In most materials when the magnetic field is removed the domains revert to their former random directions and the material is no longer a magnet. For certain alloys, however, the domains remain aligned, resulting in a permanent magnet.

What materials make the **strongest** permanent **magnets**?

Traditional permanent magnets were made of an alloy of aluminum, nickel, and cobalt, called ALNICO. Ceramic and rubber magnets use ferrites, an iron oxide material. In the 1980s the automobile companies searched for materials to reduce the weight of motors in their cars. They found an alloy of cobalt and samarium, a rare earth, made strong, lightweight magnets, but were extremely brittle and expensive. Today the strongest magnets are made from a lanthanum-iron-boron (LIB) alloy. Their strength can be as much as 20 times that of alnico magnets. They are also brittle and so are coated with a plating of nickel and copper. Their price has fallen so much that they are used to hold sunglasses to eyeglass frames, in necklace clasps, and in children's toys.

How are **refrigerator magnets made**?

Examine a refrigerator magnet. It is flexible, feels like rubber, and only one surface is attracted to metals. It doesn't stick to a stainless steel door unless the stainless has been coated with steel. It's made of rubber that has been impregnated with ferrite particles and magnetized. Small pieces, each a dipole, are then pressed together under heat to bond them into one thin sheet that can be cut, folded, and bonded to other sheets. Which of the three arrangements shown below would have the properties of a refrigerator magnet as described above?

The top two wouldn't because both surfaces would act as a magnet. The top right-hand arrangement would be a very weak magnet on both faces because the alternating poles would essentially cancel each other out.

In the third drawing the sheets have been folded and then pressed together so that the poles are at only one surface, so only that surface would act like a magnet. The alternating N and S poles attract steel and stick to it. You can check this idea by taking two refrigerator magnets and holding the magnetic surfaces together, and then try sliding one over the other. You'll find that they skip as first N and S poles touch each other and attract. Then the like poles try to touch each other but repel, making the magnets skip.

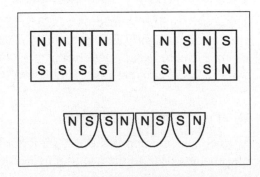

What happens when a **magnet** is cut in **two pieces**?

When a magnet is cut the atoms within the domains remain aligned. In almost

Fortunately for us, the earth generates its own magnetic field, which effectively fends off dangerous particles from the sun.

every case the cut would be between two domains, leaving aligned domains in the two halves. If you cut a domain you would create two smaller domains, each with a north pole and a south pole. So no matter where you cut the result is two magnets, each with its own north and south pole. The more domains, the stronger the magnet.

How is **Earth's magnetic field** oriented?

Because opposite poles attract, the north pole of a hanging magnet or compass must point toward a south pole. So, the south pole of Earth's magnet must be near the north geographic pole. The poles are actually far below Earth's surface, so Earth's field is not parallel to its surface.

What is the **origin** of Earth's **magnetic field**?

The source of Earth's magnetic field is its core, made of iron, so hot that it is molten. It rotates at a slightly different rate than does Earth, and this difference creates what is called a dynamo effect, generating a magnetic field. Details of how the dynamo effect works are still a matter that is under investigation.

What is **magnetic declination**?

Magnetic declination is the angular difference between north as shown by a compass and the direction to the geographic north pole, Earth's axis of rotation. Declination

> ## Has Earth's magnetic field always remained the same?
>
> The direction of magnetic poles in iron in Earth's crust demonstrates that Earth's magnetic field has reversed itself approximately nine times over the past 3.5 million years. It's not known how long the reversal lasts and what happens to the field during the reversal. The magnetic poles also wander. The magnetic north pole has moved as much as 800 kilometers toward the geographic north pole since 1831.

depends primarily on the location on Earth but, because the magnetic poles move, also on time.

Is the **magnetic field important** to **life** on Earth?

The magnetic field of Earth is very important to life on Earth because it helps deflect harmful cosmic rays and solar wind. If we were fully exposed to these charged particles the effects on us could be devastating. Communication systems would be disabled and the particles could cause damage to all living things.

How is a **compass made**?

A compass is a magnetized metallic pointer that can rotate about a low-friction pivot point. Sometimes the pointer is placed in a container of liquid to dampen the movement of the pointer. The magnetic pointer aligns itself with the north/south orientation of Earth's magnetic field, and the person using the compass can determine what direction he or she is headed by looking at the pointer.

Does a **compass sometimes point downward** along with pointing north?

For hundreds of years, navigators using compasses noticed that on occasion, the compass pointer would try to point downward in addition to pointing north. This phenomenon, which went unexplained for several hundred years, was observed by compass maker Robert Norman. He found when flying over the poles one end of the compass would point downward; he understood that the problem was that the pointer was attracted to the pole under the plane. By making the compass rotate in the vertical direction he made the first dip needle.

What is a **dip needle** and how is it similar to a compass?

A dip needle is just like a conventional compass, but instead of holding it horizontally, it is held vertically. It is a magnetic needle used for navigational purposes just like a

compass, but is used predominantly when traveling around the north and south poles. Instead of measuring horizontal magnetic deflection, the dip needle measures vertical magnetic inclination. When over the equator, the magnetic field of Earth is parallel to the surface of the Earth. The closer one gets to the magnetic poles, however, the less pilots rely on compasses, and the more they rely on dip needles to tell them how close they are to the poles. The closer one gets to a pole, the more vertical the magnetic field becomes, because it's turning into the surface of Earth. Therefore, when directly over the magnetic poles, the dip needle points directly downward.

ELECTROMAGNETISM

How was the **connection** between **electricity** and **magnetism discovered**?

The close connection between electric current and magnetic fields was discovered quite by accident. In 1820, Danish physicist Hans Christian Oersted (1777–1851) gave a lecture on the heating effects of an electric current on a wire. A compass happened to be near the wire and he was surprised to see the compass rotate when the current was on. He had been looking for connections between electricity and magnetism for several years, but expected that the compass would point away from the wire. Instead he found that the compass pointed in a circle around the wire. Above the wire it pointed perpendicular to the wire; below the wire it also pointed in the perpendicular, but in the opposite direction.

What were the **implications** of **Oersted's discovery**?

The fact that moving charge in a wire could create a magnetic field created a great deal of excitement and enthusiasm in the scientific community. A week after hearing about Oersted's discovery, French physicist and mathematician André-Marie Ampère (1775–1836) gave a presentation at the French Academy of Sciences that extended Oersted's experiments and contained detailed analyses. A day later he found that two parallel current-carrying wires would either attract or repel each other depending on the relative directions of the currents. Ampère's greatest contribution, however, was the mathematical theory he created for electricity and magnetism.

British chemist and physicist Michael Faraday's (1791–1867) philosophy led him to search for connections between phenomena like electricity, magnetism, and light. In 1821 he invented what is now called a homopolar motor. One end of a wire was suspended from a support so that it could swing in any direction. The other end of the wire contacted a pool of mercury. When Faraday put current through the wire the end in the mercury traced out a circle.

The force that Faraday had observed wasn't formalized until 1891 and then by the Dutch physicist Hendrik Antoon Lorentz (1853–1928). This force, called the Lorentz

Researching magnetic fields and electric currents, Michael Faraday and, independently, the American physics teacher Joseph Henry, invented an early form of electric generator called the dynamo. Today, generators like those pictured above use the same principles to produce electrical energy from other forms of energy.

Force Law, is proportional to the current through the wire, the magnetic field, and the length of the wire. The force, which is perpendicular to both the current and the magnetic field, is strongest when the current and field are at right angles. This force is the basis of motors and many other applications.

When Faraday published his results he failed to give credit to two other important scientists and he was given assignments to work in other fields. Nevertheless he continued to do experiments on the effects of magnetic fields. For example, he found that when dense glass was put in a magnetic field the direction of polarization of light going through the glass was rotated. He spent ten years searching for ways to create a current from a magnetic field. Finally, in 1831 he tried changing the magnetic field and made the crucial discovery that an electric current is produced by a changing magnetic field. The current, a flow of charges, is produced by an electric field exerting forces on the charges. Faraday went on to invent the dynamo, an early electric generator. The American high school physics teacher Joseph Henry (1797–1878) made the discovery at almost the same time.

What **discovery** did James Clerk **Maxwell** make that **depended** on the work of **Oersted, Faraday, and Ampère**?

In an earlier chapter we have seen that charges create electric fields. In this chapter we have seen that moving charges, that is, currents, create magnetic fields and that

changing magnetic fields produce electric fields. In the 1860s Scottish physicist James Clerk Maxwell (1831–1879) added a crucial additional connection: changing electric fields can produce magnetic fields.

With that idea Maxwell recognized that these relationships meant that electric and magnetic fields could move through space. The fields move through space as transverse waves that are perpendicular to each other. Maxwell calculated the speed and found that it was equal to the speed of light. He published his results in 1864 and a textbook on electromagnetism in 1873. In 1881 Oliver Heaviside wrote Maxwell's famous four equations in the form they are used today.

In 1888 Heinrich Hertz (1857–1894) transmitted electromagnetic waves across his laboratory, confirming Maxwell's theoretical work.

ELECTROMAGNETIC TECHNOLOGY

Why are **electromagnets**, the kind that pick up junk cars, so strong?

An electromagnet is a coil of current-carrying wire wound on a iron core that is at the center of an iron cup. The magnetic field created by current in the wire is strengthened by the iron core. The strength of the magnetic field produced by such electromagnets creates a large force, as described by the Lorentz Force Law that allows people to more easily move large metal objects, such as steel cars, from one location to another.

What is the **difference** between a **motor** and a **generator**?

In each device, a magnet and a coil of wire are employed to change one form of energy into another form. A motor consists of multiple loops of wire placed in a magnetic field. Either the loops or the magnet can rotate. The current through the wires in the field causes a force that results in rotation and thus mechanical energy. Motors in a home are used in fans, hair dryers, and food processors. There are over a hundred motors in a modern automobile. The starter motor is the largest and most powerful.

A generator does the opposite of a motor; it changes mechanical to electrical energy, but still consists of multiple loops of wire in a magnetic field. Either the loops or the magnet can rotate. In an automobile a form of a generator, called an alternator, uses some of energy from the engine to charge the battery. Backup generators use the energy from a gasoline engine to produce enough electrical energy to keep some of the lights and appliances running in a house when the electrical power fails. Electric utilities use huge generators to provide power for a city or larger area. The generators get their energy from steam turbines. The heat required to turn water into steam can come from coal, oil, natural gas, or nuclear "burners." Wind power uses generators turned by the propeller blades.

How are **magnetic materials** used in **computers**?

Magnets are used in the compact motors that turn the disks in the CD or DVD drive and that move the laser that reads the disk to the correct position. Motors rotate the disks in a hard drive. The arm on which the read/write head is mounted is rotated to the correct portion of the hard drive disk has a coil of wire on it in a magnetic field. When there is a current through the wire the force moves the arm to the correct position.

The disk itself is often made of aluminum coated with an extremely thin (10-20 nanometers) film of magnetic material that is divided into sub-micrometer thick regions that are perpendicular to the surface of the disk. Each region is magnetized one way to represent a "1" and another way to represent at "0." A tiny coil in the read/write head carries the current that magnetizes the regions. The state of the magnet is read using magnetorestriction where the magnetic field causes a change in resistance of a very thin wire in a coil in the read/write head.

How do **metal detectors** work?

Built into the frame of a metal detector are coils of wire that carry a current. When metal is close to the coils, the magnetic properties of the metal change the current in the coils of wire that is detected by the electronic circuits in the detector.

How do **traffic lights** at car intersections know when a **vehicle** is **present**?

Many traffic lights are triggered to change by the approach of a car. The

When you walk through a metal detector with metal anywhere on your person, that metal changes the current in the coils in the frame of the detector.

principle is similar to the metal detector, in that there are coils of current-carrying wire just below the road where the vehicles stop at the intersection. When a large enough amount of metal passes over the coil, it induces a change in the current that creates a signal in the electronic circuits that control the traffic light.

What are **MAGLEV trains**?

MAGLEV, or magnetically levitated trains, are different from conventional trains in that they use electromagnetic forces to lift the cars off the track and propel them along thin magnetic tracks. Some demonstration trains have reached speeds of 500 kilometers per hour (300 miles per hour). Although the United States has no MAGLEV train, nor an active research program in this technology, Germany and Japan have conducted a great deal of research in the field.

What are the two main forms of **MAGLEV transportation**?

The German system uses the attractive forces between electromagnets to lift the underside of the train 15 centimeters (6 inches) above its guide rail. The coils in the train and guide rail form a linear motor—like an ordinary motor that has been unrolled. The only commercial operation is a train in China that transports people 30 kilometers in slightly over seven minutes.

The Japanese have taken a slightly different approach toward MAGLEV technology. The track and train repel each other. Propulsion also uses a linear motor. Levitation works well at high speeds, but when starting and stopping traditional wheels must be used.

MAGNETIC FIELDS IN SPACE

What are the **Van Allen Belts**?

Charged electrons and protons from solar wind and cosmic rays entering Earth's magnetic field feel the Lorentz force that traps them into spiral orbits about the magnetic field lines. They create doughnut-shaped regions of charged particles called the Van Allen Belts. The belts are concentrated around the equator and become thinner as they approach the poles. The two belts are located at 3,200 kilometers and 16,000 kilometers above the surface of Earth.

Why aren't the **Van Allen Belts** present around the **north** and **south poles**?

At the equator, the magnetic field is parallel to the ground and the electrons and protons from the solar wind can become trapped around the field lines. At the poles, how-

ever, the magnetic field strengthens, the lines become closer together, and forces on the particles push them back toward the equator. Some of the most energetic particles are able to penetrate the atmosphere where they interact with oxygen and nitrogen atoms producing the natural light shows that are called auroras.

What causes the **northern lights**?

Disturbances on the sun can send large numbers of charged particles into space. When they reach Earth they disturb the Van Allen Belts, causing the belts to dump particles into Earth's atmosphere. There they interact with the gases in the atmosphere, causing them to emit light. The scientific name for this phenomena is "aurora."

Are there different names for **auroras** in the **northern** and **southern hemispheres**?

An aurora in the northern hemisphere, known as the "northern lights," is officially called aurora borealis, while an aurora in the southern hemisphere, or "southern lights," is called the aurora australis.

WHAT IS THE WORLD MADE OF?

What is **matter**?

Ancient people in many parts of the world believed that all matter was made of four elements: earth, air, water, and fire. No matter how small an amount of material you had, you could not separate an element into a combination of other materials. But if you kept dividing the amount of material into smaller and smaller pieces, what would you obtain?

Democritus, a Greek who lived around 410 B.C.E. and was the student of Leucippus of Miletus (ca. 435 B.C.E.), stated that all matter is made up of atoms and the void. Atoms are the smallest piece into which an element can be divided; they are uncuttable. They could be neither created nor destroyed, and thus were eternal. The void was empty space. This viewpoint was expanded by the first century B.C.E. by the Greek Titus Lucretius Carus (95–55 B.C.E.) in his epic poem "On the Nature of Things." Aristotle, on the other hand, regarded the atomist philosophy as pure speculation that could never be tested. He rejected the possibility of empty space and believed you could divide matter until it was infinitely small.

The Greeks were not the only ones to develop a philosophy of atomism. The Indian school of philosophy known as Valsesika, and in particular the philosopher Kanāda in the second century B.C.E., held that earth, air, fire, and water could be divided into a finite number of indivisible particles. These ideas were adopted by several other Indian schools of philosophy.

What happened to **Democritus's** and **Aristotle's ideas**?

For almost 2,000 years Aristotle's philosophy was taught in schools and accepted by educated people. In the sixteenth century doubts about Aristotle's science increased. A number of philosophers, including those whom today we would call scientists, actively

opposed Aristotle's dominance of the curriculum in schools. Englishman Francis Bacon (1561–1626) developed what we today would call the scientific method in opposition to Aristotle's philosophy. In 1612 Galileo (1564–1642) published "Discourse on Floating Bodies" in which he envisioned atoms as infinitely small particles, views that he later expanded in "The Assayer" (1623) and, more completely, in "Discourses on Two New Sciences" (1638). Nevertheless, the debate over whether atoms, much too small to see, really existed or were just a successful model of matter continued for another two centuries.

How did **chemistry contribute** to the **acceptance of atoms**?

Robert Boyle (1627–1691), an Irishman who wrote *The Sceptical Chymist* in 1661, is often considered the father of chemistry. He held that matter was made of atoms or groups of atoms that were constantly moving. He urged chemists to accept only those results that could be demonstrated by experiment.

The great French chemist Antoine-Laurent de Lavoisier (1743–1794) demanded that measurements be made with precision and that scientific terms be clearly defined and carefully used. With the discovery that air contained oxygen, which is necessary to support animal life, he clearly demonstrated that air was not an element, but a mixture of oxygen and nitrogen. By showing that hydrogen, discovered by Henry Cavendish (1731–1810), when mixed with oxygen formed water, Lavoisier showed that water also was not an element, but a compound of two elements. Lavoisier's care with weighing both the reactants and products of reactions allowed him to make one of the earliest statements that mass is conserved, that is, neither created nor destroyed in chemical reactions. Lavoisier's wife was a brilliant woman who assisted her husband in many ways, including translating letters from foreign scientists. He was executed during the French Revolution for being a tax collector. In supporting the guilty verdict, the judge said "The Republic needs neither chemists nor scientists."

Lavoisier met with Joseph Priestley (1733–1804) shortly after Priestley discovered oxygen in 1774. Lavoisier did extensive work on oxygen and gave it its present name. Priestley invented carbonated water and experimented with ammonia and laughing gas (nitrous oxide) but when he opposed much of the work of chemists of his generation he was pushed to the sidelines. After writing theological books that opposed traditional Christianity in England he was forced to flee to America in 1794.

John Dalton (1766–1844) was an English chemist who, because he was a Quaker, could not obtain a position in a state-run university. For a number of years he taught at a college in Manchester for dissenters from the Church of England. His strengths were his rich imagination and clear mental pictures, but especially his astonishing physical intuition.

His first interest was meteorology. He wondered how Earth's atmosphere, consisting of gases of very different densities, could have the same composition at different

altitudes. His meteorological studies led him to the conclusion that atoms were physical entities and their relative weight and number were crucial in chemical combinations. Dalton's atomic theory of chemistry was published in "A New System of Chemical Philosophy" in 1808 and 1810. Briefly, it has five parts:

- Elements are made of tiny particles called atoms that cannot be divided into smaller particles. Nor can they be created or destroyed or changed into another kind of atom.

- All atoms of an element are identical. So there are as many kinds of atoms as there are elements.

- The atoms of an element are different from those of any other element in that they have different weights.

- Atoms of one element can combine with atoms of another element to form a chemical compound (today called a molecule). A compound always has the same relative numbers and kinds of atoms.

- In a chemical reaction atoms are rearranged among the compounds; they are neither lost nor gained.

The first and last parts give an atomic basis for Lavoisier's conservation of mass that he had confirmed in many careful experiments. Two of Dalton's specifications are now known to be false. Atoms can be changed from one kind to another by the process of radioactive decay. Not all atoms of an element have the same weight. Both of these results will be discussed in the chapter "At the Heart of the Atom."

Who really **discovered oxygen**?

Three scientists are often credited with the discovery of oxygen: Carl Wilhelm Scheele, Antoine-Laurent de Lavoisier, and Joseph Priestley. The Swedish scientist Scheele discovered what he called "fire air" in 1772. The name came from the way an ember would burst into flame when immersed in the gas. Scheele wrote a book describing his work, but it took four years to be published. In the meantime, Priestley in 1774 discovered what he called "dephlogisticated air." Lavoisier, who met Priestley in 1774 and was told about Priestley's discovery, claimed to have discovered what he called "vital air." Although he was sent letters from both Scheele and Priestley describing their earlier work, he never acknowledged their receipt. Lavoisier's great contribution was to make precise studies of the role of oxygen in a variety of reactions and to give it the name oxygen.

Who introduced the **modern chemical symbols**?

Swedish chemist Jöns Jakob Berzelius (1779–1848) introduced the modern chemical notation using one or two letters to represent an element in 1813. Rather than today's notation for water, H_2O, Berzelius wrote H^2O. Berzelius did much more. He published the first accurate list of the weights of atoms.

How did **Dalton represent atoms**?

Dalton used pictographs to represent atoms. Below, in the first line, are some examples.

Dalton would represent a chemical reaction (carbon plus two oxygen to yield carbon dioxide) as shown on the second line below.

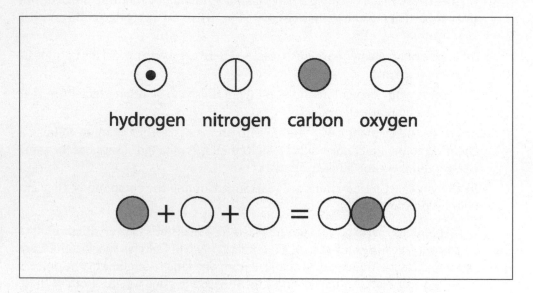

Are **atoms indivisible**?

Thanks to the invention of the electric battery in 1800 by Alessandro Volta (1745–1827) chemists had a new tool to create reactions and isolate new elements. Sir Humphry Davy was one of the most active and isolated sodium, potassium, and calcium from their salts. But it was his assistant, Michael Faraday (1791–1867), who most contributed to the discovery that the atom was not indivisible. He found that the amount of charge needed to liberate an element from a solution was proportional to the mass of the element. In modern language the amount of charge was proportional to the number of atoms liberated. It took until 1881 for the import of this result to be realized when Hermann von Helmholtz (1821–1894) pointed out that if elements are composed of atoms, then electricity could be divided into portions that could be called atoms of electricity. George Johnstone Stoney named these atoms "electrons." But what were they?

How was the "electrical atom"—the **electron—discovered**?

Further advances came not from electrolysis but from studies of gases. In the 1700s and early 1800s physicists used the vacuum pump, invented by Otto von Guericke in 1690, to reduce the pressure in glass tubes fitted with electrodes to allow electricity to pass through the tubes. In 1838 Michael Faraday passed an electric current through

such a tube and noticed a strange arc-shaped light starting at the cathode (negative electrode) and ending almost at the anode (positive electrode).

When Heinrich Geissler was able to reduce the air pressure to about 1/1,000 of an atmosphere he found that the tube was filled with a glow, like the neon lamps used today. By the 1870s William Crookes was able to reduce the pressure to 1/1,000,000 of an atmosphere. As the pressure was reduced the glow gradually disappeared. Instead the glass near the anode began to glow. Without air to disrupt their passage, rays of some sort were able to travel from the cathode to the anode. At the anode end they were going so fast that they caused the glass to glow or fluoresce. By coating the glass with zinc sulfide the glow was made brighter. The mysterious invisible rays could be shown to travel in straight lines by placing metallic objects in the tube and finding that they cast sharp shadows at the anode. Because the rays came from the cathode they were called "cathode rays."

Joseph John (J.J.) Thomson (1856–1940) conducted three experiments with Crookes tubes that showed the nature of cathode rays. His first experiment used an electrode at one side of a tube, out of the direct path, which was connected to an elec-
trometer that could detect electric charge. Thomson could deflect the path of the rays using a magnet and follow their path by observing the fluorescent glow on the tube's surface. He found that the electrometer showed a negative charge, but only when the rays were deflected on to its terminal. Thus he showed that the rays consisted of a beam of negative particles.

Using a tube with the best possible vacuum, Thomson next explored the effect of an electric field on the rays. He added two parallel metal plates to the tube, connected a battery across the plates, and found that the rays were attracted toward the positive plate and away from the negative one.

In his third, and most important experiment, done in 1897, he combined the deflection of an electric field with one by a magnetic field. In doing so he could calculate the ratio of the mass to the charge of the particles. He found that this ratio was 1,800 times lower than that of a

Modern vacuum chambers like this one are used in laboratories to study atoms, molecules, nuclei, and electrons. Otto von Guericke invented the vacuum pump in 1690 to help him study electricity in a vacuum, and since then vacuums have been used to study such things as cathode rays and electrons.

positively charged hydrogen ion. Thus the particles must be either very light or very strongly charged. He later showed that they had the same charge as the hydrogen ion, and so they were very light. Further experiments showed that the particles had the same properties no matter what metal was used for the cathode or whether the cathode was cold or incandescent. For his work Thomson was awarded the Nobel Prize in 1906.

The charge of the electron was measured in 1909 by American physicist Robert Andrews Millikan (1868–1953). Before Millikan's experiments some physicists claimed that Thomson's results could imply that electrons had an average mass-to-charge ratio given by his experiments, but that they could have a variety of masses and charges. But Millikan showed that all electrons had the same charge, and thus the same mass.

What is the **charge** and **mass** of an **electron**?

The charge of an electron is -1.602×10^{-19} C (coulombs). Its mass is 9.11×10^{-31} kg. Both values are known to 85 parts per billion.

The electron has mass, but no size! If you direct beams of very fast, high energy particles at electrons they are deflected by the $1/r^2$ force between two charges no matter how close they come. If the electron had a finite radius then when the incoming particle penetrated the electron the deflection would be different.

What is the **structure** of the **atom**?

Thomson pictured the atom as a swarm of electrons in a positively charged sphere. This model is called the "plum pudding" model, after a then favorite English Christmas treat. Americans might picture a ball of pudding filled with raisins.

The New Zealand born physicist Ernest Rutherford (1871–1937) developed a method of testing Thomson's model. Rutherford's first scientific work was done in Montréal, Canada beginning in 1898. He and Frederick Soddy conducted a study of radioactivity and radioactive materials that won Rutherford the 1908 Nobel Prize in Chemistry. Those experiments will be described in the chapter on nuclear physics, "At the Heart of the Atom." He studied the radiation emitted by thorium and uranium, which he named alpha and beta rays. He recognized that alpha rays would be ideal probes for studying materials.

Rutherford moved to the University of Manchester in Britain in 1907 where he worked with Hans Geiger (1882–1945; later to invent the Geiger counter) on ways of detecting individual alphas. They determined that the alpha particles were doubly charged. They allowed the alphas to go through a window made of very thin mica (a mineral that could be cut into very thin slices). He noticed that the rays that penetrated the mica were deflected slightly more than they should have been by a plum-pudding atom. With Geiger and Ernest Marsden, he directed a beam of alphas on extreme-

ly thin foils of gold. To their great surprise they found a significant number of alphas were deflected into very wide angles—some greater than 90°. Rutherford commented that it was as if a 15" shell from a naval cannon bounced off a sheet of tissue paper.

By 1911 Rutherford had developed his own model of an atom. It consisted of an extremely small positively-charged particle (later called the nucleus) surrounded by electrons. Although the paths of the electrons were not mentioned in

The Rutherford model, as pictured above, is used in many common symbols, like that of a nuclear power plant or the flag of the International Atomic Energy Agency.

the 1911 paper, it was later assumed that they orbited the nucleus as planets orbit the sun. The nucleus was 1/10,000 as large as the atom, but had all the positive charge and essentially all of its mass. If the atom's mass was equal to N hydrogen masses, then the nuclear charge was about N/2. The electrons carry a total charge equal and opposite that of the nucleus so that the atom would be electrically neutral. Rutherford's atom is mostly empty space!

Are there **problems** with **Rutherford's model**?

Electrons moving in circular orbits are experiencing centripetal acceleration. All accelerating charges radiate energy. As a result the electrons in Rutherford's atom would lose all their energy in a tiny fraction of a second. How then could atoms last billions of years? Rutherford offered no answer. In addition, as the electron spiraled into the nucleus it would create a smear of all colors of light, but hydrogen was known to produced only specific colors, called an emission-line spectrum.

In what ways do **atoms emit** and **absorb light**?

In the mid-1800s Robert Kirchhoff published three laws that describe how materials emit and absorb light:

1. A hot solid or a hot, dense gas produces a continuous spectrum.
2. A hot, low-density gas produces an emission-line spectrum.
3. A continuous spectrum source viewed through a cool, low-density gas produces an absorption-line spectrum.

What is a spectrum and what are **continuous** and **line spectra**?

Newton showed that when white light is passed through a prism it is split into a spectrum of all colors from violet through red. There were no gaps between the colors, so the spectrum is called continuous.

611

The emission line of sodium has only two yellow lines. Hydrogen has four lines. The spectrum of iron, on the other hand, has an extremely large number of lines.

An absorption-line spectrum occurs when the low-density gas absorbs distinct colors, leaving dark gaps in the otherwise continuous spectrum. For example, the spectrum that the German physicist Joseph von Fraunhofer (1787–1826) took of the spectrum of the sun in 1814 showed 574 dark lines. In 1859 they were explained as being absorption lines from the cooler gases in the sun's atmosphere.

Fraunhofer made the best optical glass of any glassmaker of his era. He made great improvements to the achromatic lens, which refracts light of all colors the same amount. Like most glassmakers of his era, he died young, most likely from the poisonous effects of the materials used to make the glass.

How can the **emission** and **absorption** of **light** by **atoms** be **explained**?

In 1911 Niels Bohr (1885–1962), a Dane who recently had received his Ph.D. from the University of Copenhagen, joined Rutherford at Cambridge University. He quickly began work on the Rutherford model. He published his results in 1913, basing them on three postulates.

1. Electrons only move in certain allowed orbits at discrete radii and with specific energies. That is, their radii and energies are "quantized." When in these orbits their radii and energies are constant. The atoms do not emit or absorb radiation.

2. Electrons gain or lose energy when they jump from one allowed orbit to another. Then they emit or absorb light with a frequency given by $hf = E_2 - E_1$ where E_2 and E_1 are the energies of the electrons in the allowed orbits. The constant h is called Planck's constant, 6.6×10^{-34} J/Hz (joules per hertz).

3. The correspondence principle. When the electron is very far away from the nucleus classical physics must give the same answer as the new quantum physics.

A bust of Niels Bohr is displayed in Copenhagen, Denmark. Bohr developed postulates about electron behavior, including that they orbit in discrete radii and gain and lose energy in quantized amounts when they change from one orbit to another.

He later changed the third postulate from the correspondence principle to requiring that the angular momentum of the electron be quantized, that is propor-

tional to an integer called the quantum number. The results didn't change, but the derivation of them was more straightforward. This method is presented in almost every textbook.

The two drawings below illustrate the emission of light when the electron goes from a higher-energy to a lower-energy orbit and the absorption of light when the electron's energy is increased.

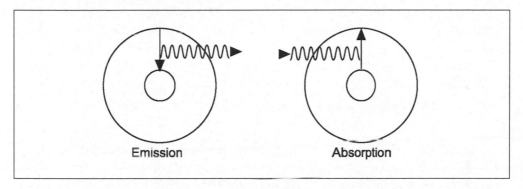

Emission Absorption

In 1885 Johann Balmer had found a formula that accurately calculated the wavelengths of the visible hydrogen spectrum. It was purely empirical—that is, there was no physics-based explanation of it. In 1888 Janne Rydberg generalized Balmer's results to allow calculation of hydrogen emission in the ultraviolet and infrared. Bohr was able to explain Balmer's and Rydberg's formulae using the results of his postulates. The equation for the wavelength of the emitted radiation is $1/\lambda = R(1/m^2 - 1/n^2)$. The numbers m and n are the quantum numbers of the two energy levels. For example, the red line would have $m = 2$, $n = 3$. The constant R is 0.01097 nm^{-1}, making the wavelength of the red line $1/(0.01097 (1/4 - 1/9)$ nm$^{-1}) = 656.3$ nm, in excellent agreement with the experiment. Thus Bohr's model is a major advance in understanding the structure of the atom.

Is **light** a **wave** or a **particle**?

Light (and other forms of electromagnetic radiation) has the properties of both a particle and a wave. As a wave it is described by its wavelength, frequency, amplitude, and polarization. It has the ability to diffract and interfere. As a particle it has energy, momentum, and angular momentum. It has the ability to be emitted and absorbed, and to scatter off other particles, transferring energy and momentum. In some experiments it acts like a wave in part of the experiment and a particle in other parts.

For example, if you put a beam of light through a pair of narrow, closely spaced slits, the so-called Young two-slit experiment, you get an interference pattern with alternating stripes of light, where the light through the two slits constructively interferes, and darkness where the interference is destructive. If you now greatly reduce

the intensity of the light and use a detector that can detect individual photons you will have regions where a large number of photons arrive and others where none arrive. The regions are exactly where the dark and light stripes were.

If the intensity is so low that there is only one photon in the apparatus at a time how can the dark and light regions be understood?

Particles can't split, with half going through one slit, half through the other so the two halves interfere. If you try to modify the experiment so you can tell through which slit the photon came you destroy the interference pattern.

Physicists have grappled with this mystery for decades. There are no easy explanations. Perhaps the fault lies with our language and thinking. We simply do not have the correct words or mental concepts to describe and understand how light works.

Does **light interact** with an **atom** as a **wave** or a **particle**?

A wave carries energy continuously over time; the more energy in the wave, the faster the energy is transferred. A particle, on the other hand, delivers its energy all at once. When an atom either absorbs or emits light, the transfer is almost instantaneous. Therefore light interacts with an atom like a particle.

The idea that light comes in packets of energy was first stated by Albert Einstein (1879–1955) in 1905. He called the packet a *light quantum*. The quantum was given the name photon in 1926. The photon has no mass or charge, but it does carry angular momentum. It always moves at the speed of light, c.

Each photon carries an amount of energy $E = hf$, where f is its frequency. Therefore a photon of blue light has more energy than one of red light. The energy carried by a beam of light depends both on the frequency and the number of photons per second leaving the source.

Are **emission** and **absorption** the **only ways** light interacts with an atom?

In 1917 Albert Einstein proposed a third way light could interact with an atom. If a photon with the correct energy struck an atom in the excited state then the atom would be stimulated to emit an additional photon and drop to the lower energy level. The two photons leave with the same energy (in terms of a wave—same wavelength) and in phase.

Stimulated emission

What are the **limits** of the **Bohr model**?

Today's model is totally different from Bohr's 1913 model. Bohr's model could explain only the spectra of hydrogen and helium from which an electron was removed. With some modifications is could also explain the spectra of the alkalis like lithium. From 1913 through 1926 physicists tried to extend the model, with some successes, but the lack of a physics-based explanation of the postulates led to research aimed at a model that was not based on classical ideas like Bohr's. One of the first steps was taken by the young German physicist Werner Heisenberg (1901–1976).

What were some of Niels **Bohr's accomplishments** as an exemplary **physicist** and **citizen**?

Bohr returned to the University of Copenhagen as a professor of physics in 1921. With the help of the government and the Carlsberg Beer Foundation he established the Institute of Theoretical Physics. Bohr's Institute attracted all the major theoretical physicists from around the world for short visits or extended appointments. When the Germans occupied Denmark, Bohr made a daring escape, first to Sweden, then England, then the United States. He was a consultant in the atomic bomb development effort, but after the war he tried to get President Harry Truman (1884–1972) and British leader Winston Churchill (1874–1965) to agree to share the secrets of the bomb with all countries, including the Soviet Union. They both rejected Bohr's proposal. But after the Soviets developed the bomb, Bohr's ideas helped found the United Nations' International Atomic Energy Agency. Until his death in 1962 he worked to reduce the threat of a nuclear war. In the centenary of his birth Denmark issued a postal stamp showing Bohr and his wife, Margarethe.

What is the **Heisenberg Uncertainty Principle**?

Heisenberg, together with Max Born and Pascal Jordan, tried a totally different approach using mathematical matrices. As part of their work Heisenberg developed a

principle that demonstrates that in the atomic world our knowledge is limited. The uncertainty principle is written as $\Delta x \times \Delta p \geq h/4\pi$. In words, the uncertainty of a particle's position times the uncertainty in its momentum is never less than Planck's constant divided by 4π. If it has a precise location, then its momentum, and thus its speed (measured at the same time), must be imprecise. Planck's constant is extremely small, and so the uncertainty principle is important only for objects the size of atoms or smaller. The position and momentum of a baseball, for example, can both be precisely known at the same time.

The uncertainty principle shows why Bohr's electron orbits cannot exist. If you know the radius of the circle precisely, then it must have some velocity along the radius—smearing out its orbit. The uncertainty principle also exists in a form linking energy and time. In this form it says that if an electron is in a state that lasts for only a short time, then its energy is not precisely defined.

How did **probability** rather than **certainty** enter into the **model** for the **atom**?

In 1926 the Austrian physicist Erwin Schrödinger (1887–1961) published an equation for a wave function that describes the probability of finding an electron at a particular position. It agrees with Bohr's model in that the most probable radius for an electron is that given by the Bohr model, and the energy of the electron is the same as Bohr calculated, but its results are fundamentally different.

The solution of Schrödinger's equation can be shown as a probability cloud that shows the most probable locations for the electron.

The $n = 1$ state of the hydrogen atom is small and spherical. There are two $n = 2$ states. The s state has angular momentum zero and another spherically symmetric cloud. The p state, with angular momentum 1 has two most probable locations, the top and bottom. The $n = 3$ state has three possible angular momenta: 0, 1, and 2. The d state, with angular momentum = 2, has four angular regions with high probability.

Red light is emitted when the electron goes from the $n = 3$ "p" state to the $n = 2$ "s" state. The lifetime of the higher-energy state is very short, less than one billionth of a second, so when many atoms emit the light, the energy they emit is spread out— the energy from any particular atom cannot be precisely predicted.

Are **electrons waves** or **particles**?

The electrons in an atom are not confined to one region of space, but are spread out. They are acting more like waves than particles. In Louis-Victor-Pierre-Raymond de Broglie's (1892–1987) 1924 doctoral thesis he proposed that electrons behave like waves with a wavelength given by $\lambda = h/mv$, where h is Planck's constant, and m and v the mass and velocity of the electron. The thesis was forwarded to Einstein, who enthusiastically endorsed the idea and recommended that the thesis be approved. De Broglie

was awarded the Nobel Prize in 1929 for this work. The de Broglie wavelength is associated with any particle, although for an object the size of a baseball it is much smaller than the diameter of a nucleus!

The de Broglie wavelength of a particle determines its wave-like properties. Just as light photons interfere with themselves in a two-slit experiment, so do particles. The interference of electrons, atoms, and even molecules as large as C_{60} (so-called Buckyballs) has been observed, and the measurements fit de Broglie's wavelength perfectly.

So, both matter and light can act like either a particle or a wave. This phenomenon is given the name "wave–particle duality."

Where do **X rays come from**?

X rays are electromagnetic waves of very short wavelength. Alternatively, they are very high-energy photons. They are emitted by atoms with many electrons, such as those high in the periodic table. The more electrons, the greater the charge of the nucleus, and the higher the energy of the electrons that are close to the nucleus (with $n = 1$ or 2). Therefore, when the atom is disturbed, as it is in an X-ray tube when the anode is bombarded by high-energy electrons, one of the $n = 1$ electrons can be kicked out. When an $n = 2$ electron loses energy and takes the place of the kicked-out electron, an X ray is emitted.

What is **quantum mechanics**?

The field of study of atoms by themselves, as well as in molecules, liquids, and solids in which the wave nature is important is called quantum mechanics. The atoms obey the Schroedinger equation, but for any atom more complicated than hydrogen the equation can be solved only by a computer. Using computers to solve equations, run complicated models, and simulate experiments is an important sub-division of the study of physics called computational physics, which now has equal status with theoretical and experimental physics.

Some of the recent accomplishments of quantum mechanics are in the areas of condensed matter physics, or the study of solids, and atomic physics. All of the integrated circuits used in mp3 players, televisions, cameras, and automobiles are designed using quantum mechanics. They are all based on diodes and transistors where quantum mechanics describes and explains their properties and guides materials scientists to select appropriate materials for their construction. One of the most exciting new materials is graphene, a film of carbon where the atoms are in hexagon-shaped arrays, but the film is only one atom thick. Graphene is being investigated as a way of constructing extremely tiny transistors, and thus powerful integrated circuits. It may also be used as a sensor to detect single atoms or molecules of selected materials or as a transparent conductor for touch-screen computer displays. Its discoverers won the 2010 Nobel Prize.

Lasers are now commonly used in industry, surgery, and communications technology, among other uses. Theodore Maiman demonstrated the first laser in 1960, but Gordon Gould was awarded the patent.

From 1924 to 1925 Einstein and the Indian physicist Satyendra Nath Bose (1894–1974) predicted that if an atomic gas were cooled enough the atoms could form a new state of matter that would exhibit quantum effects on a macroscopic scale. The first experimental confirmation of this prediction occurred in 1995 when Eric Cornell (1962–) and Carl Wieman (1952–) at the University of Colorado cooled a gas of rubidium atoms to about 1/6 of a millionth of a Kelvin. They and Wolfgang Ketterle (1957–) at MIT shared the 2001 Nobel Prize for their work. While this new state of matter, called a Bose-Einstein Condensate, has no existing applications, physicists are using it to improve their knowledge of how atoms interact at very low temperatures and to explore possible future applications to atomic clocks and computers.

How was the **laser invented**?

One of the useful applications of quantum mechanics is in each CD or DVD player in your home, or in the laser pointer. It's the device that uses stimulated emission of light predicted by Einstein so many years ago. In 1953 Charles Townes (1915–) of Columbia University (and later MIT) developed and patented the first application that he called a "maser" for microwave amplification by stimulated emission of radiation. It used a beam of ammonia molecules and later led to the hydrogen maser, now used as an extremely accurate clock. In 1958 Townes and Arthur Schawlow described how molecules could be used to extend the maser concept to optical frequencies. After

What did Einstein mean by "God does not play dice with the universe"?

As quantum mechanics was developed in the 1920s and 1930s its statistical nature became more evident. Einstein was convinced that there were variables, that could not be seen, but that actually controlled the outcomes. Einstein conducted many debates with Niels Bohr and Max Born about the statistical, or probabilistic, interpretation of quantum mechanics. In 1935 Einstein, Boris Podolsky, and Nathan Rosen wrote a famous paper that explored what they considered to be the incomplete description of the world provided by quantum mechanics. They proposed an experiment that has now been done and confirmed the predictions of quantum mechanics.

In a 1926 letter to Max Born, Einstein wrote: "Quantum mechanics is certainly imposing. But an inner voice tells me that it is not yet the real thing. The theory says a lot, but does not really bring us any closer to the secret of the 'old one'. I, at any rate, am convinced that He does not throw dice."

their paper was published a number of physicists at university and industrial labs rapidly tried to apply these ideas to working devices.

In May 1960, Theodore Maiman (1927–2007) at Hughes Aircraft Company demonstrated an "optical maser" that used a ruby crystal with a flash lamp (similar to the camera flash lamp) to put the chromium atoms in the ruby into their excited states. Maiman was involved in a court fight over the validity of his patent for the laser with Gordon Gould (1920–2005), who worked with Townes at Columbia. In 1973 Gould was awarded the patent rights. Maiman won number of awards, but never the Nobel Prize.

While the laser was first described as a "solution looking for a problem" over the past fifty years lasers have become a multi-million dollar industry. Lasers have been constructed using gases, as in the familiar helium-neon, or HeNe laser; the carbon-dioxide laser used to cut fabrics and metals; the argon-ion laser used in surgery; the ultraviolet excimer laser used for eye surgery; and the free-electron laser used in research. Lasers made of tiny semiconducting crystals are used in CD and DVD players and laser pointers, as well as optical fiber communications equipment that brings video and the internet almost to your front door. Lasers have revolutionized research in physics, chemistry, and biology.

What is a **laser tweezer**?

When a laser is sent through a microscope it creates a tiny spot of very intense light in the material on the slide. A tiny plastic sphere will interact with the light in such a

619

way that it is pulled into the center of the light. The light can be moved around the slide, dragging the sphere with it. That is the essence of a "laser tweezer." The sphere can be chemically attached to the end of a long molecule, such as DNA. When the other end of the DNA is similarly fastened to the surface of the slide, the sphere can be used to stretch the DNA, straightening it out, and measuring properties such as the force needed to stretch it. Proteins, enzymes, and other polymers can be used in place of the DNA and the forces they exert similarly measured. In addition, the tweezers can be used to sort cells, moving them to specific locations on the slide.

We'll explore other mysterious consequences of quantum mechanics in the last chapter, "Unanswered Questions."

AT THE HEART OF THE ATOM

What makes up the **nucleus**?

Ernest Rutherford (1871–1937) had determined that the charge on the alpha particle, actually the helium nucleus, was two proton charges, but its mass was four proton masses. Dmitri Mendeleev (1834–1907), in building the periodic table, had arranged the elements in order of their mass and had arbitrarily assigned them sequential numbers that he called the atomic number. The English physicist Henry Moseley (1887–1915) measured the wavelengths of X rays emitted when metals were struck by other X rays. He was able to provide a physical basis for the atomic number and, in doing so, greatly strengthened the case for Rutherford's nuclear model.

But, as is the case for helium, if the atomic number, and thus the nuclear charge, was about half the atomic mass number, what made up the additional mass of the nucleus? The first proposal was that the missing particle was a combination of a proton and an electron, which would have the correct mass and charge. But the Heisenberg uncertainty principle showed that if an electron were confined to the size of a proton its energy would be larger than ever observed. In addition, by the late 1920s the angular momentum of the nitrogen nucleus, with charge 7 and mass 14 had been measured. The result could not be obtained from a combination of 14 protons and 7 electrons.

In 1931 two German physicists found that when energetic alpha particles struck light elements a very penetrating, neutral radiation was produced. The next year Marie Curie's daughter, Irène Joliot-Curie (1897–1956), and her husband, Frederick, found that if this radiation struck paraffin protons were ejected, suggesting that the radiation was actually a neutral particle with a mass near that of a proton. The next year James Chadwick (1891–1974), working in Manchester, England, experimentally confirmed the suggestion. The particle was named a neutron, combining "neutral" with the ending of the word proton. He was awarded the Nobel Prize for his discovery in 1935.

The neutron has a mass slightly larger than that of the proton. While neutrons are stable in non-radioactive nuclei, if they are free from the nucleus they decay with a half-life of about 10 minutes. Neutrons are used extensively in creating nuclear reactions and are necessary for nuclear fission, which will be discussed later in this chapter.

Do all **elements** have a **fixed number** of **protons** and **neutrons**?

The number of protons in the nucleus of an atom determines what element it is, so the number of protons is fixed. But, the number of neutrons can vary. Nuclei with the same number of protons but different numbers of neutrons are called isotopes. For example, carbon, with six protons, can have five, six, seven, or eight neutrons. The isotopes are labeled carbon-11, carbon-12, carbon-13, and carbon-14. A more compact notation is ^{11}C, ^{12}C, ^{13}C, and ^{14}C. Chemical properties in general do not depend on the isotope. There are at least 3,100 isotopes of all the elements presently known.

How do the numbers of **protons** and **neutrons** in **nuclei compare**?

For lighter elements the number of protons and neutrons are approximately equal. For example, the most common isotope of helium with two protons is ^{4}He, so it has 4 − 2 = 2 neutrons. Oxygen, with eight protons, has eight neutrons in its most common isotope, ^{16}O.

In elements heavier than calcium (20 protons, 20 neutrons) the number of neutrons is larger than the number of protons. In uranium-238 (92 protons, 146 neutrons) the ratio is almost 3 neutrons for 2 protons.

What **holds** a **nucleus together**?

Protons, all being charged positively, will repel each other. So there must be an attractive force that holds the nucleus together. The strong nuclear force acts between protons and protons, protons and neutrons, and neutrons and neutrons, all with the same strength. Because the strong force acts the same on protons and neutrons, the two particles are frequently lumped together under the name nucleon. While the repulsive electromagnetic force acts over long distances, the strong nuclear force only acts between nucleons that are in contact. Nucleons have angular momentum, or spin, and the strong force depends on the relative orientation of the spins. The force is stronger if the spins are in opposite directions.

How were the **details** of the **strong force determined**?

Examining the kinds of isotopes that exist gives clues about the nature of the strong force. The most stable nucleus, helium-4, has two neutrons having spins in opposite directions and two protons also having spins in opposite directions. A majority of non-

radioactive isotopes have even numbers of neutrons and even number of protons, allowing them to form pairs with opposite spins. Most of the other isotopes have either an even number of protons and an odd number of neutrons or the opposite. Isotopes with both an odd number of protons and neutrons are extremely rare. So, the strength of the strong force clearly depends on the spins of the nucleons.

The mass of a nucleus is less than the sum of the masses of the protons plus the sum of masses of the neutrons. The larger the mass difference, the stronger the forces holding the nucleus together and the more energy needed to pull the nucleus apart. Studies of the mass of the nuclei can thus be used to gain further insight into the strong force. Maria Goeppert-Mayer (1906–1972) was a German-born American physicist who explained why nuclei with certain numbers of protons and/or neutrons, called magic numbers, were extremely stable. Her theory showed that the nuclear force depended on both the spin of the nucleon and its orbital angular momentum. The magic numbers are 2, 8, 20, 28, 50, 82, and 126. Thus helium-4, the most stable nucleus has a magic number of protons and a magic number of neutrons, and so is called doubly magic. Oxygen-16, calcium-40 and calcium-48, and lead-208, which is the heaviest stable nuclide, are also doubly magic. But, are all nuclei stable?

What **rays** do **radioactive materials** emit?

Among the scientists who explored radioactivity immediately after Becquerel's discovery was Ernst Rutherford, then at McGill University in Montréal, Canada. He and Frederick Soddy found that uranium and thorium emitted two different kinds of rays. One could be stopped by paper, the other required metal about a centimeter thick. Rutherford named them alpha and beta rays after the first two letters in the Greek alphabet. In 1907 he named the even more penetrating rays produced by radium gamma rays.

In 1900 Pierre (1859–1906) and Marie Curie (1867–1934), using an electroscope, found that beta rays are negative particles. Becquerel used the same kind of apparatus J.J. Thomson (1856–1940) had used (see the chapter "What Is the World Made Of?") to measure the ratio of mass to charge of an electron to determine that betas typically travel at about half the speed of light and are identical to electrons. In late 1907 Rutherford demonstrated that alpha rays were helium atoms with the two electrons removed. (He had not yet discovered the nucleus. Today we say that an alpha particle is the helium-4 nucleus.) Gamma rays were later found to be very high energy photons.

Henri Becquerel earned the 1903 Nobel Prize for his discovery of radioactivity.

In 1896 the French physicist Henri Becquerel (1852–1908) was exploring the properties of a compound of uranium that glowed in the dark. He placed the compound in a dark drawer on top of a photographic plate that he had wrapped with heavy black paper to make it light-tight. The next morning he was surprised to find that the film was already exposed, or fogged. Becquerel presumed that some unknown rays had been emitted by the uranium compound, gone through the paper, and created the same chemical reaction in the plate that light would. In further experiments he found that a thin piece of metal would block the rays. It was soon found that compounds of both uranium and thorium emitted the rays, but that they did not emit light. In 1903 he shared the Nobel Prize in recognition of his discovery of what was later called radioactivity.

Alpha, beta, and gammas all are hazardous to our health. Alphas are blocked by skin, but if a radioactive material, such as the gas radium, is inhaled, the alpha particles can cause damage to the lungs. Betas can penetrate skin and tissue and, if they strike a cell, can cause mutations to the DNA. Gammas can cause mutations and kill cells; they are used in cancer radiation therapy.

What contributions did **Marie** and **Pierre Curie** make?

Marie Skłodowska Curie, born and raised in Poland, but working in France, used an electrometer to measure the ionization of the air caused by radioactive minerals. Because the amount of radioactivity produced by a uranium compound depended only on the amount of uranium present, she concluded that the atom itself must be the source. She found that the uranium-containing mineral pitchblende was more radioactive than the uranium itself and concluded that the mineral must contain a small quantity of another element that was more radioactive than the uranium. Her husband, Pierre, stopped his own work and joined Marie in searching for the element.

They started by grinding up 100 grams of pitchblende, but by the time they had found the element they had processed tons of the mineral. In July 1898 they announced the discovery of an element they named "polonium" in honor of Poland, where she had been born. In December of the same year they announced they had found an even more radioactive element that they named radium. It took until 1902 for them to separate one-tenth of a gram of radium chloride from a ton of pitchblende. In 1910 Marie announced that she had obtained pure metallic radium.

Pierre and Marie shared the 1903 physics Nobel Prize with Becquerel for their work on radioactivity. Marie won the 1911 chemistry Nobel Prize for her discovery of polonium and radium.

The dangers of radioactivity were unknown when the Curies did their work, but both were affected by it. The radon that was produced when they were processing the pitchblende would have caused lung cancer. But, the leaky windows in their workplace and their frequent bicycle rides in the country spared them. Pierre died in 1906 when he slipped on a wet street and was run over by a horse-drawn wagon. Marie's death in 1934 was due to anemia, known now to be frequently caused by radiation.

What is a **half life**?

When will a particular radioactive nucleus decay? It's impossible to know. All that can be known is the average time between formation and decay. And we know that the number of decays will be proportional to the number of nuclei present. Now, suppose we start with a large number of nuclei. In a given time interval, say one second, a certain number will decay. At the end of that second the number of nuclei that haven't decayed will be smaller, so in the next second there will be fewer decays. At some time there will be only half as many decays in a second as there were originally. That time is called the half life. One half life later there will be only 1/4 as many decays as at the beginning. After another half life there will be half again as many, or 1/8 the number of initial decays.

How is **radioactive decay** used to **determine dates**?

Radioactive carbon-14 (^{14}C) has a half life of 5,730 years. It is produced in the atmosphere when cosmic ray neutrons strike nitrogen atoms. The ^{14}C then reacts with oxygen to form carbon dioxide in the atmosphere and dissolves into the oceans. Plants take up the atmospheric CO_2 in respiration and animals ingest it. Therefore all living things exchange both $^{12}CO_2$ and radioactive $^{14}CO_2$ throughout their lives. When they die the exchange stops and the fraction of ^{14}C to ^{12}C in their bodies is fixed. As time goes on the amount of ^{14}C decreases. Objects up to 50,000 years old can be dated by radioactive carbon as long as correction figures, agreed to by international agencies, are applied. Willard F. Libby (1908–1980), an American chemist, won the Nobel Prize in chemistry in 1960 for his development of carbon-14 dating in 1949.

There are several other dating techniques that use the half lives of radioactive isotopes in rocks including urani-

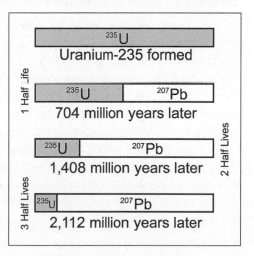

Radioactive uranium-235 decays into lead (Pb-207) very gradually. The half life is 704 million years!

um/thorium and rubidium/strontium ratios that extend dating techniques to hundreds of millions of years.

What **happens** to an **element** when it **decays** by emitting an **alpha particle**?

The nucleus that results from a radioactive decay is called the daughter. The number of nucleons in a radioactive decay does not change, and in an alpha decay the number of protons of the original must equal the number of protons in the daughter plus the number of protons in the alpha. The same is true for the number of neutrons. So, for example, when uranium-238, with 92 protons and 146 neutrons emits an alpha, the daughter has 90 protons and 144 neutrons. It is thorium-234. The alpha is emitted with a specific energy. Only very heavy nuclei decay by alpha decay.

Are there **uses** for **alpha decay**?

The decay of uranium and thorium produces all the helium that exists on Earth. Most of the helium is mixed with natural gas and is extracted from gas wells. It is expensive to separate and store the helium, but, given the increasing needs for this resource for cooling superconducting magnets used in hospital MRI machines, it is an effort that must be made.

Alpha-emitting radioactive elements are used in smoke detectors. The charged alpha particles leaving the element are collected on a metal plate where they produce a small electric current. Smoke scatters the alphas, reducing the current, and triggering the alarm.

How did the study of **beta decay** result in the **discovery** of a **new particle**?

In beta decay a nucleus emits an electron. The electron isn't in the nucleus originally, but results from the change of a neutron into a proton. Studies of the energy of the emitted electron showed that, instead of having a single energy like an alpha has, the energies of the electrons were spread from near zero to a maximum energy. Early investigators recognized that this suggested that energy was not conserved in beta decay. Austrian physicist Wolfgang Pauli (1900–1958) proposed in 1930 that a second particle was emitted along with the electron. This particle had to be neutral and zero, or extremely small mass, and he named it the neutrino, or "little neutral one." The neutrino wasn't detected experimentally until 1956. We now know that the neutrino emitted in beta decay is actually an anti-neutrino. The question of its mass will be discussed in the chapter on "Unanswered Questions."

When a nucleus undergoes beta decay the number of protons increases by one as the number of neutrons decrease by one. So, for example, carbon-14 (6 protons and 8 neutrons) becomes nitrogen-14 (7 protons and 7 neutrons) with the emission of the beta (electron) and an anti-neutrino.

What **nuclear force** is responsible for **beta decay**?

The weak nuclear force is the cause of beta decay. It is 10^{-13} (one-ten trillionth) as strong as the strong force. As a result the half life of most beta-decaying nuclei is long.

In 1968 Abdus Salam, Sheldon Glashow, and Steven Weinberg showed that the electromagnetic force and the weak nuclear force were actually different aspects of a single force, the electroweak force. How can these two forces that are so different in strength and range be unified? It only happens at extremely high energies (corresponding to a temperature of 10^{15} K), such as occurred in the first few moments after the Big Bang or in an accelerator. They received the 1979 Nobel Prize for their work.

What is the **origin** of **gamma rays**?

Gamma rays, high-energy photons or short-wavelength electromagnetic waves, are emitted from the nucleus along with an alpha or beta decay. When an alpha or beta decay produces a daughter nucleus that nucleus is often in an excited state. One or more gammas are emitted as the nucleus settles down to its lowest energy, or ground state. Gammas are like high-energy X rays, but are emitted from the nucleus, not the electrons, of an atom.

What is **antimatter**?

In 1932 Carl Anderson (1905–1991) was studying particles produced when cosmic rays struck lead sheets in a cloud chamber that was in a magnetic field. He found low-mass particles that curved the opposite direction from electrons, showing that they had positive charge. He later confirmed the existence of these particles by using a laboratory source of high-energy gamma rays. This positive electron was named the positron and was the first form of antimatter found. Anderson shared the 1936 Nobel Prize for his discovery.

When a gamma ray with sufficient energy strikes matter it can produce an electron–positron pair. Energy is converted into particles with mass. The minimal amount of gamma-ray energy needed is given by Einstein's famous equation, $E_{gamma} = m_{electron}c^2 + m_{positron}c^2$. The uncharged gamma produces a negatively charged electron and a positively charged positron, so electric charge is conserved.

Positrons are also emitted in radioactive decay of isotopes that have a deficit of neutrons. For example, stable carbon exists as ^{12}C or ^{13}C; six protons and either six or seven neutrons. As was discussed above, ^{14}C decays by emitting an electron. One of the neutrons changes to a proton with the emission of the electron and anti-neutrino. On the other hand, ^{11}C, with only five neutrons, is a positron emitter. One of the protons changes to a neutron with the emission of a positron and a neutrino.

When a positron strikes matter the positron and an electron annihilate each other, producing two or three gammas. Particles with mass are converted to energy.

Again, Einstein's equation can be used to find the total energy of the gammas: $E_{gammas} = m_{electron}c^2 + m_{positron}c^2$.

Antiprotons are created in accelerators, where the accelerated particle is slammed into a metal target, emitting gammas that create, in this case, proton–antiproton pairs.

How is **antimatter** used in **medicine**?

A three-dimensional image that shows biological activity in a person can be made using PET, or Positron Emission Tomography. PET uses a short-lived positron-emitting isotope, typically ^{11}C, ^{13}N, ^{15}O, or ^{18}F. The isotope is chemically attached to a molecule that is involved in the activity that is to be studied. Fluid containing that molecule is injected into the person and after enough time passes for the molecule to reach its target, the person is put into the PET machine. The positron that is emitted by the decaying nucleus strikes an electron and decays into two gammas that are simultaneously emitted back-to-back, that is, 180° apart. Detectors record the arrival of the two gammas, and computers extrapolate them back to the location of the gamma emission. When a sufficient number of events are recorded a three-dimensional image of the region where the biologically-active molecule accumulated can be made. PET scans can be combined with CT or MRI scans to pair information on the anatomy with biological activity for diagnostic purposes.

What **elements beyond uranium** have been discovered?

Atomic #	Symbol	Name	Longest-lived Isotope	Year Discovered	Location*	Formation Reaction
93	Np	Neptunium	^{237}Np 2.1×10^6 y	1940	Berkeley	n + U
94	Pu	Plutonium	^{244}Pu 8.0×10^7 y	1940	Berkeley	α + U

An aerial view of CERN, just northwest of Geneva, Switzerland. The Large Hadron Collider ring covers 22.4 square miles (large circle in the photo). The smaller ring at the lower right, which is the Proton Synchotron that is used to accelerate protons that are then fed into the LHC, has a circumference of 2.7 square miles.

Atomic #	Symbol	Name	Longest-lived Isotope	Year Discovered	Location*	Formation Reaction
95	Am	Americium	^{243}Am 7370 y	1944	Berkeley	n + U
96	Cm	Curium	^{247}Cm 1.6×10^7 y	1944	Berkeley	α + Pu
97	Bk	Berkelium	^{247}Bk 1380 y	1949	Berkeley	α + Am
98	Cf	Californium	^{251}Cf 898 y	1950	Berkeley	α + Cm
99	Es	Einsteinium	^{252}Es 742 d	1952	Berkeley	N + U
100	Fm	Fermium	^{257}Fm 101 d	1952	Berkeley	O + U
101	Md	Mendelevium	^{258}Md 52 d	1955	Berkeley	α + Es
102	No	Nobelium	^{257}No 58 m	1956	Dubna	C + Cm
103	Lr	Lawrencium	^{262}Lr 3.6 h	1962	Dubna/ Berkeley	B + Cf
104	Rf	Rutherfordium	^{267}Rf 1.3 h	1966	Dubna/ Berkeley	Ne + Am
105	Db	Dubium	^{268}Db 28 h	1968	Dubna/ Berkeley	Ne + Am
106	Sg	Seaborgium	^{271}Sb 1.9 m	1985	Dubna/ GSI	Cr + Pb
107	Bh	Bohrium	^{270}Bh 61 s	1981	GSI	Bi + Cr
108	Hs	Hassium	^{269}Hs 10 s	1984	GSI	Fe + Pb
109	Mt	Meitnerium	^{278}Mt 8 s	1982	GSI	Fe + Bi
110	Ds	Darmstadtium	^{281}Ds 10 s	1994	GSI	Ni + Pb
111	Rg	Roentgenium	^{281}Rg 20 s	1994	GSI	Bi + Ni
112	Cn	Copernicium	^{285}Cn 30 s	1996	GSI	Ca + U
113	Uut	Ununtrium	^{286}Uut 20 s	2003	Dubna/ Berkeley	Ca + Am
114	Uuq	Ununquadium	^{289}Uuq 2.6 s	1999	Dubna	Ca + Pu
115	Uup	Ununpentium	^{289}Uup 0.22 s	2004	Dubna/ Berkeley	Ca + Am
116	Uuh	Ununhexium	^{293}Uuh 0.060 s	2000	Dubna	Ca + Cm
117	Uus	Ununseptium	^{294}Uus 0.036 s	2010	Dubna	Ca + Cm
118	Uuo	Ununoctium	^{294}Uuo 0.89 ms	2002	Dubna	Ca + Cf

*Berkeley = University of California at Berkeley, Lawrence Radiation Laboratory, Lawrence Livermore Laboratory; GSI = Heavy Ion Accelerator at Darmstadt, Germany; Dubna = Joint Institute for Nuclear Research, Dubna (near Moscow), Russia.

Elements 113 to 118 have temporary names until the International Union of Pure and Applied Chemistry decides on the name. The number of atoms detected in the decays of elements 113–118 vary between a dozen down to even one! In the search for

element 117 a total of 10^{19} Ca ions bombarded the Californium target and resulted in three atoms of element 117.

Elements up through Californium (98) have been produced in milligram or gram quantities. They have been used as target materials for the accelerators that bombard them with ions in the search for heavier elements. The estimated cost of producing enough Einsteinium (99) to be used as a target is $50 million!

What is the **Island of Stability**?

All the isotopes of elements beyond lead are radioactive. Some have lifetimes of tens of millions of years, while others are fractions of a second. Nuclear physicists and chemists know that isotopes that have magic numbers of neutrons or protons are more stable than others. They have proposed that very heavy isotopes with a neutron number around 180 and a proton number around 110 should be more stable than those with fewer or greater neutrons and protons. A glance at the table of elements beyond uranium shows that elements around 110 have longer lifetimes than others. But researchers have not yet been able to create isotopes with enough neutrons to reach this island.

What is **nuclear fission**?

Radioactive nuclei can decay in another way—they can split in two. This process is called spontaneous fission. Fission can also be produced artificially by bombarding nuclei with low-energy neutrons. In fact, fission was discovered in this manner.

How was **nuclear fission discovered**?

Italian physicist Enrico Fermi (1901–1954) was appointed professor at the University of Rome at the age of twenty-four. Among many projects in which he and his group were involved, perhaps none was more important than his studies of the reactions produced when slow neutrons struck nuclei. Fermi had discovered in 1934 that slowing neutrons by passing them through paraffin greatly increased this ability to produce nuclear reactions. He did systematic studies of the results of bombarding a series of materials with slow neutrons.

The German chemist Otto Hahn (1879–1968) had a distinguished career that included inventing the field of radiochemistry in 1905. Using chemical techniques and measurements of half lives to study the results of nuclear reactions he had discovered dozens of isotopes and at least one element. Three times he was nominated for the Nobel Prize. Since 1907 he had collaborated with the Austrian physicist Lise Meitner (1878–1968). The teamwork between a physicist and a chemist was a great advantage.

Hahn and Meitner, together with Hahn's young assistant Fritz Strassman (1902–1980), employed Fermi's slow neutron techniques to create nuclear reactions,

and thus more isotopes. When, in 1938, they tried bombarding uranium with neutrons they expected to create new elements beyond uranium in the periodic table. But they kept finding the element barium in the bombarded uranium.

Starting in 1933, the Nazi regime forced people of Jewish origin out of all laboratories and universities. Meitner, who had Jewish parents but had converted to Protestantism in 1908, was protected because she was Austrian. But, when Austria was incorporated into Germany, she lost that protection. In July 1938, she took the train from Berlin to the Netherlands. Thanks to the intervention of two Dutch physicists she was allowed to leave Germany, but with no possessions. She soon moved to Sweden and kept up her collaboration with Hahn by mail.

On December 17, 1938, Hahn and Strassman submitted their findings for publication but admitted that they had no explanation for the appearance of barium. Meitner and her nephew Otto Frisch utilized Niels Bohr's "liquid drop" model of the nucleus and Einstein's $E = mc^2$ equation to propose that the nucleus had split into two, releasing both extra neutrons and a large amount of energy. The Meitner-Frisch paper was submitted a few days after Hahn's. Frisch returned to his laboratory in England and confirmed Hahn's result in January 1939. Hahn won the Nobel prize in chemistry for his work in 1944, but Meitner never did.

Did physicists recognize the **military uses** of **fission**?

Lisa Meitner had recognized that extra neutrons could produce a chain reaction that would produce a very large amount of energy. In early 1939 physicists from many countries attempted to create such chain reactions by slowing down the released neutrons. Among these were Enrico Fermi and a Hungarian-born physicist Leó Szilárd. They saw signs that such a reaction had occurred.

In August 1939 Szilárd drafted a letter to President Franklin D. Roosevelt (1882–1945) that the German results could lead to in an extremely powerful new weapon. To give his letter more weight he convinced Einstein to sign the letter. It worked. Roosevelt directed the government to support fission research and created the Uranium Committee. While there were several important studies during the next three years, it was the British who made the breakthrough finding that the rare isotope uranium-235

It was not long after scientists figured out how to create nuclear fusion that the Nazis began conducting research on how to turn this science into a powerful bomb. Albert Einstein and physicist Leó Szilárd urged U.S. President Franklin D. Roosevelt start a program to complete a nuclear warhead before the Germans did.

could be used in a weapon. The Americans were informed but ignored the results until a personal visit by one of the British team members convinced the Uranium Committee of the need for action. The United States then established a new office that could authorize large-scale engineering projects.

How can **uranium** be used in a **weapon**?

The British discovery that naturally occurring uranium, a mixture of uranium-238 and only 0.7% uranium-235, would have to be highly enriched in uranium-235 created a need for enrichment plants. One method chosen had been developed in California. Uranium metal would be evaporated in a vacuum. The atoms went through a narrow slit and then into a region with a strong magnetic field. Because of their mass difference the two isotopes followed slightly different paths. The atoms condensed on the surfaces of separate containers. Dozens of giant machines, called calutrons, were built in a plant in Oak Ridge, Tennessee, chosen because abundant electricity was available from the nearby hydroelectric plants. Not enough copper was available to wind the coils for the magnets so 70,000,000 pounds of silver bullion were borrowed from the U.S. Treasury to be formed into wires for the machines.

Somewhat enriched uranium from the calutrons was then combined with fluorine to produce the gas U_6. Because of the mass difference of the two isotopes $^{235}U_6$ would diffuse through porous membranes slightly faster (about 0.5%) than its more massive counterpart. Thousands of separations were needed to produce weapons-grade uranium (85 to 90% ^{235}U). The plant at Oak Ridge built to accomplish this gaseous diffusion had an area of 2 million square feet, employed 12,000 workers, and cost the equivalent of $6.2 billion in 1999 dollars. At one time it consumed 17% of all the electricity produced in the United States—more than New York City!

Why was **plutonium used** in **bombs**?

Plutonium is not found in nature, but it is produced in reactors by bombarding uranium-238 with neutrons. Plutonium-239 (^{239}Pu) can be fissioned by slow neutrons, and

so could be used in weapons. In December 1942, Hanford, Oregon, was chosen as a site for reactors that would produce plutonium. Hanford was selected because it was isolated but also on the Columbia River, which afforded a source of cooling water.

What was done in **Los Alamos**?

In September 1942, General Groves and Robert Oppenheimer chose Los Alamos, New Mexico, as the site for the top-secret laboratory at which weapons would be developed. Thirty-five miles northwest of Santa Fe, it was almost totally isolated and the site was occupied only by a school. During World War II hastily erected housing held Nobel Prize winning scientists, younger scientists and engineers recruited into the project, wives and children, and soldiers.

After determining the "critical mass," the minimal amount of enriched uranium needed to create a bomb, they designed and built the uranium-based weapon called "Little Boy." The uranium was divided into two halves and placed in a cannon-like container. An explosive charge drove the two masses together, forming a large enough mass of uranium to sustain a rapid chain reaction and explode. This weapon was never tested. It contained 64 kilograms (141 pounds) of uranium, about 2.5 times the critical mass. Less than 1 kilograms (2 pounds) of the uranium fissioned. Only 0.6 grams (0.001 pounds) was converted into energy, but the result was the equivalent of 15,000 tons of TNT. Little Boy was dropped on Hiroshima, Japan, on August 6, 1945. Over 100,000 people were killed in the blast, resulting fires, and effects of radiation.

The second task of Los Alamos was to design and build a weapon using plutonium. Originally they had expected to use the cannon-type method used with the uranium bomb, but when the plutonium was produced by the Hanford reactors it was found to

contain ^{240}Pu, and another design had to be developed. They arranged a sub-critical plutonium mass in the shape of a sphere and used specially designed explosive charges to simultaneously compress the plutonium, increasing its density above the critical point. Scientists were uncertain that the design would work, so they decided to test the device first.

When was the **first "atomic device"** exploded?

"The gadget" was a test version of the plutonium bomb. It was installed on the top of a 30-meter (100-foot) tower in the New Mexico desert at a location 35 miles southeast of Socorro, New Mexico, on the White Sands Proving Ground. The explosion, called "Trinity," occurred on July 16, 1945. The energy yield was about 20,000 tons of TNT, more than twice what had been expected. The implosion-type bomb was much safer and more effective than the cannon-style "Little Boy" design and has been used for all other nuclear weapons.

How was the **plutonium bomb used**?

The plutonium bomb, named "Fat Man" for its shape, was dropped on the city of Nagasaki, Japan, on August 9, 1945. It contained 6.4 kilograms (14 pounds) of plutonium-239. About 20% fissioned, and less than one gram was converted into energy with the equivalent of 21,000 tons of TNT. As many as 80,000 people were killed in the attack.

How many **nations** have **nuclear weapons**?

The Soviet Union exploded a nuclear device in 1949. It was similar to "Fat Man" and was built using information delivered to that country by spies. China, Britain, and France developed nuclear weapons in the 1950s.

South Africa had nuclear weapons but abandoned the program. Israel is suspected of having weapons, but has never admitted it. India and Pakistan have both tested nuclear weapons. Iran and North Korea are suspected of developing nuclear weapons.

The A-Bomb Arch in Peace Park is a memorial to those who died when a nuclear warhead was dropped on Hiroshima in 1945. The United States also dropped the bomb on Nagasaki, Japan. The war in the Pacific ended soon afterwards with Japan's surrender.

By 1953 there had been 50 above-ground tests of nuclear weapons that created radioactive fall-out, contaminating milk and animals. These effects alerted the public to the danger of such testing. The Cold War, however, created an atmosphere in which treaties could not be negotiated. In 1963 a partial test ban treaty was signed, prohibiting tests in the atmosphere, underwater, and in space. In 1968 the nuclear non-proliferation treaty was signed. Non-nuclear weapon states were prohibited from building or acquiring nuclear weapons. Many nations have signed the treaty, although some major states did not on the basis that it makes no effort to curb development by states that already have such weapons. In 1996 the comprehensive test-ban treaty was adopted by over two-thirds of the members of the United Nations general assembly. The United States has signed but rejected ratification in 1999. Nevertheless, 337 facilities around the world monitor compliance with the treaty. They send data to a center in Vienna for analysis and distribution to the states that have signed the treaty.

How is **nuclear fission** used **peacefully**?

Nuclear reactors produce electric power. The energy from uranium fission heats water that circulates through the reactor. The heated water produces steam that turns turbines connected to generators. As is the case with all electric power plants, only about 1/3 of the energy produced by the reactor is converted into electrical energy. The remaining energy heats local rivers, lakes, or the atmosphere. In the United States there are 104 reactors that provide about 20% of the electricity used by our country.

What are the **strengths** and **weaknesses** of **nuclear power**?

Electric power is produced primarily by plants using hydrocarbon fuels—coal, oil, and natural gas. These are usually called fossil fuels and are no longer being created; when they are used up these resources are gone. Nuclear power plants can reduce our reliance on such fuels. Uranium, however, is also a fossil fuel. Coal mining has significant environmental costs. Oil is used mostly for transportation. Natural gas is relatively clean and is used mostly for home and industrial heating. Another advantage of nuclear power is the reduction in greenhouse gases, primarily carbon dioxide.

One major disadvantage of nuclear power is the cost of the plant and the extremely long time scale associated with obtaining approval and constructing the facility. Costs are difficult to calculate precisely, but nuclear power and off-shore wind farms are the two most expensive methods of generating electricity, while oil from the Middle East is the cheapest. As a result of these uncertainties, factors other than costs are increasingly important.

Other disadvantages include the production of nuclear waste that poses long-term dangers to people due to its intense radioactivity. No long-term storage plans have been approved, although underground storage in salt deposits is the most likely method.

Are nuclear power plants safe?

There have been two major accidents in nuclear power plants. One was the failure of water cooling at the Three-Mile Island plant in Pennsylvania in 1979 that resulted in a partial melt-down of the reactor core. While there was a significant release of radioactive gases, studies have shown that there has been no increase in cancer that can be traced to the accident. Nevertheless, this accident has been cited as the major reason the growth in the use of nuclear power has essentially stopped in the United States.

The accident that caused the greatest loss of life and contamination was the explosion at Chernobyl—then in the Soviet Union, now in Ukraine—in 1986. The graphite-moderated reactor had a power spike during a test of the cooling system that led to explosions and fire. Radioactive material, four-hundred times the amount released by the Hiroshima bomb, was spread over a huge area of the Soviet Union and Western Europe. The estimates of the number of deaths range from 50 direct deaths to thousands due to cancers caused by the radiation.

Will **more nuclear power plants** be built?

Concerns over the build up of greenhouse gases and the environmental problems caused by coal mining has led to renewed interest in building new nuclear power plants. Advocates of construction point out that if a standardized plant could be designed, then licensing delays could be reduced and design costs minimized. In addition, several new types of plants have been suggested and undergone small-scale testing. These promise to be simpler and safer than traditional designs. While recycling nuclear fuel is an attractive option, the plutonium in used fuel rods raises issues of nuclear weapon proliferation. The problem of long-term storage of nuclear wastes still needs to be solved.

What is **nuclear fusion**?

Nuclear fusion is the opposite of fission. Two nuclei join, or fuse together, forming a more massive nucleus. The mass of the resultant nucleus is less than that of the reacting nuclei, so energy is released. Because the reacting nuclei are both positively charged, there is a large repulsive force between them. To overcome this force the reacting nuclei must have very high energy. Fusion was first observed by the British physicist Mark Oliphant (1901–2000) in 1932.

A typical fusion reaction involves two isotopes of hydrogen: ^2H, or deuterium, and ^3H, or tritium. They fuse to produce ^4He, releasing a neutron. The energy released is more than a million times larger than that released when an electron combines with a proton to produce a hydrogen atom.

637

What is the **closest fusion reactor**?

Nuclear fusion occurs naturally in stars like our sun, but reproducing a fusion reaction in the laboratory has proven to be very difficult because it takes a lot of energy to fuse nuclei together.

The sun! In stars like the sun the principal reaction is called the proton–proton cycle that was first described by the German-American physicist Hans Bethe (1906–2005) in 1939. In the first step two protons fuse into a deuterium (^2H) nucleus. The deuterium has a proton and a neutron, so the second proton changed into a neutron, releasing a positron and a neutrino. The positron annihilates with an electron, producing two gamma rays. In the second stage the deuterium fuses with another proton to produce helium-3 (^3He) plus a gamma ray. In the sun the third stage is primarily a fusion between two ^3He nuclei producing ^4He plus two protons. So the net reaction is an input of four protons and an output of two ^4He plus six gammas and two neutrinos, as well as a lot of energy due to the loss of 0.7% of the mass of the protons. In order to accomplish these reactions the protons must be moving with a large amount of kinetic energy, the equivalent of a temperature of about 10 million kelvins.

What are **fusion weapons**?

Even before the nuclear bomb was completed, some physicists at Los Alamos started work on what they called the "super," a weapon based on fusion. After the war was over there were heated discussions, both scientific and political, about the wisdom of developing a new, even more destructive weapon. Due to tensions in the Cold War, both the United States and the Soviet Union embarked on programs to create these weapons, informally called hydrogen bombs. The United States tested such a weapon in 1952; the Soviet Union in 1955. Britain, China, and France are known to have tested fusion bombs.

Some aspects of fusion weapons are known while others are still secret. What is known is that the bomb starts with a uranium or plutonium implosion bomb with deuterium and tritium gases inside its core. The neutrons released by the fusion increase the fission of plutonium or uranium, boosting the efficiency of the fission device. The energy released is transferred to a lithium-dihydride fusion fuel in a process that remains secret. That undergoes fusion, and the energy released causes fission in a surrounding layer of natural uranium. The Soviet Union exploded a fusion weapon that released the equivalent of 50 million tons of TNT. The most recent effort on weapons development is to decrease the size of the weapons so they can be deployed in smaller delivery rockets.

Can **fusion** be used for **peaceful purposes**?

The energy released in a fusion reaction could be captured and converted into electrical energy. The difficulty in creating a fusion reactor is confining the reactants, typically deuterium and tritium nuclei, at temperatures needed for fusion. There are two approaches: magnetic and inertial confinement. Most effort has gone into magnetic confinement where the positively charged nuclei are trapped in evacuated regions containing strong magnetic fields that keep the nuclei from colliding with the metallic walls of the equipment. The swarms of charged nuclei, a plasma, must then be raised to very high temperatures and held at that temperature long enough for fusion to take place. So there are three variables: number of nuclei, their energy (or temperature), and the confinement time. The product of these three variables determines whether or not fusion will occur.

What is the latest **fusion reactor research project**?

The ITER reactor project is international in scope, including the United States, Russia, the European Union, India, Japan, China, and South Korea. The plan is to spend 10 years in construction and 20 years in operation. No electrical energy would be generated. That would require a more advanced reactor. Using 0.5 grams of deuterium-tritium fuel, it is designed to produce 500 megawatts of energy over 1,000 seconds. For the first time in a fusion reactor, more energy would be produced than needed to run the reactor. In May 2010, contracts were signed to construct the first buildings in the project that are sited in the south of France. Fusion reactions are scheduled to begin in 2018.

How would **lasers produce fusion**?

The second method of producing fusion is called inertial confinement. Tiny glass, plastic, or metallic spheres containing about 10 milligrams of deuterium-tritium fuel mixture at high pressure are bombarded on all sides by extremely powerful lasers. The lasers vaporize the sphere, driving a strong inward shock wave that compresses the fuel enough to create fusion.

The National Ignition Facility, located at Lawrence Livermore Laboratory in California, has been under construction since 1997. The design goal is to create a 2 megajoule flash of ultraviolet energy that hits the target from 192 separate beamlets. All of the beamlets must strike the target within a few picoseconds. In January 2010 the laser beams delivered 700 kilojoules to a test sphere, heating the gas inside to 3.3 million kelvins. It takes hours for the lasers to cool enough to deliver another pulse. The engineering goal is to deliver one pulse each five hours. Before deuterium-tritium fusion fuel can be used neutron shields have to be built to protect the lasers. There are no accepted engineering plans to convert the energy released to electrical energy. One proposed method is to surround the bead with a blanket of liquefied lithium that would be further heated by the energy released.

When are **fusion reactors** expected to **generate electricity**?

No one knows, but the prediction of scientists working on fusion projects that has been made every year since the 1960s is "about forty years from now."

UNANSWERED QUESTIONS

BEYOND THE PROTON, NEUTRON, AND ELECTRON

What is the **"Standard Model"**?

The description of all the particles described below is called the Standard Model. A model is something like a theory in that it is intended to explain observations. But it is not as complete as a theory. The Standard Model works very well, but there are still many questions about it. Some of these will be explained below.

Why do physicists believe that there are **particles inside protons** and **neutrons**?

Ernest Rutherford (1871–1937) scattered alpha particles off gold atoms and discovered that the atom was not filled with a uniform positive material. In the same way, scattering of protons at high energies off hydrogen nuclei showed that the proton is not composed of uniform positive material. Rather, it is composed of three much smaller charged particles called quarks. The neutron is also composed of three quarks.

How are **particles accelerated** to very high energies?

The two highest energy particle accelerators are the Tevatron at Fermilab, near Chicago, and the Large Hadron Collider (LHC) at CERN (European Organization for Nuclear Research) near Geneva, Switzerland. Both machines accelerate and store protons moving in circular paths in a metallic tube, called the beam line, from which all but minute amounts of air have been evacuated. Beams of particles circulate through the tube in both the clockwise and counter-clockwise direction. The beams intersect at several places around the circle so that the particles can collide head-on. Many

superconducting magnets bend the paths of the particles into the circle while other magnets focus the particles into small beams. Electric fields created in high-power vacuum tubes provide the accelerating forces on the particles.

In particle accelerators energies are measured in electron volts (eV). One eV is the energy a particle obtains by being accelerated by a 1 volt potential difference. Modern accelerators give particles energies of hundreds of MeV (mega electron volts) or GeV (billions of electron volts). The Tevatron creates collisions between protons and antiprotons, each giving an energy of almost 1,000 GeV resulting in an energy of 2 GeV when the two beams collide. In the LHC both beams are protons. The design energy is 7 GeV in each beam for a total collision energy of 14 GeV.

An inside look at the ATLAS (A Toroidal LHC ApparatuS) at CERN in Switzlerland.

How are the results of **collisions** in **accelerators detected**?

A collision between two protons or a proton and anti-proton can produce a large number of particles of different kinds. The task of a detector is to find the direction in which each particle is going, find its charge, momentum, and energy, and identify it. Detectors are huge devices. The CDF (Collider Detector at Fermilab) weighs 5,000 tons and is 12 meters (39 feet) in each dimension. It is operated by a collaboration of about 600 physicists from 60 universities and organizations. ATLAS (A Toroidal LHC ApparatuS) at LHC is even larger. It weighs 7,000 tons, is 44 meters (144 feet) long and 25 meters (82 feet) in diameter; 2,000 physicists are involved in building and operating this experiment.

In both detectors position detectors locate the particles close to where they are produced in the beam line. Somewhat farther away from the beam line a strong magnet deflects the paths of charged particles. Outside the magnet are additional position detectors and finally detectors that measure the energy of the particles. The curved paths charged particles take in the magnet are used to find their charge and momentum.

Each collision can produce billions of pieces of data, only a small number of which are interesting. Electronic circuits and fast computers use data from the position detectors to decide whether the set of data are interesting enough to be recorded. ATLAS produces 100 megabytes of data each second. The entire LHC produces 4 gigabytes of data each second, enough to fill a DVD disk.

> ## Why have physicists given these particles the name "quark" and what do they mean by flavor and color?
>
> The American physicist Murray Gell-Man (1929–) has written that he gave the particles the name "quark" from the phrase "Three quarks for Muster Mark" in *Finnegan's Wake* by James Joyce. Flavor and color have nothing to do with their traditional meanings. The names up and down are associated with a property of protons and neutrons central to an earlier theory. While some people believe that using ordinary words in a very technical context suggests that physicists are not serious about the particles, others believe that their use suggests a whimsical approach to physics that invites people into the discussion rather than erecting barriers to keep others out.

What are the **properties** of **quarks**?

The quarks are fractionally charged, that is their charges are either 2/3 or –1/3 the charge of the proton. They have been given the names "up" and "down" respectively. The proton is composed of two up quarks and one down quark while the neutron is composed of one up and two down quarks. You can check to see that the charges of the quarks add up correctly. Up and down quarks are said to be two different quark "flavors." Because the quarks have half-integral spin (like electrons and neutrinos) there cannot be two identical quarks that have the same quantum properties. Quarks have additional property called color charge that can be red, green, or blue. A proton or neutron must have quarks with one of each of the colors so that they add to white, just like ordinary colors do.

Are there **anti-quarks** like there are antineutrinos and anti-electrons (positrons)?

Yes, there are anti-up quarks with charge –2/3 and anti-down quarks with charge 1/3. An antiproton is composed of two anti-up and one anti-down quarks. Anti-quarks have color charges that are the complementary colors to red, green, and blue: cyan (anti-red), magneta (anti-green), and yellow (anti-blue).

An up (or down) quark and an anti-up (or anti-down) quark will annihilate each other, resulting in energy being released.

What **holds the quarks together** in a proton or neutron?

Eight different massless force carriers called gluons exert the force that holds quarks together. Gluons are members of the boson family. Bosons have integral spin while quarks, electrons, and neutrinos have half-integral spins and are called fermions. Bosons can be created or destroyed while fermions can be created only if an anti-

fermion is also created. A single fermion cannot be destroyed unless an anti-fermion is simultaneously destroyed.

Can **quarks** be **free**, or are they always bound in the proton or neutron?

There have been many searches for free quarks but they have never been observed. The theory that describes the interactions between quarks and gluons, quantum chromodynamics (QCD for short), says that quarks can never break free because the more that the gluons are stretched, the stronger the force they exert. In this way they act like springs whose force also increases the more they are stretched.

Do **electrons** and **neutrinos interact** with **quarks** and **gluons**?

Electrons and neutrinos are called leptons, meaning a lightweight particle. They don't participate in the strong interaction, so they don't interact directly with quarks and gluons. They are, however, involved in the weak interaction through two additional force carrier particles, the W and Z bosons that can interact with quarks.

Beta decay involves neutrons, protons, electrons, and neutrinos. How is it explained using **quarks**?

Beta decay involves two steps. First the down quark changes to an up quark with the emission of a W⁻ boson. Then, almost instantaneously the W⁻ changes into an electron and anti-neutrino. Physicists diagram the two beta decay processes this way:

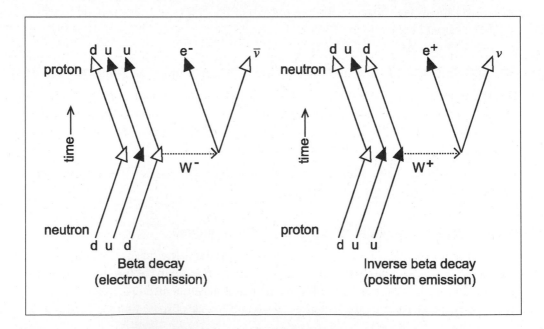

When a nucleus undergoes beta decay the number of neutrons goes down by one, the number of protons goes up by one, and an electron and anti-neutrino are emitted. In terms of quarks and leptons one of the down quarks in the neutron is changed to an up quark in the proton, and a lepton (electron) and anti-lepton (anti-neutrino) are emitted. The change from down to up quark is a flavor change and that can occur only in beta decay. When a positron is emitted in inverse beta decay, an up quark in the proton is changed to a down quark in the neutrino and a lepton (neutrino) and anti-lepton (positron) are emitted.

Are **protons** and **neutrons** the only particles containing **up** and **down quarks**?

In the 1950s new particles with masses in between those of the electron and the proton were found. They were given the name "mesotrons" where "meso" meant intermediate. This was soon shortened to meson. The most commonly produced meson in particle accelerators is the pi-meson or pion. Pions can be positively or negatively charged or uncharged.

In the quark model mesons are composed of a quark and an anti-quark. The quarks that make up the three pions are shown below.

Pion	π^+	π^-	π°
Quarks	$u\bar{d}$	$d\bar{u}$	$1\sqrt{2}\,(d\bar{d} + u\bar{u})$
Quark charge	$+2/3 + 1/3$	$-1/3 - 2/3$	$0.707(-1/3 + 1/3 + 2/3 - 2/3)$

It is also possible to create particles with different combinations of three up and down quarks. These particles have higher masses than protons and neutrons and can only be created by colliding protons and neutrons together with very high energies. Examples are the combinations uuu with charge +2 and the ddd with charge –1. These particles decay via the strong interaction. The uuu decays when its extra energy creates a $d\bar{d}$ pair. The d quark replaces one u quark in the uuu particle, resulting in a proton and the \bar{d} combines with the extra u quark to form a π^+.

Are there yet **more quarks** and **leptons**?

There are two more generations of both quarks and leptons. In the second generation the quarks are called strange and charm. The strange quark was named after particles that contain these quarks. The particles decayed in very different ways and were therefore called strange particles. The charm quark was found in a particle that had a very long, or "charmed" life. The leptons are the muon and muon neutrino. The muon was first called the mu-meson before its true identity was discovered. In the third generation the quarks are called bottom and top. The leptons are called tau and the tau neutrino. The table shows their properties.

| Generation | Quarks | | Leptons | | Anti-Quarks | | Anti-Leptons | |
	Charge +2/3	Charge −1/3			Charge −2/3	Charge +1/3		
1st	up	down	electron	electron neutrino	Anti-up	Anti-down	positron	Anti-electron neutrino
	u	d	e	ν	\bar{u}	\bar{d}	e^+	$\bar{\nu}$
2nd	charm	strange	muon	muon neutrino	Anti-charm	Anti-strange	Anti-muon	Anti-muon neutrino
	c	s	μ	ν_μ	\bar{c}	\bar{s}	$\bar{\mu}$	$\bar{\nu}_\mu$
3rd	top	bottom	tau	tau neutrino	Anti-top	Anti-bottom	Anti-tau	Anti-tau neutrino
	t	b	τ	ν_τ	\bar{t}	\bar{b}	$\bar{\tau}$	$\bar{\nu}_\tau$

What **role** do the **quarks** and **leptons beyond the first generation** quarks and leptons **play** in the universe?

The second and third generation quarks and leptons require large amounts of energy to be created. Particle accelerators like the Tevatron and the LHC have been built to create and study them. They can also be created when very high-energy cosmic rays strike Earth's atmosphere. Some astrophysicists believe that stars exist that contain the strange quark. These particles also existed at times shortly after the Big Bang when temperatures in the universe were extremely high. Thus studying high energy collisions using accelerators is a way of studying what the universe was like when it was very, very young.

What are the **masses** of the **quarks** and **leptons**?

Because quarks can't be separated their masses can only be found by using one or more theories to calculate them. The masses of the charged leptons can be measured to high precision. In the Standard Model neutrinos are all massless, but recent experimental results demand that they have mass.

Masses are given in a unit that is energy divided by the speed of light squared based on Einstein's $E = mc^2$.

Quarks	Mass	Leptons	Mass
u	$2.01 \text{ MeV}/c^2$	e	$0.511 \text{ MeV}/c^2$
d	$4.79 \text{ MeV}/c^2$	ν	$<2.2 \text{ eV}/c^2$
c	$1.27 \text{ GeV}/c^2$	μ	$105.7 \text{ MeV}/c^2$
s	$92.4 \text{ MeV}/c^2$	ν_μ	$<0.17 \text{ MeV}/c^2$
t	$171.2 \text{ GeV}/c^2$	τ	$1.777 \text{ GeV}/c^2$
b	$4.2 \text{ GeV}/c^2$	ν_τ	$<15.5 \text{ MeV}/c^2$

> ## Is there a fourth (or fifth) generation of quarks and neutrinos?
>
> **W**hile there have been many experiments searching for additional generations that have proved negative and many theoretical arguments against more, this is still an open question.

What is the **origin** of the **masses** of the **quarks** and **leptons**?

Peter Higgs (1929–), a British physicist, proposed a mechanism that gives rise to the masses of the quarks, leptons, and the two weak-interaction bosons, the W and Z. The mechanism successfully predicted the mass of the Z boson, but it requires the existence of a particle, called the Higgs boson. Despite many searches, the Higgs boson has not yet been discovered. Physicists hope that the Large Hadron Collider (LHC) that started operation in 2010 will accelerate protons to high enough energies that the Higgs will be found.

Do the **masses** of the **quarks add up** to the **mass** of the **proton**?

The mass of two up quarks and one down quark sum to 8.81 MeV/c^2, and gluons are massless, but the proton's mass is 938 MeV/c^2. How can that be? The remainder of the mass is due to the high energies of the quarks and gluons within the proton.

What are **force carriers**?

The photon is called the force carrier for the electromagnetic interaction. That means that, for example, the attractive force between two oppositely charged objects is described mathematically not by an electric field, but by an exchange of (invisible) photons. The photon has neither mass nor charge, but does have angular momentum. The gluon carries the color force which, in combination with quarks, creates the strong force. The gluon also has neither mass nor charge. The weak nuclear force is carried by the massive W^+, W^-, and $Z°$ particles. Gravity is carried by a massless particle called the graviton.

How are **neutrinos detected**?

Neutrinos hardly interact at all with matter. Some 100 trillion pass through your body every second! Yet the chance that one interacts in your body over your lifetime is only one in four. For this reason neutrino detectors must be huge and can expect to detect only an extremely small fraction of the neutrinos striking them. Most detectors are large cavities filled with extremely pure water or mineral oil. Neutrino interactions result in flashes of light that are seen by sensitive phototubes. The detectors have

identified neutrinos from the sun, from cosmic rays, a supernova, and from reactors and particle detectors. Some experiments have used beams of neutrinos that are aimed through Earth by a reactor or accelerator at a distant detector.

What is the **evidence** that **neutrinos** have **mass**?

The number of neutrinos detected from the sun is only a fraction of what should be detected if our understanding of the nuclear reactions in the sun is correct. A proposed solution to this problem is that neutrinos change from one flavor to another on their travel from the sun to Earth. This phenomenon is called neutrino oscillation. It can only occur if the neutrinos have a small mass. Most experiments that support neutrino oscillation measure the lack of neutrinos of one flavor that they interpret as an oscillation into an undetected flavor. Recently an experiment has detected tau neutrinos in a muon-neutrino beam from an accelerator at CERN and a detector, 732 kilometers away, in the Gran Sasso tunnel in Italy. This flavor change supports neutrino oscillation.

How does **gravity** fit into the **Standard Model**?

It does not fit. Gravity, explained by Einstein's General Theory of Relativity, is extremely successful on the macroscopic scale. But, all attempts to create a quantum gravity have failed. So have attempts to fit gravity into the Standard Model.

What are **possible replacements** or **additions** to the **Standard Model**?

One proposed replacement is called supersymmetry. Each boson in the standard model has a supersymmetric fermion partner particle (or sparticle). And each fermion has a supersymmetric boson sparticle. They are called sleptons, squarks, glunios, and photinos. These sparticles must be much more massive than the Standard Model particles (at least 480 billion electron volts). At this time there is no direct evidence of their existence, although the LHC might be able to reach high enough energies to find them.

A second replacement is string theory. String theory requires a ten-dimensional space-time rather than the normal four-dimensional space-time (three spatial dimensions and one time dimension). A string is a tiny closed loop (like a rubber band). In some theories the loop can break into an open length (like a piece of yarn) but in others it cannot. Strings vibrate at characteristic frequencies, like guitar strings. Each vibration frequency corresponds to an elementary particle. If a string theory is to include fermions (quarks and leptons) supersymmetry must exist.

The great advantage of string theory is that the graviton, the particle that carries the gravitational force, is naturally accommodated. But, if string theory is to be a theory of quantum gravity then the size of a string must be the size of the so-called Planck length, 1.6×10^{-35} m! That is an unimaginably small length, 10^{-20} as large as a proton.

String theories, however, contain symmetries that make their effects felt at larger distances. At this time there is no experiment that could test string theory. If supersymmetric particles are found, then string theory may garner more support.

In summary, what are some of the **unanswered questions** in **particle physics**?

What is the origin of mass? Does the Higgs particle exist? How can the mass of physical particles be completely explained based on the masses of the quarks? Are there additional generations of quarks and leptons? What are the masses of the neutrinos? Could a neutrino be its own antiparticle? How can the gravitational interaction be incorporated into particle

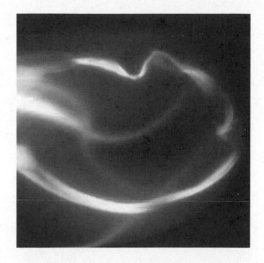

Too small for most people to even visualize in their minds, strings are theoretical objects that exist in ten dimensions and are much tinier than quarks. It is impossible to prove that strings exist using any observational methods known to humankind, but string theory helps explain how matter, energy, and forces like gravity might work in the universe.

physics theories? Are supersymmetry and string theory able to replace the Standard Model? Perhaps you will be able to find the answers to these and other questions.

ENTANGLEMENT, TELEPORTATION, AND QUANTUM COMPUTING

What is **entanglement**?

Consider what happens when a positron and electron annihilate. Two gammas (high energy photons) are produced that go off in opposite directions, 180° apart. They can be detected many meters from their source and have opposite spins, but which gamma has which spin is a random choice. That is, for each gamma there is a 50/50 chance that it will be in a particular direction. Suppose you find that the spin of one gamma is pointing up. But, the moment you detect the spin of that gamma, the spin of the other gamma must be pointing down. The result of one measurement determines the results of the other. The two detectors would measure the spins of their gammas at the same time, so there is no way that one gamma could communicate with the other gamma.

Physicists say that the spins of the two photons are entangled and that the spin state of each photon is the superposition of the two possible spin directions. When the

spin is measured the "wavefunction collapses" and gives a definitive result. Albert Einstein (1879–1955) called results like this "Spooky action at a distance." Others have called it quantum weirdness.

Similar results can be obtained with atoms or ions, in which case the photons are light quanta and may be transported through space (or the air) or by optical fibers. For example, if an atom is excited by the absorption of a photon it can emit two photons that are entangled the same way the gammas are in the example above.

What is **quantum teleportation** and how does it use entanglement?

First, what it is not. It is not "Beam me up, Scotty" where a person disappears at one place and appears at another. It involves only information transfer by either photons or atoms.

Teleportation involves an atom whose state is to be communicated from a sender, Alice, to a receiver, Bob. It also involves a source of two entangled photons.

Alice first sets or measures the state of the atom. This is the information she will send to Bob. At the same time she measures the polarization of one of the two photons. This polarization information is the encryption key that will allow Bob to decode the information. Because the two photons are entangled the polarization of the transmitted photon is fixed. Bob now has the key that allows him to decode the information Alice sent. In practice, of course, the encryption key isn't the polarization of a single photon, but many.

The longest distance information has been teleported is 16 kilometers through the air in Beijing.

What is a **qubit**?

Qubit is short for quantum bit, the basic piece of information for a quantum computer. A qubit can be the state of an atom, ion, photon, or an electron. As was the case of the polarization of the two gammas, the qubit doesn't have a value of 0 or 1, but is in a state that is a superposition of 0 and 1, so it can have any value between those two numbers. If you try to measure the value of the qubit you will get either 0 or 1, so it will act like a bit in a normal computer. The trick is to use one of two entangled photons (or atoms) to determine the qubit's state without collapsing it into either 0 or 1.

Quantum computers are by nature parallel machines that can work on many problems at once. At this time computers with 12 qubits have been demonstrated, so there is a long way to go before such a device is practical. Still, progress is being made. A company has demonstrated a way of using the kind of chip lasers used in CD players to create entangled photons, greatly reducing the size, complexity, and cost of a quantum computer.

This image from the Hubble Space Telescope shows a dark ring surrounding the CL0024+17 region of galaxies. Scientists speculate that the distorted images of these galaxies is a result of dark matter in the ring, which is five hundred million light-years wide.

failed to ignite. More likely candidates are the supersymmetric particles described above. Much discussion recently has focused on WIMPs, Weakly Interacting Massive Particles. If they exist they would be passing through Earth, and so several experiments are underway to detect them. Early results from one experiment claimed to have detected two particles. Other experiments look for indirect evidence from gamma rays or anti-matter. One result claimed to have found an excess of positrons, but not anti-protons. The composition of dark matter is one of the most active areas of investigation in astrophysics.

What is **dark energy**?

For the first ten billion years of the existence of the universe the attractive forces of gravity on matter—both ordinary and dark—slowed the expansion of the universe. But beginning about five billion years ago the universe began to expand at an increasing rate. Two studies of supernovae have documented this acceleration. The cause of this expansion has been called dark energy, but the nature of dark energy is totally unknown. It interacts only via gravity and is very dilute. One possibility is that Einstein's General Relativity has to be modified by the addition of a cosmological constant. Einstein himself considered such a constant, then discarded it, calling it his biggest blunder. The problem with such a constant is that particle physics estimates the value (in proper units) of 1, but the value required to explain the extra expansion is 10^{-120}. This huge discrepancy cannot be explained.

Will **quantum teleportation** be able to be extended to **longer distances** with **error-free results**?

At the present the encryption codes cannot be broken. Will that continue to be true? Will quantum computers become practical? At present their projected use is to factor large numbers, a task used to create encryption keys to keep electronic messages secure. What additional problems will they be able to solve that traditional computers cannot?

THE STRUCTURE AND END OF THE UNIVERSE

What **makes up** the **universe**?

If you said stars and galaxies, gas clouds, black holes, photons, neutrinos, etc. you're only partially correct. These known materials constitute only 5% of the mass-energy in universe! Dark matter comprises another 23%. Dark matter does not interact with electromagnetic radiation but does interact with gravity. Thus it is invisible and we can see right through it. The remaining 72% is made up of dark energy.

Why do **astronomers believe** there is **dark matter** in the universe?

The first hints that there is more to the universe than visible stars and galaxies came in 1933 when the Swiss-American astronomer Fred Zwicky (1898–1974) studied the motion of galaxies in the Coma cluster and estimated that in order to account for their rapid motion there must be 400 times as much mass as could be accounted for. In the 1970s the American astronomer Vera Rubin (1938–) studied the rotation of galaxies and found that at least half of the matter in galaxies must be invisible—dark matter.

Dark matter is also in evidence in gravitational lensing, where the gravitational interaction of mass with light causes the light from very distant galaxies to be bent by nearer galaxies. The result is a distortion of shape and position in the images of the distant galaxies as if they are being seen through a lens. In one set of colliding galaxies the center of mass, determined by the lensing effect, is separated from the center of optical and X-ray brightness, probably by the effect of the collisions.

Radio and infrared emissions from the initial Big Bang that formed the universe is called the 3 kelvin cosmic microwave background radiation. Understanding the details of this radiation also requires large amounts of dark matter.

What makes up **dark matter**?

Many candidates have been proposed, but there is no agreement at this point. Neutrinos with mass could make up a small portion, as could brown dwarf stars that have

Index

655

665

Viète, François, 71, 73, 76 (ill.), 77, 106
vision, mechanics of. *See* eyesight
Vitruvius, 283–85, 290, 413
voice, wind instruments' similarity to human, 514
Volta, Alessandro, 578–79, 608
voltage, 579, 582 (ill.), 582–83, 590
voltaic pile, 579
Volterra, Vito, 270
volume, 129, 517
Voronkov, Andrei, 57
Vries, Hugo de, 265

W

Wald, George, 614
Wallis, John, 69, 86
Warszawa Radio Tower, 425
water
 ability to stay level, 428
 danger of operating electrical devices in, 590–91
 freezing point of, 451–52
 lifting objects in, 434
 pressure, 427–30, 428 (ill.)
 seeing under, 544–45, 556
 submerging balloons in, 432
 towers, 429, 429 (ill.)
 using to model voltage and current, 579
 waves, 472 (ill.), 472–74
water systems, 279
Watson-Watt, Robert, 493
watt, 400–401, 584–85
Watt, James, 398, 401
wave mechanics, 221
waveform, sound spectrum relating to its, 515
wavelength, 470, 471 (ill.), 555
waves
 physics of, 469–96

properties of, 470, 470 (ill.), 613–14, 616–17
shock, 445–46
Weakly Interacting Massive Particles (WIMPs), 652
weapons
 containing uranium, 633
 fusion, 638
 nuclear, 635–36
weather prediction, 260–62
weather prognostication, 207–8
weather records, 186
Weather Research and Forecasting (WRF) model, 261, 262
websites, 317
wedge as inclined plane, 407
weight and mass, 215, 215 (ill.)
weightlessness, 378–79, 379 (ill.)
Weinberg, Steven, 627
Wessel, Casper, 137
Westinghouse, George, 587
wet measurements, 330
Wheeler, John, 374
wheels and axles, 408–10, 409 (ill.)
white light, 547–49
Widmann, Johann, 29
Wieman, Carl E., 618
Willis Tower (Sears Tower), 288, 425
WIMPs (Weakly Interactive Massive Particles), 652
wind
 increase of, in cities, 442
 speed of, and wave type, 472, 472 (ill.)
 throwing discus into, 443–44
wind chill, 254–54, 256 (ill.)
wind instruments, mechanics of, 513–14
wind speed, 254, 334
wires, grounding, 589 (ill.), 590
Wolszczan, Alekzander, 236

wood, 334–36
Wood, Thomas Nathan, 309
word problems, 75
work, 216, 397–98
workstations, 316
world, makeup of, 605–20
World Health Organization, 516
World Trade Center, 425
Wright, Orville, 445
Wright, Wilbur, 445
Wright 1903 Flyer, 445

X

X rays, 617
Xylander, Wilhelm, 28

Y

y-intercept, 134
Yates, Samuel, 19
Yeager, Chuck, 446–48
Young, Thomas, 520

Z

Zeno of Elea, 59, 104, 147
Zeno's paradoxes, 59
zEnterprise 196 (IBM mainframe), 314
Zermelo, Ernst Friedrich, 67
Zermelo's axiom of choice, 67
zero
 definition, 26
 division, 31
 fractions, 36
 placeholder, 26
 roots of a polynomial, 92
zeroth law of thermodynamics, 463
ZIP code, 332–33
zircon, 244 (ill.)
Zulu War, 534
Zuse, Konrad, 312
Zwicky, Fred, 651